Foreign Relations of the
United States, 1964–1968

Volume XXX

China

Editor   Harriet Dashiell Schwar

General Editor   David S. Patterson

United States Government Printing Office
Washington
1998

DEPARTMENT OF STATE PUBLICATION 10545

OFFICE OF THE HISTORIAN

BUREAU OF PUBLIC AFFAIRS

For sale by the U.S. Government Printing Office
Superintendent of Documents, Mail Stop: SSOP, Washington, DC 20402-9328
ISBN 0-16-048811-7

Preface

The *Foreign Relations of the United States* series presents the official documentary historical record of major foreign policy decisions and significant diplomatic activity of the United States Government. The series documents the facts and events that contributed to the formulation of policies and includes evidence of supporting and alternative views to the policy positions ultimately adopted.

The Historian of the Department of State is charged with the responsibility for the preparation of the *Foreign Relations* series. The staff of the Office of the Historian, Bureau of Public Affairs, plans, researches, compiles, and edits the volumes in the series. This documentary editing proceeds in full accord with the generally accepted standards of historical scholarship. Official regulations codifying specific standards for the selection and editing of documents for the series were first promulgated by Secretary of State Frank B. Kellogg on March 26, 1925. These regulations, with minor modifications, guided the series through 1991.

A new statutory charter for the preparation of the series was established by Public Law 102–138, the Foreign Relations Authorization Act, Fiscal Years 1992 and 1993, which was signed by President George Bush on October 28, 1991. Section 198 of P.L. 102–138 added a new Title IV to the Department of State's Basic Authorities Act of 1956 (22 USC 4351, *et seq.*).

The statute requires that the *Foreign Relations* series be a thorough, accurate, and reliable record of major United States foreign policy decisions and significant United States diplomatic activity. The volumes of the series should include all records needed to provide comprehensive documentation of major foreign policy decisions and actions of the United States Government. The statute also confirms the editing principles established by Secretary Kellogg: the *Foreign Relations* series is guided by the principles of historical objectivity and accuracy; records should not be altered or deletions made without indicating in the published text that a deletion has been made; the published record should omit no facts that were of major importance in reaching a decision; and nothing should be omitted for the purposes of concealing a defect in policy. The statute also requires that the *Foreign Relations* series be published not more than 30 years after the events recorded. The editor is convinced that this volume, which was compiled in 1993-1994, meets all regulatory, statutory, and scholarly standards of selection and editing.

Structure and Scope of the Foreign Relations Series

This volume is part of a subseries of volumes of the *Foreign Relations* series that documents the most important issues in the foreign policy of

III

the 5 years (1964–1968) of the administration of Lyndon B. Johnson. The subseries presents in 34 volumes a documentary record of major foreign policy decisions and actions of President Johnson's administration. This volume documents U.S. policy toward China, including U.S. policy toward the People's Republic of China, U.S. relations with the Republic of China on Taiwan, and U.S. policy on issues concerning Tibet. It also contains a compilation on U.S. policy with regard to Mongolia.

Principles of Document Selection for the Foreign Relations Series

In preparing each volume of the *Foreign Relations* series, the editors are guided by some general principles for the selection of documents. Each editor, in consultation with the General Editor and other senior editors, determines the particular issues and topics to be documented either in detail, in brief, or in summary.

The following general selection criteria are used in preparing volumes in the *Foreign Relations* series. Individual compiler-editors vary these criteria in accordance with the particular issues and the available documentation. The editors also tend to apply these selection criteria in accordance with their own interpretation of the generally accepted standards of scholarship. In selecting documentation for publication, the editors gave priority to unpublished classified records, rather than previously published records (which are accounted for in appropriate bibliographical notes).

Selection Criteria (in general order of priority):

1. Major foreign affairs commitments made on behalf of the United States to other governments, including those that define or identify the principal foreign affairs interests of the United States;

2. Major foreign affairs issues, commitments, negotiations, and activities, whether or not major decisions were made, and including dissenting or alternative opinions to the process ultimately adopted;

3. The decisions, discussions, actions, and considerations of the President, as the official constitutionally responsible for the direction of foreign policy;

4. The discussions and actions of the National Security Council, the Cabinet, and special Presidential policy groups, including the policy options brought before these bodies or their individual members;

5. The policy options adopted by or considered by the Secretary of State and the most important actions taken to implement Presidential decisions or policies;

6. Diplomatic negotiations and conferences, official correspondence, and other exchanges between U.S. representatives and those of other governments that demonstrate the main lines of policy implementation on major issues;

7. Important elements of information that attended Presidential decisions and policy recommendations of the Secretary of State;

8. Major foreign affairs decisions, negotiations, and commitments undertaken on behalf of the United States by government officials and representatives in other agencies in the foreign affairs community or other branches of government made without the involvement (or even knowledge) of the White House or the Department of State;

9. The main policy lines of intelligence activities if they constituted major aspects of U.S. foreign policy toward a nation or region or if they provided key information in the formulation of major U.S. policies, including relevant National Intelligence Estimates and Special National Intelligence Estimates as may be declassified;

10. The role of the Congress in the preparation and execution of particular foreign policies or foreign affairs actions;

11. Economic aspects of foreign policy;

12. The main policy lines of U.S. military and economic assistance as well as other types of assistance;

13. The political-military recommendations, decisions, and activities of the military establishment and major regional military commands as they bear upon the formulation or execution of major U.S. foreign policies;

14. Diplomatic appointments that reflect major policies or affect policy changes.

Sources for the Foreign Relations Series

The *Foreign Relations* statute requires that the published record in the *Foreign Relations* series include all records needed to provide comprehensive documentation on major U.S. foreign policy decisions and significant U.S. diplomatic activity. It further requires that government agencies, departments, and other entities of the U.S. Government engaged in foreign policy formulation, execution, or support cooperate with the Department of State Historian by providing full and complete access to records pertinent to foreign policy decisions and actions and by providing copies of selected records. Many of the sources consulted in the preparation of this volume have been declassified and are available for review at the National Archives and Records Administration. The declassification review and opening for public review of all Department of State records no later than 30 years after the events is mandated by the *Foreign Relations* statute. The Department of State and other record sources used in the volume are described in detail in the section on Sources below.

Focus of Research and Principles of Selection for Foreign Relations, 1964–1968, Volume XXX

The editor of the volume sought to include documentation illuminating the foreign policymaking process of the U.S. Government, with emphasis on the highest level at which policy on a particular subject was determined. The documents include memoranda and records of discussions that set forth policy issues and show decisions or actions taken. The emphasis is on the development of U.S. policy and on major aspects and repercussions of its execution, but not details of policy execution.

Lyndon Johnson made the major foreign policy decisions during his presidency, and the editor sought to document his role as far as possible. Although the foreign policy record of the Johnson administration is voluminous, many internal discussions between Johnson and his advisers were not recorded. The record of Johnson's involvement in the policy process must often be pieced together from a variety of sources. Secretary of State Dean Rusk's role is perhaps even more elusive. The editor sought to document Johnson's and Rusk's roles in the policy process as far as possible.

The volume focuses on the issues that primarily engaged high-level U.S. policymakers. Major topics include: 1) U.S. anticipation of the first Chinese nuclear explosion and the U.S. reaction when it took place in October 1964; 2) the attempts of U.S. policymakers to deal with the issue of Chinese representation in the United Nations; 3) U.S. relations with the Chinese Nationalists on Taiwan, especially the question of possible Nationalist operations against the mainland; 4) the ambassadorial meetings at Warsaw; 5) proposals to liberalize U.S. restrictions on travel to and trade with the China mainland; 6) the U.S. response to French recognition of the People's Republic of China; and 7) U.S. policy concerning Tibet.

The absence of U.S. diplomatic representation in the People's Republic of China increased the importance of intelligence on China. The editor included a selection of intelligence estimates and analyses seen by high-level policymakers, especially those that were sent to President Johnson, and made a particular effort to include a sampling of reports and analyses on the Cultural Revolution. Selected intelligence estimates and analyses on internal developments in Taiwan were also included.

Editorial Methodology

The documents are presented chronologically according to Washington time or, in the case of conferences, in the order of individual meetings. Memoranda of conversation are placed according to the time and date of the conversation, rather than the date the memorandum was drafted.

Editorial treatment of the documents published in the *Foreign Relations* series follows Office style guidelines, supplemented by guidance from the General Editor and the chief technical editor. The source text is reproduced as exactly as possible, including marginalia or other notations, which are described in the footnotes. Texts are transcribed and printed according to accepted conventions for the publication of historical documents in the limitations of modern typography. A heading has been supplied by the editors for each document included in the volume. Spelling, capitalization, and punctuation are retained as found in the source text, except that obvious typographical errors are silently corrected. Other mistakes and omissions in the source text are corrected by bracketed insertions: a correction is set in italic type; an addition in roman type. Words or phrases underlined in the source text are printed in italics. Abbreviations and contractions are preserved as found in the source text, and a list of abbreviations is included in the front matter of each volume.

Bracketed insertions are also used to indicate omitted text that deals with an unrelated subject (in roman type) or that remains classified after declassification review (in italic type). The amount of material not declassified has been noted by indicating the number of lines or pages of source text that were omitted. Entire documents withheld for declassification purposes have been accounted for and are listed by headings, source notes, and number of pages not declassified in their chronological place. The amount of material omitted from this volume because it was unrelated to the subject of the volume, however, has not been delineated. All brackets that appear in the source text are so identified by footnotes.

The first footnote to each document indicates the document's source, original classification, distribution, and drafting information. This note also provides the background of important documents and policies and indicates whether the President or his major policy advisers read the document. Every effort has been made to determine if a document has been previously published, and, if so, this information has been included in the source footnote.

Editorial notes and additional annotation summarize pertinent material not printed in the volume, indicate the location of additional documentary sources, provide references to important related documents printed in other volumes, describe key events, and provide summaries of and citations to public statements that supplement and elucidate the printed documents. Information derived from memoirs and other firsthand accounts has been used when appropriate to supplement or explicate the official record.

Advisory Committee on Historical Diplomatic Documentation

The Advisory Committee on Historical Diplomatic Documentation, established under the *Foreign Relations* statute, reviews records, advises, and makes recommendations concerning the *Foreign Relations* series. The Advisory Committee monitors the overall compilation and editorial process of the series and advises on all aspects of the preparation and declassification of the series. Although the Advisory Committee does not attempt to review the contents of individual volumes in the series, it does monitor the overall process and makes recommendations on particular problems that come to its attention.

The Advisory Committee has not reviewed this volume.

Declassification Review

The final declassification review of this volume, which was completed in 1997, resulted in the decision to withhold about 1.3 percent of the documentation selected. Three documents were denied in full. The remaining documentation provides an accurate account of U.S. policy toward China, including policy concerning Tibet, and U.S. policy toward Mongolia during this period.

The Information Response Branch of the Office of IRM Programs and Services, Bureau of Administration, Department of State, conducted the declassification review of the documents published in this volume. The review was conducted in accordance with the standards set forth in Executive Order 12356 on National Security Information and applicable laws, which was superseded by Executive Order 12958 on April 20, 1995.

Under Executive Order 12356, information that concerns one or more of the following categories, and the disclosure of which reasonably could be expected to cause damage to the national security, requires classification:

1) military plans, weapons, or operations;
2) the vulnerabilities or capabilities of systems, installations, projects, or plans relating to the national security;
3) foreign government information;
4) intelligence activities (including special activities), or intelligence sources or methods;
5) foreign relations or foreign activities of the United States;
6) scientific, technological, or economic matters relating to national security;
7) U.S. Government programs for safeguarding nuclear materials or facilities;
8) cryptology; or
9) a confidential source.

The principle guiding declassification review is to release all information, subject only to the current requirements of national security as embodied in law and regulation. Declassification decisions entailed concurrence of the appropriate geographic and functional bureaus in the Department of State, other concerned agencies of the U.S. Government, and the appropriate foreign governments regarding specific documents of those governments.

Acknowledgements

The editor wishes to acknowledge the assistance of officials at the Lyndon B. Johnson Library of the National Archives and Records Administration, especially David C. Humphrey, Regina Greenwell, and Charlaine Burgess, who provided key research assistance. The editor also wishes to acknowledge the assistance of historians at the Central Intelligence Agency, particularly Kevin Ruffner; officials at the Department of Defense, especially Sandra Meagher; at the National Defense University, particularly Susan Lemke, and officials at the Library of Congress, Manuscript Division, who assisted in the collection of documents for this volume.

Harriet Dashiell Schwar collected, selected, and edited the volume, under the general supervision of Edward C. Keefer and former General Editor Glenn W. LaFantasie. Gabrielle S. Mallon prepared the lists of names, sources, and abbreviations. Vicki E. Futscher, Deb Godfrey, and Rita M. Baker did the copy and technical editing. Do Mi Stauber prepared the index.

William Z. Slany
The Historian
Bureau of Public Affairs

May 1998

Johnson Administration Volumes

Following is a list of the volumes in the *Foreign Relations* series for the administration of President Lyndon B. Johnson. The titles of individual volumes may change. The year of publication is in parentheses after the title.

Print Volumes

I	Vietnam, 1964 (1992)
II	Vietnam, January–June 1965 (1996)
III	Vietnam, July–December 1965 (1996)
IV	Vietnam, 1966 (1998)
V	Vietnam, 1967
VI	Vietnam, 1968
VII	Vietnam, 1968
VIII	International Monetary and Trade Policy (1998)
IX	International Development and Economic Defense Policy; Commodities (1997)
X	National Security Policy
XI	Arms Control and Disarmament (1997)
XII	Western Europe
XIII	Western Europe Region (1995)
XIV	Soviet Union
XV	Berlin; Germany
XVI	Cyprus; Greece; Turkey
XVII	Eastern Europe; Austria; Finland (1996)
XVIII	Arab-Israeli Dispute, 1964–1967
XIX	Six-Day War
XX	Arab-Israeli Dispute, 1967–1968
XXI	Near East Region; Arab Peninsula
XXII	Iran
XXIII	North Africa; Congo
XXIV	Africa
XXV	South Asia
XXVI	Indonesia; Malaysia-Singapore; Philippines
XXVII	Mainland Southeast Asia; Regional Affairs
XXVIII	Laos (1998)
XXIX	Korea; Japan
XXX	China (1998)
XXXI	Central and South America; Mexico
XXXII	Dominican Crisis; Cuba; Caribbean
XXXIII	United Nations; Organization of Foreign Policy; Vatican
XXXIV	Scientific and Humanitarian Affairs

Contents

Preface III

Johnson Administration Volumes XI

Sources XV

Abbreviations XXV

Persons XXXI

China 1

Questions pertaining to Tibet 731

Mongolia 745

Index 757

Sources

The editors of the *Foreign Relations* series have complete access to all the retired records and papers of the Department of State: the central files of the Department; the special decentralized files ("lot files") of the Department at the bureau, office, and division levels; the files of the Department's Executive Secretariat, which contain the records of international conferences and high-level official visits, correspondence with foreign leaders by the President and Secretary of State, and memoranda of conversations between the President and Secretary of State and foreign officials; and the files of overseas diplomatic posts. When this volume was being compiled, all Department of State records consulted were still under the custody of the Department, and the footnotes citing Department of State files suggest that the Department is the repository. By the time of publication, however, all the Department's indexed central (or decimal) files for these years were permanently transferred to the National Archives and Records Administration (Archives II) at College Park, Maryland. Many of the Department's decentralized office (or lot) files covering this period, which the National Archives deems worthy of permanent retention, will also be transferred from the Department's custody to Archives II over the next several years.

The editors of the *Foreign Relations* series also have full access to the papers of President Johnson and other White House foreign policy records. Presidential papers maintained and preserved at the Presidential libraries include some of the most significant foreign affairs-related documentation from the Department of State and other Federal agencies including the National Security Council, the Central Intelligence Agency, the Department of Defense, and the Joint Chiefs of Staff.

In preparing this volume, the editor made extensive use of Presidential papers and other White House records at the Lyndon B. Johnson Library. Numerous White House memoranda, including memoranda to the President, testify to President Johnson's concern with issues relating to China, especially China's nuclear development, the Chinese representation issue, and internal developments in China during the Cultural Revolution. The bulk of the foreign policy records at the Johnson Library are in the country files and other component parts of the National Security File. The China Country File includes records on issues concerning the China mainland and also on relations with the Chinese Nationalists on Taiwan. Material pertaining to the ambassadorial talks at Warsaw is in the Poland Country File.

The Department of State arranged for access to the audiotapes of President Johnson's telephone conversations, which are held at the Johnson Library. The first audiotapes became available to the editors in late

1994, after this volume was completed. Others became available after the declassification process was well underway. The editor did not consider that the small portion of material in those tapes pertaining to U.S. policy toward China justified delay in the publication of the volume. Information concerning a few conversations pertaining to China is included in the volume.

Second in importance only to the White House records at the Johnson Library were the records of the Department of State. The Department's central files contain the cable traffic recording U.S. diplomatic relations with the Republic of China on Taiwan and the ambassadorial talks at Warsaw, memoranda of diplomatic conversations, and memoranda proposing action or providing information. Some important documents are found only in Lot Files. The Conference Files maintained by the Executive Secretariat contain briefing materials as well as records of conversations. Documentation on initiatives that were not approved is often found only in desk or bureau files. The Rusk Files contain records of Secretary Rusk's telephone conversations.

The Central Intelligence Agency provides access to Department of State historians to high-level intelligence documents from those records in the custody of that Agency and at the Presidential Libraries. This access is arranged and facilitated by the History Staff of the Center for the Study of Intelligence, Central Intelligence Agency, pursuant to a May 1992 memorandum of understanding. Department of State and CIA historians continue to work out the procedural and scholarly aspects of identifying the key portions of the intelligence record.

The China volume has an important intelligence component, including finished intelligence and some covert operations. In CIA records, the files of the Directors of Central Intelligence, especially John McCone's, were especially useful. Retired files of the Department of State's Bureau of Intelligence and Research contained National Intelligence Estimates, and the INR Historical Files provided records of the meetings of the 303 Committee, the interdepartmental committee that reviewed and authorized covert operations, and related material.

The records of the Department of Defense (DOD) at the Washington National Records Center at Suitland, Maryland, particularly the records of the Secretary of Defense and the Assistant Secretary of Defense for International Security Affairs, provided important documents. The papers of W. Averell Harriman at the Library of Congress include some valuable material relating to China not available elsewhere. The papers of Maxwell D. Taylor at the National Defense University contain records of White House staff meetings for the early part of 1964.

All of this documentation has been made available for use in the *Foreign Relations* series thanks to the consent of the foregoing agencies, the assistance of their staffs, and especially the cooperation and support of the National Archives and Records Administration.

The following list identifies the particular files and collections used in the preparation of this volume. The declassification and transfer to the National Archives of these records in process. Many of the records are already available for public review at the National Archives. The declassification review of other records is going forward in accordance with the provisions of Executive Order 12958, under which all records over 25 years old, except file series exemptions requested by agencies and approved by the President, should be reviewed for declassification by 2000.

Unpublished Sources

Department of State

Central Files. See National Archives and Records Administration below.

Lot Files. These files are either transferred or in the process of being transferred to the National Archives and Records Administration at College Park Maryland, Record Group 59.

Bundy Files: Lot 85 D 240

> Files of William P. Bundy, 1962–1970; largely covering the period when he was Assistant Secretary of State for Far Eastern Affairs, 1964–1969.

Conference Files: Lot 66 D 110

> Records of official visits by heads of government and foreign ministers to the United States and international conferences attended by the President, the Secretary of State, and other U.S. officials, 1961–1964, maintained by the Executive Secretariat.

Conference Files: Lot 66 D 347

> Records of official visits by heads of government and foreign ministers to the United States, and international conferences attended by the President, Vice President, or Secretary of State for 1965, maintained by the Executive Secretariat.

Conference Files: Lot 67 D 305

> Records of international conferences attended by the President, Vice President, or Secretary of State from January to October 8, 1966, maintained by the Executive Secretariat.

Conference Files: Lot 67 D 586

> Records of international conferences attended by the President, Vice President, or Secretary of State from October 1966, to May 10, 1967, maintained by the Executive Secretariat.

EA Files: Lot 73 D 8

> Correspondence on East Asia Advisory Panel and China Advisory Panel Meetings for 1967–1968, maintained by the Bureau of East Asian and Pacific Affairs.

EA/ACA Files: Lot 71 D 144

> Files of Paul H. Kreisberg, Officer in Charge of Mainland China Affairs, 1965–1970, maintained by the Office of Asian Communist Affairs, Bureau of East Asian and Pacific Affairs

EA/ACA Files: Lot 72 D 175

> Subject Files: Administrative and economic files for 1962–1969, maintained by the Office of Asian Communist Affairs, Bureau of East Asian and Pacific Affairs.

EA/ROC Files: 71 D 517

> Top Secret files relating to China for 1954–1964, maintained by the Office of Chinese Affairs and later by the Republic of China desk in the Office of East Asian Affairs.

EA/ROC Files: Lot 72 D 140

> Top Secret files, including briefing materials and records of visits, for 1961–1968, maintained by the Office of Chinese Affairs, later by the Republic of China desk in the Office of East Asian Affairs, and later by the Office of Republic of China Affairs, Bureau of East Asian and Pacific Affairs.

EA/ROC Files: Lot 74 D 25

> Political files for 1964–1972, maintained by the Republic of China desk in the Office of East Asian Affairs and later by the Office of Republic of China Affairs, Bureau of East Asian and Pacific Affairs.

EA/ROC Files: Lot 75 D 76

> Political files for 1954–1973 and miscellaneous Top Secret files for 1955–1973, maintained by the Office of Chinese Affairs, later by the Republic of China desk in the Office of East Asian Affairs, and later by the Office of Republic of China Affairs, Bureau of East Asian and Pacific Affairs.

EA/ROC Files: Lot 79 D 120

> Top Secret files for 1961–1972, maintained by the Republic of China desk in the office of East Asian Affairs, and later by the Office of Republic of China Affairs, Bureau of East Asian and Pacific Affairs.

FE/IRG Files: Lot 70 D 56

> Files of the Far East Interdepartmental Regional Group from March 1966 through December 1968, maintained by the Special Assistant to the Assistant Secretary of State for East Asian and Pacific Affairs.

Geneva Talks Files: Lot 72 D 415

> Files relating to the Sino-American ambassadorial talks at Geneva and Warsaw for 1955–1968, maintained by the Office of Chinese Affairs, later by the Office of East Asian Affairs, and later by the Office of Asian Communist Affairs.

INR/EAP Files: Lot 90 D 99

> National Intelligence Estimates, Special National Intelligence Estimates, Telegrams, and Memos for 1952–1985, maintained by the Office of Research and Analysis for East Asia and the Pacific, Bureau of Intelligence and Research.

INR/EAP Files: Lot 90 D 110

> National Intelligence Estimates, Special National Intelligence Estimates, Telegrams, and Memos for 1952–1985, maintained by the Office of Research and Analysis for East Asia and the Pacific, Bureau of Intelligence and Research.

INR/IL Historical Files

> Intelligence files, including records of the 303 Committee, containing records from the 1950s through the 1970s, maintained by the Office of Intelligence Liaison, Bureau of Intelligence and Research.

Policy Guidelines: Lot 67 D 396

Master file of Guidelines for Policy and Operations papers, 1961–1966.

Rusk Files: Lot 72 D 192

Files of Secretary of State Dean Rusk, 1961–1969, including texts of speeches and public statements, miscellaneous correspondence files, White House correspondence, chronological files, and memoranda of telephone conversations.

S/P Files: Lot 70 D 199

Files of the Policy Planning Council for 1963–1964.

S/P Files: Lot 71 D 382

Top Secret files of the Policy Planning Council, 1964–1970.

S/P Files: Lot 72 D 139

Top Secret files of the Policy Planning Council, 1963–1971; country files, 1965–1969.

S/S–NSC Files: Lot 70 D 265

Master set of papers pertaining to National Security Council meetings, including policy papers, position papers, administrative documents, but not minutes of the meetings, for 1961–1966, maintained by the Executive Secretariat.

S/S–NSC Files: Lot 72 D 316

Master file of National Security Action Memoranda (NSAMs), 1961–1968, maintained by the Executive Secretariat.

Visit Files: Lot 67 D 587

Records of official visits by heads of government and foreign ministers to the United States from October 1966 to May 10, 1967, maintained by the Executive Secretariat.

Warsaw Talks Files: Lot 73 D 210

Files relating to the U.S.–China ambassadorial talks at Warsaw for 1958–1971, with some material concerning the 1955–1957 talks at Geneva, maintained by the Embassy at Warsaw and later by the Office of People's Republic of China and Mongolia Affairs.

Warsaw Talks Files: Lot 75 D 342

Files relating to the U.S.–China ambassadorial talks at Warsaw for 1961–1968, maintained by the Office of Office of Chinese Affairs, later by the Office of East Asian Affairs, later by the Office of Communist Affairs, and later by the Office of People's Republic of China and Mongolia Affairs.

National Archives and Records Administration, College Park, Maryland

RG 59, General Records of the Department of State

Subject-Numeric Indexed Central Files

AID (US) CHINAT, U.S. economic aid to the Republic of China
AID (US) 15 CHINAT, P.L. 480 assistance to the Republic of China
CSM 1 CHICOM, Chinese Communist doctrine, objectives
CSM 1–1, Communist schisms, deviation
DEF CHICOM, military affairs, People's Republic of China
DEF CHINAT, military affairs, Republic of China

DEF 1 CHINAT, defense policy, plans, readiness, Republic of China
DEF 1 CHINAT–US, defense policy, plans, readiness, Republic of China–U.S.
DEF 1–4 CHINAT, air defense, Republic of China
DEF 6 CHINAT, armed forces, Republic of China
DEF 6–5 CHINAT, paramilitary forces, Republic of China
DEF 12–1 CHICOM, nuclear testing, People's Republic of China
DEF 15 CHINAT, bases and installations, Republic of China
DEF 15 CHINAT–US, bases and installations, Republic of China–U.S.
DEF 15 HK, bases and installations, Hong Kong
DEF 15–3 CHINAT-US, status of forces, Republic of China–U.S.
DEF 19 US–CHINAT, U.S. military assistance to the Republic of China
DEF 19–8 US–CHINAT, U.S. provision of military equipment and supplies to the Republic of China
FT CHICOM–1 US, general policy on the question of trade with the People's Republic of China
FT CHICOM–US, question of trade with the People's Republic of China
ORG 1 OSD–STATE, State–Defense coordination
ORG 3–2, chiefs of mission and principal officers
ORG 7 FE, travel by officials of the Bureau of Far Eastern Affairs
ORG 7 S, travel by the Secretary of State
POL CAN–CHICOM, political affairs and relations, Canada and the People's Republic of China
POL CHICOM, political developments, People's Republic of China
POL CHICOM–JAPAN, political affairs and relations, People's Republic of China and Japan
POL CHICOM–US, political affairs and relations, People's Republic of China and the United States
POL CHICOM–USSR, political affairs and relations, People's Republic of China and the U.S.S.R.
POL CHICOM–CHINAT, political affairs and relations, People's Republic of China and Republic of China
POL CHINAT, political developments, Republic of China
POL CHINAT–CHICOM, political affairs and relations, Republic of China and People's Republic of China
POL CHINAT–FR, political affairs and relations, Republic of China and France
POL CHINAT–US, political affairs and relations, Republic of China and the United States
POL HK, political affairs and relations, Hong Kong
POL HK–US, political affairs and relations, Hong Kong and the United States
POL MONG–US, political affairs and relations, Mongolia and the United States
POL 1 ASIA SE–US, U.S. general policy toward Southeast Asia
POL 1 CHICOM, U.S. general policy toward the People's Republic of China
POL 1 CHICOM–FR, general policy, People's Republic of China and France
POL 1 CHICOM–US, U.S. general policy toward the People's Republic of China
POL 1 CHINAT–FR, Republic of China general policy toward France
POL 1 CHINAT–US, U.S. general policy toward the Republic of China
POL 1 CHINAT–VIET S, Republic of China general policy toward South Vietnam
POL 1–3 CHICOM, general policy evaluation, People's Republic of China
POL 2 CHICOM, general reports and statistics, People's Republic of China
POL 2 CHINAT, general reports and statistics, Republic of China
POL 2 US, general reports and statistics, United States
POL 7 CHINAT, travel and visits by high-level Republic of China officials
POL 7 JAPAN, visits of Japanese leaders
POL 7 ROM, travel and visits by high-level Romanian officials
POL 7 US/BUNDY, travel by McGeorge Bundy

POL 7 US/GOLDBERG, travel by Arthur Goldberg
POL 7 USSR, travel and visits by high-level Soviet officials
POL 13–2 CHICOM, People's Republic of China students and youth groups
POL 15–1 CHINAT, Republic of China head of state
POL 15–1 CHICOM, People's Republic of China head of state
POL 15–1 US/JOHNSON, President Johnson's meetings and correspondence with heads of state
POL 16 CHICOM, independence and recognition, People's Republic of China
POL 16 CHINAT, independence and recognition, Republic of China
POL 16 MONG, question of recognition of Mongolia
POL 17 CHICOM–FR, diplomatic and consular representation, People's Republic of China and France
POL 17 CHINAT–FR, diplomatic and consular representation, Republic of China and France
POL 17 CHINAT–US, Republic of China diplomatic and consular representation in the United States
POL 17 CHINAT–CONGO, diplomatic and consular representation, Republic of China-Congo
POL 17 FR–CHICOM, French diplomatic and consular representation in the People's Republic of China
POL 17 ROM–POL, Romanian diplomatic and consular representation in Poland
POL 19 TIBET, political issues concerning Tibet
POL 19 TIBET/UN, the Tibet issue in the United Nations
POL 19 TIBET/US, U.S. policy with respect to Tibet
POL 23–8 HK, demonstrations, riots, protests, Hong Kong
POL 23–10 COMBLOC, travel controls, Communist Bloc countries
POL 27 CHICOM–CHINAT, military operations, People's Republic of China–Republic of China
POL 27 VIET S, military operations, South Vietnam
POL 27–7 CHICOM–US, U.S. prisoners of war, hostages, civilian internees in the People's Republic of China
POL 29 CHINAT, political prisoners, Republic of China
POL 30–2 TIBET, Tibetan exile political activities
POL 31–1 CHICOM–US, air disputes and violations, People's Republic of China and the United States
POL 32–1 CHICOM–USSR, territory and boundary disputes, violations, incidents, People's Republic of China and the U.S.S.R.
SP 1 US, U.S. general policy on space
STR 13–3, strategic trade controls on trade with the People's Republic of China
UN 3 GA, United Nations General Assembly
UN 6 CHICOM, Chinese representation question in the United Nations

Lyndon B. Johnson Library, Austin, Texas

Papers of President Lyndon B. Johnson

National Security File

Agency File: Central Intelligence Agency, United Nations

McGeorge Bundy Files

Country File: China, France, Poland, United Nations, U.S.S.R.

Head of State Correspondence File: China

International Meetings and Travel File

Robert W. Komer Files

Memos to the President: McGeorge Bundy, Walt W. Rostow

Name File: Jenkins Memos, Jorden Memos, Senator Mansfield, Moyers Memos, Thomson Memos

National Security Council Meetings File

Walt W. Rostow Files

Special Head of State Correspondence File: China, Tibet

White House Central File

Confidential File

Subject File: Nuclear Testing, China

Intelligence File

Special Files

Tom Johnson's Notes of Meeting

Meeting Notes File

Office of the President File

President's Daily Diary

Recordings and Transcripts of Telephone Conversations and Meetings

Other Personal Papers

George Ball Papers

Dean Rusk Papers, Personal Appointment Books

Central Intelligence Agency, Langley, Virginia

ODDI Registry of National Intelliegnce Estimates and Special National Intelligence Estimates, Job 79–R01012A

DCI Files, Job 80–B01285A

Files of Directors of Central Intelligence John A. McCone (1961–1965), William F. Raborn (1965–1966), and Richard M. Helms (1966–1973.)

DCI Executive Registry, Job 80–B01676R

Library of Congress, Manuscript Division, Washington, D.C

Harriman Papers

Papers of W. Averell Harriman, Special Files: Public Service, Kennedy and Johnson Administrations, 1958–1971.

National Defense University, Washington, D.C.

Taylor Papers

Papers of Maxwell D. Taylor, Military Adviser to the President, 1961–1962, and Chairman of the Joint Chiefs of Staff, 1962–1964.

Washington National Records Center, Suitland, Maryland

Record Group 330, Records of the Office of the Secretary of Defense

OASD/ISA Files: FRC 68 A 306

Files of the Assistant Secretary of Defense for International Security Affairs, 1964.

OASD/ISA Files: FRC 70 A 3717

Files of the Assistant Secretary of Defense for International Security Affairs, 1965.

OASD/ISA Files: FRC 70 A 5127

Top Secret files of the Assistant Secretary of Defense for International Security Affairs, 1965.

OASD/ISA Files: FRC 70 A 6648

Files of the Assistant Secretary of Defense for International Security Affairs, 1966.

OSD Files: FRC 69 A 7425

Top Secret files of the Secretary of Defense, Deputy Assistant Secretary of Defense, and Special Assistants, 1964.

OSD Files: FRC 70 A 1265

Top Secret files of the Secretary of Defense, Deputy Assistant Secretary of Defense, and Special Assistants, 1965.

OSD Files: FRC 70 A 1266

Secret files of the Secretary of Defense, Deputy Assistant Secretary of Defense, and Special Assistants, 1965.

OSD Files: FRC 70 A 4443

Files of the Secretary of Defense, Deputy Assistant Secretary of Defense, and Special Assistants, 1966.

OSD Files: FRC 72 A 2468

Files of the Secretary of Defense, Deputy Assistant Secretary of Defense, and Special Assistants, 1967.

OSD Files: FRC 73 A 1250

Files of the Secretary of Defense, Deputy Assistant Secretary of Defense, and Special Assistants, 1968.

OSD Files: FRC 91–0017

Top Secret files of the Secretary of Defense, Deputy Assistant Secretary of Defense, and Special Assistants, 1949–1969.

Abbreviations

AA, Afro-Asian
AB, Air Base
ABM, anti-ballistic missile
ACA, Office of Asian Communist Affairs, Bureau of Far Eastern Affairs (East Asian and Pacific Affairs after November 1, 1966, Department of State
ACDA, Arms Control and Disarmament Agency
ACDA/IR, International Relations Bureau, Arms Control and Disarmament Agency
AEC, Atomic Energy Commission
AF, Bureau of African Affairs, Department of State
AICBM, air-launched intercontinental ballistic missile
AID, Agency for International Development
Amb, Ambassador
AmConsul, American Consul
ANZUS, Australia, New Zealand, United States
APD, high-speed transport
ARA, Bureau of Inter-American Affairs, Department of State
ASAP, as soon as possible

CA, circular airgram
CAF, Chinese Air Force (Republic of China)
CanDel, Canadian Delegation
CAS, Controlled American Source
CAT, Civil Air Transport
CBC, Canadian Broadcasting Corporation
CCA, Chinese Communist Army
CCK, Chiang Ching-kuo; also Ching Chuan Kang Air Base
CCN, Chinese Communist Navy
CCNE, Chinese Communist nuclear explosion
CCP, Chinese Communist Party
ChiCom, Chinese Communist(s)
ChiDel, Chinese Delegation
ChiNat, Chinese Nationalist(s)
ChiRep, Chinese representation
CHMAAG, Chief, Military Assistance Advisory Group
CIA, Central Intelligence Agency
CINCPAC, Commander in Chief, Pacific
CJCS, Chairman, Joint Chiefs of Staff
COCOM, Coordinating Committee on Export Control
COMINT, Communications intelligence
COMUSMACV, Commander, U.S. Military Assistance Command, Vietnam
COMUSTDC, Commander, U.S. Taiwan Defense Command
ConGen, Consulate General
CONUS, Continental United States
CPR, Chinese People's Republic
CU, Bureau of Educational and Cultural Affairs, Department of State

DCI, Director of Central Intelligence
DCM, Deputy Chief of Mission
DDCI, Deputy Director of Central Intelligence
DDP, Deputy Director for Plans, Central Intelligence Agency

DefMin, Defense Minister
Del, delegation
Dept, Department of State
Deptel, Department of State telegram
DOD, Department of Defense
DOD/ISA, Office of the Assistant Secretary of Defense for International Security Affairs, Department of Defense
DRV, Democratic Republic of Vietnam (North Vietnam)

EA/RA, Office of Regional Affairs, Bureau of Far Eastern Affairs (East Asian and Pacific Affairs after November 1, 1966), Department of State
EA/ROC, Republic of China Affairs, Office of East Asian Affairs, Bureau of Far Eastern Affairs (East Asian and Pacific Affairs after November 1, 1966), Department of State
ECAFE, Economic Commission for Asia and the Far East (UN)
ECOSOC, Economic and Social Council (UN)
Embtel, Embassy telegram
EST, Eastern Standard Time
EUR, Bureau of European Affairs, Department of State
EUR/CAN, Country Director for Canada, Bureau of European Affairs, Department of State
Exdis, Exclusive Distribution

FAC, Foreign Assets Control
FBI, Federal Bureau of Investigation
FBIS, Foreign Broadcast Information Service
FE, Far East; also Bureau of Far Eastern Affairs, Department of State
FonMin, Foreign Minister
FRG, Federal Republic of Germany
FSO, Foreign Service officer
FY, fiscal year
FYI, for your information

GA, General Assembly (UN)
GIMO, Generalissimo Chiang Kai-shek
GNP, Gross National Product
GOC, Government of Canada; Government of the Congo
GOI, Government of India
GOJ, Government of Japan
govt, government
GRC, Government of the Republic of China
GVN, Government of Vietnam (South)

HK, Hong Kong
HKG, Hong Kong Government

IBMND, Intelligence Bureau of the Ministry of National Defense (Republic of China)
IC, Indochina
ICBM, intercontinental ballistic missile
ICC, International Control Commission
ICFTU, International Confederation of Free Trade Unions
ICJ, International Court of Justice
ICRC, International Committee of the Red Cross
ILO, International Labor Organization
info, information
INR, Bureau of Intelligence and Research, Department of State

INR/RFE, Office of Research and Analysis for Far East, Bureau of Intelligence and Research, Department of State
intel, intelligence
INTELSAT, International Telecommunications Satellite Corporation
IO, Bureau of International Organization Affairs, Department of State
IQ, important question
IRG, Interdepartmental Regional Group
ISA, Bureau of International Security Affairs, Department of Defense
ITU, International Telecommunications Union (UN)

JCRR, Joint Commission on Rural Reconstruction
JCS, Joint Chiefs of Staff
JCSM, Joint Chiefs of Staff Memorandum
JOC, Joint Operations Center

KMT, Kuomintang (Nationalist Party, Republic of China)
KT, kilotons

L, Office of the Legal Adviser, Department of State
Limdis, Limited Distribution

MAAG, Military Assistance Advisory Group
MAP, Military Assistance/Aid Program
MIG, A.I. Mikoyan i M.I. Gurevich (Soviet fighter aircraft named for designers Mikoyan and Gurevich)
MinDef, Minister of Defense
MisOff, Mission Office
MLF, Multilateral force
MND, Ministry of National Defense (Republic of China)
MOD, Minister of Defense
MOFA, Ministry of Foreign Affairs
MPR, Mongolian People's Republic
MRBM, medium-range ballistic missile

NATO, North Atlantic Treaty Organization
NEA, Bureau of Near Eastern and South Asian Affairs, Department of State
NFLSV, National Front for the Liberation of South Vietnam
NIE, National Intelligence Estimate
Noforn, No foreign dissemination
NSAM, National Security Action Memorandum
NSC, National Security Council
NVN, North Vietnam
NW, Northwest

OASD/ISA, Office of the Assistant Secretary of Defense for International Security Affairs
ONE, Office of National Estimates, Central Intelligence Agency
OSD, Office of the Secretary of Defense

PACAF, Pacific Air Force (U.S.)
para, paragraph
PL, Public Law; also Pathet Lao (Communist Party in Laos)
PLA, People's Liberation Army (People's Republic of China)
POL, petroleum, oil, and lubricants
POLAD, political adviser
PRC, People's Republic of China

Pres, President
PZPR, Polish United Workers' Party

reftel, reference telegram
Res, Resolution
RG, Record Group
RLG, Royal Laotian Government
ROC, Republic of China
ROK, Republic of Korea
R&R, rest and recuperation
RVN, Republic of Vietnam (South)
RVNAF, Republic of Vietnam Air Force

S, Office of the Secretary of State
SAC, Strategic Air Command
SAM, surface-to-surface missiles
SC, Security Council (UN)
SCA, Bureau of Security and Consular Affairs, Department of State
SCI, Bureau of International Scientific and Technological Affairs, Department of State
SEA, Southeast Asia
SEATO, Southeast Asia Treaty Organization
SecDef, Secretary of Defense
Secy, Secretary of State
Secy Gen, Secretary-General (UN)
septel, separate telegram
SIG, Senior Interdepartmental Group
SNIE, Special National Intelligence Estimate
Sov(s), Soviet(s)
S/P, Policy Planning Council, Department of State
SVN, South Vietnam
SVNLF, South Vietnam Liberation Front
SYG, Secretary-General (UN)

TDC, Taiwan Defense Command

U, Office of the Under Secretary of State
UK, United Kingdom
UN, United Nations
UNESCO, United Nations Educational, Scientific and Cultural Organization
UNGA, United Nations General Assembly
UNTS, United Nations Treaty Series
UPI, United Press International
UPU, Universal Postal Union
USAF, United States Air Force
USG, United States Government
USIB, United States Intelligence Board
USIS, United States Information Service
USN, United States Navy
USRO, United States Mission to European Regional Organizations (in Paris)
USSR, Union of Soviet Socialist Republics
USUN, United States Mission at the United Nations

VC, Viet Cong
VN, Vietnam

VOA, Voice of America
VP, Vice President

WDC, World Disarmament Conference
WHO, World Health Organization (UN)
WMO, World Meteorological Organization (UN)

YCL, Young Communist League

Persons

Aldrich, George, Assistant Legal Adviser for East Asian and Pacific Affairs, Department of State, from July 1965

Alphand, Hervé, French Ambassador to the United States until October 1965

Bacon, Leonard L., Acting Director, Office of East Asian Affairs, Bureau of Far Eastern Affairs, Department of State, until July 1964

Ball, George W., Under Secretary of State until September 1966; Representative to the United Nations, June–September 1968

Barnett, Robert W., Deputy Assistant Secretary of State for Far Eastern Economic Affairs until October 1966; Deputy Assistant Secretary of State for East Asian and Pacific Affairs, November 1966–June 1968

Bennett, Josiah, Deputy Director, Office of East Asian Affairs, Bureau of Far Eastern Affairs (East Asian and Pacific Affairs after November 1, 1966), Department of State, July 1964–June 1966; Officer in Charge of Republic of China Affairs, June 1966–October 1967

Berger, Samuel D., Deputy Assistant Secretary of State for Far Eastern Affairs (East Asian and Pacific Affairs after November 1, 1966) from July 1965 until January 1968

Bohlen, Charles E., Ambassador to France until February 1968; thereafter Deputy Under Secretary of State for Political Affairs

Brown, Winthrop G., Deputy Assistant Secretary of State for East Asian and Pacific Affairs from May 1968

Buffum, William B., Director, Office of United Nations Political and Security Affairs, Bureau of International Organization Affairs, Department of State, until August 1965; Deputy Assistant Secretary for International Organization Affairs, September 1965–December 1966

Bundy, McGeorge, Special Assistant to the President for National Security Affairs until February 1966; Executive Secretary of the Special Committee of the National Security Council, June–August 1967

Bundy, William P., Assistant Secretary of State for Far Eastern Affairs (East Asian and Pacific Affairs after November 1, 1966), March 1964–May 1969

Cabot, John M., Ambassador to Poland until September 1965

Carter, Lieutenant General Marshall S., Deputy Director of Central Intelligence until April 1965

Chase, Gordon, staff member, National Security Council, until January 1966

Chen I, Foreign Minister of the People's Republic of China

Chew, Vice Admiral John L., Commander, U.S. Taiwan Defense Command

Chiang Ching-kuo, General, Defense Minister of the Republic of China from January 1965

Chiang Kai-shek, President of the Republic of China

Chou En-lai (Zhou Enlai), Premier of the People's Republic of China

Chow Shu-kai, Ambassador of the Republic of China to the United States from February 1966

Ciccolella, Major General R. G., Chief, Military Assistance Advisory Group, Taiwan

Cleveland, J. Harlan, Assistant Secretary of State for International Organization Affairs until September 1965

Cline, Ray S., Deputy Director for Intelligence, Central Intelligence Agency, until January 1966

Clough, Ralph N., Counselor of Embassy, Consul General, and Deputy Chief of Mission at the Embassy in Taiwan until August 1965

Couve de Murville, Maurice, French Foreign Minister until May 1968; thereafter Minister of Finance and Economic Affairs

De Gaulle, Charles, President of France

Dean, David, Officer in Charge of Mainland China Affairs, Bureau of Far Eastern Affairs, Department of State, until May 1965; Deputy Director, Office of Asian Communist Affairs, May 1965–July 1966

Dobrynin, Anatoliy F., Soviet Ambassador to the United States

Fearey, Robert A., Acting Deputy Director, Office of East Asian Affairs, Bureau of Far Eastern Affairs, Department of State, until July 1964; Director until July 1966

Felt, Admiral Harry D., Commander in Chief, Pacific, until June 1964

Forrestal, Michael V., staff member, National Security Council, until April 1964

Freeman, Orville L., Secretary of Agriculture

Gaud, William S., Administrator, Agency for International Development, from August 1966

Getsinger, Norman W., Officer in Charge, Republic of China Affairs, Bureau of Far Eastern Affairs, Department of State, August 1964–June 1966

Gleysteen, William H., Jr., Deputy Director, Office of United Nations Political Affairs, Bureau of International Organization Affairs, Department of State, from August 1966

Goldberg, Arthur J., Representative to the United Nations, July 1965–June 1968

Grant, Lindsey, Acting Director, Office of Asian Communist Affairs, Bureau of Far Eastern Affairs, Department of State, until April 1964; Director, May 1964–July 1965

Green, Marshall, Deputy Assistant Secretary of State for Far Eastern Affairs, September 1963–June 1965

Gromyko, Andrei A., Soviet Foreign Minister

Gronouski, John A., Ambassador to Poland, December 1965–May 1968

Harriman, W. Averell, Under Secretary of State for Political Affairs until March 1965; thereafter Ambassador at Large

Helms, Richard M., Deputy Director for Plans, Central Intelligence Agency, until April 1965; Deputy Director of Central Intelligence, April 1965–June 1966; thereafter Director

Hilsman, Roger, Jr., Assistant Secretary of State for Far Eastern Affairs until March 1964

Holdridge, John H., Deputy Director, Office of Research and Analysis for East Asia and Pacific, Bureau of Intelligence and Research, Department of State, August 1966–April 1968; thereafter Director

Hummel, Arthur W., Jr., Deputy Chief of Mission at the Embassy in Taiwan, August 1965–November 1967

Humphrey, Hubert H., Vice President of the United States from January 1965

Jacobson, Harald W., Director, Office of Asian Communist Affairs, Bureau of Far Eastern Affairs (East Asian and Pacific Affairs from November 1, 1966), Department of State, August 1965–August 1968

Jenkins, Alfred LeS., staff member, National Security Council, from July 1966

Jessup, Peter, staff member, National Security Council, from January 1964

Johnson, Lyndon B., President of the United States

Johnson, U. Alexis, Deputy Under Secretary of State for Political Affairs until July 1964; also November 1965–October 1966; thereafter Ambassador to Japan

Jorden, William J., staff member, National Security Council, from May 1966 until May 1968

Katzenbach, Nicholas deB., Under Secretary of State from October 1966

Kiang Yi-seng, Minister of the Republic of China to the United States until December 1964

Kohler, Foy D., Deputy Under Secretary of State for Political Affairs, November 1966–December 1967

Komer, Robert W., staff member, National Security Council until September 1965; Deputy Special Assistant to the President for National Security Affairs, October 1965–March 1966; Special Assistant to the President, March 1966–May 1967; thereafter Special Assistant to the President for Peaceful Reconstruction in Vietnam

Kreisberg, Paul H., Officer in Charge of Mainland China Affairs, Bureau of Far Eastern Affairs (East Asian and Pacific Affairs after November 1, 1966), Department of State, from May 1965

Li Kwoh-ting, Minister of Economic Affairs of the Republic of China from February 1965

Lin Piao (Lin Biao), Deputy Premier and Minister of Defense of the People's Republic of China

MacArthur, Douglas, II, Deputy Assistant Secretary of State for Congressional Relations, March 1965–March 1967

Mao Tse-tung (Mao Zedong), Chairman of the Central Committee of the People's Republic of China

Martin, Edwin W., Consul General in Hong Kong from September 1967

Martin, Paul, Canadian Secretary of State for External Affairs until April 1968

McConaughy, Walter P., Jr., Ambassador to the Republic of China from June 1966

McCone, John A., Director of Central Intelligence until April 1965

McNamara, Robert S., Secretary of Defense until February 1968

McNaughton, John T., Assistant Secretary of Defense for International Security Affairs, July 1964–July 1967

Meeker, Leonard C., Legal Adviser, Department of State, from May 1965

Moyers, Bill D., Special Assistant to the President, 1964–1967

Pearson, Lester B., Prime Minister of Canada until April 1968

Popper, David H., Deputy Assistant Secretary of State for International Organization Affairs from September 1965

Popple, Paul M., Officer in Charge, Republic of China Affairs, Bureau of Far Eastern Affairs, Department of State, until July 1964

Read, Benjamin H., Special Assistant to the Secretary of State and Executive Secretary of the Department of State

Rice, Edward E., Consul General in Hong Kong and Macau, January 1964–September 1967

Ritchie, A. Edgar, Canadian Ambassador to the United States from March 1966

Roche, John P., Special Consultant to the President, 1966–1968

Rostow, Eugene V., Under Secretary of State for Political Affairs from October 1966

Rostow, Walt W., Counselor of the Department of State and Chairman of the Policy Planning Council until March 1966; thereafter, Special Assistant to the President

Rusk, Dean, Secretary of State

Sharp, Admiral U.S. Grant, Commander in Chief, Pacific, June 1964–August 1968

Sharp, W. Mitchell, Canadian Secretary of State for External Affairs from May 1968

Shen Chang-huan, Foreign Minister of the Republic of China until May 1968

Shen, Sampson (Shen Chi), Vice Minister of Foreign Affairs of the Republic of China until June 1968

Shoesmith, Thomas P., Officer in Charge of Republic of China Affairs, Bureau of East Asian and Pacific Affairs, Department of State, from October 1967

Sisco, Joseph J., Assistant Secretary of State for International Organization Affairs from September 1965

Smith, Bromley K., Executive Secretary, National Security Council

Stevenson, Adlai E., Representative to the United Nations until July 1965

Stoessel, Walter J., Jr., Deputy Assistant Secretary of State for European Affairs, September 1965–July 1968; thereafter Ambassador to Poland

Thompson, Llewellyn E., Ambassador at Large until December 1966

Thomson, James C., Jr., Special Assistant to the Assistant Secretary of State for Far Eastern Affairs until July 1964; staff member, National Security Council, July 1964–September 1966

Tsiang Ting-fu, Ambassador from the Republic of China to the United States until June 1965

Tyler, William R., Assistant Secretary of State for European Affairs until May 1965

Valenti, Jack, Special Assistant to the President until May 1966

Vance, Cyrus R., Deputy Secretary of Defense, January 1964–June 1967

Wang Kuo-ch'uan (Wang Guoquan), Ambassador of the People's Republic of China to Poland; representative of the People's Republic of China in ambassadorial talks with the United States from July 1964

Wang Ping-nan (Wang Bingnan), Ambassador of the People's Republic of China to Poland; representative of the People's Republic of China in ambassadorial talks with the United States until April 1964

Wei Tao-ming, Foreign Minister of the Republic of China from June 1966

Wheeler, General Earle G., Chief of Staff, U.S. Army, until July 1964; thereafter Chairman of the Joint Chiefs of Staff

Wright, Admiral Jerauld (Ret.), Ambassador to the Republic of China until July 1965

Yen Chia-kan, Prime Minister and Vice President of the Republic of China

Yu Ta-wei, Defense Minister of the Republic of China until January 1965

Zhou Enlai, *see* Chou En-lai

China

1. **Telegram From the Department of State to the Embassy in France**[1]

Washington, January 15, 1964, 6:01 p.m.

3539. For Ambassador Bohlen. Alphand called on Harriman under instructions 2:15 pm January 15. Said he was instructed see Harriman because Secretary not available.

Alphand reviewed recent history US-French conversations regarding possible French recognition Communist China recalling fact de Gaulle had told Secretary French would be in touch with US before carrying out any decision[2] and mentioned January 7 Bohlen–Couve conversation[3] where Couve said decision made to recognize Red China but this would be confirmed later. This was reason Alphand now seeing Harriman.

Alphand said French Cabinet has decided to recognize Communist China. Announcement will be made in "next several weeks". Exchange of Ambassadors will take place three months after communiqué. Alphand said he had been instructed to stress:

(1) France would not accept conditions from Peiping. This means France will not break relations with Taiwan. He professed not to know what would happen but said there will probably be a unilateral statement from Peiping saying that government represents all of China. France does not accept this version but is not required to make a public statement. French relations with Taiwan will remain unchanged unless Taiwan chooses to break relations.

(2) France made no concession or decision regarding the position it will take in the UN. France has reserved its freedom of decision on this matter although clearly a position must be taken in the next General Assembly.

Alphand emphasized Paris had not "yielded to any demand from Peiping" and requested the matter remain secret until public announcement made.

---

[1] Source: Department of State, Central Files, POL 16 CHICOM. Secret; Immediate; Exdis. Drafted by Director of the Office of Western European Affairs Francis E. Meloy, and approved by Harriman.

[2] Rusk reported the conversation in telegram Secto 25 from Paris, December 16, 1963; see *Foreign Relations*, 1961–1963, vol. XXII, pp. 409–410.

[3] Reported in telegram 3177 from Paris, January 8. (Department of State, Central Files, POL 16 CHICOM)

Harriman said report had just been received from Ambassador Bohlen of his talk today with Couve on this same subject.[4] Bohlen had made clear and Harriman wished to underline this decision by France was very disturbing to the US and to other governments as well. Harriman emphasized he was speaking personally and without instructions but as well-known long-time warm friend of France. Response of President and US government would no doubt be forthcoming in due time. French action would be in direct conflict with fundamental US interests. It could not help having cooling effect on US popular feeling towards France. This was not an action we would have expected from an ally. It would seem the only gain to France is the assertion of its independence for the sake of asserting independence. This was an act on the part of France which can do no good to anyone and can do great harm to many.

Harriman continued still on personal basis saying de Gaulle must have known the effect of such a decision on the US. There was little to gain for France and there would be great damage to the US. The Ambassador must realize what the effect would be if US and French roles were reversed.

Alphand said he did not understand Harriman's reaction. Others have recognized Communist China. Harriman reminded him these actions had been prior to Korean war.

Alphand said he also would speak personally and unofficially. He failed completely to understand this reaction. Harriman said Alphand was one of ablest and cleverest diplomats he knew. Alphand knew exactly what he meant. Harriman said French action would create doubt in Asia and would give a boost to Communist China. French action would create great difficulty for people and government and President of US. It was clear decision had been taken with total disregard of important US interests. France will be throwing away a great deal of good will and affection here in the US only for the sake of demonstrating its independence of US policy.

Harriman pointed out US has great responsibilities in the Far East, although we welcomed France taking more responsibility in such places as Laos and Cambodia. However, basic problem is containing Communist China and France can contribute very little as far as this basic problem is concerned. Burden rests squarely on US and France is strengthening our enemy. The Korean war has never been settled. Other areas of Asia are seething with Communist-supported conflicts. France has chosen the moment when our enemy is weak to help him.

---

[4] Bohlen reported the conversation in telegram 3344 from Paris, January 15. (Department of State, Central Files, POL 17 FR–CHICOM)

Harriman closed by reminding Alphand his reactions had been personal and unofficial but he felt they would be shared by many Americans.

Rusk

---

2.   **Editorial Note**

In a telephone conversation between President Johnson and Senator Richard Russell at 4:30 p.m. on January 15, 1964, Johnson told Russell that "de Gaulle's going to recognize Communist China" and that the question was whether he should send a personal message to de Gaulle with a strong protest or send a lower-level protest for the record. His inclination was to do the latter. Russell told the President he "wouldn't go too strong on it" because de Gaulle would not pay much attention. Russell added, "The time's going to come when we might well—can't talk about it now—the time's going to come when we're going to have to recognize them." Johnson replied, "Yeah, I think so—don't think there's any question about it." Russell went on, "I ain't too sure but what we'd have been better off if we'd recognized them three-four years ago." Johnson replied, "I think so. It's the only thing Bill Douglas [Supreme Court Justice William O. Douglas] said—" Russell broke in, "Politically, right now it's poison, of course." The conversation then turned to other subjects. At the end of the conversation, Johnson returned to the subject of how to respond to the French action: "About this de Gaulle thing, you just think we ought to play it as low key and just make a little protest for the record." Russell agreed. (Johnson Library, Recordings and Transcripts, Recording of a Telephone Conversation Between Johnson and Russell, January 15, 1964, 4:30 p.m., Tape F64.06, PNO 1)

In a conversation between the President and his Special Assistant for National Security Affairs McGeorge Bundy later that day, Bundy told the President, "The one chance that we can frustrate de Gaulle is to get Chiang to stand still for a week or so. If he would not break his relations with the French, which is what he's always done when people recognize Peking before, this would put the monkey right back on Peking's back, because they have maintained a position that they can't recognize anybody who also recognizes Formosa. What the French hope is that Chiang will break relations right away, and that is probably what he'll do. We want to advise him to stand still for a week. Is that all right with you?" Johnson agreed. (Ibid., Recording of a Telephone Conversation Between Johnson and Bundy, January 15, 1964, 6:30 p.m., Tape F64.06, PNO 2)

---

3.   Telegram From the Department of State to the Embassy in the Republic of China[1]

Washington, January 16, 1964, 5:46 p.m.

587. Please deliver soonest following letter to President Chiang from President Johnson:[2]

"My dear Mr. President:

Your Government has been informed of reliable indications we have that the French Government intends to recognize the Chinese Communist regime in the near future. We have also learned that the Chinese Communists are prepared to accept French recognition without imposing any condition and that France intends to maintain its diplomatic relations with your Government.

I want you to know that the United States has done everything possible to deter the French Government from this ill-advised action. We have told the French at the highest levels that French recognition of the Peiping regime can only damage free world interests. We have asked France to reconsider its intention. We know that other governments are doing the same.

Despite our efforts, there is no indication of change in France's attitude. We understand that Paris and Peiping intend to exchange Ambassadors three months after announcing diplomatic ties. In this situation it is vitally important for our two Governments to work closely together to reduce by all means the ill effects of this event.

It is clear that the Chinese Communists will strongly resent continued French relations with your Government, and hope that your Gov-

---

[1] Source: Department of State, Central Files, POL 16 CHICOM. Secret; Immediate; Exdis. Drafted by Green and Officer in Charge of Republic of China Affairs Paul M. Popple, cleared by Harriman and the President, and approved by Rusk.

[2] Telegram 600 from Taipei, January 18, reported that Ambassador Wright had delivered the message that day. Chiang told him that he was awaiting a message from de Gaulle responding to a message Chiang had sent asking whether there was any truth to rumors that France might establish a trade mission in Peking or recognize the Communist government. (Ibid.)

ernment will take the initiative in severing relations with France as a result of French recognition of their regime. Mao Tse-tung is undoubtedly gambling on your Government doing just this, thereby relieving him from the burden of appearing to accept a 'two China' situation. Therefore, I believe it would be extremely wise for you to refrain from retaliatory action against France at this time. Your patience will cause Mao Tse-tung the greatest possible embarrassment. It will greatly reduce the advantages which the Chinese Communists expect to gain by the establishment of relations with France.

Finally, I wish to give you my personal assurance that we shall continue to stand by you and your Government and to provide all possible support in our common endeavors.

Warmest personal regards.

Lyndon B. Johnson"

Rusk

---

4.   **Circular Telegram From the Department of State to the Embassy in France**[1]

Washington, January 18, 1964, 3:28 p.m.

1291. For Ambassador. Alphand called on Secretary at his own request 6:30 PM January 17. Alphand said US had presented note previous day saying French decision recognize Communist China "against security and political interests of free world."[2] He had note in response (which he presented) saying France thinks its action not against interests of free world.[3] In Harriman/Alphand conversation January 15, Harriman had said he saw no reason for French action except assert independence and embarrass US. This was not so. Alphand pointed out Western nations which recognized Communist China prior to Korean war had

---

[1] Source: Department of State, Central Files, POL 17 CHICOM–FR. Secret; Priority; Exdis. Drafted by Meloy on January 17, cleared by Tyler, and approved by Rusk. Repeated to London, Bonn, Rome, Tokyo for the Attorney General, Taipei, Brussels, Ottawa, and Saigon.

[2] Dated January 16; the text is quoted in telegram 3545 to Paris, January 15. (Ibid., POL 16 CHICOM)

[3] Filed as an attachment to telegram 3614 to Paris, January 18. (Ibid.)

not broken relations during war. It was now twelve years later and France believed it should act. First point he wished to make was France did not consider recognition meant approval. Second point was Soviet Union and Communist China no longer monolithic bloc. Previously there was no need to talk to Peiping. One could talk to Moscow as the master of Peiping. There is now a split in the bloc and one must talk directly to Peiping. Contrary to US belief France may be able to achieve something useful through this channel, speaking especially of Asia and Southeast Asia in particular. Alphand stressed establishment diplomatic relations France has in view is without commitment. There is no requirement to break relations with Taiwan and nothing is said about the United Nations.

Alphand said he was surprised by text of US note. France hopes US will not think its action done as a gesture against US but that there are other reasons.

Secretary said Harriman had pointed out he was speaking personally and as old well-known friend of France. Secretary would now speak officially. Recognition will increase the prestige of Peiping. Since Korean war no country comparing in prestige to France has recognized Communist China. France must consider the effect of its action. If France finds American people react strongly, France must realize we are taking casualties every day. Just a short time ago we found 7 tons of Chinese Communist made arms south of Saigon. We are spitting blood.

Secretary continued we do not believe agreement can be reached with China through means adopted by France. Communist China does not respect its agreements. President Kennedy felt we took French views into full account over Laos. We expect our views to be considered by France now.

Secretary said Alphand had claimed recognition does not mean approval but it will be so interpreted. He had reviewed with Alphand many times our views on Communist China. US is aiding India resist Chinese Communist aggression. Chicoms are active in subversion in Latin America. Secretary pointed out if French action leads to Chinese Communist subversive centers in Africa, this will be more of problem for France than for US.

Secretary said Alphand had mentioned no conditions imposed on France by Peiping. He emphasized there were also no conditions imposed by France on Peiping, such as even minimum requirement for Chinese Communists to honor commitments in Southeast Asia.

Alphand protested French position not taken to oppose US. France believed its action might be beneficial to all. France was doing only what others have long since done. French recognition might be useful in obtaining agreement at conference to neutralize Cambodia. Secretary said 1954 Agreement already exists which Chicoms are not honoring. It is possible to have contacts with Chinese Communists without recognizing them. There is very slight chance US would attend a conference on Cambodia.

Tyler asked if French Government had assessed probable effect on Taiwan. Alphand said relations with Peiping did not prevent relations with Taiwan. Secretary said Peiping may be gambling on Taiwan breaking relations. If Taiwan does not break relations is France not exposing itself to rebuff by Peiping?

Secretary said he would not judge how France regards its national interest, but he would think French relations with NATO, SEATO, the United States and Southeast Asia would be worth more than its relations with Peiping because all these other relations would be affected.

Alphand said he could not control US press, public or congressional reaction, but US Government could at least say French action not taken against US. As to timing there comes a time when one must do what one has long felt is right.

Secretary inquired how France intends to handle Africa. Alphand said France does not intend to dictate but does not know if French African states will follow example of France.

Secretary said two things will erode attitude of American people toward alliance in coming months: 1) recognition of Communist China; and 2) Western European trade with Cuba. If Western European countries consider these problems as matters for each alone to decide, then US attitude will be seriously eroded. Secretary was very much concerned over alliance in next three months.

Secretary said we can understand that our allies do not give same priority as US to matters in Pacific. US however is bearing burdens both in Europe and in Far East. If we find in carrying out our responsibilities our position is being weakened or undermined, this is bound to affect our relations. Secretary said if French decision irrevocable then it is duty both governments to circumscribe and attempt to limit damage which will inevitably be caused.

Alphand said he would report Secretary's views to Paris.

Rusk

5.   Telegram From the Department of State to the Embassy in the Republic of China[1]

Washington, January 18, 1964, 5:01 p.m.

607. Following is FYI Noforn subject to amendment upon review based upon uncleared memcon:

1. Secretary called in Amb. Tsiang January 18 to discuss French intention recognize Chinese Communists. Secretary told Tsiang:

a. That it our impression de Gaulle has made personal decision which not likely be changed, although we have not completely abandoned hope.

b. That USG regards de Gaulle's action this matter almost intolerable for many reasons, but particularly in light Chicom involvement South Vietnam where US troops incurring almost daily casualties.

c. That USG had lodged strong protest with France requesting reconsideration and had asked allies do same. In this connection, Secretary cited support from Germany and Italy, but particularly emphasized vigorous efforts Japanese had made on behalf GRC and in attempt to forestall French recognition Chicoms. Secretary told Tsiang it was most important that GRC aware these Japanese efforts and that it would be helpful if GRC could find some way express its appreciation, particularly in light recent acrimony over Chou Hung-ching case which has led to deterioration GRC-GOJ relations.

d. That there was absolutely no two-China sentiment in USG. That to cast doubt on USG firm opposition two-China concept could have most serious repercussions at this stage, particularly in Africa.

e. That USG understood GRC concern over two-China connotations, but felt best course for GRC to follow at present juncture was to stand fast and to take no immediate retaliatory action against France.

f. That if GRC sits tight, Peiping may find situation intolerable, since there good chance both French and Chicoms gambling on provoking GRC into breaking off relations with France.

g. That USG not suggesting GRC make definitive decision at this time but merely put Chicoms to maximum test.

h. That should Chicoms go ahead with exchange of Ambassadors without GRC-French break, then GRC would have to make own decision in light prevailing circumstances.

i. That GRC should avoid giving France any normal pretext, e.g. anti-French demonstrations in Taipei, for severing relations with GRC.

---

[1] Source: Department of State, Central Files, POL 17 CHICOM–FR. Secret; Priority; Exdis. Drafted by Popple, cleared by Bacon and Tyler, and cleared and approved by Don T. Christensen of S/S. Repeated to Paris and Tokyo.

2. Ambassador Tsiang said he agreed that GRC should stay its hand for the moment.

3. In reply to question on level of GRC representation in Paris, Tsiang said GRC for many years had been unsuccessful in effort get French to accept GRC Ambassador. Most recent request made last fall during ForMin Shen's visit France. Secretary suggested GRC give thought to renewing such request now as means testing French. If France refused we would then be in a position puncture bubble of French willingness give GRC and Chicoms equal treatment. Secretary pointed out that it may be two or three months before exchange of Ambassadors between France and Chicoms took place, and that in meantime France may have to put certain conditions on Peiping in connection with French plans for South Vietnam. In any event, Secretary stressed it was important to make the recognition matter as difficult as possible for both Paris and Peiping.

4. In reply to Amb. Tsiang's question re French motives, Secretary said very difficult to answer but felt motives could be found more in peculiar psychological make-up of de Gaulle rather than in serious analysis French interests.

Rusk

---

6.   **Memorandum of Conversation**[1]

Washington, January 24, 1964, 11–11:28 a.m.

SUBJECT

   Japanese Political Questions; French Recognition of Communist China

PARTICIPANTS

   Tingfu F. Tsiang, Chinese Ambassador
   Yi-seng Kiang, Chinese Minister
   Johnson Cheng, Counselor of Embassy

   The Secretary
   Robert W. Barnett, Deputy Assistant Secretary for Far Eastern Affairs
   Robert A. Fearey, Acting Deputy Director for East Asian Affairs

---

   [1] Source: Department of State, Central Files, POL CHICOM–JAPAN. Secret; Limit Distribution. Drafted by Acting Deputy Director of the Office of East Asian Affairs Robert A. Fearey. Approved by Rusk on January 27 in Tokyo. The time of the meeting is taken from Rusk's Appointment Book. (Johnson Library)

Ambassador Tsiang said that he had been instructed to take up with the Secretary two matters relating to Japan.

First, his Government wished him to call the Secretary's attention to certain developments in Japanese politics. During the last several years Prime Minister Ikeda had, willingly or unwillingly, associated himself with and promoted the political influence of Ichiro Kono, Kenzo Matsumura, Tatsunosuke Takasaki and Takeo Miki. As a result, the political influence of these individuals had increased. With the development of trade with the mainland, Kono particularly had been able to acquire considerable funds for political purposes. Kono was building up a political organization of his own in hopes of promoting a different type of governing coalition in which he, Kono, would be the Prime Minister while Ikeda became the honorary chief of the coalition. The GRC wished to warn the Secretary that Japanese trade with the mainland would not only help Communist China but would also, on the Japanese side, corrupt Japanese politics in the direction of the left. The Secretary said that he would bear in mind what the Ambassador had said.

Second, Ambassador Tsiang said that the Japanese Government was considering establishing a permanent trade mission in Peiping, reciprocated by a Chinese Communist permanent trade mission in Tokyo. The Ambassador said that his Government hoped that the Secretary would use his influence to prevent this. The Secretary said that he planned to discuss the mainland trade question in Tokyo and would see what could be done.

The Secretary said he was very disappointed and disturbed over news of the manner in which the GRC is handling the French-Communist Chinese recognition matter.[2] There appears to us to be overwhelming evidence that if the GRC refuses to break relations with France this would have a major impact on Peiping in its attempt to establish diplomatic relations throughout the world. The Secretary said that we have no wish to interfere in the GRC's business in giving them advice. However, the United States' future relations with the GRC, its relations with NATO and Southeast Asia are all very much involved. We need the cooperation of the GRC. If there were only a 50 percent or even a 33 percent chance that the French-Communist Chinese move could be frustrated it would be of the greatest importance that that chance be taken. The consequences of failure are such that we should take any step that might assist in frustrating the Paris-Peiping action. If France succeeds in establishing relations with Peiping in circumstances where the GRC has made it easy

---

[2] Telegram 616 from Taipei, January 21, reported that Foreign Minister Shen had told Wright that Chiang had received a letter from de Gaulle that had convinced him that de Gaulle intended to formalize relations with Peking swiftly and that it would be impossible to keep an Ambassador in Paris even for a short time. (Department of State, Central Files, POL 17 FR–CHICOM)

for them to do so, we will not be able to commit our prestige in other cases, in other capitals. We need maximum assistance from the GRC to deal with this problem.

The Secretary said that the GRC should not only continue to protest France's action—the GRC should in addition make it just as hard as possible for Paris and Peiping to carry their plan out. Our information and strong belief is that France would be unwilling to take the initiative in breaking relations with the GRC. The Secretary said that he hoped the GRC and people of Taiwan saw the gravity of the matter as we see it in our own national interest. As he had said, ours is not just the advice of a friend. We too have an important stake and need the GRC's help. If it becomes clear that we are not able to work together in an effort to make the establishment of relations between France and Communist China as difficult as possible, the loss of interest in the U.S. in the effort to support the GRC will be very severe. The Secretary said that he had been reading records of Congressional discussions of the matter which clearly confirmed this. This is an extremely important matter. If we cannot work together on this, it would be very difficult to work together effectively as we have for so many years in support of GRC interests. He was not pointing a finger at the Ambassador personally since he knew the Ambassador had correctly reported their discussions. But he wanted to be sure that the Government at Taiwan understands the utter gravity of the problem. He understood that Ambassador Wright had not been afforded opportunity to discuss the matter personally with President Chiang.

Ambassador Tsiang said that his information was scanty. He was not personally familiar with all aspects of the problem and was not in a position to say anything at the moment. He would report with all clarity to his Government what the Secretary had said.

The Secretary said he wished to add a further point. There had been intimations that in Taiwan there were some who suspected that we were trying to booby-trap the GRC into a false position. This was not true. Such an interpretation would be very badly received here.

Ambassador Tsiang said that it was hard for the GRC to distinguish official from unofficial views and comment in Washington. So many people wanted to speak their minds on the problem, including, for example, Mr. Lippmann. The Secretary said that Mr. Lippmann had held the same position for 15 years. He could understand the difficulties President Chiang had in dealing with a man like deGaulle. He could show the Ambassador his own wounds. DeGaulle is a very complex man, almost impossible to persuade. The Secretary reiterated that our information is that Paris is very worried over the possibility that the GRC will not break relations.

Ambassador Tsiang said that his personal recommendation to Taipei had been that the Government should sit tight through the announcement of recognition, but should withdraw after completion of an exchange of ambassadors. He had warned his Government not to talk about future steps. The Secretary said that the GRC should give no indication of intention to withdraw in any circumstances. He made plain that the GRC should not give any indication that it would withdraw its Paris Embassy if a Chinese Communist Ambassador arrived, or the GRC's whole position will be undercut.

The Secretary said that looking ahead, we are in a major battle of a long campaign. If Paris goes ahead we will be faced probably quite soon with a danger of recognition of Peiping by some African countries, by Belgium, by Canada, by Japan and by other countries. It is true that 42 UN nations recognize Peking. But France is a special case—if this hole is made in the dam the prospect is that the water will flood through. The Secretary said that he could not emphasize too strongly the importance of doing all we can to frustrate Paris' and Peiping's move.[3]

---

[3] Wright reported in telegram 648 from Taipei, January 26, that he had reviewed Rusk's conversation with Tsiang in detail with Chiang that morning. (Ibid., POL CHINAT–US)

---

7.   Memorandum From Robert W. Komer of the National Security Council Staff to President Johnson[1]

Washington, January 25, 1964.

Here are the instructions we've sent out to Ray Cline in our back-door effort to bring the Gimo around. You'll note we've gone no further than to say he's coming at your request.

His instructions (attached)[2] take a fairly tough line, as Rusk did with the GRC Ambassador. This includes implied threat that if GRC won't listen to us, we may not be able to work so closely with it

McCone favors a softer line, even promising the Gimo again what Kennedy did at the time of the 1962 Outer Mongolia flap, i.e. that we'd

---

[1] Source: Johnson Library, National Security File, Country File, France, Recognition of Communist China, Vol. II. Secret.

[2] Telegram 648 to Taipei, January 24, stated that Cline was going to Taipei at Johnson's request to talk to Chiang Ching-kuo and, if it appeared desirable, to President Chiang; he was to explain the U.S. position and give advice but not to make deals or negotiate. (Department of State, Central Files, POL 17 CHICOM–FR)

use every means, including the veto, to keep Chicoms out of the UN.[3] But State thinks this would rob us of any freedom of action if things went sour and we wanted to pursue a flexible strategy at the UN.[4]

R.W. Komer[5]

---

[3] Reference is to an oral message to Chiang, delivered by Ambassador Drumright on October 17, 1961, in which Kennedy stated that "if at any time a U.S. veto is necessary and will be effective in preventing Chinese Communist entry into the U.N., the U.S. will use that veto." See telegram 259 to Taipei, October 16, 1961, in *Foreign Relations, 1961–1963*, vol. XXII, p. 160.

[4] McCone stated his views in a January 24 telephone conversation with Harriman and in messages that Acting DCI Carter transmitted in letters of January 24, 25, and 27 to Harriman. (Library of Congress, Manuscript Division, Harriman Papers, Kennedy–Johnson Administrations, Subject Files, Cline, Ray S.; also Central Intelligence Agency, McCone Files: Job 80–B01285A, Box 5, Folder 3, DCI European Trip, January 1964) Harriman told Ball in a January 26 telephone conversation that McCone was "quite upset" but that Harriman, Rusk, and Komer agreed that it was impossible to give Cline any negotiating authority. (Johnson Library, Ball papers, China (Taiwan))

[5] Printed from a copy that bears this typed signature.

---

8.   **Telegram From the Embassy in the Republic of China to the Department of State[1]**

Taipei, January 27, 1964, 8 p.m.

658. Deptel 648.[2] Department pass CIA. Following from Ray Cline:

Following my early morning talk with Chiang Ching-kuo [*less than 1 line of source text not declassified*][3] Ambassador, DCM, [*less than 1 line of source text not declassified*] and I went over file and Deptel 648 instructions. At 1130 Chiang requested another meeting with me where he said he had briefed Gimo on basic points of earlier talk and also discussed subject with Premier and FonMin.

He said Gimo understood US view that GRC should lodge protest when French recognize Peiping and should issue strong statement

---

[1] Source: Department of State, Central Files, POL 17 CHICOM–FR. Secret; Immediate; Exdis. Repeated to Tokyo for the Secretary.

[2] See footnote 2, Document 7.

[3] The message under reference, January 27, along with two January 28 messages from Cline concerning the other two meetings reported in this telegram, are filed with a memorandum of McCone's January 24 telephone conversation with Harriman; see footnote 4, Document 7. A copy of the first message is in Department of State, Central Files, POL CHINAT–FR.

against "two China" policy but should await further developments before breaking off relations. Gimo felt that GRC action and its timing would depend on content and timing of French announcement. If de Gaulle announced he breaking with GRC nothing could be done. If French statement equivocal GRC would consider possible responses aiming at US objectives.

Chiang said in any event GRC and US mutually affected by French action and grave consequences likely to follow made it essential GRC and US work together on Asian problems. GRC plans to recover mainland would have helped prevent this situation if they had been carried out. Now necessary to talk about how to save GRC and US position in Asia, not just in Paris. He felt serious political troubles would arise in Taiwan if prospects for return to mainland become remote.

Chiang said Gimo wanted to know what US would do if GRC maneuvers in Paris won some time before GRC ouster. Replied that time would permit moral and political pressure on France not to consummate full diplomatic relation, would assist in urging other nations not to follow French lead, and would permit strong US effort to rally support for defense Southeast Asia and free China against Chicom thrusts to dominate area.

Chiang said he hoped all points made in our talks would be got across to Gimo. At this point upon request of Ambassador I said Ambassador would want to accompany me for talk with Gimo and we would be ready anytime. Chiang said he would report to his father and get in touch with me later.

In third meeting with me on January 27, Chiang said he had reported second meeting to Gimo. Gimo wished me to know that GRC reaction to French recognition had been thoroughly discussed between two countries and given deep consideration by Gimo. The Gimo's decision had been passed to Ambassador Wright. Up to this point the GRC still held to this position in principle but the government was willing to study French recognition statement and reconsider their decision if nature of statement allowed it. Gimo did not deem French recognition as most important point but rather effects it would have on world situation, in Asia and particularly Southeast Asia. He hoped that while I was here I would discuss fully implications of French recognition especially on US and GRC interests in Asia. The Gimo felt that two matters of principle should be discussed after the French announcement:

1) The future of the GRC and
2) This future as related to the recovery of the mainland.

The President had therefore instructed FonMin Shen to discuss these problems with Amb Wright and me. After these discussions the President would be happy to meet with me.

In ensuing discussion Chiang Ching-Kuo expressing his own views hoped US would consider GRC problems. He catalogued restraints placed by US on GRC action against the mainland. He said GRC would never "sell the soul of its people" on the mainland. Later in emotional voice he said "We may smile on the surface but our hearts are heavy." The GRC would not go against US interests but they were afraid that Taiwan might fall to Chicoms without a fight.

He said news stories from Washington that the US pressuring GRC on French recognition issue were giving government bad time in party.

I said GRC can count on support from US but that support would be stronger if it clear that de Gaulle to blame for breaking relations, not GRC. I emphasized that US not asking GRC to accept "two-China" policy but to stay and fight at same time forcing de Gaulle's hand to take responsibility if he made it impossible for GRC to continue in Paris.

Chiang said he would get in touch with me after French statement available.[4]

Wright

---

[4] Telegram 660 from Taipei, January 27, reported that after the French announcement that evening, Chiang Ching-kuo gave Cline a draft statement protesting the French action but with no indication that the GRC would break diplomatic relations. Telegram 662, January 28, reported that Chiang Kai-shek had approved the draft statement with only minor changes. (Ibid., POL 17 CHICOM–FR)

---

9.   National Intelligence Estimate[1]

NIE 13–64   Washington, January 28, 1964.

ECONOMIC PROSPECTS FOR COMMUNIST CHINA

The Problem

To assess the problems and performance of Communist China's economy, and its prospects over the next few years.

---

[1] Source: Department of State, INR/EAP Files: Lot 90 D 110, NIE 13–64. Secret; Controlled Dissem. According to a note on the cover sheet, the estimate was submitted by the Director of Central Intelligence and concurred in by the U.S. Intelligence Board on January 28. The Central Intelligence Agency and the intelligence organizations of the Departments of State, Defense, the Army, the Navy, the Air Force, and the National Security Agency participated in the preparation of the estimate. All members of the U.S. Intelligence Board concurred, except the Atomic Energy Commission Representative and the Assistant to the Director of the Federal Bureau of Investigation, who abstained on the grounds that the subject was outside their jurisdiction.

Note

Firm information on Communist China remains so sparse that precise economic analysis is not possible and even broad judgments are subject to error. The Estimate should be read in the light of this general caution. Annex A[2] gives a brief description of our information on the Chinese Communist economy.

Conclusions

A. The Chinese economy has recovered somewhat from its 1960–1961 low, but its prospects are considerably worse than in 1957.[3] Any Chinese government would face monumental economic problems resulting from the huge and growing population, inadequate arable land, and the low level of technology. The problems of the Chinese Communists are compounded by their own past errors, their ideological compulsions, the break with the Soviet Union, and extreme nationalism. (Paras. 1–10)[4]

B. Grain output in 1963 was no greater than in 1957, when there were some 75 million fewer people to feed. Peiping's mismanagement and the post-1960 decline of Soviet support have grievously hurt the industrial sector; total output in 1963 remains far below the 1959 peak. A few priority industries, such as those supporting agriculture and the petroleum industry, are operating at close to capacity, but many suffer from unbalanced development, technological deficiencies, and shortages of parts and raw materials. Foreign trade is at the lowest point since 1954. That with the Soviet Union has declined more than 60 percent since 1959, and China has become a substantial importer of food from the Free World. (Paras. 11–26)

C. We believe that the Chinese Communists will seek and obtain additional credits and technical assistance from the Free World, but in relatively modest amounts. We do not believe that diplomatic recognition by France and other Free World countries will alter this picture substantially. (Para. 27)

D. We believe that agricultural production in the next few years is unlikely to grow much faster than the population, and that industry will grow at a rate well below what was achieved in the mid-1950s. The Chinese are likely to continue to devote more attention to agriculture in both

---

[2] Attached but not printed.

[3] In the following discussion we use 1957 as a base year for comparison because it was the eve of the Great Leap Forward, and because the per capita grain output in that year represents a level of production that provided farmers and factory workers an adequate diet, made grain imports unnecessary, and permitted the export of modest amounts of grain and other agricultural products. [Footnote in the source text.]

[4] The paragraph numbers refer to the discussion portion of the estimate, which is not printed.

their domestic and import programs, but will probably not divert enough resources from industry and the arms program to put agriculture on a sound footing. We believe that the Chinese will be anxious to revert to a policy favoring industrial development, and will be prone to do so prematurely. We believe that difficulties will accumulate in the economy, within the leadership, and between the regime and the people. We thus do not believe that China can become a modern industrial state for many years. China's direct military threat to the West will remain limited, but China will continue to be a major force in Asia, and a crucial menace to its Asian neighbors and to Western interests in the area. (Paras. 29–39)

[Here follows the Discussion portion of the estimate.]

---

10.   Telegram From the Embassy in Poland to the Department of State[1]

Warsaw, January 29, 1964, 5 p.m.

1273. Cabot–Wang Talks. 119th meeting 1 hour 45 minutes.[2] Deptel 1150.[3]

(1) I opened along lines paragraphs 3, 4 and 5 reference telegram followed by substance all numbered paragraphs reference telegram plus inquiry re *Blue Goose*.[4]

---

[1] Source: Department of State, Central Files, POL CHICOM–US. Confidential; Priority; Limit Distribution. Repeated to Taipei, Hong Kong, Stockholm, Moscow, and Geneva.

[2] Cabot commented on the meeting in telegram 1277 from Warsaw and reported it in detail in airgram A–630, both dated January 30. (Ibid.) For records of previous meetings in the series of Ambassadorial talks between representatives of the United States and the People's Republic of China, see *Foreign Relations*, 1955–1957, volume III; 1958–1960, volume XIX; and 1961–1963, volume XXII.

[3] Telegram 1150 to Warsaw, January 21, transmitted guidance for the meeting. (Department of State, Central Files, POL CHICOM–US)

[4] Paragraphs 3, 4, and 5 stated that the United States sought to promote a relaxation of tensions and to seek a just and enduring peace and that it had refrained from responding in kind to the hostility which appeared daily in the Chinese press. Paragraph 2 stated that the "United States cannot tolerate a situation where your side continues to introduce arms into Viet-Nam and seeks to increase the level of insurrectionary activity in South Viet-Nam." Other numbered paragraphs requested release of four U.S. nationals held as prisoners in China and gave Wang information on three deportee cases. The *Blue Goose* was a plane missing since October 1, 1958; information concerning it had been requested at several previous meetings.

(2) Wang expressed disappointment nothing new or positive in my opening statement. Said hope for relaxation tensions Taiwan Straits and Far East and improvements in our relations in the New Year depend on Washington not Peiping. Said China was victim of aggression. Said USG must [garble] change in its erroneous China policy of aggression and mil encirclement. This policy leads to blind alley. US seizure Taiwan by armed force is root of bad relations. If this key issue were resolved other questions would not be difficult. Converse all attempts resolving side issues of no avail until key issues solved. Two-China policy will not be tolerated. Quoted recent statements Secretary and Undersecretary Harriman in attempt prove we had assumed proprietary air in saying US would never "turn over" Taiwan. Wang complained of trade and travel restrictions, our UN policy, mentioned 272nd through 276th serious warning, complained of spy aircraft penetrating deeply into mainland and support of Chiang attempt invade [or] harass mainland for which we held answerable. "Big Dipper" exercise was military provocation. Complained our activities South Vietnam and Laos and masterminding of aggression and subversion in Cambodia, of military bases Thailand, and alleged we were resurrecting Japanese militarism to use for our purposes. Complained of aid to India and activities attempting encirclement in crescent from India to Japan.

(3) I pointed out once again we were not occupying Taiwan but fully intended fulfill our treaty obligations to GRC. Gave brief examples historical sequences indicate our posture in Asia was reaction to Chicom hostility. Said if his side believed any Chinese being prevented from returning to Mainland we would like to know of case. Followed with paragraph (G) paragraph reference telegram serious warnings[5] plus some of third paragraph Deptel 1154[6] and paragraph (B) reference telegram re Seventh Fleet.[7] Gave obvious rebuttals to South Vietnam and Laos charge staying it was Chicoms who were aiding Pathet Lao and sending arms to South Vietnam.

(4) Wang gave standard upside-down version post-war history FE ending with assertion Chicom policy was winning sympathy and support all over world.

(5) Refuting charges our insistent hostility to China I pointed out warm feelings American people had had for Chinese for many decades,

---

[5] It stated that serious warnings 270–275 (concerning alleged U.S. violations of Chinese territory or territorial waters) related for the most part to the Hsi Sha islands and that the United States did not recognize Chinese Communist sovereignty over those islands but would be willing to check into claimed violations in other areas.

[6] Telegram 1154 to Warsaw, January 22, provided additional details for Cabot's guidance. (Department of State, Central Files, POL CHICOM–US)

[7] It stated, with reference to Seventh Fleet maneuvers in the Indian Ocean, that U.S. fleet maneuvers on the high seas were a matter of U.S. concern.

when we had helped China in its need on more than one occasion including in World War II when we fought as allies. I said it was clear from recent public statements Wang's side felt free to subvert governments which did not happen to like. Chicoms had urged Soviet Union intervene in Hungary and there were more recent examples to be noted. Asked whether his side believed in non-intervention or whether it believed in toppling other governments which it may not agree with.

(6) Wang gave as proof of our constant hostility lack of diplomatic recognition, blockade and trade embargoes, UN policies, and occupation Taiwan. Said his side believed in ability each country manage own affairs and was against outside interference. Much of world's trouble due to interventionist policies of US. Said had no information re *Blue Goose*. Said our intention toward other interested parties re disarmament discussion was matter for us to entertain.

Date of next meeting April 8.

Cabot

---

11.   **Telegram From the Embassy in the Republic of China to the Department of State**[1]

Taipei, January 29, 1964, midnight.

680. At two and one half hour meeting with President this evening, Ambassador, visitor, FinMin, Ching-kuo and interpreter Shen. After generalities President asked how we viewed the future. We replied three steps: first, prevent French-Communist [China] consummation of their proposed establishment relationships, second, urge other nations not to follow, third, support GRC, and fourth, strengthen and develop backing for GRC in United Nations.

Asked President if he had any proposals. President answered, under US policy of open door and accommodation very little to suggest. If commie regime not overthrown or destroyed PM [PRC?] will swallow up GRC and all others opposed.

---

[1] Source: Department of State, Central Files, POL 16 CHICOM. Secret; Immediate; Limdis.

After discussion President said first step to study French objectives. Three years ago de Gaulle sent emissary to President who suggested GRC abandon exclusive reliance on USA and make France third partner. Quid pro quo would be exchange of Ambassadors. This first unmistakable indication French motives to expel US and UK, restore French influence all Southeast Asia and to pursue alliance with Chicoms for this purpose. Latest attitudes towards Laos and Cambodia neutralization, and Chicom recognition all verify.

President said US failed to realize the effect on morale of GRC people and forces caused by deteriorating situation in East. State of mind frail and brittle. Danger Chicom will seize and capitalize on this and overcome his country by infiltration and subversion.

President said he must have some way of reassuring his people that he will never agree to two-Chinas situation. So long as there is no two-Chinas there will be hope for return to mainland and high morale in his people and forces. If we had taken steps to recover mainland three years ago, French recognition would not have happened. If we move against the mainland French recognition of us would be of no importance. Once we take this action it will have reassuring effect on morale of people and forces. He said if GRC had been left alone they would have taken such action to restore the mainland three years ago. However, he is well aware of US attitude and has no intention to act at present time.

If we fail to take some action which will have a similar effect on maintenance of morale we will open the gates to infiltration and subversion in which the people and forces would be demoralized and the Chicoms could take over without the use of force and by their well-known tactics of "peaceful liberation", in which the Seventh Fleet would be helpless.

Knowing US policy well, could not the GRC ask the United States come forth some formula to maintain morale of people and armed forces?

The President said he had some views on this subject. There are three interrelated war zones: South Vietnam, Korea, GRC. Collapse of one will affect the other two. French recognition creates a new situation in South Vietnam where commies will use French influence to sabotage US actions with view to forcing US to pull out. Effect of pull out would be such that US prestige would suffer so much that no reassurances would prevent demoralization in Korea and the GRC.

The President said he would submit three proposals: Plan one. US take the lead to establish a four-nation alliance of US, Korea, South Vietnam and GRC, such that armed forces of one would be at disposal of others for movement to troubled areas.

Plan two. A three-nation alliance of Korea, South Vietnam and GRC with US to give only its blessing, air cover and naval support.

Plan three. The GRC make separate bi-lateral agreements with South Vietnam and Korea with same US support which would permit exchange of forces for mutual support.

Note that in plans two and three US could officially stand aside providing only support. He said plans two or three were a minimum requirement for the maintenance of stability and morale in the area. Frankly he does not see how US can maintain position in South Vietnam without some such alliance which would permit use of GRC troops. There followed detailed discussion three plans including effect on Laos, Burma and Thailand.

Asked about Japan. President said Japan was out. Her constitution would not permit it. Communism and infiltration have gone too far and her country is now divided in two, one under Ikeda and one under communists. US should not overestimate role of Japan in the East.

President said at his last meeting with General Marshall that if US persists in its policy mainland will fall to communists. Same applies today to all Southeast Asia and GRC.

Discussion concluded with assurances of careful US consideration and generalities.

Foregoing is a brief of long discussion much along previously reported lines.

Comments:

1.   President appears to think French-Chicom relations an eventual fact.

2.   President seems deeply concerned over morale of nations in area and particularly people and military forces of GRC.

Wright

12.   Telegram From the Embassy in the Republic of China to the Department of State[1]

Taipei, February 10, 1964, 9:17 a.m.

736. Embtel 735.[2] At a twenty minute meeting with the President at 1800 today he confirmed the arrival of the French communication delivered orally to the Foreign Minister by French Chargé Pierre Salade this morning. He considered this as an official communication from the French Government.

President said he had cooperated with the United States in his handling of the January 27 announcement and the January 31 press conference but he considered that the French message delivered by the French Chargé had ended the period of manuever. He said that at a meeting of his government after arrival of the message he had decided that the relations of the GRC and the Government of France had been terminated by the French communication. I said that in speaking for the United States all our efforts had been bent on forcing the French to take the initiative and I hoped that in handling this matter the GRC would assure by all means available that the responsibility for this action in the eyes of the world rested squarely on the French. The President replied that there was no doubt in his mind that the French Government with the delivery of the French Chargé message had in fact taken the initiative.

The President then asked that I convey to the Secretary of State and President Johnson that relations between the GRC and the Government of France had by French action ceased to exist.

There will be an emergency Cabinet meeting at 2100 to decide on the form in which the French action will be announced. The Premier stated there would be an announcement to the press tonight.

I have urged the Premier and Foreign Minister to get the French message in writing to facilitate a clear public understanding but both have stated that they considered that the meaning of the French message was clear and unmistakable and therefore a written statement would not be requested. I repeated to Premier and Foreign Minister the need for wording of their announcement so as to make it clear that the initiative for breaking relations had been taken by the French.

Wright

---

[1] Source: Department of State, Central Files, POL 1 CHINAT–FR. Secret; Flash; Limdis. Received at 9:04 a.m. Repeated to Paris, Tokyo, Hong Kong, and USUN. Passed to the White House, OSD, Army, Air Force, Navy, and CIA.

[2] Telegram 735 from Taipei, February 10, reported a conversation with Shen, who stated that the French Chargé had made an oral statement to him that day that France would exchange diplomatic representatives with Peking soon and that once the Chargé from Peking arrived in Paris, the French would consider him as the representative of China; consequently, the Republic of China diplomatic mission would lose its raison d'etre. (Ibid., POL 1 CHICOM–FR)

13.   Telegram From the Department of State to the Embassy in the
       Republic of China[1]

Washington, February 12, 1964, 7:46 p.m.

727. Taipei's 753 Dept; rptd Paris 55, Tokyo 223, Hong Kong 272,
USUN 23.[2] Dept. shares your disappointment with manner GRC handled severance relations with France, and agrees that maximum advantage of tactical maneuver was lost through GRC failure put onus for
break clearly on French.

On other hand, press here has learned of French action which led to
GRC announcement of break. As result, over past two days editorials
and news analyses have presented facts fairly accurately.

Under circumstances, Dept. feels that little to be gained by raising
issue directly with President Chiang at this time. However, you might
consider bringing to GRC's attention informally and at lower level our
concern over lack of adequate consultation as described reftel and consequent adverse effect on ability U.S. provide maximum support in maintenance GRC international position.

Rusk

[1] Source: Department of State, Central Files, POL 17 CHINAT–FR. Secret; Limdis.
Drafted by Popple, cleared by Bacon and in the Bureau of Public Affairs, and approved by
Green. Repeated to Hong Kong, Paris, Tokyo, and USUN.

[2] Telegram 753 from Taipei, February 12, recommended that Wright be authorized to
express to President Chiang the U.S. disappointment that the GRC announcement of February 10 failed to place the onus on the French for the break in diplomatic relations. (Ibid.)

---

14.   Memorandum From Robert W. Komer of the National
       Security Council Staff to the President's Special Assistant for
       National Security Affairs (Bundy)[1]

Washington, February 26, 1964.

Mac—

I've been sitting on attached Chicom nuclear paper,[2] on assumption
you'd hardly find it urgent business.

[1] Source: Johnson Library, National Security File, Komer Files, China (CPR), Nuclear
Explosion/Capability. Secret.

[2] Reference is to a draft policy statement of October 15, 1963, prepared in the Policy
Planning Council of the Department of State. (Ibid.) For information concerning it, see *For-
eign Relations*, 1961–1963, vol. XXII, p. 399, footnote 1. For the summary portion, see the
Supplement to that volume.

Walt's first hope is that LBJ will look at the conclusions (at my suggestion he summarized them in letters to McNamara, McCone, etc.).[3] LBJ really should be told about these, because they reduce the problem to proper perspective, i.e. not much of a military threat but of some political "scare" potential. If you agree I'll do a *one-pager* for weekend reading.[4]

Walt also wants a NSAM. This seems quite unnecessary at this point, and you'll agree when you see horrendous draft attached.[5] Paper is mostly of educational value, and has already largely served its purpose. If a high level ad hoc group is really needed for follow-up action (I'm of two minds),[6] why couldn't this be discussed in SG and then set up by Rusk (with WWR as chairman).

JCS have done some comments, which further complicate picture.[7]

WWR is also poking around in pre-emptive action field. Do we want this?[8]

RWK

---

[3] A January 24 letter from Rostow to Bundy enclosed a copy of his January 21 letter to McNamara. (Both Johnson Library, National Security File, Komer Files, China (CPR))

[4] A marginal note in Bundy's handwriting next to this sentence reads, "Yes." The word "weekend" was crossed out and the word "night" added in Bundy's handwriting.

[5] A marginal note in Bundy's handwriting next to this sentence reads, "Not needed yet." The draft NSAM, with a drafting date of January 24, is in Johnson Library, National Security File, Komer Files, China (CPR).

[6] A marginal note in Bundy's handwriting connected to the words "ad hoc group" reads, "Not now, in my view. Ad hoc groups are over employed on more urgent stuff."

[7] The JCS comments on the October 15 draft statement have not been found. A JCS memorandum to McNamara (JCSM–986–63), December 14, 1963, responded to a memorandum of July 31 from Acting Assistant Secretary of Defense for International Security Affairs William Bundy to the JCS Chairman requesting a contingency plan for an attack with conventional weapons on Chinese Communist nuclear weapons production facilities designed to cause severest impact on and delay in the Chinese nuclear program. The JCS memorandum of December 14 indicated that such an operation was feasible but recommended consideration of the use of nuclear weapons for such an attack. Both memoranda are in Washington National Records Center, RG 330, OSD Files: FRC 91–0017, 471.61 China Reds.

[8] A marginal note in Bundy's handwriting connected to this sentence reads, "I'm for this."

15.   **Memorandum From the Central Intelligence Agency's Deputy Director for Intelligence (Cline) to Director of Central Intelligence McCone**[1]

Washington, March 2, 1964.

SUBJECT

U.S. Relations with Republic of China (Taiwan)

1. My trip to Taipei last month succeeded in getting the Government of the Republic of China (GRC) to postpone breaking relations with France for two weeks, thus forcing both Peiping and Paris to make clear that France was obliged to drop its diplomatic support of the GRC in Taiwan as the price of establishing relations with Peiping. This was a gain for the U.S. since many nations would recognize Peiping if they thought they could maintain diplomatic relations with "Two Chinas." Few nations have followed the French lead because it became clear that any nation recognizing Peiping had to go all the way and recognize its right to take over Taiwan and its twelve million non-Communist people.

2. President Chiang Kai-shek agreed to this delay out of respect for President Johnson's direct request to do so, but pointed out (correctly) that the French had sold out to Peiping and would force a break between Paris and Taipei. He also said this would be a shattering blow to morale in Taiwan, particularly among the Mainland Chinese element in his Armed Forces and Government.

3. President Chiang requested that his views be conveyed to Washington, along with his recommendations for actions to restore morale in Taiwan and build up U.S. prestige in Southeast Asia. I summarized these views in the form of an oral message for President Johnson and provided it to Secretary Rusk, Under Secretary Harriman and McGeorge Bundy about three weeks ago. A copy is attached.[2]

4. This memorandum is intended to call to your attention some information on which I orally briefed Governor Harriman and McGeorge Bundy. It is that (a) I found the morale of GRC officials exceptionally and dismally low; (b) a senior Chinese General had attempted on 21 January 1964 to lead the crack 1st Armored Division against Taipei

---

[1] Source: Department of State, Central Files, POL CHINAT–US. Top Secret. Filed with a covering memorandum of March 2 from McCone to Rusk, McGeorge Bundy, and Harriman suggesting that a warm communication be sent to Chiang Kai-shek promptly "in the interests of rekindling confidence."

[2] Not attached to the source text. A copy is filed with a covering memorandum of February 8 from Cline to Harriman, which states that he had left the original with Bundy for the President. (Library of Congress, Manuscript Division, Harriman Papers, Kennedy–Johnson Administrations, Subject Files, Cline, Ray S.)

to overthrow the Government (of course, he failed); (c) President Chiang told me personally in highly emotional tones that a continuation of present U.S. policy in Asia, which he feels will end in Chinese Communist control or domination of all East and Southeast Asia, will create a situation in which the GRC cannot survive; (d) many officials in addition to President Chiang felt that present trends would bring a military coup in Taipei against the present Government within two years because of frustration with inability to return to the Mainland and a feeling that U.S. military, economic and political support was weak and waning.

5. In view of the seriousness with which these views were impressed upon me, I feel that they should be seriously considered by the U.S. Government. My own feeling is that a strong U.S. initiative in Vietnam would buck up morale in Taipei, but I think it would be dangerous to assume that we can always take stability and friendly cooperation on the part of the GRC for granted.

Ray S. Cline

16. Memorandum From Robert W. Komer of the National Security Council Staff to President Johnson[1]

Washington, March 3, 1964.

Here is a proposed telegraphic reply to Chiang Kai-shek's letter of 1 February (Tab B).[2] He also sent an informal message via Ray Cline (Tab C).[3] The Gimo is of course very worried by what he sees as the eroding of the GRC's position because of French recognition of Peiping and our troubles in Vietnam.

The Gimo seizes the occasion to urge some of his favorite ideas, such as a new GRC-ROK-South Vietnam security pact, stepped up GRC action against the mainland, and perhaps sending GRC troops to help out in Vietnam. Chiang also feels strongly that serious US setbacks in the Far East would bring a military coup on Taiwan within two years.

---

[1] Source: Johnson Library, National Security File, Head of State Correspondence File, China, Vol. I. Secret.

[2] Attached but not printed; the letter was transmitted in telegram 700 from Taipei, February 2. (Department of State, Central Files, POL 16 CHICOM)

[3] Not attached, but see footnote 2, Document 15.

US reactions to Chiang's fears vary widely. Cline takes them quite seriously. On the other hand, a senior State official who visited Taiwan about the same time reports that GRC officials below the very top level are quite pleased with their undoubted success in making a going concern of Taiwan.[4] We doubt in any case that a GRC-SVN alliance or an overt GRC troop commitment would help enough to counteract the real risk of justifying Chicom counteraction.

So the best bet seems to be a friendly response showing Chiang that we take his concerns seriously and are studying them, but not committing us in any way as yet. Such a message is at Tab A.[5] Rusk, Harriman, and Cline concur, and I've edited it for suitable warmth.[6]

R.W. Komer

---

[4] A memorandum entitled "Recent Observations in Taipei," with name and date removed, was sent from Harriman to Michael V. Forrestal of the NSC Staff on March 4 and from Forrestal to Bundy on March 5. (Johnson Library, National Security File, Country File, China, Vol. I) A copy of the memorandum from Deputy Assistant Secretary for Far Eastern Economic Affairs Robert W. Barnett to Harriman, March 3, is in Department of State, FE/EA Files: Lot 66 D 225, R.C. 1964, POL 2. Barnett visited Taiwan February 5–8. The Embassy's report on his visit was transmitted with airgram A–738, March 6. (Ibid., Central Files, ORG 7 FE)

[5] Not attached to the source text, but see Document 17.

[6] A notation on the source text in Komer's handwriting states, "Approved by Pres 6 Mar. in my presence. RWK."

---

17.   Telegram From the Department of State to the Embassy in the Republic of China[1]

Washington, March 6, 1964, 3:53 p.m.

820. Please deliver following letter to President Chiang from President Johnson:

"March 2, 1964. Dear Mr. President: I greatly appreciate your letter of 1 February, which I have most carefully studied. I should also like to

---

[1] Source: Department of State, Central Files, POL 15–1 US/JOHNSON. Secret; Limdis. The telegram indicates that it was drafted by Popple on March 3, cleared by Harriman and McGeorge Bundy, and approved by Green, but an attached note of March 6 from Bundy to Read states that it was approved by the President. See also footnote 6, Document 16. The original draft, attached to the source text, indicates that it was cleared by Cline, Green, and Harriman, and approved by Rusk.

thank you for the cordial reception given Mr. Ray Cline. He has reported fully on your strategic concerns and recommendations with respect to the situation in Asia.

Your views on world problems are always much valued here. We too are actively concerned over possible trends in the Far East, though I can assure you that we intend to meet our responsibilities squarely and are confident that the forces of freedom will not be found wanting.

I am also confident that through continual close consultation and coordination our two governments will find mutually acceptable solutions to the problems which particularly concern us. As to steps which might be taken to offset the adverse effects of France's deplorable recognition of the Chinese Communist regime, some of the suggestions which you and your officials have made are already being carried out and others are under intensive study. I am asking Ambassador Wright to discuss them with you in detail, and to keep in closest touch with your representatives so as to ensure full coordination.

As a matter of primary urgency, I believe it essential to mount an intensified diplomatic effort to strengthen your country's international position, especially within the United Nations. We want to cooperate fully with you in this effort, but you must take the laboring oar.

We further intend to take steps to cope more effectively with Communist aggression in Southeast Asia, which, as you emphasize, poses grave risks to all free world countries whether or not they acknowledge it. In this connection we have again reviewed our bilateral and multilateral defense arrangements in Asia, along the lines you have suggested. Our tentative conclusion is that these arrangements are basically sound and can effectively deter Communist encroachment in the area. We do intend, however, to take steps to improve their practical effectiveness.

We recognize that your Government is already making a significant contribution to assist the valiant people of South Vietnam, and we believe that there may be additional areas for cooperation between your Government and the Government of the Republic of Vietnam.

Finally, Mr. President, I should like to reiterate the view endorsed by President Kennedy in March, 1962, that the United States would regard with great satisfaction developments on mainland China in which freedom might be restored to the Chinese people. I hope that through further close consultation and planning our Governments can agree on actions which will demonstrate to people everywhere the inevitable defeat of Communist aggression. Secretary Rusk will discuss these matters with you when he visits Taipei in April.

I recall my visit to Taiwan with great pleasure. I hope that your health continues to be excellent and that Madame Chiang has recovered safely from her recent illness.

Warmest personal regards,

Sincerely,

Lyndon B. Johnson"

Rusk

18.   Telegram From the Embassy in the Republic of China to the Department of State[1]

Taipei, March 12, 1964, 4 p.m.

852. Deptel 812 and 820.[2] I delivered Pres Johnson's letter of Mar 2 to Pres Chiang on Mar 10. Others present were FonMin Shen, Chiang Ching-kuo, James Shen (interpreter) and DCM. He had already seen translation made from advance copy we delivered to Foreign Ministry. He asked whether I had any comments to make on the letter.

I said I had no comments to make on President Johnson's letter, but I had received instructions from the Department concerning proposals he had made in conversation with Ray Cline and me on January 29 and certain other proposals subsequently made by Foreign Minister.

I then gave him US reaction to his three alternative proposals as instructed paras A, B, and C, Deptel 812.[3] I wanted to avoid implying that, by suggesting he explore feasibility bilateral arrangement with Seoul, US was prepared to support such arrangement in terms his original suggestion. Consequently, I added that I was not authorized to state

---

[1] Source: Department of State, Central Files, POL 1 CHINAT–US. Secret; Limdis. Repeated to Saigon, Seoul, and Paris.

[2] Telegram 812 to Taipei, March 4, transmitted guidance for Wright's discussions with Chiang Kai-shek and other GRC officials on the U.S. reaction to recent GRC proposals. (Ibid., POL 16 CHICOM) For telegram 820, see Document 17.

[3] The reference paragraphs provided responses to Chiang's plans one, two, and three, which he proposed during his meeting with Cline and Wright on January 29; see Document 11. The responses were negative, except for the suggestion that Chiang might consider exploring the feasibility of a bilateral arrangement with South Korea.

that US would be prepared to provide air, naval, or logistic support to any bilateral arrangement that might be reached.

I then outlined support US giving to GRC international position citing EEC, Tunisia, Ethiopia, Senegal, Congo, (Brazzaville) and FRG.

President then asked what was meant by statement in President Johnson's letter that "there may be additional areas for cooperation" between GRC and GVN.

I responded with substance of para G, Deptel 812 on subject of financial assistance and land reform, saying I believed this probably represented part of what President Johnson had in mind, although I had been given no interpretation.

The President asked whether he was correct in inferring US was not in favor GRC sending a representative to Viet-Nam at present to discuss possibility of alliance as we had suggested he do with respect Seoul.

I repeated our view that situation in Viet-Nam is too sensitive at present for such action and we hoped he would defer undertaking any such initiative.

I told President that I had reported to Washington what Foreign Minister Shen had told me March 8 concerning difficult situation faced by GRC in Brazzaville. We hoped GRC would find it possible to keep mission there until situation clarified. If withdrawal should be considered advisable, we hoped onus could be placed on Brazzaville and that GRC would closely consult with us on steps considered necessary. I then read to him Dept's 833.[4]

President said he had nothing particular to say at this time. He believed he understood the meaning of what I had told him and asked whether the Secretary was definitely coming on April 16.

I replied that I had reported that the President would be glad to see him on April 16 and I believed that he was now definitely planning to come.

President said that matter we had discussed could be gone into fully with the Secretary.

Wright

---

[4] Dated March 9. (Department of State, Central Files, POL 17 CHINAT–CONGO)

19.   **Memorandum From Robert W. Komer of the National
Security Council Staff to President Johnson**[1]

Washington, March 16, 1964.

Relations with the Chinats. Your reply to Chiang's messages and our
other actions appear to have calmed Taipei for the moment.

The Gimo will naturally keep talking up his pet ideas for a stronger
anti-Chicom posture: (1) a US-backed alliance of Vietnam, S. Korea, and
the GRC; (2) a Chinat landing on Hainan; and (3) sending GRC and ROK
troops to help in Vietnam. However, we should be able to fob off these
ideas, all of which have serious drawbacks on present reading. Rusk's
mid-April stopover in Taipei after Manila SEATO meeting will be a further safety valve.

Meanwhile we're doing our best to prevent further erosion on the
Chirep issue. Fortunately, the French Africans have not all followed
DeGaulle. The GRC itself is also playing a cannier game, which is encour-
aging.

Chiang keeps talking of the risk of military coup on Taiwan if the
GRC's international position collapses. But our new NIE on GRC prospects (43–64)[2] is more reassuring. Its chief conclusion is that:

"A. French recognition of Communist China, together with fears
about the strength of the US position in the Far East and the firmness of
US Far Eastern policy have further damaged the morale and confidence
of the Government of the Republic of China (GRC). *However, we believe
that, unless the GRC leadership becomes convinced that the US is abandoning
Taiwan and the anti-Communist cause in the Far East, the GRC will live
through this setback relatively intact and that it is also likely to survive subsequent blows arising from recognition of Peiping by other important powers and
from a bitter struggle over the UN China seat.* The possibility cannot be
excluded, however, that a crisis might precipitate a radical change in the
makeup or policies of the GRC."

R.W. Komer

---

[1] Source: Johnson Library, National Security File, Country File, China, Vol. I. Secret. A
notation on the source text reads: "President read. 3/19."

[2] NIE 43–64, March 11, is entitled "Prospects for the Government of the Republic of
China." (Department of State, INR/EAP Files: Lot 90 D 110)

20.   Letter From the Ambassador to the Republic of China (Wright) to the Assistant Secretary of State for Far Eastern Affairs (Bundy)[1]

Taipei, March 30, 1964.

DEAR BILL: I am sure you are familiar with the "Blue Lion" Committee organized for the purpose of examining Chinese capability plans for operations against the mainland under conditions of a mainland uprising. The Committee was specifically excluded from examining plans for employment of U.S. forces in support except for Taiwan defense.

The Blue Lion Committee work has been largely responsible for getting across to the President and the GRC a factual and realistic evaluation of their chances of success in such operations. This realization has resulted in the relatively quiescent period of propaganda and effort by the GRC in "mainland recovery" plans and for this reason has done a splendid job.

Recently the GRC, entirely on their own initiative, has expanded their planning to operations against Hainan Island. This goes beyond the Blue Lion terms of reference inasmuch as their plans assume:

1) A U.S. requirement for the operation,
2) The employment of U.S. air, naval and logistic support forces.

To clarify the situation I called a meeting of the Blue Lion Committee and have attached hereto the minutes of the meeting.[2]

If you or Defense have any views that we should proceed with requirements planning, please advise and we will act accordingly.

Sincerely,

Jerauld Wright

---

[1] Source: Department of State, Central Files, DEF 1 CHINAT. Secret. The source text is stamped, "Mr. Bundy has seen."

[2] The meeting is recorded in an enclosed March 27 memorandum of conversation. Wright stated at the meeting that the U.S. representatives were not authorized to study and comment on any plans that presupposed the use of U.S. forces except in the defense of Taiwan.

21.   Memorandum for the Record[1]

Washington, April 2, 1964.

SUBJECT

NSC Meeting[2]

1. I briefed the NSC on the following items as per the attached briefing notes:[3]

[Here follow a list of subjects of the briefing and discussion of matters not related to China.]

5. Rusk stated that it was his and the Department's opinion that CIA was in no way overstating the depth of the Sino-Soviet split, indicating that the Department was studying carefully any evidence of actions by one party of the controversy against the other. He said no physical actions were discernible as yet but Rusk raised the question of the possibility of the abrogation of the Soviet-ChiCom Mutual Defense Treaty.[4]

Action: We should continue to study this problem in depth and confer from time to time with State. I should be kept informed for personal discussions with Rusk.

[Here follows discussion of matters not related to China.]

---

[1] Source: Central Intelligence Agency, DCI (McCone) Files: Job 80–B01285A, Box 6, Folder 7, DCI Mtgs with the Pres, Jan–Apr 1964. Secret; Eyes Only. Drafted by McCone.

[2] The meeting was held from 12:10 to 12:35 p.m. (Johnson Library, President's Daily Diaries)

[3] Attached but not printed.

[4] The Treaty of Friendship, Alliance, and Mutual Assistance, signed at Moscow on February 14, 1950; for text, see UNTS 226:5.

22.   Telegram From the Department of State to the Embassy in Poland[1]

Washington, April 2, 1964, 8:59 p.m.

1533. EmbTel 1622.[2] We believe the Chinese Communists will seek to avoid any move that would make it appear that they responsible for breaking off Warsaw talks in view of considerable propaganda advantage that would accrue to our side. Moreover, ChiComs may well wish to continue talks, bearing in mind that Chou En-lai and Chen I during recent African tour made several public references to Warsaw talks to illustrate reasonableness of their position.

Although it appears unlikely, possibility nevertheless exists that ChiComs, perhaps carried away by bitterness of their dispute with Soviets, may decide break off talks or to have them indefinitely deferred. In that event, Wang might behave in manner you suggest hoping to provoke us to suspend talks (Deptel 138, July 26, 1963, para 10).[3] Also possible ChiComs, without necessarily intending to break off talks, may instruct Wang to dramatize ChiCom charges and punctuate his departure by in effect throwing book at you and stamping out.

If any of these situations arise, we want to leave you free to play it by ear as you are so able in doing. For your general guidance, however, you should make it clear the Chinese Communists are responsible for any break or interruption in talks and that the US, in its search for a peaceful settlement of dispute, has been willing and continues willing explore every avenue to this end. We welcome Warsaw talks as effort reduce tension in Far East and lessen threat of war. As relevant to situation, you authorized make statement to press along above lines. If you are asked by press for US position on continuation of talks, merely state US awaiting word from Wang's side concerning talks.

If ChiComs have decided to break off or suspend talks, it seems most likely that they would do so by delaying naming replacement for Wang. This bridge we will cross when we come to it. If Wang does not agree re date of next meeting, you should not press but merely state US presumes his side intends continue talks and that we await proposal from his side as to date.

Rusk

---

[1] Source: Department of State, Central Files, POL CHICOM–US. Confidential; Priority; Limit Distribution. Drafted by Dean and Green, cleared by Popple and U. Alexis Johnson, and approved by Green.

[2] Telegram 1622 from Warsaw, April 1, requested any thoughts the Department might have about Cabot's response in case Wang should "throw the book at me and then stamp out without waiting for my reply." (Ibid.)

[3] Telegram 138 provided guidance for Cabot's meeting with Wang on August 7, 1963. (Ibid.)

23.   **Telegram From the Embassy in Poland to the Department of State**[1]

Warsaw, April 8, 1964, 7 p.m.

1684. Cabot–Wang Talks.[2] Deptel 1509.[3]

(1) Wang opened saying he was being recalled and this would be last meeting this series of talks in which he would participate. Wanted to review Chinese efforts over nearly nine years he has been representing his government in talks. Said his side had made five reasonable proposals for relaxation tension, on October 27 and December 1, 1955, on May 11, 1956, and on September 15 and September 22, 1958. In addition his side presented series of draft agreements designed remove obstacles to trade and travel, exchange newsmen, promote judicial systems and lifting nuclear threat from China. Today he wanted present yet one more effort his side in form of draft agreed announcement (text next following telegram).[4] Essence is mutual agreement for peaceful co-existence, renunciation use of force against each other, and withdrawal US forces from Taiwan area. Repeated position agreements of principle must be reached before concrete issues can be solved. Accused us not only lacking sincerity in talks but throughout talks carrying on hostile acts. Enumerated these in substantially same form as in many previous meetings. Asked USG study draft carefully saying five principles conform to UN principles and should be acceptable to all peace-loving peoples.

(2) I responded with expression appreciated Wang's personal courtesy and regret this was last meeting with him. Said his remarks, however, seemed in their contradiction to echo same differences between words and deeds noted during my Shanghai service, record of which I recently reviewed. Same twisting of facts and concealed aggressions attributed to others. Chicom record throughout had been one of aggression around perimeter of territory they hold. Said while talks not wholly fruitless certainly no spectacular results. Nonetheless peace has been preserved within measure in Far East except for aggression in Korea which was before talks started. Said I could not give categorical answer to proposal before referring my government but pointed out we could hardly renounce certain treaty responsibilities which in effect proposals called for.

---

[1] Source: Department of State, Central Files, POL CHICOM–US. Confidential; Priority; Limdis. Repeated to Geneva, Moscow, Stockholm, Hong Kong, and Taipei.

[2] The meeting was the 120th in the series of Ambassadorial talks. Cabot commented in telegram 1686 from Warsaw, April 9. (Ibid.) He reported the meeting in detail in airgram A–900, April 9. (Ibid.)

[3] Telegram 1509 to Warsaw, March 30, provided guidance for the meeting. (Ibid.)

[4] Document 24.

(3) I continued with attack on duplicity re talk of adherence to five principles peaceful co-existence and other statements and actions expressing intention aid revolutionary movements against legitimate governments non-Communist countries. I continued with bulk of paragraphs 2, 3, 4, and 5 reference telegram[5] with slight deletions and additions. I called particular attention last sentence Rusk quote[6] reminding Wang we had consistently advocated renunciation force but his side would not agree.

(4) Wang attempted explain Chicom double talk by saying while they believed socialism would eventually triumph in entire world it was matter for given country to decide whether its revolution should be violent or not. No foreign country can ever concoct revolution in another country nor can revolution in given country be stopped from outside. Claimed one principle in foreign policy his government called for peaceful co-existence between countries of different social systems. Said Secretary Rusk revealed hostility toward China even in speech quoted. Said if USG willing, as Chinese Government is, practice five principles peaceful co-existence between us, he was sure we could find common ground and could have peaceful and friendly relations. Said dispute between China and US must be settled and he saw no other way except to agree on draft such as presented today.

(5) I referred to statements his authorities indicating they considered peaceful transition to socialism impossible. Bearing this out was long record trying export revolutions. This has forced on USG its policies in the Far East. Korea had led inexorably to present condition existing Taiwan Straits. Said I believed his side could stop the fighting immediately in Laos and South Vietnam if it chose.

(6) Wang quoted American constitution re right of people institute new government. Said they stand for revolution but object to export of revolution and it was USG which conducted subversion throughout world. Said they had not sent single soldier to South Vietnam. It was United States carrying on inhuman war there to convert South Vietnam into colony and in disregard Geneva agreement.

(7) I said presence North Vietnamese troops in both Laos and South Vietnam had been proved. They were there in defiance Geneva accords

---

[5] Paragraphs 2, 3, and 4 set forth U.S. views in general, declaring that the United States sought a lessening of tensions and that the major problem in Asia was "Peiping's expansionist aims." Paragraph 5 stated that Chinese nationals were free to leave the United States, but that U.S. nationals were not permitted to travel to Communist China because the U.S. Government was unable to extend protection to U.S. citizens in China.

[6] Telegram 1509 to Warsaw quoted at length from a February 25 speech by Rusk. The reference is to the following sentence: "When mainland China has a Government which is prepared to renounce force, to make peace, and to honor international responsibilities, it will find us responsive." For text of the speech, see Department of State *Bulletin*, March 16, 1964, pp. 390–396.

and with obvious Chicom connivance because supplied to substantial extent with Chinese weapons. Said their polemics with Soviets made clear their reliance on violent resolutions. Quoted from paragraph 4 CA–4523[7] and from June 14 letter[8] to effect it was wrong make peaceful co-existence generally line of Socialist countries.

(8) Wang said quote was correct—there was difference between opposing peaceful co-existence and in advocating it not be made general line. Point was foreign policy Socialist countries should contain something more than peaceful co-existence.

(9) Wang said it not known exactly when new Ambassador would arrive and it would take him some time to familiarize self with previous negotiations. I offered let him suggest date and accepted July 29.

Cabot

---

[7] Circular airgram CA–4523, October 23, 1963; not printed. (Department of State, Central Files, CSM 1 CHICOM)

[8] Reference is to a letter of June 14, 1963, from the Central Committee of the Chinese Communist Party to the Central Committee of the Soviet Communist Party. The text was transmitted to Warsaw in circular airgram CA–1789, August 13, 1963. (Ibid., CSM 1–1)

---

24.   Telegram From the Embassy in Poland to the Department of State[1]

Warsaw, April 8, 1964, 7 p.m.

1685. Cabot–Wang Talks. Embtel 1684.[2] Following is text draft agreed announcement mentioned reference telegram.

Begin Verbatim Text.

Agreed announcement of the Ambassadors of the Peoples Republic of China and the United States of America on easing the relations between China and the United States and promoting their normalization (draft) in order to ease the relations between China and the United States

---

[1] Source: Department of State, Central Files, POL CHICOM–US. Confidential; Priority; Limdis. Repeated to Hong Kong, Taipei, Geneva, Moscow, and Stockholm.

[2] Document 23.

of America and promote their normalization, and also to safeguard peace in the Far East and the world,

Ambassador Wang Ping-nan, on behalf of the Government of the Peoples Republic of China, and Ambassador John M. Cabot, on behalf of the Government of the United States of America, have agreed to announce the following:

1. The Governments of the two countries agree that the two countries will co-exist peacefully on the basis of the five principles. The five principles are:

Mutual respect for sovereignty and territorial integrity,
Mutual nonaggression,
Noninterference in each others internal affairs,
Equality, and
Peaceful coexistence.

2. The Governments of the two countries agree that they will settle their disputes through peaceful negotiations without resorting to the threat or use of force against each other. Consequently, the Government of the United States of America undertakes to withdraw all its armed forces from China's Taiwan province and the Taiwan Straits area.

The Ambassadors of the two countries will continue their talks on the concrete implementation of the two above-mentioned agreements of principle.

April 8, 1964.

End verbatim text.

Cabot

25.   Paper Prepared in the Policy Planning Council[1]

Washington, April 14, 1964.

AN EXPLORATION OF THE POSSIBLE BASES FOR ACTION
AGAINST THE CHINESE COMMUNIST NUCLEAR FACILITIES

I. Conclusions

1. It is evident on the basis of analysis in this paper and the basic paper on the implications of a ChiCom nuclear capability[2] that the significance of such a capability is not such as to justify the undertaking of actions which would involve great political costs or high military risks.

2. Direct action against the Chinese Communist nuclear facilities would, at best, put them out of operation for a few years (perhaps four to five).

3. A general threat of overt U.S. action to destroy the ChiCom nuclear production facilities in the event of major Chinese aggression would probably not be desirable. Threat of action in response to a specific instance of actual or threatened Chinese aggression would be preferable to a general threat, but would also have significant disadvantages. Whether it would be desirable would depend a good deal upon the circumstances surrounding a particular situation. If, for example, the ChiComs were threatening nuclear action, a threatened response limited initially to nuclear production facilities might be desirable.

4. Action against the ChiCom nuclear facilities which was incidental to other military actions taken against Communist China in response to Chinese aggression would generally be preferable to actions directed against nuclear facilities alone. Similarly, threats designed to deter ChiCom action should probably not be directed solely against nuclear facilities. (However, as stated in par. 3 there may be circumstances in which action limited to nuclear facilities may be preferred.)

5. It seems most unlikely that we can develop, through negotiations in the arms control field, a politically viable basis for action against

---

[1] Source: Johnson Library, National Security File, Country File, China, Vol. I. Top Secret. Filed as an attachment to an April 22 covering memorandum from Rostow to Bundy. The source text does not indicate the drafter, but Rostow's memorandum states that it was prepared by Robert Johnson of the Policy Planning Council with the help of informal comments from State, CIA, and DOD and that it had been revised to reflect the consensus of an interdepartmental discussion in February. No record of the discussion has been found. Copies were sent to Rusk, McNamara, McCone, and ACDA Director William C. Foster.

[2] See Draft Policy Planning Statement on "A Chinese Communist Nuclear Detonation and Nuclear Capability", October 15, 1963. [Footnote in the source text. The October 15 draft statement is cited in footnote 2, Document 14.]

the ChiCom nuclear facilities. The USSR is also most unlikely to agree explicitly or implicitly to U.S. action against ChiCom facilities or to cooperate in helping lay the political basis for such action. But arms control negotiations can further isolate the Chinese on this issue and can thus help prepare the way for possible action taken in other ways and on other grounds against the ChiCom facilities.

6. Covert action seems to offer the politically most feasible form of action. Such action would present least problems if undertaken as part of a reaction to Chinese Communist aggression. Political costs of action in the absence of ChiCom aggression are difficult to estimate. They could be considerable if Peiping reacts strongly; small, if it does not. [3 *lines of source text not declassified*] Technical feasibility continues to be a real question and requires continued analysis.

7. There are a number of technical and technical-related questions which would require an answer before a decision for any of the possible forms of action were made. These include the following:

a. It is doubtful whether, even with completion of initial photographic coverage of the mainland, we will have anything like complete assurance that we will have identified all significant nuclear installations. Thus, even "successful" action may not necessarily prevent the ChiComs from detonating a nuclear device in the next few years. If an attack should be made, some installations are missed and Communist China subsequently demonstrates that it is continuing to produce nuclear weapons, what is likely to be the reaction to the half-finished U.S. effort?

b. It seems to be the case that a relatively heavy non-nuclear air attack would be required to put installations "permanently" out of business (i.e., destroy them so completely that any rebuilding effort would have to start virtually from scratch). If complete destruction is unattainable without a large attack, how effective a job could be done with various alternative levels of attack?

c. Could the U.S. mount an effective counterforce operation, should that prove necessary, without employing nuclear weapons?

[Here follow 28 pages of discussion.]

26.   Memorandum of Conversation[1]

Taipei, April 16, 1964, 4–6 p.m.

SECRETARY'S VISIT TO TAIPEI
April 16–17, 1964[2]

SUBJECT

U.S. and GRC Policies in East Asia

PARTICIPANTS

President Chiang Kai-shek
Madame Chiang
Shen Chang-huan, Minister of Foreign
    Affairs
James Shen, Director, Government
    Information Office, Interpreter

The Secretary
Ambassador Jerauld Wright
William P. Bundy
Ralph N. Clough

After an exchange of pleasantries, the President remarked that the time was short and suggested that the Secretary open the conversation.

Sino-Soviet Dispute

The Secretary responded that he appreciated the opportunity of meeting with the President and wanted to hear him speak on the questions that were on his mind. But, the Secretary said, at the top of his own mind now was the feeling that we were at the beginning of large events in the world. The situation was beginning to show mobility. It was too early to see what the final results of this would be, but it appeared that important changes were in the making. He therefore very much wanted to discuss with President Chiang what was going on inside the Communist world, the implications of the dispute between Peiping and Moscow, and what all this means to the security problems which we and the GRC have in the Western Pacific.

The Secretary said the quarrel between Moscow and Peiping seems to us very deep. Personal relations between Mao and Khrushchev could not be worse. They were using stronger language about each other than the Communists had ever used regarding free world leaders.

---

[1] Source: Department of State, Conference Files: Lot 66 D 110, CF 2384/E. Secret; Limit Distribution. Drafted by Clough, and approved in S on May 6. The meeting was held at President Chiang's Shihlin residence.

[2] Rusk visited Taipei April 16–17. He sent a telegram briefly summarizing his visit as Secto 60 from Saigon, April 17. (Ibid., Central Files, POL 1 CHINAT–VIET S) A record of his initial conversation with Chiang Kai-shek on April 16 is ibid., POL 15–1 CHINAT. Other documentation pertaining to his visit is ibid., Conference Files: Lot 66 D 110, CF 2375, 2380, and 2384/E. A record of an NSC meeting on April 22, during which he reported on his trip to Manila, Taipei, and Saigon, is printed in *Foreign Relations*, 1964–1968, vol. I, pp. 258–262.

In one sense this was a quarrel over the leadership of the Communist world, but it also affected state relations, border problems, trade and security questions. It must, of course, be kept in mind that it is always possible for two dictators to reverse their positions completely and come together as Hitler and Stalin had done prior to the Second World War. In another sense, the Moscow-Peiping dispute may be a family quarrel which may not affect relations with the free world. If one or the other came into military conflict with the free world, there was still a question whether either could afford not to support the other. This is a question we cannot yet answer. However, we may get the answer in the course of this year.

The Secretary said that he knew the President had given a great deal of thought and study to Soviet affairs, including recent developments between Peiping and Moscow and would be much interested in hearing the President's analysis of the situation.

The President said that the Secretary had briefly outlined two possibilities. First, that Peiping and Moscow might each go its own way, and second, that this was a family quarrel and the two might come together again. Which development did the Secretary consider most likely?

The Secretary replied that he frankly didn't know the answer to that question. As late as yesterday Khrushchev had said that this quarrel would bring no benefit to the free world and that the Communist bloc would come out of it stronger than ever. U.S. experts on Communist affairs believe that the dispute goes much deeper than personal relationships. It involves party relations, ideology, state relations and questions relating to nuclear weapons. This combination of differences points in the direction of a complete break. However, the Secretary said he didn't think we could predict now what would happen. The whole problem of what to do about the dispute is now being discussed within the Soviet world. There is a great reluctance to permit a complete break to occur. A complete break would be a great advantage to the free world, but we cannot yet say what will happen.

The President said he was glad that the Secretary had mentioned Khrushchev's statement. He said his own general yardstick for interpreting Communist statements was to look for the opposite meaning from what was said. If the Communists alleged there would be no split, then there probably would be one. The words of Communist leaders cannot be taken at face value. The more they talk in terms of possible rapprochement, the more likely there is to be continued conflict.

The President said it was also significant that Khrushchev should have referred to his conflict with Mao as a family affair. Historically Communists would rather compromise with an outside enemy than one inside the party. The cases of Trotsky, Hitler and Molotov all demonstrated this. A struggle inside the party would be fought out to the very end. The President concluded that since the Secretary had indicated to Ambassador Tsiang that he would like to discuss Sino-Soviet affairs, he had put down some of his ideas in writing, and would have an English translation read (see Document A attached).[3]

The Secretary commented that these were interesting observations concerning the largest problem we had before us in the world today. He inquired whether there was any evidence of traditional regional differences within the Peiping regime, or was the leadership relatively united?

Possibility of GRC Operations Against China Mainland

The President responded that there were ample signs of distrust among middle echelon cadres in the provinces toward the Central Government. There was not the same degree of confidence as before between the regions and the Central Government, but things were kept under control by stringent measures. The President said he knew that within the central leadership a small number of persons had come increasingly in recent years to distrust Mao, but there was still no outward manifestation of this.

The Secretary said that elementary arithmetic demonstrates that the problem of feeding the Chinese people is becoming more difficult year by year. The situation must eventually develop to the point where these strains will become almost impossible to handle.

The President said this was but one of the Communists' numerous weaknesses. In addition to economic weakness, there were political and social weaknesses too numerous to cite. There were also signs of wavering and disloyalty within the armed forces, whose rations were being steadily reduced.

As evidence of differences within the regime, the President referred to the liquidation of Kao Kang and Jao Shu-shih, and the opposition to Mao of Peng Te-huai and his associates. Lin Piao, the present Chief of Staff of the armed forces, was practically paralyzed by illness. The President said he knew that Lin in his heart was opposed to Mao. Lin was a graduate of the fourth class of the Whampoa Academy, where he had been a classmate of General Liu An-chi, commander of the GRC Army. During the Japanese War, Lin had lived for some time in Chungking.

The Secretary said he would like to comment on the question of possible operations against the mainland which the President had raised. He would like to repeat his opening remark that we were at the beginning of a period of great change and could not be certain what the outcome would be. But his judgment today would be that in the face of the large

---

[3] See A-942 attached—Tab 2, page 3. [Footnote in the source text. Airgram A-942 enclosed GRC records of Rusk's three conversations with Chiang, which the Foreign Ministry had provided to the Embassy. The four documents that Chiang and his interpreter read during this session were incorporated into the GRC record of the conversation.]

Chinese Communist forces on the mainland the GRC could not establish itself militarily on the mainland without large-scale assistance from other countries, particularly the United States, and involving U.S. military forces and possibly nuclear weapons. He said, if he had to make a judgment today—who knows what might happen in six months—he would say that Khrushchev would have to support Mao. This could lead to the whole Northern Hemisphere going up in flames.

Nevertheless, the Secretary said it was essential to follow most closely the Sino-Soviet dispute because of its implications for the security situation in Asia, as well as Europe, Africa and Latin America. If either Khrushchev or Mao should die the situation could change suddenly and dramatically. There might be a complete reshaping and realignment of the situation.

The President said that he was opposed in principle to the use of nuclear weapons, particularly in settling the China problem. He didn't want to give the impression that he was advocating immediate action against the mainland. He had a concept he would like to explore. It was not his intention to request U.S. aid to go back to the mainland right away.

The Secretary said it was important for the United States and the GRC to keep in close touch in assessing the situation so as not to miss an opportunity which might be provided by the rapidly changing situation. Think of the difference if the free world had done what was needed in China in 1931! Subsequent history would have been entirely changed.

The President said, as he had stated, he had a concept as to how to proceed against the China mainland which he would have read in English translation (see Document B attached).[4]

The Secretary commented that these were very important and far reaching proposals. He was sure the President would not wish him to comment on them offhand, as they were deserving of careful study. The Secretary went on to say that the reason he had asked the President about the possible existence of regional differences within the Communist regime was related to the President's own interest in South China. A major crisis could develop with Communist China in Southeast Asia. He wanted to tell the President seriously that if the situation in Vietnam deteriorated, the United States course of action would not be to pull out, but to take additional measures. These additional measures might very well involve danger and damage to South China. In view of the pressing internal economic problems in South China, perhaps something could be offered if that area wished to pursue a policy of peace. A combination of opportunity, pressure and danger might cause South China to break

---

[4] See A–942 attached—Tab 2, page 8. [Footnote in the source text.]

away and cooperate with the GRC. The Secretary said he didn't know whether this was possible, but these are things we should be thinking about.

The President responded that he felt very strongly that without the active participation of the GRC no movement in China's southern provinces could arise. The people in these provinces might suffer from bombing and other measures, but the end result would only be more hatred of the United States rather than a move for independence. The key factor would be participation of the GRC.

The President said he had mentioned earlier that the GRC would need U.S. support and assistance in initiating a large-scale anti-Communist movement on the mainland. Opportunities must be created rather than waited for. Guerrilla activity in certain provinces needed to be started. All this must be done first. Any help given by the United States would involve no risk to the United States. The President felt opportunities could be created in the southwest provinces bordering Vietnam, Laos, Thailand, Burma and India. This area was too far away for the USSR to take any interest in and therefore there should be no concern regarding Soviet intervention. The President then said he would like to know exactly what U.S. policy, strategy and tactics were in South Vietnam.

U.S. Policy in South Vietnam

The Secretary replied that the most immediate purpose is to help South Vietnam deal with the Viet Cong insurrection which is supported by and to some extent supplied by North Vietnam. We estimate there are 25 to 30 thousand hard core Viet Cong and 60 to 70 thousand irregulars. The Viet Cong have more strength than these numbers would indicate because they interfere through terror with the villagers' cooperation with the government. They come by night, terrorize the villages and leave the people fearful of cooperating with the government. North Vietnam is providing four types of assistance to the Viet Cong. These are (1) full support in stimulating and agitating through political and propaganda means to try to create the impression that the Viet Cong are the winning side. (2) We have very good information demonstrating that the operating control of the Viet Cong forces is centered in Hanoi. (3) Relatively small numbers of cadres are being infiltrated from the north into the south. Last year perhaps 1800 of such highly trained individuals were sent. Each is worth 25 to 30 times his own weight because of his ability to train and organize local bands. (4) The north is also supplying relatively modest amounts of arms, particularly some of the most sophisticated weapons introduced to deal with the tactics of the Vietnam Army. These include anti-aircraft machine guns for use against helicopters, a few 75 mm recoil-less rifles and communications equipment. Arms are not being supplied in large amounts. Most arms used by the

Viet Cong come from the stock of English, French, Chinese, U.S. and other weapons accumulated over the past 20 years.

Vietnamese Government forces are much larger than the Viet Cong forces, consisting of 200,000 regular troops and 170,000 irregulars. Government forces have superior weapons and equipment, mobility and unlimited economic support. Nevertheless, their task is very difficult because they need not only to deal with the Viet Cong but also to pacify areas. The Viet Cong hit and run tactics are very hard to cope with.

The President interjected "You say, in other words, the Chinese Communists are not directly involved?"

The Secretary replied that no Chinese Communist personnel had ever been found in South Vietnam. There was not even evidence of large numbers of Chinese Communist military or technicians in North Vietnam. Some weapons had been captured which were made in China in 1959, 1960 and 1961, but there was no evidence of direct Chinese Communist involvement in South Vietnam at present.

The Secretary referred to the substantial Chinese community in South Vietnam and said we were very grateful for the work the GRC had done with this community. There might be a few of these people who have been influenced by Peiping, but on the whole, they support the government and are no problem.

The Secretary said that we were trying very hard on the political front to deny Laos as an infiltration route from North to South Vietnam. All signatories to the 1962 agreements on Laos agreed that Laos would not be used as an avenue for this purpose. Of course, this agreement has been violated. We have been working with the signatory countries trying to get compliance with the agreements. If Laos could be stabilized the situation in Vietnam could be improved. Not all of our action is political. We are also engaged in certain activities on the ground to increase the difficulty of using Laos as a route to South Vietnam. Not all of these activities appear in the press. We are working very hard on this problem.

The President said with regard to the situation in South Vietnam, the important thing is to know the real enemy. The enemy is not the Viet Cong in South Vietnam, but the Communists in North Vietnam. This must be recognized before tactics to be used can even be discussed. To move a step further, we should know that the real masters of North Vietnam are the Chinese Communists. They pull the strings. If there were no Chinese Communist regime on the mainland there would be no North Vietnam, and if there were no North Vietnam there would be no Viet Cong. Regarding the question of how to win the war in Vietnam, the President said he had put his thoughts down in a paper which he asked be read (see Document C attached).[5]

---

[5] See A–942 attached—Tab 2, page 11. [Footnote in the source text.]

Madame Chiang said she understood the strategic hamlets had not been very successful.

The Secretary said it depended on the area. In the south the GVN had tried to go too far too fast. Its tactics were now being changed. The Secretary assured the President that his suggestions would be given very careful study. The United States was deeply concerned regarding the security of Southeast Asia. We could assure the President that we did know who our real enemies were. A great deal of sober thought would be given to this problem in the weeks ahead, and as the President knew, he was himself going to Saigon the next day for a first-hand look. He said we would be in touch with the GRC concerning the President's suggestions.

The Secretary continued that since World War II the United States had taken over 160,000 casualties in the cold war against the Communists, most of these in the Far East. We are not going to deal with large masses of men on the Asia mainland with conventional U.S. forces. We cannot ask that of our people. This means frightful destruction if the United States becomes involved militarily in this area. Consequently, we are not prepared to move too far or too fast in the direction of precipitating that kind of war. It may be that Southeast Asia cannot be made secure unless the Chinese Communists are hurt and hurt badly, but this would build up a legacy of hate against the United States. Even many of those who hate Castro advise us not to invade Cuba and kill 40 or 50 thousand Cubans, because of the scar this would leave on our relations with Cuba.

The Secretary said he could not quarrel with the President's identification of the enemy and his analysis of cause and effect. The question is, at what point do we face up to the costs involved, costs which may be frightful? This we must consider most carefully.

The President said he had earlier indicated his objection to the use of nuclear weapons in this part of the world. He was also sure that other people in this area would object. Their use was wholly unnecessary. Vietnamese manpower should be used in Vietnam, and Chinese manpower in China. U.S. military manpower would not be required. Even to think of using nuclear weapons was open to question. It was unwise. It would hurt the United States more than anything else and it was unnecessary. He said he was speaking very frankly to an ally and his desire was to be helpful.[6]

Chiang's Views of U.S. Policy

The President added that it was for the sake of the real interests of the United States that he spoke the way he did and he had also put down

---

[6] This is apparently the exchange that Rusk described in *As I Saw It*, pp. 288–289, although Rusk states that it occurred in his "final meeting with Chiang Kai-shek" in 1968. Rusk's last meeting with Chiang was in December 1966; he did not visit the Republic of China in 1968.

on paper some thoughts regarding U.S. policy. He was afraid these were rather critical, but if the Secretary did not object, he would have them read.

The Secretary said that we value the criticism of a friend.

The President said he had taken into consideration the real interests of the United States. He hoped the criticism would be taken in the spirit it was offered, as the views of a friend. He wanted to emphasize that only the armed forces of the GRC could liquidate the Chinese Communists (see Document D attached).[7]

The President said he was afraid he had overdone his criticism. The Secretary replied that he took no offense, because the President's criticisms were directed at some very fundamental questions. He said the United States does not want to take any action on behalf of others if others are able to take care of their own independence and security. If you scratch the skin of any American you find beneath it an isolationist who would rather be home than anywhere else, but we feel we have learned since 1931 that aggression, if unchecked, becomes a threat to all, and free peoples must stand together to resist it. It was not until 1948–1949 that we began really to learn the lesson of the period beginning in 1931. We now have 48 allies in various parts of the world. Yet we don't control one of them. Sometimes we have the feeling that others control us.

The President said the Secretary must not misunderstand. It was Chinese Communist propaganda which alleged that the United States controlled the policies and actions of others. Take, for example, the United States presence in Taiwan. The United States certainly did not control things here, but this was the Communist propaganda line and it was sometimes taken seriously. Neither did the President have the slightest intention of suggesting that the United States return to isolationism. The world needs the United States, but the United States need not be directly involved in fighting. It should support others to do the fighting.

The President continued that it seems to be present U.S. policy to help nations fighting Communism to maintain the status quo. This indirectly enables Communist regimes to maintain control of the people. The resentment of the people that the U.S. is taking no steps to free them is bound to increase. Chinese Communist propaganda can then exploit this resentment against the United States by accusing the United States of aggression.

The Secretary said that if what the President had in mind was the capability of engaging in military action against the Communists without U.S. participation, this needed to be looked at with great professional

---

[7] See A–942 attached—Tab 2, page 16. [Footnote in the source text.]

competence to determine the capability. However, the United States cannot escape responsibility for assisting such action. No United States Government could accept supporting such an action and then backing away in the face of failure.

The President said he was glad to hear the Secretary's comments. To make a long story short, the results would depend upon U.S. policy and the methods employed. He hoped in the evening to have an opportunity to discuss the matter further. He also wanted to take up certain questions which President Johnson had said in his letter could be taken up with the Secretary.

The Secretary expressed his appreciation at the great thought which the President had put into his preparation for today's meeting.

---

27.   Memorandum of Conversation[1]

Taipei, April 16, 1964, 9:30–10:30 p.m.

SECRETARY'S VISIT TO TAIPEI
April 16-17, 1964

SUBJECT

GRC Relations with U.S. and Free World Nations of Far East

PARTICIPANTS

President Chiang Kai-shek   The Secretary
James Shen, Director, Government   Ambassador Jerauld Wright
    Information Office, Interpreter   Ralph N. Clough, DCM

After dinner the President opened the conversation by stating that one point President Johnson in his letter had said might be discussed with the Secretary was the matter of the proposals made by President Chiang for alliances among anti-Communist nations in the Far East.

Alliance of Anti-Communist Far Eastern Nations

The Secretary said on that matter he had no final, categorical views. Things were in motion. It was relevant to observe that the United States

---

[1] Source: Department of State, Conference Files: Lot 66 D 110, CF 2384/E. Secret; Limit Distribution. Drafted by Clough and approved in S on May 6. The meeting took place at President Chiang's Shihlin residence.

has alliances with the Republic of China, the Republic of Korea and, in effect, the Republic of Vietnam, which was a protocol state under the SEATO Treaty. We are inclined to believe that joint action by these three powers is only likely to become effective should there be a general war with mainland China. Under such circumstances, the United States presumably would be a party. The Secretary didn't quite see what the three powers could do without the United States. Of course, the U.S. was grateful for certain assistance which the GRC was providing to the GVN and he expected to discuss this matter further in Saigon. He thought it unlikely that the Senate would permit the United States to join another alliance arrangement in the Far East. Without United States' participation, whether such an arrangement could be effective was a matter for consideration.

The Secretary said that in connection with their common enemy, Communist China, there was real substance in an arrangement between the GRC and Korea. Both had substantial, well-trained forces which would make a real difference in a struggle with Communist China. He doubted that Vietnam could contribute much. The question now was what could be done to help Vietnam. The GVN did not want foreign combat troops, not even from the U.S.

The President said he recognized the existence of the bilateral U.S. treaties and he knew that the proposed tripartite arrangement might not mean much in practical terms. Nevertheless, it would mean much psychologically to the people concerned and would serve to counter Communist China's treaties with North Korea and North Vietnam.

Effect on Asia of Chinese Communist Nuclear Explosion

The Secretary inquired what the President's views were concerning the effect on Asia should the Chinese Communists explode a nuclear device by the end of this year or next. He was not thinking of the military significance of such an event because it would be many years before Peiping could develop any significant nuclear power and the United States had plenty of nuclear force to counter it. What he was wondering about was the psychological effect of such an event. It might be necessary to take additional steps to counter it.

The President said that on the basis of information at the GRC's disposal he did not believe that the Communists would be able to explode a nuclear device in the next three to five years. Of course, he said, it is necessary to be prepared for that possibility.

Alliance of Anti-Communist Far Eastern Nations

Reverting again to the alliance, the President said this would be a good thing in the light of French recognition of Peiping and it would result in strengthening the confidence in the future of the people in this area.

The Secretary inquired what was the attitude of the other two countries toward an alliance.

The President replied that the South Koreans were most enthusiastic. He said it was they who first brought up the idea. The GRC has had some talks with the Koreans on this subject but not with the Vietnamese. He had brought the matter up only for the Secretary's reference and because he wanted to coordinate his action with the United States.

The Secretary said he would not wish to say at this time that we are opposed to such an alliance. It would have to be studied further. There are, of course, other important countries in this area such as Japan, Thailand and the Philippines. We have given tentative thought to ways in which closer relations can be established among the anti-Communist countries of the western Pacific. In the North Atlantic there is the North Atlantic community. Would it be possible to establish in the Pacific a Pacific community? Naturally, he meant a community excluding Communist China.

The President said all would be in favor of such a community but there was a question as to how to obtain Japanese participation. The Japanese constitution prohibited participation in any form of alliance. Furthermore, Japan was heavily infiltrated with leftists, who could at any moment mount a demonstration against such a project.

The Secretary said, regarding the possible explosion of a nuclear device by Peiping, the Soviets' estimate agreed with that of the GRC. We knew that the Chinese Communists had had a plutonium plant in operation for some time and thought it possible that they might be able to detonate a device this year or next. However, we hoped the GRC estimate was correct. If the Chinese Communists did explode a device, we might see a rapid evolution in Japanese policy, as the Japanese would see this development in Communist China as a major threat to them.

The President said that his view of possible Japanese reaction to the explosion of a nuclear device by the Chinese Communists was the opposite of the Secretary's. He thought it might cause the Japanese to move away from the Free World.

The Secretary said the Japanese were aware of the enormous nuclear power possessed by the United States and would not dare to move to the side of its enemies.

The President said he found the Secretary's comments very interesting and hoped some day they might be able to discuss them again.

U.S. Nuclear Strength

The Secretary said he wanted to impress upon the President the almost unimaginable power in nuclear weapons possessed by the United States. He said we cannot take too much comfort in this, because it is almost unusable. However, he wanted the President to understand the order of magnitude of U.S. nuclear power in order to reassure him and also to help him understand why we were reluctant to risk a general war which the human race might not survive.

The President commented that he thought the Soviet Union knew this only too well.

The Secretary replied that Khrushchev knew it but Mao did not.

The President said that in his opinion the likelihood of nuclear war was remote because of this realization on the part of the USSR. The Soviet Union would not dare to take on the United States.

The Secretary replied that the problem was one of rationality. If people could remain rational, of course, they would not do so, but the question was, at what point does irrationality take over?

The President indicated he appreciated this point.

Warsaw Talks

The Secretary said there was one point on which he wanted to be very clear and direct so there could be no misunderstanding. This concerned the talks in Warsaw. These talks were initiated by President Eisenhower and Secretary Dulles because they had an obligation to U.S. citizens held prisoner on the China mainland. We felt an obligation to attempt to get them released. For seven years these talks have had a single pattern. Peiping says the United States must get out of Taiwan and turn the island over to Peiping. We say we cannot do this. This has become a sort of phonograph record which is repeated over and over.

The Secretary said he could assure the President that we were not negotiating with Peiping for a détente, for trade, or for recognition of the Peiping regime. He understood that the GRC was unhappy about the existence of the talks. He could understand this. The talks would now be suspended for several months as Wang was being transferred. He wanted to assure the President that nothing was going on between the United States and Peiping that the GRC didn't know about.

The President said he doesn't feel unduly exercised about the matter. He knows that there is nothing in the talks. Nevertheless, he hopes they will be discontinued. The man in the street doesn't know what is going on and these talks boosted the prestige of the Chinese Communist regime, particularly after French recognition. The Chinese Communists' propaganda machine takes full advantage of the situation.

The Secretary said that we have similar problems elsewhere. For example, two Americans were shot down in a helicopter and are held by the North Koreans. The United States public demands that we get them back. So we go to Panmunjom and talk with the North Koreans about it. As for the Warsaw talks, there would be none for several months and we will keep in touch with the GRC concerning them.

The President said he was not himself at all exercised about the talks. He knows the United States cannot possibly reach a compromise with the Chinese Communists. If the United States really wanted to do so, it would not have to so publicly. There are many other ways.

The Secretary said that the talks have served a useful purpose. When people accuse the United States Government of being too harsh and inflexible on the Chinese question, we just point to the record of the Chinese Communist position in the Warsaw talks. There it is in the record for seven years.

GRC's UN Position

The President repeated that he had full confidence in the United States. He went on to say that another matter he was not losing sleep over was the GRC's position in the United Nations. President Johnson had called for an intensive effort to support that position and the GRC was prepared to do all it could. At the same time he had absolute confidence in the United States' determination to support the GRC position.

The Secretary said the principal battle would be in the General Assembly. He was not concerned about the Security Council. A number of countries which had recognized Peiping still supported the position that the seating of Peiping in the UN was an important question. The British, for example, had been very helpful. He was reasonably optimistic that the position could be held in the General Assembly, and this is where difficulties might be encountered. However, we both must continue to work hard.

Shen inquired whether the Secretary was referring to the situation this fall, and the Secretary replied he was and to the next two or three years.

The President said he thinks the Chinese Communists are predominately interested in the Security Council and not in being seated in the General Assembly, as such. Unless they can be seated in the Security Council, they are not interested in getting into the UN. Therefore, we must pay attention to the Security Council.

The Secretary said he was not absolutely convinced that the USSR really wants the Chinese Communists in. Sometimes they played their hand with great awkwardness, as if they wished to lose.

The President said that he personally feels assured that so long as the U.S. is determined to keep the Chinese Communists out, they will not be able to get in. However, ordinary people see that three out of the five permanent members of the Security Council now recognize Peiping and feel that their side no longer has the upper hand.

GRC-Japan Relations

The Secretary said that he realized there had been certain differences between the GRC and Japan. There were also differences between the

United States and Japan. He hoped the President would realize how very helpful Japan had been to the United States and the GRC in supporting the GRC's UN position. The U.S. had been an occupying power in Japan, but we were no longer in that position and could not command the Japanese. There were some policies on which we and they did not agree. We hoped the President realized that for the GRC to lose Japanese friendship and support would be a very serious thing. We hoped the GRC and Japan could find a way to compose their differences.

The President said he understood the question very well and appreciated the Secretary's remarks. He understood the importance of Japan's support for the GRC's international position. Had the GRC severed relations with Japan, it would be even more isolated than by the French action. He said that so long as the Japanese did not actually aid the Chinese Communists, he would try to work for improved relations. Since the Yoshida visit to Taiwan, the atmosphere in this respect had improved.

The Secretary said we are constantly in touch with the Japanese and we have discussed this problem with Ikeda. We will continue to pay close attention to it.

In taking leave of the President, the Secretary said he was grateful for this exchange of views which he thought had strengthened and further developed the close relationship which had grown up over many years between the United States and the GRC.

---

28.   Memorandum From the Ambassador to the Republic of China (Wright) to Secretary of State Rusk[1]

Taipei, April 17, 1964.

The following three points were omitted from the record of your after dinner conversation with President Chiang the evening of April 16 because of their extremely high classification.

(1) In describing the almost unimaginable power of the United States nuclear arsenal, you told the President that the United States had

---

[1] Source: Department of State, Conference Files: Lot 66 D 110, CF 2384/E. Top Secret; No Distribution. Drafted by Clough. Filed as an enclosure to a note from Wright to Rusk, stating that it covered three highly classified points from his after dinner conversation with Chiang.

in place in Western Europe weapons with a destructive power 150,000 times the capacity of those used in the course of World War II. This was only a fraction of the total U.S. arsenal. You mentioned to the President that this figure was very highly classified.

(2) In connection with his expression of confidence in U.S. support for the GRC position in the UN, President Chiang stated that he relied on the promise President Kennedy had made that in case of absolute necessity the United States would use the veto to keep the Chinese Communists out of the UN. You later assured the President that although there had been a change of Presidents in the United States, the U.S. position remained unchanged. President Chiang replied he had full confidence in that.

(3) At the end of the conversation, President Chiang said he wanted to express his appreciation to President Johnson for having reiterated the seven points which President Kennedy had made to him in the spring of 1962.[2] He was gratified and would continue to proceed on that basis.

---

[2] The reference is to the seven points set forth in a memorandum of March 31, 1962, to Cline; see *Foreign Relations, 1961–1963,* vol. XXII, p. 206–207. Airgram A–943 from Taipei, April 27, noted that according to the GRC record of the conversation, Chiang stated that Johnson had reiterated the seven points in his letter. (Department of State, Central Files, POL 15–1 CHINAT)

---

29.   Memorandum for the Record[1]

Washington, April 20, 1964.

SUBJECT

Daily White House Staff Meeting, 20 April 1964

1. Mr. Bundy presided throughout the meeting.

[Here follows discussion not related to China.]

5. *National Policy Papers.* Today Bundy's staff had another of its periodic discussions on national policy papers, this one prompted by

---

[1] Source: National Defense University, Taylor Papers, Box 25, Chairman's Staff Group, April 1964. Secret; Eyes Only. Prepared by NSC staff member Colonel William Y. Smith, USA.

Rostow's insistence that he will be able to get a China policy paper out which will be agreed and which will offend no one.[2] Some people believe that if the paper can be agreed to, it will not say much, and thus hardly will be worth the effort. There are others who believe that if there is sharp disagreement over the paper, focusing on the issue of the Off-shore Islands, the whole matter might become a campaign issue.

The government faces a basic dilemma with respect to the policy papers. If they can be used as campaign fodder, that is not good; and everyone feels they will be leaked if they have potential political value. On the other hand, it would be equally unwise for the White House to send the word out that no one is to do any thinking for the next year.

This dilemma was openly recognized at the meeting, and some discussion resulted on ways to deal with the matter. There was general agreement that it would be very useful, and indeed almost necessary, for the government to focus on policies and programs for use by the government in 1965. These papers would, of course, be useful to either the same or a new Administration. Cooper would handle this problem by setting small study groups to deal with particular problems. He was virtually the only one, however, who believed such work could be kept secret. Amory suggested that perhaps the groups like the Council of Foreign Relations could be useful. Bundy, who believed that the Council suffered essentially from the same inhibitions as the government in either getting a small group together or in keeping the discussion secret, preferred a more informal approach. He is thinking in terms of isolating some problem areas, e.g.—Cuba, East-West trade, perhaps China—for discussions among selected individuals. He wants problems that seem manageable and people that are knowledgeable. He asked the staff for any suggestions on either that they might have.

Brubeck made an interesting point when he said that what often starts out as a new look at an old policy often ends up with the people who support existing policy being provided another opportunity to get a restatement. Bundy added that not only was that true, but that for most high level people in government, you could tell what door they would come out of by watching which one they went in.

One other point worth mentioning came up. Forrestal and Bundy both believe the Rostow paper on the consequences of a ChiCom nuclear

---

[2] At the April 15 staff meeting, Bundy and Komer briefly discussed Rostow's desire to get approval of a policy paper on the Republic of China; Komer thought it was "not much of a paper" and that "now is just not the time to decide policy on China." At the April 17 meeting, Bundy told Komer to tell Rostow not to seek approval of the policy paper on China because it "would raise more problems than it would solve, particularly this year." (Memoranda for the Record by Smith, April 15 and 17; ibid.)

capability[3] have defused the issue too much. They believe such a development would have far greater political consequences than does Rostow, and they are probably right since they are in a key position to influence our reaction. In the discussion today, however, the only consequence was that it seems clear the matter will be looked at again.

WYS

---

[3] Reference is apparently to an undated paper entitled "The Implications of a Chinese Nuclear Capability," attached to a memorandum of April 17 from Rostow to the President. (Johnson Library, National Security File, Country File, China, Volume I) It was evidently not sent to the President. Document 30 is a revised version.

---

30.   Paper Prepared in the Policy Planning Council[1]

Washington, undated.

THE IMPLICATIONS OF A CHINESE COMMUNIST NUCLEAR CAPABILITY

I. Summary and Key Issues

1. *Timing and Character.* A first nuclear test could occur any time; it is likely to be in late 1964 or later. With their one known plutonium reactor, the ChiComs could produce only one or two crude weapons per year. A substantial program would require completion of a plant started with earlier Soviet assistance. While initial nuclear delivery means may be obsolescent aircraft, the Chinese are apparently concentrating on medium-range missiles.

2. *Military Effects.* The ChiComs have demonstrated prudence in the use of military force. Their capability will be more important for its political-psychological than for its direct military effects—primarily because of the great disparity between U.S. and Chinese nuclear capabil-

---

[1] Source: Johnson Library, National Security File, Country File, China, Vol. I. Secret. Filed as an attachment to a memorandum of April 30 from Rostow to the President, which states that it summarized a "major planning exercise" conducted over the previous year on an interdepartmental basis by Robert Johnson of the Policy Planning Council and that issue 4–b was the subject of "further intensive staffing on a particularly secure basis."

ities and vulnerabilities. The Chinese could eventually do significant, but not crippling, damage to U.S. forces in Asia, while the U.S. will have the ability to destroy Communist China. This makes Chinese first-use of nuclear weapons unlikely—unless the regime were already threatened with destruction—and greatly reduces the credibility of its nuclear capability as a deterrent. A limited ChiCom intercontinental capability would not eliminate this basic disparity.

3. *Political-Psychological Effects.* The ChiComs will hope that their nuclear capability will weaken the will of countries resisting insurgency; inhibit requests for U.S. assistance; put political pressure on the U.S. military presence in Asia; and muster support for Chinese claims to great power status. They may hope that it will deter us in situations where our interests seem only marginally threatened.

4. *U.S Counter-Actions.* No major policy changes are required. Specific action proposals are developed in another paper. Policy issues include the following:

a. *Military posture.* Does the Sino-Soviet split deprive Communist China of the Soviet nuclear umbrella and make a lower U.S. nuclear threshold a desirable policy in Asia? Dependence upon nuclear weapons should not increase. Future emphasis should be upon dual-capable and seaborne forces.

b. *Pre-emptive Military Action.* Would military action against ChiCom nuclear facilities be desirable? Would be undesirable except possibly as part of general action against the mainland in response to major ChiCom aggression. Study of covert action should continue.

c. *Nuclear Proliferation.* What U.S. actions might reduce the likelihood of development of additional national nuclear capabilities (e.g., by India)? No combination of actions may be adequate; the following offer best prospects: (i) broad public declaration of willingness to provide nuclear defense; (ii) assurances to allies under existing security commitments; (iii) offers to neutrals of declaratory commitment to consult; (iv) offers to engage in bilateral planning for nuclear defense; (v) offers to deploy nuclear weapons in event of nuclear threats; (vi) exploration of possible forms of joint declarations with Soviets.

d. *Additional Assurances.* If the ChiComs exploit both the sense of threat and the desire for peace, what other U.S. actions might provide relevant assurance to Asian states? Such actions as deployment of mobile air defense units to advance bases in Asia; stimulation of Asian military and non-military cooperation; selective token increases in military assistance; positive statement of U.S. interest in involving Communist China in disarmament negotiations; development of Asian components of our arms control plan; etc.

31.   Letter From the Chargé to the Republic of China (Clough) to the Assistant Secretary of State for Far Eastern Affairs (Bundy)[1]

Taipei, May 22, 1964.

Dear Bill:

The Chinese Communist shelling of Matsu on May 16, which clearly seems to have been a reaction to GRC artillery fire from Matsu covering a raiding party launched from Matsu against Lienchiang (FCT 8622), caused me to give consideration to repeating to the GRC the warning we gave them last spring that they should not assume the US would assist the GRC should the Chicoms attack the smaller offshore islands in retaliation for raids mounted by the GRC from such islands. (Dept's CA–10363, March 22, 1963, and Embassy's A–1091, June 21, 1963.)[2]

While the raid in question was not launched from one of the smaller offshore islands, some of the GRC's recent raids have been launched from Tungyin. Of course, these have not been of the size that we were afraid the GRC might launch last spring, nor has there been any evidence that the GRC is deliberately seeking to provoke a Chinese Communist reaction against the offshore islands. On the contrary, the lack of success of the raids appears to have deterred the GRC for the present from any further activity in that general area (FCT 8622).

I assume our policy continues to be to oppose any action which might heighten the risk of the US becoming involved in military action in the Taiwan Straits area. We have not objected to the small scale raids the GRC has been running recently and I do not believe actions on that scale significantly increase the risk of a Chinese Communist reaction which would involve the US. However, if the GRC should continue to use Tungyin or other minor offshores as a base for raids against the mainland, it would be easier for the Chinese Communists to build up a case in the eyes of the world justifying a military assault by them against these islands. Consequently, I believe we should consider repeating our warning of last year, if raids from the offshores should be resumed.

The timing of any such action would be influenced by measures we may take to cope with the serious situations in Laos and Vietnam, which might ultimately involve the Chinese Communists. It would be untimely, I think, to be warning the GRC against their minor harassing activities against the China mainland, just at the moment we were undertaking strong measures in Southeast Asia.

---

[1] Source: Department of State, Central Files, POL 27 CHICOM–CHINAT. Secret; Limit Distribution.

[2] Not printed. (Ibid.)

I have been in touch with Bill Nelson and other members of the Country Team on this matter, and will, of course, discuss it with the Ambassador.[3]

Sincerely,

Ralph

---

[3] Wright raised the subject of the May 16 clash at Matsu with Shen on June 19. He warned him that launching raids from the offshore islands was dangerous because it invited retaliation against the islands and that it would be unwise of the GRC to rely on U.S. assistance in such a situation. Shen said this was the first he had heard of the episode but that he would pass on what Wright had told him. (Memorandum of conversation, enclosed with airgram A–1110 from Taipei, June 26; ibid.)

---

32.   Memorandum From the Central Intelligence Agency's Deputy Director for Plans (Helms) to the President's Special Assistant for National Security Affairs (Bundy)

Washington, May 25, 1964.

[Source: Johnson Library, National Security File, Country File, China, Volume I. Top Secret. 4 pages of source text not declassified.]

33.   Memorandum From the Deputy Assistant Secretary of State for Far Eastern Economic Affairs (Barnett) to the Director of the Office of Asian Communist Affairs (Grant)[1]

Washington, May 28, 1964.

SUBJECT

Transfer of "Warsaw Talks" to Paris

After Tuesday's Assistant Secretaries meeting with Gov. Harriman, he held me back for a while to talk about China, particularly the Greene film. In the course of our conversation, he indicated that he was inclined to go along with transfer of the "Warsaw Talks" from Warsaw to Paris, and believed also that Cabot had made a good suggestion in offering hope that we might get a quid pro quo from this move which presumably Peking very much wants. In addition to asking the release of our prisoners, he threw out the possibility that we ask Peking to alter its present policy with respect to U.S. scholars and newspapermen desiring to go to Communist China.

Paul Popple rightly points out that there are certain risks in negotiating with Peking over the locus for the Warsaw talks; we might even lose the contact in Warsaw itself. My own view is that we should welcome the transfer, notwithstanding Bohlen's warnings.

---

[1] Source: Department of State, Central Files, POL CHICOM–US. Confidential. Copies were sent to Green, Popple, McNutt, and Thomson.

34.   National Intelligence Estimate[1]

NIE 10-2-64   Washington, June 10, 1964.

PROSPECTS FOR THE
INTERNATIONAL COMMUNIST MOVEMENT

The Problem

To examine the situation and probable developments in the world Communist movement.

Conclusions

A. The international Communist movement is now openly split into majority and minority factions oriented respectively toward the Russians and the Chinese. It is also disturbed by other factors, such as the weakening of Soviet authority in Eastern Europe, the example of Yugoslavia, and the independent inclinations of a number of Communist parties, notably the Communist Party of Italy. (Paras. 1–16)

B. The Sino-Soviet dispute will probably continue to have its ups and downs, and in certain circumstances relations between the two states might improve considerably. However, the rift is so deep and the national interest of each party so heavily engaged that there is now virtually no chance of reconciliation under the present leaders. The international movement may now be on the eve of a formal split, but whether or not this step is taken, the bitter struggle for control and influence over the Communist parties will continue. Further tension in state relations between China and the USSR also seems likely, especially on the common frontier. The demise of either or both of the present leaders would offer some prospect of temporary amelioration of the dispute, but we believe that the fundamental differences between the two powers would remain. (Paras. 2–5)

C. The international Communist movement as a whole is likely to be characterized by increased dispersion of authority and by more independent conduct by various parties. Although Soviet power remains a major factor in Eastern Europe, further manifestations of autonomous and nationalist behavior will probably occur. Among the parties out of

---

[1] Source: Department of State, INR/EAP Files: Lot 90 D 110, NIE 10–2–64. Secret; Controlled Dissem. According to a note on the cover sheet, the estimate was submitted by the Director of Central Intelligence and concurred in by the U.S. Intelligence Board on June 10. The Central Intelligence Agency and the intelligence organizations of the Departments of State and Defense, the National Security Agency, and the Federal Bureau of Investigation participated in the preparation of the estimate. All members of the U.S. Intelligence Board concurred, except the Atomic Energy Commission Representative, who abstained on the grounds that the subject was outside his jurisdiction.

power, we foresee a trend toward regionalism—as in the Far East, but also perhaps in Western Europe and Latin America. The Sino-Soviet competition for influence will in some cases lead to further splits within individual parties. At the same time, Moscow and Peiping will remain powerful sources of material support for their followers, and will retain considerable operational influence on a bilateral basis. (Para. 11, 24–25, 29–33)

D. For the non-Communist world this situation offers important advantages and some dangers. The assertion of divergent national interests by Communist powers offers an opportunity for the West to deal profitably with some of them individually. The Sino-Soviet conflict is increasingly absorbing the energies of the USSR and Communist China and diverting them from sharp contentions with the major Western powers.[2] Among the nongoverning parties, a few have already suffered severe setbacks as a result of the conflict. On the other hand, some Communist parties will become more effective and will gain greater freedom of action and respectability because of their more independent status. While in some countries the parties will tend to lose their rationale and elan, in others they will probably emerge as more formidable revolutionary organizations, though more national than international in character. Regardless of internal quarrels, Communists will retain an underlying enmity toward the West if only because their convictions are in so many respects incompatible with traditional Western concepts of political and economic life. (Paras. 37–40)

E. In general, we foresee the emergence of a variety of Communists and Communist parties, some chiefly influenced by Moscow or Peiping, some largely autonomous. In conducting their relations with Communist states and forming their policies toward revolutionary movements, the principal non-Communist powers will probably find it increasingly advantageous to judge each particular situation on its own merits, rather than on the assumptions which generally prevailed when Moscow unquestionably dominated the international movement. This situation offers new opportunities and advantages to Western policy, but it presents new dangers and difficulties as well. (Paras. 40–43)

[Here follows the Discussion portion of the estimate.]

---

[2] For discussion of the impact of the conflict on Soviet and Chinese foreign policy, see NIE 11–9–64, "Soviet Foreign Policy," dated 19 February 1964, and NIE 13–63, "Problems and Prospects in Communist China," dated 1 May 1963. [Footnote in the source text. NIE 11–9–64 is scheduled for inclusion in *Foreign Relations, 1964–1968*, volume XIV. NIE 13–63 is printed in part in *Foreign Relations, 1961–1963*, vol. XXII, pp. 365–367.]

35.   Memorandum From James C. Thomson, Jr., of the National Security Council Staff to the President's Special Assistant for National Security Affairs (Bundy)[1]

Washington, July 15, 1964.

SUBJECT

Warsaw Talk with the Chicoms, July 29

The attached cable from Ed Rice in Hong Kong[2] offers a persuasive U.S. line for the re-opened Warsaw talks with Peiping's new Ambassador July 29.

Rice argues that:

(1) We have here a good opportunity to clarify our various signals to the Chicoms on Southeast Asia.
(2) We should do this in strictly non-polemical fashion—and thereby attempt to alter the tone of the Warsaw meetings for future discussions with the new man.
(3) We should re-invoke the "Bandung principles".
(4) We should avoid squeezing debater's points from the literature of Sino-Soviet polemics.

It seems to me that such an approach might help to raise the tone and usefulness of the Warsaw channel. This presentation would be impressive as well to Warsaw's keyhole listeners, the Poles and the Russians.

May I urge my pals at State to follow this approach in their instructions to Cabot?[3]

James C. Thomson, Jr.[4]

---

[1] Source: Johnson Library, National Security File, Country File, Poland, Cabot–Wang Talks. Secret. A note in Komer's handwriting on the source text reads as follows: "Jim Thomson and Rice make sense on this one! We may want to use Warsaw channel for *real* signals, so better not to clog it with a lot of useless noise. RWK."

[2] Telegrams 48 and 52 from Hong Kong, July 13 and 14 respectively, are attached but not printed. Both are in Department of State, Central Files, POL CHICOM–US.

[3] A note in Bundy's handwriting next to this sentence on the source text reads as follows: "Yes, indeed."

[4] Printed from a copy that bears this typed signature.

36.   Memorandum From William E. Colby, Chief, Far East
       Division, Plans Directorate of the Central Intelligence Agency
       to That Agency's Deputy Director for Plans (Helms)

Washington, July 15, 1964.

[Source: Johnson Library, National Security File, Agency File, Central Intelligence Agency, Volume I. Top Secret. 4 pages of source text not declassified.]

37.   Telegram From the Department of State to the Embassy in
       Poland[1]

Washington, July 23, 1964, 6:54 p.m.

160. Cabot–Wang Talks: 121 Meeting Guidance. Following guidance is provisional and not fully cleared. It is provided to permit you to begin to organize your presentation. Changes or confirmation will follow.

FYI: ChiComs in June held major party meeting and apparently consulted with North Vietnamese and other friends. Result has been deeper ChiCom commitment to come to assistance North Viet-Nam if attacked. (See July 9 *People's Daily Editorial*.) While ChiComs thus more committed to meet major US attack, they have avoided committing selves to explicit action in response US actions at lower level. We presume they will reiterate threats contained July 9 editorial. We are particularly interested to see whether their private statements to us differ in any way from the public utterances. We are also interested in determining whether they press strongly for reconvened Geneva Conference, and on what terms. Intensity of pressure in this direction probably would reflect degree of ChiCom concern at likelihood escalation in Southeast Asia. We do not have indications that ChiComs presently anticipate US attack on North Viet-

---

[1] Source: Department of State, Central Files, POL CHICOM–US. Confidential; Priority; Limit Distribution. Drafted by Dean and Grant. Cleared in substance by William Bundy, and in draft by Carl Salans of L/FE, Allen Whiting of INR/RFE, William C. Trueheart of SEA, Special Assistant to the Secretary for Vietnamese Affairs Michael Forrestal, and Thomson. Approved by Grant. Repeated to London, Stockholm, Taipei, and Hong Kong.

Nam. First session with new ChiCom representative affords good opportunity both to clarify US signals on SEA and to indicate our desire to keep open Warsaw channel. End FYI.

1. Suggest you open meeting by greeting Ambassador Wang Kuo-chuan and introducing staff. Then proceed on following lines:

2. "While we cannot boast of many successes or much agreement reached in these talks, hope you agree that they have served useful purpose in permitting contact and providing channel in case of need. We believe it is to advantage both our sides to have clear understanding of each other's intentions, particularly in situations where there is serious threat of a major confrontation.

"In Southeast Asia we presently face just such a serious situation. We have read your statements as to obligation which you feel to support Communization of other nations. We see a confrontation between your ambitions and our resolve to prevent non-Communist governments of Southeast Asia from being overturned by infiltration and subversion supported and led from outside their borders.

"If in fact we stand perilously [close] to a confrontation, it is no pleasure to us. We have too much affection and respect for Chinese people to enjoy possibility of becoming involved in hostilities involving them. Nevertheless, if we correctly read your intentions, the possibility exists. If we have misread your intentions, we should be informed."

3. Make following points, paraphrased from Depcirtel 49:[2]

a. US has vital interest and commitments in Asia as well as Europe, and does not intend to treat our Asian commitments more lightly than European ones.

b. Our specific commitment to the Republic of Viet-Nam goes back a decade. Systematic violation of 1954 Geneva Accords by Communists has forced us to respond.

c. Our consistent policy has been to assist South Viet-Nam in its efforts to maintain freedom and independence in the face of covert Communist aggression directed from outside SVN, and in violation of Geneva Accords. We intend to maintain that policy.

d. This battle is being fought by Vietnamese, with aid sent by US and other free nations, at request of Republic of Viet-Nam. So long as Viet Cong, supported and directed by DRV and encouraged by your side, continues its attacks on GVN, US will find it necessary to lend GVN such help as it needs to restore peace.

e. Secretary Rusk said on July 1 "peace ought to be possible in Southeast Asia without any extension of the fighting .... First objective of

---

[2] Circular telegram 49, July 7; not printed. (Ibid., POL 1 ASIA SE–US)

our policy and our desire in SEA is to exploit that possibility."[3] We are well aware of serious consequences that could flow from an expansion of war beyond the borders of SVN. We do not desire it and will seek to avoid it, but we shall not abandon our objectives or commitments out of fear of it.

f.   As to negotiation, neutralization, or a political settlement to bring peace to Southeast Asia: we would like nothing better than an end to terror and killing. Negotiated settlements have been spelled out in Geneva Agreements of 1954 and 1962, and we believe present need to be for Communist observance of those accords, rather than negotiation of new arrangements.

4.   In Laos a similar situation obtains. We shall continue our support for RLG. We support Geneva Agreement of 1962 and Government of National Union headed by Prince Souvanna Phouma. PL and DRV have endeavored to undermine arrangements. North Vietnamese troops have never left Laos as provided in Geneva Agreement and they continue use Laotian territory as route of infiltration to South Viet-Nam, in violation 1962 Agreements. With assistance of DRV, PL has taken over Plaine des Jarres, traditional base of neutralist forces under Kong Le. It has done so on fiction that neutralist forces in possession that area had suddenly become no longer "true neutralists," apparently because PL decided they were not amenable to Communist control. So long as these Communist efforts destroy Tripartite Government continue, we shall continue to respond to requests for assistance by the legitimate government of Laos recognized by all participants in Geneva settlement.

We read in *People's Daily* of July 6 that "US and Laotian right wing ousted Prince Souvanna from power by force, put him under house arrest, announced his removal from Premiership, etc." You have fabricated your own version of events by ignoring explicit US condemnation of April 19 coup and continued US support for Souvanna, and by attempting to create a US announcement which does not exist. A policy based on unreality constitutes a peril for all involved. It is unfortunate enough for you to make such misstatements. We hope that you do not believe them. Similarly, we hope that you understand correctly the firmness of our resolve to support the RLG, and that you are not acting on basis of a willful underestimate of our seriousness and ability to assist RLG to defend its independence and neutrality.

5.   Lest there be any misunderstanding of our policy in Far East, we wish to repeat what President Kennedy said on June 27, 1962: "purposes

---

[3] For the transcript of the July 1 press conference at which Rusk made this statement, see Department of State *Bulletin*, July 20, 1964, pp. 82–88.

of the US in this area are peaceful and defensive."[4] We believe your side is aware that our presence in SEA is intended to help free nations there protect themselves against externally-directed subversion, and is not aimed at your destruction or at destruction of authorities in North Viet-Nam. We have no interest in maintenance of US presence in SEA beyond defense of those free governments. If US military presence is onerous to your side, simplest means of achieving its withdrawal would be for you and North Vietnamese to terminate pressures upon those governments.

6. Wang Kuo-chuan will probably start with lengthy series of complaints about US "aggressive acts" in FE. This will include *People's Daily* editorial on 300th serious warning (FBIS 128) and editorial on U–2 (FBIS 139). Wang may then reiterate ChiCom serious warnings concerning attacks on North Viet-Nam (see July 9 *People's Daily* editorial, FBIS 133, and ChiCom Government statement July 19, FBIS 141). He may repeat that "Chinese people cannot be expected to look on with folded arms in face of aggression in North Viet-Nam" and that a US attack on North Viet-Nam would pose threat to China's peace and security.

7. Suggest you respond to warning re ChiCom actions in event US attack on NVN by referring to your statements para 4 d&e and para 6 above, and observing that his side's peace and security not at stake, but rather his side's ambitions.

8. Wang may press strongly for Geneva meeting on Laos. You should respond that such meetings seem desired by Communists to legitimize military conquest. Note Souvanna's statement that meeting dependent upon restoration of neutralist position in Plaine des Jarres and an effective ceasefire. We favor negotiation among Lao leaders, or with other participants as proposed by Poland. If Wang presses this point or makes an official request for such a meeting tell him that you will refer request to Department.

9. Suggest you ignore routine "serious warnings." If pressed, state that in past complaints have been without foundation but volunteer to submit specific complaints to Department. On U–2s, ignore unless Wang charges that we broke word in supplying further U–2s to GRC after first two were lost. In latter case, observe that US never made such commitment. US spokesman on September 9, 1962 said GRC had contracted purchase two U–2s.[5] On September 13, 1962 President Kennedy said we had no plans to sell any further ones.[6] We have subsequently had ample reason to change decision.

---

[4] For the transcript of the press conference on June 27, 1962, at which Kennedy made this statement, see *Public Papers of the Presidents of the United States: John F. Kennedy, 1962*, pp. 509–517.

[5] See *Foreign Relations, 1961–1963*, vol. XXII, p. 318, footnote 2.

[6] For the transcript of the press conference on September 13, 1962, at which Kennedy made this statement, see *Public Papers of the Presidents of the United States: John F. Kennedy, 1962*, pp. 674–681.

10. Wang may ask for US view on draft joint statement presented 120th meeting requesting US adhere Bandung principles and withdraw from Taiwan. Suggest you tell Wang US favors these principles, but we have observed that his side seems to have no scruples of conscience in pronouncing such principles, and then announcing support of Communist insurrection in free world. We believe in non-interference, and wished that his side really shared the belief. As for "withdrawal" from Taiwan US has treaty obligation with Republic of China. We will not abandon this obligation. There are a few thousand US military advisors on Taiwan. It requires a remarkable imagination to say that these men seized Taiwan by force of arms and are controlling the Republic of China and its army of several hundred thousand.

11. It is just possible that ChiComs may raise substance Mao July 11 interview with Japanese Socialist Party delegation concerning Taiwan. (See Hong Kong 57 to Department being repeated you.)[7] Mao reportedly said if US would agree to withdraw forces from Taiwan China would guarantee not to install its own forces on island. You should respond that you presume this means ChiComs prepared renounce use of force against Taiwan provided US withdraws its military advisors. If response affirmative say you will report to Department. In any case, draw Wang out as to specifics of proposal.

12. If Wang raises question of transferring site of talks, tell him you will refer suggestion to Department.

13. When Wang suggests date for next meeting you should, if necessary, suggest that interval until next meeting not exceed two months.

14. In view sensitivity of topics, you are particularly urged to make detailed telegraphic report covering this meeting.

Rusk

---

[7] Dated July 14. (Department of State, Central Files, POL 7 JAPAN)

38.   Memorandum for the Record[1]

Washington, July 24, 1964.

SUBJECT

Meeting with the President—11:15 a.m., 24 July 1964.

[Here follows discussion of unrelated matters.]

3. With respect to the Chinese atomic program, I said we could not foretell when the Chinese would explode a device. However, we had observed five installations associated with the Chinese Atomic Energy Program in various stages of assembly and operation and hence I concluded they had overcome some, if not all, of their problems associated with the Soviet's withdrawal of technical assistance and were now making progress.[2]

[Here follows discussion of unrelated matters.]

---

[1] Source: Central Intelligence Agency, DCI (McCone) Files: JOB 80–B01285A, DCI Mtgs with the Pres, May–Oct 1964. Secret; Eyes Only. Drafted by McCone.

[2] An attached paper dated July 22, entitled "Chinese Communist Nuclear Weapons Capabilities," is apparently the briefing paper that McCone used to brief the President on this subject. It states that the evidence was "still insufficient to permit confident conclusions as to the likelihood of Chinese Communist nuclear detonation in the next few months."

---

39.   Telegram From the Department of State to the Embassy in Poland[1]

Washington, July 25, 1964, 9:42 p.m.

169. Cabot–Wang Talks: 121st Meeting Guidance. Deptel 160[2] rptd London 569, Stockholm 66, Taipei 74, Hong Kong 98.

Guidance in reftel is confirmed, with following amendments:

Section 2. Introduce presentation with brief review of purposes of talks and their successes and failures. Revise first two paragraphs sec-

---

[1] Source: Department of State, Central Files, POL CHICOM–US. Confidential; Priority; Limit Distribution. Drafted by Grant, cleared by William Bundy and in substance by Harriman and Thomson, approved and initialed by Rusk. Repeated to London, Stockholm, Taipei, and Hong Kong.

[2] Document 37.

tion 2 as necessary to accommodate your general introduction. Eliminate third para section 2. Close section with statement that a clear statement of our position seems desirable to avoid possibility of misunderstanding.

Section 3 para d. Expand closing phrase to read "to lend SVN such help as it desires and needs to restore peace."

Section 5. Expand conclusion of your presentation along following lines: We have presented our position in SEAsia in some detail as means insofar as possible of avoiding danger of conflict based upon misunderstanding. Given our understanding that your ultimate intention is Communization SEAsia by any means, we are not confident that confrontation between us is avoidable. However, we welcome an expression from you of your side's intentions concerning area.

Rusk

---

40.   Telegram From the Embassy in Poland to the Department of State[1]

Warsaw, July 29, 1964, 8 p.m.

223. Department telegram 160. Cabot–Wang talks.[2]

(1) Wang asked say a few words first in which he affirmed in pursuance directive his government he wished to continue maximum efforts through talks to achieve peaceful solution Sino-American problems and work toward change in stagnant state of them. I reciprocated hope talks may prove fruitful. Then made lengthy opening statement based closely on first five sections reference telegram with changes desired Department telegram 169.

(2) After Wang's rejection my "absurd distortion facts and groundless charges" against his government he mentioned draft agreed announcement of last meeting, saying it would open way to find settle-

---

[1] Source: Department of State, Central Files, POL CHICOM–US. Confidential; Priority; Limdis. Repeated to Hong Kong, Taipei, Geneva, Moscow, and Stockholm.

[2] Telegram 160 is Document 37. Cabot commented in telegram 227 from Warsaw, July 30, "I think it fair to say there appeared to be something of a 'collision course' atmosphere." He reported the meeting in further detail in airgram A–112, August 3. (Both in Department of State, Central Files, POL CHICOM–US)

ment Sino-American disputes and conforms to common desire improve relations. Agreement would carry immense significance. Wang then reviewed totals serious warnings with break-down recent ones saying provocations not confined to coastal regions but extended deep into hinterland. Mentioned "incessant instigation and support of 'Chiang gang raids' and spy aircraft." Since November of last year until June of this, nine groups of Chiang agents captured in raids on mainland and two more spy planes shot down since last meeting. U–2 nominally Chiang's but "control US". Said recently Admiral Felt in Taiwan clamored for risking war with Communist China and President Johnson openly declared US must be prepared risk war. All these facts point to utter unwillingness seek peaceful settlement disputes or practice peaceful coexistence. Said at last meeting I had tried justify US seizing Taiwan and our rejection agreed announcement by revoking treaty with Chiang government. This completely untenable since Chiang long ago overthrown by Chinese people and did not represent anyone. Treaty illegal, null and void. Said we had concocted treaty of December 2, 1954 more than four years after our seizure Taiwan.

(3) Wang continued we had slandered his side in accusing it of violation principles peaceful coexistence. Said "we are Communists. It goes without saying we shall propagate revolutionary doctrine but unlike you we do not have single soldier in any foreign territory anywhere in world. We have never advocated export of revolutions in propagating our revolutionary doctrine. We only publicize objective truth." Continued our armed intervention many areas of world was aggression. Said we and not they unscrupulously meddled in affairs other countries. Seizure Taiwan and interference Chinese internal affairs gave rise Sino-American dispute. These facts can in no way be bypassed and account must be settled at some time.

(4) Wang continued tension Indo-China caused by our planning new military adventures there which aroused concern people of China, Asia and rest of world. Said after assassination Foreign Minister Laos we had again instigated rightists to stage coup and our intervention had known no bounds. Geneva accords in danger being completely scrapped. On June 11 our fighter bombers bombed Khang Khay. Our brutal atrocity caused heavy losses among Lao and killed one, wounded five in Chinese Economic and Cultural Commission. Chinese Government and people expressed great indignation at this and Wang instructed lodge serious protest to US through me. Chinese Government reserves all rights pursue responsibility in this case (*sic*). Said we had long since thrown overboard Geneva agreements South Vietnam and even clamoring spread war to North Vietnam. Present situation Indo-China exceedingly grave. There is danger flames of war will spread even to whole of SEA. China is signatory to both Geneva agreements and these

matters have direct bearing on Chinese security. China cannot look on with apathy in face grave situation we have created in Indo-China. Chen Yi has made clear Chinese people absolutely will not sit idly by while Geneva agreements torn up and flames of war spread. Chinese people cannot be expected look on with folded arms in face any aggression against DRV. Said he hoped these statements had received our full attention. China had advocated conference fourteen signatory nations seek peaceful settlement Laos question basis Geneva accords. Many among fourteen endorsed proposal but we obstructing holding conference, putting blind faith in force of arms, believing we can act with impunity. Said we must understand revolutionary people cannot be cowed into submission through force of arms. This policy would ultimately bring ignominious fiasco.

(5) I responded I was astonished and dismayed at Wang's statements and must state categorically many of them inaccurate. For instance we had nothing do with bombing Khang Khay. Re Taiwan I made clear US has no intention abandoning treaty obligations. Followed with substance latter half section 10 reference telegram then first half re draft statement. I then spoke of peaceful coexistence and exportation revolutions, quoting from ChiCom Central Committee letter to Soviets June 14 last year re general line including concept "to support and assist the revolutionary struggles of all the oppressed peoples and nations." Said this policy has caused ChiComs give support contrary Geneva agreements to wars being waged by PL in Laos and Viet Cong in both Laos and South Vietnam. Asked how in face this quote issued by highest authority and in face ChiCom deeds Laos and Vietnam they could expect us let SEA fall through ChiCom use of force against wishes people of area. Said we agreed most unfortunate for everyone if war expanded such as to North Vietnam but on other hand surely ChiComs must realize if their gross interference Laos and South Vietnam continues there is danger war might spread and it is that we wish avoid. If we are agreed on necessity upholding Geneva agreements that is great step forward. Unfortunately complete discrepancy between ChiCom words spoken here and deeds SEA.

(6) I continued saying re 14-power conference we had encouraged consultation Vientiane and we prepared accept Polish proposals but all this refused by Wang's side.

(7) Wang returned to Taiwan theme in familiar well worn terms saying we tried use pretext GRC was sovereign state to cover up our serious crime of seizing Chinese territory. We would not succeed in this scheme.

(8) Wang continued I had made clear US determined continue intervention Indo-China and even made threat extending war to North Vietnam. Said this was making mockery of Sino-American ambassadorial level talks. Said he wanted tell me bluntly 650 million Chinese people

cannot be bullied easily. Indomitable Chinese nation cannot ever be cowed into submission. We would do well ponder matter carefully as to serious consequences for ourselves which will arise as result our irresponsible behavior. Said despite our lawlessness Indo-China his government had consistently exercised self-restraint. Should we make miscalculation and take this attitude as sign weakness and think we can act as we please with impunity, going on with present course, we would find ourselves "licked by the fire with which you have been playing." Said Indo-China is next door to China and DRV and other IC states related to China "like lips and teeth" and fraternal feelings exist. Chinese people by no means would sit idly by while US expanded war. Whatever Chinese Government and people say will count and we would do well bear this in mind. Evident US should be held fully responsible for daily worsening situation Indo-China. We were trying to play trick of thief crying "stop thief" and make wild allegation Chinese support DRV in aggression. Said it was known to whole world DRV firmly abided by all provisions Geneva agreements. There was no single foreign military base or single foreign soldier on territory DRV. Said our call for them abstain from exerting pressure on neighbor was putting foot in wrong shoe. Tension IC created solely by US. US instead of China should do some intensive soul-searching rectifying our misdeeds and rein up horse before precipice. Said could not see indications we willing for relaxation tension IC. On contrary every sign we plotting fresh military adventures.

(9) Wang then put following questions:

What are you up to in sending Chairman JCS to South Vietnam? What is your purpose in giving $125 million aid to bogus South Vietnam Government? What is your purpose in reinforcing forces South Vietnam with several hundred more so-called military advisers? What are you up to in despatching several hundred Sky Raider aircraft and other types to South Vietnam? What are your intentions in sending flagship *Oklahoma City* to Saigon? Said if we were really sincere we would immediately call off aggression and intervention.

(10) I replied remarks re seizure Taiwan so wide of mark I need not review again. Fact is a government exists there recognized by more governments than recognize Chinese Communists and important armed forces are there. Have been no hostile military operation by US there. As for Wang's series of questions my opening statement really answered them. I said I had no desire issue threats but wished make our intentions clear and could scarcely consider some of Wang's comments anything but a threat. I then followed guidance section 7 reference telegram, adding could not help but note Wang gave no explanation for extraordinary and revealing statement Chinese Communist Central Committee which I quoted and said we had ample proof war South Vietnam and Laos both backed by North Vietnam with Chinese Communist help.

(11) After another Taiwan tirade Wang said leaders USG had publicly admitted aggression and intervention Vietnam affairs. US has grossly violated sovereignty, independence, unity and territorial integrity IC states. Said we would be fostering reactionary forces Laos and instigated them in repeatedly overthrowing legal governments Laos thus undermining national unity. We could not shift responsibility recent bombing there.

(12) I said we seemed to have reached a point where further discussion almost useless. I profoundly disagreed with practically everything he said. Important thing was ask Wang transmit to his regime what we had said here today and hoped his regime would study it carefully.

(13) Wang mentioned their unacceptable earlier proposal re newsmen saying in view our extremely hostile attitude toward China our proposal re newsmen made them suspicious of ulterior motive. Said prior meetings had made clear Chinese position re American "criminal offenders" and he would not go into that. Said Central Committee article was correct but this sort of thing not chief subject we called on to settle in these meetings and did not propose go into that. Complained of my discourtesy in calling the government of the great PRC a "regime."

Next meeting September 23.

Cabot

---

41. Memorandum From James C. Thomson, Jr., of the National Security Council Staff to the President's Special Assistant for National Security Affairs (Bundy)[1]

Washington, August 5, 1964.

SUBJECT

Possibility of an Emergency Warsaw Meeting

Regardless of how Peking and Hanoi respond to our air strikes, I think we should consider the advisability of an emergency Warsaw meeting as soon as possible between Cabot and Wang. (A precedent: the

---

[1] Source: Johnson Library, National Security File, Country File, Poland, Cabot–Wang Talks. Secret.

Chicoms called for a special session in the Taiwan Straits build-up of 1962.)

The purpose of such a meeting would be to make clear to the Chinese once again that we have no desire to expand the war but are willing to do so if forced by their actions and those of Hanoi. I realize that we have tried to make this point in a number of ways over the past few months. However, our air strikes and our dramatic and visible build-up in Southwest Pacific may well combine, despite our best intentions, to communicate a significantly different message: one of U.S. determination to destroy the North Vietnam regime and even to strike Hainan and South China.

So far, the Chinese have appeared to be opposed to escalation of the conflict; they also appear to have believed that we are similarly opposed. Their relatively cautious pattern of response seems to bear this out. Once they conclude that our objectives have changed, however, this can produce a basic shift in their own thinking and actions. In such altered circumstances, they might well consider taking any pre-emptive actions available to them (i.e. air or naval attacks against vessels in the Gulf of Tonkin and a full-scale southward thrust of their own armed forces) on the assumption that all-out war was in the offing anyway.

In short, it seems to me imperative that where misinterpretation and miscalculation may well produce rashness rather than caution, we should move to use any channel of communication available to us. With such potential targets as Port Wallut so close to the Chinese border, the burden of communication rests with us. We have communicated to all other governments; we should not neglect our prime adversary.

The Warsaw channel was re-opened on July 29th; Ambassador Cabot is now in Washington. He could be thoroughly briefed and flown right back to Warsaw, if we decided to call such a meeting.[2]

JCT Jr.

---

[2] A note in Komer's handwriting on the source text reads as follows: "Mac—I'm less concerned than Jim that Chicoms or Hanoi will misinterpret. Nor do I see merit in reassuring them just now. But I do see value in using Warsaw for communicating our *real* purposes. RWK."

42.   Memorandum for the Record[1]

Washington, August 8, 1964.

SUBJECT

Meeting of 303 Committee[2] on 6 August 1964

[Here follows discussion of unrelated subjects.]

6. I then brought up the question of a U–2 flight over high priority targets in South China, presented a flight plan and a weather map. Pointed out that a weather phenomena would occur over the next two days because of the approaching hurricane and that we could expect reasonably good weather—categories 2 and 3—over the area of interest in the next two days. For that reason I recommended that CIA be authorized to fly a U–2 [less than 1 line of source text not declassified] with a CIA civilian pilot, utilizing a cover story which was discussed in its broad outline. Messrs. Vance and Thompson expressed approval. Bundy saw the advantages but withheld judgment. Vance reported that Secretary McNamara opposed. Thompson reported that he felt that Secretary Rusk opposed, but was not sure of his position. Bundy stated this was a matter for Presidential decision and that the President should meet with McCone, McNamara and Rusk to hear the arguments and make the decision and he agreed to arrange such a meeting immediately. I stated this was not possible from my standpoint because of the necessity to go to Gettysburg to brief General Eisenhower. It was agreed, therefore, that the subject would be discussed separately with Secretary McNamara and Secretary Rusk and then Mr. Bundy would approach the President. However, he called the President on the telephone in the meeting room, outlined the problem to him; the President indicated he desired to think the matter over and would render a decision later in the day.

I then went to Vance's office and reviewed the program with Secretary McNamara. In this discussion I made the specific recommendation that the flight be conducted on one or both of the next two days, taking advantage of the break in the weather, and that if it was not so conducted, we probably would not have another opportunity for some time because

---

[1] Source: Central Intelligence Agency, DCI (McCone) Files: Job 80–B01285A, 303 Committee Meetings (1964). Secret; Eyes Only. Drafted by McCone.

[2] The 303 Committee was an interdepartmental committee that reviewed and authorized covert operations. Established under NSC 5412/2, December 28, 1955, it was known as the Special Group or 5412 Committee until National Security Action Memorandum No. 303, June 2, 1964, changed its name to the 303 Committee. In 1964–1968, it consisted of the Assistant to the President for National Security Affairs, the Deputy Secretary of Defense, the Deputy Under Secretary of State for Political Affairs, and the Director of Central Intelligence.

of the weather which would close in. I told the Secretary there was a very definite intelligence gap that worried me and that I felt the risk of the flight was worth it. The Secretary said he was unalterably opposed on the grounds that the flight would become known to the ChiComs and it would exacerbate the situation and he wished to take a "wait and see" attitude before making any further move which could be construed by Hanoi or Peiping as a further United States provocation. McNamara said he was quite agreeable for me to present my views to the President and he felt that, from the standpoint of my responsibilities, this should be done, but from his standpoint he was opposed.

I left for Gettysburg feeling that Bundy would follow through as agreed and discuss the subject further with the President.

The next morning Bundy called me and said that Thompson had talked to Rusk and Rusk was unalterably opposed to the flight despite Thompson's recommendation, and the fact that the flight involved a comparatively "low risk," and since both Rusk and McNamara were definitely opposed to the flight, he, Bundy, felt it would serve no useful purpose to bring my recommendation again to the attention of the President as he would undoubtedly look to his two Secretaries for advice and would be governed accordingly. Therefore Bundy had, on his own initiative, decided not to present the matter to the President.

---

43.   Special National Intelligence Estimate[1]

SNIE 13–4–64   Washington, August 26, 1964.

THE CHANCES OF AN IMMINENT
COMMUNIST CHINESE NUCLEAR EXPLOSION

The Problem

To assess the likelihood that the advanced stage of construction at a probable nuclear test site in Western China indicates that the Chinese

---

[1] Source: Central Intelligence Agency, NIE Files. Top Secret; Ruff/[codeword not declassified]. According to a note on the cover sheet, it was submitted by the Director of Central Intelligence and concurred in by the U.S. Intelligence Board on August 26. The Central Intelligence Agency and the intelligence organizations of the Departments of State and Defense, AEC, and NSA participated in its preparation. All USIB members concurred, except the FBI Assistant Director who abstained because the subject was outside his jurisdiction.

Communists will detonate their first nuclear device in the next few months.

Conclusion

On the basis of new overhead photography, we are now convinced that the previously suspect facility at Lop Nor in Western China is a nuclear test site which could be ready for use in about two months. On the other hand the weight of available evidence indicates that the Chinese will not have sufficient fissionable material for a test of a nuclear device in the next few months. Thus, the evidence does not permit a very confident estimate of the chances of a Chinese Communist nuclear detonation in the next few months. Clearly the possibility of such a detonation before the end of this year cannot be ruled out—the test may occur during this period. On balance, however, we believe that it will not occur until sometime after the end of 1964.

Discussion

1. Overhead photography of 6–9 August shows that the previously suspect facility near Lop Nor in Sinkiang is almost certainly a nuclear testing site. Developments at the facility include a ground scar forming about 60 percent of a circle 19,600 feet in diameter around a 325-foot tower (first seen in April 1964 photograph), and work on bunkers near the tower and instrumentation sites at appropriate locations is underway. [1-1/2 lines of source text not declassified] the outward appearance and apparent rate of construction indicate that the site could be ready for a test in two months or so. The characteristics of the site suggest that it is being prepared for both diagnostic and weapon effect experiments.

2. Analysis of all available evidence on fissionable material production in China indicates—though it does not prove—that the Chinese will not have sufficient material for a test of a nuclear device in the next few months. The only Chinese production reactor identified to date is the small, air-cooled reactor at Pao-t'ou. As of September 1963, [less than 1 line of source text not declassified]. Construction was continuing throughout the site, including some fairly substantial work around the building which houses the reactor. Photography of March 1964 indicated that major construction at the site—including service roads, [less than 1 line of source text not declassified] and additional security provisions—had apparently been completed. Thus we believe the reactor went into operation possibly in the latter part of 1963 but more probably in early 1964. We estimate that, even if no major obstacles were encountered, it would take at least 18 months, and more likely two years, after the starting up of the Pao-t'ou reactor before a nuclear device would be ready for testing. Thus, if the Pao-t'ou reactor started operation no earlier than late 1963 and if it is China's only operating production reactor, the earliest possible date for testing is mid-1965.

3.   It is, of course, possible that the Chinese have another source of fissionable material. Such a facility might have been started with Soviet aid as a result of the 1957 Soviet-Chinese aid agreement, probably about the same time as the Lanchou gaseous diffusion building. We would expect this reactor to be a fairly large water-cooled production reactor. There are areas, particularly parts of Szechwan, which are suitable for such a reactor and have not been photographed. Since it is doubtful that a reactor of this type could have been finished before the withdrawal of Soviet technicians in 1960, its completion would have depended on a native Chinese effort, a difficult but not impossible task. Such a reactor might have started operations in 1962 or 1963, thus making available sufficient plutonium for a test by the end of this year.

4.   On the other hand we have photographed much of the area around virtually all locations where A-E activity is indicated [*less than 1 line of source text not declassified*] about half of all locations that might be geographically suitable for reactor sites. Apart from Pao-t'ou, no operating production reactor or isotope separation plant has been found. We believe it unlikely—though clearly not impossible—that such an operating facility exists.

5.   It is also possible that the Chinese may have acquired fissionable material from a foreign source, [*9 lines of source text not declassified*]. As for the Soviets, we do not believe that in the past they have transferred appreciable amounts of weapon-grade material to the Chinese. In the current state of their relations with the Chinese, they would almost certainly not furnish fissionable materials to them.

6.   Obviously, it is incongruous to bring a test site to a state of readiness described in paragraph 1 without having a device nearly ready for testing. It would be technically undesirable to install much of the instrumentation more than a few weeks before the actual test. We cannot tell from available photography whether the installations have yet reached this point—it seems unlikely that they have, mainly because some heavy construction is still going on. However, it is possible that the basic work will soon be completed, and that final preparations could be made this fall.

7.   On the other hand, in such a complex undertaking as advanced weapons development—especially when it is almost certain that there is heavy political pressure for at least some results—it would not be surprising if there were uneven progress among various phases of the program. In a number of instances in the past, Peiping has been unable to prevent—and has seemed willing to tolerate—uneven development in various important programs. Indeed, in other parts of their advanced weapons program we have already observed this. Some facilities seem to be behind schedule—notably the incomplete gaseous diffusion plant at Lanchou; others are larger and more elaborate than present Chinese

capabilities warrant—for example, the possible nuclear weapons complex near Koko Nor.

8. As for the test site itself, Lop Nor is extremely remote, with poor transportation and communication facilities, and we might expect to see the Chinese taking a long leadtime in preparing this installation. They have relatively few men with the necessary scientific competence and they cannot be fully confident that unexpected difficulties will not appear. We believe the Chinese would do everything in their power to prevent a last minute hitch on the testing facility from delaying, even briefly, China's advent as a nuclear "power."

9. The evidence and argument reviewed above do not permit a very confident estimate of the chances of a Chinese Communist nuclear detonation in the next few months. Clearly the possibility of such a detonation before the end of this year cannot be ruled out—the test may occur during this period. On balance, however, we believe that it will not occur until sometime after the end of 1964.[2]

---

[2] [Footnote in the source text (1 line) not declassified.]

---

44.   Letter From the Ambassador to the Republic of China (Wright) to the Under Secretary of State for Political Affairs (Harriman)[1]

Taipei, August 26, 1964.

Dear Averell:

I well recall our conversations of a little over a year ago in which the subject of "return to the mainland" was given extensive coverage. I recall also that Ambassador Kirk's principal concern was the possibility of a move towards a channel crossing by the GRC which might get underway without our knowledge. Following my several conversations with you, I explored this problem in considerable detail with him with a view to continuation of the informative and preventative measures which he proposed.

---

[1] Source: Library of Congress, Manuscript Division, Harriman Papers, Special Files: Public Service, Kennedy–Johnson Administrations, Subject File, Wooe–Wz. Secret; Eyes Only.

Over the past year a noticeable change has taken place in the attitude of the GRC toward "mainland recovery". There has been a very definite quiescence on the extensive preparations and planning which took place in late 1962 and early 1963. During this period you will recall the planning agencies of the Ministry of National Defense were burning the midnight oil to crank out plans for operations toward this objective.

During the past six months there has been a noticeable slacking off, if not disappearance, of this intensive effort and in its place we find a rather keen and increasing interest in developments in Southeast Asia, particularly in Laos and South Vietnam.

I have covered in greater detail the changes which I have noted and the reasons therefor in my Embassy A–138,[2] of which I am enclosing a copy in the event you care to examine these details.

I could summarize the situation by relating two circumstances which have deviated the attention of the GRC from across-the-channel amphibious operations to developments in Southeast Asia as follows:

1) The very excellent step taken by Ambassador Kirk in setting up the "Blue Lion" planning committee, consisting of the Ambassador and the Minister of National Defense, in which the GRC detailed plans for cross channel operations were examined by our staff and their inadequacies and deficiencies thoroughly developed. These shortcomings, I am sure, reached the eyes and ears of the President and were instrumental in convincing him of the gargantuan nature of such an operation and the need for massive U.S. support.

2) The worsening situation in Southeast Asia has, I believe, revealed to the President the possibilities of getting into China by the Southern route rather than by the route of direct amphibious assault.

This change in their approach does not signify in any sense a reduction in their desire to return to the mainland but rather a change in the method and approach as to how this might be accomplished.

I am sending a copy of this letter to Bill Bundy in order that he may know of my communication with you.

Best wishes,

Sincerely,

Jerry W.

---

[2] Airgram A–138 from Taipei, August 21, noted that GRC infiltration attempts and commando raids had not revealed any weak spots in the mainland coastal defenses; on the contrary, the loss well out to sea of two commando teams in July had been a severe setback to the program and had forced a reevaluation of GRC strategy. (Department of State, Central Files, POL 1 CHINAT–US)

45.   Letter From the Assistant Secretary of State for Far Eastern Affairs (Bundy) to the Ambassador to the Republic of China (Wright)[1]

Washington, September 4, 1964.

Dear Jerry:

Thank you for your letter of August 7 sending us the report on "Blue Lion" planning.[2] We are glad to have your comments and, as you suggested, are transmitting a copy of the report as well as a copy of your letter to CIA.

I believe there are few, if any, on our side who would be surprised at the conclusion reached by COM US TDC that the various operations contemplated in this planning exercise are beyond GRC capabilities with present forces. In my opinion the greatest value of this planning exercise is the point noted in your letter, i.e. that it has brought home to the GRC the magnitude of such operations and its own deficiencies in resources for carrying them out. This has no doubt reduced any tendency the GRC may still have toward irresponsible military ventures and, perhaps even more significant, it should help place GRC political thinking on a more realistic foundation. I am glad to see that the "Blue Lion" Committee is to continue since it has served, and I think can continue to serve, a very important purpose.

In conjunction with the "Blue Lion" report, I was interested in seeing the further amplification of the mainland recovery subject which you sent us in your A–138.[3] The shift in emphasis in GRC planning which you traced is a natural one in the circumstances, though it is not something we can welcome wholeheartedly. Obviously GRC objectives in Southeast Asia differ widely from our own and we must continue to watch closely everything it does there, even while we continue to encourage suitable GRC activities in those limited areas where our interests coincide.

With best regards,

Sincerely yours,

William P. Bundy[4]

---

[1] Source: Department of State, ROC Files: Lot 75 D 76, Blue Lion Consultations. Top Secret. Drafted by Officer in Charge of Republic of China Affairs John B. Dexter on August 31.

[2] Wright's letter enclosed a letter of June 30 to him from Admiral Melson reporting on the work of the "Blue Lion" committee. (Ibid., Central Files, POL CHINAT–CHICOM)

[3] See footnote 2, Document 44.

[4] Printed from a copy that bears this typed signature.

46. Telegram From the Department of State to the Embassy in the Republic of China[1]

Washington, September 4, 1964, 5:15 p.m.

210. For Ambassador from Secretary. I have reviewed recent exchange messages concerning approaches to GRC proposed by Dept in connection reported GRC activities Thailand and Burma. In view of recent conversations Gen Yeh and Chiang Ching-kuo in which US views on GRC-sponsored paramilitary activities SEA reaffirmed, I agree with you that we have probably done enough for the present to make our position clear to the GRC. However, I still believe it would be useful bring to GRC attention at highest level two points which apparently have not been mentioned or stressed in conversations with Yeh and Chiang. We should report to GRC fact that Burmese Foreign Office has expressed to our Embassy Rangoon its concern over resumption what they refer to as "legitimate KMT" activities in Thai-Burma border area under direction GRC officials in Thailand; and we should mention our belief, based upon various reports, that these activities were probably a subject of discussion during Chou En-lai's visit Rangoon last July. Both points I believe would be of legitimate interest to GRC even apart from opportunity they provide to restate our position on irregulars.

In connection Burmese Foreign Office approach to us, you might wish say that Burmese did not present evidence of activities in question and our Embassy did not express any opinion as to basis Burmese concern. However, our Ambassador did reaffirm to Burmese our continuing opposition to any recurrence unfortunate Chinese irregulars issue which has left lasting legacy misunderstanding between US and Burma.

I believe it should be possible to bring these points to President Chiang's attention in manner which would subtly complement rather than offensively duplicate recent conversations with Chiang and Yeh. I suggest further that you introduce these points during next appropriate occasion when you meet with President on other business, rather than seek special meeting to discuss them.

You are of course aware that Chinese irregulars question continues to be of concern to us. We are determined to do everything possible assure that GRC does not undertake excessive or indiscreet actions, as they have in past, which could needlessly complicate our problems in SEA. In this we recognize that GRC has its own axes to grind in SEA. In pursuing its objectives against the mainland, it has a natural tendency to

---

[1] Source: Department of State, Central Files, POL CHINAT–US. Secret; Exdis. Drafted by Dexter, cleared by SEA Director William C. Trueheart and Bundy, and approved and initialed by Rusk. Repeated to Bangkok and Rangoon.

go beyond what we consider limits of prudence and to be less than candid with us in doing so.

Rusk

---

47.   Circular Telegram From the Department of State to Certain Posts[1]

Washington, September 5, 1964, 8:02 p.m.

446. Personal for Chief of Mission. I trust that you will do all in your power to ensure that countries now recognizing the GRC will continue this policy and that those not now recognizing Peiping will not move closer to Communist China. It is clear that the Chinese Communists are mounting a subtle, persistent offensive, particularly in Africa, with a view to improving their international position at the expense of the GRC. An official Chinese Communist goodwill mission now touring West Africa is trying to undermine the GRC position there. Malawi and Northern Rhodesia appear disposed to establish relations with Peiping.

I am sure you realize, as we move into the weeks preceding the General Assembly, that the GRC's status in the United Nations depends upon a solid international position. Moreover, it would be particularly dangerous for the peace of the world if Peiping were to be rewarded with recognition and admission to the UN at a time when the Chinese Communists are inciting aggression in Asia, encouraging rebellion in Africa and extolling militant revolution in much of the world. This point should be of particular concern in those areas of the world where the Chinese Communists are now actively supporting revolutionary and subversive movements which seek to topple duly constituted authority.

I leave to your judgment what measures will be best suited to the situation in each of your posts. You may find CA–4523, October 23, 1963,[2]

---

[1] Source: Department of State, Central Files, POL 16 CHINAT. Secret. Drafted by Green and William J. Cunningham of the ROC desk, cleared by UNP Director William B. Buffum, and approved and initialed by Rusk. Sent to all U.S. diplomatic missions except those in the Soviet bloc and to Hong Kong, Lusaka, Valletta, USUN, the Mission at Geneva, and USRO Paris.

[2] See footnote 7, Document 23.

and CA–10131, April 3, 1964,[3] helpful in this regard. If you desire additional guidance, the Department is prepared to supply background and talking points.

Rusk

---

[3] Not printed. (Department of State, Central Files, POL 2 US)

---

48.   National Policy Paper[1]

Washington, September 11, 1964.

THE REPUBLIC OF CHINA

[Here follow a preface and table of contents.]

PART ONE: U.S. POLICY

[Here follows an introduction comprising 9 pages.]

II. U.S. STRATEGY FOR THE NEXT FIVE YEARS

A. General

1. Desired Course of Free China's Evolution

An understanding of what progress should be made in Taiwan in the next five years can best be obtained by looking beyond this period and considering what situation we would like to see there in the mid-1970's. The following outline of the hoped-for Taiwan of 1975 necessarily reflects judgments on what is possible as well as on what is desirable. It must be emphasized, however, that it is not an intelligence estimate.

---

[1] Source: Department of State, S/P Files: Lot 70 D 199, National Policy Paper, Republic of China. Secret. Portions of the paper, entitled "Future U.S. Role in External Defense" and "Present U.S. Role in External Defense," are filed ibid. under a cover sheet dated June 1964. Drafted by Joseph A. Yager of the Policy Planning Council and approved by Rusk on September 11. The preface states: "All agencies with major responsibilities affecting U.S. relations with the Republic of China participated in drafting the paper and concur in the Strategy and Courses of Action which it sets forth."

The assumptions used below are those stated in Section I. E., above, which imply the further assumption that Taiwan in 1975 would still be cut off from significant contact with mainland China.

a. *Social.* By 1975, one might hope that the line between Taiwanese and mainlanders would have become somewhat blurred through increased inter-marriage, expanded cooperation in a wide range of common enterprises, and the unifying effect of a common educational system. Knowledge of Mandarin would have become widespread, and communication between Taiwanese and mainlanders would no longer be a problem. A substantial Taiwanese-mainlander middle class and a Taiwanese-mainlander intellectual elite would have appeared, thus promoting a greater sense of communal unity.

A significant increase in educational standards would have occurred and the body of technically skilled workers greatly expanded. The present nearly stagnant academic life on Taiwan's university campuses would have been replaced by an upsurge of intellectual activity, although some inhibitions would persist in sensitive political areas. Something approaching a cultural renaissance would be underway in literature and the fine arts.

b. *Economic.* By 1975, Taiwan would have experienced a generation of continuous economic growth. The island would have been free for a number of years from dependence on all forms of concessional economic aid. Growth would be concentrated in a thriving private sector of the economy, operating with little government interference and under rationalized systems of commercial law and taxation.

The rate of population growth would have leveled off to between one and two percent annually, thereby easing the problem of maintaining an adequate rate of investment.

Price levels would have been reasonably stable for at least a decade and interest rates would have fallen to levels only moderately above those prevailing in advanced countries. An efficient money market would have been created

The government would have adopted a liberal trade policy based on the improved competitive strength of the export industries. The new Taiwan Dollar would have become fully convertible.

c. *Security.* The armed forces would have been reduced in size, but some improvements in fire power and mobility would have avoided a proportionate decrease in combat effectiveness. Taiwanese would form perhaps one-fifth of the officer corps and a few Taiwanese would have risen to general or flag rank.

MAP grant aid would have been significantly reduced in the early 1970's and procurement of military goods and services from the United

States shifted in part to a Military Assistance Sales basis, including liberal loan and credit arrangements.

The military situation in the Taiwan Strait would have been stabilized and a cease-fire tacitly established.

No serious threat to internal security would have arisen.

d. *Political.* Political stability would have been maintained, in part as a consequence of a timely Kuomintang decision to permit greater freedom of political action within the framework of the party itself and to give Taiwanese a growing role in party councils and in government. A non-vocal, but independent, opposition party would have been permitted to organize and function. This party, however, would not be purely Taiwanese in its membership or outlook.

Communications media would be operating more freely and with a greater sense of responsibility.

The Taiwan Provincial Government would have been granted considerably greater autonomy, but the central government would still make the basic decisions, at least in the fields of foreign relations, internal and external security and fiscal and monetary policy. The governor of Taiwan would be popularly elected.

The GRC would not have abandoned its claim to be the government of all China and recovery of the mainland would still be proclaimed to be its primary national objective. However, actual preparations for action aimed at recovery of the mainland would have fallen to a low level and major attention would be focused on development of Taiwan and the maintenance of the GRC's international position. The credibility of the mainland recovery policy would have been seriously eroded by the passage of actionless decades, the deaths of many party elders and the emigration of many others to the United States and elsewhere, as well as by the introduction of a significant Taiwanese element into the KMT leadership.

As a consequence of its economic, educational and cultural achievements, the GRC would have won increasing international recognition as a progressive force in the Far East and would continue to be recognized by a large number of non-Communist nations.

2. Dimensions of U.S. Influence During the Next Five Years

As in the past, the GRC's dependence on the U.S. for its very existence will continue, in the final analysis, to provide the principal basis for U.S. influence. We face, however, the problem of adjusting to the declining importance of two of the specific instruments—our economic and military aid programs—through which we have made our influence felt. We must make the best possible use of these instruments while we still have them. We must also learn to work more effectively through international organizations and private U.S institutions.

During the next few years, direct U.S. influence will probably be most effective in influencing specific GRC economic development tactics, diplomatic activities and defensive military policy. We shall have less influence on fiscal policy, military force levels, the missions and tasks of the armed forces, propaganda and clandestine operations. We shall probably be least effective in the field of political reform.

Fortunately, our direct means of exercising influence are reinforced by indirect influence flowing from the continued pervasive penetration of U.S. standards and methods throughout society and from the delayed social and political repercussions of the economic progress which we have supported.

3. General Description of U.S. Strategy

The next five years should see as much progress as possible toward the kind of Taiwan described in section II.A.1, above. The U.S. strategy to bring about this kind of progress will be more fully developed in subsequent sections, but its key ingredients should be:

a. A carefully planned, step-by-step effort to gain broad acceptance of our view of the desirable long-term future of Taiwan among GRC leaders and private leaders of opinion.

b. Continued observance of and reiteration of our commitment to the defense of Taiwan and the Penghus.

c. Continued economic and military aid in amounts and for periods of time needed to ensure: (1) sustained economic growth without concessional aid, (2) maintenance of armed forces needed to support U.S. security objectives, and (3) preservation of the necessary degree of U.S. influence in key elements of Government and society.

d. Reduction and eventual elimination of concessional economic aid as a means of encouraging the GRC to stand on its own feet and adopt self-help measures essential to realization of the economy's full potential for growth.

e. Attachment of explicit or implicit conditions on aid designed to induce adoption of: (1) rational economic policies, including appropriate economic development policies and (2) levels and composition of armed forces consistent with the U.S. view of the missions and tasks of those forces.

f. Encouragement of the GRC—largely through private persuasion—to: (1) relax its political controls, permitting development of more effective opposition activity, (2) bring more Taiwanese into positions of responsibility, (3) promote joint Taiwanese-mainlander enterprises, (4) adopt a rational population policy and a comprehensive manpower program and (5) promote cultural and intellectual activities in a free atmosphere.

g. Identification and appropriate cultivation of future leaders.

h. Continued diplomatic support of the GRC in the UN and elsewhere.

4. Principal Contingencies

Any of the following contingencies would probably require a major change in one or more aspects of the US strategy:

a. Major hostilities in the Far East involving the U.S., the GRC or Communist China; especially: hostilities between the U.S. and Communist China, the U.S. and the USSR; hostilities caused by a Chinese Communist attack on Taiwan, the Penghus or one of the major offshore islands; or hostilities precipitated by a GRC invasion of the mainland.

b. A drastic increase in the vulnerability of the Chinese Communist regime to GRC military or paramilitary operations resulting from economic disaster, internal revolt, a split in the regime or involvement of the regime in major hostilities on another front.

c. A deal between the GRC and the Chinese Communists.

d. The rise to power on Taiwan of a more repressive militaristic regime as a consequence of a succession crisis, suppression of a Taiwanese uprising, military defeat or economic stagnation.

e. Loss by the GRC of its UN seat either through expulsion or through voluntary withdrawal in protest over a UN decision to offer membership to the Chinese Communists.

These contingencies will not be treated explicitly in this paper, but are properly the subject of separate contingency plans.

B. US Political Strategy

1. Political Stability and Political Reform

For the past decade, the U.S. has operated on the assumption that the GRC could maintain political stability on Taiwan if it were protected from Communist military pressures and assisted in the development of the island's economy. This assumption has proved correct, but something more is likely to be required in the years ahead. The stability that has prevailed on Taiwan rests on a balance of opposing forces that cannot easily be maintained. Unless change comes gradually and peacefully, there is a danger that it will come with a disorderly rush, threatening all that the US, the GRC and the people of Taiwan have achieved since the loss of the mainland.

Peaceful change is everywhere a matter of timing, pace and style. This is particularly true of Taiwan where ill-considered, precipitate reform would be as dangerous as blind reaction. In this complex and delicate situation, we must move with caution and deliberation, constantly keeping in mind the limits on both our understanding and our capabilities.

The weight of our influence should be thrown behind the general proposition that a gradual relaxation of political controls, greater observance of civil rights (including giving trade unions freedom of activity and functions usual in democratic countries) and increased Taiwanese participation in responsible levels of government are essential conditions of political stability. We should make our views to the GRC clear whenever appropriate opportunities arise in connection with specific instances in which we feel GRC observance of political or civil rights has been dangerously deficient.

Use should be made of the good offices of prominent Americans outside the government who are known to be sympathetic to the GRC. On occasion, the ILO, the ICFTU and other international organizations might be encouraged to call violations of political or civil rights to the attention of the GRC. Public information media could lend indirect support to the campaign by publicizing advances in popular government in other countries and by applauding constructive steps taken by the GRC. In the field of labor rights, public and private American employers on Taiwan could set a good example by recognizing and dealing with unions of their Chinese employees.

Our campaign for political and civil reforms should be conducted in a low key and largely behind the scenes. Great care should be taken to avoid either unduly whetting Taiwanese and other oppositionist political appetites or frightening GRC leaders into more repressive policies.

The layering of the national and provincial government lends itself to a gradualist approach to the problem of political reform. Increasing the autonomy of the provincial government and the authority of both its legislative and executive branches would automatically lead to more effective popular participation in government and to a more influential role for Taiwanese. At the same time, the mainlander leadership could retain control over defense and international relations and a share in the making of domestic policy that might be adequate for their purposes. U.S. agencies on Taiwan should seek to promote this development by gradually increasing their dealings with the provincial government and seizing appropriate opportunities to build up its prestige and influence.

2. The Possibility of a Presidential Succession

An orderly, constitutional transfer of power upon the death or incapacity of Chiang Kai-shek is strongly in our interest. During the period before Chiang's departure, we should do what we can in all fields—political, psychological, economic and military—to create favorable conditions for a smooth transition at the time of the succession.

3. Return to the Mainland

We should continue to discourage the GRC from military or paramilitary operations against the China mainland which might provoke a dangerous Chinese Communist reaction or damage our prestige and that of the GRC. We should encourage the GRC to rely more on political and psychological efforts in seeking to undermine Communist control of the mainland.

When appropriate and necessary, we should remind GRC leaders of their obligation under the exchange of notes of December 10, 1954, to obtain our prior agreement to any offensive actions by their armed forces. If the GRC appears intent on taking such actions without our prior agreement, we should make clear that we would be under no obligation to help contain any Communist military counteraction and that our continued economic and military aid to the GRC would be placed in jeopardy. At the same time, we should not foreclose the option of assisting the GRC in playing an effective role on the mainland in the event of a drastic increase in Chinese Communist vulnerability to GRC pressures.

A sharp and damaging confrontation with the GRC, on the return to the mainland issue can probably be avoided, if we maintain our present intimate knowledge of GRC's plans and thinking, and if we continue to be successful in persuading the GRC of our view that, under present circumstances, operations on a scale larger than those we have accepted to date would almost certainly fail with seriously adverse consequences for GRC interests.

4. The International Status of the GRC

We should continue to oppose the admission of the Chinese Communists to the UN and other international organizations by using the abundant evidence disqualifying the Peiping regime from admission to the society of peace-loving nations. We should continue to support the resolution of the 16th General Assembly declaring Chinese representation an important question requiring a two-thirds vote. We should not abandon the possible option of using the veto as the final defense against admission of the Chinese Communists to the Security Council.

In the immediate future, our main task will be to dampen down the repercussions of the recent French recognition of Peiping. Over the longer-run—assuming that the French action does not lead to rapid erosion of the GRC's international position—the main threat to our ability to protect the status of the GRC as the representative of China in international organizations will come from the existence of sentiment in many governments for seating both GRC and Chinese Communist representatives. This sentiment might eventually result in the passage of a "two Chinas" resolution in the UN which would seriously undermine the GRC's status as the legitimate representative of China and would probably lead many countries to recognize Communist China and officially proclaim a "two Chinas" policy. This threat would become even more serious if the Chinese Communists reversed their present position and indicated their willingness to sit in international organizations with representatives of the GRC, or if the GRC were to react to a mere invitation to the Chinese

Communists to join an international organization by themselves withdrawing. The first of these possibilities is fortunately remote. We should guard against the second by continuing to urge on the GRC the merits of a pragmatic, as opposed to a rigidly doctrinaire, approach to the Chinese representation problem.

We should continue to support GRC efforts to maintain its relations with governments now recognizing it and to establish relations with newly independent governments. We should also continue to encourage the GRC to use its small technical assistance program as a valuable adjunct of its diplomacy, particularly in Africa.

We should view sympathetically the GRC tendency to tighten its ties with other strongly anti-Communist Asian governments, in part to compensate for diplomatic reverses received or feared in other areas. But at the same time we should not now support GRC proposals for new regional alliances. To do so under existing circumstances would add little or nothing to our strength in the Far East and would complicate our efforts to cope with several major problems, notably those in Vietnam and Laos.

5. Two Chinas

Since both the GRC and the Chinese Communists strongly oppose the separation of Taiwan from China, it is most unlikely that an independent state could be created on Taiwan during the next five years—or indeed for a considerably longer period of time. Under present circumstances, adoption by the U.S. of a "two Chinas" policy (i.e., recognition of the Chinese Communist regime as the government of China and the GRC as the government of Taiwan) would be futile and would involve serious losses and risks. The value of the GRC as a diplomatic counter to the Chinese Communists would of course be largely, if not entirely, lost. But beyond this, U.S. adoption of a "two Chinas" policy would have a deeply unsettling effect on political stability on Taiwan, conceivably including opening the door to a deal between KMT leaders and the Chinese Communists. We would also risk arousing the bitter and lasting enmity of many patriotic Chinese who would interpret our action as an effort to separate off part of the national territory.

In the absence of any diminution of the Chinese Communist threat, the governments of South Korea, South Vietnam and Thailand would regard any U.S. moves toward a "two Chinas" posture with considerable apprehension. This feeling would probably be shared by leaders in the Philippines and Malaysia and to some extent even in Burma, Indonesia and India. Pressures for accommodation with the Chinese Communists would increase throughout the area.

We should, therefore, not adopt a "two Chinas" policy. At the same time, we should pursue economic, political, and security policies which will in fact facilitate the survival of Taiwan as an independent national entity if, as now seems possible, this proves to be the ultimate consequence of further prolonged isolation of the island from the mainland of China.

[Here follow the remainder of section II, which concerns U.S. economic and military policy, section III, Courses of Action, and Part Two, Factors Bearing on U.S. Policy.]

49.   Memorandum for the Record[1]

Washington, September 15, 1964.

We discussed the question of Chinese nuclear weapons today, first in a lunch at the State Department given by Secretary Rusk for McNamara, McCone, and myself, and later at a meeting with the President in which Rusk, McNamara and I were with him in the Cabinet Room (McCone having left at a time when we thought the President would not be able to join us).

At the luncheon we developed the following position:

(1) We are not in favor of unprovoked unilateral U.S. military action against Chinese nuclear installations at this time. We would prefer to have a Chinese test take place than to initiate such action now. If for other reasons we should find ourselves in military hostilities at any level with the Chinese Communists, we would expect to give very close attention to the possibility of an appropriate military action against Chinese nuclear facilities.

(2) We believe that there are many possibilities for joint action with the Soviet Government if that Government is interested. Such possibilities include a warning to the Chinese against tests, a possible undertaking to give up underground testing and to hold the Chinese accountable if they test in any way, and even a possible agreement to cooperate in preventive military action. We therefore agreed that it would be most desirable for the Secretary of State to explore this matter very privately with Ambassador Dobrynin as soon as possible.

(3) We agreed that it would be much preferable to conduct any overflight of Chinese nuclear test facilities in a plane [*less than 1 line of source*

---

[1] Source: Johnson Library, National Security File, Memos to the President, McGeorge Bundy, Vol. 6. Top Secret; Sensitive.

text not declassified]. In the course of the afternoon, Director McCone produced a proposal that such a flight be staged [*less than 1 line of source text not declassified*].

These preliminary decisions were reported to the President in the Cabinet Room, and he indicated his approval. The Secretary of State now intends to consult promptly with the Soviet Ambassador.

McG. B.[2]

---

[2] Printed from a copy that bears these typed initials.

---

50.   Memorandum for the Record[1]

Washington, September 15, 1964.

SUBJECT

Memorandum of Discussion at Luncheon—September 15th Secretary Rusk's Dining Room[2]

ATTENDING

Secy. Rusk, Secy. McNamara, McGeorge Bundy, Mr. McCone

1.   Reviewed the needs for photographic [intelligence on] Lop Nor Chinese Communist nuclear test site.[3] I explained the need for the U–2 mission as discussed and recorded in USIB meeting of September 10th.[4] Rusk took the position that finite intelligence on when a ChiCom test

---

[1] Source: Central Intelligence Agency, DCI (McCone) Files: Job 80–B01285A, DCI (McCone) Memo for the Record, 11 Sept–31 Oct 1964. Secret; Eyes Only. Dictated by McCone on September 17.

[2] See also Document 49.

[3] In a September 12 meeting with Rusk, as recorded in McCone's September 13 memorandum for the record, McCone stated that the "status of the Lop Nor site and certain clandestine reports indicated a test was imminent." Rusk told him that "Dobrynin had told Thompson at lunch that the ChiComs 'would get off a test at any time.'" (Central Intelligence Agency, DCI (McCone) Files: Job 80–B01285A, DCI (McCone) Memo for the Record, 11 Sept–31 Oct 1964)

[4] No record of the meeting has been found. In the September 12 meeting between Rusk and McCone cited above, Rusk told McCone that he opposed the proposed mission because the political consequences of the loss of a plane outweighed the advantages.

might be made was not of importance to him from a policy standpoint, as he knew it was inevitable and he knew of no political action he would take if finite information was given to him. Bundy seemed to agree. After extended discussion, I stated that I could not conceive of our failing to take some actions if finite information was in our hands, i.e., Rusk might contact Gromyko or Dobrynin; the President might communicate with Khrushchev privately; we might discuss the subject with our Allies, both in Europe and the Far East; and we might take some position in the press through leaks or planted information. Certainly we should discuss the subject with Thailand, Laos and South Vietnam. It was agreed that the embarrassment and consequences of failure outweighed the advantages and therefore, while the final decision was up to the President, Rusk would not recommend the mission. Bundy agreed. McNamara indicated his concurrence but was non-committal.

Note: In a 5:00 o'clock meeting, I suggested that the mission could be accomplished [*3 lines of source text not declassified*]. All immediately agreed that this plan was a good one and should be approved. Subsequently at a meeting with the President (which I did not attend because of another appointment) the President approved the Takhli–Lop Nor plan and this was reported to me by McGeorge Bundy in a telephone call.

[Here follows discussion of other subjects]

---

51.   Memorandum From Robert W. Komer of the National Security Council Staff to the President's Special Assistant for National Security Affairs (Bundy)[1]

Washington, September 18, 1964.

Mac—

September 17 Planning Lunch (regular members only) again took up question of how to cope with *ChiCom nuclear explosion.*[2] Rowen gave a

---

[1] Source: Johnson Library, National Security File, Nuclear Testing—China. Top Secret. A marginal note in Bundy's handwriting reads: "*Very* interesting. McGB."

[2] Rostow's report of the meeting is in a memorandum of September 21 to Rusk. (Ibid.) A paper by Robert H. Johnson entitled "Some 'Unorthodox' Approaches to the Problem of Nuclear Proliferation," drafted on May 28, was sent to Planning Group members with a September 11 memorandum from Rostow. (Library of Congress, Manuscript Division, Harriman Papers, Special Files: Public Service, Kennedy–Johnson Administrations, Chronological File, Schedules and Briefing Material) Rostow's memorandum states that a memorandum by Henry Rowen of the International Security Affairs Office in the Department of Defense was to be circulated. A copy of Rowen's paper, entitled "Doing Something About Communist China's Nuclear Program," September 15, was sent to Rostow on September 16. (Department of State, S/P Files: Lot 70 D 199, China)

powerful counter-argument to the "temperate" approach proposed by the interdepartmental planning group chaired by Bob Johnson. Rowen saw many people taking an "excessively cheery" view, primarily because they were thinking too much in short-run terms. True, the Chi-Coms wouldn't have much of a nuclear capability for a long time; true, they wouldn't suddenly launch new aggressions simply because they had a rudimentary capability; true, there might not be any profound panic reactions from other Asians.

But the longer term implications, say over a 15-year period, were horrendous. Harry noted that the first Soviet nuclear explosion had occurred 15 years ago this month; look at the growth in Soviet power in the following 15 years. Even the first Soviet test might have affected Stalin's decision to launch the Korean war. In any event, the staggering growth in Soviet capabilities over the last 15 years had had an immense effect on our policies, postures, defense budget, etc. Granted that China today has a much feebler resource base than the USSR had in 1949; on the other hand the ChiComs might be even more adventuresome once they went nuclear than the Soviets had been. There was no reason why the ChiComs could not develop even crude ICBMs in 15 years. As for the external effects of Peiping's going nuclear, these would entail greatly increased pressure on us for new aid commitments, and major counter-efforts on the part of those Asians who felt themselves menaced. Most immediately, India could probably go nuclear in a year. As for the US, a growing ChiCom capability might be the deciding factor driving us into a $30 billion AICBM program or a huge civil defense effort. Yet another risk was that the ChiComs might be freer than we or the Russians in handing around nuclear technology; they had already hinted at this to Nasser.

What could we do? Rowen thought it technically feasible to destroy the two key ChiCom installations by a limited non-nuclear air attack. We could (a) handle this as a completely open matter and justify it at the time; or (b) seize on any opportunity created, say by a major blow-up in SEA; or (c) make a secret attack. In the latter case, it was quite possible that Peiping would prefer to say nothing about it. Such a spoiling operation would gain us a 2–5 year delay, and also deter ChiCom rebuilding. How valuable were 2–5 years? To Rowen they could be quite important.

What about reactions? The Soviets would approve privately, but might have to raise a to-do publicly. However, there was a chance we could bring them around in advance. The ChiComs might go for a tit-for-tat response, though it wasn't clear where they could do so effectively. In the rest of the world there would be considerable fear—also some feeling that the US was punishing a smaller power for getting into the nuclear business. Was this necessarily bad, however? Moreover, initial fears might quickly turn to relief once the crisis seemed to pass.

Rostow suggested that if we and the Soviets had just moved toward some big arms control agreement (say an unlimited test ban), the fact that we were going in this direction would create an optimum atmosphere for US pre-emption to forestall nuclear proliferation by Peiping.

Bob Johnson's rebuttal was that the Soviet-ChiCom analogy was weak; the ChiComs were a lot less further along today than the Soviets were 15 years ago. Moreover, the ChiCom explosion wouldn't change much, except psychologically. The US would still have great nuclear superiority as a deterrent, and perhaps an effective counter-force capability. The ChiComs would have to take into account possible pre-emptive US action if they brandished missiles in a crisis or at the least assume a disproportionate US retaliation if ChiComs used nucs. He queried whether US decisions on civil defense or ALCBMs were so sensitive to a ChiCom capability as Rowen indicated. (I commented that the more likely problem was that a ChiCom capability might trigger Soviet CD or ALCBM programs, which in turn might trigger us.)

Johnson found the stimulus to proliferation the strongest argument for pre-empting the ChiComs. But we should look at what other options we had besides pre-emption. Various arms control and propaganda programs, as well as new US commitments, could greatly limit the ChiCom impact. Moreover, would pre-empting the ChiComs prevent proliferation by other powers? Countries such as Israel would have their own reasons for going nuclear regardless of what China did. Finally, a one-time attack wouldn't do the job. It would only buy us some delay. To repeat the performance two or three times would be very difficult for the US.

Harriman's contribution was that we ought to have serious discussions with the Soviets on the ChiCom nuclear problem right after the election.

It was also brought out that the ChiComs already have overwhelming conventional superiority over their neighbors. So would other Asians be materially more scared of ChiCom power than they are already? Rostow and I mentioned the "precedent" problem. Would preemption of ChiComs encourage Nasser to take out Israeli nuclear facilities? Would it encourage the Soviets to play similar games?

Rostow questioned Rowen's proposition that the ChiComs might become much more aggressive once they had A-bombs. With nuclear weapons comes caution. The Soviets advanced less after they had gone nuclear than before. They were more cautious in the 1959–61 Berlin crisis than in 1948–49. As soon as the ChiComs got nuclear weapons, they'd have to worry lest we might be more inclined to use nucs against them in a local conflict. So a ChiCom nuclear capability might actually operate to make the ChiComs more cautious. Others present thought Rowen had taken the best case for our pre-emptive capability, and the worst case for what the ChiComs would do if we didn't pre-empt. Rowen gladly conceded the point.

Rostow summed up by saying that if the ChiComs attacked in SEA, then we had an overwhelming case for pre-emption. As to the other case, we should keep looking at it, particularly in the context of whether we could arrive at a broader modus vivendi with the Soviets about Germany, arms control, etc. If we and the Soviets could isolate the ChiComs in this way, by getting world opinion on our side, then the reaction to pre-emption would be considerably less. However, WWR didn't see Khrushchev prepared to go this far for quite a while yet.

There was an interesting aside when WWR asked Helms his view. Dick said he had raised this question several times at the White House and had been told to "keep his mouth shut." He pointed the finger at me and I said that I'd in effect been shut up too, but that you seemed to have no objection to PG discussion. I suspect that several of those present concluded that some planning was probably afoot on this matter. If so, or if there ought to be, the best cover for it might be simply to put out the word that we've taken a negative decision on the matter.

RWK

---

52.   Telegram From the Embassy in Poland to the Department of State[1]

Warsaw, September 23, 1964, 7 p.m.

645. Cabot–Wang Talks.[2] Deptels 557, 568, 581, 582.[3]

(1) Wang opened by reminding me I had said at last meeting we were well aware of serious consequences which could come from extension war beyond borders South Vietnam and seek avoid it. Yet we had

---

[1] Source: Department of State, Central Files, POL CHICOM–US. Confidential; Priority; Limdis. Repeated to Hong Kong, Taipei, Geneva, Moscow, and Stockholm.

[2] This was the 122d meeting of the Ambassadorial talks. Cabot reported the meeting in detail in airgram A–363 from Warsaw, September 28. (Ibid.)

[3] Telegram 557 to Warsaw, September 18, transmitted guidance for the meeting; telegram 568, September 19, and telegrams 581 and 582, September 22, provided supplementary guidance. (Ibid.)

fabricated second Tonkin Gulf incident as pretext expand war in Indo China. US surprise attack against DRV had met head on blow and even so-called allies failed give US active support in Vietnam. This illustrative of isolation in which we find ourselves in world. Said virtually every day US aircraft, warships invaded territorial waters other nations in Far East and large reinforcements being sent South Vietnam. It is well known USG working on operational plan for North Vietnam in further expansion war. Particularly serious that on September 18 we concocted another alleged Gulf of Tonkin incident as excuse to expand war. CPR strongly supports serious warning already served US by DRV. Alleged trend of opinion in US assumed Chinese reaction to August 4 incident was not strong and so there was suggestion we could "try it again". Debt of blood to DRV not yet repaid. Should we make another adventure, it could be said with certainty the situation in Vietnam and whole of SEA would be beyond repair. Mentioned recent serious warnings saying he directed to launch serious protest against such unscrupulous violation sovereignty of China. Mentioned increased support Taiwan and visits there of US "brass hats". Said Secretary Rusk was calling white black when he said China and DRV must come to decision leave neighbors alone. Trick of thief shouting "stop thief" can fool no one. He said if we bent on war then Chinese people have no alternative but to keep us company to the end. Hoped USG would take note of this.

(2) I said I shared hope he had expressed that peace could be reestablished in SEA but regretted say did not think his statements today had in any way contributed to that result. Spoke of detailed account first two incidents Tonkin Gulf as taken from log books American vessels involved. I gave facts of incidents and emphasized Hanoi should be made to realize its actions must inescapably involve other powers. Then restated at length our policies SEA adding our response would continue to be restrained but it was important his side not misread our intentions.

(3) Wang repeated at length his accusations our words inconsistent with our deeds, saying Chinese knew true facts Tonkin Gulf incidents and futile for me try argue otherwise. Called second Tonkin Gulf incident "a lie" saying on August 4 DRV did not have single war vessel in waters where US ships were and whole world knows this attack never occurred. Announcements by US Defense Department officials contradictory and full of loopholes and description so called encounter contrary to elementary military sense. Spoke further of alleged intrusions and claimed US on 30 July shelled two DRV islands. Alleged USS *Maddox* on 2 August intruded into territorial waters DRV. Concocted incident September 18 was attempt repeat farce of August 4 with view creating fresh excuses expand aggression. Since we had not been able piece together coherent story how did we expect fool others. Repeated it was clear USG simply lying. Implied we could not [be] well aware serious

consequences extending war as we had said since our recent actions appeared designed to expand war in SEA. Gave long tirade about alleged US aggressive action in Far East and whole world saying PRC supported national liberation movements in world because these movements are just ones. Communists have never tried to conceal their position. Had always stood by side with oppressed nations and people throughout world. This was honorable and no attack could ever check their determination. Spoke at length of the law of the development of history saying revolutions could neither be exported nor imported but it was also impossible for anyone to put down by force a genuine revolution. Said he thought it was a fraud when I said we would be restrained and would take limited action. Asked whether it could be said aggressive action became legitimate if limited.

(4) I said I considered his remarks a deplorable contribution to our talks. I said Wang seemed imply that any US presence in Tonkin Gulf impermissible. I denied American warships had penetrated what we considered under international law to be territorial space or waters of any nation Wang mentioned. Certainly three incidents in Gulf all took place many miles from territorial waters. I then reviewed in greater detail facts first two incidents. Also denied US warship attack on islands. I referred to ChiCom Central Committee statements supporting liberation movements, saying could not see how this could be reconciled with support of five principles, one of which was noninterference internal affairs other countries. Fact was North Vietnam had interfered in both Laos and South Vietnam long before we extended help to either. Mentioned North Vietnam prisoners captured Laos and assured Wang North Vietnam Government was playing very dangerous game.

(5) Wang then lectured on sovereign right establish territorial limits and launched into tedious but vitriolic repetition most of themes he had broached earlier, including pious lecture on nature of revolution in modern times, emphasizing theme it was international duty as well as a right for all fair minded people in world to support just cause (national liberation struggles).

(6) I assured Wang that search lights, torpedos and automatic weapons aimed at our vessels were not imaginary and that second Tonkin incident was not "lie" as he alleged. Said must insist on right my government question excessive claims to territorial waters. Objected to Wang's reference to "puppet regime" of South Vietnam, pointing out that government recognized by overwhelming number governments of world and if there is puppet regime in that area, it is Government North Vietnam, which he said at last meeting was closely connected to China as teeth and lips. Again spoke of unreconcilability support of liberation movements and support five principles. Mentioned confirmation North Vietnam troops in Laos according Peking Radio. Referred to his lecture on resist-

ance to oppression and asked whether enormous numbers Chinese liquidated by his side did not constitute oppression.

(7) Wang followed with long lecture of "facts" in South Vietnam situation centering around theme government there hated by broad masses South Vietnamese people. Alleged I had again referred to his government as a "regime".

(8) I denied I had used word regime in connection with his side in this meeting.[4] (Wang was reading from prepared statement when he made this accusation.)

(9) There followed several exchanges re Vietnam mostly tedious repetition on Wang's part and I finally said his statements were so ridiculous I saw no reason to continue argument. Wang blandly stated difference was his statements were in accordance with facts, and facts are facts. I reviewed points on which we simply disagreed as to facts almost as much as we disagreed on conclusions to be drawn from them. Wang closed saying of course we held different views but USG should be held responsible for tensions SEA at present. Next meeting November 25.

Cabot

---

[4] Telegram 557 to Warsaw suggested that since Wang seemed sensitive over Cabot's use of the word "regime," he should substitute "your side."

---

53.   Telegram From the Embassy in Poland to the Department of State[1]

Warsaw, September 24, 1964, 3 p.m.

650. Cabot–Wang Talks. Reference: Embtel 645.[2] Comments and recommendations following 122 meeting.

1.   This was one of longest and on Chinese side by far most vitriolic meeting in many months. Wang was loud, tendentious, impolite and arrogant, virtually spitting out his accusations, often with finger wag-

---

[1] Source: Department of State, Central Files, POL CHICOM–US. Confidential; Priority; Limdis. Repeated to Hong Kong, Taipei, Geneva, Moscow, and Stockholm.

[2] Document 52.

ging. We were subject to lengthy lectures delivered from an offensively professorial height. He almost invariably referred to me as "you," whereas long habit in the talks had been use "Mister Ambassador" or "Your Excellency." He used such phrases as "I want to tell you." He called not only me, but USG "liars." He expressed cocky contempt for our allegedly unavailing efforts in SEA, and made clear he thought we were seeing beginning of end for us there. After I pointed out that while he objected to use of word "regime" as applied to Peiping, he used it re SVN and "Chiang clique" for GRC, he seemed to take pleasure in using those terms more frequently. On side rustled papers quite unnecessarily while I was talking.

2.   There was a "Panmunjom" flavor to this meeting. Repetitious sermons, full of invective and pompous Communist "axioms" were delivered with no regard for factor logic, in a spirit of contemptuous one-upmanship seemingly designed to arouse anger. I answered firmly but not provocatively, and was careful not to let my anger show. Wang obviously wanted to prolong the meeting and engaged in lengthy ad libs before and after his prepared papers ran out—one of which he used twice. We believe he hoped I would leave the meeting with angry or at least glum mien. I therefore emerged to meet the larger than usual number of newsmen with relaxed, smiling aspect. Last evening one reporter told Narding press consensus based on length meeting and aspect two principals on emergence was that we had read riot act to Chinese due Tonkin Gulf incidents, and had derived satisfaction from meeting.

3.   The new Wang was entirely different in comportment from his first meeting in July. To limited extent this may be attributable his settling in saddle and hence emergence his own nature as provincial, blindly dedicated cadre who has made good through intelligence and loyalty with "know nothing" contempt for reason or logic. I am inclined believe, however, temper of his approach largely set by direction Peiping and doubtless had ChiComs worried. Notable that our retaliatory actions per se scarcely mentioned by Wang. Instead he assumed posture of heady confidence combined with threatening warnings. Believe this is his character. This is not time to expect them mention our successes or their weaknesses, even if they saw chance needling us in process. (Not surprising defector Tung not mentioned, even to advance excuse of kidnapping charges.)

4.   Particularly interesting is fact Wang readily admitted ChiComs supported "just" revolutions in other countries, implying all true communists should do so. He saw no inconsistency in this and coexistence line, since revolutions could not be exported, but inevitably arose indigenously in the face of local or foreign imposed oppression. In such instances, he maintained, communist support was "honorable."

5.   Wang pointedly denied both second and third Tonkin Gulf incidents took place, claiming we had concocted them as pretext more aggressive plotting against NVN. When I pointed out Wang had not denied first incident took place in international waters, Wang did not return to this point.

6.   Wang made no response on subject NVN prisoners Laos, despite fact their assignment would come under his label of "honorable" support.

7.   I believe at next meeting we should continue phraseology of confident great power, rather than swapping invective for invective, at least yet. If character of exchange is to alter for worse it should be of their making. At same time within this frame there is room for bluntness, and among other things we may wish indicate we not interested in elementary course in Marxist maxims in these serious talks.

8.   Wang has penchant for ad libbing, and I may be forced to do more of this myself than has been necessary in past, although I have all along tried to tailor my remarks to the requirements of the moment.

9.   Vientiane's 491 to Department[3] arrived after meeting.

Cabot

---

[3] Dated September 23. (Department of State, Central Files, POL CHICOM–US)

---

54.   Memorandum of Conversation[1]

Washington, September 25, 1964, 1–3:30 p.m.

Memorandum of conversation with Ambassador Dobrynin, Friday, September 25, 1964, 1:00–3:30 p.m.

I had a long and cordial lunch with Ambassador Dobrynin in which we touched lightly on a large number of topics of only casual interest. The points of principal importance are as follows:

[Here follows discussion not related to China.]

---

[1] Source: Johnson Library, National Security File, Country File, USSR, Dobrynin Conversations, 11/63–4/68, Vol. I. Secret.

3. My own principal effort was to direct the Ambassador's attention to the problem of Communist Chinese nuclear weapons. I made it very plain that in our judgment the Chinese nuclear weapons would be real dissemination, while the MLF was nothing of the sort. I also made it plain that we would be ready for private and serious talk on what to do about this problem if there were any interest in the Soviet Government. The Ambassador gave no direct reply, but he gave me clearly to understand that in the thinking of the Soviet Government the Chinese nuclear capability was already, in effect, taken for granted. He argued that Chinese nuclear weapons had no importance against the Soviet Union or against the U.S., and that therefore they had only a psychological impact in Asia, and he implied that this impact had no importance for his government.

4. On China in general, the Ambassador admitted and indeed emphasized the depth and strength of the existing split between Moscow and Peking, but he took the view that the primary cause of this split was the personal megalomania of Mao. He said that Stalin at his worst had never insisted upon the kind of personal worship which was now accorded to Mao. He said that while in the Soviet Union younger men (like himself) were coming into positions of responsibility, and were able to argue openly and honestly with Khrushchev, in Communist China the older generation and, above all, Mao himself, were still in full charge and were inaccessible to reasonable argument. He told me at some length of the dismal experience of Soviet advisers trying to warn against the technological nonsense of the Great Leap Forward. But he asserted calmly, but strongly, his conviction that in the long run there would be a restoration of harmony between the two countries. And at one point, in discussion of our American differences with Communist China, he gently remarked on the continued existence of the treaty between the USSR and the ChiComs.

[Here follows discussion of an unrelated subject.]

McG. B.

55.   Memorandum for the Record[1]

Washington, October 5, 1964.

SUBJECT

> Discussion with the President, Secretary Rusk, Secretary McNamara and
> Mr. McGeorge Bundy—Monday, 5 October—4:45 p.m.

[Here follows discussion of unrelated matters.]

3. The Takhli–Lop Nor flights were discussed. I presented KH–4 photography and stated that U–2 photography would give us more precise information on the final stages of construction at Lop Nor from which we might estimate the probable time of a nuclear detonation. I said that unless information concerning the time of a detonation was of significant importance to the President and Secretary Rusk, I could not recommend the flight, pointing out it was a deep penetration extending the U–2 to the full limit of its range during which time no other important targets would be traversed. Secretary Rusk opposes the flight on the grounds the information is not of significant importance to him and the flight carried us over Burma and India which was undesirable.[2]

4. I then said that the units were deployed [*less than 1 line of source text not declassified*] and suggested we fly some southern China missions covering critical targets. This was agreed.

Action: Mr. Bundy asked that we present flight plans and other information through the usual Special Group (303) channel, which I agreed to do promptly.

---

[1] Source: Central Intelligence Agency, DCI (McCone) Files: Job 80–B01285A, DCI Mtgs with the Pres, May–Oct 1964. Secret; Eyes Only. Drafted by McCone on October 7.

[2] CIA telegram ADIC 5332 to Taipei, October 8, stated that the primary reason for cancelling the Lop Nor mission was the risk of an incident in the month preceding the presidential election. In addition, information obtained from a satellite and a September 29 statement by Rusk that a Chinese nuclear explosion might be imminent had both tended to diminish the importance of the mission. (Ibid., Job 80–B01676R, DDCI Trip to the Far East, 17–31 October 1964)

56. **Memorandum From the Assistant Director for Scientific Intelligence of the Central Intelligence Agency (Chamberlain) to the Deputy Director of Central Intelligence (Carter)[1]**

Washington, October 15, 1964.

SUBJECT

Estimated Imminence of a Chinese Nuclear Test

1. This memorandum is for your information.

2. In a Special National Intelligence Estimate issued in August 1964[2] it was concluded that, on balance, a Chinese nuclear test probably would not occur before the end of 1964. At that time available information indicated that the Chinese nuclear test site near Lop Nor was under active construction and could be ready for a nuclear test by about October 1964. On the other hand, continuing construction in September 1963 at the only known Chinese plutonium production site indicated a probable startup of the reactor at that site in early 1964. This in turn indicated a date around mid-1965 for first availability of sufficient plutonium for a nuclear test. Although neither the possibility of an earlier startup of this plant nor the existence of an unidentified plutonium production facility could be wholly discounted, it was felt unlikely that plutonium would be available in 1964. The U–235 plant at Lanchou is only partially complete and thus could not contribute fissionable material for a nuclear test in the near future.

3. More recent information on the Lop Nor test site has confirmed the earlier estimate of its probable readiness date. Preparations for a test were essentially completed at the Lop Nor nuclear test site by October 1964. Included in these preparations is a 340 foot shot tower that was installed prior to April 1964 and is now surrounded by a double fence. Arrays for instrument emplacement are located around the tower. These include arcs at 9,800, 16,000, 23,000 and 33,000 feet respectively and a number of radial lines from the tower with bunkers and platforms emplaced along the lines. Two small towers, approximately 50 feet high, are located on the arc at 9,800 feet from the shot tower and at 90° from each other. Available information does not permit determination of

---

[1] Source: Central Intelligence Agency, DCI (McCone) Files: Job 80–B01676R, DDCI Trip to the Far East, 17–31 October 1964. Top Secret. Concurred in by the Deputy Director for Science and Technology, with the notation that a memorandum to holders of the estimate was planned for the following week. A paper entitled "Indications Relating to a Chinese Communist Nuclear Test in the Near Future," neither signed nor dated, is attached to the source text, along with a second memorandum of October 15 from Chamberlain to Carter entitled "The Chinese Atomic Energy Program."

[2] Document 43.

whether or not instruments have actually been emplaced on the platforms and towers. The high priority apparently given to the completion of site construction suggests that a test is scheduled in the fairly near future since it would not be desirable to establish the parameters of an initial nuclear experiment much in advance of the test.

4. A high level of flight activity to and from the area was noted throughout this very active construction period. The activity halted in September 1963 when the site was essentially complete. Subsequent resumption of this activity in late September may reflect final preparations for testing.

5. A restudy of the Pao-t'ou reactor site indicates that adequate primary and backup electric power circuits for reactor operation had been installed by March 1963. Thus, our confidence has been reduced in the August 1964 judgment that the reactor probably did not start operation until early 1964. Another prospect for a fissionable material supply is a facility in a large complex near Chih-Chin-Hsia (Yumen) which might contain a small operational reactor, but this identification is uncertain.

6. We no longer believe that evidence on plutonium availability justifies the on-balance judgment reached in August 1964. We believe the Lop Nor evidence indicates that a test could occur at any time. In any case we believe a test will occur sometime within the next six to eight months.

Ernest J. Zellmer[3]

---

[3] Zellmer signed for Chamberlain above Chamberlain's typed signature.

---

57.   Memorandum for the Record[1]

Washington, October 16, 1964.

SUBJECT

Meeting of an Executive Group of the National Security Council, 16 October 1964

1. A special meeting of a small group of members of the National Security Council was convened at the White House at 1030 on 16 October

---

[1] Source: Central Intelligence Agency, DCI (McCone) Files: Job 80–B01285A, DCI Mtgs with the Pres, Oct–Dec 1964. Top Secret.

1964 to discuss the change of government in Moscow. In attendance were the President, Secretary Rusk, Secretary McNamara, Under Secretary Ball, Under Secretary Thompson, McGeorge Bundy, the DCI, and the undersigned. [Here follows the remainder of paragraph 1 and paragraphs 2–5 on other subjects.]

6.   During this meeting preliminary reports about the explosion of a nuclear device in Communist China arrived, and there was a good bit of discussion over the kind of statement that should be released from the White House. Bundy had a draft of a "stand-by statement" which had been prepared in an interdepartmental committee earlier,[2] and this was revised during and shortly after the meeting for release,[3] along with the preliminary views provided by JAEIC as to the size and location of the explosion. There was a general discussion of the meaning of the Chinese Communist acquisition of a nuclear capability and a recollection of Secretary Rusk's statement of 29 September[4] based upon new data provided by the Intelligence Community concerning the test site that had pretty well prepared the world for expecting this event and not becoming unduly alarmed by it.

Ray S. Cline
Deputy Director (Intelligence)

---

[2] Read sent a copy of the draft statement to Bundy with a covering memorandum of September 30. (Department of State, Central Files, DEF 12–1 CHICOM) A copy of a draft program of action to minimize the impact of the anticipated Chinese nuclear test, prepared by the interdepartmental committee, is filed with a September 25 covering memorandum from Rostow to Bundy. (Johnson Library, National Security File, Subject File, Nuclear Testing, China)

[3] The statement that Johnson read to the press at 1:20 p.m. that day is printed in *Public Papers of the Presidents of the United States: Lyndon B. Johnson, 1963–64*, Book II, p. 1357.

[4] For text of Rusk's September 29 statement, see Department of State *Bulletin*, October 19, 1964, pp. 542–543.

58.   Memorandum for the Record[1]

Washington, October 17, 1964.

SUBJECT

Meeting of the National Security Council—Saturday—12:00 o'clock—17 October 1964[2]

With the President—all members present (except Secretary Dillon) plus Secty. Vance, Secty. Ball and Amb. Thompson

1.   DCI opened the meeting with a briefing on the background of ChiCom nuclear capability. I reviewed briefly the Soviet-Chinese collaboration in the mid- and late '50's,

(a) the nuclear energy institute at Peiping with a small heavy water reactor, duplicate of one which I had seen in Moscow (Seaborg had also seen it);

(b) the existence of a suspected U–235 plant at Lanchow which was not completed and we did not expect would be in operation for 2 to 3 years;

(c) the existence of a small air-cooled reactor at Pao Tou with capacity to produce about 10 kilograms of plutonium per year which we thought went into operation in late '63 or early '64 or it might have gone into operation earlier though that is unlikely;

(d) the existence of a suspected graphite-moderated water-cooled reactor in the vicinity of Yumen which was first photographed in 1962 and again in February 1964; at the latter date the reactor apparently was not operational however I stated it may have been shut down for change of fuel elements and hence it was possible, though by no means certain, that the reactor might have been operational in 1962.

I said that the existence of the reactor was not surprising as both we and the Russians had built a small graphite-cooled reactor prior to the construction of our large reactors at Hanford. This reactor had a capacity of between 30 and 35 kilograms plutonium per year.

The test site at Lop Nor which we have observed over the past 2 or 3 years, during recent months had seen considerable activity on the basis of photography of this site, that I had stated in my briefing of the heads of eight Western European Governments that we could expect a nuclear test based on the evidence of the completion of this site within 30 to 60 days from the time of my briefing which was mid-September, and the

---

[1] Source: Central Intelligence Agency, DCI (McCone) Files: Job 80–B01285A, Box 6, Folder 10, DCI Mtgs with the Pres, Oct–Dec 1964. Secret; Eyes Only. Dictated by McCone.

[2] Summary notes of the meeting by Bromley Smith are filed in Johnson Library, National Security File, NSC File, NSC Meetings, Vol. 3, Tab 25. For AEC Chairman Glenn T. Seaborg's notes of the meeting, see *Journal of Glenn T. Seaborg, Chairman, U.S. Atomic Energy Commission, 1961–1971*, Vol. 9, pp. 254–258.

activities we noted just prior to the explosion such as the stand-down of all aviation in the area and unusual sampling of weather.

2.   I then said the known facilities could, if one assumed the earliest operational dates, produce plutonium for the device and some more. Pao Tou alone could not do so, but Pao Tou plus Yumen would give them sufficient plutonium. The two reactors could produce between 40 and 45 kilograms of plutonium per year which would be enough for 6 or 7 crude devices. I noted that both the United States and France had used about 6 kilograms or more plutonium in their initial devices and assumed that the Chinese Communists would use about the same.

3.   With reference to delivery capability, I said that the ChiComs had 290 IL–28's with a range of 600 nautical miles and a lift capacity of about 6,000 pounds. The bomb bay however was limited to a 36" diameter bomb although it was 14' long. I said we must wait the diagnosis of the radioactive debris to determine the degree of sophistication of the Lop Nor device and thus make a judgment as to whether the ChiCom present technology would permit them to develop an implosive device small enough to fit into the IL–28 bomb bay. Pointed out they had a few "B–29" types and that they had made a considerable effort in missiles and had an elaborate missile range but it was our observation that their success had been marginal. Therefore it seemed to us that many years would pass before the ChiComs would have a sophisticated delivery capability against nearby territory and we did not see them developing any intercontinental capability at this time.

4.   I stated that while we had extensive U–2 and satellite photography over ChiCom, there was an important area in and about Chungking and east on the Yangtze River on which the photography was unsatisfactory and hence there might exist there or elsewhere in China, a reactor or a production complex which we did not know about.

Note: Action: Information received from NPIC on Sunday evening was in sharp variance with this above statement given to me by Jack Smith and Wally Howard on Saturday morning. It is important that I receive a comprehensive evaluation of this situation prior to briefing Leadership.

[Here follows discussion not related to China.]

6.   There followed a general discussion and adoption of the general line followed by the President's speech.[3] It was agreed that the President should withhold political trips for a few days; that he should address the public; that he should meet the Leadership and that he should meet with

---

[3] For text of Johnson's radio and television address of October 18 on the Chinese nuclear explosion, the Soviet change of leadership, and the British elections, see *Public Papers of the Presidents of the United States: Lyndon B. Johnson, 1963–64,* Book II, pp. 1377–1380.

the Cabinet. The sequence of these events to be decided after careful consideration by Messrs. Bundy, Rusk, McNamara and the President himself.

[Here follows discussion not related to China.]

---

59.   **Telegram From the Embassy in the Republic of China to the Department of State**[1]

Taipei, October 19, 1964, 11 p.m.

328. Met President this afternoon [*1 line of source text not declassified*].[2]

[*less than 1 line of source text not declassified*], present were President, Madam and interpreter. President asked if I had any news for him. I stated that at Saturday meeting with FonMin I had passed all available information and guidance on ChiCom atomic event and on Soviet change of leadership.[3] I said no developments but we were evaluating carefully statements of *Izvestia* and *Pravda* and world reaction. I then gave him sanitized version of State and CIA analysis.

I then asked him if he could give me any views these two events I could pass USG.

President passed by specific comment on Soviet shift and concentrated on ChiCom event.

President stated that event of such far reaching importance that he had been unable up to the present to make any detailed or specific statement or comment. He stated however that he would like to pass to me "as US Ambassador and friend" his own personal views on impact on Asian peoples. He said that psychological reaction was enormous and far reaching. He said it was a turning point in the attitude of people of this part of the world and that their views on world affairs would henceforth be different from those of the past. He said the psychological effect could not be overestimated.

President stated that Americans at home and abroad were not capable of truly appraising the psychology of Asian people. He said this event

---

[1] Source: Department of State, Central Files, DEF 12–1 CHICOM. Secret. Repeated to Hong Kong, Tokyo, and CINCPAC for POLAD. Received at 1 p.m.

[2] [*text not declassified*]

[3] On October 15 Khrushchev was removed as Chairman of the Council of Ministers and replaced by Alexei N. Kosygin.

required special efforts by US to see the change in its true light and urged that we do all possible to this end.

I said the US was studying the situation with all resources in Asia and at home. I agreed with inadequacy of Americans in true appraisal of Asian thought and stated that we respected his judgement more than any other in his position as true leader of Chinese people.

President then said that Asia henceforth would never be the same as it was in the past. He said the United States and the Republic of China should at this point reevaluate their policy toward Mainland China based not on the past but the present and future and work jointly for a new solution. This latter point emphasized by the Madam.

Wright

60.   Memorandum for the Record[1]

Washington, October 19, 1964, 1:30 p.m.

SUBJECT

President's meeting with Congressional Leadership, Oct. 19

The President met with the bipartisan Congressional Leadership on Monday, October 19, at 1:30 p.m. The President worked from the attached briefing memorandum (Tab A),[2] and the discussion at the meeting generally followed the attached agenda.

The President opened the meeting by giving his welcome to the Leadership and his thanks for their return from their homes and whatever else they were doing. He then asked Director McCone to explain what we know of the Chinese nuclear effort.

Director McCone gave a general explanation of the capabilities of the United States in satellite reconnaissance, and then described our current understanding of their capabilities. A copy of the notes from which he worked is attached (Tab B). The Director was followed by Chairman

---

[1] Source: Johnson Library, National Security File, Bundy Files, Miscellaneous Meetings, Vol. I. Secret. The memorandum is dated October 20.

[2] The tabs are attached but not printed.

Seaborg who gave a general discussion of the problems of the technology of nuclear weapons. Chairman Seaborg indicated the probability but not the certainty that the Chinese weapon was made of plutonium (an assumption that was challenged by evidence from debris later in the day). He indicated his belief that the Chinese would begin with a device and that it would take sometime to "weaponize" such a device. Chairman Seaborg indicated that the speed of the Chinese development would depend on how much the Chinese knew about the technical details—quality of material and design details—in weaponmaking. He thought that if they had been fully cut off from what the Soviets knew for several years, it might be a matter of about 4 or 5 years before they would have a thermonuclear device. On the other hand, if they wished to make a thermonuclear explosion simply for its political and psychological impact, they could use the bulk of their production for this specific purpose and produce such an explosion considerably sooner.

The President asked Secretary McNamara to give an account of the military position of the United States vis-à-vis the Chinese bomb. Secretary McNamara began by discussing the dangers in the spread of nuclear weapons. He pointed out that there are half a dozen countries which could move rapidly in this direction if they made the political decision to do so, and that the cost of developing a nuclear device was now on the order of $120 million—not a prohibitive figure. He underlined the importance of finding ways and means to limit nuclear spread.

Secretary McNamara then turned to the strategic position of the U.S. and pointed out that Chinese targets as well as Soviet targets were included in our strategic planning. He explained that we had 2700 nuclear weapons in our survivable alert force, and said that 800 of these weapons would suffice to inflict unacceptable damage on the Soviet Union. The additional weapons were important for their damage-limiting capability.

Ambassador Thompson discussed the developments in the Soviet Union, along the lines of the attached memo of his talking notes (Tab C).

Senator Hickenlooper asked if the immediate meaning of the Chinese bomb was not more important in its psychological impact than in its military meaning. Secretary Rusk replied that we were taking every possible measure in consultation with interested nations to limit this psychological impact. We had given important assurances in the President's statements. The Secretary reported that a number of Ambassadors had told him that his warning of September 29 had been very useful in limiting the impact of this event.

[Here follows dicussion not related to China.]

McG. B.

61.   Memorandum of a Conversation[1]

Washington, October 20, 1964, 6:10 p.m.

SUBJECT

Chinese Communist Nuclear Detonation

PARTICIPANTS

Ambassador Anatoliy F. Dobrynin—USSR
The Secretary
Ambassador Adlai Stevenson—USUN

After discussing other matters, Ambassador Dobrynin asked what else could the US and USSR do to improve relations. Mention was made of the explosion of a nuclear device by the Chinese Communists. Ambassador Dobrynin stated that it would take some time before the Chinese Communists would become a nuclear power. He suggested the extension of the test ban treaty to all environments as a possible next step. The Secretary stated the US position with respect to the need for adequate and effective verification. Ambassador Dobrynin reiterated the standard Soviet position.

---

[1] Source: Department of State, Central Files, DEF 12–1 CHICOM. Secret. Drafted by Polansky. The conversation took place in the Secretary's office. A handwritten notation on the source text reads "Uncleared. Never distributed." The source text indicates it is Part 3 of 4.

---

62.   Report of Meetings[1]

Taipei, October 23–24, 1964.

Report of Meeting Between Chinese Nationalist Officials and Dr. Ray S. Cline

Dr. Cline held two briefings in Taipei[2]—one on 23 October was attended by Foreign Minister Shen, Defense Minister Yu, and Chiang

---

[1] Source: Johnson Library, National Security File, Agency File, Central Intelligence Agency. Secret; Eyes Only. No drafting information appears on the source text. Filed with a covering note of October 24 from McCone's Executive Assistant, Walter Elder, to McGeorge Bundy stating that McCone asked that it be brought to Bundy's personal attention.

[2] According to a record of a telephone conversation between McCone and Ball on October 20, McCone gave Ball the gist of Carter's report of his conversation with Chiang and told him Cline was planning to go to Taipei, stating that because of Cline's "background and relationship with those people, it would be useful to get his appraisal of the attitude of the people." (Johnson Library, Ball Papers, China (Taiwan))

Ching-kuo. The second session on 24 October was with President Chiang Kai-shek and Madame Chiang Kai-shek, Foreign Minister Shen, and Chiang Ching-kuo.[3] Both briefings were extremely well received. Ambassador Wright and Mr. Nelson were present at both sessions.

At first Shen made strong point of the anxiety of the ordinary man in Taipei who feared that three small bombs could destroy Keelung, Taipei, and Kaohsiung. It would be small consolation to him to know that after he was dead, U.S. would retaliate on ChiComs. Yu warned that nuclear deterrent credible assurance only when facing rational men and Chi-Coms were not rational. All Chinese in first briefing concerned re U–235 content of test blast and implication that ChiComs might have much greater production capacity of fissionable material than first estimated. Gimo also said this information most important.

Gimo after briefing in fairly emotional response said U.S. assurances for defense of Taiwan inadequate to calm fears aroused by explosion. U.S. policy of isolation of ChiComs was no longer enough. ChiComs merely felt immune to this policy which would enable Chi-Coms perfect their nuclear capability undisturbed. He said primary Chi-Com aim was to destroy him and GRC and when this happened all of Asia would be threatened. In reference to ChiCom atomic bombs which could be carried in present ChiCom air force planes, he said "we are the target". He brushed aside stated U.S. assurances of defense support and probable ChiCom reluctance invite retaliation. U.S., he felt, would be deterred from nuclear retaliation by European allies. It would be useless come to support of GRC once it destroyed. He said explanations of how U.S. would come to GRC aid left him "unconsoled".

He said if U.S. real friend it would [2 *lines of source text not declassified*]. Present U.S. assurances could have adverse reaction toward U.S. on part of people. They would believe that American friends asking that they wait for death. He said if Chinese Communists successful in destroying GRC, they might well compromise with Soviets. In past U.S. worried about GRC counter attack for fear of Soviet reaction and subsequent world conflict. No matter who in power in Russia, they know only Gimo can bury Mao Tse-tung. Russians know this. Do Americans know it? Now time for U.S. to review its policy and choose either Mao or Gimo as friend.

---

[3] The Embassy reported Cline's meeting with Chiang Kai-shek in telegram 347 from Taipei, October 24, and in more detail in airgram A–358, October 27. (Department of State, Central Files, DEF 12–1 CHICOM and POL 1 CHINAT–US respectively)

63.   **Memorandum From James C. Thomson, Jr., of the National Security Council Staff to the President's Special Assistant for National Security Affairs (Bundy)[1]**

Washington, October 28, 1964.

SUBJECT

The U.S. and Communist China in the Months Ahead

I return to my Far Eastern cable traffic with some thoughts on China policy that may well derive from the heady brew of speech-writing for an optimist. I pass them on to you not because they are particularly original, but because recent events seem to me to give them new validity.

To begin with, I am struck by the quantity of the U.S. Government's time, energy, and resources now focused on South Vietnam/Laos, as against all the rest of Asia. This is perhaps an inevitable consequence of our preoccupation with the major Communist challenge at hand. But the fact of our concentration on the tail of the dog, rather than the dog itself, has been dramatized anew by recent developments. (I might add that I am not even sure that this tail belongs to that particular dog; there is danger in pushing too far the thesis of Peking's responsibility for the South Vietnam crisis.)

Given the Chicom nuclear blast, the new Soviet leadership, de Gaulle, Wilson, et al, we are now moving into a period when Communist China's world position will probably change quite rapidly, regardless of what we do. To what extent can we influence these changes so as to minimize the damage to our security? Also, to what extent can we preserve appearances—i.e., not seem to lose our shirts in the process of these changes?

I have in mind, of course, two virtual certainties: that Communist China will be voted into the United Nations sometime during the life of the new Administration—probably not this year (although that still seems to me an open question), but very probably next year; and that Communist China will soon—one way or another—be brought into international negotiations regarding the control of nuclear weapons. I also have in mind the fact of fast increasing free world trade and travel contacts with mainland China.

Faced with these developments, we can either sit tight in increasingly lonely isolation; or we can seek ways to cut our losses.

So far, we have chosen to sit tight, waiting for Peking to "shape up." The Kennedy press conference response of last November 14 and the

---

[1] Source: Johnson Library, National Security File, Country File, China, Vol. II. Secret. A copy was sent to Komer.

Hilsman China speech of December 13 are the clearest articulation of this approach at its best. During 1963–4, our gradual détente with the USSR certainly gave it added impetus; our Kremlinologists have urged us not to rock the boat.

It seems to me increasingly clear, however, that our present approach actually serves Peking's interests—and that Peking has no intention of "shaping up" in terms of taking tension-relieving initiatives with us, either now or in the foreseeable future. On the contrary, Peking is seriously intent on isolating us—while we, in turn, are generally blamed for trying (unsuccessfully) to isolate Peking.

I would therefore urge consideration of a different approach—one designed to cut our losses, to reduce our isolation, and to improve our look as a confident, realistic, and responsible world power.

My objective would be to try to bring our China policy into line with both reality and our long-term interests. Our aim has always been the "domestication" of Communist China. A strategy of containment plus moral preachment has achieved little success in this regard. So why not try modified containment—plus subversion? By the latter, I simply mean the careful use of free world goods, people, and ideas—instruments which have proven their long-term corrosive value in our relations with other totalitarian societies.

The following ingredients seem to me appropriate to a revised China policy over the next several months:

1. After the election, we should indicate anew our willingness and even desire to discuss the problem of nuclear arms control in a forum that includes Communist China sometime during 1965–6.

2. At the UNGA session in December we should base our opposition to Communist China's membership primarily on Peking's threat to the independent existence and UN seat of the 12 million people of Taiwan. (Our aim would be to hold the line on Chirep during the present session but to prepare for acquiescence in a "one-China one-Taiwan" seating arrangement at the next GA.)

3. Sometime in January the Secretary of State should find an occasion, ideally during a press conference, to note casually that "of course, the United States has accorded de facto recognition to the Peiping regime ever since President Eisenhower authorized the Geneva and Warsaw conversations of 1954–5; our real problem, however, is Communist China's continuing threat to Formosa and to its neighbors." Such a low-key remark would move us toward "one-China one-Taiwan" without igniting public concern over imminent de jure recognition of Peking (a move that I would regard as of little value and of very low priority as long as we maintain our commitments to the security and independence of Taiwan).

4. Early in the year, the Department of State should announce revised travel regulations for American citizens which would in effect

permit them to journey to nations we do not recognize, on the understanding that the U.S. Government cannot provide protection for such travellers. (As you know, this travel package was cleared through State last January; the one chief difficulty seems to relate to Cuba, a point on which I have no views.)

5. Depending upon responses here and abroad to the above moves and depending upon new international developments, we should move quietly to place our trade in non-strategic goods with Communist China on the same basis as our trade with the Soviet Union.

6. At the time of the next UNGA meeting in the autumn of 1965, we should focus our energies on the retention of Taiwan's seat in the General Assembly (and perhaps on preventing Peking from occupying a seat in the Security Council). If we play our cards right—and if the Chinats don't commit political suicide—we might even succeed in shifting the onus for Peking's continued exclusion to the Chicoms.

At the same time that we take the above moves, we should maintain all aspects of our present *military containment* of Communist China—our assistance to Vietnam, Laos, India, and other nations of the region; also, our resistance to Chicom activities in Africa, etc. In other words, we should move toward treating the Chinese much as we treat the Russians: an appropriately tough response wherever or whenever they seriously cause us harm; but otherwise, a groping toward coexistence on the basis of mutual self-interest.

I am under no illusion that the above moves would produce a change in Communist China's behavior or its view of the United States. I strongly believe, however, that these moves would give us a greater look of maturity and self-confidence, far greater rapport with our major allies, increased respect from the "third world," a greater degree of maneuverability, and the basis for long-term leverage with the Chicoms. We would also have less the look of a defeated obstructionist by the end of 1965.

I would argue, in addition, that the U.S. political climate can bear the weight of such moves—particularly if the President wins big next week. (Press and Congressional reaction to the Hilsman China speech last year revealed a dramatic ebbing of passions on the China issue over the past decade.)

I might add that I am well aware that much of this strategy is dependent upon early decisions that must be taken with regard to the situation in South Vietnam. I assume that we will have to choose roughly between escalation towards negotiation on the one hand, and a muddle-through towards negotiation on the other.

Even if we were to elect the first alternative, my China suggestions might still make sense. On the basis of my own limited knowledge of the Vietnam situation, however, I would hope that our choice would be the second alternative. If so, my suggestions would hardly run counter to this strategy.

Jim

---

64.   Memorandum From the Assistant Secretary of State for International Organization Affairs (Cleveland) to Secretary of State Rusk[1]

Washington, November 5, 1964.

SUBJECT

China and the UN

After some consultation around here, and a good deal of brooding, I offer the attached analysis of the Chinese representation issue and its ramifications into Southeast Asia and a good many other related subjects.

This is not a "solution" but an essay which tries to take a fresh look at a tired old problem. I think it would be worthwhile to have a small seminar with a very limited number of people, to discuss how we tackle our ChiRep problem before we are dragged to unsatisfactory outcomes by some of our best friends and allies.

I have given copies of this only to George Ball (who originally asked for it), Averell Harriman, Llewellyn Thompson, Bill Bundy, and Walt Rostow.[2]

Attachment[3]

THE TAMING OF THE SHREW:
COMMUNIST CHINA AND THE UNITED NATIONS

There is a good deal of talk these days about the erosion of support for excluding the Chinese Communists from the United Nations, and

---

[1] Source: Department of State, Central Files, UN 6 CHICOM. Secret. A handwritten notation on the source text indicates that it was seen by the Secretary.

[2] Cleveland sent a copy of the attachment to Ball with a covering memorandum of October 31, a copy of which is attached to the source text but not printed.

[3] Drafted by Cleveland. The drafting date is October 31.

about the related problem of how to accomplish U.S. objectives in Southeast Asia. On both situations we are in something of a box. This paper will argue that the same box contains both problems; and while it is something of a Chinese puzzle, we can escape from the box we are in.

I.

Erosion and Opportunity

Contrary to widespread belief, the central problem in the Far East is the military and political behavior of the Chinese Communists, not our military and political response to that behavior.

On the military side we are doing what we can to contain ChiCom power without expanding the Southeast Asian war or unleashing the Chinese Nationalists for an invasion of the Chinese mainland. We have created something close to a stalemate around the whole periphery of Chinese power from Korea to India. But the Viet Nam salient of that stalemate is precarious in the extreme.

The ChiComs do not yet have reason to believe they cannot win in Southeast Asia by applying patience, pressure, and the principles of indirect aggression. They know how fragile the Saigon government is—they are helping make it that way. And they hear vocal elements in American politics proposing that we get out of Vietnam, and get the United Nations in.

On the political side, the most recent soundings place the vote on Chinese representation in the 19th General Assembly on the ragged edge of losing by simple majority. Of our friends in this battle we can say only, as Thurber said of his early colleagues at *The New Yorker,* that "some of them helped, with left hand and tongue in cheek."

Canada, Italy and many others are impatient to get on some new track that is not vulnerable to the political charge they are "ignoring" the world's most populous nation. The Africans are increasingly wobbly. The French are increasingly unhelpful. Even so strong an opponent of ChiCom admission as Paul-Henri Spaak has now told us this Assembly is the last time around for him in the face of mounting public and parliamentary pressure at home.

If we make enough of an issue of it, the British and a few others who recognize Peking will probably stick with us in insisting a two-thirds majority is required to change the representation of China in the UN. But at best we can hope to hold the line on the traditional basis only through the present General Assembly. If the line up of power in the Far East remains about the way it is, and we do not change our UN tactics, we face a serious defeat on the issue in the 20th General Assembly.

Studying these facts, virtually every government in the world now believes that we are gradually losing both the guerilla war in South Viet Nam and the parliamentary trench war in the UN.

And a growing number of governments now seem convinced (a) that there is a better chance of taming the aggressive behavior of the Chi-Coms if they are admitted to the UN and subjected to peaceful persuasion in its precincts; and (b) that the rigid posture of the United States is somehow preventing an accommodation with the ChiComs.

(The evidence that the ChiComs can be tamed by the application of sweetness and light is wholly lacking. They are still mobilizing on India's northern border, stirring up the Pathet Lao, subverting Cambodia, supporting the attack by North Viet Nam on South Viet Nam, and threatening Formosa—and they are still at war with the UN itself in Korea. They have exploded a nuclear device and will doubtless now add nuclear blackmail to their kit of tools.)

This picture of our friends and allies leaving the sinking ship of U.S. policy is not overdrawn; but what it reveals is not their defection from the anti-Communist cause, but their defection from our existing policies. After all, most of the relevant political leaders in the world do not favor Chinese Communist influence; they fear it. They do not want Southeast Asia to become a peninsula of China; they just don't believe we can prevent that outcome in the way we are trying to prevent it. They do not look forward to the day the Chinese enter the United Nations; they merely regard it as historically inevitable.

In other words, *what is eroding is not the opposition to Communist China's behavior, but the support of our traditional tactics for dealing with it.*

[Here follows Section II, "Military Firmness and Political Flexibility," and the first 9 pages of Section III, "Political Perspective."]

Even to get started on this political escalator would require enormous changes in the attitudes and ambitions of the Chinese Communists. In steps 2 and 4, it would also require far-reaching changes in the attitudes and ambitions of the Government of the Republic of China—in return for the maintenance of its name and identity, and its control over Formosa, it would be abandoning the "return to the Mainland," liquidation of its own Security Council veto, and acceptance of the People's Republic of China as, in effect, the senior one of the two Chinas.

It is not likely that we will have to cross many of these difficult bridges any time soon. Indeed, the danger of getting started down this somewhat slippery road at all is made remote by the implacable hostility of the Chinese Communist leadership. They will surely insist for quite a while that they won't come into the UN unless Taipei is thrown out and Peking gets not only the China seat in the General Assembly but the veto in the Security Council as well. Moreover, the Chinese Communist leaders, who are still the veterans of the Long March, have some reason to believe that their kind of toughness pays off: French recognition, Western trade credits, Khrushchev's fall and the political fall out of their own nuclear test all bear witness.

But if we were to indicate to the world our willingness to move down a peaceful road by negotiated steps at a negotiated speed (while increasing our military pressure to demonstrate that we do not regard fighting and talking as alternatives but as mutually reinforcing policies), we would place on the Chinese Communists, where it belongs, the onus for delaying its own acceptance into the community of nations and the United Nations peace system.

Indeed, we should not at first have to do more than (a) insist that changes in Chinese behavior are an essential to an accommodation of the ChiComs on its relationship to the UN; and (b) indicate that Laos and the Nuclear Test Ban are the obvious places to start testing China's willingness to be in fact a part of the world community. Later, while the ChiRep item is being discussed in the 19th General Assembly, we could (c) indicate our willingness to join in setting up a "study committee" on ChiRep, to report to the 20th General Assembly in 1964. (Such a tactic was approved for possible use in last year's General Assembly, but was not used since we clearly had the votes to beat the Albanian resolution on its merits.)

Clearly the traditional structure of the ChiRep issue, which has (remarkably) served us well for a decade-and-a-half, is eaten away at its very foundations. Our major allies, France and Britain, will not help us maintain it and most of our other significant allies, from Italy and Belgium around to the Philippines and Japan, are hanging on only for fear of what it would do to their relationship with us if they were to let go.

Our cue, surely, is to find a way of mobilizing all of the world's nations that oppose the way the Chinese Communists are using their power, in a new strategy that puts the primary stress on future improvements in Chinese behavior.

65.   Memorandum of Conversation[1]

Washington, November 14, 1964, 4:30 p.m.

SUBJECT

Canadian Views on Chinese Representation at the UN

PARTICIPANTS

Ambassador Charles S.A. Ritchie of Canada
Mr. Gary R. Harman, First Secretary, Embassy of Canada

The Secretary
Harlan Cleveland, Assistant Secretary, IO
William B. Cobb, Jr., EUR/BNA

Ambassador Ritchie began by saying that he had talked with the Canadian Foreign Minister and had been asked by him to convey to the Secretary the Foreign Minister's present thinking on the problem of Chinese representation at the UN. The Canadians, on the basis of extensive checking, are of the opinion that on an Albanian-type resolution the General Assembly would vote 53 in favor, 45 against, with 15 abstentions. This possibility argues for taking a long look at the China representation question between now and the beginning of the General Assembly session rather than between the 19th and 20th sessions of the General Assembly, as had been suggested earlier. The Canadians are aware of the importance of America's relations with the free countries of Asia and, of course, recognize domestic sentiment in the United States. They are also aware of domestic considerations in Canada which are more favorable toward the ChiComs. Because of these factors, the Canadians feel that they would not oppose an Albanian-type resolution as they had in the past. With respect to the "important question," Canada would vote affirmatively despite uncertainties that the resolution would carry. The Canadians under the circumstances are considering the possibility of introducing a declaratory resolution which would support a two-China solution at the UN.

The Secretary said that he would like to speak with the President about the Canadian views and accordingly would withhold full comment until after he could do so. Nevertheless, he thought it should be pointed out that the problem is not so much with the domestic reaction in the United States or the UN reaction as it is with Peiping. If the ChiComs continue on their present aggressive course, there will be war in the Pacific. Unless they realize there is opposition to their present course,

---

[1] Source: Department of State, Central Files, UN 6 CHICOM. Confidential. Drafted by Cobb and approved in S on January 5, 1965. The meeting was held in the Secretary's office.

they will conclude that they are doing fine. So far as we know not one of the free world countries represented in Peiping has expressed to the Chi-Coms criticism of their actions during the past two years. Paradoxically, it is now argued by some that the Chinese explosion of a nuclear device is a reason for admitting them to the United Nations, yet the same voices would loudly condemn the United States and seek to throw us out of the UN had we done so.

Ambassador Ritchie said that the problem in part was based on the mathematics of the vote. The Secretary noted that in this connection Article 19 comes into play since a number of votes counted one way or another by the Canadians "have to be paid for." Ambassador Ritchie gave the Secretary the Canadian analysis of the country-by-country vote. The Secretary said that we would check the Canadian figures against our own for there may be different views on certain ex-French-African countries and others. Our assessments can be compared on November 17 when Assistant Secretary Cleveland goes to Ottawa for discussions there. The Secretary again emphasized that the reaction in Peiping was in our view of central importance. Looking ahead we could see the possibility that the NATO and Warsaw Pact countries could work out their problems without war. We are not so sure about Peiping.

Assistant Secretary Cleveland asked if the views expressed by Ambassador Ritchie reflected the joint Belgian-Italian-Canadian assessment. The Ambassador said that they did not and that, in point of fact, the Canadian view reflected the Minister's present thoughts on the subject rather than a firm policy decision of the Government of Canada.

---

66.   Memorandum for the Record[1]

Washington, November 18, 1964, 1 p.m.

MEETING WITH THE PRESIDENT ON UNITED NATIONS MATTERS

PARTICIPANTS

The President, Secretary Rusk, Assistant Secretary Harlan Cleveland, Ambassador Stevenson, McGeorge Bundy, George Reedy, Samuel Belk

[Here follows discussion not related to China.]

---

[1] Source: Johnson Library, National Security File, Bundy Files, Memoranda of Conversation, Bundy. Secret. Prepared by Samuel E. Belk of the National Security Council staff.

Chinese Representation

Stevenson then told the President that we faced a difficult problem with ChiRep. This year our position was badly eroded; next year it would be irretrievable. The Canadians, for instance, were deserting us for the first time. As of now, we had a slight simple majority on our side, and we might have to revert to asking for a 2/3 majority ("important question").

Bundy then reminded the President that there was more to it than just what we might do this year: Could we get support for a 2-China policy? What was to be done about the seat in the Security Council where the U.S. has the veto? Peiping certainly would not come into the UN unless it got the Security Council seat. This was the matter of seeing how things look that are not going to happen this year.

Stevenson said that unless we start to shift our policy this year, Taiwan would be, at any rate, totally replaced in a few years. We could just allow this to happen or we could begin to shift toward a 2-China policy. The ChiNats might withdraw on their own initiative. He recalled that the ChiNats refused to accept recognition from France when France recognized Communist China.

Stevenson thought we must study the alternatives: admit the ChiComs and throw the ChiNats out; adopt a 2-China policy; get somebody to propose a study group (which is bitterly opposed on Taiwan as the beginning of the end); get the ChiComs into disarmament talks. Stevenson told the President that we would need guidance as to how to go about it. He did not think we should continue frozen, which would in the near future damage our prestige. We could move toward a 2-China policy, which the ChiComs won't accept anyway.

The President asked what would happen to the Security Council seat if Communist China got into the UN. Ambassador Stevenson said the ChiComs would get it.

Bundy reminded the President that we could keep the ChiComs out by using the veto which was what President Kennedy had said he would do. But the U.S. never had used the veto and did we actually want to use it in the Security Council year after year to keep the ChiComs out.

The Secretary stated to the President that the matter of war and peace lay in the Pacific. If we appeared to falter before the Soviet Union and Communist China this would be interpreted as a reward for the track they have been following, and this would increase the chance of war. If we were to make a move that would signal to Peiping that we were weakening, this would increase our danger. The Secretary agreed with Stevenson that something must be done—perhaps the establishment of a study committee that would allow the matter to fall into complete confusion for an indefinite period.

Stevenson said the sooner we moved the better. He recalled President Kennedy had said that President Eisenhower had told him that "the only thing that will bring me back into politics is to bring China into the UN."

Bundy suggested that President Kennedy might have been using President Eisenhower's remark as an umbrella for his own policy.

The Secretary thought that it might be necessary for the President to telephone Prime Minister Pearson and impress upon him that we must not make a move that will be interpreted as weakness in the Far East.

The President agreed. He then turned to the Philippines and recalled that there had been offers from the Philippines to give us support in South Vietnam, but that our military leaders had regarded this offer as embarrassing because, if it were accepted, the Chinese would come in. The President recalled that we had been appealing for more flags and more units instead of ambulance units and that this was an offer of what we wanted and the military had turned it down.

Bundy and the Secretary remarked that Max Taylor and McNamara would be very disappointed to hear this.

Stevenson repeated that the U.S. must be prepared for a loss of prestige unless we were willing to move forward on a 2-China policy in this session—the ChiComs would not accept it anyway. To stand fast with people dropping away right and left—especially the French Africans—was not right. We should not stand still and be overwhelmed by the waves. Stevenson noted, however, that the matter would not come before the UN until January.

The President said that Secretary Rusk's remarks impressed him; that perhaps better than abandoning our policy and inviting strong partisanship in Congress, the President said that what gave him pause was Secretary Rusk's statement that to change would be a pay-off for the Soviet and ChiCom hard line.

Stevenson said that he and others had felt for a long time that we should get the ChiComs into the community of nations—then you could manage them better.

The President noted that he did not pay the foreigners at the UN to advise him on foreign policy, but that he did pay Rusk and that he was inclined to listen to him.

The Secretary noted that there was no real basis for some of our allies wanting to get the ChiComs in the UN. There had been no effort on the part of our friends to level off with the ChiComs on the problems that we jointly faced with Peiping. There had been no effort on the part of the French, for instance, to get at the heart of the matter.

Stevenson said that nevertheless there were 700 million people not represented in the UN as against a few million of the Kuomintang on Taiwan.

Cleveland pointed out that, while it was true that our position in the UN was eroding, it was important to remember that it had lasted for fifteen years. The Secretary said this was correct; that he had invented it fifteen years ago.

Cleveland thought one approach we should make would be to go to those who favor admission and emphasize the behavior of the ChiComs on the international scene and say, in effect, "unless your behavior is better, you can't get in." Many UN members say we are standing in the way of ChiCom admission but it is the Chinese Communists themselves.

The President remarked that it was just as we are being blamed now for denying the USSR its vote in the GA.

Secretary Rusk agreed that this would be the last General Assembly in which we could use the standing tactic on ChiRep.

Cleveland thought we could succeed this year only if we indicated that there was movement in some way toward a new approach.

The President wondered why Martin would wish to change the Canadian vote. Both Bundy and Cleveland said it was because it would be politically popular.

Stevenson said that he had travelled into nine states during the fall and that he had found the people far ahead of the Congress on ChiRep. Rusk thought it a far less domestic problem than an international one. Stevenson said that, as he travelled through the country, the people asked him about Article 19 and ChiRep. He said it was difficult to give out all the old answers—there were often bad editorials. Stevenson recalled that there had been movement on ChiRep under President Kennedy when he agreed to abandon the Eisenhower position of a moratorium and, instead, to discuss the problem—this had been a step forward. He said he did not know how much longer we could hold the line.

Samuel E. Belk

67.   **Telegram From the Department of State to the Embassy in the Republic of China**[1]

Washington, November 20, 1964, 4:21 p.m.

493. Embtels 393[2] and 381.[3] Department considers Chiang Kai-shek visit to US inadvisable at this time. Chiang clearly plans seek stronger US support for GRC activities against mainland than we could agree to and would go home disappointed. Visit prior to 19th GA vote on Chirep would stir unhelpful speculation and could appear as desperate step taken in weakness. Effect on GRC position during upcoming critical GA could be seriously adverse.

Chiang visit to attend inauguration (Embtel 393) not feasible. White House seeking restrict attendance inaugural ceremonies to diplomatic Chiefs of Mission resident Washington in accordance past practice.

Suggest you take appropriate opportunity tell Chang Chun we pleased to learn President Chiang might be prepared come to US to confer with President Johnson and that we of course share desire for closest possible top level consultation between our two Governments, especially in difficult days that may lie ahead. However, timing of visit of utmost importance. We fear that Presidential visit US when crucial Chirep vote impending in GA would be misconstrued as sign of weakness and hurt GRC position. If Chang Chun presses matter, you might tell him it difficult to foresee at what precise time it will be possible to extract maximum advantage from visit but this should be clearer after 19th GA over.[4]

Ball

---

[1] Source: Department of State, Central Files, POL 7 CHINAT. Secret; Limdis. Drafted by Bennett on November 17; cleared by Fearey, Samuel L. King of O/CPR, Sisco, Llewellyn E. Thompson, Green, and Komer; approved by William Bundy. Also sent to USUN.

[2] Telegram 393 from Taipei, November 10. (Ibid.)

[3] Telegram 381 from Taipei, November 7. (Ibid., DEF 12–1 CHICOM)

[4] Wright reported in telegram 468 from Taipei, November 26, that he had given Chang the Department's views. (Ibid.)

68.   Memorandum From Robert W. Komer of the National Security Council Staff to the President's Special Assistant for National Security Affairs (Bundy)[1]

Washington, November 23, 1964.

Mac—

ChiRep Thoughts. The real problem we face on ChiCom policy is far less one of *substance* than of *tactics.*

Most people agree that, after 15 years of sustaining a rigid policy against Peking (and rather successfully at that), the erosion of our position is forcing us to take a different tack. Even the general nature of this tack is not really at issue—we want to retreat gracefully from an increasingly isolated position toward a stance which puts the onus for continued friction more on Peiping and less on us. In effect, we want to make our ChiCom policy more like that toward the USSR—tough where they push us but flexible where there's something to be gained, if only in terms of willingness to talk.

So the real question is no longer whether to disengage from the more rigid aspects of our China policy but *how and when.* On this essentially tactical question, the two extremes are either to take the initiative ourselves in order to minimize the loss and maximize our control over the consequences, or to let ourselves be pushed reluctantly by the pressures of the international community. By and large, however, it is simply unrealistic to expect us to say boldly we were wrong about our China policy. This isn't good domestic politics, and great nations don't win kudos abroad by admitting mistakes and saying mea culpa. So our posture must be one of saying that, although we haven't changed our views on the ChiCom threat, we reluctantly accept the verdict of the international community that China should be admitted to the club. Even so, we're still confronted with the question of how long to hold out before confessing, and what terms, if any, we can exact in return. Our decision on this when and how should take into account a whole series of factors, including those discussed below.

A. *How much domestic backlash?* I'm one of those who feel that the China question has tended to become de-politicized with time. It's hard to tell how much residual emotion it can yet arouse, or how much the Republicans could exploit it. Not only does the President's new mandate

---

[1] Source: Johnson Library, National Security File, Country File, China, Vol. II. Secret. Filed with a covering memorandum from Komer to Bundy, also dated November 23, noting that for reasons of space he had not discussed the Quemoy/Matsu problem but that "This little time bomb is still there ticking away, and none of us know how to defuse it." He concluded, "In short, a close look at Quemoy/Matsu bidding better be on our agenda too."

itself give him some room to maneuver, but this mandate was partly a vote for cautious responsibility in a nuclear world. So what the President does under the "peace" rubric generally nets out at a big plus. In this sense Peiping's nuclear test actually serves as a reason why we *should* enter into a dialogue with Peiping on such issues as arms control.

Peiping's test also dramatically underlines that *Red China is here to stay*. It destroys what's left of the Gimo's thesis that the civil war is still on (he knows it, too, poor man). Even *Time* has read this lesson. Moreover, the Sino-Soviet split (which will continue even if in muted form) provides further public justification for dealing with both Communist centers, not only one.

Despite all this, however, there's no blinking the fact that *a shift in our policy will look like a defeat*—whenever it occurs. This is the price we have to pay for having successfully maintained a fixed position for so long. Peiping is wholly unlikely to change its spots sufficiently to justify our shift on these grounds. To the contrary, one of the best arguments for shifting our policy is to pin the onus for its own intransigence more squarely on Peiping.

B. *So the real issue is when and how to shift our China policy in a way which will minimize our losses—both domestically and abroad.* And the real argument against doing so is that we can't afford it when we face a crunch with Peiping over Vietnam. To me, this was the central point in LBJ's 18 November talk with Rusk and Stevenson. Rusk's argument was that easing up on ChiRep now would make us appear to "falter" in the Pacific at just the wrong time.

C. *Thus our decision on ChiRep, etc. turns largely on how we play Vietnam.* If we appear to cut and run or to be losing, it will be domestically and internationally impossible to "make concessions" on ChiRep too. Nor would it be possible if we were "negotiating" (except theoretically as additional frosting on a negotiated settlement). But isn't the corollary also true? If we take a tougher stance in VN, if there is widespread fear abroad of US escalation—it can hardly be taken as a sign of undue weakness to be flexible on ChiRep. In fact, we could use this counterpoint as a justification for our VN policy; it would demonstrate that while we were determined to resist Communist aggression, we were simultaneously prepared to deal with the ChiComs wherever there was some peaceful purpose to be served.

In effect, I see increased pressure in VN as permitting greater flexibility on ChiRep—as supporting our contention that we don't seek a US/ChiCom war, and even that we are "escalating to negotiate." Paradoxical as it might seem, we could walk both sides of the street, thus helping to protect ourselves both from accusations we're seeking to do in Peiping and from complaints we're faltering in the face of the enemy.

D. *How does the Article 19 Fight fit in?* If we succeed in facing down Moscow on this issue (which means stemming panic among the neutralists), we will have started off the 19th GA with a crashing victory. To a degree at least, this too would provide a shield behind which we could be more flexible on ChiRep without seeming to falter. Indeed, the bigger our Article 19 victory, the more the neutralist majority will want to demonstrate non-alignment by voting against us on something else. Let's not ask too much.

E. *How do we best preserve the position of Taiwan?* To be coldly realistic, Taiwan is our ultimate card in any eventual modus vivendi with Peiping, and by the same token the bargaining counter to be preserved at all costs. But we can no longer tell ourselves with any conviction that trying to ostracize Red China is the best way to protect Taiwan. To the contrary, the longer we insist on an "either-or" choice, the more we will force the wrong choice from our point of view. What we need to do is to stem the rapid erosion of Taiwan's international position by getting it internationally recognized that China is a divided country (like Germany, Korea, and Vietnam). To do this we have to pay the price. I'm not suggesting we opt for "Two Chinas" yet;[2] what we want to do is to get others on a "Two China" kick as the tacit price for our ostensible willingness to let Peiping into the UN. It's the only real counter to an Albanian-type resolution.

Peiping has recently made clear again that it won't come in unless Taiwan goes out. Fine—this will buy us another few years of maneuvering room if only Taipei will play it smart and not withdraw. I'm not optimistic, however, as the Gimo (at his advanced age) is more interested in face than in practical politics. So appealing to Chiang's finer sensibilities would get us exactly nowhere. Ergo, once we decided to move, I'd put it hard and cold to the Gimo—if he pulled out of the GA, we'd regard ourselves as relieved of our commitment to veto ChiCom admission to the SC.

The above doesn't really get to the tactics of when and how to alter our China policy. It merely gives my slant on some of the key variables. I have some thoughts on tactics and timing but I'll not overload the circuit for the moment. My main point is that our ability to be flexible on ChiRep may well turn largely on our decisions re Vietnam. Since the latter will almost certainly be upon us first, time enough for the latter later.

RWK

---

[2] The word "yet" is a handwritten insertion on the source text.

69.   Memorandum From Robert W. Komer of the National
       Security Council Staff and the President's Special Assistant
       for National Security Affairs (Bundy) to President Johnson[1]

Washington, November 25, 1964.

When Chiang Kai-shek handed the attached long rambling letter[2] to
our Ambassador he asked that you be told of his feeling that with the
ChiCom test the situation in Asia had entered a critical stage—more critical than at any previous time.

The gist of the letter itself is that (1) the ChiComs, not the Soviets, are
the greatest threat today; (2) they are engaged in a protracted war of attrition in Southeast Asia, the only answer to which is a quick US victory;
and (3) the ChiCom nuclear test poses a new dimension of threat, chiefly
to the morale of Free Asians.

The Gimo then calls on the US to: (1) urgently develop a strategy for
quickly winning the war in Vietnam; (2) take leadership in developing an
"overall plan" for concerted action by the Free Asian peoples themselves
to overthrow the ChiComs before it is too late (e.g. equip and unleash the
GRC); and (3) if this is not possible just now, immediately give the GRC
the wherewithal to destroy the ChiCom nuclear installations. He asks for
an urgent reply.

We see this letter as essentially aimed at reminding you of the
Gimo's well-known views at a time when he senses we must be rethink-
ing our China policy. While he couches his letter in terms of a series of
proposals he knows we can't accept, his chief aim is probably to forestall
any weakening of our position on the ChiRep issue in the UN. State will
draft a proposed answer.

R.W. Komer
McG. B.

---

[1] Source: Johnson Library, National Security File, Head of State Correspondence File,
China, Vol. I. Secret. A handwritten "L" on the source text indicates Johnson saw it.

[2] Telegram 452 from Taipei, November 23, transmitted the text of the letter. Telegram
456, November 24, reported Chiang's comments to Wright when he gave him the letter.
Both are attached to the source text. Copies are also in Department of State, Central Files,
POL 15–1 US/JOHNSON.

70.   Telegram From the Embassy in Poland to the Department of State[1]

Warsaw, November 25, 1964, 6 p.m.

1174. Cabot–Wang talks.[2] Deptel 980.[3]

(1) I opened with substance most points reference telegram except paragraph one and contingency items and appealed for avoidance polemics far as possible.

(2) Wang replied with review Chinese position on number issues often discussed before plus lengthy reiteration position on nuclear weapons. Nothing in this not already made known through Chou letter to President,[4] enclosed statement, and recent press accounts of Chinese position. Wang read aloud and passed to me draft agreed announcement saying in effect two governments determined make joint effort eliminate nuclear weapons and effect thorough destruction of them. Both governments to undertake not to use such weapons and the two Ambassadors, on behalf their governments, solemnly declare that at no time and under no circumstances will either government be first to use nuclear weapons. Two governments propose governments of all nations of world hold summit conference as proposed in Chou letter (text in tomorrow's pouch).[5]

(3) Wang continued UN had proved incapable handling question of disarmament and in any event so long as UN fails restore legitimate rights Chinese Government and does not nullify illegal status Chiang clique his government would have nothing to do with UN. Spoke of increased reconnaissance provocations including pilotless craft and said he hereby demands US immediately stop these provocations and threats.

(4) I promised transmit draft announcement, assuring him it would receive attention it merited, but observed question of verification and

---

[1] Source: Department of State, Central Files, POL CHICOM–US. Confidential; Priority; Limdis. Repeated to Hong Kong, Taipei, Geneva, Moscow, and Stockholm.

[2] This was the 123d meeting of the Ambassadorial talks. Cabot reported the meeting in more detail in airgram A–544, November 30. (Ibid.)

[3] Telegram 980, November 19, provided guidance for the meeting and stated that the deterioration of language at the last meeting might have been a deliberate effort to taunt Cabot into breaking off the talks; if so, and for the record, "it seems desirable at this time to recapitulate our stance in broadest terms." (Ibid.)

[4] Chou's October 17 letter to Johnson was delivered to the Embassy in Warsaw on October 19; the text was transmitted in telegram 885 of that date from Warsaw. (Ibid., DEF 12–1 CHICOM) The letter enclosed a copy of the PRC Government's announcement on October 16 of China's first nuclear test. The text of the statement is printed in *American Foreign Policy: Current Documents, 1964*, pp. 882–884. The text of the letter, also sent to other heads of government, is printed ibid., p. 1077.

[5] Not found.

control obviously vital consideration in any disarmament proposal and noted no mention made of conventional armament which is intimately related question.

(5) Wang observed we had no competence speak of contamination of atmosphere on part others when we were first to test and use nuclear weapons. Said tripartite treaty designed to tie hands of peace loving countries and his government continued oppose treaty.

(6) Wang asked for careful, sober-minded consideration before we attempted link China question with that of Vietnam by using Chiang troops in South Vietnam.

(7) I reviewed sequence developments in Far East since World War II in refutation Wang's accusation aggressive intentions USG because of alleged arms build up. I said it was clear Viet Cong was armed, trained and financed by ChiCom connivance with North Vietnam and his side was playing very dangerous game. I continued with substance paragraph six A and Rusk quote paragraph 18.

(8) Wang continued with lengthy tirade on alleged US aggressions worldwide and said we should stay home, asking who has committed aggression against US—the Congolese? I said his government had done so in Korea when we were opposing under UN banner North Korean aggression. Lengthy discussion of who supporting whom in Southeast Asia and where charges of aggression properly lay. This was chiefly repetition worn themes on Wang's part.

Next meeting December 24.

Cabot

---

71.   **Telegram From the Embassy in Poland to the Department of State**[1]

Warsaw, November 26, 1964, noon.

1176. Cabot–Wang talks. Embtel 1174.[2] Comments and recommendations following 123rd meeting.

---

[1] Source: Department of State, Central Files, POL CHICOM–US. Confidential; Priority; Limdis. Repeated to Hong Kong, Taipei, Geneva, Moscow, and Stockholm.
[2] Document 70.

1. Wang's tone better than last time, and never so severe that I considered terminating meeting. However it was at times a bit contemptuous, often patronizing and always ex cathedra.

2. No mention of Khrushchev political demise.

3. Wang spoke smugly of their development of nuclear device. Draft agreed announcement re Summit, non-use of and eventual destruction nuclear weapons so patently unacceptable do not believe Chinese themselves take it seriously. Fact Wang proposed next meeting at three-month interval would seem indicate lack of interest in response. I did not refer to obvious unacceptability their proposal, but did point out crucial aspect controls and intimate relation conventional arms and force levels to whole question.

4. At one point Wang said in effect if Geneva agreements were adhered to, there would be no trouble in Indo-China area. I expressed interest in this statement, and said we would be glad conform meticulously to these agreements if only others would do same.

5. I took liberty some omissions and some changes in guidance for opening statement, partly because I wanted emphasize absence polemics and desire for constructive proposals and partly because we could not find references for some of quotes paragraph 1, and feared Wang might ask who said them and when. Hope Department can give documentation all quotes in subsequent guidance.

6. Wang obviously unprepared for moderate tone my opening statement, since he misquoted me three times in his response, assuming that I would naturally say things which in fact I did not say. He paid no attention to my plea for no polemics.

7. As for next meeting, I see no value in lengthy and sterile polemics. I think both sides really know the score, so there is little to gain in propagandizing each others home offices—ostensibly our only audiences until the historians come in. Since two sides differ so basically on so many issues this admittedly leaves little room on constructive side of ledger. Hence if Department agrees, I would propose simply give somewhat shorter responses than has been our habit, adequate to keep record straight, but leaving lengthy preachments up to Wang (he enjoys them so). This would preserve inherent value of holding talks per se, and retain them for time when they can again serve specific useful purpose. For present, Chinese clearly interested in talks only as propaganda forum.

8. Believe we should not go on record as rejecting draft agreed announcement, but ask questions re implementation and control, and reaction conventional force levels.

9. Chinese made no attempt take extensive notes this time, whereas we believe past habit was take seemingly verbatim notes in English shorthand. Do not know whether they have decided it not worth the

effort, or whether they now have access to Polish tapes which may emerge from newly activated Mysliewiecki Palace—i.e., we may indeed have a third audience.

Cabot

72.   Memorandum of Conversation[1]

SecDel/MC/4   New York, November 30, 1964, 11 a.m.

SECRETARY'S DELEGATION TO THE NINETEENTH SESSION OF
THE UNITED NATIONS GENERAL ASSEMBLY
New York, November 1964

SUBJECT

Chinese Representation

PARTICIPANTS

US
The Secretary
Assistant Secretary Cleveland
Mr. Foster, Director, ACDA
Mr. Givan, EUR

Canada
Secretary for External Affairs Martin
Ambassador Tremblay, UN Mission
Mr. H. Basil Robinson, Deputy
    Undersecretary for External
    Affairs
Minister Cox, UN Mission
Mr. William Barton, OIC, UN Affairs

Minister Martin said that, although he opposed a postponement of the UNGA over Article 19, he would be happy to see a postponement to delay a showdown on the Chinese question. The Secretary said he could see some advantage from that point of view and also to let certain aspects of the Congo question cool off. With regard to the Hanoi–Peiping situation, we will see what the other side is up to in the coming dry season. We feel strongly that anything that causes the Chinese Communists to think they are on the right track is a step toward war.

---

[1] Source: Department of State, Conference Files: Lot 66 D 110, CF 2447. Secret; Exdis. Drafted by Givan on December 1, and approved in S on December 2. The source text is labeled "Part II of II." Part I is ibid. The meeting was held at the U.S. Mission to the United Nations in New York.

Martin said he understood the Secretary's feelings and, because they get along well, they can be frank with each other. The Chinese issue has gone beyond the point where he could do anything to turn back his government. The Canadians are, however, resolved not to do anything without the fullest disclosure and consultation. Although their talks with the Belgians and the Italians have been serious, these are not at all as thorough as they undertake to carry on with the United States. Martin said they would not be honest if they did not say they had reached the point where they must speak out. They cannot delay action any longer.

The Secretary asked what action could not be delayed. We certainly want to delay a war with China if possible. Martin agreed. The Secretary said something that deeply distresses us but which may have the seeds of a suggestion is the fact that in the past two years apparently no country with relations with China has expressed concern to Peiping over its policies in Southeast Asia. Perhaps when Canadian diplomats are in touch with Communist Chinese, they could express the Canadian attitude toward Chinese aggression. When the Chinese react negatively, the Canadian Government could draw the obvious conclusions.

Martin said his government had no contact at all with Peiping, which is symptomatic of the unreality of the present situation. When the Canadian Broadcasting Company planned to do a series on China, Martin asked the CBC representative to pass on unofficially some thoughts to the Chinese leaders. The man saw Chou En-lai three times and told him forcefully that the Canadians hoped the Chinese attitude on Indochina would enable Canada to do what it believed right in the interests of universality in the UN. Chou replied that this was an old argument, that no one is taking over Indochina, but that no one could stop the march of events; in any case, Canada is merely a satellite of the United States and will do nothing without the US approval. Members of the wheat mission to China had also tried to talk to the ChiComs but the latter said they did not want to talk politics with wheat experts. This illustrates that the GOC has done what it can to convey its views to Chinese leaders. Martin said that, speaking as a friend, he must say that if the Chinese question comes up at this GA and if the vote on substance is close, within perhaps two votes of a majority, the Canadian position as a nation would be impaired for a long time if it did not vote favorably. On the Important Question, Canada would be with the United States.

Martin said that Mr. Cleveland had been in Ottawa when Conservative MPs had asked why the government did not act on China, and if the government was afraid of the United States. Martin had talked with Barbara Ward, who reflected State Department thinking on this issue. She, however, seemed to see something in a parity proposal to protect Formosa's position. The GOC recognizes the difficulties in making any such proposal but feels that if the Chinese question comes up Canada should say something to protect the rights of Formosa. Martin recalled in this regard that Secretary Rusk had asked in a television speech what should be done for Formosa and whether it was to be thrown to the wolves. The Secretary commented that if Canada maintained diplomatic relations with Formosa, Peiping would not allow Canada to establish relations.

Martin said that his government's assessment of the voting alignment in the GA on ChiRep is not good. The Secretary asked what Canada would like to see in Southeast Asia and on the western rim of the Pacific. Martin replied that Canada would naturally want to see peace all over the world, but none of us can avoid recognizing that the Chinese will exert increasing influence. This is not in Canada's interest, nor is it in Canada's interest to have a Communist regime in Russia. But there it is. To make an ideological identification of one's enemies is not the right approach. Coming into the UN will not alter the aggressive tendencies of any state, but it will provide that much more contact. The Secretary commented that inclusion in the UN might confirm the aggressive tendencies of Peiping. He could understand, however, if Canada helped the ChiComs in this way if they were willing to put a division into Southeast Asia to help contain Peiping's expansion. Martin said this was an unfair argument to use with "little fellows" such as Canada that could not put its troops in NATO, Cyprus and everywhere else. If there should be a war, it is axiomatic that Canada would be alongside the United States.

Martin said he had recently asked the Russian Ambassador to Canada what the Soviets would do if the Canadians supported admission of China, and had commented that Chinese admission would pose some difficulties for the USSR. The Ambassador had nodded at this statement.

With regard to the Soviet attitude, the Secretary said that if the Russians had become more cautious lately, it was not because of their contacts in the UN but because of their direct contacts with the United States, and because NATO solidarity had convinced them that they must stop pressing. In addition, since the beginning of the cold war the U.S. defense budget had totalled some 700 billion dollars. With regard to China, Secretary Rusk said he was disturbed by the view that Chinese domination of Southeast Asia is unavoidable. Would Martin say this was equally true of the USSR and Iran? Martin said that it was inconceivable that a nation of 700 million people would not share the authority and influence of Japan and India in Southeast Asia.

The Secretary asked whether the same relationship held between the United States and Canada. Martin said it did indeed, so much so that he had hesitated to speak in this frank way despite his great personal esteem for Secretary Rusk. The Secretary commented that we would never object to a relationship between China and Southeast Asia along the lines of the United States-Canadian relationship.

The Secretary asked what the public reaction in Canada would be if the GOC published an account of what the CBC man had reported of his conversation with Chou En-lai. Secretary Martin said that this would make no difference. People in Canada would tell the government to show that Canada is not a satellite.

The Secretary said he would be in touch further on the subject and it would certainly be discussed in NATO. It would be of some importance to NATO since US interests could easily swing to the Pacific if the situation there grows more serious. He would also be giving Martin data on increased infiltration in South Vietnam.

Martin recalled that Defense Secretary McNamara had told him that the situation in South Vietnam could go on a thousand years. He could not believe it. Secretary Rusk said that we certainly believe our contribution to security in Europe might have to go on a thousand years, or as long as it is needed. We see no terminal date for it. Martin said that he had suggested to Mr. Cleveland, as he could not suggest to a Secretary of State, that he should not use such arguments because they do not touch reality. Bringing China into the UN would not affect these issues one way or the other. They would affect many people in Southeast Asia; for example, Catholics would be offended beyond words, but this would be temporary.

The Secretary said he appreciated Minister Martin's frankness. It should be quite clear, however, that if all of our allies in NATO do not feel deeply concerned about how China may be turned away from aggression, there could be bad results in NATO as we are forced to turn to problems of the Pacific. Martin said that the difficulty for the Canadians is that they do not believe entry into the UN would affect this situation. It would be a long process, but it cannot start until we "mingle." He had talked with Ikeda six weeks ago in Tokyo. The Japanese want to take part when the Chinese question is resolved, although perhaps the new government will have a different idea on timing. He had also talked with Spaak recently who does not go quite as far as the Canadians but feels that resolution of the Chinese question cannot be delayed much longer. The Canadians are not much concerned about the recognition issue, but would want to overcome this at the same time as ChiRep. They would probably regard UN admission as constituting recognition.

73.   Telegram From the Embassy in the Republic of China to the Department of State[1]

Taipei, December 10, 1964, 4 p.m.

504. A–1110, June 26, 1964.[2] Present were [*less than 1 line of source text not declassified*] General Chiang Ching-kuo, and interpreter in connection with briefing of President Chiang today on highly classified matters reported [*less than 1 line of source text not declassified*] separately. President called attention to IL–10 planes recently reported at Foochow. He stated that these planes gave ChiComs considerable added capability for attacks on Taiwan, offshore islands and China shipping. He asked that I recommend speeded delivery of programmed MAP equipment not yet delivered as a means to counter this threat. Asked if request was general or for any specific equipment. President replied that principal fear was raid on shipping by PSA class boats and that Bull Pup would give a capability to handle this threat. I agreed to transmit his request.[3]

I stated that Dept has recently expressed concern that ChiNat raids launched from off shore islands would stimulate retaliation by ChiComs and that I had so advised FonMin. President stated that US should not be concerned about this matter.

Wright

---

[1] Source: Department of State, Central Files, POL CHICOM–CHINAT. Secret; Limdis.

[2] See footnote 3, Document 31.

[3] Telegram 583 from Taipei, January 7, stated that the U.S. military evaluation was that the IL–10 aircraft did not represent a significant increase in the threat to Taiwan, and that expedited delivery of Bullpup missiles was therefore not warranted; it recommended that Wright should discuss this with Chiang. (Department of State, Central Files, DEF 19 US–CHINAT) Telegram 745 to Taipei, February 9, concurred. (Ibid., POL CHICOM–CHINAT)

74.   Telegram From the Department of State to the Embassy in the Republic of China[1]

Washington, December 21, 1964, 9:52 a.m.

593. Embtels 490[2] and 452.[3] Deliver to President Chiang following letter from the President:[4]

"Dear Mr. President:

Thank you very much for your letter of November 23 and for your congratulations on my election. I greatly value your views on the present situation in Asia and have given them close attention.

The aggressive policies being pursued by the Chinese Communists are indeed a grave menace to all free nations. As both our countries have learned through the years, they are a menace which has many facets—psychological and political as well as military—assuming different forms and dimensions in different parts of the world. Our task must be to bring about the highest possible degree of Free World vigilance and solidarity in defense against the Communists' designs.

The United States is fully alive to the Chinese Communists' aggressive designs against Taiwan. You may be assured that the American people regard their Mutual Defense Treaty with the Republic of China as one of their basic international commitments, and that their determination to stand by it would in no way be weakened by Chinese Communist development of nuclear weapons. I believe that the continuing strength of our alliance will deter the Chinese Communists from any thought of a nuclear attack on Taiwan, as the NATO alliance has deterred the Soviet Union from an attack on Western Europe. We are considering the deployment of additional fighter aircraft to Taiwan from time to time to enhance the strength of our defense posture, if you agree this would be of value.

The United States is fully conscious of the Chinese Communists' plan to deprive the Republic of China of its place in the United Nations, to destroy the Republic of China and to seize Taiwan. Against these

---

[1] Source: Department of State, Central Files, POL 15–1 US/JOHNSON. Secret; Priority; Exdis. Drafted by Bennett; cleared by Green, Fearey, Grant, William Bundy, McGeorge Bundy, and the President; and approved by Harriman. A December 19 memorandum from Komer to the President, with the draft telegram attached, noted that the proposed answer to Chiang "gives him such general assurance as we can and simply avoids joining the argument on the things we cannot help him with." Johnson checked the "Let it go" line on Komer's memorandum. (Johnson Library, National Security File, Head of State Correspondence File, China, Volume I)

[2] Telegram 490 from Taipei, December 4. (Department of State, Central Files, POL 15–1 US–JOHNSON)

[3] Telegram 452 from Taipei, November 23, transmitted the text of Chiang's letter; see footnote 2, Document 69.

[4] Telegram 542 from Taipei, December 24, reported the delivery of the letter. (Department of State, Central Files, POL 15–1 US–JOHNSON)

threats too the United States will continue to give your Government full support.

I greatly appreciate your sharing with me your thoughts as to actions we might take to meet the Communist threat. So far as the objective of restoring the mainland of China to freedom is concerned, I believe we should continue to be guided by the principles you and the late Secretary Dulles set forth in the communiqué of October 23, 1958. As was agreed then, success against the Communists is to be won principally by political means, not by force. The United States Government has no evidence of increased popular restiveness on the mainland or of a weakening of the Communists' internal controls; and it doubts that present political conditions favor the taking of military initiatives.

I do not believe the United States can presume to assert leadership in Asian affairs; but I agree with you that closer consultation among Asian countries could bring important benefits to the Free World cause. The United States would welcome an Asian initiative for such a purpose. In this regard, the United States, as you know, attaches the highest importance to normalization of relations between Japan and Korea. I greatly appreciate what your Government has done to foster the establishment of friendly relations between these two countries and hope you will continue your efforts.

You mention your deep concern for the situation in Southeast Asia. The United States has just ended a review of the situation there and of the policies best suited to frustrate the Communists' aggressive policies. We feel we must take steps to improve the politico-military situation in the area; yet the fragility of political conditions in South Viet-Nam hampers us. As your Government was recently informed in confidence, we are undertaking moderate increases in air activity directed at the infiltration problem and are prepared to take certain other measures in retaliation against Viet Cong actions of any special nature. It is our purpose to impress upon Hanoi that the United States Government is not moving in the direction of retreat but is prepared to respond to Communist pressures by stepping up the level of its activity in Viet-Nam. The United States is of course looking beyond the immediate future, but we must bear in mind that additional actions in Viet-Nam must be based upon a reasonably secure situation in the south of that country.

In the years ahead I look forward to a further strengthening of the friendship between the Republic of China and the United States and to many future exchanges of views between us.

Mrs. Johnson joins me in sending our warm regards to you and Madam Chiang for Christmas and the New Year. Sincerely yours,

Lyndon B. Johnson"

Rusk

75.   **Memorandum From the President's Special Assistant for National Security Affairs (Bundy) to President Johnson**[1]

Washington, January 10, 1965.

You may have heard of the Red Chinese announcement that a Chinese Nationalist U–2 was shot down over the Chinese Mainland early today. Our intercepts and other data confirm this report, and the Chiang government is now announcing that one of its aircraft is missing and presumed lost.

This is the fourth shoot-down over a period of 2-1/2 years (September '62, October '63, July '64, and January '65). [*1-1/2 lines of source text not declassified*]

We believe the Chinese are using surface-to-air missiles, but we have less information than we would like on how many there are and where.

[*1 paragraph (5 lines of source text) not declassified*]

McG. B.

---

[1] Source: Johnson Library, National Security File, Memos to the President, McGeorge Bundy, Vol. 8. Top Secret. A handwritten "L" on the source text in Johnson's handwriting indicates that he saw the memorandum.

---

76.   **Memorandum From the Joint Chiefs of Staff to Secretary of Defense McNamara**[1]

JCSM–41–65   Washington, January 16, 1965.

SUBJECT

Possible Responses to the ChiCom Nuclear Threat

1.   By a memorandum, I–30032/64, dated 11 December 1964,[2] subject as above, the Assistant Secretary of Defense (ISA) requested an anal-

---

[1] Source: Washington National Records Center, RG 330, OASD/ISA Files: FRC 70 A 5127, 471.6 Communist China. Top Secret. Filed as an attachment to a letter of February 18 from Deputy Assistant Secretary of Defense for International Security Affairs Peter Solbert to William Bundy.

[2] Not found.

ysis of possible responses which the US Government might make to the threat of Chinese communist nuclear blackmail, to include consideration of certain specific points which were expressed as questions.

2. Answers to the specific questions posed are attached hereto as Appendix A.[3] The analysis made by the Joint Chiefs of Staff, which could provide the basis for further interdepartmental studies, is attached as Appendix B. This memorandum and its appendices are based on and supplement the military appraisal of Chinese acquisition of nuclear weapons forwarded by JCSM–1013-64, dated 3 December 1964.[4]

3. The Joint Chiefs of Staff conclude that:

a. There is no military requirement to modify US commitments at this time. The present ChiCom nuclear capability has not materially affected the existing balance of military power between the United States and Communist China; however, the expansion of this capability will pose difficult problems in the future. Maintaining and using in forward areas, as appropriate, flexible forces with both a conventional and nuclear capability becomes most important to provide visible evidence to our allies, as well as to the ChiComs, that the US defense commitment is firm. We should anticipate pressures which would result in requests by threatened countries for more definitive guarantees, including increased nuclear support.

b. With the exceptions of Japan and probably India, the Free World nations in Asia cannot develop a capability for defending themselves without US support. Japan should be encouraged to increase its defense efforts, providing improved conventional forces for use in the common defense of Asia and providing military assistance to other nations in Asia. Asian nations should continue to provide conventional forces.

c. Should pressures build up to the point that our Asian allies believe the development of a national nuclear capability to be clearly in their national interest, refusal to provide some form of nuclear assistance would put the United States in a position of denying to valued allies a nuclear capability possessed by the common enemy. The United States, therefore, should not rule out the possibility of increased nuclear support including some form of nuclear sharing with our allies in Asia when such is required in the US national interests.

d. In view of the foregoing, some program of positive US action may become necessary. The following appear sufficiently advantageous to warrant further study:

(1) Improvements to our system of alliances oriented at the threat of Communist China. The Joint Chiefs of Staff endorsed studying the feasi-

---

[3] The appendices are attached but not printed.
[4] Not found.

bility of related concepts in JCSM–1013–64, dated 3 December 1964, subject: "A Military Appraisal of Chinese Acquisition of Nuclear Weapons." (2) [13 *lines of source text not declassified*]

e. Specific military courses of action to implement the concepts outlined in subparagraph d, above, should await determination of US policy.

4. It is recommended that interdepartmental studies be initiated to recommend US national policy with regard to:

a. Improvements to our system of alliances in Asia and the Pacific.

b. Increased nuclear support of our allies in Asia, including some form of nuclear sharing.

> For the Joint Chiefs of Staff:
> **Earle G. Wheeler**[5]
> *Chairman*
> *Joint Chiefs of Staff*

---

[5] Printed from a copy that indicates Wheeler signed the original.

---

77.   National Intelligence Estimate[1]

NIE 13–2–65   Washington, February 10, 1965.

COMMUNIST CHINA'S ADVANCED WEAPONS PROGRAM

CONCLUSIONS

The Problem

To assess the current state of Communist China's nuclear weapons and missile program and, insofar as possible, estimate the future course and size of that program.

---

[1] Source: Department of State, INR/EAP Files: Lot 90 D 110, NIE 13–2–65. Secret; Controlled Dissem. According to a note on the cover sheet, the estimate was submitted by the Director of Central Intelligence and prepared by the CIA and the intelligence organizations of the Departments of State and Defense, Atomic Energy Commission, and the National Security Agency. All members of the U.S. Intelligence Board concurred on February 10, except the FBI representative, who abstained on the grounds that the subject was outside his jurisdiction.

NIE 13–2–65 was originally issued on January 27. It included a discussion section not included in the later version here printed. The conclusions of the later version are slightly revised but similar in substance. (Central Intelligence Agency, NIE Files)

Note

Although we have obtained a considerable amount of new information in the past year or so, there remain serious gaps in our information and we are therefore not able to judge the present state or to project the future development of the Chinese program with any high degree of confidence. The specific judgments in this paper should be read in the light of this general caution.

Conclusions

A. Communist China's first nuclear test on 16 October 1964 was of an implosion fission device with U–235 as the fissionable material [*less than 1 line of source text not declassified*]. We cannot estimate with confidence its weight or dimensions but believe it was relatively large and heavy. The most likely source of the U–235 was uranium first brought to partial enrichment in the gaseous diffusion facility at Lanchou and then further enriched by the electromagnetic process. We cannot, however, rule out the possibility that the U–235 was of Soviet or other non-Chinese origin though we believe this to be highly unlikely.

B. Although we have no good basis for estimating the current level of production of fissionable material, we believe that the Chinese will have enough material during the next two years to conduct a test program, with enough left over to stockpile at least a few bombs. The Chinese could now build bombs based on the results of their first test which could be carried by their two TU–16 medium jet bombers or their 12 or so TU–4s.

C. The evidence leads us to estimate that the Chinese Communists are developing a medium-range ballistic missile (MRBM). We believe this system is essentially a Soviet design, probably the SS–4, perhaps with some Chinese modifications. It is possible that the Chinese could have a few MRBMs ready for deployment with compatible fission warheads in 1967 or 1968. A weapon in bomb configuration could be available somewhat earlier and could be delivered by the Chinese air force's light jet IL–28 bombers of which they have about 290.

D. The Chinese have a submarine closely similar in outward appearance to the Soviet G-class submarine which is designed to launch 350 n.m. ballistic missiles while surfaced. We do not know whether the Chinese built this submarine or assembled components supplied by the USSR, or what missile they expect to put in it. We have no evidence that the Chinese are constructing any more of this type submarine and it would be at least several years before any units could be operational with Chinese-produced missiles.

E. The Soviets provided the Chinese with some surface-to-air missiles (SAMs) by mid-1960. We have no evidence to confirm or deny that the Soviets have furnished any more since then and we do not know how many such missiles are now in China. The Chinese have an urgent requirement for SAMs and we believe are working hard on a production program. There are indications that the Chinese are now producing some kind of surface-to-air missile, either Soviet-type SAMs or proto-types of a Chinese version. The evidence is not sufficient to permit a firm judgment but we think it highly unlikely that either will be produced on a large scale for two or three years.

F. It is unlikely that the Chinese will develop a deliverable thermonuclear weapon for several years, and there is little chance of an intercontinental capability until after 1970.

---

78.   Telegram From the Embassy in Poland to the Department of State[1]

Warsaw, February 24, 1965, 7 p.m.

1744. Cabot–Wang talks.[2] Deptel 1446.[3]

(1) Wang opened saying because of defeats suffered in Viet-nam we had recently sent planes to raid North Viet-nam, against the Geneva Agreements and thereby spreading the war. These criminal actions jeopardize peace, arousing condemnation all peace-loving peoples of the world. The Chinese Government made two statements on February 9 and 13 which make clear action against Viet-nam is action against China. U.S. defeat in South Viet-nam is foregone conclusion. Outcome Viet-nam war must be decided on the ground. In Chinese view long as U.S. continues present course Viet-nam people will continue deal heavier and heavier blows until U.S. is kicked out. It is U.S. which has invaded South Viet-nam and taken the lead in breaking up the demarcation line. Only one way out for U.S.: withdraw and let the people of Indochina settle

---

[1] Source: Department of State, Central Files, POL CHICOM–US. Confidential; Priority; Limit Distribution. Repeated to Geneva, Moscow, Stockholm, Hong Kong, and Taipei.

[2] This was the 124th meeting of the Ambassadorial talks. Cabot reported on the meeting in detail in airgram A–779, March 1. (Ibid.)

[3] Telegram 1446 to Warsaw, February 20, provided guidance for the meeting. It instructed Cabot that in response to Wang's anticipated charges, he should restate U.S. policies on Vietnam and disarmament. It noted that the wording had been carefully chosen to avoid polemical arguments but that he should endeavor to present it in a crisp and declaratory manner, without any suggestion that he was attempting to open negotiations on Vietnam. (Ibid.)

their own problems. Up to U.S. to decide road to be taken. Wang said the more we go on expanding war, the surer is our defeat.

(2) Wang continued, claiming tension Far East is caused by U.S. occupation Taiwan, mentioning Polaris subs in Asian waters and aircraft capable carrying nuclear weapons in area. Said press was saying purpose was destroy all main cities of China. Chinese Government has long pointed out nuclear blackmail will not intimidate Chinese people. Mentioned serious warnings since last meeting and "spy planes" shot down. Said seven groups comprising 196 men of the Chiang clique had raided mainland and no good could come from our support such actions.

(3) I responded with guidance para 3, A through F.[4]

(4) Wang said my statement was prevarication to cover up our aggressive acts. Everyone could see we had violated Geneva Agreements in moving U.S. troops to South Viet-nam and spreading flames of war so as to carry out armed aggression to slaughter large numbers Vietnamese people. Facts cannot be covered by pretext. Said we claimed Hanoi was masterminding. This is nonsense. Obviously aggression will cause struggle against aggression. It is United States who forced people South Viet-nam to take up arms. Only correct way to settle this question is for U.S. to implement Geneva Agreements in good faith. U.S. must immediately stop war of aggression, withdraw troops and armament, and let South Vietnamese people settle own problems by selves. Said we lied in saying we came into South Viet-nam to protect freedom and have no selfish aims.

(5) I said Wang knew as well as I what he said untrue and I had stated true U.S. position. U.S. clearly prepared observe Geneva Agreements if others would. Reminded Wang had spoken of closeness between China and North Viet-nam and in such case believed could not avoid all responsibility for what was going on. Problem could be simply resolved if North Viet-nam authorities called off their aggression. We cannot abandon South Viet-nam. We willing leave South Viet-nam if North Viet-nam would stop interfering in South Viet-nam.

(6) Wang said China and DRV are fraternal countries and at same time close neighbors and rely on each other. Therefore U.S. aggression against DRV is just like aggression against China. Said if we insist on spreading war flames to North Viet-nam, China will definitely not sit idly by. China does not want war but must make clear its determination. If U.S. continues its aggression China is prepared to carry on to the end. If U.S. really means to abide by Geneva Accords it must first withdraw its troops.

---

[4] Paragraph 3 covered U.S. policy on Vietnam.

(7) I then gave guidance para 4 A through E.[5]

(8) Wang then gave repetitious account Chinese/Viet-nam views. Said we blamed North Viet-nam for fighting in both Viet-nam and Laos and asked what we were doing in Laos. Asked what is the reason U.S. launched attacks in Cambodia. Is this also fault North Viet-nam. Said that we had spread war to North Viet-nam. North Viet-nam has right to strike back and signatories Geneva Agreements also have right to act against United States aggression. The situation really grave now and if U.S. refuses withdraw it will be held fully responsible for all the consequences.

(9) Wang continued with meaningless statement concerning reasonableness Chinese draft agreed announcement, saying if we really wanted peace we should find no difficulty in agreeing to it.

(10) I said Wang's side seemed to call those governments it did not like "puppets" and seemed to feel it was all right for them to pursue so-called wars of liberation but not right for us to support free governments against such aggression.

(11) Wang said scale of war in North Viet-nam had developed with scale of U.S. aggression there. Wang said it was our usual practice to call all revolutionary movements Communist-backed, but this is simply attempt cover up our own aggression. Only way out is to withdraw troops from South Viet-nam. Said only practical thing was for countries having nuclear capability to agree not to use it on each other.

Next meeting April 21.

Cabot

---

[5] Paragraph 4 covered U.S. policy on disarmament.

79.   Paper Sent to President Johnson[1]

Washington, February 25, 1965.

Cabot–Wang Talks

Ambassador Cabot's Comments on His Talk with Chinese Ambassador Wang in Warsaw yesterday:

In the one hour and forty minute meeting nothing new of significance was noted. In both content and delivery, Wang's statements were less heated than they might have been expected to be under the circumstances—less, for instance, than after the Tonkin Gulf incidents.

Still, he claimed that an attack on North Vietnam was the same as an attack on China and made it clear, as he had previously, that China supports "wars of liberation," including this one.

Wang did use some intemperate language, such as at one point, he called what I said re US policy in Vietnam "lies." In view of my guidance, I did not respond in kind to the degree I might have otherwise. Also, in view of the tenor of the guidance, I conformed this time to its wording almost verbatim.

In this meeting, Wang predictably put on record Chinese views designed to justify intervention in case of future need. (In addition to the above, his claim is that we have now destroyed the demarcation line, and our bombing of North Vietnam has legitimized retaliation by the signatories of the Geneva agreements.)

I scarcely think his statement indicated that intervention is planned for the moment, at least. In fact, the most notable feature of the meeting was the relative lack of bluster or any show of confidence. Wang did not even attempt to prolong the meeting as he has done in the past, presumably to cause press speculation he had read the riot act to us. Upon entering the meeting room, too, Wang was, if anything, a little more friendly than usual.

The Chinese immediately accepted the April 21 date.

---

[1] Source: Johnson Library, National Security File, Country File, Poland, Cabot–Wang Talks. Confidential. Filed as an attachment to a covering note of the same date from Bromley Smith to the President. A handwritten "L" on the source text indicates that it was seen by Johnson. The paper summarizes Cabot's comments on the meeting, which he transmitted in telegram 1753 from Warsaw, February 25, a copy of which was also sent to the President with Smith's covering note. (Department of State, Central Files, POL CHICOM–US)

80.   National Intelligence Estimate[1]

NIE 13–3–65   Washington, March 10, 1965.

COMMUNIST CHINA'S MILITARY ESTABLISHMENT

The Problem

To assess the character and present effectiveness of Communist China's armed forces, and to estimate trends which would affect their future capabilities.

Note

This estimate is the first to attempt a comprehensive analysis of the broad range of questions pertaining to Communist China's military establishment. The Chinese Communist regime's intensive and highly effective security measures make China, in general, a difficult intelligence target. Estimating the nature and scope of the Chinese military production effort is made more difficult because much of the program is still in the developmental and factory construction stages. We are thus unable to make confident judgments on many important matters concerning the nature, scope, and prospects of Chinese Communist military developments and this paper should be read in the light of this general caution.

Conclusions

A. Communist Party influence permeates all levels of the Peoples Liberation Army (the entire Chinese Communist military establishment). The senior political and military leaders are united by ties of comradeship in a long revolutionary war. Political commissars are assigned to every command down to company level. Although the troops are conscripts, they are selected for political reliability and receive constant political indoctrination. (Paras. 12–13, and para. 1 of Annex B)

B. The Chinese Communists continue to proclaim the military doctrine of Mao Tse-tung which stresses self-reliance, the dominance of men and politics over weaponry, and the concept of a protracted "people's war." This doctrine, deemed applicable to "wars of national liberation,"

---

[1] Source: Department of State, INR/EAP Files: Lot 90 D 110, NIE 13–3–65. Secret. Controlled Dissem. According to a note on the cover sheet, the estimate was submitted by the Director of Central Intelligence and prepared by the CIA and the intelligence organizations of the Departments of State and Defense, Atomic Energy Commission, and the National Security Agency. All members of the U.S. Intelligence Board concurred on March 10, except the Assistant to the Director of the Federal Bureau of Investigation, who abstained on the grounds that the subject was outside his jurisdiction.

is also applied to a potential conflict with the US. Communist China is apprehensive regarding the possibility of a US nuclear attack followed by a large-scale invasion, but holds that in such a case China could accept nuclear devastation and still overwhelm the invaders in a protracted "people's war." The Chinese leaders hope that this prospect will deter the US. (Paras. 6–10)

C. The Chinese leaders, however, cannot derive much comfort from this rationalization of their present strategic situation. Since coming to power in 1949, they have steadily sought to modernize their military establishment. They have considered it a matter of first importance to develop an independent nuclear capability. (Paras. 1, 11)

D. Communist China's military power derives primarily from the numerical strength of the Chinese Communist Army (CCA), some 2.3 million men, and tremendous reserves of manpower. Although the CCA is essentially an infantry force, its capabilities for combat are formidable. In open warfare against modern opposition, it would be hampered by shortages of armored equipment, heavy ordnance, mechanical transport and POL. In mountainous or jungle terrain, these shortages would be of less importance. In 1961, many Chinese units had serious shortages of equipment and were understrength. The Chinese have sought to ameliorate this situation by bringing up to strength and fully equipping selected divisions. We estimate that as many as one-third of the combat divisions have been so improved, and are distributed throughout most of China's military regions. We lack the information to make any confident estimates of present production rates of specific items of army equipment, but Communist China has sizable facilities for the production of such matériel. We believe that the production at land armaments plants has increased over the low 1960–1963 level and that it will continue to increase. (Paras. 15–17, 28, 38, and paras. 1–10 of Annex B)

E. The mainstay of the Chinese Communist fighter force in the air force and navy is the some 1,600 MIG–15s and MIG–17s. There are also about 150 MIG–19s and 25 to 35 MIG–21s. Except for the MIG–21s, these aircraft are obsolescent and probably less than 10 percent of these fighters have airborne intercept equipment. The backbone of China's air offense would be the 270 or so IL–28 jet light bombers. They also have 12 or so TU–16 medium bombers capable of carrying a bulky nuclear weapon. Attrition has taken its toll of aircraft in service and the Chinese aircraft industry is only now approaching the capability to arrest this decline. The Chinese have been adding to all of their aircraft development and production centers, and there are indications that they are getting ready to produce the MIG–19, or the MIG–21 and may, indeed be in the early stages of production. We believe the chances are less than even that production of bombers will begin during the next two or three years. (Paras. 22, 27, 41–43, and paras. 1–7 of Annex A)

F. The primary mission of the Chinese Communist Navy (CCN) is coastal defense. Its major combatant units are 21 operational W-class submarines, 4 Gordy-class destroyers, 4 Riga-class destroyer escorts, and 14 patrol escorts. The CCN also has about 155 motor torpedo boats. The capabilities of the CCN against modern opposition would be limited by obsolescent equipment and probably by substandard combat proficiency of its crews. We believe the Chinese have placed a high priority on construction of submarines. We estimate that by mid-1966 the Chinese Communist naval order of battle will include 25 W-class submarines. (Paras. 15, 25, 44, and paras. 8–11 of Annex A)

G. The Chinese have given top priority to their nuclear weapons and missile programs. On the basis of our scanty evidence, we estimate that the Chinese, over the next two years, will be able to carry out a nuclear test program and stockpile about 10 bombs. In the ballistic missile field, we believe the Chinese are developing a medium-range missile (1,000 n.m.) modeled on the Soviet SS–4. It is possible that by 1967 or 1968 the Chinese could have a few such missiles with compatible fission warheads. The Chinese almost certainly are determined to develop a nuclear strike capability against US territory. This determination could be reflected in the initiation of programs in the near future looking toward longer run development of a limited number of ICBMs and the construction of a small fleet of missile carrying submarines. Even if the Chinese have already begun work on such programs, we believe that they could not pose a threat to the US until sometime after 1970. (Paras. 51–52, 56)

H. During the last year or two, Communist China's industry has begun to revive from the severe setbacks it suffered when the Great Leap Forward collapsed and the Soviets withdrew most of their assistance in 1960. We believe the Chinese leaders will sustain substantial military production even at the risk of serious economic difficulty. However, China's economy will not be able to support anything approaching a maximum production effort by all sectors of military industry and in coming years the Chinese will have to make a number of difficult decisions regarding priorities. We cannot predict in what quantities Peiping may decide to turn out the various items of equipment, and there is a good chance that the Chinese themselves do not yet see their way clearly. (Paras. 31, 34, 56)

I. Nevertheless, barring some major setback, Communist China's military power will gradually grow and this growing power will almost certainly increase Peiping's political leverage against its Asian neighbors—whether or not Chinese Communist leaders actually engage in direct hostilities or commit armed forces abroad. (Paras. 53, 55)

[Here follow the Discussion portion of the estimate and two annexes.]

81.   **Telegram From the Embassy in the Republic of China to the Department of State**[1]

Taipei, March 23, 1965, 4 p.m.

869. On March 20 President Chiang held special meeting for discussion MAP and requested Ambassador to attend. Present were Admiral Gentner, COMUSTDC; General Sanborn, CHMAAG; General Peng, Chief of General Staff; Minister of National Defense Chiang Ching-kuo and Major General Hu, liaison.

This message in three parts. First deals with possible second nuclear explosion and GRC concern of shortage of ADC equipment. Second part (MAP programs, priorities and deliveries). Third part—conclusions.

Part 1. President stated all intelligence indications are that second atomic blast by ChiComs is about to take place. It is possible that this will be delivered from the air. This possibility brings our attention to area of air defense. President indicated ChiComs have 15 TU4 aircraft. Our air defense system just cannot afford even one of them to come through and deliver the weapon. After looking into present status of missiles, President not satisfied with number of missiles (Nike–Hercules and Hawk) on hand. President noted that at present we have only a few missiles per launcher. This certainly will not be adequate. Fortunately this fact is not known to general public. If it were it would cause feeling of panic among general public to know that we only have a small number of missiles on hand. Therefore, President requests that ground-to-air missiles (Nike–Hercules and Hawk) which are already programmed be delivered expeditiously. If possible we would like to have some extra missiles stored here in reserve. President also mentioned need for more air-to-air Sidewinder missiles.

In addition to missiles the President also mentioned the importance of maintaining aircraft support. He referred particularly to spare parts program. Some of them, he stated are at very low stock level.

Part 2. President referred to FY65 Military Aid Program. He mentioned some of the items, funds for which have already been approved and their delivery has been programmed, such as Bull Pup missiles and F 100 modification kits, M113 (APD), and M 41 tanks. President feels that these items, since they are already programmed should be delivered with the highest priority.

President hopes thorough review be held with regard to equipment and weapons status of 15 forward look divisions in the five-year program.

---

[1] Source: Department of State, Central Files, DEF 12–1 CHICOM. Secret. Repeated to CINCPAC For POLAD.

Part 3. In conclusion, President mentioned during the past he has asked the Ministers and Agencies to discuss problems of economic aid and military aid with American counterparts and he has not previously discussed these with Ambassador himself. He is not satisfied with attention given Military Aid Program in Washington. He does not understand why items already appropriated for and programmed have not been delivered. ROC should receive highest priority in military aid next after South Vietnam. President feels Military Aid Program is critical and US Govt has not, so far, given ROC enough priority in delivery of military priority items. He urged Ambassador to convey his view to US Govt.

First meeting with Defense Minister Chiang took place Monday, March 22, to discuss shortages mentioned by President and get into priorities for 15 forward look divisions. Will be reported through military channels.

Comment: Following should be noted: First, that these are view of President not subscribed to by US Embassy or military commanders. Second, this is first time detailed military requirements have been placed on echelon of President to Ambassador. Third, we believe that President is concerned with what he considers deteriorating situation in South Vietnam. His greatest concern, however, is with propaganda effect of prospective second CCNE, particularly if it is an air drop.

Specific comment on part 1: We have on several previous occasions emphasized to President and his principal supporters that GRC's best air defense is US nuclear deterrent. However, President has consistently downplayed its effectiveness against ChiCom probable intentions, particularly toward GRC. He states need for a military air defense system as only defense his people will understand. We believe US deterrent is better understood and appreciated by his principal subordinates, political and military.

President states desire for more ground-to-air missiles although he has a full battalion allowance. They do not have trained personnel to handle more at present.

Parts 2 and 3: It is obvious President has not been kept up to date by his subordinates on details of programs and deliveries, although MAAG has made all pertinent information available to them. The five-year program is under constant review and discussion by MAAG and MND representatives.

Recommendations: It is obvious that we must continue our efforts to sell President on US nuclear deterrent as his best air defense, emphasizing our defensive commitment to GRC which is as strong as that to any other free nation. We cannot provide complete air defense for all nations liable to nuclear attack.

With respect to remaining points on shortages and delays in delivery, I have directed MAAG to prepare detailed presentation of present status all items, which will be delivered direct to President. MAAG will contact Dept of Defense for up-to-minute information.

A special ROC–US committee will be established in MND to study Communist nuclear threat and how best to meet it. COMUSTDC will coordinate US participation. Any recommendations which committee may produce as to accelerated deliveries will be forwarded through military channels.

Unless Dept desires action different from above or has amplifying information not available here, I do not see any instructions needed in addition to current MAP programs. Would appreciate any views Department may wish to convey to President in addition to above, particularly with respect to his comments on Washington policy.[2]

Wright

---

[2] Telegram 927 to Taipei, March 25, replied that the Department concurred in the measures Wright had taken in response to Chiang's comments and that he could assure Chiang that his comments on priority for GRC military assistance deliveries were being given careful consideration. (Ibid.)

---

82.   Airgram From the Embassy in the Republic of China to the Department of State[1]

A–801   Taipei, April 14, 1965.

SUBJECT

Conversation with Minister of Defense on U.S. Nuclear Deterrent

On Friday, April 9, I had the following at the Residence for lunch: the Minister of Defense, General Chiang Ching-kuo; Chief MAAG General Sanborn; CG 13th Air Force General Wilson; and interpreter S.K. Hu. The purpose of the lunch was to discuss certain important military matters with the Defense Minister.

I stated that at our March 20 meeting with the President he had expressed very grave concern over the condition and capabilities of the

---

[1] Source: Department of State, Central Files, DEF 1–4 CHINAT. Secret. Drafted by Wright. Repeated to CINCPAC.

Republic of China's air defense. I said the President had stated the Communists had 14 TU4's and when they had developed a nuclear weapon these 14 planes could be used for an attack on Taiwan. The President stated that with the current state of air defenses it would be impossible to assure that at least one of these planes would not penetrate the air defense net for a nuclear attack on the Island. The President had asked that a missile allowance be increased to guard against this contingency and that the current status of aircraft spares be increased to provide more effective employment of intercept aircraft. The President had requested also that the Republic of China be given high priority in MAP allocations, particularly in air defense. The President had stated that his principal concern was public consciousness of the vulnerability of air defenses and their apprehension about air defense weaknesses if the present shortages of equipment were publicly known.

I told the Minister of Defense that we appreciated the President's thoughts in this matter. I said that no air defense system, however elaborate, could guarantee against the penetration of a small number of planes. I stated that even the air defense system of the United States was inadequate to give this assurance. I stated also that having no anti-missile capability, U.S. defense against a missile attack was probably non-existent. I stated that in realization of this fact the United States had placed the maximum air defense reliance on the Strategic Air Command and that retaliatory capability of this organization was the principal contributing factor to our deterrence against such a nuclear attack against the United States. I stated that by far the largest component of our military expenditures in the air defense field were allocated to the Strategic Air Command.

I stated also that the deterrent effect of this nuclear capability was equally applicable and effective in the air defense of Free World nations which were associated with or allied with us in opposition to the Communist threat. I stated that our strong defensive alliance with the Republic of China has certainly placed them in this category and that the entire retaliatory capability of our nuclear forces would be equally effective in deterring an attack against Taiwan. Recognizing the possibility of penetration of Taiwan air defenses by Chicom aircraft, I said that this was most unlikely in the face of the probability of large-scale U.S. retaliation against the Communist mainland.

I stated that I shared the President's concern in the ability to convince his people of the strong defensive potential of our retaliatory forces and that I would do anything I could along these lines to assist him in informing and educating his people of the unlikelihood of any nuclear attack on Taiwan against the possibility of retaliation by the United States.

Generals Sanborn and Wilson seconded my thoughts and, in addition, added the thought that Chinese defense systems as they were were in excellent shape and although many more forces could be used, those which we had would make a good showing for themselves in the event of an attack. Both emphasized the need for good organization and coordination with the forces and facilities which the United States might make available.

The Minister expressed appreciation for our thoughts and said that the President was principally concerned with the factors of time and space. He said the Formosa Strait was a very narrow body of water and therefore the time interval in which an attack could be conducted was extremely short. He said it was his opinion an active joint study should be conducted which would develop the maximum coordination of Chinese and United States efforts in the matter of air defense.

I replied that the committee recently established and consisting of the Minister, Admiral Gentner, General Sanborn and their respective assistants had been charged with a detailed study on air defense matters and that the findings of this committee would be available to both our governments. I assured him that the United States would give very careful consideration to anything this committee might propose.

Comment: I think the meeting was extremely useful in bringing to an important member of the Government and a close associate of the President our thoughts on the value of our nuclear capability in deterring an attack on Taiwan. In our previous contacts with the President he has tended to ignore this deterrent and has concentrated on getting more military hardware for air defense. We will continue to keep the facts of air defense life before both the President and all of his principal military and political advisors with the hopes of generating a greater appreciation of the unlikelihood of Chicom nuclear attack on Taiwan against the likelihood of United States retaliation.

I then raised the question of the 20 per cent increase in the military budget. I stated that the military budget was a matter entirely internal to the Republic of China. I stated, however, that an increase in the budget must be at the expense of funds available for the economy. We of the United States sincerely hoped that the economy could continue to grow at the rate which over the past two years has made such a tremendous impression on the outside world and be of such enormous benefit to the people of the Republic of China. I said any slow-down in economic growth of the ROC would be sure to have an adverse effect in their world position, both politically and commercially, and particularly would affect their ability to borrow needed funds in the international money market. I sincerely hoped, speaking for the U.S. Government, that military expenditure would not prevent a continuation of this very satisfactory economic growth.

The Minister of National Defense stated that he appreciated my thoughts on the matter and that the effect on the economy of the increased military budget had been carefully considered by the economic branches of the Government. It has been decided that the effect would not be damaging.

Comment: In the minds of myself and my assistants I believe it is inevitable that there will be increased inroads into funds otherwise available for economic growth in order to meet the demands of the military establishment, particularly in those fields in which U.S. military aid is being reduced. We will continue to observe this important matter and bring it up with the higher echelons of the government as necessity and occasion arise.

Jerauld Wright
Ambassador

---

83.   Memorandum From James C. Thomson, Jr., of the National Security Council Staff to the President's Special Assistant for National Security Affairs (Bundy)[1]

Washington, April 15, 1965.

SUBJECT

The Taiwan Situation

As a follow-up to my preliminary travel report of March 29,[2] I offer the following comments and recommendations on the situation in Taiwan. I must stress that these views reflect only a 48-hour visit; they also reflect, however, extensive conversations in Washington and elsewhere in the field, both before and after my trip.

The key word in Taiwan's present apparent health and longer-term sickness is "stability". Most of our current actions—and all of our current

---

[1] Source: Johnson Library, National Security File, Komer Files, China (GRC). Secret. The source text is a copy sent to Komer; a copy was also sent to NSC staff member Chester Cooper.

[2] In his March 29 memorandum, Thompson reported briefly on a 2-week trip to the Philippines, Hong Kong, Taiwan, Okinawa, and Japan. (Ibid., Name File, Thomson Memos)

inaction—are explained in terms of the maintenance of stability. Where, one is asked, can one find a more stable nation in all East and Southeast Asia than the Republic of China? Why upset the apple cart?

The problem is that underneath the surface lie major factors of instability. As long as we minimize them or pretend that they don't exist—and as long as the GRC does the same—we are courting bad trouble in the very near future.

I identify three chief problem areas, all of which are interrelated:

1. The Problem of Morale

From both Chinese and Americans (I talked to no Taiwanese) I developed a disturbing impression of a severe and deepening crisis of morale on the part of most elements of the island's population. It is a new and particularly significant factor among the mainlanders. Its ingredients appear to be:

(a) *The growing awareness, on the part of most of the émigrés, that a return to the mainland is simply not in the cards.* It is probable that a good many have doubted the feasibility of return for sometime now; but the Chicom nuclear explosion has confirmed their doubts.

(b) *Poverty and corruption.* The present low ceiling on civil service salaries cuts across the bureaucracy, the military and all teachers, thereby forcing educated mainlanders to scrape along at below-subsistence levels of income. For officials, this makes corruption essential to survival. My Chinese informants tell me that corruption has spiraled over the past two years, and there is no end in sight. To quote one fortunate mainlander, whose salary is double the civil service norm because he works for a joint Sino-American outfit: "All my friends in the bureaucracy are doing it; and if I were in their place, I would be doing exactly the same thing." As for academics, they have had to support themselves by holding down two and three jobs simultaneously for some years now. One additional by-product of low civil service salaries is inadequate police pay, hence poor police protection and a very high rate of petty crimes.

(c) *Conspicuous consumption and the condition of the KMT.* Meanwhile, the party apparatus suffers from two familiar maladies—a general lack of vigor, youth and ideas, and a high level of luxurious living at the top. The fat, heavy hand of the party is an obstruction to creative talent in the bureaucracy; the big black limousines and the 30-course feasts of the party bigwigs add to the demoralization of their impoverished underlings. Although the Generalissimo continues to live and preach austerity, his retinue are prime offenders (and have outdone themselves in building a rumored 16 largely unused villas for their Chief at scenic points on the island).

(d) *The flight of talent.* Twenty-five percent of all Taiwan's college graduates leave the country, mainly for the United States; and over 95 percent of these young people never return.

(e) *Feather-bedding.* The processes of government are further obstructed by the excessively large number of bureaucrats kept on the job in one province to maintain the paraphernalia of a national government. My informants suggest that a solution to this problem would be to lay off at full salary the 4 out of 6 men in every office who are extraneous, so that the two remaining officials can perform their functions with efficiency.

(f) *Communal relations.* Those Embassy officers who keep in close touch with mainlander-Taiwanese relations report that little has been accomplished to bridge the gap between the two groups. The apparent political docility of the Taiwanese is a result of the relative prosperity of the farmers and businessmen as well as their sense of the futility of political action; it is not a result of increased support for the GRC or of rapport with the mainlanders. Taiwanese resentment remains a potentially dangerous force on the island.

2.   *The Malaise of Our Embassy*

In our own diplomatic establishment we face a classically dangerous situation. I talked at length with seven of the younger Embassy and Agency China specialists. They were all bright and articulate, largely free of visionary zeal. They were unanimous in their bitter complaint: that the upper echelons of the Embassy will not permit reporting of the facts of life in Taiwan. When I pressed them to clarify their meaning, I was told that reporting which tends to contradict the current U.S. "line" on the stability and prosperity of Taiwan is suppressed. In particular, the reporting of group attitudes, as detected by these younger officers—the attitudes of enlisted men, of mainland lesser bureaucrats, of mainland intellectuals, and of various Taiwanese groups—is strongly discouraged, either through the blue pencil or a refusal to pass such papers forward (a "gentleman's agreement" that such things are not helpful to report).

I regarded this as a very serious charge and said so; but my informants stood their ground.

As far as I can determine, this Embassy gap between young Turks and their seniors has been a Taiwan problem for some years. In its currently acute form, it is largely a reflection of the attitude of the present Ambassador, as implemented by his senior associates. There are also, of course, certain factors endemic to Taiwan: the exploration of group attitudes, particularly among Taiwanese, inevitably causes concern on the part of the GRC security establishment, and this concern is passed to the top Embassy personnel. If your primary purpose is not to "upset the apple cart", it is safer to discourage such snooping.

Needless to say, however, there is a rather more urgent objective to be served: that policy makers in Washington be adequately informed of what underlies the surface stability of Taiwan. That objective is not now being served. The dangers are compounded by the inevitability of political change once Chiang Kai-shek is removed from the apparatus he has controlled and balanced so skillfully for 35 years—and by our unpreparedness for those changes.

3.   *The High Costs of Ambiguity*

I came away from Taiwan deeply disturbed by the debilitating effects on both Chinese and Americans of a non-credible but unquestioned myth: the myth of return to the mainland.

On the face of it, the situation is rather eerie: the GRC knows that we don't believe it; and we know that they know we don't believe it; and we suspect that some of them don't believe it; *but no one says it*. The result is that our every relationship is affected by the unmentionable dead cat on the floor.

I am most concerned by two costs that are paid out for continued ambiguity: the emotional and intellectual cost, and a more tangible cost in the allocation of economic resources.

In the first category, the general effect of any over-riding myth is to make most serious discussion impossible. In the case of Taiwan, the ambiguity is a breeding ground for continuing suspicion of the U.S. and for latent anti-Americanism. As long as we make a pretense, by silence, of sharing their myth, we are subject continually to the charge that we are *not* true believers—and, by extension, that we are going to betray their interests. In permitting the ambiguity to linger, we hand to the GRC a considerable instrument of leverage against us: leverage to force us regularly to prove what cannot be proven, i.e., that our hearts are in the right place on this issue. To assuage our guilt and sustain the ambiguity, we have to keep offering up bits and pieces of concessions. Finally, I might add, ambiguity permits *some* U.S. officials to begin to believe in the myth.

The second category of cost relates to the first. As long as the GRC is tacitly encouraged to honor the myth, its economic planning will be geared to implementing that myth through the maintenance of a foolishly massive defense establishment. One of the tragedies of Taiwan is the fact that the resources do indeed exist to make it a "garden spot", a "beacon of free Chinese development", and a "showcase" for the mainland and the rest of Asia. As one Chinese friend told me, "This place is obviously a paradise relative to the mainland; but the tragedy is that it could have been and could be so much more—a free, dynamic and prosperous alternative to the mainland."

Recommendations

On the basis of the foregoing analysis, I would conclude that the U.S. has a major interest in assuring that Taiwan's apparent stability and prosperity become real stability and prosperity. I would also conclude that we have certain instruments to achieve this result which we are not now using. Specifically, I suggest the following actions:

(1) That we replace Ambassador Wright at the earliest possible moment with an experienced, tough, politically sensitive and shrewd insider. My three top choices for this assignment would be Bill Bundy (if available), Marshall Green, and Henry Byroade. State's tentative candidate, Walter McConaughy, would be an improvement over the present incumbent; but I do not believe that he would be capable of curing the Embassy's present malaise or of moving with skill and swiftness in the fluid situation that may develop after the Generalissimo's death.

(2) That the present DCM be replaced by a Foreign Service Officer of strong economic background. It will be essential in the months ahead to bring to bear on the GRC as much persuasion as we can to make rational use of its economic resources in the development of Taiwan and to edge away from unjustifiable expenditures on the military establishment. (Our AID Mission is closing down this year.) For this job I would suggest the names of Edwin Cronk (Economic Counselor in Bonn) or David M. Bane.

(3) That we explore on an urgent basis ways in which our heavy accumulation of Taiwan counterpart funds could be put to use at once to supplement the GRC's civil service salaries. There are precedents for such a move in the long-standing Joint Commission on Rural Reconstruction (JCRR), whose salaries are now double the normal bureaucratic level. The GRC currently hopes to increase civil service salaries by 15 percent next year; but this is clearly inadequate in terms of the current need.

(4) That whoever our new Ambassador in Taipei may be, he be given a Presidential mandate to:

(a) press for a continuation of Taiwan's economic growth;
(b) use every occasion possible to reduce the size of the GRC military establishment; and,
(c) end the present U.S. ambiguity regarding mainland return in his dealing with top GRC officials. (Such a move should be coupled with absolutely firm assurances of our proper unambiguous commitment: support for the continued free existence of Taiwan and the Pescadores. We have many friends and allies with regard to whose grandiose aims we have agreed to disagree; it is high time to do the same with the GRC— it would be a far healthier arrangement, both for them and for us.)

James C. Thomson, Jr.[3]

---

[3] Printed from a copy that bears this typed signature.

84.   Telegram From the Embassy in Poland to the Department of State[1]

Warsaw, April 21, 1965, 1932Z.

2153. Cabot–Wang talks. Deptel 1805.[2] 125th meeting. 3 hours 5 minutes.[3]

1) In opening statement I covered all guidance subjects except American prisoners and contingency items. At point where I said I wished pass him copy our reply to 17-nation appeal, he waved it away and would not receive it, saying they already clear on that and did not need it.

2) After consultations on Chinese side Wang replied saying he absolutely did not agree with my statement. Said he had learned about the President's speech. Said we claimed be ready for unconditional discussions for peaceful settlement but he thought this was simply a swindle. Said we had torn up Geneva Agreements and launched aggression and were now trying to play with peace hopes to save ourselves from defeat, but this impossible. When we were bombing day and night, how can we claim to be ready for peaceful negotiations. President said US must be prepared for long conflict. 24 hours after President's speech there was large-scale bombing. In week following there were new landings of forces and more planned. Wang claimed President actually laid down three preconditions, according to what I said:

1) Independent South Viet-nam with its security guaranteed, which Wang said ruled out Vietnamese union; 2) South Viet-nam must have freedom from attacks; and 3) US would not withdraw under the cloak of meaningless agreement. Wang said this was aimed at legalizing our aggressive actions; also aimed at forcing Viet-nam people recognize we have right to act as we please, that is, US demands equal unconditional surrender to which we would never get agreement. Also claimed US plan spend $1 billion was gross insult. US would meet with failure attempting to buy over people with a few stinking dollars. US should listen carefully to the voice of Vietnamese people who determined fight to the end if US forces are not withdrawn.

3) Wang continued Ho Chi Minh declared US imperialistic acts will not prevent Vietnamese people from carrying on patriotic struggle to

[1] Source: Department of State, Central Files, POL CHICOM–US. Confidential; Priority; Limit Distribution. Repeated to Hong Kong, Taipei, Stockholm, Moscow, and Geneva.

[2] Telegram 1805 to Warsaw, April 16, provided guidance for the meeting. It was modified by telegram 1811, April 17. (Both ibid.)

[3] Cabot commented in telegram 2159 from Warsaw, April 22, that Wang was "rougher this time in both word and manner than at the last meeting." (Ibid.) He sent a detailed report of the meeting in airgram A–966, April 26. (Ibid., POL 27 VIET S)

final victory. US must first withdraw from South Viet-nam. End of Nazi Germany and Japanese militarists was lesson for US. Command of war in Viet-nam was not in Hanoi or Peking but in Washington. On behalf Chinese people Chou En-lai had said Chinese would send South Vietnamese people all their needs, including arms, and would send own men when South Vietnamese people want them.

4) Wang spoke of air engagement Hainan, calling it act of direct military provocation against China. Said he would like launch strongest protest. Said when engagement made public US Defense Department had guilty conscience and tried to hide true meaning. Wang handed to me two photos as evidence of "crime." These showed alleged wreckage downed US plane (forwarded with verbatim text). But this was not only case of military provocation against China. Since last meeting 365th through 377th serious warnings issued, indicating US had stepped up its provocations. Had intruded several times into airspace Hainan Island, fired on Chinese fishing boats near Hainan and given pursuit into territorial waters. US had repeatedly sent spy planes over China and Wang made strongest protest, demanding US put immediate end to military provocations.

5) Wang claimed US actively instigating Chiang clique to raid mainland and mentioned joint maneuvers, delivery newest weapons, and visits of brass to Taiwan. Said US even had plans let Chiang gang occupy Hainan Island and brag about breaking through Chinese coastal defenses. Said If US linked up Chinese civil war with its war of aggression, more disastrous developments were in store for US.

6) I replied saying US had offered enter discussions without conditions. Said at same time we made clear what we expected get out of discussions but these were not conditions. I stressed firmness American purpose wage war for sake of people South Viet-nam. I suggested lesson of Germany and Japan could apply Wang's side if they continued present policies. Re Hainan engagement, I quoted Sylvester press replies with additional sentence from guidance telegram. Then spoke of American prisoners as instructed. Again stressed importance of 17-nation appeal, asking when Chinese reply could be expected.

7) Wang said while we spoke of wanting peaceful negotiations my remarks indicated we would continue war at any cost or risk; US attempting intimidate peoples by war threats but this would not succeed. Repeated favorite phrase about Viet-nam and China being interdependent and close as teeth and lips; two peoples were brothers sharing same weal or woe, and aggression against North Viet-nam was aggression against China. China as one of signatories Geneva Agreements had right to safeguard them. US has torn them up. Wang followed with long description of US alleged aggression in South Viet-nam over past years. Said recently we had carried out all manner atrocities including burning people alive and taking out their internal organs. We are not

only using conventional weapons but poison gas and napalm. Said US more cruel than Hitler. These acts could not be permitted by Vietnam, China and world's people. Root cause of war was US aggression and futile try shift blame on others. Only way settle problem was withdrawal US troops from South Viet-nam. If aggression continued debt of blood must be repaid in blood. U–2 and pilotless planes often intrude Chinese airspace and three of them shot down were now on display in Peking. Warned once again if US did not end violation Chinese sovereignty it would certainly be punished. US also had sole responsibility for acts of Chiang clique. Wang said "we do not fear you." Added if Chiang wants to come, let him; all his men will be annihilated.

8) Concerning 17-nation appeal Wang said Chinese completely agreed to the propositions made by the DRV, and he had nothing to add.

9) I gave obvious answers to Wang's points concerning Geneva Agreements, alleged US atrocities, adding I knew of no indication we encourage Chiang attack mainland. I said did not know what two photos he handed me proved and repeated our planes had orders not enter Chinese territory. I said it was of interest that Wang claimed Chinese entirely approved North Vietnamese response but I had not seen text of that and did not wish comment now. Repeated I trusted his side would make suitable reply. I then spoke at some length of chronology aggression in Southeast Asia, saying our support to South Vietnamese had come long after North Vietnamese had aggressed against South, which proceeded even before ink dry on Geneva Agreements.

10) Wang then gave another long tirade on "out-and-out imperialistic policies of US." Said even in Washington large number of people had risen up against our policies demonstrating before the White House. Wang listed number of alleged violations Geneva Agreements on our part but these have all been covered before. Claimed we had turned South Viet-nam into experimental ground for practicing special warfare. Re American prisoners said they had offended Chinese law and of course must receive sanctions of that law. This was question Chinese sovereignty. Said exchange newsmen had always been opposed by USG and while basic problem between us unresolved, discussion specific questions could not come about. Said war in Indochina must also be settled from foundation by withdrawal US troops.

11) I spoke of Communist demonstrations and attacks on embassies and answered Wang's allegations concerning Geneva Agreements and why elections could not be held in 1956 etc. etc.

12) There followed futile exchange concerning motivations both sides' actions in Congo and implications support world opinion each side. Wang again accused US of being world's gendarmes, of using gangster's logic in our policies. Wang said Chinese never engaged in subversive activities in other countries but certainly would support liberation movements which were just, because people of world had had enough of

imperialistic oppression and were determined stand up against it. Re Sino-Indian dispute said no Chinese government had ever recognized McMahon line and China had not made single step outside its legal territory. It was futile for US use India as base from which launch attacks on China. Said Chinese did not like to make relations between China and US tense, but if US compelled them they had no other way out.

13) I observed today's talks had made it clear Chinese planned continue abetting of North Vietnamese aggression and continue stir up trouble where they could in other parts of world.

14) Wang said Chinese security was directly threatened by US aggression South Viet-nam. We were now committing aggression not only against others but also against China. Chinese share same destiny with people all over world and must join hands with them.

15) Wang suggested July 7 as date next meeting. I said view so many serious things happening in Southeast Asia might be wise for us meet earlier. Wang then suggested June 30. I replied while I was aware it was Chinese turn to set date, I would still prefer a much earlier date than that suggested. Wang said he still would like to plan for June 30 as date next meeting but of course if need arose earlier than that time, meeting could always be called by either side. I said with that provision I would accept date on which he was insisting. (I shall of course be happy to return for earlier meeting if this is indicated.)

Cabot

---

85.   National Intelligence Estimate[1]

NIE 13–9–65   Washington, May 5, 1965.

COMMUNIST CHINA'S FOREIGN POLICY

The Problem

To analyze the principles and forces which shape the formulation and conduct of Communist China's foreign policy and to estimate the probable course of that policy over the next two or three years.

---

[1] Source: Department of State, INR/EAP Files: Lot 90 D 110, NIE 13–9–65. Secret; Controlled Dissem. According to a note on the cover sheet, the estimate was submitted by the Director of Central Intelligence and prepared by the CIA and the intelligence organizations of the Departments of State and Defense, and the National Security Agency. All members of the U.S. Intelligence Board concurred on May 5, except the Atomic Energy Commission Representative and the Assistant to the Director of the Federal Bureau of Investigation, who abstained on the grounds that the subject was outside their jurisdiction.

Conclusions

A. We believe that the principal aims of Chinese Communist foreign policy over the next few years will be as follows: (a) to eject the West, especially the US, from Asia and to diminish US and Western influence throughout the world; (b) to increase the influence of Communist China in Asia; (c) to increase the influence of Communist China throughout the underdeveloped areas of the world; and (d) to supplant the influence of the USSR in the world at large, especially in the presently disunited Communist movement. (Para. 1)

B. These objectives, and the method and style with which they are pursued, are shaped by ideology, by Chinese tradition, by the apparatus of power which the present Chinese Communist leaders can bring to bear to achieve their ends, and by the personalities and experience of these leaders. As a result, their foreign policy in some ways resembles an international guerrilla struggle which attempts to wear down the enemy's strength by attacking the weak points. (Paras. 2–16)

C. For both ideological and nationalistic reasons, China regards the US as its primary enemy. Peiping's immediate security interest and the short reach of its military power lead it to concentrate its main foreign policy efforts on undermining the US position in the Far East, though in other parts of the world the Chinese Communists are also using such means as they have to weaken the US. Among other "capitalistic" nations, which Peiping sees as in some sense victims of US exploitation, Peiping tries simultaneously to build up recognition of China as a major power and to weaken the US position of leadership. (Paras. 17–20)

D. The USSR has come increasingly to rival the US as a dominant problem for Chinese foreign policy. China recognizes the USSR as a pioneer Communist nation and as the most powerful member of the Communist camp. Yet nationalistic and ideological factors join to create a strong enmity. The Chinese leaders will continue to seek the overthrow of the present Soviet leadership, but without great hope of seeing the emergence of new men who would follow the Peiping line. Elsewhere in the Communist world, Peiping will seek to dilute or supplant Soviet influence and to win over or split Communist parties and front movements. (Paras. 21–24)

E. Peiping has chosen the underdeveloped, ex-colonial world as its most advantageous arena of conflict. In this "Third World," the Chinese not only aim to erode US strength but to displace Soviet influence; they seek to establish themselves as the champions and mentors of the underdeveloped nations. The greatest impact of Peiping's policy is felt in Southeast Asia. The theater of primary interest is Indochina, where Peiping is seeking a decisive and humiliating defeat of the US. To date, the Chinese leaders have not made risky countermoves to the limited US attacks in North Vietnam, and they almost certainly seek to avoid a wider war. Nevertheless, they have been making preparations for at least limited engagement, and we believe that they would be prepared to risk a major military conflict with the US should they feel China's vital security interests threatened by US actions. (Paras. 25–28)

F. In the rest of Southeast Asia, unless the situation alters sharply, Peiping is likely to support policies designed to maintain and increase pressure against the US. Peiping seems to look on Africa as a second great area of opportunity and is likely to increase both its overt and subversive efforts on that continent. (Paras. 29–33)

G. As long as the present group of leaders remains in control, which is likely to be well beyond the period of this estimate, Peiping's dynamic and aggressive attitudes will persist. Moreover, though we have little information concerning the next generation of leaders, there are many reasons to believe that China's foreign policy will be assertive and uncompromising for a long time to come. (Para. 39)

[Here follows the Discussion portion of the estimate.]

---

86.   Telegram From the Embassy in the Republic of China to the Department of State[1]

Taipei, May 18, 1965, 0320Z.

1132. Deptel 1140.[2] GRC has no capability for taking any effective independent action against Hainan except for covert air drop or sea infiltration of few individuals. Even these actions unlikely to succeed without US technical assistance. Any larger scale action would require US support. Hainan is far beyond range of GRC fighters, and without air cover, no GRC air-borne or sea-borne attempt on any significant scale could succeed. GRC leaders, including President Chiang, are well aware of this.

While Vietnam situation undoubtedly has brought Hainan more into forefront of GRC's strategic thinking recently, no GRC official has

---

[1] Source: Department of State, Central Files, POL CHICOM–US. Secret; Limdis. Repeated to Hong Kong.

[2] Telegram 1140 to Taipei, May 14, instructed the Embassy to raise with the GRC the recent calls in the Taiwan press for an invasion of Hainan Island, conveying the feeling that, "while there probably some virtue in keeping ChiComs guessing re GRC intentions toward Hainan, US would be strongly opposed to such an attack." (Ibid.)

proposed to us GRC action against Hainan. We would prefer not to go to GRC on basis of press stories to urge them not to take action which they have not indicated to us they intend to take, and which they well know they could not undertake anyway without US support.

Possibility remains that ChiComs might be misled by statements in Taiwan press, particularly should GRC undertake infiltration attempt or even leaflet drop against Hainan. Recommend that if démarche considered necessary for this reason, it be directed toward discouraging press statements and those small-scale actions which GRC capable of taking on its own. We would not say to GRC there may be virtue in keeping Chi-Coms guessing, but rather place emphasis on danger of misleading Chi-Coms and thus provoking undesirable ChiCom reaction toward Vietnam. If such démarche is made while bombing of North Vietnam suspended, GRC likely to attribute significance to timing. We cannot judge here whether this desirable or not and request further instructions, both as to line proposed above and timing of démarche.[3]

Wright

---

[3] Telegram 1167 to Taipei, May 20, replied that the Department did not have a démarche in mind but an informal indication of U.S. views; it requested that the Embassy find an appropriate time and channel to convey U.S. concern. (Ibid.) Telegram 1151 from Taipei, May 21, reported that this had been done. (Ibid.)

---

87.   **Memorandum From James C. Thomson, Jr., of the National Security Council Staff to the President's Special Assistant for National Security Affairs (Bundy)[1]**

Washington, June 2, 1965.

SUBJECT

U.S. Initiatives on (1) Travel to China, and (2) Mongolia Recognition

On May 14th the Zablocki (Far East) Subcommittee of the House Foreign Affairs Committee issued a report on the Sino-Soviet conflict which includes, inter alia, the following recommendations:

"The United States should give, at an appropriate time, consideration to the initiation of limited but direct contact with Red China

---

[1] Source: Johnson Library, National Security File, Country File, China, Vol. III. Secret. The handwritten notation "Staff mtg. McGB" appears on the source text.

through cultural exchange activities with emphasis on scholars and journalists;"

and,

"The recognition of Outer Mongolia should be considered."

These two thoughts are tired old chestnuts that have been kicked around in the Government since at least the first months of the Kennedy Administration. As you know, inter-agency agreement has been achieved more than once on a lifting of the travel ban (either specifically for Red China, or across the boards; also, either for special groups—scholars, etc.—or for all citizens). Similar agreement has been reached more than once on recognition of Mongolia. But both proposals have foundered because "now is not the time."

I am convinced that "now" is never going to be the right time—and that *right now* is actually as good a time as we may ever find for making one or perhaps even both moves.

This conclusion was reinforced by my Far East trip in March. At Baguio, in Hong Kong, in Taiwan and in Japan I discussed possible U.S. initiatives towards Communist China and Mongolia with many of our leading State and CIA specialists. In all cases there was general agreement—as there has been in the U.S. Government since 1961—that our national interest would be served by recognition of Mongolia and by a unilateral freeing of U.S. travel to Communist China. More important, I also found general agreement that the present climate of U.S. firmness in Asia—our Vietnam air strikes, the dispatch of ground forces, etc.—was ideal for such moves that might be judged superficially to be "soft". (Typically, such proposals had not been sent to Washington by any of the people with whom I talked; the fact of the matter is that no post abroad considers itself an "action desk" for U.S. relations with Communist China—a situation that is costly to our Government, I fear.)

In the weeks since my return to Washington, I have found similar views here at the working levels of State and CIA on the conduciveness of the present climate to such initiatives.

Now, to my great interest, we have fresh support for such moves, not only from the Zablocki Subcommittee, but also in part from the U.S. Chamber of Commerce in its 1965 Annual Meeting (it urged us to "open channels of communication with the people of Mainland China"). In addition, I have just talked to our Taipei DCM, who assures me that the necessary advance consultations with the GRC on both of these matters would go far more easily in the present climate and would be successful.

In view of the fact that our Asian posture is tougher than ever before, that the Congress has given us a gentle boost, that the GRC is judged to be persuadable, and that we face no election this autumn, I would strongly urge that we get moving on both these items at long last.

Present status of these items: A favorable Mongolia recommendation has been sitting on Secretary Rusk's desk for two months now. He has just asked that FE "update" its recommendation.[2] Meanwhile, Marshall Green was pressed by Fulbright yesterday, at his confirmation hearing, for action on lifting the China travel ban (this item remains buried at State since the 7th Floor got cold feet in January 1964).

We may shortly face the usual State worry as to whether to try one or the other, both, or neither (with the neither-boys probably destined to prevail unless we can give some encouragement from over here).

Question: Can we give such encouragement? In this regard, would you like to see fuller papers on these items?

Jim

_____

[2] See Document 344 and footnote 9 thereto.

_____

88.   **Memorandum From the President's Special Assistant for National Security Affairs (Bundy) to President Johnson**[1]

Washington, June 4, 1965, 11:10 a.m.

SUBJECT

Item in CIA daily brief[2]

1. The CIA daily brief last night had a very important annex on Chinese Communist policy toward Vietnam, but they did not make it wholly clear that this account was part of a direct effort to send a message from Chou En-lai to the U.S. Government. This is so interesting that I think you will want to read it yourself in the British telegrams which have been pro-

_____

[1] Source: Johnson Library, National Security File, Memos to the President, McGeorge Bundy, Vol. 11. Confidential. A handwritten "L" on the source text indicates that it was seen by the President. Another handwritten notation reads: "Rec'd June 4, 1965, 11:25 a.m."

[2] The daily briefs are ibid., Intelligence Briefings.

vided to us.[3] The first two pages of the attached give a brief summary, and there follows a long reporting telegram which is worth reading in full.

2. Dean Rusk's first impression is that this is a relatively defensive message.[4] My own feeling is more mixed. The basic trouble with the message is that it does not tell us at all at what point the Chinese might move in Vietnam itself in a way which would force us to act against China. And that of course is the $64 question.

McG B

---

[3] Telegrams 720 and 722 from the British Embassy in Peking to the Foreign Office, May 31 and June 1. The former summarized a meeting with Foreign Minister Ch'en Yi, largely about Vietnam, in which he asked the British to deliver the message from Chou. The latter reported the portion of the meeting relating to Vietnam, including the message, in detail. Copies of the telegrams were sent to William Bundy with a June 2 covering note from British Minister of Embassy Michael N.F. Stewart, asking whether there would be any U.S. objection if the British Chargé in Peking told the Chinese that the British had delivered the message. No reply to the note has been found. (Washington National Records Center, RG 330, OASD/ISA Files: FRC 70 A 3717, 092 Communist China)

[4] Telegram 720 stated that Ch'en said Chou En-lai had asked Pakistan President Ayub Khan, when he visited Peking in March, to give a message to the U.S. Government, but since Ayub's visit to the United States had been postponed, the message might not have been delivered. Ch'en therefore asked if the British would pass on the message. The message reads as follows: "(I) China will not provoke war with United States; (II) what China says counts; (III) China is prepared; and (IV) if United States bombs China that wd mean war and there wd be no limits to the war."

---

89.   **Action Memorandum From the Assistant Secretary of State for Far Eastern Affairs (Bundy) to Secretary of State Rusk**[1]

Washington, June 16, 1965.

SUBJECT

Travel of Scholars and Representatives of Humanitarian Organizations

Discussion:

The time appears to be at hand to broaden somewhat the categories of Americans entitled to travel to Communist China. I believe we should

---

[1] Source: Department of State, EA/ACA Files: Lot 72 D 175, Travel Controls (Gen), June–July 1965. Confidential.

broaden the categories to include scholars and graduate students with a legitimate professional requirement to visit the area.

We have an unusual opportunity here to put the Chinese Communists on the defensive and to nullify domestic criticism of both the right and the left. Given our stand in Viet-Nam, our critics on the right can hardly accuse us of going soft on Communist China. Since the Chinese Communists will probably not permit any increase in travel at this time, we can demonstrate that we are acting out of boldness, not timidity, and that it is the Chinese Communists rather than ourselves who fear the exchange of ideas. On the other hand, there are few gestures which would better serve both to further our own policy interests and to reassure the academic community that we are interested in the flow of information to and from Communist China.

Even if the Chinese in the future should allow some scholars to enter China, we do not believe there is a significant chance of adverse incidents or ill-treatment of these Americans. We would continue to warn of the inability of the government to provide protection, and to make clear that we are removing restrictions on, rather than promoting, such travel.

Further, a relaxation of certain travel restrictions will show that the Department is exercising the authority, upheld in the *Zemel* case, in a reasonable and responsible manner.

We have had recommendations for increased efforts at contact from various quarters, including the U.S. Chamber of Commerce and the Zablocki subcommittee. You may recall that the proposal to authorize scholars' travel to Communist China was made formally to us by the Joint Committee on Contemporary China and was seriously considered in 1962, but was laid aside in favor of the decision to press for a more general relaxation of our travel rules. A proposal for a general relaxation was made to the White House in January 1963, but was not acted upon at that time. We do not believe that the present situation justifies the resurrection of the more general proposal, but to act now on scholars has many advantages, among which is the circumstance that the scholarly community has been largely mollified by the awareness that we were sympathetically considering their interest in a revision of the rules, but this situation cannot be indefinitely extended if we do not take action.

If after such consultation with the White House as you deem appropriate you decide to authorize such a broadening, it might be worthwhile at the same time to consider whether the President might take advantage of this move, and make the idea of "improved communication" one of the themes for his forthcoming UN commemorative speech in San Francisco. If authorized, FE, SCA and L will draw up and issue appropriate Department regulations and notification of the change. In addition, in announcing the change, we might note the existence of the "national interest" category, which we now use, and explain the terms whereby persons might be eligible to travel in Communist China on the grounds that such travel would be in the national interest. I would propose to cite representatives of bona fide humanitarian, cultural and educational organizations as potential examples of persons entitled to be considered under "national interest" considerations.

Recommendations:[2]

1.   That you authorize the broadening of the categories of Americans eligible to travel in Communist China, as above.

2.   That you authorize FE to pursue with IO the possibility of writing the theme of "improve communication" into the President's forthcoming San Francisco speech, calling for a greater exchange of visits between the Communist countries and the free world.

---

[2] Rusk initialed his disapproval of both recommendations on June 24.

---

90.   Memorandum From James C. Thomson, Jr., of the National Security Council Staff to the President's Special Assistant for National Security Affairs (Bundy)[1]

Washington, June 29, 1965.

SUBJECT

China Travel Problem

In the event that State's China travel paper[2] (which I have not seen but have heard about) is raised at your luncheon with the President today, the following points seem to me pertinent:

---

[1] Source: Johnson Library, National Security File, Country File, China, Vol. III. Confidential. A handwritten notation on the source text reads: "Staff mtg Fri. McGB."

[2] Reference is to a June 28 memorandum from Rusk to the President that recommended adding a new category, medical doctors and public health specialists, to the existing categories of Americans entitled to receive passports valid for Communist China and stated that if the President approved, Rusk proposed to instruct Cabot to mention it at the June 30 Warsaw meeting. It is filed as an attachment to a June 28 memorandum from Bundy to the President with an agenda for his Tuesday lunch meeting with his top advisers. (Ibid., Memos to the President, McGeorge Bundy)

1. The current proposal that we permit doctors and public health specialists to travel to Communist China is irrelevant and inadequate. It is irrelevant because we have had only two requests in the past several years for validated passports from such types (from Paul Dudley White and the famous ear specialist). In both cases the Chicoms have refused visas. State's proposal is inadequate because it fails to meet our basic 2-fold need on this subject: to shift the onus to the Chinese dramatically, and once and for all, for obstinacy, rigidity and self-isolation; and to be responsive to persistent pressure from bona fide American scholars who for years have patiently accepted State's assurance that the travel ban will be shortly lifted. (These scholars have been very cooperative, but their cooperation has predictable limits.)

2. State's proposal that we give the Chinese at Warsaw tomorrow a preview of this mouse makes no sense. The Chinese reaction is utterly predictable (they will reject the idea as a pure propaganda ploy). Furthermore, State's request for Presidential decision on this matter today creates a false sense of urgency on a subject whose full dimensions should receive unhurried Presidential consideration.

For your information. Abba Schwartz, Meeker, and the FE specialists all favor a considerably broader lifting of the travel ban for scholars, scientists and journalists to Red China and Albania. In my view, it would be far better procedure to defer any Presidential action on the present proposal until State can present the President with the full travel picture, including alternatives which the 7th floor has rejected.

Jim

---

91.   Telegram From the Embassy in Poland to the Department of State[1]

Warsaw, June 30, 1965, 1900Z.

2614. Cabot–Wang talks. Deptel 2224.[2] 126th meeting.[3] Content of meeting relatively routine except for occasional outbursts of tough and

---

[1] Source: Department of State, Central Files, POL CHICOM–US. Confidential; Priority; Limit Distribution. Repeated to Hong Kong, Taipei, Geneva, Moscow, and Stockholm.

[2] Telegram 2224 to Warsaw, June 24, modified by telegrams 2245 of June 28 and 2261 of June 29, provided guidance for the meeting. (All ibid.)

[3] Cabot commented on the meeting in telegram 6 from Warsaw, July 1 (ibid.), and sent a detailed report in airgram A–16, July 5. (Ibid., POL CHINAT–US)

intemperate language from Wang. Next meeting is scheduled for September 15. Wang opened with condemnation U.S. "occupation" Taiwan. He claimed U.S. using Taiwan as "ever-floating aircraft carrier" from which to attack mainland, that U.S. plotting create two Chinas, that U.S. crimes of aggression against Taiwan beyond description. He said Taiwan inalienable part of Chinese territory. Chinese people will strive to end to liberate Taiwan. Claimed U.S., while expanding war in Indo-China, also intensifying efforts make military provocations against China in Taiwan Straits area and that U.S. trying draft Chiang gang into war by ordering them place airfields at U.S. disposal etc. Cited serious warnings 378 to 387.

Wang said he instructed lodge strong protest April 24 presidential executive order which included Paracel Islands in combat waters. Wang said Paracels are Chinese. U.S. Govt must be held responsible for all grave consequences arising therefrom.

Second part Wang's opener devoted to U.S. actions Viet-nam. Wang stated U.S. openly declaring war on Vietnamese people and embarking on fighting major war. He repeated standard line on 17th parallel and that all Vietnamese people including those in North have right hit back at U.S. aggressors. Since U.S. has sent own and lackey's troops Chinese have secure right to do all in their power to hit back at U.S. aggressors. U.S. attempting cover up crimes by playing peace hoax. All peace talks doomed to failure. U.S. should never be able to get by political deception what U.S. cannot get on battlefield.

I responded by strongly refuting Wang's argument on U.S. aggression against Taiwan. Also denied ChiCom claim to Paracel Islands. Followed with text Department's instruction. Wang retorted with at times intemperate but familiar attack on U.S. position claiming U.S. on one hand pursuing war and on other giving lip service to peace. He said empty words alone cannot alter atmosphere between our two countries. Wang claimed U.S. instead of ending aggressive acts was redoubling aggression. Claimed every time U.S. said prayer for peace we add fagot to fire of aggression.

Wang said U.S. suffering one defeat after another in war of aggression, hence desire to talk about peaceful settlement. Peace talk plot a vicious one but it impossible pull wool over eyes of people of world. Wang gave standard ChiCom position on Indian proposal, 17-nation appeal, and Wilson mission (but for once in more temperate language). Repeated line only way settle Viet-nam problem is for U.S. Govt to stop war of aggression against South Viet-nam, withdraw all U.S. lackey forces from South Viet-nam, stop acts of war against DRV, implement Geneva Agreements of 1954 and let Vietnamese people settle own affairs. Claimed Front, as true representative South Vietnamese people, must have decisive voice. Referring to Front's March 22 statement as only way settle problem.

Wang then became impassioned and, after saying U.S. hands stained with blood South Vietnamese people, he departed from text and referred to our comments that Chinese youth should be steeled in war. Wang said "We should deal with your unjust war with a just war. You are not only committing aggression against Viet-nam but are also posing threat to China every day." He then quickly shifted subject to repetition U.S. aggression against Taiwan. Wang said as long as U.S. refuses to give up policy of aggression we will continue have struggle. If this root cause not removed, no way to settle problem. If U.S. has sincere desire for peace, U.S. must immediately withdraw forces and stop aggression. Otherwise, all other talks of peace are useless and nothing but a swindle.

I told Wang his side had rejected numerous efforts towards peaceful discussions but had offered no suggestions in return. Wang made weak retort that Hanoi's four points and Front's March 22 position constituted only basis for settlement.

Wang then discussed standard line on atomic explosion. Accused U.S. of crime in using atomic bombs against Japan. Wang repeated at length ChiCom claim to Paracels; gave standard line on Cambodia and Laos conferences (smoke screen to fool peoples of world). Wang also recited usual line on U.S. interference in Dominican Republic, Congo, and referred to comments in U.S. press (including Senators Morse and Gruening) critical of U.S. actions.

Wang toward end of meeting stated, "Should you impose war on Chinese people we will fight back. We are not warlike. This is shameless slander. If others wish to impose war on Chinese people we are not afraid to fight a war. We shall resolutely strike back to end. Should anyone dare to extend his tentacles to China we will cut them off." At another point Wang said, "we will not watch U.S. riding roughshod in world, particularly in neighboring countries, without doing anything on our part."

Meeting lasted 2 hours 35 minutes.

Cabot

92.   Memorandum for the Record[1]

Washington, July 6, 1965, 4 p.m.

PARTICIPANTS

The Secretary
U—Mr. Ball
G—Ambassador Thompson
FE—Mr. Bundy; Mr. Dean
S/P—Mr. Yager; Mr. Goodby
G/PM—Mr. Kitchen; Mr. Weiss; Col. Lewis

SUBJECT

China Study[2]

1.   The purpose of the meeting was to exchange views with the Secretary on the above subject study.

2.   Ambassador Thompson reviewed the activities leading to the study, the organizational arrangements for supervision, and the major policy issues brought to light by the study.

3.   The Secretary commented that the study appeared not to have taken into account sufficiently the total capability of the other side to react in *other* areas to a crisis in Southeast Asia. He cited Berlin as an example. In the event of Soviet pressure in Berlin he foresaw a possible worldwide adverse reaction, but particularly on the part of our European allies, on the grounds that the U.S. had precipitated the European crisis. It was pointed out that the consensus in the intelligence community was that the Soviets preferred to handle one crisis at a time in view of the escalatory potential of concurrent widely spaced crises. Moreover, Ambassador Thompson thought the Soviets would have available a wide range of opportunities to retaliate against the U.S. in Southeast Asia, e.g. against U.S. naval forces, without the same degree of danger that a direct confrontation with the U.S. in Europe would inevitably involve. The Secretary responded that there is considerable latitude with respect to Berlin within which the Soviets could bring pressure before the problem got out of hand.

---

[1] Source: Department of State, Central Files, ORG–STATE. Top Secret. Drafted by Seymour Weiss and Colonel William F. Lewis of G/PM. The meeting took place in Rusk's office. Filed as an attachment to a July 29 memorandum from Thompson to McNamara enclosing papers that he thought Rusk would want to discuss "at our meeting on problems arising out of the China confrontation study."

[2] Not attached to the source text. A copy of the study, prepared by a State–Defense study group, entitled "Communist China (Short Range Report)," April 30, is filed as an attachment to a May 4 letter from Thompson to Ambassador Kohler in Moscow, requesting his comments. (Ibid.) For a summary, see Attachment B, Document 94.

4. The Secretary indicated his agreement with Ambassador Thompson that the study tends to underestimate the forces which might impel the Soviets to earlier and more extensive participation in a Southeast Asian crisis. He asked what the reactions of our Ambassadors were to this question, especially that of Ambassador Kohler. Ambassador Thompson and Mr. Weiss quoted from Ambassador Kohler's letter[3] which strongly argued that the study had underestimated probable Soviet involvement.

5. In connection with Far Eastern attitudes, Mr. Kitchen cited the view of Ambassador Reischauer that even a prolonged conventional war in Southeast Asia is likely to have an adverse effect on U.S. objectives in Japan. Mr. Weiss added that some of our overseas representatives feel that the Japanese are totally out of sympathy with U.S. policy in Southeast Asia. They reason from their own experience in attempting to conquer China that it is a losing proposition. Moreover, the Japanese, as do other Asians, doubt the ability of the Chinese to extend their sovereignty over all of Southeast Asia. They believe the area is too vast and the indigenous populations too hostile to permit this. Thus the Japanese dislike seeing a deepening U.S. involvement. The Secretary responded that it is misleading for the Japanese to argue that their experience was so unsuccessful. At least until Japan made the mistake of attacking the U.S. it was not doing too badly in Asia.

6. Turning to the matter of the longer-range ChiCom study, the Secretary stated that the Study Group should work on alternative hypotheses. This would recognize that some changes are inevitable, e.g., changes in present ChiCom leadership. What happens if China continues to be militant? How do we proceed? On the other hand, what happens if China moves toward peaceful co-existence? Are there other alternatives? In essence, the Secretary believes we should not tie a review of policy to *one* assumption. Ambassador Thompson agreed and commented that we should not overlook the influence of changes in the USSR. The Secretary went on to cite other variables that need consideration, including the effect of population growth; the ability to arm and feed an increased population; the effect on Chinese policy if attitudes hardened against them, e.g., in Africa or somewhere else; the impingement of Chinese and Japanese policy; and the effect of Sukarno passing from the scene. In concluding these comments, the Secretary asked that he be furnished recent intelligence studies of worldwide Communist party reactions to the

---

[3] Kohler's May 22 letter commenting on the study is filed as an attachment to a June 9 memorandum from Thompson to Rusk. (Department of State, Central Files, ORG 1 OSD–STATE) Letters of May 24 from Rice and May 28 from Reischauer are also attached. A June 4 letter from Maxwell Taylor conveying his views and those of U. Alexis Johnson is filed as an attachment to a June 16 memorandum from Thompson to Rusk. (Ibid.) JCS comments are set forth in JCSM 437–65, June 7. (Ibid.)

Sino-Soviet split. Finally, the Secretary suggested that the long-range study be checked out with McGeorge Bundy. Mr. Yager indicated that he had already been in touch with the White House staff.

7. The Secretary indicated that he wished a meeting to be established with Mr. McNamara and McGeorge Bundy to discuss the China Study. He asked that they be given an opportunity to look at the "Résumé" and the "Critical Policy Issues" papers[4] before the meeting. Ambassador Thompson agreed to set up the meeting.[5]

---

[4] The papers to which Rusk was referring are filed with a May 26 memorandum from Thompson to Rusk. (Ibid.) For revised versions, see the attachments to Document 94.

[5] See Document 99.

---

93.   Memorandum From the Deputy Assistant Secretary of State for Far Eastern Affairs (Green) to Chester Cooper and James C. Thomson, Jr., of the National Security Council Staff[1]

Washington, July 9, 1965.

A personal disappointment in leaving FE after almost two years has been our inability over that period of time to strengthen and modernize our China policy by lifting restrictions on travel of Americans to Communist China and by taking certain other measures such as easing the administrative application of FAC controls and recognizing Mongolia. We were unable even to include in our last Warsaw instruction the limited suggestion of informing the Chinese representative that we would be authorizing travel of American medical and public health officials to mainland China. This was a small step in the right direction, although it fell far short of what I hoped would be our position by 1965.

Attached is a talking paper which Lindsey Grant and I prepared almost two years ago providing the argumentation on liberalization of travel regulations governing American citizens.[2] Those arguments are just as valid today although I appreciate that the intensified war in Viet-

---

[1] Source: Johnson Library, National Security File, Country File, China, Vol. IV. Confidential. Drafted by Green. Filed as an attachment to an August 21 memorandum from Thomson to Bundy.

[2] Not attached to the source text.

Nam might make it difficult to liberalize travel to North Viet-Nam and possibly to North Korea. But why not Communist China?

Over the past four years, both in Hong Kong and in Washington, I have spoken to many members of Congress and the press and have given hundreds of speeches and briefings. Oftentimes the subject of taking new initiatives on travel and recognition of Outer Mongolia has arisen and I have not heard one voice raised in dissent when this issue has been discussed. On the contrary, I feel that the overwhelming opinion amongst our countrymen is in favor of doing that which broadly advertises our freedom and our confidence and of dramatizing Peiping's self-isolation. Clearly the liberalization of our policies, taken at the very moment we are showing toughness in Viet-Nam, would *not* be misunderstood. It would be widely applauded in the U.S. and elsewhere. And it would do much to cope with criticisms in our scholarly community of US policies in Asia.

I feel that this is a real opportunity for the Johnson administration.

---

94. **Information Memorandum From the Acting Deputy Under Secretary of State for Political Affairs (Thompson) to Secretary of State Rusk**[1]

Washington, July 15, 1965.

SUBJECT

China Study

1. Pursuant to your request I have proceeded with the arrangements for a meeting on the above subject. The exact date is not yet settled because of uncertainties and conflicts in the schedules of the senior participants in the meeting but I expect that a mutually satisfactory date can be set after Secretary McNamara returns from Viet Nam. In addition to yourself, the Secretary of Defense, and Mac Bundy, I have alerted Bus Wheeler and Cy Vance (who together with me formed the Board of Directors for the China Study), Bill Bundy and John McNaughton.

---

[1] Source: Department of State, Central Files, ORG 1 OSD–STATE. Top Secret; Exdis. Drafted by Weiss and James Goodby of S/P.

2. I have also made available to Defense and to Mac Bundy a list of "Critical Policy Problems" (Attachment A), a résumé of the China Study (Attachment B), and a precis of the views which we received from Kohler, Reischauer, Rice and Taylor/Johnson (Attachment C).[2]

3. You may find it useful, as a means of orienting the discussion, to establish at the outset the purpose for convening the meeting. In this connection, I see the following objectives:

A.   *A Discussion of the "Critical Policy Problems."*

It appears to me that these issues are intrinsically of great significance and to the extent that they are deemed valid, it would be extremely useful to have both an understanding of their nature and a consensus about their significance at the top levels of the government. My own impression, I am bound to make clear, is that both field comments and the study itself seem to suggest that further escalation of our military operations against the DRV (as opposed to prosecuting the war in the RVN) would not have the result of winning the war in which we are presently engaged but would seriously risk changing the character of the war, possibly to the point where the costs are out of proportion to the gains. By and large, it seems to me that the comments on the study which we have received from key U.S. Missions abroad have indicated a preference for the thesis that "the war must be won in the South." Obviously, this issue has been through the crucible of debate many times but perhaps not with the advantage of the "look down the road" which is furnished by the Study Group's report.

B.   *Discussion of Next Steps.*

(1) Long Range Study.

The short range study laid no claims to being a definitive analysis of the problem, nor does it purport to represent a plan of action for the future. We are, of course, committed to undertake a longer range study, in which State will take a leading role, of US-Chinese relations looking through 1975. You may wish to solicit views as to areas of investigation which that study might seek to analyze.

(2) Short Range Politico-Military Planning.

It was my feeling in initiating the China Study that pressures inevitably force too much of a concentration on very immediate objectives and courses of action without permitting the full recognition of longer range implications and without necessarily permitting a relating of individual actions to a comprehensive, long-range politico-military concept. A rather provocative, but trenchant, observation made in the Report epitomizes the concern I think we all share:

---

[2] Attachment C is not printed.

"With or without a decision on our part to increase the level of such military pressure, the history of past conflicts worldwide suggests that there is some danger that punitive military operations may acquire a momentum of their own and may be allowed to continue beyond the point of any real military or political utility."

To the extent that the discussion of the study, and more specifically, consideration of the "Critical Policy Problems" and the comments from the Missions identify points which you, the Secretary of Defense and Mac Bundy deem to be significant, you may wish to suggest that these points be taken into account in our current and continuing Southeast Asia politico-military planning.

An INR memorandum responding to your request for the results of recent intelligence studies of world-wide Communist party reactions to the Sino-Soviet split is at Tab D.[3]

Attachment A

CRITICAL POLICY PROBLEMS

1.   Degree of Soviet Involvement.

With respect to Soviet interests in Southeast Asia, it has been pointed out that the Chinese did not invent nor have they been in the past the principal supporters of the doctrine of national liberation. The Soviets are equally committed to the concept of wars of national liberation.

The study however appears to underestimate the degree of Soviet involvement and of Soviet reaction to U.S. actions, particularly in the stage where U.S. military operations are confined to the DRV, and consequently overestimates the possibility of reaching a tacit understanding between the U.S. and USSR to avoid a major conflict as each side seeks to defend its own interests. Because of the public commitment which the USSR has made to defend the interests of North Viet Nam, escalation or even continuation of our attacks on North Viet Nam will make it increasingly difficult to maintain any serious dialogue with the USSR for the purpose of trying to influence it to moderate its support of that regime. Moreover, the type of assistance which Moscow has already supplied Hanoi could lead to a confrontation with the United States. As the amount of equipment increases, the possibility of mutual miscalculation or accident also increases.

---

[3] Not attached to the source text.

In general, the assumption that Soviet involvement would be minimal has the effect of making the military equation less difficult for the U.S. If a major Soviet involvement of matériel and perhaps of volunteers was in prospect, the effect this would have on the size, nature and consequences of the U.S. commitment, is a matter not explored by the study.

With respect to U.S. actions against Communist China, the study does say that "in the event of U.S. attacks against South China, the USSR would probably feel compelled to provide the ChiComs, after some period of delay, with military equipment, e.g., advanced fighters and missiles." "Soviet first line aircraft and SAMs might have a critical effect on control of the air over the DRV and China." A threat to the existence of a Communist regime in Peiping would probably force the Soviets to become involved militarily to a highly dangerous degree: "An objective that includes the destruction of the Communist regime in China would be most costly and would carry grave risks of general war with the USSR." This would illustrate a situation in which military activities would have far out-run fundamental U.S. national security interests.

2.   *The Nature of the Communist Chinese Threat.*

While the Chinese are utterly opposed to the U.S. presence in Southeast Asia, they expect to use subversion and infiltration of supplies to achieve their objectives, and not direct military force unless their own immediate lines of defense are threatened. The study does not indicate what, if any, level and intensification of U.S. military operations in North Viet Nam will bring the Chinese into the war but it does indicate that at some point Chinese interests and prestige will become increasingly committed to some sort of participation. It has been suggested that the Communist Chinese might become actively involved in the war if the Communist regime in North Viet Nam were threatened, if Chinese borders were placed in jeopardy, or if large Chinese Nationalist forces were brought to the Southeast Asia mainland.

One form of Chinese intervention, well prior to any land action, might be the commitment of fighters from Chinese bases to the air defense of the DRV. The Study suggests that the U.S. would be at a serious disadvantage if it failed to neutralize bases from which the Chinese fighters were employed. It is hard to believe that such an attack on China could result in anything other than the signal for war with that country. Indeed, a special NIE recently completed estimates that if the Chinese actually commit their aircraft to defend the DRV from Chinese bases they must be assumed to be prepared to fight a major conflict with the U.S. Already we have reports that the Chinese are evacuating various executive offices and factories from certain cities and are also installing large numbers of AA units in key areas apparently in anticipation of an escalation of conflict to the Chinese mainland.

3. *The Use of Nuclear Weapons.*

The study suggests that military requirements for nuclear weapons will be especially acute in two circumstances: (1) if the ChiComs/DRV launched a massive invasion of Southeast Asia before U.S. forces were deployed there in large numbers; ("It is quite likely that the U.S. would be faced with the decision to use nuclear weapons . . . perhaps the second or third day of the invasion.") (2) if the U.S. were to bombard Communist Chinese military or industrial facilities on any military significant scale; ("The comparable effects of a conventional attack are very much less because the time required to achieve the same level of destruction is very much longer, thus, permitting repair of damage . . ."). There is an inference in the study that planners are also counting heavily on the psychological effects of nuclear weapons to break the ChiCom will to resist. However, the report emphasizes that the use of nuclear weapons by the U.S. would produce an "overwhelmingly adverse reaction from U.S. allies as well as the Communist world and the uncommitted powers" and that "lasting resentment against the U.S. might be generated." It is suggested that U.S. use of nuclear weapons might mean the loss of key military bases in the Far East, the disassociation of NATO countries from U.S. actions in Asia, and the reduction or termination of the U.S. presence in many parts of the non-aligned world.

While it seems highly improbable that the Soviets would turn over nuclear weapons to the Chinese, and at least in the relatively short run the Chinese will not have an inventory of their own, it is not quite so inconceivable that the Soviets might support the Chinese with their own nuclear arsenal by some expedient method. Though this would obviously be very dangerous for the Soviets, they might feel forced to it, and might even devise techniques which were sufficiently ambiguous, such as provision of Soviet volunteers with nuclear capability, which the Soviets might calculate would avoid a direct confrontation with the U.S. In any event, if the enemy did have nuclear weapons for use in the theater, for example, against U.S. and allied bases and forces, is it entirely clear that introduction of nuclear weapons would even be militarily advantageous to the U.S.?

4. *Escalation of Political Objectives.*

The study lays considerable stress on the upward pressure on U.S. objectives which would result from a major military confrontation with Communist China (e.g., "initial U.S. objectives . . . would appear wholly inadequate to the large-scale hostilities going on and some adjustment would have to be made.") One objective which is frequently mentioned is the reunification of Viet Nam. Others mentioned are the destruction of ChiCom nuclear facilities, the ChiCom industrial base, and even the elimination of the Communist regime in Peiping. "But enlarged objectives also mean enlarged costs, and perhaps a war in Asia which might be decisive only when large-scale strategic nuclear attacks against China were carried out." Since military domination of China by the U.S. seems impractical in military terms, would almost assuredly involve war with the Soviet Union, and seems otherwise to present enormous problems for the U.S., consideration should be given to such questions as how readily we should be prepared to expand political objectives, how insistent we should be on maintaining limited objectives in the face of major hostilities, and whether, in fact, we should not insure that military operations do not create an undesired upward pressure on national objectives.

Attachment B

RÉSUMÉ

The China confrontation study was undertaken on March 8 under the direct supervision of Mr. Vance, General Wheeler and Ambassador Thompson. It was completed on April 30. The staff work was done by a State/DOD/JCS team under the direction of Lt. General Spivy, newly appointed head of J-5. The study is largely focused on the military implications of a rising crescendo of hostilities with the Red Chinese, the scenarios in some cases being intentionally forced in order to bring out the aforementioned military implications.

The study assumes that the broad political objective of the US in the Far East is to seek the containment of Communist China, working over the longer run and as occasion permits for a softening of the present militant approach of the Chinese Communist leadership. Within this broad framework, the group examined the more immediate and specific political objectives which the US might wish to pursue, assuming that under alternative potential contingency situations the US could find itself faced with the possibility of a military confrontation with Communist China. The study was to examine these political objectives in relation to existing and projected military plans and capabilities. Points of particular concern were to be how to discourage Soviet support for the ChiComs in event of hostilities; how to keep the level of hostilities as low as possible consistent with attainment of objectives; the proper role for our nuclear capability; and what political and military adjustments were indicated by the study.

Essentially the study moves through five basic military situations, starting from the position in which we found ourselves in Southeast Asia in March 1965, through a major nuclear war with the Chinese.

In *Situation A*, US air attacks (2500 sorties) on military targets well removed from urban industrial areas have not produced the results we desire. A number of military installations have been destroyed or damaged; about 20% of the DRV's ammunition storage capacity has been destroyed; and the movement of supplies south of the 20th parallel has been restricted. Despite this limited impact, the bombings have had a cohesive effect on the populace of North Vietnam and there has been no significant reduction in DRV supply and support of the continuing Vietnam operations. Therefore, the US elects to increase the scale and scope of bombing within North Vietnam, to include *peripheral* industrial targets, such as *selected* electric power plants.

Situation B represents one step up the ladder of escalation. At this point, a total of 4500 sorties have been flown by US/RVN forces which include the increase in scale and scope as a result of Situation A. However, the Viet Cong have intensified their activity and expanded their control despite the increased bombing; ChiCom volunteers are now operating in North Vietnam with limited numbers of aircraft (50–70) and surface to air missiles; and Soviet missile technicians have manned the SA–2 SAM installation in the vicinity of Hanoi. The US response is to increase the level of bombing again, including more general attack of industrial targets and all categories of transportation, but excluding Hanoi; deploy to South Vietnam the remainder of the Marine division which has elements already there, one Army Division, and one Free World Division (presumed to be ROK); and develop plans and prepare to blockade North Vietnam.

In *Situation C*, the US response described in Situation B has checked deterioration of the military and political situation in South Vietnam and the DRV gives some indications of wavering. At this point, ChiCom aircraft operating from bases in Hainan and South China engage the US/GVN aircraft which are bombing North Vietnam, and large numbers of ChiCom ground forces are deployed in North Vietnam. The USSR has continued to send "volunteer" units to set up and man missile sites. It has announced also the forming of a "volunteer" division which it implies will be sent to North Vietnam if the US does not halt aggression and agree to negotiations.

The postulated US response in *Situation C* is to: increase military activity against the Viet Cong; include targets in Hanoi in air attacks; bomb ChiCom air and naval bases on Hainan Island and in South China, as well as the DRV ports; and mine ports of DRV, in South China, and on Hainan. Additional naval units are introduced into the South China Sea and two Army divisions are deployed to Thailand.

The marked improvement in South Vietnam assumed to have been produced by the measures taken by the US in Situation C, causes Communist China and the DRV in *Situation D* to launch a major attack at the beginning of the dry season. This involves operations by 22 divisions in South Vietnam, Laos and Thailand. Rather than postulating a US response in this situation, the study examined the political and military implications of a variety of courses of action.

The final situation (*Alternative Situation A*) departs from the forced escalation of Situation A through D by assuming ChiCom/DRV initiation of large scale ground attack prior to the significant build-up of friendly forces which is assumed had been achieved in Situation D as by-product of progressive escalation. Thus the situation when the attack commences is assumed to be that at the outset of the study, i.e., Situation A. The treatment in Alternative Situation A generally parallels that in Situation D: an examination of the political and military implications of a variety of courses of action.

Both Situation D and Alternative Situation A include assessment of the impact of nuclear weapons on ground and air operations. Some interesting comparisons of nuclear and non-nuclear force requirements for the same operations appear in summary charts opposite pp IV–60 and IV–80.[4]

---

[4] Not printed.

---

95. Memorandum From James C. Thomson, Jr., of the National Security Council Staff and the President's Special Assistant for National Security Affairs (Bundy) to President Johnson[1]

Washington, August 5, 1965.

SUBJECT

Ray Cline's Talks with Chiang Kai-shek

Ray Cline, CIA's Deputy Director for Intelligence and formerly Taipei station chief, visited Taiwan this week at the urgent personal request of Chiang Kai-shek.[2] Cline had two long talks with the Gimo, the first in

---

[1] Source: Johnson Library, National Security File, Memos to the President, McGeorge Bundy, Vol. 13. Secret. A handwritten note on the source text reads: "For information only." A handwritten "L" on the source text indicates that the President saw it.

[2] Wright reported Chiang's request for Cline's visit in telegram 16 from Taipei, July 7, and commented that he thought the request meant that Chiang wanted to use an alternate channel to send a policy proposal to Washington and recommended against such a visit. (Department of State, Central Files, POL CHINAT–US) Telegram 31 to Taipei, July 13, cleared by Bromley Smith and Rusk, stated that Cline should accept Chiang's invitation but not until after Wright's departure and that the visit should be portrayed as having a reporting rather than a policy context. (Ibid., INR/IL Historical Files, Roger Channel Telegrams, Taipei)

the presence of our Chargé, the second one alone on August 3 for five hours at the Gimo's mountain retreat.[3]

Chiang's aim was to use Cline, whom he trusts, in order to communicate a "message" directly to you. (Chiang feels that more normal "diplomatic channels" have distorted and disregarded his views in recent years.)

The Gimo's message, in brief: The Chinese Communists and their Vietnamese allies are about to engage the U.S. in a long ground war of attrition which we cannot hope to win; Chiang stands ready to provide troops to Vietnam if we want them; but most important, he urges that now is the time for an amphibious Chinese Nationalist landing on the South China (Kwangtung) coast in order to cut Peking's supply lines to Vietnam and to begin the reconquest of the mainland. The Gimo believes that it is now or never; the Sino/Soviet dispute assures that the U.S.S.R. will not intervene, and the Chinese Communists have not yet achieved a sufficient nuclear buildup to deter a Nationalist invasion.

Regardless of our views on such undertakings, the Gimo asks that we do some coordinated strategic planning for such a move. He intends to spell out his proposals more fully in a letter to you that will be carried by his son Chiang Ching-kuo, the Defense Minister, when he comes to Washington in late September.

Ray Cline comments that the Gimo was more emotional than the situation warrants and probably fears that his control of Taiwan will weaken unless he appears to be doing something active about fighting the Chinese Communists. Hence the revival of the "counter-attack" theme. In balance, Cline's visit seems to have provided a boost to the Gimo's ego—and a healthy escape-valve for his pent-up feelings that the U.S. had written him off.

JCT Jr.
McG B

---

[3] [*text not declassified*] telegram [*text not declassified*], August 1, conveyed a message from Clough to Bundy reporting Cline's first meeting with Chiang. (Ibid.) [*text not declassified*] telegram [*text not declassified*], August 3, transmitted a message from Cline summarizing his meeting that day with Chiang. (Johnson Library, National Security File, Country File, China, Vol. XIII) A second message from Cline with a more detailed account of the meeting is filed as an attachment to an August 4 memorandum from Walter Elder to McGeorge Bundy. (Ibid.)

96.   National Intelligence Estimate[1]

NIE 13–7–65   Washington, August 5, 1965.

POLITICAL PROBLEMS AND
PROSPECTS IN COMMUNIST CHINA

The Problem

To analyze Communist China's most significant political problems and to estimate its political character over the next few years.

Conclusions

A.   The dedicated, narrowly doctrinaire men who rule China initially gained the support of the Chinese people by swiftly unifying a country in chaos. But their adventurist "Great Leap Forward" program failed disastrously, substantially reducing popular faith in the leadership and popular support of its programs. Despite their failures, the dwindling group of elderly leaders remain determined to carry through political and social programs that will produce a modernized China, and a "new Communist man."

B.   This policy is the work of a remarkably small and stable group of men. Mao and his lieutenants have, over the past three decades, avoided major internal schisms and refused to admit younger blood into their ranks. In recent years the leadership has turned inward upon itself; it has virtually dispensed with formal party meetings and congresses while cloaking its operations in ever greater secrecy.

C.   The party can exact obedience and compliance, but, despite its recurrent campaigns, the people attempt to improve their material lot and to avoid politics. These attitudes have widely infected the lower levels of the party apparatus as well. The regime is currently engaged in massive campaigns to "reform" or weed out errant party cadres and to "educate" the people to accept the regime's collectivist programs. It has announced that it will launch another production upsurge, but this is likely to differ significantly from the ill-fated Great Leap Forward. The outlook is for increased tensions.

D.   Mao is 71, and most of his dozen or so closest lieutenants are in their 60s. Mao's departure probably will not split the leadership, and

---

[1] Source: Department of State, INR/EAP Files: Lot 90 D 110, NIE 13–7–65. Secret; Controlled Dissem. According to a note on the cover sheet, the estimate was submitted by the Director of Central Intelligence and prepared by the CIA and the intelligence organizations of the Departments of State and Defense, and the National Security Agency. All members of the U.S. Intelligence Board concurred on August 5, except AEC and FBI representatives, who abstained on the grounds that the subject was outside their jurisdiction.

policy is likely to continue along present doctrinaire lines. His successors will not have Mao's authority, however, and this may in time open the door to the growth of factionalism inside the party.

E. Mao's lieutenants will be succeeded in their turn by a generation of party veterans, now in their 50's. Although these men give no evidence of a broader, more moderate viewpoint, they will have to deal with a host of accumulated pressures and may perforce be more flexible and pragmatic. At least for the next several years, however, political and social problems within China are unlikely to prevent economic and military development or to force a softening of Chinese foreign policy.

[Here follows the Discussion portion of the estimate.]

---

97.   Action Memorandum From the Assistant Secretary for Far Eastern Affairs (Bundy) to Secretary Rusk[1]

Washington, August 23, 1965.

SUBJECT

Request for Authority Under Circular 175 to Sign a Status of Forces Agreement with the Republic of China

Discussion:

Article VII of the Mutual Defense Treaty between the United States and the Republic of China, which entered into force on March 3, 1955, provides for the stationing of United States forces in and about Taiwan "as determined by mutual agreement." Discussions with the GRC concerning a status of forces agreement were begun in 1955 but were interrupted by the Taipei riot of 1957 and the Straits crisis of 1958. In 1959 authority to negotiate an agreement was granted by the Acting Secretary to the Ambassador to China, with the understanding that authority to sign the agreement would be sought when negotiations were concluded (Tab A).[2] On July 30, 1965 the United States and the Republic of China jointly announced the conclusion of negotiations.

---

[1] Source: Department of State, Central Files, DEF 15–3 CHINAT–US. Confidential. Cleared by Fearey, Deputy Legal Adviser Richard D. Kearney, Eleanor C. McDowell of L/T, G.H. Aldrich of L/FE, George L. Warren of G/PM, Deputy Assistant Secretary for Congressional Relations John P. White, in draft by Eugene T. Herbert of L/FE and Colonel Ramundo of DOD/ISA/FMRA, and in substance by Rubin of DOD/OSD/GC.

[2] The tabs are attached but not printed.

Attached (Tab B) is the English text of the agreement which will be the basis for final agreement.

The twenty article agreement is modeled on the basic NATO status of forces formula, tailored to fit the particular situation in Taiwan. It provides that the United States will bear the cost of the maintenance of its forces, while the Republic of China will furnish facilities and areas and rights of way. The United States is to receive utilities and services at rates and under conditions which are no less favorable than those of any governmental agency of the Republic of China. United States personnel are to enjoy freedom of entry and exit, exemption from local taxes, and exemption from customs duties provided that personal items are brought into the agreement area (Taiwan and the Pescadores) within six months of the person's initial arrival, or are purchased or obtained thereafter through a United States operated exchange, commissary, or military post office, or under certain other specified conditions.

The jurisdiction article is patterned after the Supplementary Agreement between the United States and Germany. In the minutes to be published with the agreement the Republic of China agrees to waive its primary jurisdiction but reserves the right to recall such waiver in specific cases where major interests of Chinese administration of justice make the exercise of Chinese jurisdiction imperative, particularly in cases of security offenses against the Republic of China, offenses causing the death of a human being, robbery and rape.

In a separate exchange of letters, the cases in which the Chinese Government could recall its waiver are limited solely to the following: security offenses against the Republic of China, offenses causing the death of a human being, narcotics offenses, robbery, rape and arson. By limiting Chinese jurisdiction to these offenses, the United States personnel are protected against the operation of the Special Laws (tantamount to martial law) presently in effect in Taiwan. It is also provided that United States personnel will not be tried in Chinese military courts.

The jurisdiction article provides further that the United States shall have the right to custody of an accused person until the completion of all judicial proceedings. The Chinese have agreed to comprehensive trial safeguards and to the conclusiveness of United States duty certifications in determining primary jurisdiction. Under the agreed minutes the adequacy of Chinese confinement facilities will be a matter of joint agreement between United States and Chinese authorities. A Joint Committee is to be formed by the two governments to assist in implementing the agreement.

The claims article provides for unilateral settlement of claims by the United States, with the Chinese having the option to turn to the standard NATO claims formula should they find United States unilateral settlement procedures unsatisfactory.

A memorandum summarizing the provisions of the agreement was transmitted to the staffs of the Senate Foreign Relations and the House Foreign Affairs Committees on July 28.

Recommendation:

That you authorize signature by our Ambassador at Taipei, or by the Chargé d'Affaires, of the Status of Forces Agreement which has been negotiated with the Republic of China, based on the attached text and subject to approval of the final text by the Assistant Secretary for Far Eastern Affairs or his deputy with the prior concurrence of the Office of the Legal Adviser, Congressional Relations, and the Department of Defense.[3]

---

[3] Thompson initialed his approval on August 24. The agreement was signed at Taipei on August 31; for the text, see 17 UST 373.

---

98.   Memorandum From the President's Special Assistant for National Security Affairs (Bundy) to President Johnson[1]

Washington, August 24, 1965, 9:45 a.m.

SUBJECT

Paul Dudley White and Mainland China

1.   Last week you sent me for comment a letter from White[2] in which he offered his services in any way that might be useful "in helping to break our deadlock with China."

2.   It turns out that Dr. White has had a long interest in this problem! He was invited to China by the President of the Chinese Academy of Medicine in July 1962. The Department of State agreed to his visit, but at the last minute the Chinese withdrew their invitation on the ground that the U.S. "has persistently adopted a reactionary policy against New China, and blockaded every possible channel of communication between the peoples of our two countries."

---

[1] Source: Johnson Library, National Security File, Memos to the President, McGeorge Bundy, Vol. 13. No classification marking.

[2] Dated August 10; attached but not printed.

3. This is a characteristic example of the way in which the Red Chinese have tried to pin on us a responsibility which is really their own. I bet that 80% of those interested in the problem think that the reason more Americans cannot go to Red China is U.S. intransigence—while the fact is that it is mainly the Red Chinese themselves who have prevented such travel.

4. Under our own current policy guidelines, I know of no way we can use Dr. White at this time. If we were to give official backing to a White visit to China, it is predictable that the Red Chinese would turn it down. This would not gain us much.

5. On the other hand, the White case does raise the question whether we are smart to let it appear that we are the people who block communication between our two countries. Our Chinese experts have recommended for some time that we should ease our present travel restrictions and make a general rule that doctors and public health specialists—or perhaps all workers in the fields of health, education, and welfare—would be authorized to receive visas. (Our present rule includes (1) authorized news correspondents, (2) families of the four imprisoned Americans, and (3) individual cases in which the national interest is served—Dr. White's visit would have come under this third category.)

6. We discussed this matter at a Tuesday luncheon earlier this winter [summer?],[3] and you felt then that it would not be wise to change our current policy. But perhaps if we were to change it in response to an appeal by Paul Dudley White—and at a time when our policy in Vietnam has reached a new level of clarity and firmness—we might make a useful stroke in all directions. I will put this matter on the agenda for our next Rusk/McNamara meeting.[4] Meanwhile, I have given Dr. White a cordial interim acknowledgment, as attached,[5] and protected your right to answer him yourself when you are ready.

McG. B.[6]

---

[3] See Document 90.

[4] A September 2 memorandum from Thomson to Bundy states that a proposal on modified travel restrictions had been on Rusk's desk for several days and that Rusk reportedly had doubts about its "breadth" and would probably avoid action for a while. Thomson asked Bundy whether the attached proposal conformed with Bundy's "understanding of what the President authorized" and whether they could do anything to encourage faster action. (Johnson Library, National Security File, Country File, China, Vol. IV) A September 8 memorandum from Thomson to Bundy attached a new draft Department of State memorandum to Rusk and noted that it was "an outgrowth of your phone call to Ben Read last Friday." (Ibid.)

[5] Dated August 24; attached but not printed.

[6] Printed from a copy that bears these typed initials.

99.   Memorandum of Conversation[1]

Washington, August 27, 1965.

SUBJECT

Meeting on China Study[2]

PARTICIPANTS

State	Defense
The Secretary	The Secretary
G—Ambassador Thompson	Mr. Vance
FE—Mr. Berger	ISA—Mr. McNaughton
S/P—Mr. Yager	JCS—General Wheeler
G/PM—Colonel Lewis	JCS—General Spivy
White House—Mr. Bundy	JCS—General Hightower

1.   The Secretary opened the meeting by commenting that the study was a very useful piece of work. He stated, however, that there are certain aspects which require further thinking through. In this connection, he mentioned to Ambassador Thompson that the Soviet position requires further thought. It is possible the Soviets may not prefer to see a settlement in Southeast Asia. The struggle with Peiping is very deep-rooted and as a result may force the Soviets to take a stronger position than might otherwise be the case. He said he questions whether the Soviets would be willing to suffer another missile crisis setback considering the very major effects this could have upon the Soviet world position. Putting himself in their shoes, were he a Soviet leader he would be inclined to be sure that the US was presented with threats elsewhere in the world but tied to Southeast Asia, for example, by renewed pressure on Berlin. Such action, the Secretary believed, would raise very difficult alliance problems. The US would be blamed. The Secretary said he would be pleased to be proven wrong, but be doubted it. He thinks the study may have been too optimistic concerning Soviet policy, though we would do everything possible on the diplomatic side to avoid a confrontation with the Soviets. Nevertheless, the longer the hostilities continue, the bigger the problem with the Soviets will become.

2.   The Secretary went on to say that the second major problem that bothered him was the time factor. He pointed out that the US is con-

---

[1] Source: Department of State, Central Files, POL 1–3 CHICOM. Top Secret; Limdis. Drafted by Weiss and Lewis. A note on the source text reads: "S Clearance not required on Memo for the Record. EJStreator." Another record of the meeting is in a September 21 memorandum for the record prepared by Yager and Hightower, dated September 21. (Washington National Record Center, RG 330, OSD Files: FRC 70 A 1265, China Reds 092 China Study)

[2] See Documents 92 and 94.

cerned with the need "for something to support in Vietnam." The US effort would be very difficult in Southeast Asia if the political position in Vietnam erodes. However, the same might well be applied to the other side. There would be a great advantage to an all-out effort in South Vietnam, perhaps in September, if this could bring the other side to the conclusion that there was too little left for it to support in South Vietnam; too little from which to construct a viable political position. With a basis in military success, a concurrent peace offensive would give us a possibility of effective action *before* the other side makes the major decision to ask for more support.

3. Thirdly, the Secretary said that the problems of the use of nuclear weapons was perhaps understated in the paper. He noted that the use of nukes is not a line of action which we are going to abandon. He pointed out that the US has been careful not to foreclose this possibility, particularly in the Pacific against China. However, this problem may affect our whole position in the world and could even be influenced by domestic attitudes. The gravity and difficulty of the decision should be recognized.

4. Finally, the Secretary said he was pleased to see that a State-DOD group had been set up to take a longer, more careful look at the problem and that this should be helpful.

5. Secretary McNamara stated that his understanding was that the study was directed at the longer range problem and in this connection he would hope to have more analyses of the way the Communist Chinese are likely to move in their foreign policy, especially in Asia. From this we would be able to derive how the US should move in response. He cited India and Japan as two key areas. Mr. Vance commented in response to Mr. McNamara that the Senior Policy Group (Vance–Wheeler–Thompson) had decided that such a look was not practical in the initial short-range effort, but quite agreed that the longer range study should encompass such considerations.

6. In response to Mr. McNamara's question, General Spivy said the longer-range study was due for completion next June, but with internal wrap-ups on various actions from time to time. He commented that the study is not a planning document per se, but an independent look at the problem. Mr. McNamara asked if an outline of the longer-range study could not be developed. General Spivy indicated that an initial outline is available (and passed out copies)[3] noting that the outline is still being revamped. Mr. Yager said that the outline is considered as a checklist of points to be covered at this stage.

7. The Secretary stated that some of the matters covered in the outline are already operational and others may become so even before next

---

[3] Not found, but see Document 161.

summer, when the report will be completed. It might therefore be most useful if the study group were to look at certain specific problem areas more immediately. For example, if one were to try to influence Peiping toward accepting a more peaceful coexistence attitude then certain problems such as those presented by the India-Pakistan conflict are not very helpful. On the other hand, in Africa things are going very well and we might wish to capitalize on our position there. He said he could think of nothing more important in our longer range relations with Communist China than getting the Kashmir dispute settled so that India and Pakistan can live peacefully. Mr. McNamara agreed fully, and suggested an immediate effort by a very small group to get down on paper in about ninety days some of the more important considerations. It is less important that this be a completed and fully coordinated job, than that it reflect the thoughtful work of a limited number of good minds. Mr. Bundy agreed. He said we need in hand not an interdepartmental coordinated draft but a useful analysis.

8.   The Secretary stated that it might be useful for him to dictate the thoughts on his mind as to how events, as he sees them developing, might affect the longer-range problem. He emphasized that this would be a casually dictated paper over a weekend, stressing questions and problems which trouble him, rather than a directive. General Wheeler commented that this would be excellent and just what the study group needed. Mr. McNamara also agreed.

9.   Ambassador Thompson agreed that the Secretary's offer would be very useful and suggested that Mr. McNamara, General Wheeler and others might wish to do the same. He commented that the problem is vast. For example, he cited as just one possibility the consideration that China and the Soviet Union could some day get back together again. Leadership in the various countries will eventually change and particularly if the US suffers severe setbacks in Vietnam this could attract the Soviets and Chinese together. The implications of this should be considered. Another thought that he had was the possible utility of attempting to bring pressure on China through the use of wheat, capitalizing on their difficult food problem. In this connection, he noted the problem of the dearth of good intelligence on China, commenting for example that we had little information on Chinese atomic capabilities. He stated he personally doubts that it will be significant soon, though he anticipates an attempt by the Chinese to make maximum use of the political potential of their having become a nuclear power.

10. General Wheeler commented that they are making a major effort in the intelligence community to lay out what we do and what we do not know. For example, he thinks that there is a need for a study in depth on the Chinese economy. He said that the DIA project on the military economy showed a greater capability than what most of the "economists"

have been saying. He said doubtless this reflects a dual economy in China, one for peace and one for military use, but that we need a better analysis. Mr. McNamara tended to disagree, stating that he believes a report could be drawn up now. He doubts, for example, that a study in depth of the economy would have much affect upon the results of such a report. In the relatively short run of from five to seven years, China will be able to skim from the top of its economy base whatever is needed for military purposes.

11. Ambassador Thompson said he is struck by the concern of the present Chinese leadership with the possible disaffection of the next generation of Chinese leaders. He believes that the present leadership is taking precisely the wrong measures by insisting on more rigid indoctrination. We might well look at the possibility of capitalizing on this.

12. The Secretary said that we should look at the possibility of a food crisis in China and how the US might capitalize on that. He wondered whether a study by the Department of Agriculture might be useful. Ambassador Thompson said Agriculture had done some studies, but he finds them rather incredible. They tend to show that the Chinese could easily expand their agriculture and feed their population, but this was based on the assumption that US agricultural methods could be used. This was the big hooker. The Secretary agreed that this is a questionable assumption. Ambassador Thompson suggested that perhaps a study independent of the Agriculture Department might be useful.

13. The Secretary asked if the Study Group were in touch with Professor Taylor and his group at the University of Washington. He commented that they were doing work on the economy of China. The response was negative, but that the contact would be made. General Spivy commented that ISA is contracting with IDA for a long run study on China, the information from which would be of interest to the study group.

14. The Secretary suggested that one device which might be used would be to develop a loose leaf study. On some parts we might be able to write useful pieces immediately, developing the other parts as more information becomes available.

15. Mr. Bundy asked if CIA had been involved in the study. It was pointed out that they had been.

16. Ambassador Berger stated that two additional problems particularly interest him. One has to do with the possible admission of Communist China to the UN, and the range of problems which that would present. He suspected that this is a matter which we will have to face up to in the not distant future. The second issue is the possibility of Indonesia being taken over entirely by the PKI.

17. The Secretary stated that the central question, as he sees it, is the need to influence a half-dozen key people in China on the question of how China is doing, and whether its present policy is or is not on the right track. Such actions as the recognition of China by France or its future admission into the UN would, of course, be very bad in that it would persuade the Chinese that they were being successful. Unless other things demonstrate to the Chinese that they are not on the right track we will be faced with much greater danger in the future, not to mention that which we face today.

18. Mr. McNamara agreed, saying in addition that if the US takes positions in opposition to the Chinese which it cannot successfully back up, this only makes things worse. Mr. Bundy agreed, stating there is no point in opposing the Chinese in areas where we do not have the power to influence events.

19. The Secretary pointed out that successful opposition to the Chinese would create a terrific burden. He noted that it required a trillion dollars in NATO defense budgets to stop the Russians in Europe (but noted parenthetically that they still risked the Cuban missile adventure). It is going to require a major decision on the part of the US and its allies to stop the Chinese. Mr. McNamara agreed but stated that as a government we have not really faced the problem of generating sufficient power to convince the ChiComs of their error.

20. Ambassador Thompson raised a question as to how our studies and analysis might be used outside of the US, perhaps in some sanitized version. He stated that he has been impressed as to the lack of serious thought about the Chinese problem on the part of our allies and others. Mr. McNamara agreed and pointed out that since others do not think about the problem, and he doubts the US ability to stop the Chinese unless others are prepared to help, he wonders whether we will not have to say this to them at some point. This applies especially to India and Japan.

21. The Secretary stated that he thought the meeting had been useful and that it perhaps provided sufficient guidance for the next steps to be taken.

100.   Telegram From the Commander in Chief, Pacific (Sharp) to the Chairman of the Joint Chiefs of Staff (Wheeler)[1]

Honolulu, September 15, 1965, 0212Z.

150212Z. Exclusive for Gen Wheeler from Sharp. CHINAT/US planning and visit of Defense Minister Chiang Ching-kuo (U).

A. CINCPAC 110234Z.[2]

1. In the ref, I commented upon my visit with President Chiang and also upon Ray Cline's talks with him.

2. I have received further information from COMUSTDC which is of interest in connection with the forthcoming visit of Defense Minister Chiang Ching-kuo. You will recall that ChiNat/US planning for the "return to the mainland" has the nickname "Blue Lion."

3. Ray Cline's conversation indicates that the Generalissimo felt there was insufficient Blue Lion planning. COMUSTDC has informed me that Blue Lion planning on TMH TDC/MND level has been reasonably active. During the past two years, twelve Blue Lion meetings have been held as follows:

Month	Year	Number of Meetings
October	1963	2
December	1963	1
March	1964	2
April	1964	1
June	1964	1
September	1964	1
November	1964	2
December	1964	1
August	1965	1

4. The same MND planners who work on Blue Lion were involved in the TDC/MND war game in January 1965 and the major CPX of Plan Rochester in April 1965. This accounts for the lapse in Blue Lion activity during the first half of this year. At present, the MND planners are working on two planning projects; one an amphibious assault and drive inland in a northwest direction from the coastal area west of Canton to seal off Vietnam, and second, the logistic plan to support a northwesterly breakout from the lodgment area in the vicinity of Amoy. The first project is scheduled for a TDC/MND meeting later this month.

5. I have been informed that the DCM at Taipei has suggested in a message to State that during Chiang Ching-kuo's visit, the President

---

[1] Source: Department of State, Central Files, DEF 1 CHINAT–US. Top Secret; Exdis; Specat; Exclusive.

[2] Not found.

might propose that a general officer planner from the joint staff be sent to Taiwan from time to time to review Blue Lion planning. COMUSTDC objected to this on the basis that first, it is not necessary and further, it would bypass CINCPAC. I concur with COMUSTDC. If Blue Lion planning should be reviewed, it is obviously a job for CINCPAC.

6. During Chiang Ching-kuo's visit to Honolulu next week, I intend to discuss frankly with him the ChiCom defenses in the south China area which are available to counter an amphibious landing. I will point out to him in general terms the kind of force which would be required to support an amphibious landing and let him know that we are thoroughly aware of the size of the task. I am sure he will get this kind of information in Washington also. But it seems appropriate to speak frankly with him during his visit here.

101.   Telegram From the Embassy in Poland to the Department of State[1]

Warsaw, September 15, 1965, 1837Z.

396. Cabot–Wang talks.[2] Deptels 315, 339.[3]

1.   127th meeting. I opened with substance instructions in Deptels 315, 339. Wang's prepared reply contained no substantive change in Cjio-ChiCom position. Next meeting scheduled for December 15.

2.   Wang devoted his initial reply to my opening comments by restating well-known Chinese position on Vietnam: "The only way to

---

[1] Source: Department of State, Central Files, POL CHICOM–US. Confidential; Priority; Limit Distribution. Also sent to Taipei, London, Hong Kong, Saigon, New Delhi, Karachi, and Moscow.

[2] This was the 127th meeting of the Ambassadorial talks. Cabot commented in telegram 412 from Warsaw, September 16, and reported on the meeting in detail in airgram A–271, September 20. (Ibid., POL CHICOM–US and POL 1 CHICOM–US, respectively)

[3] Telegram 315 to Warsaw, September 10, conveyed guidance for the meeting. (Ibid., POL CHICOM–US) Telegram 339, September 13, added a paragraph referring to recent Chinese notes to India. It stated that unfounded Chinese allegations in the most recent note appeared to be designed to convey a threat of Chinese military action and stated that the U.S Government deplored "even the making of such threats, which if pursued, could create a most dangerous situation, which it would be difficult to confine to the areas or parties initially affected." A note from William Bundy to Rusk, attached to the telegram, states, "I understand this conforms to the discussion at the White House meeting today." (Ibid.) Telegrams 332 and 345, dated September 11 and 14, transmitted additional guidance. (Ibid.)

settle Vietnam question is for US to stop aggression in Vietnam, withdraw all its forces and let Vietnamese people solve their own problems." This formula was repeated several times during the meeting. Wang followed with list of US acts of "aggression" against China, including alleged overflight Hokou, US warships bombarding ChiCom fishing vessels, ramming of Lebanese vessel by US sub in Chinese waters, overflights of pilotless planes, serious warnings, etc.

3. Wang then departed from his written text and discussed Lin Piao's article. Said "We communists have never tried conceal our views," and that "Chinese experience over past decades told us it was necessary to use revolutionary war against counter-revolutionary wars to get rid of imperialist aggression." Wang said Chinese are compelled to take up arms for purpose of self defense.

4. I told Wang US had repeatedly sought means establish peace in SEA. I said tide of battle now seems to have changed. Said we prefer to seek peaceful solution rather than lengthy war. I told Wang his side seemed to reject Geneva Agreement as basis for making peace. Said we are committed by our national faith to the defense of the SVN people. I stated most firmly that we will fulfill that commitment.

5. Wang returned to Vietnam question. Said "reason why you shout so loudly for peace talks is that you have come to grief in battlefield . . . and met powerful rebuff. . . ."

6. Wang then read long article from *People's Daily,* Sept. 9, on India's "frenzied provocative activities," along the whole Sino-Indian border. Said that after India provoked large scale armed conflict in 1962, the situation on Indian border eased as result series efforts made by Chinese side. But India never stopped intrusions in Chinese territory. Incidents by no means accidental. Also charged India with carrying out aggression against people of Kashmir. Said India–Pak conflict entirely provoked by Indian Government. Claimed India's attacks on Pak "could not be separated from backing USG." I said this charge was nonsense and told Wang our principal aim was to restore peace between our Indian and Pakistani friends.

7. I reiterated our strong determination to support GVN against aggression and stressed that American public firmly supports USG policy in Vietnam. I told Wang that Lin Piao's article looked like blueprint for Communist aggression and that it reminded me of Hitler's *Mein Kampf.* This stung Wang who retorted that American actions since WW II resembled those of Hitler, Mussolini, and Japanese aggressors. Wang charged large numbers of US troops deployed all over world and repeated familiar line that US has committed aggression against Korea, Vietnam, Dominican Republic and Congo.

8. Wang reiterated support for Vietnamese people. Said US "aggression against Vietnam also jeopardizes security of whole Indo-

China and our own country," and "no force can shake our determination to support Vietnamese people." Wang said everybody can see clearly who does not want peace. While US talks of peace it continues send troops and wantonly carries out bombings.

9. Wang also said, "not only are we ready to settle Taiwan and Taiwan Straits matters in peaceful way, we are also ready settle peace in South-East Asia, but if you still refuse to withdraw your forces this question can not be settled." Wang replied to my charge of Chinese aggression in Korea by stating China was defending own national borders. He repeated VNA statement that 325 Division not in South Vietnam. I refuted this statement saying we had prisoners.

10. I told Wang that I agreed that SVN should be liberated, that they should be liberated from aggression from the North and that was what we were trying to do. I said they should settle their own affairs, and should be free to do so by withdrawal of North Vietnamese as well as by American and other forces, and by the withdrawal of very substantial aid and arms given to the Viet Cong. I concluded by saying that I hoped these talks would have more result in the future than they have had in recent sessions.

11. Following the meeting I made the following statement to the press: "I have, as you know, participated in these talks for the past three and one-half years, first with Ambassador Wang Ping-nan and more recently with Ambassador Wang Kuo-chuan. I believe that the talks have served a useful purpose in providing a ready channel of communications. I regret, however, that during this time there has been little progress towards the achievement of a deduction of tensions in the Far East. I am sure that my successor will continue our efforts to reach a peaceful solution for the grave problems confronting Asia."

12. The meeting lasted two hours thirty-six minutes.

Cabot

102.   Letter From the Ambassador to Poland (Cabot) to the Assistant Secretary of State for Far Eastern Affairs (Bundy)[1]

Warsaw, September 16, 1965.

Dear Bill:

Thank you for your letter of September 10[2] concerning my final session at the Warsaw talks and the letters from Senator Fong and Vermont Royster.

After some consideration I decided not to suggest an informal session with Ambassador Wang Kuo-chuan because our previous relationship had been rather cold and distant. I was agreeably surprised after the meeting when he shook hands all around and wished me smooth sailing. This was the first time Wang has unbent and acted naturally in my presence. I hope he will continue to exhibit this new side in the future.

I sent David Dean to the Chinese Embassy on the day before the meeting to discuss the letters from Senator Fong and Royster. Chinese Counselor Li agreed to consider forwarding the letters. He said he would refer the matter to the appropriate authorities. Two days later Mr. Li told us that he had consulted the responsible authorities and regretfully could not accept the letters for transmission. He suggested they be mailed directly. I am enclosing memoranda of conversations for these visits.[3]

It seems to me that if we can maintain as reasonable a position as possible during these meetings, we may achieve a long-range educational impact, at least on those who read the transcript of the meetings in Peking. However, it appears unlikely that the Chinese will abandon their position that major matters, such as Taiwan, must be settled before minor problems can be resolved.

I hope to have a chance to discuss the talks more thoroughly with you when I return to Washington.

Sincerely yours,

John M. Cabot

---

[1] Source: Department of State, Central Files, POL CHICOM–US. Official–Informal; Limited Official Use.

[2] Not found.

[3] Attached but not printed.

103. Memorandum of Conversation[1]

Washington, September 20, 1965.

SUBJECT

China

PARTICIPANTS

The Secretary
Madame Chiang Kai-shek
Chinese Ambassador Shu-Kai Chow
Dr. Kung
Secretary of Defense McNamara
Senator Dirksen
Senator Sparkman
Ambassador Jerauld Wright
Later—Mr. Cooper

The Secretary opened the conversation by stating that he knew there were many things on Madame Chiang's mind and he hoped she would use this occasion to give him her views on any aspect of the world situation as she saw it.

Madame Chiang replied by stating that she would first prefer to hear the Secretary's views.

The Secretary stated that he believed one of the things foremost in the minds of President and Madame Chiang was the Chinese Communist nuclear explosion and he would appreciate her views on this matter.

Madame Chiang stated that the CCNE had a decidedly powerful influence not only on adjacent Asian states but on the entire world. As a result of this development the Chinese Communists' prestige and influence throughout the entire world had been vastly increased. She stated that this development was a matter of considerable concern to Asiatic nations including her own people in the Republic of China.

The Secretary said that France had a far greater nuclear capability than the ChiComs. France had in 7 years only three megatons, a very small arsenal compared to the enormous power of the U.S. The ChiComs could not approach French capabilities. The Secretary said we should

---

[1] Source: Department of State, Central Files, POL CHINAT–US. Secret; Exdis. Drafted by Ambassador Wright and approved in S on September 30. The conversation took place at a dinner given by Rusk for Madame Chiang. Ambassador Chow called on Chief of Protocol Lloyd Nelson Hand on September 9 to state that Madame Chiang's visit, although private, was to be considered a return visit for President Johnson's 1961 visit to Taipei. Hand stated that since the Department had been notified that her visit was private, it had made arrangements accordingly, but that the arrangements that were made for a White House tea on September 14 and the Rusk dinner were beyond those normally made for private visits. (Telegram 239 to Taipei, September 18; ibid., POL 7 CHINAT)

assume that we are dealing with rational men not lunatics and that no rational men would employ nuclear weapons against the certainty of their own obliteration by the retaliatory power of the U.S. Any such action would be purely suicidal.

Madame Chiang replied that the Chinese Communists are not rational men. They are insane with power and will resort to any means to accomplish their objectives. She stated that ChiCom nuclear weapons had been developed at enormous expense to the people of China and created extreme hardship and in many cases starvation. She stated that their nuclear capability was a threat not only to the surrounding Asian nations but to the United States. She said that if two men faced each other, one armed with a weapon that shot 50 bullets and the other with a weapon that shot only 2 bullets, the man with the lesser weapon could destroy the other before he could use the greater weapon.

Secretary McNamara stated in substance, that the man with the 2-bullet weapon would never shoot if he realized it meant his own death. He said that deterrent power rested not only in superior weapons but on the willingness to use them if necessary in retaliation.

Madame Chiang stated that in the present situation of increasing ChiCom nuclear power the only course of action for the United States under the increasing ChiCom nuclear capability was for the United States to (provide the means) to take out the ChiComs nuclear installations now by the employment of conventional forces, to destroy now their nuclear capability before it reached dangerous proportions.

The Secretary then asked what action the ChiComs would take if such an operation were undertaken. Madame Chiang replied they would raise a terrific uproar.

The Secretary then stated that in his opinion the ChiCom reaction would be violent and would result essentially in the employment of their principal weapon, their enormous manpower, in offensive retaliatory operations beyond their borders. In this connection we could not employ U.S. manpower to resist such action and would have to resort to nuclear weapons. In such case the United States would be condemned by all the nations of the world, including those on the periphery of China, for starting a nuclear war. The Secretary stated that if the Nationalists were in Peking and such an attack were made in China they would certainly react with all their strength.

Madame Chiang stated that nuclear weapons would not have to be used; that the ChiComs could not go far in operations beyond their borders.

The Secretary then stated that the United States had only 190 million people whereas China had over 600 million and that he hoped Madame Chiang appreciated the impossibility of employment of U.S. manpower in Asia against such odds.

Madame Chiang replied that she hoped that it was thoroughly understood that the Republic of China did not propose the use of any American troops against the ChiComs.

Dr. Kung stated that in the development of nuclear weapons the Chinese Communists were "winning" in the eyes of the world; that by this accomplishment their prestige had been enhanced in the views of the Asian and African nations.

There followed a general conversation on ChiCom chances in the UN, and whether they actually desired entering.

The Secretary stated he believed their condition of entry would be the acquisition of Formosa.

The Secretary stated that the meeting had been fruitful in the frank exchange of views and expressed the hope that that discussion might be continued at a later time.

104.   Memorandum of Conversation[1]

I–26204/65   Washington, September 22, 1965, 9:15–11 a.m.

SUBJECT

Call on the Secretary of Defense by the Chinese Minister of Defense

PARTICIPANTS

Chinese Side
Chinese Defense Minister—Chiang Ching-kuo
Chinese Ambassador—Chow Shu-kai
Chinese Information Minister—James Shen

United States Side
Secretary of Defense—Robert S. McNamara
Assistant Secretary of Defense (ISA)—John T. McNaughton
Desk Officer Far East Region—Colonel Austin L. Berry, USAF

1. Opening Remarks

Secretary McNamara welcomed Minister Chiang and party to the US. Minister Chiang said they were happy to be here and that he brought

---

[1] Source: Washington National Records Center, RG 330, OASD/ISA Files: FRC 70 A 3717, 333 China, Rep of. Secret. Drafted by Berry on September 23 and approved by McNaughton on September 24. The meeting was held in McNamara's office at the Pentagon.

personal greetings to Secretary McNamara from President Chiang Kai-shek. Secretary McNamara replied that he had always admired Chiang Kai-shek and was especially pleased to note the economic development that has taken place under Chiang Kai-shek's leadership. Minister Chiang suggested at this point that they dispense with translation from English to Chinese.

2.   *GRC Assistance to Vietnam*

Minister Chiang said President Chiang had asked him to seek Secretary McNamara's views on how the GRC can help the US in Vietnam. Secretary McNamara responded, first by explaining to Minister Chiang with the use of maps, the situation as the US views it. Secretary McNamara pointed out the Viet Cong had apparently undertaken what was intended to be a decisive campaign to cut South Vietnam in half and to destroy the RVNAF but that the added weight of US forces had frustrated VC plans and forced them to revert to small scale guerrilla tactics. Secretary McNamara then went on to say that the RVN is grateful for GRC economic and technical aid and that the RVN wants it increased; that the RVN needs help especially in increasing agricultural production. Secretary McNamara said the RVN also needs help in the field of transportation, especially water transportation such as commercial ships and that the RVN needs medical assistance. Secretary McNamara stated that the war will be ultimately won or lost by how well the government takes care of its people and that this is the area in which they need help the most. Minister Chiang thanked Secretary McNamara for his briefing on the situation and stated that the GRC would be happy to do anything they could to help, noting that Premier Ky had also talked to him in the same vein.

3.   *Overall Asian Situation*

Minister Chiang said he wished to discuss the overall Asian situation and Secretary McNamara responded that he was anxious to hear Minister Chiang's views on the subject. Minister Chiang stated that three areas are of great interest to Communist China: Korea, Taiwan Straits and Southeast Asia (now extended to include India). Korea and the Taiwan Straits being strongly defended, the ChiComs were devoting their attention to the south. In an effort to expand southward the ChiComs had two areas in mind, Vietnam and India, where it had felt US power could not reach effectively. As a result of the stepup in US military effectiveness in Vietnam, the ChiComs feel they can do little more there now and will shift their focus of activity to the Indian border, and perhaps Thailand. The ChiCom objective is to spread and scatter US resources like "ten fingers extended." Minister Chiang continued that he greatly admired the way Secretary McNamara had implemented US policy in Vietnam, that he believed the ChiCom strategy had been frustrated in

Vietnam, but that he did not feel the ChiComs would give up their expansionist policies in South and Southeast Asia.

4. *Seizure of 5 "Southwest Provinces" (Kwangtung, Kwangsi, Yunnan, Kweichow, Szechwan)*

Minister Chiang said President Chiang had asked him to discuss the historic development of certain things, and that what he was about to discuss were things which need not be done immediately but which nevertheless should be given consideration now. Again saying that he saw little chance of a ChiCom thrust in Korea or the Taiwan Straits, hence a ChiCom focus toward the south, Chiang said that from a strategic viewpoint the 5 southwest provinces of China are the most important because due to terrain they form a natural barrier between "China proper" and SE Asia. If seized (by the GRC) they can shield SE Asia from China proper. For this reason, President Chiang wants to stress the importance of seizing the 5 SW provinces. He again said Chiang Kai-shek was discussing only policy and strategy, not operational proposals. Minister Chiang said Russia has never in history been involved with respect to the 5 Southwest provinces, that ChiCom control is weakest in these same 5 provinces, that resentment against the Communists is strongest and popularity of Chiang Kai-shek is greatest in these provinces. At this point Chiang left a small brochure to explain further this concept.[2]

5. *Stronger ChiCom Action Foreseen*

Minister Chiang said he foresaw stronger ChiCom action against the US and the GRC; the US because it is the ChiComs' strongest military obstacle and the GRC because it is the ChiComs' greatest political threat.

6. *Need for US and GRC to Work Together*

Chiang said the US and the GRC must continue to work together; that US wealth and Chinese manpower, in which should be included the millions of Chiang supporters on the mainland, constitute a force the ChiComs must respect.

7. *High Level Consultations*

Chiang said suspicions that the GRC seeks more military aid, or seeks to involve the US in their return to the mainland are superficial and that what is really important is that we consult more closely at high levels of government on matters of Asian policy and strategy. Our common problems will be with us a long time; they require constant contact and joint consideration from a longer range point of view.

---

[2] The reference is to a paper entitled "A Problem of Common Interest," undated. A copy is filed as an attachment to an October 13 memorandum from McNaughton to JCS Chairman Wheeler, referring to it as Chiang's "concept paper" and requesting JCS comment. (Ibid., 381 Rep of China)

8. *ChiCom Military Buildup in Coastal Area*

Minister Chiang said GRC intelligence showed the ChiComs are increasing their military strength in the coastal areas opposite Taiwan. Ground force buildup is chiefly replacement of units with other units better trained and equipped. Air buildup consists of increased training, more SAMs, more and better radars although conventional AAA had been reduced somewhat to provide weapons for Vietnam.

9. *GRC Forces "Available"*

Minister Chiang said Chiang Kai-shek had asked him to say that GRC forces are "available" to support free world interest in Asia but that if we anticipated they might be needed the GRC should be given a little notice so they could have their forces ready when an emergency arose.

10. *Immobilizing ChiCom Forces*

Minister Chiang said that larger numbers of ChiCom forces could be immobilized in Fukien province (opposite Taiwan) thereby making them unavailable for ChiCom use elsewhere such as SE Asia. He said he felt this was an important possibility worthy of joint study by the US and the GRC.

11. *US Military Assistance Program*

Minister Chiang expressed GRC appreciation for the US military assistance over past years which had enabled the GRC to build up strong forces. Minister Chiang pointed out that if we want to keep these forces strong it is necessary that they be given some new equipment every year to replace equipment that becomes obsolete. Minister Chiang stated that he is aware that reduction of military assistance is a part of US policy but that he hopes that without increasing the total amount, certain things can be done to strengthen GRC forces. He stated to save time he had prepared a memo which he wished to leave with Sec Def. Sec Def said he would be delighted to have the memo.[3] (A separate comment will be prepared on the memo.)[4]

12. *Proposed GRC Attack on the Mainland*

[*less than 1 line of source text not declassified*] renewed discussion of the GRC proposal for seizure of 5 southwestern provinces. [*less than 1 line of source text not declassified*] President Chiang, in his November 1964 letter to President Johnson,[5] had pointed out that in any advance on mainland China it would be unwise for US forces to be involved; [*less than 1 line of*

---

[3] Dated September 16, this memorandum is attached to a letter of June 16, 1966, from McNamara to Chiang; see Document 159.

[4] Not further identified.

[5] See Document 69.

source text not declassified] the US agrees. [*less than 1 line of source text not declassified*] President Chiang had also stated that nuclear weapons should not be used to support GRC forces. [*less than 1 line of source text not declassified*] then asked whether, in the GRC-proposed seizure of 5 southwestern provinces, it was thought that either US ground forces or nuclear weapons would be needed to support the GRC. Minister Chiang replied that the GRC would not favor the use of nuclear weapons and that they would not want US ground forces. Minister Chiang said that the presence of US ground forces would change the nature of the attack from an internal Chinese war to a foreign war, a change which would aid the Communists. Minister Chiang said the GRC would need US transportation and also US planes. Minister Chiang said the GRC would need US air and navy *cover* (protection from ChiCom air and sea attack) but would not need or want US air or naval strikes.

13.   Bay of Pigs Comparison

Secretary McNamara said the proposal for seizure of 5 southwest provinces looked somewhat like the Bay of Pigs plan in that it obviously contemplated large scale popular uprising against the Communists. Secretary McNamara asked what evidence the GRC had that the people would rise. Minister Chiang replied that in the 5 SW provinces resistance to the Communists was strongest, hatred of the Communists was greatest, Communist force deployments were weakest, popularity of Chiang Kai-shek was greatest. Minister Chiang said he had studied the Bay of Pigs operation and felt that it was inadequately organized and lacked an established government to lead it, both conditions which would not be true in the seizure of the SW provinces.

14.   US–GRC Consultations

Secretary McNamara said the discussion had been very helpful and that he thought it would be well for the US and the GRC to study together the intelligence relating to proposed seizure of 5 SW provinces, particularly intelligence relating to the possibility of popular support for GRC forces. Secretary McNamara said that, without in any way committing the US to provide any forces, we would be glad to participate in joint studies. Secretary McNamara said the US would be glad to resume the "Blue Lion" consultations when our new ambassador arrives. Secretary McNamara said he would be happy to arrange for senior CINCPAC and DOD officers to visit Taiwan for studies and consultations. Secretary McNamara said he recognizes US–GRC common interests. Secretary McNamara said it is important for the GRC to understand that the US is firmly committed to defend Taiwan, and that it is important for the US and the GRC to understand each other's views.

15. Military Assistance

Secretary McNamara said the US believes that countries which are able should increase their contribution to their own defense and that the US believes this applies to the GRC.

16. Reduction of Forces

Secretary McNamara said that he believes that, in the long run, it will be to the GRC advantage to reduce its forces to relieve costs that don't contribute much. Secretary McNamara noted that the GRC defense budget had increased this year; that we understand the need but that the US believes it would be unwise for the GRC defense budget to exceed about 9% of GNP. Minister Chiang responded that he felt that what matters most is how GRC defense capabilities can be kept satisfactory. Secretary McNamara replied that he agreed but that he felt the GRC should consider carefully whether its forces are too large in view of the cost of maintaining them.

17. Role of Japan and India

Secretary McNamara asked what was the GRC view of the role of Japan and India in Asian affairs over the next 5–10 years. Minister Chiang replied that with respect to India he did not feel the ChiComs were able to engage in large scale operations, but that they intended to stir up internal trouble in India by making trouble on the border. Minister Chiang said that with respect to Japan he felt the ChiComs would limit themselves to political and diplomatic moves and that the ChiComs are trying hard to arouse more anti-US feeling in Japan. Minister Chiang did not, in fact, respond to the question about the future role of Japan and India.

18. Joint Communiqué

Secretary McNamara then proposed that a joint communiqué be issued and offered a proposed text. Minister Chiang agreed to issuing a joint statement and after minor changes, the proposed text was agreed upon.[6]

---

[6] The text of the joint statement issued that day was transmitted in telegram 293 to Taipei, September 22. (Department of State, Central Files, POL 7 CHINAT)

105. Memorandum of Conversation[1]

Washington, September 23, 1965, 11 a.m.

PARTICIPANTS

U.S.
Mr. McGeorge Bundy
Mr. Chester Cooper
Mr. Calvin E. Mehlert, Interpreter

Republic of China
General Chiang
Ambassador Chou
Minister Shen

General Chiang introduced the discussion by stressing the need for close collaboration between the U.S. and the GRC. He felt that a thorough joint study of the Chinese Communists was a necessary prelude to a common policy.

Although the United States had global responsibilities, he hoped that we could proceed on a common path with respect to the Chinese Communists. "Public relations are one thing", but in our "serious discusions", we should adopt a "joint policy".

The Generalissimo felt that any joint studies that were undertaken should be "penetrating and sustained". The Chinese strength on Taiwan should be used effectively to help with the problem of the Chinese Communists. It is now time "to put our heads together to work out a joint plan". We may have different views, but we must find a common meeting ground. The Chinese Communists have an integrated policy toward both Taiwan and the U.S. and this means that *we* should have "an integrated policy". This is the essence of President Chiang's position.

Mr. Bundy agreed that the Chinese Communist problem is a critical one for both our governments. Although it is not the *only* problem the U.S. faces, it is a growing one. He also agreed that the two governments must consult and work together. We probably have difference in assessment "at least at the margin" both within our own society and between our two governments and this is an important reason for close consultation.

The U.S. has an immediate problem in Vietnam and Southeast Asia and we are fully aware of the hostility of Peiping to the Republic of China. Nonetheless, we cannot reach a decision that full-scale conflict with the ChiComs is inevitable. Our policy is to contain Peiping and

---

[1] Source: Johnson Library, National Security File, Country File, China, Vol. IV. Secret. Drafted by Cooper on September 24. The meeting was held in Bundy's office.

attempt to avoid full-scale war. We have many alliances in Asia, but our closest ally is the Republic of China; within our own overall policy we desire to conduct the closest kind of consultation and partnership with Taipei.

We have kept the situation on the mainland under close scrutiny because if we ever felt that limited operations against Communist China could, in fact, be successful we would want to examine those carefully. Thus far we have not undertaken such actions—wisely. In any case, we are anxious not to undertake actions which will enlarge hostilities in Vietnam or lead to a full-scale conflict on the mainland.

Chiang reiterated his view that the basic question is how Chinese Nationalist strength can be used without touching off a wider war.

The meeting concluded at 11:25.

CLC

106. Memorandum of Conversation[1]

Washington, September 23, 1965, 11:45 a.m.

PARTICIPANTS

> *U.S.*
> The President
> Mr. William Bundy, Dept. of State
> Mr. Chester L. Cooper, White House
> Mr. Calvin E. Mehlert, Interpreter
>
> *Republic of China*
> General Chiang
> Ambassador Chou
> Minister Shen

General Chiang presented a letter from Generalissimo Chiang Kai-shek (attached).[2]

---

[1] Source: Department of State, Central Files, POL CHINAT–US. Secret. No drafter appears on the source text, but it was drafted on September 24, and approved in the White House by Thomson on October 22. The meeting was held in the President's Office at the White House.

[2] Not found attached to the source text. The text was transmitted to Taipei in telegram 354, October 6. (Ibid., POL 15–1 CHINAT)

The President expressed his pleasure at having recently seen Mme. Chiang Kai-shek and recalled with pleasure his visit to Taiwan in 1961.

General Chiang noted that he had had useful conversations with Secretaries McNamara and Rusk and Messrs. William and McGeorge Bundy.[3] He said that President Chiang was especially interested to learn from the President what U.S. policy is in the Far East and in what way the Republic of China can help the U.S.

The President expressed appreciation for what the Chinese have already done and the example they have set in the area. He informed the General that the U.S. is proceeding with a military buildup in Vietnam which we think can arrest the present dangers and, at the same time, avoid provoking an all-out war in the Far East.

The reports of the past month give us reason for cautious optimism. The results during the monsoon season were especially encouraging. The U.S. plans to stay in Vietnam until the aggression stops. There are some people who feel the U.S. should undertake unlimited military measures, but the Government feels that this will result in increasing the help being given to the other side and that this would be unwise. On the other hand, there are some who feel that the U.S. should pull out altogether. The U.S. does not plan to pursue either of these extreme courses.

The President indicated his pleasure with the UN-initiated cease-fire in the Indian-Pakistan dispute. We will do everything appropriate to encourage them to negotiate their differences. The Chinese Communists, for their part, have done a great deal of talking in the past week or so, but have not acted, and they have probably lost a great deal of prestige in many quarters.

There promises to be difficulties in the UN on the China question, but Ambassador Goldberg thinks it will come out satisfactorily. The President hoped that all countries would hesitate to reward Peiping for their conduct in the last several days, but one never knows how other countries feel about such questions.

The President asked General Chiang to tell President Chiang that we appreciate all the GRC has done in support of our common objectives and that the U.S. remains a loyal ally of the Republic of China.

The President expressed his high regard for President Chiang and his hopes for close collaboration with him. He once again expressed his admiration for Madame Chiang.

---

[3] Records of Chiang's September 22 meetings with Rusk and William Bundy are in the Johnson Library, National Security File, Country File, China, Vol. IV. A record of a September 24 meeting with McNamara is ibid. A record of a September 23 meeting with Harriman is in Department of State, Central Files, POL CHICOM–USSR. A record of a September 27 meeting with McNaughton is in Washington National Records Center, RG 330, OSD Files: FRC 70 A 1266.

General Chiang said that his Government joined the U.S. in the desire to avoid general war in Asia. The basic question is how "to reduce or, if it is possible, to destroy Chinese Communist power without a general war." He had discussed this with Messrs. Rusk and McNamara and had raised a number of proposals for a coordinated U.S.–GRC effort. The General emphasized that this question was the essence of President Chiang's message to President Johnson.

General Chiang also noted that he had been asked to pass on the Generalissimo's belief that the Chinese Communists would not intervene "massively" in Vietnam or on the Indian sub-continent. Instead, they will try to create turmoil through "revolutionary warfare" all over the world. These tactics can last a long time and will dissipate U.S. strength and efforts. They could have more dangerous implications for the U.S. than massive intervention. He felt our common effort should be a long-term one. There is a need for continued joint study. Although we may differ in our interpretations, we should have common objectives.

The meeting concluded at 12:15 with an exchange of gifts (an autographed picture and some books from the President; two porcelain plates with portraits of the President and his family from General Chiang). The President then took General Chiang into the press lobby.

---

107.   Memorandum of Conversation[1]

Washington, September 26, 1965.

SUBJECTS

    (1) U.S. Policy on Travel to Communist Countries
    (2) Current U.S. Thinking on Outer Mongolia
    (3) Chinese Representation Issue at Current General Assembly
    (4) U.S.–GRC Consultation and the August 6, 1965 Sea Clash Between GRC and ChiCom Naval Units

PARTICIPANTS

    Chiang Ching-kuo—Defense Minister of the Republic of China
    Chow Shu-kai—Ambassador of the Republic of China
    James Shen—Director, Chinese Government Information Office
    William P. Bundy—Assistant Secretary for Far Eastern Affairs
    Calvin E. Mehlert—Interpreter

---

[1] Source: Department of State, Central Files, POL 23–10 COMBLOC. Secret. Drafted by Mehlert. A Top Secret memorandum of conversation provided addenda to paragraphs 6, 9, and 12 of this memorandum of conversation. (Department of State, Central Files, POL CHINAT–US)

1. In response to a request made September 23 by General Chiang for a second opportunity to meet with Mr. Bundy, Chiang was invited to call at Mr. Bundy's home at 6:30 September 26 for drinks. The meeting lasted until 8:15.

U.S. Policy on Travel to Communist Countries

2. After an exchange of greetings, Mr. Bundy said that he wished to inform Minister Chiang that the U.S. would announce in the near future a change in its passport policy which would permit doctors and public health workers to be issued passports with no restrictions as to destination of travel. Thus, doctors and public health personnel with legitimate cause for travel to Cuba, countries in Eastern Europe or Communist China, and who have reason to believe they would be admitted, would be issued passports. Mr. Bundy pointed out that this did not represent a change in actual practice, noting that Drs. White and Rosen had been issued passports for travel to Communist China, although in neither case had travel taken place. Mr. Bundy explained that the President feels that the humanitarian considerations involved should be separated from political problems. Mr. Bundy said also that this change would tend to take one issue away from those who criticize our policies toward travel to Communist countries as being too restrictive. He also noted that, if any travel should take place, it might produce useful intelligence; this, however, was secondary.

3. Mr. Bundy observed that, although the announcement will be worded in a general way, some people may take particular note of its applicability to Communist China and draw unwarranted conclusions therefrom. We do not anticipate that this will be a problem because 1) as in the case of news correspondents, there will probably be very little travel resulting from this announced change and 2) the U.S. attitude toward Communist China is clearly shown by our actions in the Far East and by the recent strong statement by Ambassador Goldberg at the UN on the Chinese representation issue.

4. Minister Chiang said that the travel of a few doctors was not in itself an important matter, but that such actions as this often are viewed as highly significant by people in the Far East who might see in it a dilution of American firmness toward Communist China. The timing, close to the opening of the General Assembly, was not too good.

5. Mr. Bundy replied that we also had had to examine carefully the considerations raised by the Minister, but in sum had concluded that 1) now was a suitable time for such an announcement and 2) this move would probably strengthen our overall position vis-à-vis Communist China. Mr. Bundy appreciated, however, that it might not to be appropriate to make the announcement during the Minister's visit to the U.S. and

said that he would look into the possibility of having it issued after the Minister's departure.

Current U.S. Thinking on Recognition of Outer Mongolia

6. Mr. Bundy recalled the discussions which had taken place in 1961 between the U.S. and the GRC on the subject of possible U.S. recognition of Outer Mongolia. He wanted to inform the General that while we did not now have recognition of Outer Mongolia under active consideration we did review the problem periodically with special emphasis on two factors: 1) possible impact on the Sino-Soviet dispute of U.S. recognition of Outer Mongolia; and 2) possible intelligence benefits. The first factor did not seem important at this time, given the extremes to which the split between Peiping and Moscow has already gone. As far as the intelligence factor is concerned, this could become significant, and it is possible that in the future, perhaps a few months, this matter may come up for more active consideration.

7. General Chiang (apparently not understanding fully) replied that as the matter involved only intelligence collection and not the political recognition of Outer Mongolia, he saw no problem. Mr. Bundy said that the two matters in this case were inseparable. Chiang suggested that in that case this was a matter for our two governments to discuss. Mr. Bundy emphasized that in raising the issue at this time he simply wanted to be sure the GRC understood our exact state of thinking on a matter that had once been active between us.

Chinese Representation at the General Assembly

8. Mr. Bundy noted the importance of the African votes in the Chinese representation issue at the UN, complimented the GRC on its active foreign policy in Africa, remarked on how much he had learned about Africa during Deputy Foreign Minister Yang Hsi-k'un's visit to the U.S. earlier this year, and said that we regarded as astute the GRC handling of the recent problems with Mauritania and Dahomey.

9. Mr. Bundy said that we believe we have a favorable margin of about five votes, at this time, against a resolution calling for the seating of Peiping and expulsion of the GRC, and a margin of some 15–18 votes supporting the Important Question. Mr. Bundy emphasized the special importance of the closest liaison possible between us on this problem.[2]

---

[2] The Top Secret memorandum of conversation cited in footnote 1 above stated with reference to paragraph 9: "Mr. Bundy informed Minister Chiang that the commitment made in May 1961, and reaffirmed by Secretary Rusk in 1964, concerning U.S. action were the Chinese representation issue to be raised in the Security Council still stood."

U.S.–GRC Consultation and the August 6, 1965 Sea Clash Between GRC and ChiCom Naval Units

10. Mr. Bundy noted the general excellence of communication between us, and referred to specific proposals made during Minister Chiang's visit for strengthening the mechanisms by which mutual consultation is accomplished. He referred to the August 6 GRC operation which resulted in a sea clash between GRC and ChiCom naval units and to which the attention of an element of the U.S. Seventh Fleet had been drawn. He noted that the U.S. had not been informed beforehand of this operation and indicated that the significance of such clashes for our Seventh Fleet made closer liaison on such matters important to us.

11. Minister Chiang noted in reply that this had not been an "amphibious operation" (as he had understood from an error in interpretation) but only an attempt at landing 16 men for intelligence-gathering purposes. Mr. Bundy remarked that the problem apparently lay in the fact that ChiCom naval reaction and capabilities had not been anticipated. General Chiang agreed and said that it would be possible to strengthen liaison in these matters.

12. Minister Chiang asked concerning the new U.S. Ambassador, emphasizing the importance of his arrival in Taipei as soon as possible. Mr. Bundy reviewed the factors which had delayed this matter and indicated that within a short time we expected to have more definite information.

13. On leaving, Minister Chiang expressed appreciation for the courtesies shown him by the Department of State during this visit.

---

108.   Telegram From the Embassy in the Republic of China to the Department of State[1]

Taipei, October 28, 1965, 0925Z.

489. 1. DefMin Chiang Ching-kuo asked me in today to discuss message I passed to FonMin Oct 23 reported Embtel 467.[2] His purpose was to clear up some garbles in notes passed to him by MOFA which had puzzled both CCK and Pres Chiang.

---

[1] Source: Department of State, Central Files, POL 15–1 CHINAT. Secret; Limdis.

[2] Telegram 467 from Taipei, October 23. (Ibid.)

2. I took the opportunity to probe further on his proposal for high level exchange of views (para D Deptel 369 [396?]).[3] I said Dept probably wondering whether an additional formal mechanism was necessary, and whether it would not be preferable to have periodic informal exchanges between Ambassador on one hand and Pres Chiang and/or DefMin on the other.

3. CCK said that was what he had in mind, that meetings should be informal and should take place whenever either side wished them, and that no formal committee required. He said purpose in his mind was to make an opportunity for exchanges of views between friends, with no commitments on either side. He said sometimes diplomatic channels (by which I think he meant all occasions when close records and close following of policy guidance is required) too constraining, and that GRC was seeking easier and less formal ways to discuss what each side was thinking.

4. I asked for examples of subject matter, and he said that he hoped discussions could deal with the general situation in Asia, and with opinions, private or official, about future trends. He said that few if any details or specific intelligence reports would be discussed, only general principles and trends.

5. CCK today discussed with [*less than 1 line of source text not declassified*] plans for exchanging appraisals of situation on mainland (para C Deptel 369).

6. *Comment:* Believe this is significant retreat from previous request for high level committee structure, possibly occasioned by my statement that Dept may be having problems with formal aspects of proposal. Seems likely that CCK and his father realize that closer communication with USG is highly desirable, and that it has been hampered by Chinese desire, and US unwillingness, to discuss such deeply held articles of faith as return to mainland, knocking out ChiCom nuclear capability, etc. CCK visit designed among other things to show greater flexibility and accommodation to US views, which they understand very well. They are now asking for discussions and better communication between friends and assured us that they do not wish to press for specific actions to be taken. Strongly recommend that Dept instruct me to reply that USG is pleased at prospects for closer exchanges of views and agrees that periodic informal meetings between Amb and high level GRC officials will be very useful. Also would like to say that Amb will carry special instructions from Pres Johnson or SecState relating to these meetings, and that we

---

[3] Telegram 396 to Taipei, October 15, instructed Chargé Arthur W. Hummel, Jr., to inform the Foreign Minister of the Department's preliminary thoughts on actions it might take concerning U.S.–GRC consultations to follow up Chiang Ching-kuo's conversations in Washington. (Ibid., POL 7 CHINAT)

hope the meetings can be supplemented from time to time by discussions with visiting high level US officials. Any other forthcoming and cooperative noises I can be empowered to make will be helpful.[4]

7. At this point would be useful to demonstrate that US attitude is one of desire to have better understandings with GRC. Realize that such exchanges are not going to be easy to keep within bounds. We have sharply divergent views of the world, which I believe stem from GRC conviction that there is a war on already and has been for many years, while USG is committed to exploration of steps toward peace. Because of this, high level discussions here are curiously constrained by unwillingness either side to expose different views and cause impasse. CCK has taken significant steps to open up broad-scope substantive conversations which have been rare in recent years.

8. CCK has asked me to go with him on overnight trip to Quemoy about Nov 10 which should give opportunity for further probing.

Hummel

---

[4] Telegram 463 to Taipei, October 30, authorized Hummel to reply along the lines he suggested, except that it did not say the Ambassador would have special instructions from the President or Secretary of State. (Ibid., POL CHINAT–US)

---

109. Memorandum From Gordon Chase of the National Security Council Staff to the President's Special Assistant for National Security Affairs (Bundy)[1]

Washington, November 3, 1965.

SUBJECT

ChiRep

1. Attached is a cable from USUN[2] which recommends that if the substantive vote on ChiRep looks intolerably close (as we get nearer to it), we not take a chance on losing. Instead, we should avoid the vote on

---

[1] Source: Johnson Library, National Security File, Country File, United Nations, Chinese Representation, 10/65. Secret.

[2] Telegram 1734 from USUN, November 2.

substance (which would be politically disastrous if we lose—even if we win on the "important question") and put up a resolution designed to shift the issue into a study committee.

2. State feels that USUN is excessively jumpy on ChiRep and intends to instruct USUN that we will proceed as already agreed. Among other things, State believes that we will win on the substantive question and that USUN is over-estimating the psychological losses involved even if we do have to take the "important question" route. Moreover, if anybody now gets wind of the idea that we are thinking of a study committee (and it would get out), we would improve our chances of getting to the intolerably close vote that USUN fears.[3]

GC

---

[3] A note in Bundy's handwriting on the source text reads, "Let State handle it. McGB."

---

110.   Memorandum From the Joint Chiefs of Staff to Secretary of Defense McNamara[1]

JCSM–825–65   Washington, November 16, 1965.

SUBJECT

GRC Proposal for Landings on Mainland China

1.   Reference is made to a memorandum by the Assistant Secretary of Defense (ISA), I–26555/65, dated 13 October 1965, subject as above, which requested the position of the Joint Chiefs of Staff with regard to a proposed concept for Government of the Republic of China (GRC) landings on mainland China which was submitted to the Secretary of Defense by GRC Minister of Defense Chiang Ching-kuo on 22 September 1965.[2]

2.   The proposed concept depends for its success on massive US naval, air, and logistic support and large-scale popular uprisings and

---

[1] Source: Washington National Records Center, RG 330, OASD/ISA Files: FRC 70 A 3717, 381 China, Rep of. Secret. Filed as an attachment to a December 20 letter from Deputy Assistant Secretary of Defense for International Security Affairs Alvin Friedman to Fearey.

[2] Chiang's proposal and the ISA memorandum are cited in footnote 2, Document 104.

defections once a landing has been accomplished. The use of US air and naval forces, as proposed, in a cover role only, without air and naval strikes on mainland targets, is unrealistic. The GRC has only a limited capability to strike airfields in south China. A concept which commits US forces to protecting the invasion force against Chinese Communist air and naval attacks without being permitted to strike the supporting bases is militarily unsound. Further, available intelligence provides no evidence that the mainland population would support a GRC invasion. Therefore, there appears to be no possibility of successfully executing the concept as proposed.

3. The timing and the circumstances of the proposal by the GRC Minister of Defense and the fact that it was submitted as a matter for discussion and not as an operational proposal mark it as a vehicle for increasing the scope and volume of US–GRC consultations. However, US involvement in a comprehensive bilateral study of a GRC offensive concept requiring US logistic, air, and naval support would imply a degree of US interest and encouragement to the project greater than warranted by the facts.

4. On the other hand, there are features of the concept which lead to discussion and consultation without implying US commitment. These include:

a. Concepts and strategies for dealing with the Communist threat in Southeast Asia.
b. Intelligence assessments of the mainland China situation, with particular reference to the prospects for popular uprisings and defections.
c. Critique of GRC unilateral plans, with emphasis upon factors required for success which lie outside GRC resources and control.

5. Although various aspects of the proposed concept can profitably be discussed with the GRC, existing restrictions against joint planning should be maintained. Joint planning conceivably could be considered under conditions of expanded hostilities in Asia. However, the circumstances presently pertaining in Asia and those which attend consideration of the concept at hand do not now justify joint planning for operations against the mainland.

6. Consultations concerning the proposed concept and related matters should do much to satisfy President Chiang Kai-shek that his views and experience are being given due consideration by the United States. Such consultations should serve to maintain the GRC as a fully cooperating partner rather than as a course of potential disruption to our policies and objectives in Asia. If discussions were limited to those aspects of the concept indicated above, the existing US–GRC "Blue Lion" Committee would appear to be the most appropriate forum for carrying

on these consultations, as well as conducting critiques of GRC unilateral plans.

7. In summary, it is the position of the Joint Chiefs of Staff that:

a. There is no apparent possibility of successfully executing the concept as proposed.

b. The United States should not engage in a comprehensive bilateral study of the proposed concept for GRC landings on the mainland of China.

c. The United States should, by means of the "Blue Lion" Committee:

(1) Examine with the GRC the concepts and strategies for dealing with the Communist threat in Southeast Asia.

(2) Endeavor to arrive at agreed intelligence assessments of the mainland China situation, with particular reference to the prospects for popular uprisings and defections.

(3) Conduct critiques of GRC unilateral plans, with emphasis upon factors required for success which lie outside GRC resources and control.

d. These consultations should be conducted without committing the United States to involvement in planning for, encouragement of, or support for the proposed GRC landing on the mainland.

> For the Joint Chiefs of Staff:
> **A.H. Manhart**
> *Major General, USA*
> *Vice Director, Joint Staff*

---

111.   **Letter From the Deputy Assistant Secretary of State for Far Eastern Affairs (Berger) to the Consul General in Hong Kong (Rice)**[1]

Washington, November 24, 1965.

Dear Ed:

At the time of Chiang Ching-kuo's visit to Washington last September we discussed with him means of tuning up our machinery for mutual

---

[1] Source: Department of State, ROC Files: Lot 75 D 76, Blue Lion Consultations. Secret; Eyes Only.

consultations. We on our side felt this was necessary because of unmistakable indications that Chiang Kai-shek felt excluded from U.S. thinking on Viet-Nam and other Far Eastern policy problems. We found our thoughts on this confirmed by Chiang Ching-kuo's repeated mention while in Washington of the need for closer U.S.–GRC consultations on policy matters.

We told Chiang Ching-kuo that we would be ready to resume the Ambassadorial level consultations of the "Blue Lion" committee, of which I think you are aware from the time you were in Washington, when our new Ambassador arrives in Taipei. At the same time we made no suggestion that the frame of reference for "Blue Lion" be relaxed and we intend to adhere strictly to "Blue Lion" ground rules in future consultations. These ground rules are:

(a) that the Chinese planners should develop detailed plans for landing on the China coast on the assumption that uprisings had occurred on the mainland;

(b) that planning is to be based upon the GRC's *current* capabilities, without any additional matériel support or participation by U.S. forces;

(c) that completed plans would be reviewed by the U.S. side, which would make appropriate criticisms and suggestions to the GRC.

In general the purpose of these restrictions has been to obviate any participation by us in joint military planning with the GRC in connection with operations against the mainland.

One other proposal that we made to Chiang Ching-kuo was an exchange of intelligence appraisals of conditions on the mainland. We hoped in this way to stimulate more realistic thinking by the Chinese on the possibility that widespread dissidence on the mainland would permit a successful GRC counterattack against the Communists. As by-products we might also gain additional intelligence on the Communists and further insight into GRC thinking. There has been a continuing exchange of intelligence on the Communists [*less than 1 line of source text not declassified*] and the GRC on a piece-by-piece basis; however, there has not been the more searching and comprehensive type of intelligence exchange which we have in mind.

The plan is that CIA will produce a study which, after a review in the Department and in Defense, will be submitted to the Chinese; the Chinese will produce a similar study for our review. There might then be a meeting in which we and the Chinese would discuss our studies and compare notes as to conclusions. We think it would be helpful if someone from Hong Kong's political section could participate in such discussions and we have made this suggestion to Embassy Taipei for comment.

I would very much appreciate your own thoughts on this.[2] We wil
in any case see that you receive copies of all materials on mainland China
which are generated as a result of this exchange.

With all best wishes,

Sincerely,

Samuel D. Berger[3]

---

[2] Rice replied in a December 13 letter to Berger that he had "some qualms" about this.
Predicting that the Chinese Communists would hear of it, perhaps in a distorted form, he
commented, "Some may argue it would be useful to make the ChiComs believe we are
working with the GRC on plans for attacking the mainland, but I would consider this a
highly dubious and danger-fraught exercise."

[3] Printed from a copy that bears this typed signature.

---

112. Action Memorandum From the Assistant Secretary of State for Far Eastern Affairs (Bundy) to the Under Secretary of State (Ball)[1]

Washington, December 4, 1965.

SUBJECT

Proposed New Policy Initiatives for December 15 Warsaw Meeting

1. At the December 15 Warsaw meeting we propose to give the Chinese Communists clear warning of our intention to intensify our efforts in Vietnam with full realization of the possible consequences. To balance this strong warning we propose to say that it is incumbent upon both sides to take some steps away from a direct confrontation in the direction of a peaceful settlement. We propose to tell the Chinese that we are taking certain unilateral steps in this direction.

2. We suggest that present U.S. policy be modified to allow for the following new initiatives:

a. We would state *our readiness to admit Chinese journalists to the United Sates without reciprocity.* Our present policy is to issue validated

---

[1] Source: Department of State, Central Files, POL CHICOM–US. Confidential. Drafted by Dean.

passports to American newsmen and to press for either a formal or informal agreement on the exchange of newsmen. We have asked the Chinese Communists for such an exchange since 1959. Our efforts to secure an exchange are well known as is the Chinese refusal to agree. The offer to allow Chinese Communist journalists to come to the United States would almost certainly be rejected by the Communists, but when it became known we believe that this step would be welcomed by the American press community and the public as evidence of our desire to bring about an eventual exchange. In the unlikely event that the Chinese did accept such an acceptance would signal a major change in Peking's attitude towards the United States. We would not plan to publicize this offer until some time after the meeting.

b. Provided our travel package on doctors and scientists in the fields of public health and medicine is cleared in time for the talks, we propose telling the Chinese of the new travel regulations[2] and informing them of *our willingness to allow Chinese doctors and scientists in the same fields to come to the United States* as a reciprocal aspect of such a move. While we do not plan to publicize this reciprocal aspect, we envisage at some point it will have to be made clear that we would have no objection to reciprocal visits on the part of the Chinese. We are virtually certain that the Chinese under their present policy will reject visits of Americans and will refuse to allow Chinese to come to the United States.

c. We propose suggesting to the Chinese that *we jointly examine their charges of air and sea violations of their territory and attacks on Chinese vessels on the high seas.* If the Chinese were to accept, which is possible but unlikely, we would plan to examine with them in Warsaw each new charge. We would not plan to publicize this suggestion. It is unlikely the Chinese would reveal it to the press. If they did, it would enhance our own image of reason and responsibility.

3. I believe that these moves are important to indicate to the Chinese that we still seek to avoid a major confrontation. The moves suggested will not be interpreted as a sign of weakness since our power position in the Far East is steadily growing. But if the Chinese eventually decide to look for a way out, this approach may ease the way.

4. In the event we wish to make public the record of this talk, it would prove that we warned the Chinese of the dangers of a major confrontation and that we took several unilateral steps to hold out the possibility of an alternate solution.

---

[2] On December 29 the Department of State announced the relaxation of travel controls to permit doctors and scientists in the fields of public health and medicine to travel to countries under travel restrictions for purposes directly related to their professional responsibilities. For the text of the announcement, see Department of State *Bulletin,* January 17, 1966, p. 90.

5. Additionally, I believe that we should maintain a policy of firmness but transfer to Peking the opprobrium of being intransigent and hostile. Chinese rejection of the U.S. moves proposed above would serve to isolate them still further from world opinion.

6. Clearances for these three proposals have been obtained in draft from P, L, SCA, CU and SCI and are shown on the attached telegram.

7. The telegram containing instructions for the Warsaw talks is attached (Tab B) for your approval.[3] It may be advisable to send the instructions for attached translation purposes before a decision is reached on the policy decisions listed above. In the telegram, you will note that it is recommended:

1. That you approve a modification in present policy to permit Ambassador Gronouski to say that we will allow Chinese Communist journalists to visit the United States without an exchange agreement.

2. That you authorize Ambassador Gronouski to affirm our willingness to allow Chinese doctors and scientists in the fields of public health and medicine to come to the United States as a reciprocal aspect of our move to permit similar professional men to travel to mainland China.

3. That you authorize Ambassador Gronouski to suggest to the Chinese Communists that we jointly investigate their charges of air and sea violations of their territories and attacks on Chinese vessels on the high seas.[4]

---

[3] The draft telegram, not attached, was sent to Warsaw as telegram 863, December 10. It stated that it was an uncleared preliminary draft and that final approval would be sent subsequently. (Department of State, Central Files, POL CHICOM–US) Telegram 873 to Warsaw, December 11, cleared by McGeorge Bundy, approved the instructions in telegram 863 with some revisions. (Ibid.)

[4] The source text bears no indication of approval or disapproval.

113.   Memorandum From the Deputy Director for Intelligence of the Central Intelligence Agency (Cline) to the Director of Central Intelligence (McCone)[1]

Washington, December 6, 1965.

SUBJECT

Chinese Nationalist Military Forces vis-à-vis Vietnam

1.   One element in the balance of military forces in Southeast Asia is seldom mentioned, for reasons I find difficult to understand. This element is the half-million or so Chinese Nationalist ground forces supported by qualitatively good though small air forces and naval forces. The Chinese Nationalists are reasonably well trained and equipped and are highly motivated against the Chinese Communists and in favor of US objectives in Southeast Asia. They have argued strongly for an assault on the South China coast on a scale that would threaten logistic lines to Vietnam and probably would supply a considerable number of ground forces for employment in South Vietnam if requested to do so by the US.

2.   Reluctance to use this Free World military asset stems from fears of *provoking* or at least providing a public excuse for Chinese Communist intervention in Vietnam. Now that some Chinese Communist troops (albeit probably logistic ones) are already in Vietnam, this nicety on our part may be somewhat anachronistic. In any case, I think we should do some serious thinking about when, if ever, and how we might employ Chinese Nationalist forces.

3.   My own recommendations would be:

a.   do some contingency planning jointly with the GRC for landing Chinese Nationalist forces in South China, since this will undoubtedly leak and frighten the Chinese Communists as it did in 1962; this is probably the greatest deterrent (short of US nuclear attack) we can bring to bear to keep Communist China from intervening directly and massively in Vietnam.

b.   add realism to this contingency planning exercise by accepting a 10,000 man Special Forces unit from Taiwan to engage in search-and-destroy operations in the highlands area of South Vietnam.

c.   in fact decide and work out realistic plans for a Chinese Nationalist landing on the South China coast (supported by US Navy and US Air Force elements) when and if Chinese Communist military commitments of troops to North Vietnam pass the 50,000 mark or result in Chinese Communist combat troop contacts with US forces in South Vietnam or friendly forces in Laos or Thailand.

---

[1] Source: Johnson Library, National Security File, Country File, China, Vol. XIII. Secret. Sent to Bundy with a January 11, 1966, covering note from Cline.

4. Somehow or other the admittedly delicate politics of using Chinese Nationalist forces always suppresses serious inquiry into this subject. My own feeling is that the kind of Communist threat we face in Vietnam makes this particular political delicacy a luxury the US can ill afford. If the Chinese Communists are forcing us into a war of attrition on the ground in Southeast Asia, we should feel free to use Chinese Nationalist troops against them.

Ray S. Cline

---

114.   Telegram From the Embassy in Poland to the Department of State[1]

Warsaw, December 16, 1965, 1527Z.

1003. Gronouski–Wang talks. Deptels 863 and 873; Embtel 998.[2]

1. 128th meeting. Prior to meeting I was introduced to Ambassador Wang and his staff. Wang regretted that he had been unable to accept my earlier invitation to have an informal conversation and tea after the meeting. He said he really had another diplomatic engagement so he could not have tea but suggested that we might get together at another time. Wang took this opportunity to mention that there had been a lot of "rumors" about the Warsaw talks lately. I assured him that neither I nor my staff would divulge contents of talks. It possible that Wang made this observation because of press commentary about my visit to Paris prior to talks or because he thought we might have used his acceptance of my invitation as basis for more "rumors".

2. Wang started meeting with some polite phrases of welcome. In brief review of talks he said Chinese government has always stood for peaceful settlement of Sino-US dispute through negotiations and that his side would continue to take positive and reasonable attitude towards peaceful settlement. He soon marred this auspicious start by expressing

---

[1] Source: Department of State, Central Files, POL CHICOM–US. Confidential; Priority; Limdis. Repeated to Hong Kong. A copy of the telegram, omitting paragraph 11, was sent to the President. (Johnson Library , National Security File, Country File, Poland, Gronouski–Wang Talks)

[2] Regarding telegrams 863 and 873 to Warsaw, see footnote 3, Document 112. Telegram 998 from Warsaw, December 15, reported briefly on the meeting. (Department of State, Central Files, POL CHICOM–US)

hope that I would persuade USG to change its wrong position and give up its aggression against China.

3. Wang's attitude throughout the meeting apparently was milder than his previous behavior. He read 20-minute long list of alleged US provocations in quiet restrained voice. He did not raise his voice when registering his government's strong protest and serious warning concerning these incidents.

4. Wang listened attentively to my statement. His interest was obviously aroused by our offer to jointly investigate Chinese claims of Chinese fishing boat incidents on high seas, but he later rejected this initiative. He also finessed our offer concerning Chinese journalists and our statement concerning validated passports for doctors and scientists in the fields of public health and medicine by labeling my statements about doctors and journalists as old problems that could not be solved until problem of Taiwan was solved.

5. Wang only became heated when, during his rebuttal, he asked what threat Chinese fishing vessels which had been attacked on the high seas offered to the US. He asked, "what right have your planes to dive and strafe. . . . We have right to fish on high seas. What threat can such small fishing boats pose? How can they prevent you from your rescue work? What right have you to kill these fishermen?"

6. Wang was careful not to make any new commitments concerning Viet-Nam. However, he repeatedly stressed Peking's firm intention to maintain its support for Hanoi. He emphasized China's defensive rather than aggressive intent and said they would fight to defend themselves. Unlike last session, Wang did not dwell at any length on opposition of American public to administration policy in Viet-Nam.

7. I believe our position at this meeting demonstrated our concern about Viet-Nam and our desire to move towards a peaceful settlement. We also indicated reasonable flexibility in our efforts to obtain some meaningful contact with the Chinese. In both my opening statement and in my rebuttal I asked Wang if his side doubted our sincerity about unconditional negotiations why didn't they put us to the test?

8. I was impressed by inflexibility of Chinese position and their refusal to give any indication of willingness to resolve the Viet-Nam crisis or anything else on any terms other than their own. I believe that others who listened to the talks will also get same impression. In this context our SY officer has tape recorded this session of talks which were broadcast by Polish transmitter concealed in or near the meeting room. (I understand our British colleagues were also aware of the transmitter in the meeting room. We may find that others also listened in.) PZPR Central Committee Plenum, now in session, may have received prompt report of our talks. If so, I suspect they also must have been impressed by our attempts reach some agreement and by Chinese inflexibility.

9. I was also impressed by Wang's evident belief that US really was hostile and had aggressive intentions towards China. He was particularly eloquent on these points during his rebuttal when he was free wheeling and not reading from his text. He appeared genuinely to believe US harbors aggressive intentions towards Communist China and inter alia twice cited US assistance to Chiang "gang" in slaughtering millions of Chinese as proof of US hostility.

10. Wang seemed to be trying to drag out length of meeting by reading long statement on ChiCom position on disarmament (largely a repeat of previous stand). At end of meeting I suggested that because of critical situation Viet-Nam, we meet next January 19. After some discussion I agreed to March 16 date. Possible that delay until March 16 may be further evidence Chinese desire to extend interval between talks but we subsequently learned Ambassador Wang and interpreter Chien will leave before Christmas for 2 months home leave plus 20 days travel time.

11. I note that Dept instructions sent only to Warsaw. Dept may wish to repeat them to interested posts together with this telegram and Embtel 998. In briefing GRC both in Dept and at Taipei suggest use of paras 5 through 17 of Deptel 863 with changes in Deptel 873, plus Wang's statements our 998, omitting Wang's comments about joint investigation para 5 and doctors and journalists para 10.[3]

Gronouski

---

[3] Paragraph 5 of telegram 998 stated that Wang rejected the offer of joint investigations of Chinese fishing boat incidents. Paragraph 10 reported that Wang said concerning doctors and journalists, "We have repeatedly made clear our position—no problems can be settled until major problem (Taiwan) settled."

---

115.   Memorandum of Conversation[1]

Taipei, December 29, 1965.

PARTICIPANTS

President Chiang Kai-shek
General Earle G. Wheeler, CJCS

1. I called on President Chiang Kai-shek on the afternoon of 29 December 1965. The conversation lasted from 1705 hours until 1855

---

[1] Source: Johnson Library, National Security File, Country File, China, Vol V. Secret. Wheeler sent the memorandum of conversation to the President under a January 11 covering letter. (Ibid.)

hours. The conversations were continued both before and after a dinner which the President gave for me that evening; however, nothing of substance arose additional to the areas covered during the afternoon call. Chinese present were: President Chiang Kai-shek; Minister of Defense Chiang Ching-kuo; Admiral Ni Yue-si, Chief of the General Staff; and General Yu Pak-Chuan, Vice Chief of the General Staff; Mr. James Shen, Interpreter. On the U.S. side, in addition to General Wheeler, were Chargé d'Affaires and Ambassador Ad Interim A. W. Hummel, Jr.; Vice Admiral William E. Gentner, Commander, Taiwan Defense Command; and Major General D. B. Johnson, Chief, Military Assistance Aid Group, Republic of China.

2.   This long conversation was conducted in a friendly atmosphere and the President was calm and courteous although frank and direct (I understand from Mr. Hummel unusually so). Moreover, the President repeated several times that he desired that I convey his views to President Johnson, Secretary Rusk and Secretary McNamara.

3.   After the usual amenities and serving of tea, the President questioned me closely regarding our strategy in Vietnam. I responded by quoting President Johnson as to the limited nature of our political objectives (no territorial ambitions; no bases; want predator nations of SE Asia to permit their neighbors to seek their own destinies unhindered by outside forces) and our consonant military strategy in South Vietnam and North Vietnam. The President stated that not to go into North Vietnam did not make military sense; however, he understood the political reasons behind this American decision. The fact is that the Americans do not recognize the North Vietnamese as merely puppets of the Chinese Communists; the ChiComs are your enemy and must not be left untouched if there is to be a lasting settlement in Vietnam. You are already fighting Communist China by proxy; indeed, you are fighting forces trained and supported by the ChiComs. There are Chinese troops now in North Vietnam. It is time for a basic plan to be formulated to deal with the ChiComs; such a plan is entirely lacking. Some time ago MOD Chiang Ching-kuo gave the U.S. Government a plan for seizing and holding the five southwest provinces of China, thereby severing the lines of communication by which the Communists supply the North Vietnamese. To date, I have received no reaction to this proposal.

4.   I replied that we knew there are Chinese railroad engineer units in North Vietnam and, probably, some anti-aircraft units. The MOD had told me that electronic intercepts revealed four infantry regiments had been deployed there also. [*less than 1 line of text not declassified*] As to the plan for invading mainland China, General Yu had briefed me earlier that afternoon on the concept. The requirements for such an operation were very large, as I had pointed out to the MOD the needed naval and air effort would be great. The President then made the following points:

a. I am convinced you cannot achieve any lasting conclusion of the Vietnam problem until you have settled the problem of Communist China;

b. In reaching this settlement you should use local troops to a much greater extent. You should not send U.S. troops into North Vietnam or Thailand. You should think of ways to use GRC forces, and the best way to use GRC forces is the plan I have proposed to seize and hold the five southwest provinces of China. This plan would require no U.S. ground forces; GRC ground forces could do the job and effectively sever ChiCom support to the trouble spots in Southeast Asia.

c. We know that the people of the mainland would welcome our forces. If you were to use one-half the power you are using in South Vietnam and help put GRC troops on the mainland, you could solve your Southeast Asian problems. The ChiComs are in no degree as strong as the Germans were in Europe; you would not need to involve yourselves on anything like the scale of Normandy.

d. We should make greater efforts to arrive at common understandings and common plans for action. In dealing with Asian problems, you should consult with Asians more than you do. In dealing with the Chinese Communists, you should listen more to the GRC; we have knowledge and experience which could help you.

e. I am speaking very frankly and honestly as to my convictions. I am speaking as a long-time friend of the United States, not exaggerating here and holding back a little there.

f. Please inform President Johnson, Secretary Rusk and Secretary McNamara of my views.

5. To the foregoing statements, which were not delivered in that order or in one declaration, I replied substantially as follows:

a. The planning by the GRC for invasion of mainland China should, as already discussed, be continued. I would hope that we would continue to be informed.

b. The reason I was in Taiwan was to consult with GRC officials, to attempt to see Asia through Asian eyes. I pointed out that the forthcoming visit of Vice President Humphrey would give the President the opportunity to present his views directly to the second-ranking elected official of the United States.

c. I had no doubt but that he was speaking from the heart; no one who heard him could think otherwise.

d. I would, of course, convey his views to President Johnson, Secretary Rusk and Secretary McNamara as he requested.

6. *Comment:* An interesting sidelight on my conversations with President Chiang Kai-shek is provided by the context of my earlier meeting that day with Minister of Defense Chiang Ching-kuo and certain senior officers of the Chinese General Staff. This meeting lasted one hour and twenty minutes. The greater portion of that time was devoted to a general discussion of the situation in Vietnam, deficiencies in GRC forces and a discussion of Chinese proposals for additional military assistance in critical areas such as modern radars, submarines, and an accelerated F–5 program. Only about ten minutes was consumed by a briefing by

General Yu, Vice Chief of the General Staff, on the plan for the invasion of mainland China to seize the five southwestern provinces and sever Chi-Com lines of communications into North Vietnam. General Yu made the remarkable statement that "99 per cent of the population of the five southwestern provinces" would adhere to Chiang Kai-shek's cause. Other than that, I gained the distinct impression that the presentation was pro forma and that the military had a far better appreciation of the difficulties of transportation and air support required for such a considerable operation. At any rate, when I pointed out the logistic and other problems involved, very little rebuttal was attempted by the Chinese officers except for the implication that I overestimated the difficulties and underestimated the degree to which the Chinese people would welcome Chiang Kai-shek's return to the mainland of China. On the other hand, President Chiang Kai-shek made two demands for action in straight forward language. These were: (a) An explicit request for the United States to put GRC forces ashore to reconquer the five southwestern provinces; and (b) a complaint that the U.S. Government fails to consult him with sufficient frequency or to heed his advice when it is offered.

7. *Recommendations:* If one considers the age and background of President Chiang Kai-shek, his remarks are perfectly understandable. He probably recognizes that the Vietnamese War provides him with his last opportunity to return to mainland China with any hope of establishing and maintaining himself there. Moreover, he probably believes that if he were consulted more frequently he would gain influence in U.S. Government Councils which, over time, would lead to the adoption of the plan for the invasion which he advocates. In view of the fact that his military staff continues unilateral planning for the invasion, keeping our Embassy and our military personnel in Taiwan informed, we can adopt one of two tactics in dealing with him. First, we can tell him frankly that an invasion supported by United States forces is out of the question at this time; or, second, we can continue our present posture of being interested but uncommitted onlookers. I, myself, advocate the first course of action, although it would have to be done tactfully and perhaps sweetened by some addition of military assistance to assuage his pride. As to additional consultation, I believe it would be in the best interests of continued amity and cooperation for the U.S. Government to consult with President Chiang Kai-shek frequently on many aspects of Asian problems. After all, we would not be committed to accept his views anymore than the views of other Asian leaders whom we do consult on a regular basis.

Earle G. Wheeler
Chairman
Joint Chiefs of Staff

116. Telegram From the White House Situation Room to President Johnson in Texas[1]

Washington, January 2, 1966, 1745Z.

CAP 66018. For the President from the Vice President. Report on conversation with President Chiang Kai-shek[2] and Foreign Minister Yi Tong-won of Republic of China; Prime Minister Chung Il-kwon and President Park of Korea.

1. The meeting with Chiang Kai-shek went about as predicted, in that he stressed the need for the United States to recognize that the real enemy in Southeast Asia was not the Viet Cong or North Vietnam, but was Communist China. He stressed as he has before that we could not expect to match Communist manpower in Asia, and that it would be a mistake to think that sophisticated weapons could replace manpower, the objective should be to utilize Asian manpower with American logistics support. He again stressed that the Soviet Union would not intervene in a situation in which a civil war would be created by a Chinese "return to the mainland," on the grounds that the USSR commitment was in the event of a U.S. attack. He would not go into detail as to the plans for returning to the mainland, or for further cooperation with the United States in combatting Communism in Asia, but said that if we can come to a consensus on the question of who is the real enemy, we can work out such details.

Rather surprisingly Chiang commented that your peace offensive was a wise and effective effort. He also commented that the Russian moves were especially significant, and should be watched very closely.

As all Asian leaders have stated, there has been a measure of concern about the U.S. intentions in South Vietnam stirred by the peace program. But I reassured him strongly that we had no intention of seeking a peace that left our friends unprotected. I parried his question as to what you would do if the peace effort failed, by saying only that this was a matter for the highest policy level, and would of course be up to you to decide. But we would undoubtedly take all measures necessary to defeat the aggression.

---

[1] Source: Johnson Library, National Security File, International File, Vice President Trip, Far East, 12/27/65. Top Secret; Exdis. A handwritten "L" on the source text indicates that the President saw it.

[2] Vice President Humphrey met with Chiang Kai-shek on January 1. A record of the meeting by Special Assistant to the President Jack Valenti is ibid., President's Office File, Valenti, Jack, Memoranda of Conversations, Japan, the Philippines, Taiwan, Korea, December 1965–January 1966. Another, sent in telegram 722 from Taipei, January 3, is ibid., National Security File, Country File, China, Vol. V. A January 5 memorandum from Humphrey to Johnson pertaining to his visit to Taipei is ibid., NSC Files, NSC Meetings, Vol. 3, Tab 37.

Chiang looks rather old, but very healthy, with ruddy complexion and obviously in full command of himself. There are no signs of senility that I could detect. He, of course, asked particularly after your health and asked me to extend to you his best wishes. The conversation was extremely friendly and cordial, and there was no effort to press for decisions, nor any hint of chagrin that he has not been consulted lately. I gave him your warm personal greetings, as I did to the Chinese people both on arrival and departure at the airport.

[Here follows a report of the Vice President's conversations in Korea.]

---

117. Telegram From the Embassy in the Republic of China to the Department of State[1]

Taipei, January 12, 1966, 1020Z.

761. Ref: Deptel 707.[2]

1. Embassy has been kept informed by military [*less than 1 line of source text not declassified*].

2. We know of no order such as that reported UPI story.

3. Jan 10 depth charge attack by GRC Navy on alleged sonar contact in straits is evaluated by US naval authorities as unlikely to be against real target but is rated as "possible". Sonar contact reportedly made at depth of 33 fathoms (198 feet) which is beyond depth ChiCom subs likely to be maneuvering. COMUSTDC advises no US or known friendly subs in vicinity.

4. There is no question that the GRC has lost prestige in this and other incidents. President Chiang is reportedly provoked and has directed Minister Chiang and Admiral Ni to conduct an investigation into the HU–16 incident.

---

[1] Source: Department of State, Central Files, POL 27 CHICOM–CHINAT. Secret; Priority; Limdis. Repeated to Hong Kong and to CINCPAC for POLAD.

[2] Telegram 707 to Taipei, January 11, reported that the Department had received reports of a GRC Navy attack on January 10 on a suspected Chinese Communist submarine in the Taiwan Strait and a January 10 UPI report that President Chiang, angered by the Communist downing of a plane carrying defectors, had ordered a full military alert and ordered ships and planes in the Strait to shoot on sight. It requested Embassy's views. (Ibid.)

5. On day after shooting down of amphibian, Air Force C in C Gen Hsu approached C in C PACAF General Harris (who was visiting Taiwan) and ATF–13 Commander, General Wilson. Hsu indicated continued ChiCom provocations such as the destruction of the amphibian and recent ship sinking would require a "change in GRC policy". This was later developed as meaning GRC would have to take reprisal actions. Hsu cited knocking out a radar site and harassment of ships, as possible examples of limited actions intended. Both US officers declined to consider proposal and said this sort of action must be taken up at govt to govt level.

6. Embassy reasonably confident that GRC does not plan unilateral military action at this time. Chiang Ching-kuo had direct request for prior consultation from Asst Secretary Bundy in Washington in September, and indirectly from me in November.[3] He has clearly stated [*less than 1 line of source text not declassified*] that military actions (as opposed to intelligence raids) will be consulted upon before execution in accordance US–GRC Defense Treaty. We also have independent confirmation that Ching-kuo is saying same thing to MND officers. General Hsu démarche, as well as GRC Chief of General Staff Ni démarche to COMUSTDC Admiral Gentner Dec 17 (reported separately) are also indications GRC intention to consult.

Hummel

---

[3] A briefing paper of June 22, 1966, prepared for Rusk's July visit to Taipei, states that on November 27, 1965, after intelligence reports indicated impending GRC military actions against the mainland, Hummel, acting on instruction, emphasized to Vice Foreign Minister Sampson Shen the U.S. expectation of consultation before any such operations were undertaken. (Ibid., Conference Files: Lot 67 D 305, CF 59) Further documentation on this episode is ibid., INR/IL Historical Files, Country Files, China, 1965.

118.   National Intelligence Estimate[1]

NIE 13–5–66   Washington, January 13, 1966.

COMMUNIST CHINA'S ECONOMIC PROSPECTS

The Problem

This estimate focuses on the two factors which dominate the economic scene in Communist China: a huge and rapidly growing population living close to the margin of bare subsistence, and the regime's determination to invest in costly weapons programs.

Note

We noted in NIE 13–64, "Economic Prospects for Communist China" (28 January 1964), that the information available for an appraisal of the Chinese Communist economy is fragmentary, uneven in coverage, and uncertain as to reliability. There has been no significant improvement; although open-source information is currently supplying somewhat more data on production trends, these data are still spotty and consist mainly of percentage increases over an unknown base. A major intelligence collection effort is focused on this target, and continuing efforts are made to increase its effectiveness.

Conclusions

A. Communist China has managed in the past five years to pull the economy back from the brink of catastrophe and has made progress in its programs to acquire modern weapons.

B. The Vietnam conflict has not yet added serious strains to the Chinese economy. However, a sustained increase in the level of fighting in Vietnam, if accompanied by a comparable rise in Chinese assistance as well as significant defensive measures within China itself, would add greatly to China's economic problems.

C. In any event, the Chinese economy faces slow growth, at best, over the next few years. The primary causes will be lagging agricultural production and a burgeoning population, but these problems will be complicated by the ambitious military program and by the inefficiencies brought on by Peking's ideology. In agriculture, despite somewhat

---

[1] Source: Department of State, INR/EAP Files: Lot 90 D 110. Secret; Controlled Dissem. According to a note on the cover sheet, the estimate was submitted by Director of Central Intelligence Raborn and prepared by the CIA and the intelligence organizations of the Departments of State and Defense, and the National Security Agency. All members of the U.S Intelligence Board concurred on January 28 except the AEC and FBI representatives, who abstained on the grounds that the subject was outside their jurisdiction.

greater support in the last few years, the regime is still not doing enough to achieve the yields necessary for sustained economic growth. Since Peking's birth control program will have little early effect, population pressure on the food supply will increase over the next decade. This narrow food margin makes the economy highly vulnerable to bad crop conditions. Moreover, growing competition for resources in China's sluggish and nonresilient economy seems likely gradually to undermine economic stability.

D. In the face of even a critical food emergency, the present regime would probably make only grudging and piecemeal cuts in its military programs. Although China will continue to be a dangerous and growing military threat, we believe that some future Chinese leadership will be forced to a fundamental concentration on China's economic problems.

[Here follows the Discussion portion of the estimate.]

---

119. Telegram From the Embassy in the Republic of China to the Department of State[1]

Taipei, January 25, 1966, 1040Z.

797. Ref: A. Deptel 728;[2] B. Depcirtel 1387, 1390, Deptel 741.[3]

1. Yesterday evening Jan 24 I delivered messages contained reftels to Chiang Ching-kuo. Meeting lasted over one hour. I took along COM-USTDC VAdmiral Gentner.

2. Would not have been advisable follow instructions Ref B which stated I should try to convey substance Pres. Chiang, because to do so would have invited reiteration of Great Torch Five (GT–5) as solution for Vietnam. I considered it important, therefore, to deliver message Ref A first, and decided to deliver Ref B to Chiang Ching-kuo at same time, making clear that two instructions not directly related.

3. CCK showed considerable disappointment and irritation. Stated that GRC had tried to make helpful suggestion in honest belief

---

[1] Source: Department of State, Central Files, POL CHINAT–US. Secret; Immediate; Limdis. Passed to the White House.

[2] Telegram 728 to Taipei, January 19, transmitted U.S. comments on the proposal that Chiang Ching-kuo gave to McNamara on September 22 and instructed Hummel to convey them to Chiang Ching-kuo. (Ibid.)

[3] Circular telegrams 1387 and 1390, January 22 and 23, and telegram 741 to Taipei, January 23; not printed. (Ibid., POL 27 VIET S)

that US has no way to solve Vietnam without solving ChiCom problem. Said it is not good that US refuses to discuss GT–5 and stops the planning; it will have bad effect on GRC morale and won't help USG. Said US is making mistake, and that someday such a plan might be used, even if not now, and that planning now for the eventual contingency would be useful.

4. Gentner and I several times pointed out that we wish to broaden Blue Lion consultations to include discussion of concepts and strategies, even though we do not wish to discuss "plans". CCK replied that he understood US position very well. Said that if USG unwilling even consider this kind of operation, in light USG view of weakness number one (Ref A, para 4–A)[4] there was little point in continuing discussion.

5. I pointed out that exchange of intelligence appraisals should continue since it had bearing on weakness number two (para 4–B), but CCK said he saw little point in this. When I asked if he did not wish to continue plans for exchange of appraisals, he seemed to reconsider. Said that everyone should know that there could be no significant rebellions on mainland without outside pressures and without a place to defect to. Said when time came and GRC forces landed with US backing there would be defections. I agreed that we would not expect actual rebellion or defections at present time, but that intelligence appraisals might show some indications which could be used in estimating likelihood of defections. CCK doubted there could be such indications, but insisted that defections would occur when mainland attacked. Cited recent IL–28 and LCM defections as evidence and pointed out that both had occurred even in absence of battle conditions. Stated that in wartime many more defections inevitable. Said that ChiComs obviously fear their own people and that GRC is best judge of state of mind of people on mainland.

6. On para 5, CCK brushed aside as useless any further discussions of unilateral GRC plans in Blue Lion framework. Said that without US help no plan could succeed. Said that while GRC does not want or need US ground forces would obviously need other help. Therefore unilateral planning is pointless.

7. He repeated at some length arguments we have heard before. Said that ChiComs only fear strength, and that US show of weakness only encourages aggressive acts. Said that ChiComs have stated that US forces total only 2 million, which must be divided into half million for US itself, half million for eventual use Vietnam, half million for other areas, leaving only half million for use on mainland China, which would not be nearly enough and which ChiComs do not fear.

---

[4] The statement in paragraph 4 of the two fundamental weaknesses of the plan is similar to the statement in paragraph 3 of telegram 762, Document 120.

8. CCK asked if US answer to Great Torch Five was related to present Vietnam peace offensive. I repeated my earlier statement that two instructions coincidental, and pointed out that answer on GT–5 was result of Washington examination over several months. GT–5 and peace offensive related only in general sense that they both involve Vietnam, and that US is not at war with ChiComs and therefore cannot consider the air strikes against mainland that would be necessary under GT–5.

9. CCK said he would convey request for views on Vietnam (Ref B) to his govt, but said GRC had already given its views on recommending GT–5 as only long-term solution to Vietnam problem.

10. CCK calm and controlled throughout, but obviously disappointed and irritated that proposal which GRC had hoped would open door to joint consideration of future contingencies had been turned down flatly. He came close to saying that exchange of intelligence appraisals useless, and he did say he saw no point in further Blue Lion plans. He brushed aside suggestion for broadening scope of Blue Lion to include discussion of concepts and strategies. How much of this was quick reaction that will be reconsidered later, we will have to wait and see.

11. At lunch today Jan 25 which CCK hosted in honor of Senator Miller and Congressman Dorn CCK got me aside and said he had not yet reported to Pres. Chiang. Said that when he did he wanted to be sure he was conveying accurate summary of USG reaction, and asked if I could furnish informal written summary. He said next day would be soon enough, and went on to say he thought we should continue discussions these topics. I replied I would try to furnish written document, perhaps morning of Jan 26, and that I thought it very important for us to continue discussions.

12. Believe that CCK may now be worried about Gimo reaction, and hoping for some softening of language Reftel A which would minimize reaction. Also probably wants to be sure he is accurately conveying US intentions, although his aide and interpreter Col. Pat Wen took notes, and there should be no confusion.

13. Recommend that Dept send me soonest text of summary of Ref A which could be passed as informal document, unheaded, undated and unsigned. If possible summary should contain insertion of words "at this time" in appropriate spots, and should amplify para 7 to indicate what is meant by broadening of Blue Lion concept.

14. We are still faced with strong advisability, if not necessity, of having some future contingencies in mind which we can talk to GRC about. So far our responses, when viewed from GRC perspective, have been entirely negative except for assurances of future discussions of general strategy, and exchange of intelligence on mainland. CCK's reaction shows that the day is past when we can give GRC sensation of being con-

sulted and having its plans seriously considered without some demonstration of "give" in US views. Blue Lion framework served very useful purpose in previous years, but is inadequate now.

15. Believe Dept not willing to consider discussions of specific contingencies under which GRC forces might be used, and I also believe this is wise. However would be very helpful if we can say something along following lines: "Vietnam situation still contains several unused US options for further US pressure and suasion. Until we have explored these we are unwilling to consider any significant action against Chi-Coms, even through agency of GRC. At some later time, after more US options have been exercised and if there is still no hope for a settlement in Vietnam, we would re-examine our premises. In meantime we are still anxious to exchange views on present situation, and to discuss basic concepts and strategies."

16. This telegram not repeated info CINCPAC because of exdis Pinta slug on some references. Dept please repeat appropriate portions.

Hummel

---

120. Telegram From the Department of State to the Embassy in the Republic of China[1]

Washington, January 28, 1966, 4:30 p.m.

762. Ref A—Embtel 797 (being repeated CINCPAC); B—Deptel 728.[2]

1. Following is summary requested Ref. A of guidance contained Ref. B for conveyance in writing to Chiang Ching-kuo:

2. *Begin summary.* The concept to seize five southwest provinces of China which Minister of National Defense Chiang Ching-kuo left with Secretary McNamara last September has been studied with the greatest care by the highest military authorities in the United States Government.

---

[1] Source: Department of State, Central Files, POL CHINAT–US. Secret; Immediate; Limdis. Drafted by Bennett; cleared by Fearey, Jacobson, Smith in CIA, Friedman and Admiral Blouin in DOD/ISA, and Colonel Reichner in J–5; and approved by Berger. Repeated to CINCPAC and CINCPAC for POLAD.

[2] See Document 119 and footnote 2 thereto.

Although the terms of reference for Blue Lion consultations do not provide for U.S. critique of military plans which are based on the assumption of U.S. participation or matériel support, this fact did not prevent us from giving it the most serious consideration, because we value the views of the Republic of China and because we recognize the need for our two governments to exchange views at the highest level.

3. Regarding the feasibility of the concept, which appears to us the basis of Great Torch 5, the plan in our view has two fundamental weaknesses:

(a) It contemplates a commitment of U.S. forces to protect a GRC invasion force against Chinese Communist air and naval attack but not U.S. air strikes against the supporting Chinese Communist bases. We regard this as militarily unsound. On the other hand, air strikes against the mainland would initiate war between the U.S. and Communist China, which we are not prepared to do.

(b) Intelligence on mainland conditions available to US intelligence authorities is deficient in evidence that the population—or even a substantial portion—of the five southwest provinces of mainland China would rise in support of a GRC invasion. The concept proposed appears to be impractical without such support and concomitant military defections to the GRC. We therefore conclude that there is at present no possibility of executing Great Torch 5 under such conditions.

4. We continue to stand ready to examine and prepare critiques of GRC unilateral plans for actions against the mainland in the Blue Lion Committee on the basis of the agreed terms of reference.

5. Since an understanding of the intelligence picture in mainland China is essential to any plan for military action against the mainland, we wish to push on with the project we have agreed on to exchange intelligence appraisals. These appraisals would include study of the dissidence potential in the five southwest provinces as well as elsewhere in mainland China. We understand that these intelligence appraisals are now being worked on within our two governments and that the exchange will be effected [*less than 1 line of source text not declassified*].

6. We would like to broaden our Blue Lion consultations with the GRC to include examination with the GRC of concepts and strategies (but not plans) for dealing with the Communist threat in Southeast Asia.

7. We would also like to hear GRC ideas on means of making our consultations, both in the military and political fields, more responsive to the needs of the existing Far East situation. *End Summary.*

8. We have serious reservations about statement proposed para 15 Ref. A. Statement would not only encourage further GRC mainland attack plans along the lines of Great Torch 5 but would also be subject to misinterpretation and possible anticipatory action by ChiComs should they learn of statement, as is entirely possible. Suggested statement should accordingly not be used.

9. We are unable to expand usefully on para 7 Ref B. You may nevertheless tell Chiang Ching-kuo that we hope through broadened Blue Lion consultations to benefit on regular basis from President Chiang's and GRC's views on Southeast Asian situation, while at same time acquainting GRC with our own thinking particularly in respect to Viet-Nam.[3]

Rusk

---

[3] Telegram 813 from Taipei, January 29, reported that the summary in telegram 762 had been given to Chiang's aide, Colonel Wen, that morning. (Department of State, Central Files, POL CHINAT–US)

---

121. Memorandum From James C. Thomson, Jr., of the National Security Council Staff to the President's Special Assistant for National Security Affairs (Bundy)[1]

Washington, February 3, 1966.

SUBJECT

Moment of truth with GRC regarding Mainland counter-attack?

You asked me about the significance of Chargé Hummel's account of his conversation with Chiang Ching-kuo last week regarding U.S. views of the GRC's most recent counter-attack proposal (Taipei's 797, attached).[2]

Here is the background:

1. On September 22, Chiang Ching-kuo submitted to McNarmara a GRC proposal for ChiNat landings on the mainland with a view to seizing China's five Southwest provinces (a proposal generally identified as "Great Torch-5"). McNamara said that we would give the proposal careful study. [3 lines of source text not declassified] The same proposal was

---

[1] Source: Johnson Library, National Security File, Country File, China, Vol. V. Secret. A note in Bundy's handwriting reads, "Thanks; a good memo. McGB".

[2] The reference telegrams are not attached to the source text, but see Documents 119 and 120.

pressed on General Wheeler by Chiang Kai-shek in his conversation on December 29.

2.   On November 16, the JCS passed to McNamara its views of the GRC proposal.[3] In brief, the Chiefs concluded that (a) "there is no apparent possibility of successfully executing the concept as proposed"; (b) "the U.S. should not engage in a comprehensive bilateral study of the proposed concept"; and (c) the U.S. should [*less than 1 line of source text not declassified*] examine GRC concepts and strategies for the Southeast Asian situation, to compare assessments of the mainland situation with particular reference to the prospects of popular uprisings and defections," and to critique GRC unilateral plans. The central point of the JCS paper was that the GRC proposal would depend for its success on *massive U.S. naval, air and logistic support*, and on *large-scale popular uprisings and defections* once a landing had been accomplished.

3.   On January 19, State and Defense instructed Hummel to give a polite but negative oral response to Chiang Ching-kuo along the lines of the JCS recommendation (Deptel 728 to Taipaei, attached).

4.   On January 24, Hummel conveyed this message to young Chiang, and the latter's response was "disappointment and irritation." On the 25th, Ching-kuo requested a written precis of Hummel's message, to be passed to his father.

5.   On January 28, the Department came through with a written precis which Hummel gave to young Chiang on the 29th (Deptel 762 to Taipei, attached). To date, we have had no further response from the GRC.

Comment: This four-month exchange is bringing to a head a fundamental but usually submerged issue—the basic divergence between U.S. and GRC objectives in the conflict with Asian communism. We have long understood that GRC desire for war with mainland China and U.S. desire to avoid such a collision run at cross purposes; but we have usually been able to mute and disguise these differences.

The GRC's present proposal has the Gimo's personal imprimatur. We have met it head on with the JCS's best judgment. The result has made Chiang Ching-kuo unhappy, and it is predictable that Chiang Kai-shek himself will explode. Such an explosion may take the form of a private letter to the President or, more likely, a blunt and passionate unburdening on the next high-level American visitor to Taiwan; also, conceivably, some attempts to complain to sympathetic Congressional leaders.

We should anticipate any such moves and apply soft soap generously; but there is little we can do to provide the assurance Taipei seeks on an issue on which our military and civilian thinkers are firm and

---

[3] Document 110.

united. The immediate price we may have to pay for exercising our realistic best judgment is some foot-dragging by the GRC on expanded use of Taiwan facilities in connection with the Vietnam war.

In brief, the GRC has pushed us harder than ever on our central point of divergence and has received, politely, the response it feared and expected. The result will further complicate U.S.–GRC relations in a year when they are already clouded by the ChiRep issue and the 7-month non-appearance of a U.S. Ambassador in Taipei.

Jim

122. Memorandum From James C. Thomson, Jr., of the National Security Council Staff to the President's Special Assistant for National Security Affairs (Bundy)[1]

Washington, February 4, 1966.

SUBJECT

Seventh-Floor Assignment for Ambassador Reischauer?

1. Recommendation

I have a rather simple proposal that would serve our national interests in the Far East and also preserve a rare talent within government service: *that Ambassador Reischauer be appointed a Special Assistant to the Secretary of State (or Ambassador-at-Large), with responsibility for China operations coordination and China policy planning.*

As you know, Ed Reischauer plans to leave his Tokyo post this summer for a new chair at Harvard; he intends to announce his resignation in April.

What I am proposing is that Ed be asked to postpone his departure from Government for at least one year in order to serve, in effect, as "Ambassador to Peking in Exile." From what I know of his long and deep

---

[1] Source: Johnson Library, National Security File, Name File, Thomson. Secret. Filed as an attachment to a February 6 memorandum from McGeorge Bundy to William Bundy, endorsing Thomson's suggestion and stating that if he went to Saigon and if the idea was attractive to Bundy and the Seventh Floor, he might go to Tokyo and "try it out on Reischauer."

concern with the China problem, I regard the odds as better than even that he would accept such an assignment.

2. *Rationale*

There seems to me a clear and compelling need for such a figure at State. Our highest-placed full-time China expert in Washington is currently Allen Whiting of INR, who will probably move either to an overseas post or a university this summer. Within FE there is no one of deeply rooted China experience above the rank of Office Director (Harald Jacobson, who runs Asian Communist Affairs; an exception is Bob Barnett, whose job as economic Deputy provides little opportunity for China planning). Nor is there anyone on the Seventh Floor who would claim China expertise, much less time for intensive China thinking. This leaves only the handful of high-level China types abroad and in other agencies: [*less than 1 line of source text not declassified*] and Ray Cline of the Agency (the one now in [*less than 1 line of source text not declassified*] and the other apparently scheduled for reassignment); Marshall Green in Djakarta; and Ed Rice in Hong Kong—a very thoughtful observer and analyst, but not an operator or planner.

What we are confronting here is a shortage and generation gap produced by the sealing off of the mainland, McCarthyism, and the Dulles–Robertson years. There are wise and tough younger China specialists coming along in the Service; but the Tommy Thompsons, Chip Bohlens, and Foy Kohlers simply don't exist as yet.

In the circumstances, with China a permanent problem, and with no U.S. diplomatic mission in Peking, we are in some danger of succumbing in Washington to at least three types of unavoidable distortion in conducting a Far Eastern policy. There is the distortion bred by our own China experience (the "loss of China", Korean war, public and Congressional opinion, etc.); the Southeast Asian distortion (a narrowly Saigon or Bangkok perspective on China); and finally the Soviet distortion (a Kremlinological view of China that may be shaped both by the demands of our "détente" with the USSR and by Moscow's own distorted view of Peking).

In addition to whatever distortions may color our approach, we are also endangered by the fragmentation of our present China operations. By this I refer to the considerable number and variety of intelligence-type mechanisms that have been set in motion over the past fifteen years on China's frontiers and are now compounded by our Vietnam-related activities. There is no one in Government at a senior policy level who has within his daily ken the full sweep of our China activities from Tibet through Southeast Asia, North Vietnam, the Taiwan Straits, and Korea—not to mention matters of travel and trade. Such a review point is particularly important to the extent that however much we may regard China as a series of separate problems (i.e., Tibetan rebels, KMT irregulars, overflights from Taiwan, medical travel, etc.), China regards us as *one* single problem—and is highly sensitized to all the "signals" we may inadvertently be sending through a variety of unrelated acts.

Ideally, what is needed is a *China coordinator and China advocate* of the stature of Tommy Thomson. Ideally, too, such a man should come from the career Service and should be unscathed by the McCarthy era. I have combed the ranks of the career Service, however, and although there are some vaguely promising names (perhaps Henry Byroade or Fulton Freeman), none seems to me more logical than that of Reischauer. Ed is a man whose roots, training, experience, and thinking cover China as well as Japan, Korea, and Southeast Asia; his first and foremost field of scholarship was pre-modern China (T'ang history), and he has applied himself both as an academic and as an operator to modern and Communist China, also to the broad questions of U.S.–China strategy. In addition, he has clearly earned his spurs within the FSO Club and in his press, public, and Congressional relations. Finally, his standing with both Defense and the CIA is uncommonly high.

I am convinced that Ed could be persuaded to put off his Harvard chair for at least one year and take on such an assignment—provided that the Administration made it clear that his services were needed. If he were appointed, I would urge, for obvious reasons, that his role be publicly described as that of a general adviser on Far Eastern affairs—*not* a China watcher.[2]

Jim

---

[2] A March 19 letter from William Bundy to Reischauer states that Rusk shared Bundy's feeling that it would be difficult to devise a position that would make full use of Reischauer's talents. Whereas Thompson was constantly involved with immediate policy problems and direct dealings with the Soviets, a comparable job concerning China would not have the practical immediate high-level decisions or contacts at the same frequency. (Department of State, Bundy Files: Lot 85 D 240, Ambassador's Private Correspondence)

123.   Telegram From the Consulate General at Hong Kong to the Department of State[1]

Hong Kong, undated.

1448. 1. Classification and channel used because several items below so require, but I hope it will be distributed to those in Department and other agencies who are involved in the matter discussed.

2. I have had a growing feeling that we are reaching the point when the USG (including the ConGen) must give more attention than in the past to what might be called the question of how much the traffic will bear in Hong Kong. In other words,there is some optimum level of US activities, requests and pressures, both direct and indirect, which if exceeded would detract from rather than advance over-all US interests. This level is difficult to define, but I believe it is important that we all make a conscious effort to recognise that a potential problem exists. Otherwise, we may inadvertently step across the line and be suddenly confronted with a major problem. The purpose of this message is to share some of our thoughts; it is not intended to make specific recommendations regarding specific matters.

3. My concern has been prompted by a variety of matters, some mundane in isolation, others of major importance in themselves. The list includes the R & R program from Vietnam; liberty visits (which have been increasing) by Seventh Fleet ships, including nuclear-powered ships and carriers which conduct air strikes against the DRV; a considerable [2 *lines of source text not declassified*]; strong pressure on the Brit Govt to take whatever steps are necessary to prevent Hong Kong registered ships from going to the DRV; almost constant pressure on the HKG on textile matters; GRC use of Hong Kong as a base for sabotage attempts against the mainland; and an expanding US official population (such as the currently active questions of the FBI liaison officer, the AID-requested position for monitoring trade in items that might end up in DRV or Viet Cong hands, and the second FAS officer position). Each of these can probably be justified in itself, but we may be reaching the point where a decision on one may adversely affect our interests regarding another—or all of them.

4. In trying to determine the optimum level of our activities and pressures, there are a number of unknown, variable, and related factors. One is the ChiCom attitude, which in turn may increasingly become a function of the Vietnam situation. Even if we were to assume that the

---

[1] Source: Department of State, Central Files, POL HK–US. Top Secret; Priority; Roger Channel. The telegram does not indicate the date and time of transmission; it was received at 9:52 a.m. on February 5.

leaders in Peking were wholly rational, trying to estimate their tolerance level would be difficult; the problem is compounded by what is apparently an element of irrationality in their outlook. We do not mean to suggest that ChiCom thinking is on the verge of a conclusion that some drastic action should be taken against HK, but we do judge that the Chi-Coms are thinking more about Hong Kong and how it fits into the overall confrontation between them and the US and the West as a whole. This is, of course, at a time when the Chinese Communists have suffered repeated frustrations in their efforts to put pressures on us elsewhere in hope of indirectly affecting the course of events in Vietnam.

5. A second factor is of course the attitude of the HKG and the Brit Govt. This is to a large extent, but not entirely, directly related to ChiCom attitude and actions. HKG and the Brits have about as much difficulty as we do in predicting ChiCom reactions to matters affecting HK, so we can not take much comfort in the idea that if the HKG concurs in some matters, our problems are over. The HKG attempts to be as cooperative as possible, but obviously insists upon retaining the option of reviewing a situation after the event even though it has previously concurred.

6. A third factor is the attitude of the people of Hong Kong, particularly the press, businessmen and other leaders of influence. In general, Hong Kong has been remarkably insulated from political problems of the area, but we sense the beginning of uneasiness, accompanied by the initiation of Chinese Communist efforts to use labor unions and other organizations as sounding boards for propaganda directed against our activities here. The HKG is no democracy, but it is acutely conscious of the need to maintain an atmosphere of stability and confidence. Apart from its relationship to law and order, such an atmosphere is essential to Hong Kong's economic well-being. Hong Kong is something of an economic miracle, but its success has been largely the result of intangibles, which are not the soundest base for continued stability.

7. There is also the possibility that events in the area and our military use of Hong Kong are almost inexorably leading us towards some sort of commitment for the defense of Hong Kong against any ChiCom action. (In fact, local press has on several occasions suggested that continued visits of USN ships is to demonstrate such a commitment.) As far as we know, this has not been subject of any recent US–UK discussions. Nevertheless, it is a point we need to keep in mind.

8. In sum, we think that Peking, the HKG and the HK people are giving increased attention to the future of HK, and that we must do the same in order to avoid jeopardizing the usefulness which we now derive from Hong Kong. This may mean at times foregoing something in one field in order to protect our overall interests, and this may cause an outcry from those involved primarily in that field. We will of course try to exercise this overall judgment within the ConGen, and we hope that all

developments which may significantly affect our interests in Hong Kong will be similarly coordinated in Washington.

Rice

124.   Letter From Secretary of State Rusk to the Ambassador to Poland (Gronouski)[1]

Washington, February 5, 1966.

Dear John:

I was very interested in your initial impressions of the Chinese Communists at your first meeting with them.[2] I agree the Chinese seem to believe that the U.S. is hostile to Communist China. It is also clear they are inflexible in their outlook. Their experience over the past forty years, their deep-seated beliefs, their dispute with the Soviets and their projection of Viet-Nam as a test-case, their vision of the future, and their nationalistic aspirations have combined to convince them that their current policies are right regardless of the consequences. It is highly unlikely that the present leadership will alter its views.

Given these circumstances I believe that our present course of action—firm resistance to Chinese Communist expansionism while at the same time searching for means to establish more contacts and a reduction of tensions—is the best course that we can pursue. Your role in this search for more meaningful contact is most important. At your last meeting with Wang I think you scored several points—particularly in telling him of the removal of the travel ban on doctors, our willingness to admit their journalists without reciprocity, our willingness to meet with them in an exploratory committee to discuss the World Disarmament Conference and finally our proposal to jointly investigate their claims of attacks on the high seas. We hope to propose more of these small steps for the next meeting. We realize that Peking will reject them as well. Never-

---

[1] Source: Department of State, Central Files, POL 1 CHICOM–US. Secret. Drafted by Dean on January 29. Cleared by Stoessel, Thompson, Berger, U. Alexis Johnson, and Assistant Legal Adviser for Far Eastern Affairs George H. Aldrich.

[2] A note on the source text refers to an incoming letter from Gronouski in the Exdis file. The letter has not been found.

theless, when these moves gradually become known they will reflect our own reasonableness and our desire to move towards some lessening of tensions. The Chinese rejections will prove they are intransigent and their unreasonableness will cause them to become more and more isolated.

I think you will be interested in the following recent observations from Hopson, the British Chargé in Peking.

"It is supposed to be axiomatic that China does not listen to reason. Certainly that has been my humble experience at this post so far. The arguments of power and bitter experience are more likely to move her. Nor shall we tame her by just giving her what she wants. It would be folly for the Americans to dismantle the defensive system which is at present their only means of deterring China from adventures outside her frontiers. She must be taught that her present policies will not pay. At the same time real efforts must be made to lead China back into the international community and to show her the advantage of peaceful co-existence. There is no magic formula for this. It will require strength, patience and understanding, particularly from the United States and from the Soviet Union; and it will be a long business. There is not much prospect of changing the attitudes of the present Chinese leadership. We may even have to wait for a new generation. Meanwhile we would be wise to keep our powder dry."

Your report on the eavesdropping of the last session of the talks raises the question whether we should consider suggesting to the Chinese that we hold the talks alternatively in each other's Embassy rather than at the Museum. I should appreciate your views on making such a move. On the other hand, there may be some benefit in letting the Poles and Russians know about the contents of our talks at the present time.

In view of the present situation in the Far East I think it would be best not to have Sir George discuss our long term plans in that area with Michalowski at this time.

With warm regards,

Sincerely,

Dean[3]

---

[3] Printed from a copy that indicates Rusk signed the original.

125. Telegram From the Consulate General at Hong Kong to the Department of State[1]

Hong Kong, February 19, 1966, 0731Z.

1539. Country Team message. Subject: Indicators of genuine Chi-Com fears of US/GRC invasion and suggested U.S. policy response.

1. We have become convinced, in watching the current Communist Party campaign telling the people the U.S. is planning to attack China, that the motive power behind the campaign is no longer primarily precautionary. Rather it is a widespread belief which has grown and which stems from the top, that we will soon launch major operations against the mainland. Apparently it is conceived that these operations may involve both aerial attacks and amphibious landings. We do not believe this conviction can be dismissed as irrational, given the premises on which it probably is based. It certainly cannot be dismissed as unimportant since, in human affairs, acceptance of an outcome as inevitable tends to make it so: leaders will not take with conviction steps which might stave off an outcome they regard as fatalistically certain, nor will they be so likely to forego actions which might make it so.

2. A propaganda campaign of this sort, begun for precautionary purposes and to gain certain side benefits (such as harder work from the people and removal to the countryside of people who have no employment in the crowded cities), can gain its own momentum which carries along those who started it. But this factor, in our opinion, can at most help marginally to explain the growing atmosphere of crisis which surrounds some reports we now get from areas near Hong Kong.

3. The most rational explanation of how war might come about was that contained in Chou En-lai's Dec 20 speech in Peking at a reception for the NFLSV mission. In brief, he portrayed the U.S. strategy as one of escalating our forces and capabilities in South Vietnam while endeavoring to isolate our opponents there from access to outside support. He asserted we were preparing implement this sealing-off strategy by carrying out a sea blockade of the DRV; bombings of Hanoi, Haiphong and parts of Laos; occupying, in collaboration with the Thai and South Vietnamese, areas of Laos between Thailand and South Vietnam; and instigating our two allies to attack Cambodia.

4. Chou did not say whether and how China would respond, though recent intelligence reports suggest the Chinese Communists anticipate Phnom Penh may during the next six months request Chinese help in

---

[1] Source: Department of State, Central Files, POL CHICOM–US. Top Secret; Limdis. Repeated to CINCPAC, Bangkok, Moscow, Saigon, Taipei, and Vientiane.

defending Cambodia, that China would send Chinese "volunteers", and that we can be expected to react by attacking China. This would add to Vietnam another theater—or possibly two, since Chinese access to Cambodia might have to be via Laos—for the possible employment of Chinese volunteers (selected men for possible use in Vietnam have already undergone training near Kweilin). (FCH–6010)

5. However, Chou merely said our efforts would fail and that we might react by extending war to the whole of Indochina and to China itself. Indeed, he charged we were even then making preparations for such an eventuality. He described this as a "possible" outcome, basing his conclusion on the "objective laws governing the development of aggressive wars."

6. There is a considerable gap between the "possible" of Chou's analysis in December and the growing belief in inevitability we get, from recent reports, and it carries with it a sense of conviction which must, we think, derive from more than mere objective analysis. Indeed, the areas we are evidently expected to attack are quite specific, and they seem to carry the inference of GRC participation.

7. [1-1/2 lines of source text not declassified] the local Chinese Communists in Hong Kong are preparing for the expected American attack and have even been told by the Chinese Communist party that the southern provinces of China may be lost to the Americans before the situation can be reversed and China can successfully counterattack. This fatalistic acceptance of an initially successful American attack reoccurs in FCH–6017 in the party discussion in Canton.

8. We have endeavored to catalogue the probable additional facts, circumstances and assumptions on which the Chinese Communist leadership may have based its conclusions. They could include numerous statements by official and unofficial Americans; plans involving the Khmer Serei, whose activities and intentions the ChiComs have long been able to follow in considerable detail; and information derived from top-level penetrations of the GRC. (We have long accepted that such penetrations exist and the experience of the troop build-up in Fukien, and its correlation to the "Blue Lion" planning in Taipei seems too obvious to be dismissed; similar concern may well have been aroused by its reactivation if indeed this has happened.) Finally, there is the list of policy defeats, too long to be recounted here, which the ChiComs have suffered in their efforts to isolate us and create troubles elsewhere which would divert our efforts from Vietnam.

9. Clearly things have gone badly wrong in the external field, giving China a sense of encirclement and isolation. This sense of isolation appears to have carried the leadership into irrationality at one point: fear of attack also from other quarters, including the USSR. Thus [less than 1 line of source text not declassified] a conversation between a senior Chinese

Communist leader and a member of the Communist Party of New Zealand (a party long associated with the ChiComs), indicating the Chinese believe the Soviet Union will give support to "revisionist Chinese" in the western areas of China and that the Soviets might actually attack and occupy parts of these areas of China should a war between China and the U.S. break out. This irrationality, which equates containment to aggressively hostile encirclement, assumes that India and the Japanese "imperialists" would also act in concert with the U.S.

10. The concept of the Japanese imperialists joining in suggests that the top Chinese Communists are operating in an atmosphere which reminds them of 1937, and expecting developments to take a similar course [2 lines of source text not declassified]. This also suggests to us that Mao, as is the way with aging men, has been looking to the past for guidance for the future. Given the extent he is deified and his works are being regarded as the gospel, it is clear that his thinking is playing a major part. This could be so whether he is ill—he has not appeared publicly for six weeks—or issuing ill-tempered directives from some rustic retreat. We are tempted, in this connection, to search for parallels in the last years of Stalin. We are also tempted to conclude he would half-welcome a U.S.–GRC invasion, believing his two old enemies could, before he dies, be drowned in the sea of Chinese manpower once they were sucked inland. This would also deal a mortal blow to the revisionism he sees affecting China (and perhaps the DRV too, as Le Duc Tho admitted in his speech this week). Perhaps most important of all, it would ensure that the next generation of Chinese Communist leaders would become steeled in struggle, and become worthy successors of his own generation of leaders.

11. We do not know what full range of conclusions should be drawn from the foregoing speculation, but we can offer several:

A. We should abandon any intention we may have for "Blue Lion" or similar exercises—confining our joint consultations with the GRC to a mere exchange of information and analysis;

B. We should increase our efforts to ascertain what GRC leaders may be planning on their own—independent GRC capabilities have increased, but the quietness of GRC leaders of late makes us curious;

C. Reservations about our basing B–52's on Taiwan deserve to be strengthened;

D. We should rethink our policy of allowing hot pursuit from South Vietnam into Cambodia, if we have not already done so;

E. We should not only be stern with South Vietnam and Thailand about activities against Cambodia, but try to have our opposition to those activities be bruited about among the Khmer Serei (in hopes that the ChiComs and Sihanouk may both learn of it); and

F. We should resolutely resist pressures to permit hot pursuit into ChiCom airspace.

12. Other measures may well occur to the Dept whereby dangerous ChiCom delusions about our intentions could be corrected—perhaps at Warsaw and by public statements. Our policy objective surely is a mainland China willing to live at peace with its neighbors and with US. We here assume containment is only a subordinate and interim element supporting pursuit of that goal. It is dangerous for Communist China's leaders to believe otherwise.

Rice

---

126. **Telegram From the Embassy in the Republic of China to the Department of State**[1]

Taipei, February 22, 1966, 0311Z.

905. Ref: Hong Kong's 1359 [1539] to Department.[2] Following is joint Embassy/TDC/[less than 1 line of source text not declassified] message:

1. Blue Lion planning since its inception in 1962 has not changed ground rules, which ChiComs almost certainly realize involve only unilateral GRC plans within GRC's own capabilities. USG refuses to comment on any GRC plans that do not fit this framework. On Jan 24 we bluntly rejected a GRC request to consider a contingency plan for large scale landings in South China with US logistic assistance. Believe it possible that ChiComs know of this rejection. We doubt that ChiComs have any rational grounds for thinking that USG and GRC are jointly planning aggressive moves against mainland.

2. Ref para 11 B unusually good and extremely sensitive sources give us considerable information on GRC plans and high level deliberations. We have taken suitable occasions to remind GRC of its treaty obligation to obtain prior USG agreement before using force against mainland, and our sources confirm that GRC is taking obligation seriously. When Ambassador arrives we shall open up more overt channels for discussing GRC desires and obtaining additional information on GRC intentions. At present above reports on high level GRC delibera-

---

[1] Source: Department of State, Central Files, POL CHICOM–CHINAT. Top Secret; Limdis. Repeated to Hong Kong, CINCPAC, Bangkok, Moscow, Saigon, and Vientiane.
[2] Document 125.

tions reveal no GRC intention embroil US in war with ChiComs, but of course this motivation could become significant element of GRC policy later.

3. Independent GRC air and naval capabilities have not increased but have actually decreased in recent years in comparison with Chi-Coms. This is particularly noticeable in ChiNat Air Force where relative tactical superiority in 1958 Quemoy crisis is demonstrably diminished because of better ChiCom tactics and equipment. ChiCom successes in air and naval clashes in recent months should have result of increasing ChiCom confidence. ChiComs are probably well enough informed on modest state of GRC readiness and capabilities so that they do not see significant threat of unilateral GRC action.

4. Emphatically agree with para 11 C that this is not the time to be thinking of basing B–52's on Taiwan.

5. Peking has at various times in last few years shown extreme sensitivity to imagined attacks in situations where no such attacks were in offing. This may be the case at present, but we are inclined to believe that (a) ChiCom moves of recent months are precautionary in the main, occasioned by concern that US might expand air war in North Vietnam and into south China; and (b) reftel analysis tends to take scattered lower level indicators (as in para 7) and assume they represent high level ChiCom policies.

6. There is certainly cause for concern about ChiCom fears of US action against them, and it may be advisable to consider appropriate channel for conveying calming message to Peiping. Seems to us here, however, that ChiCom fears should have effect on preventing adventurous or provocative actions in Vietnam, and also should diminish chance of ChiCom provocation against offshore islands if we, and GRC also, refrain from actions Peiping could consider provocative.

Hummel

---

127. **Memorandum From the Deputy Director for Coordination in the Bureau of Intelligence and Research (Koren) to the Director of the Bureau (Hughes)**

Washington, February 23, 1966.

[Source: Department of State, INR Files, 1966 FE Weekly Staff Meetings. Secret. 3 pages of source text not declassified.]

128.   Letter From the Deputy Assistant Secretary of State for Far Eastern Affairs (Berger) to the Assistant Secretary of State for Far Eastern Affairs (Bundy)[1]

Washington, February 23, 1966.

Dear Bill:

The Secretary had me in not long after you left over the ChiRep memo.[2] (Joe Sisco was called, but not immediately available.)

The Secretary did not approve the memo, and does not want to take this issue up with the President at this time. In your talks in Taipei he does not want you to go further than:

a. discussing the close last vote;
b. the gradual shift in the General Assembly toward abstention or opposition;
c. the growing tendency in the General Assembly to use majority rule on substantive questions. He thought this should be strongly stressed;
d. the serious problem that may confront us in the next General Assembly.

With this as a setting, he wants you to throw the question to them as to their views in the event it appears impossible to hold the line. He does not want any reference made to two Chinas.

He said the GA is still eight months away, and it is too early to come to conclusions. If, as we begin to approach the Assembly, we find that we are in real trouble, he said he had various ideas that could tie up the issue for a year or more. He mentioned in particular the study committee idea.

Sincerely yours,

Sam

---

[1] Source: Department of State, EA/ROC Files: Lot 75 D 76, Bundy Visit to ROC, March 10–12, 1966. Secret; Official–Informal.

[2] A copy of a February 16 memorandum from Bundy and Sisco to Rusk is attached. It states that they considered it highly unlikely that the General Assembly would sustain its past votes on the important question issue and that they needed to begin at once to develop an alternative strategy. They proposed that as a first step, when Bundy visited Taipei in March, he should explain to the GRC leadership the need to think of an arrangement that would "reaffirm Taipei's seat" but "permit—by the initiative of others—some form of proposal involving an offer of membership for Peiping as well."

129. Memorandum From James C. Thomson, Jr., of the National Security Council Staff to the President's Special Assistant (Valenti)[1]

Washington, March 1, 1966.

SUBJECT

Some Propositions on a China Strategy

In response to your request, here are some informal thoughts on the China problem:

1. One highest priority task for American policy-makers in the years ahead is to help domesticate the Chinese Communist revolution in its relations with other nations—or, to put it another way, to help reclaim the Chinese mainland to responsible membership in the world community.

2. The importance of the task is self-evident: 700 million people; the key to stability in Asia; the grandiose belligerent aims of Chinese Communist doctrine; Peking's development of a nuclear capability.

3. This task demands not merely "containment", but a multiple strategy. Three chief aspects of such a strategy should be: (a) traditional military containment—the deterrence of overt and covert Chinese aggression, and resistance to such aggression wherever it may occur (as in Vietnam or Laos on the one hand, India on the other); (b) generous assistance to the fragile societies on China's perimeter in the process of nation-building; and (c) systematic efforts to help erode the Chinese totalitarian state, to influence Chinese behavior, and to combat Chinese ignorance and fear of the outside world.

4. All three aspects, simultaneously, are essential to a broad-gauged policy. With the first two, we seek to prevent a disturbed China from inflicting harm on its weaker neighbors; with the third, we attempt to induce more rational patterns of behavior on the part of China's leaders and/or their successors.

5. The first two of these aspects have received much attention since the Korean war. They underlie our network of military alliances and our aid program; they are reflected in the Vietnam war today. But the third aspect has been very largely neglected.

---

[1] Source: Department of State, Central Files, POL CHICOM–US. Confidential. Filed with a note of March 3 from Thomson to Read. A copy is filed with a July 25 memorandum from Thomson to Alfred Jenkins, which stated that "we have made some significant moves in this direction since early March" and "the new rhetoric has moved toward 'containment without isolation' and now 'reconciliation'—or a policy of 'firmness and flexibility' (a phrase the President likes)." (Johnson Library, National Security File, Country File, China, Vol. VI)

6. By the third type of strategy, I mean essentially the familiar array of flexible initiatives—of instruments of leverage and erosion—that we have brought to bear on the Soviet Union and Eastern Europe for many years now: a freeing of the flow of ideas, people, and goods—the instruments of contact, of communications, travel, and trade.

7. One primary reason for failure to develop this second approach has been the residue of bitterness and suspicion here at home over the "loss of China" and the Korean war; "flexibility" toward China has seemed politically risky, and the Democratic Party has felt especially vulnerable. In addition, the existence of an alternative claimant to Chinese sovereignty—Taiwan—has acted as a brake against China initiatives.

8. A second chief reason of this failure has been the policy pursued by the Chinese Communists themselves since the Korean war, and particularly since the failure of the Great Leap Forward (roughly 1959–60). It has been and still remains evident that any and all U.S. initiatives in the areas of communications, travel, trade, and the like, would be currently spurned by the Chinese Communists; Peking has made clear that for the foreseeable future the U.S. is a useful Public Enemy, still Number One (with the USSR now running a close second).

9. However, the primary U.S. domestic arguments against a flexible approach are today of greatly diminished significance. The leadership of the so-called "China Lobby" has largely passed from the political scene; public opinion polls show a high degree of public tolerance for coexistence with Communist China (see especially the newly issued Council on Foreign Relations study by A. T. Steele); and recent conciliatory moves such as the Hilsman "Open Door" speech of December 1963 and State's medical travel package of December 1965 elicited widespread press support and no Congressional criticism whatsoever. (Note the Zablocki Sub-Committee recommendation last May for increased non-diplomatic contacts with the China mainland. Note also the total non-success of Mme. Chiang's recent public relations trip to the U.S.)

10. At the same time, the argument of Chinese intransigence or non-responsiveness is only marginally relevant. The strategy of flexible initiatives is based *not* on expectation of a favorable Chinese response but rather on several near-term and longer-term objectives.

11. Among the near-term objectives are: (a) a signalling to the Chinese people that we are not eternally and implacably hostile to China (despite their leaders' propaganda to the contrary); (b) a rebuttal of the widely held view, among many of our allies as well as neutrals, that Americans are obsessive and irrational on the subject of Communist China; and (c) a shifting of the onus for Peking's belligerence and isolation to the Chicoms, where it rightly belongs.

12. The major longer-term objective is the offer of alternative patterns of relationships with the U.S. to China's leaders, to their successors,

and to doubting elements within the Chinese elite. Simultaneously, the objective is gradually to help break down China's acutely distorted view of the outside world that plots her encirclement and destruction.

13. The specific ingredients of a flexible "third" approach *might* ideally include the following items: (this list is only *illustrative*)

(a) unilateral termination of the present travel ban to Communist China (we now bar all Americans except bona fide journalists and, since December, specialists in medicine and public health);
(b) a renewed invitation to Chinese journalists, scholars, artists, etc., to visit the U.S.;
(c) licensing of commercial sales of medicines and foodstuffs to China;
(d) eventual further modification of the present trade embargo to permit trade in non-strategic goods, as with the USSR;
(e) inclusion of China in disarmament talks;
(f) a shift in our UN strategy from exclusion of Peking to inclusion of Taipei;
(g) A proposal that the now sterile Warsaw dialogue be reinvigorated through transfer of these talks to a major European or Asian capital (Paris?).

14. Two points should be made about the preceding list:

(a) All these initiatives will almost certainly be rejected outright by the Chinese Communists in the present circumstances.
(b) Such initiatives may have only the most marginal and very long-term effects on Chinese outlook and behavior.

15. Despite these cautionary comments, the pursuit of a third strategy of flexibility commends itself as a low-risk imaginative policy worthy of a strong and confident power in its dealings with the China problem.

16. It is a strategy that can be implemented most easily at a time when our toughness and firmness in opposition to Chinese Communist aggressiveness is being manifested in Southeast Asia as never before.

James C. Thomson, Jr.[2]

---

[2] Printed from a copy that bears this typed signature.

130. **Letter From Secretary of State Rusk to the Ambassador to Poland**[1]

Washington, March 4, 1966.

Dear John:

I have inquired about Bob McNamara's reply to your inquiry which you mentioned in your letter of February 12.[2] I understand that a close check has been made of the Chinese charges of incidents on the high seas and that Bob will be writing to you shortly.

In view of your recommendation[3] we have decided to drop the idea of shifting the talks with the Chinese to each other's Embassy in Warsaw. The Chinese are undoubtedly aware of the Polish microphones and may be talking to the Poles and the Russians as well as to us. Nevertheless, until we detect any sign of change in the Chinese attitude we may as well continue with the present venue.

The instructions for the next meeting are being prepared and they will get to you in sufficient time to allow you to make any comment or suggestion you may desire. I hope the next meeting goes off well. While I don't expect any basic change in the Chinese position, it will be interesting to see if Wang brings back any new attitudes from his recent meetings in Peking.

With best regards,

Sincerely,

Dean[4]

---

[1] Source: Department of State, Central Files, POL CHICOM–US. Secret; Official–Informal. Drafted by Dean. Cleared by Jacobson, Berger, Stoessel, and Colonel Cowherd in FE for Defense.

[2] In Gronouski's February 12 letter (ibid.) he referred to a December 17 letter to McNamara, in which he observed that Wang had referred repeatedly, and with emotion, to incidents of strafing of Chinese fishing boats on the high seas by U.S. planes and asked whether steps could be taken to avoid or at least minimize such incidents. (Filed with McNamara's interim reply of December 30; Washington National Records Center, RG 330, OASD/ISA Files: FRC 70 A 3717, 381 Communist China)

[3] Gronouski commented in his February 12 letter that he thought it was "useful" that the Poles and the Russians had first-hand knowledge of the substance and tone of the talks and that the United States should as much as possible gear its presentations to the Poles and Russians.

[4] Printed from a copy that indicates Rusk signed the original.

131. Telegram From the Department of State to the Embassy in the Republic of China[1]

Washington, March 9, 1966, 6:50 p.m.

884. Ref: Taipei's 837.[2] Joint State/Defense message.

1. Country Team's concern expressed in reftel fully understood and appreciated here. We recognize some lessening of overall GRC capabilities is implicit in the revised MAP dollar guidelines. It has been judged here however that this is consistent with established US objectives and security.

2. The revised MAP guidelines are based on the Secretary of Defense draft Memorandum for the President on MAP FY 67–71, elements of which will be reflected in forthcoming revision to Military Assistance Manual. Following planning guidance derived from draft Memo to President has State Department concurrence and is expected to be published in revision of Part I, MAM:

"a. The size and nature of the forces which the US would support through MAP can be properly determined only after comprehensive analysis of (1) the US ability to augment local forces against the threat, and (2) the types of forces that can be more effectively produced and maintained by the recipient country than by the US.

b. Our major MAP programs should take larger account of the growing mobility and combat power of US general purpose forces, while realistically reflecting the degree of commitment of those forces. This should, of course, be done in the context of other US objectives, particularly those of a political nature.

c. US military assistance will not be designed to support the GRC objective of returning to the mainland.

d. Estimates regarding the type and size of GRC forces required to defend Taiwan and the Penghus against serious attack should be based on the firm premise of major participation, from the opening day of hostilities, by US naval and air forces.

e. While the US is firmly committed to the defense of Taiwan and the Penghus, US policy leaves to Presidential discretion whether to treat an attack on the offshore islands as an attack on Taiwan. The US is not committed to the defense of the offshore islands.

---

[1] Source: Department of State, Central Files, DEF 19 US–CHINAT. Secret; Priority. Drafted by Colonel Berry in DOD/ISA/FER and by George L. Warren in G/PM; cleared by Fearey, Director for Operations in G/PM Howard Meyers, and in draft by Adam Yarmolinsky in DOD/ISA; and approved by Berger. Also sent to CHMAAG CHINA and COMUSTDC and repeated to CINCPAC and CINCPAC for POLAD.

[2] Telegram 837 from Taipei, February 4, urged reconsideration of proposed reductions in the military assistance program for the GRC. (Ibid.)

f.   It would be in the US interest to maintain a continually modernized GRC air force of roughly the current size, and a navy similar to the one now in existence but with a reduced amphibious capability. Such forces are necessary both to supplement US capability and, in the event of a limited ChiCom challenge or probe, to provide the GRC with a capability to engage alone, permitting the US time to assess the situation and determine whether to commit its own forces or reserve them for a more serious challenge.

g.   Planning will be based on reducing the GRC force level from the present 612,000 to 458,000 at the end of FY 1971. The major change from the present will be a reduction in the Army of 146,000 men. Particular emphasis should be put on modernization of the GRC Air Force and the pattern of expenditures for the services should work toward the proposed force goal of 458,000 men. Such a force can be sustained and kept reasonably modern, particularly as to its Air Force, with MAP aid in the range of $90–100 million for the early years of the planning period. Thereafter a total grant military assistance of $70 million will be sufficient, particularly if combined with a relatively modest sales program. During this entire period, efforts will be made to integrate grant military assistance with the sales program.

h.   We should make clear to the GRC our view that their forces are too large in relation to the threat, and that the US is not prepared to underwrite modern GRC forces at their present level, in part owing to the stringency of military assistance funds. It is recognized that the GRC will probably attempt to maintain a larger force structure than we deem desirable, and may well increase their defense spending in order to purchase additional military equipment. We should, as appropriate, argue the merits of a smaller GRC force.

i.   The GRC will be encouraged to assume some of the operating costs presently borne by grant military assistance so that a higher proportion of grant military assistance can be applied to force investment."

3.   The dollar guidelines are based on the assumptions that: (1) MAP investment, starting with FY 67, will be limited to that required in support of end-FY 71 objective levels of forces, (2) adequacy of current inventories of equipment will be judged against end-FY 71 force objectives, and (3) MAP operating cost support will be phased down on straight line basis from actual MAP-support levels of FY 66 to end-period objective levels in FY 71.

4.   In context of above guidance, dollar guidelines are deemed sufficient to (1) provide MAP support for operating costs of the reduced numbers of supported forces on same basis as contemplated for forces in current MAP plan, (2) provide complete replacement of F–86F and C–46 aircraft, (3) provide average of about six million per year FY 67–71 for

investment in Army/Navy/Marine forces. This, plus modest sales program, would seem to provide adequate support for GRC forces.

5. Also of significance is the outlook presented by delivery figures as contrasted to program figures used in reftel. Total deliveries FY 64–67 estimated $390 million for four-year shortfall of $110 million from NPP objective, rather than $152 million shortfall between NPP and program figures shown in reftel. Looking to future, deliveries expected to average about $95 million through FY 70 with shortfall of deliveries against NPP averaging $30 million per year FY 63–70.

6. Impact on GRC militarily, politically, and economically of a reduced MAP is likely to be gradual since the reduction itself is spaced over a number of years and MAP level for FYs 66–69 would still be higher than FYs 63–65. Consequently, we do not expect GRC reaction to take extreme or dramatic form.

7. We agree that as reduced MAP gradually becomes apparent, GRC would probably seek offset by increase in its own military expenditures. We also agree that economic effect this added expenditure would be increased by MAP shift and disappearance of military budget support. Yet, leaving aside the question of desirability of supplying under US military sales program military hardware which we were unwilling supply under MAP, the question remains whether extent of additional GRC military spending would actually cause serious economic setback or extensively undermine economic development achievements. We believe that regime is sufficiently aware of importance of economic viability to security of state that it would seek to avoid this. In final analysis of course, there is little US could do to prevent GRC from allocating whatever funds it believed necessary to maintain its military establishment but this is a choice the GRC itself must continually make and not a choice which we force upon it.

8. We do not believe gradual reduction MAP will cause GRC reluctance to support Viet-Nam related proposals. GRC leadership has consistently identified Viet-Nam conflict as matter of vital GRC national interest. Stationing of US aircraft and visits to Taiwan of R&R personnel provide substantial economic windfall. Improvement of US facilities and additional US deployments all contribute to GRC security.

9. We do not believe that reduction of GRC MAP combined with increasing commitment US military forces in area to Viet-Nam conflict would necessarily lead to increased ChiCom aggressiveness in the Taiwan Straits as long as military assistance to GRC continues at a level adequate to insure defense in combination with available US forces. In view of general US military buildup in Pacific area we believe US military strength will remain sufficient to insure ability of US to continue to meet obligations under Mutual Defense Treaty.

10. We recognize that cost estimates which form basis for dollar guidelines have not had benefit of comprehensive analysis by country team and CINCPAC and we look forward to such analysis in planning cycle now underway. While policy remains firm that MAP dollar levels must be minimum required to serve US security interests, your comprehensive evaluation will be given full consideration in our continuing reviews. Many questions and details remain to be resolved such as what strength in armor is to be MAP supported, to what extent will MAP support the modernization of GP vehicle fleet, etc. In meantime, MAP planning should proceed in such way as to enable all concerned to identify easily those forces and programs which are and those which are not MAP supported. For example, we consider it essential to base computations on adequate support for specific divisions and none for others, rather than to plan inadequate and indefinable level of support for all divisions.

11. We appreciate your comprehensive analysis set forth in reftel and assure you that your opinions will be given continuing consideration as US objectives and total strategy are constantly under review.

12. It would be useful for Country Team to explore with Bundy question level credit sales program. Taiwan may well be one of the candidates for early application of President's policy (1 Feb 66 Foreign Aid Message) to shift gradually from grant to sales basis in military assistance program when this can be done without jeopardizing security interests or progress of economic development. GRC has substantially increased foreign exchange reserves in recent years. According to DOD, GRC has under current consideration significant purchases of items from Germany, including matériel to support objective of returning to mainland. Would therefore seem appropriate that US should seek to influence GRC to direct foreign exchange matériel procurement toward high-priority items included in grant MAP short-fall list.

Rusk

132. Telegram From the Embassy in the Republic of China to the Department of State[1]

Taipei, March 12, 1966, 0707Z.

964. For Berger from Bundy.[2]

1. Central theme of talks with Gimo and CCK has been alleged threat of ChiCom action against Taiwan in near future. [*less than 1 line of source text not declassified*] will report intelligence aspects, which so far as we can see do not add up to any clear likelihood or imminence as of now.[3]

2. I have of course assured both that in event of such action our treaty commitment would come into play and there could be no doubt of our action. I also said that I was sure ChiComs knew as much. Nonetheless, after long discussion during my talk with Gimo yesterday, CCK came in briefly this morning to say new evidence just received [*less than 1 line of source text not declassified*] and to urge that we include in next Warsaw conversation clear reminder to this effect.

3. I told him I thought this would present no problem to us, but that I would refer to Department and Embassy could let him know. We must have covered topic many times, and I urge we do so again, probably in low key and without indicating we have any special indication such action likely. Please advise Embassy of action taken.[4]

Hummel

---

[1] Source: Department of State, Central Files, POL CHICOM–CHINAT. Secret; Priority; Exdis.

[2] Assistant Secretary Bundy visited Taiwan March 10–12 and transmitted a brief summary of his talks in telegram 965 from Taipei, March 12. (Ibid., POL CHINAT–US) Detailed reports of his conversations with Chiang Kai-shek on March 11 and with Chiang Ching-kuo on March 11 and 12 are in telegrams 972, 973, and 974, all dated March 14. (Ibid., POL 7 US/BUNDY) Briefing material for his visit is filed ibid., ROC Files: Lot 75 D 76, Bundy Visit to ROC, March 10–12, 1966.

[3] [*text not declassified*] telegram [*text not declassified*] to the Department of State, March 12, stated that the GRC had a report that the Communists were considering a surprise airborne attack against Taiwan as a preemptive measure to prevent the use of Nationalist troops in Vietnam. (Ibid., Central Files, POL CHICOM–CHINAT)

[4] Telegram 899 to Taipei, March 12, reported that a U.S. statement at the next session of the Warsaw talks would include a specific reference to the continuation of U.S. defense commitments to allies in the Far East, including the GRC on Taiwan. (Ibid., POL CHICOM–US)

133.   **Information Memorandum From the Assistant Secretary of State for Far Eastern Affairs (Bundy) to Secretary of State Rusk**[1]

Washington, March 14, 1966.

SUBJECT

From Lee Kuan Yew to Chiang Kai-shek: Far East—March 1966

Around our Chiefs of Mission Conference, I paid visits to Japan (briefly), Viet-Nam, Thailand, Singapore, Malaysia, the Philippines, and the Republic of China. This memorandum gives the highlights of my observations, drawing briefly on some of the broader policy points already covered in the "highlights" summary of our Baguio meeting, but primarily on my own observations.

[Here follows discussion of the area in general and of specific countries.]

7.   *Republic of China.*

a.   *Fear of Basic Change in US Policy.* Although the travel regulation on scholars[2] was calmly received while I was there, the current US discussion is doubtless stirring some fears.

b.   *Chinese Representation.* This is the real touchstone. I delivered our message of "deep concern" and laid out the negative factors fully. They got the message, and it was certainly wise not to take it further at this stage. I suspect we will be hearing from them, and that the argument must be raging in high quarters as to whether they should pull out if the worse comes to the worst and some formula is presented that offers the possibility of membership to Peiping. If they are to come to the right answer, they must deeply believe that we are doing everything possible to help them (e.g., in Vanguard below) and that, at least for the present, we are doing our utmost to prevent unwise initiatives (e.g., as has already been done with Canada).

c.   *The Gimo.* The Gimo is currently in a state of mild jitters, reflected in excessive dwelling on the ChiCom threat to Taiwan but more conspicuously in the most unwise proposals for drastic emergency powers that we know (from highly sensitive sources) that he has been putting forward. I believe we can cushion his fear of ChiCom action—if indeed it is

---

[1] Source: Department of State, Central Files, ORG 3–2. Secret; Exdis. Drafted by Bundy. A handwritten notation on the source text indicates that it was seen by Rusk.

[2] On March 10 the Department of State announced that it would consider on an individual basis applications from scholars for travel to restricted areas. For text of the announcement, see Department of State *Bulletin*, March 28, 1966, pp. 491–492.

real—and his reaction to our continued negative attitude on the Mainland planning seemed resigned. The internal reorganization could be more serious, although the final proposal—apparently much modified by C.K. Yen and others—will not be too hard to present to the world, especially in view of its pairing of reorganization with possible elections within Taiwan. The underlying problem apparently is the Gimo's fear that his death could produce a chaotic succession situation. Although the succession has now become much more uncertain than we had supposed—with Chiang Ching-kuo's stock down and health uncertain, and C.K. Yen's elevation—it is hard to see why it should be so chaotic as the Gimo appears to believe. Ching-kuo and Yen are personally close and both strike me as being at heart "realists" who do not really accept the Mainland mystique. As to the reorganization, all will depend on what is actually done under it, and we need to do some talking in the right places when the plan is surfaced.

d. *MAP and Military Facilities.* I encountered moderate pressure on MAP, but I think this can be met if we maintain roughly the planned levels. They fully expect to spend more money of their own, including $5–10 million of military sales from us. They know we want them to reduce their forces, but unless the economic pinch gets much worse it seems wholly out of the cards that they will do so. There must be a latent argument within the GRC on military spending, and this could indeed break into the open if the Gimo departed. For now, his voice is decisive on the military side of the argument, and my judgment is that—having made our basic view quite clear—we would be wasting credit to no good purpose to hammer any harder. The whole MAP argument now has additional coloration from the fact that the GRC is giving us significant air and naval facilities, to the point where our air transport squadrons will shortly be taking over the Chinese areas of their major air base. So far, my visit gave no indication that they would use this leverage overtly, but the time may come.

e. *Economic Planning and Vanguard.* This is our most important action decision. I was tremendously impressed both by their internal agricultural policy and by their expanded plans for Africa. They have now appealed specifically for our support of the latter through the use of PL–480 wheat to generate local currency. We ourselves would get a proportion of the currency, and, since our local currency supply runs out in the fall, this would substitute for gold flow. But, more basically, the "exchange of resources" (K.T. Li's phrase) involved in our assisting a significant technical assistance program for food in Africa seems to me a good buy in its own right, with the major additional factor of its relation to the UN problem. While it can be argued that the Chinese have the money themselves, their external accounts are now slightly adverse. In short, I would recommend favorable consideration of the PL–480 proposal.

f. *New Ambassador.* Hummel's excellent performance and their satisfaction with our nominee have somewhat muted the official concern over the delay, although one must assume that recent newspaper attacks have been to some extent inspired. The situation is deeply unsatisfactory on balance, and particularly so with the kind of talking that we may soon have to do on the UN and other issues.

---

134. Memorandum From the President's Acting Special Assistant for National Security Affairs (Komer) to President Johnson[1]

Washington, March 14, 1966, 7:30 p.m.

Staying Loose on China Policy. I'm convinced that China is fast becoming a major foreign and domestic issue again, and needs careful watching. Though I gather that the VP's "hint" of flexibility was strictly his own (and rather premature, to say the least), why not let it serve as a sort of *trial balloon?*

To withdraw from what was rather grossly overplayed by the press would only start another debate with our VN critics, and also force us to eat crow later if, as Secretary Rusk has twice indicated, we may yet be forced to make a virtue of necessity and accept an adverse Chirep vote in the UNGA.

On the other hand, to start shifting our China policy now—before we've carefully assessed all the implications, would be risky. We still lack any firm feel for where the electorate stands, or for how our Vietnam enterprise might be affected.

Yet there may be a way to have our cake and eat it too. It is to move gradually to the same stance toward Peiping as we now have toward Hanoi—i.e., if these people will only stop their subversion and aggression and live peacefully with their neighbors, we are prepared to re-examine co-existing peacefully with them. It is not we who are isolating Red China, but Red China which is isolating itself. If we're going to be

---

[1] Source: Johnson Library, National Security File, Memos to the President, McGeorge Bundy. Confidential. A handwritten "L" on the source text indicates that the President saw it.

forced to adjust our China policy sooner or later anyway, there is virtue in doing so in a way which puts the monkey on Peiping's back.

I don't want to overdo this prickly issue, only to urge the case for staying loose till we can sort it out better. Signs of US flexibility would offend Korea, the GVN, and above all Taiwan, but be quite a plus with most other friends. More important is whether such signs would tend to undermine our Vietnam stance or serve rather as a diversion protecting our Vietnam flank.

R.W. Komer

---

136. **Memorandum From James C. Thomson, Jr., of the National Security Council Staff to the President's Special Assistant (Moyers)**[1]

Washington, March 15, 1966.

SUBJECT

The China Hearings and the Vice President's TV Remarks

At the suggestion of Hayes Redmon, here are some thoughts on how to handle both the Fulbright China hearings and Humphrey's remarks on China as highlighted in today's newspapers:

1. The Administration is in luck, so far, on both China and Vietnam during the present phase of the Fulbright hearings. Two of the country's top Asian specialists, Fairbank and Barnett, *have supported us on Vietnam* and *have offered constructive suggestions rather than sharp criticism on China*.

2. The Fairbank/Barnett central thesis on China policy is *"containment—yes, isolation—no"*. This is a useful and memorable shorthand for describing a rational policy.

3. As of this morning's papers, the Administration, through the Vice President, appears to have adopted both (a) a friendly and positive approach to the China hearings, and (b) the Fairbank/Barnett thesis itself, i.e., "containment—yes, isolation—no".

---

[1] Source: Johnson Library, National Security File, Name File, Moyers Memos. Confidential. A typed notation on the source text reads "Revised Version." A handwritten notation on the source text reads "Bill—note p. 2." Subparagraph 4(b) begins the second page.

4. *Recommendation:*

I would urge that we now make the VP's line the official Administration position. It gives us just the room for maneuver that we will need in the months ahead. It should also help to avoid an unhealthy polarization on China policy. *Furthermore, it need not be billed as a new policy.*

In talking to the press, our stress should be that:

(a) *Of course we welcome such hearings on the problem of China,* a matter of continuing concern to all the nations of the world, and one on which dispassionate discussion and public education can only be useful; and

(b) *We do indeed pursue a policy of containment but not isolation*—in fact, we have attempted to pursue such a policy for a number of years now, and as the situation permits, we will attempt to find new ways to reduce China's isolation, *despite the fact that China has been responsible in large degree for isolating itself from us.*

On this latter point, it should be noted that:

(a) We have sought an exchange of journalists with China since 1959—over 80 American newsmen now have valid passports, but the Chinese won't let them in (only Edgar Snow, admitted as a "writer", not a journalist);

(b) We have authorized various categories of Americans to travel to Communist China—most recently specialists in medicine and public health last December and scholars as of last week—but again the Chinese won't let them in (case of Dr. Samuel Rosen, ear surgeon, in 1964);

(c) We have expressed our willingness to see China participate in international disarmament talks;

(d) We have left the door open since 1962 to the commercial sales of grain to Communist China, if application should be made (despite Peking's denunciation of any trade relations with the U.S.);

(e) We have privately made clear our willingness to admit to this country Chinese journalists and other specialists (scientists), but none have applied; and, of course,

(f) We talk to the Chinese regularly at Warsaw—the latest meeting is this Wednesday.[2]

In other words, the Vice President's statement does not indicate a "new policy"; it is rather a description of our continuing and expanding efforts to find ways to lessen the belligerence of the Chinese Communist regime and to bring the people of the mainland into a more peaceful relationship with the world community.

Jim

---

[2] March 16.

137. Telegram From the Embassy in Poland to the Department of State[1]

Warsaw, March 16, 1966, 2050Z.

1536. Ref: Embtel 1535.[2] Prior to opening of meeting I asked about Wang's home leave and welcomed him back. He seemed reasonably relaxed and courteous. In course of conversation I mentioned he had missed Governor Harriman's visit when he was on home leave. Wang laughed and said perhaps it was just as well. An army of photographers which had been lurking at the door was admitted by mutual agreement. They left ten minutes later and I opened with an expression of my personal sympathy for the victims of the recent earthquake in Hopei. I used Department's guidance in Deptel 1331 [1303].[3] Wang listened with considerable attention, despite length of statement, and took extensive notes.

Wang's response seemed short and almost perfunctory. He read it with a calm and almost detached air quite different from his more emotional charges of the December meeting. Part of his problem may have been the lack of substance in his charges of US military provocations against China. He could only muster up serious warnings 397 and 398 (without details), a GRC plane and two US robot planes shot down and March 2 attack on Chinese fishing vessel which caused no damage. Wang threw in Taipei SOFA agreement, Kung Kuan Airbase, and US Air Force activities and lodged what he termed a strong protest and serious warning through me to the USG. He said he wanted to tell us in all seriousness that the Chiang clique had been long repudiated by the Chinese people. "Taiwan will certainly be liberated by Chinese people and US will never succeed in perpetuating its occupation of Taiwan."

Wang then charged that US since last meeting had taken grave steps to expand its war of aggression in Viet-Nam. He listed resumption air raids, Honolulu Conference, increase US troops in South Viet-Nam, allied assistance, building bases round the clock in SVN, and Thailand, to accommodate more troops "to slaughter SVN people." Said US mopping up operations in SVN burned, killed and destroyed. Claimed US used poison gas and toxic chemicals. Said US was using more barbarous means than those of Hitler and was not only expanding effort in Viet-

---

[1] Source: Department of State, Central Files, POL CHICOM–US. Confidential; Immediate; Limdis. Repeated to Taipei and Hong Kong and passed to the White House.

[2] Telegram 1535 from Warsaw, March 16, reported briefly on the 129th meeting of the Ambassadorial talks that day. (Ibid.) Gronouski reported in detail in airgram A–697, March 21. (Ibid., POL 1 CHINAT–US)

[3] Telegram 1303 to Warsaw, March 10, conveyed guidance for the meeting. (Ibid., POL CHICOM–US)

Nam, but was trying to spread war flames to Laos and Cambodia in attempt save self from defeat in SVN. Said if US dared spread war flames to all of Indochina, its efforts will only meet with more disaster, defeat and nothing else.

Wang then lodged protest about bombing Chinese Consulate Phong Saly, saying it was deliberate act of provocation and that he was instructed once again to lodge strong protest to USG. Wang said US actions proved US, not China, is aggressor. He repeated claim China does not have single soldier stationed in foreign land. Said US can solve no problem by attacking China and continued with comments reftel on Chinese determination to fight to end.

Wang mentioned US peace talks plot and said test of US sincerity is whether or not US honors Geneva Agreements with withdrawal all troops, US must accept DRV's four points, Front's five points, and recognize Viet Cong as sole legal representative of SVN people.

Wang then dredged up and dusted off April 1964 draft-agreed announcement on Taiwan Straits. Repeated it and said US acceptance was only way to effect improvement in Sino-US relations. "If USG really has sincere desire for better relations it should accept the draft-agreed announcement."

Wang ended his initial presentation with this parting thrust. I responded by reiterating that we had no hostile or aggressive intent towards his country. Said we had treaty obligations protect Taiwan against attack and said we hoped for peaceful solution this and other problems in Far East. If we could agree to renunciation of force in Taiwan Straits this would be major stride towards peace. I also dwelt at some length on US sincere desire for peace in Viet-Nam. I told Wang that I would request a further investigation by DOD on Phong Saly charge and would let him know if there were any results of further investigation at next meeting.

Wang responded by repeating charge focus US strategy has shifted to Far East. He said "aggression against our fraternal neighbor is also a threat to our country so we can by no means sit idly by.... These are facts and you cannot deceive others by lies ... so long as you refuse to change your policy it is impossible to improve relations." Wang said US has no right to say that there should be renunciation of force in Taiwan Straits. "As everyone knows, it is an internal affair and US has no right to interfere.... The only means to improve relations is for US to withdraw forces from Taiwan and Taiwan Straits."

Wang said that his side not fundamentally opposed to talks but in problems like Viet-Nam it impossible have talks because US aggression in Viet-Nam absolutely unjust and violation Geneva Agreements. He said as long as US refuses to change its policy our talks about a relaxation of tensions is false. Also said it impossible for his side take part in disarmament discussions because US not sincere. In mentioning prisoners, Wang said his government's policy was to give time off for good behavior. But said this a matter for Chinese Government to decide. Made no mention of Captain Smith.[4]

I made brief reply to Wang's statement. Wang then ended by complaining about leaks of the talks by USG officials. He cited three instantly (including that reported in Embtel 1535). I think it is advisable when mentioning the talks in the future to avoid any reference to substantive content. Wang proposed next meeting for June 22. I told him I extremely busy in mid-June with Poznan Fair and other travel, and suggested mid or late May. Wang suggested May 25 and I agreed. Meeting lasted three hours. After meeting I gave Wang copy of testimony on China before Zablocki committee and then asked him, in interest of becoming better acquainted, to dinner at my home with his staff during week of April 3. He did not reject invitation, but received it courteously. After deliberating he said he would let me know.

As reported Embtel 1534[5] our security officer has again taped broadcast of meeting. During meeting strange whirring noises occurred occasionally in nearby closet attracting attention of Chinese as well as ourselves.

After the meeting I gave brief, very general press statement. NBC and CBS then taped a television interview in my office.

Gronouski

---

[4] Reference is to Captain Philip E. Smith, USAF. The New China News Agency reported on September 20, 1965, that a U.S. F–104 plane had been shot down by PRC aircraft over Hainan that day and that Smith had been captured. Telegram 406 to Warsaw, September 21, instructed Cabot to send a letter to Wang Kuo-ch'uan stating that the plane's navigational equipment had malfunctioned, expressing regret for any intrusion it might have made inadvertently into Chinese airspace, and requesting that Wang's government facilitate Smith's release and return. (Ibid., POL 31–1 CHICOM–US) Cabot reported in telegram 445, September 22, that he had done so. (Ibid.)

[5] Not found.

138.   Telegram From the Embassy in the Republic of China to the Department of State[1]

Taipei, April 6, 1966, 0813Z.

1086. For Bundy.

1. In last week or so Embassy has encountered serious concern in GRC about eventual drift of US policy toward greater accommodation with Communist China. This is result of estimate of long-range effect of domestic US policy debate, not conviction that administration has decided or intends to decide to change its attitude. However, those GRC officials with long memories, and this includes all the senior people, seem to suspect that US fear of war with ChiComs, coupled with what they believe is manipulation of US debates by subversive elements, will result during coming months in relaxation of US determination to prevent UN admission of ChiComs. In short, they seem to think that we may reenact some events of 1945–50 when, in their view, Communist and leftist elements cleverly and successfully manipulated US policy. This is nonsense of course, but there are, it seems to me, some compensations in this belief, since it may be better for US officials to be considered dupes than thought to be knaves.

2. My own recent exposure to this has come April 2 in conversation with Premier, April 4 in meeting with group of Legislative Yuan members (both memcons pouched),[2] and yesterday when accompanying Ray Cline in call on President Chiang. Other Embassy officers report similar concerns, and newspaper comment and speculation has also reached high level. Phrase "containment without isolation" has been center of much of this discussion, with newspapers using Chinese word for "containment" that means something close to "isolation" and then complaining about faulty US logic.

3. Cline's conversations being summarized separately,[3] but mention should be made here of unusual tenor of Pres Chiang conversation yesterday. This was only meeting Cline had with Gimo. Chiang seemed glum and discouraged; he made little effort to be communicative, which struck us as strange in light his long friendship with Cline and energetic and forthcoming atmosphere of previous talks. Cline's talks with CCK were much more relaxed and friendly. They showed little CCK concern over ChiRep.

4. Chiang accepted gracefully our assertions that US policy is firm, but clearly believed some change will occur whether USG now intends it

---

[1] Source: Department of State, Central Files, POL 1 CHICOM–US. Secret; Exdis.

[2] Enclosed with airgram A–807 from Taipei, April 6. (Ibid., POL 1 CHINAT–US)

[3] Not found, but see Document 142.

or not. Said he believed elements in US were doing to US Govt what had been done to GRC on mainland by ChiCom subversives. Appeared much concerned by recent alleged Japan Gaimusho spokesman statement that US problem this year would be to keep GRC in after ChiComs voted in. Said "if that occurs, how can we stay in the UN?"

5. Chiang declined to give his views on Southeast Asia when asked by Cline, saying only "I have nothing to say; I said it all in my letter to President Johnson after his election[4] and I've said it on many other occasions."

6. I realize problems of trying to give unequivocal assurances to GRC in light of probable UN situation this fall, and of other factors involving US domestic scene and Peiping reaction. However I strongly recommend we attempt some reassurance. This could be done in two ways: (a) through continued high level public denials of change in US attitude toward ChiComs entering UN, and (b) personal and private message, preferably from President Johnson to Chiang Kai-shek. Latter message should if possible refer to recent public discussions among Americans who are not in administration, and express resolve not to allow true USG position be misunderstood in third countries.

7. Also desirable would be beginning, if it has not started already, of intensive consultations on UN estimates with GRC officials in Wash and N.Y. Conclusions about US domestic pressures now being drawn by GRC are detrimental to our objective of convincing GRC that any change in US tactics in UN will be result not of USG desire for change but of our hard estimate of UN situation.

8. Ray Cline and [less than 1 line of source text not declassified] have seen this cable.

Hummel

---

[4] See Document 69.

139. Telegram From the Department of State to the Embassy in the Republic of China[1]

Washington, April 14, 1966, 5:41 p.m.

1048. 1. Assistant Secretary Bundy April 14 called in Chinese, Korean and Japanese ambassadors to explain that Marvin Kalb CBS broadcast morning of April 14 citing statement by Secretary before Zablocki committee as evidence that US–China policy changing is completely without foundation.[2]

2. Bundy said it had been our plan give text Secretary's statement to ambassadors prior publication originally planned for next week. Since press leak had occurred we making it available to the ambassadors' governments at once and will send copies to embassies later in day. (Text of statement being transmitted addressee posts by septel.)[3]

3. Bundy flatly denied there any change in US–China policy, as he said would be clear on reading text of Secretary's statement. Said there no implication whatever in Secretary's statement that US, as claimed in Kalb broadcast, moving toward two Chinas. Referring to Kalb mention of Secretary's reference to invitations to Chinese Communist scholars to travel to the US, Bundy said no policy change involved as reciprocal travel always considered implicit in categories authorized by Dept travel to restricted areas, namely newsmen, doctors, and scholars.

4. Australian and New Zealand embassies also informed.

5. Embassy requested convey ASAP to Foreign Ministries full text Secretary's statement, making foregoing points.

Rusk

---

[1] Source: Department of State, Central Files, POL CHICOM–US. Secret; Priority. Drafted by Bennett, cleared by Dean and FE Public Affairs Adviser Richard L. Sneider, and approved by Fearey. Also sent Priority to Tokyo, Seoul, Wellington, and Canberra.

[2] The texts of Kalb's broadcast and Rusk's March 16 statement before the Subcommittee on the Far East and the Pacific of the House Committee on Foreign Affairs are attached to a memorandum of April 16 from Read to Walt Rostow. The memorandum stated that Rusk had made revisions in the statement before giving it to the Subcommittee for publication; Kalb had seen the original version and had drawn inferences from a revision concerning the Chinese representation issue. (Ibid., POL 1 CHICOM–US)

[3] The text was transmitted in circular telegram 2012, April 14. (Ibid.)

140.   Memorandum From the Consul General at Hong Kong (Rice) to the President's Special Assistant (Rostow)[1]

Washington, April 15, 1966.

SUBJECT

United States Policy Towards Communist China

You asked me for comments on things we might do and say now in the hope of reaching a better relationship with mainland China.

Our Policy Objectives

I think we should have as our objective not only avoiding hostilities with Communist China—hostilities which are likely if past and recent trends are extended much farther. We should also have the objective of reaching a live-and-let-live relationship with China. If we do not begin to pursue the latter objective we are much more likely to get into war with China. And if we are to maximize chances of achieving a live-and-let-live relationship we obviously need a strategy for achieving it and a program to implement that strategy. The possibility for a better relationship must be made evident if it is to be considered a realistic option by Mao's successors when he passes. The standard Chinese Communist line is that we are China's irreconcilable enemy. If we do not now plant the seeds of doubt that this is so, we are unlikely to gather their fruit. If we wait till Mao dies and then make efforts to influence the succession we may only ensure the elimination of those among potential new leaders who were inclined towards more pragmatic policies.

Obstacles to a Better Relationship and US Courses of Action

From our point of view, a China which we can live with should be one which pursues live-and-let-live policies towards other governments whose overthrow it now seeks. We cannot expect Chinese Communist leaders publicly to disavow the doctrines which call for such overthrow. We can hope for emergence of leaders who may concentrate more on solving China's enormous internal problems and divert fewer resources to pushing world revolution. Meanwhile we must seek to see Communist China contained. Some countries will be more disposed and better able to deal with threats posed by Communist China without our interventions than with them. They may also be clearer-eyed about China if they have first-hand experience with the Chinese Communists. Our seeking to isolate them from the relevant contact, expecting them to take

---

[1] Source: Johnson Library, National Security File, Country File, China, Vol. 6B. Secret. Rice was in Washington on consultation.

our evaluation of Chinese Communist objectives at second-hand, may be no more appreciated by the non-Communist leaders of those countries than by those of Communist China itself. Thus we must pursue a policy of containment for the indefinite future as in Vietnam, conceivably but not necessarily by similar means.

There are other obstacles in the way of a better relationship. One is the fact that, according to Communist dogma and by definition, we are China's main enemy because we are the strongest non-Communist power. We cannot change the dogma but we can undermine its credibility, and challenge the validity of Chinese Communist views that war between us may be inevitable and, perhaps, ultimately necessary.

Our standing in the way of Chinese Communist acquisition of Taiwan is another obstacle. The mainland regime cannot be expected overtly to accept this separation as final: When China has been divided, nationalistic feelings always have created pressures for reunification. But we can hope the Chinese may learn to live with the situation.

There are other obstacles we can do something about. One is the fact that we still are apparently committed to the overthrow of the Chinese Communist regime. We appear committed to such a policy by virtue of our alliance and intimate relationship with a Government on Taiwan which proclaims return to power on the mainland its overriding objective. We should seek publicly to disassociate ourselves from the GRC objective of reconquest of the mainland. We lend credence to our own presumed commitment to overthrow of the mainland regime by a whole set of courses of action, overt and covert. Pursuing the policy of seeking the overthrow of European Communist regimes ended a decade ago. Such a policy is probably no more realistic towards China.

But courses of action designed to support it have not been reviewed, evaluated and—where counterproductive—modified or abandoned. Speeches going in a contrary direction will in any case evoke a hostile propaganda response from the present Chinese leadership. They may be believed by some in the world audience, which would be helpful in taking the monkey from our backs and putting it on the backs of the Chinese Communist leaders. But speeches accompanied by concrete actions may favorably affect the viewpoints of numbers of Chinese Communists, including some who will succeed to leadership before long.

An inventory of the overt and covert actions we have been taking against China can be supplied (e.g. by the Department's Bureau of Intelligence and Research). These courses of action should be evaluated from the standpoint of their utility. Those which do not produce results which justify their costs, or which stand in the way of attaining the objectives we should now set for ourselves, should be modified or abandoned.

Illustratively I might mention some I am dubious about:

1. Our naval vessels sometimes cruise up and down through Communist China's claimed territorial waters. If we and the Soviets do something similar with each other, neither of us feels humiliated, but the Chinese Communists remember all China's own past humiliations, know China cannot do to us what we do to them, and distrust us more than the Soviets do. If the situations were reversed—a good touchstone of judging our international conduct—we would feel the same. I find it hard to believe that cruising ten miles from China's coast is necessary either to uphold our reservations to a 12-mile limit, which we nearly accepted at one point ourselves, or for other good reasons.

2. During the past century the West forced China to recognize that no country can refuse to trade with the rest of the world. We now enforce an opposite stand in our own embargo policy. With even the Chinese Government on Taiwan allowing at least some indirect trade with the mainland, we are being more Catholic than the Pope.

3. We are considering a project which, according to some of the planners, would "assault" mainland China by radio. Initiation of such a program would be regarded by the Chinese Communists as another step in our pursuit of a policy of seeking the overthrow of their regime. If it were conducted in the spirit of an assault, their beliefs that we were conducting political warfare to that end would be confirmed. This factor should be placed on the losses side of the ledger in evaluating the project, which should be judged on the basis of its utility in serving the policy objective of reaching a live-and-let-live relationship with China. And unless we had a clear Government policy towards China controlling such a radio project, its personnel would of necessity formulate their own and pursue it. I am not optimistic it would, in such circumstances, serve the national interest.

4. India serves itself ill by not trading territory in dispute with China which it cannot use or defend for similar territory it can use and defend. An undefined, disagreed border is like broken skin; it invites the entry of dangerous foreign bodies. A fair settlement would erect an obstacle to Chinese expansion in its place. We publicly supported India in its quarrel, and might now privately encourage it to try for a dignified and fair settlement.

Communist China, in short, has national interests, both pretended and genuine—perhaps even a valid legitimate interest in exerting such regional leadership as it peacefully earns through cultivating relationships of mutual helpfulness with its neighbors. We would do well to recognize by word and deed those of its interests which are legitimate.

Edward E. Rice

141. Memorandum From the President's Special Assistant (Komer) to President Johnson[1]

Washington, April 19, 1966, 7:30 p.m.

Goldberg's Ideas on China. Last weekend I passed Arthur Goldberg your message that you were "fascinated" by his 8 April memo to you suggesting you write Mao proposing a Sino-US foreign ministers meeting or write all the Big Five proposing all meet together.[2] I also told him you wanted him to come back on what more could be done in New York.

He is happy to do so, but feels we should reach a meeting of minds here before he talks with any of our friends in New York or probes the SYG's views. I quite agree, since I'm not at all sure (nor is Walt Rostow) that Arthur has hit on the best idea. At any rate the time is not yet ripe.

Moreover, Arthur talked with Dean Rusk, whose reaction he described as "noncommittal." If anything, Rusk preferred the 5-power approach (Tommy Thompson thought the Soviets wouldn't want to be left out). Since Peiping wouldn't buy anyway (and the whole virtue of the letter is to show our flexibility and its inflexibility), I see little reason to risk three negative replies (Mao, Brezhnev, De Gaulle) rather than only one. Goldberg too prefers a more cautious approach to Peiping alone first (he also points out that when the Warsaw talks began, Peiping itself proposed they be at foreign minister level—thus giving us a precedent to cite).

Goldberg also fears we're in real trouble on the ChiRep issue this year. He sees the Japs and Canadians as ready to leave us. Nor will we gain African votes in his view. So "we'll go down to defeat if we pursue our present posture."

He urges that we switch to a "Two Chinas" policy, which will show that "LBJ is not a stick-in-the-mud", and carries only limited risk because Peiping won't buy anyway. The real problem, he admits, is Taiwan.

I urged that if he felt this strongly he should re-state his case to you and Rusk. I personally agree with him, and note that all the hints about new flexibility in our China policy have netted out a big plus so far.

In any case, Goldberg and I recommend that the next step be to set up a *small high level action group* to work out across the board recommendations to you. He suggests Ball, Komer, and himself. But I'm Vietnam so this is more Walt Rostow's baby (suggest Ed Rice—a talented old China

---

[1] Source: Johnson Library, National Security File, Agency File, United Nations, Vol. 3. Secret. A handwritten notation on the memorandum indicates that the original was returned to Komer and a copy was sent to Rostow. The source text is the photocopy sent to Rostow.

[2] Not found.

hand now back from Hong Kong—as chief legman). There's nothing to lose if we can only keep the matter from leaking. But it will take your proposing such a group to get it off the ground.

I'll discuss with Rusk

Rostow see me[3]

R.W. Komer

---

[3] Both recommendations are checked on the source text.

---

142. Memorandum for the Files[1]

Washington, April 25, 1966.

SUBJECT

Ray Cline's Observations on Taiwan

1. The following is a summary of the more important points made by Ray Cline in conversation with Mr. Bundy April 19:[2]

U.S. Attitude toward Asian Allies

2. Mr. Cline said President Chiang made the point to him that the U.S. should take greater care in its relations with its Asian allies to ensure that they not appear as U.S. puppets. There was, Cline thought, in this an implied criticism of our treatment of Vietnamese Prime Minister Ky and of the handling of the Honolulu Conference. Cline thought there was also probably an implication, which Chiang did not wish to make specific, that the U.S. should take greater care with respect to the GRC itself to let it appear that GRC actions were those of an independent country, not responses to Washington's bidding.

---

[1] Source: Department of State, EA/ROC Files: Lot 79 D 120, Exdis Material, 1965–1966. Secret; Exdis. Drafted by Bennett.

[2] Cline visited Taipei as part of a trip to several countries in the area. He sent Rostow notes of his impressions of the psychological climate in the area with a covering memorandum of April 13. His notes on Taiwan were headed "Free Chinese Government in Taiwan Tragically Low in Morale About U.S. China Policy." Rostow sent the package to the President on April 18. (Johnson Library, National Security File, Agency File, CIA, Vol. II)

State of Morale

3.   Cline said that he found the state of morale in the upper echelons of the GRC very bad. He found President Chiang and Chiang Ching-kuo dispirited and discouraged. They seemed to have lost the dynamism and drive which he had always found in them in the past. During his conversation with Cline, President Chiang did not argue the GRC point of view but told Cline that he had already made his points to American officials from President Johnson on down, that they all knew his points of view, but that he had failed to persuade them.

Viet-Nam Policy

4.   Chiang Ching-kuo told Cline that he doubted that our present military course in Viet-Nam could succeed. Chiang took the view that manpower was one thing the Communists had plenty of, and that we could not hope to defeat them solely by draining off their manpower. Cline said that this all led to the usual GRC argument that the only real solution to the Southeast Asian situation was an attack on the mainland of China; but he thought that Chiang in advancing his comments was sincerely persuaded that we were not on the right track in Viet-Nam.

Chinese Representation

5.   Cline talked to certain Chinese officials, including a former Ambassador to Australia, Chen Chih-mai, about the prospects for the Chinese representation issue in the UN. These felt that, if the U.S. made an all out effort, it would be possible to get through the next General Assembly by a margin of possibly 3 or 4 votes. Cline said that the fundamental GRC attitude toward the UN was that, while there was some prestige in membership, it was not really essential. Chinese take the view that the UN problem is really more a U.S. problem than one for the GRC. They are willing to cooperate with us on it, but they feel a defeat in the UN would be more a U.S. defeat than a GRC defeat. In answer to a question by Mr. Bundy, Cline said he thought the GRC would go along with a tactic designed to preserve its seat by making the minimum necessary gesture in the direction of a seat for Communist China while safeguarding the position of the GRC—but only if the GRC was persuaded that we were doing this for the purpose of helping the GRC, not simply to avoid embarrassment to the U.S.

The Air Force

6.   Cline said he found morale in the armed forces poor, and especially in the Air Force. Air Force officers are afraid that they are being rapidly outstripped by the competition on the mainland and they no longer have confidence that they are a first-class fighting force. Our MAP has not been sufficient to keep the Air Force in modern condition. A high number of planes have been lost and a high percentage are deadlined for

repairs. He said that some 25 F–86s had been lost last year. (On checking with DOD we found the correct figure to be 11.)

Chiang Ching-kuo's Health

7. Mr. Bundy wanted to know whether Chiang Ching-kuo's somewhat unresponsive attitude might not be a result of poor health. Cline believed not; in fact, Chiang Ching-kuo's health was about as good as it has been in recent years. Cline said that the younger Chiang is suffering from diabetes. So long as he takes care of himself and does as the doctor orders, his health is good; and in the last several months he has been very careful. Chiang is now 55 and the doctors give him another 8 or so years of good health.

Election of C.K. Yen

8. Cline observed that the election of C.K. Yen is being interpreted as President Chiang's solution of the succession problem. President Chiang is thought to have realized that it was necessary for a person of the younger generation to be named as Vice President. At the same time, he did not wish to set up as Vice President a person of sufficient political power to rival Chiang Ching-kuo. The future pattern, as Cline sees it, is that C.K. Yen will occupy the titular position while Chiang Ching-kuo holds the substantive power.

Madame Chiang

9. Cline said he heard gossip in Taiwan that there is an estrangement between President Chiang and Madame Chiang and that Madame Chiang will not be returning for the inaugural ceremonies May 20.

(*Intelligence Exchange*—In a separate conversation Cline told me that the intelligence exchange with the GRC on mainland China conditions was proceeding. The GRC had no great enthusiasm for it, but he (Cline) felt it was worth carrying on with it.)

Recommendations:

10. Cline said there were two things which we could do to improve the situation in Taiwan: (1) appoint a new Ambassador and (2) increase MAP for the Air Force. He felt these two steps were urgently needed to repair the eroded morale of the GRC leadership. When the new Ambassador is installed in Taipei, Cline said his first concern should be to reestablish a policy and strategy dialogue with Chiang Kai-shek.

143. Action Memorandum From the Assistant Secretary of State for International Organization Affairs (Sisco) to Secretary of State Rusk[1]

Washington, April 27, 1966.

SUBJECT

Alternatives on Chinese Representation in UN

You will recall that in your last luncheon meeting with Ambassador Goldberg there was a preliminary discussion regarding the future strategy and tactics of the United States on the Chinese representation issue at the coming 21st General Assembly. The discussion was inconclusive, and I indicated that IO was in the process of preparing a paper canvassing certain of the principal possibilities. Since then, the President has expressed his desire to find a way of handling the Chinese problem, including the Chinese Representation question at the next General Assembly, which would get the U.S. off the defensive.

This paper discusses the principal possibilities open to us at the General Assembly. None of them would, I believe, lead to Communist China's taking a seat at the 21st Assembly. In the first place, it is not at all certain that any of them would receive the necessary support for adoption, particularly if the Assembly continues to uphold the requirement for a two-thirds majority. Moreover, even if an invitation to Peiping were adopted, it would be in the framework of a two-China approach. It is extremely unlikely that Communist China would take a seat as long as the GRC remained in the Assembly, and we believe it should be possible to persuade the GRC to continue to remain as long as its presence prevented the ChiComs from taking a seat.

We assume that for this year at least the Security Council situation can be controlled and that our principal strategy must be directed to the Assembly and only thereafter to other UN technical bodies where the question has arisen in one way or another in the past. The risk would nevertheless exist that Assembly rejection of any new approach or action that resulted in no real change in the situation, might well lead to increased pressure for action in some other UN bodies.

There are several ways in which we could alter our strategy in order to help place the onus for Chinese Communist exclusion on them, and to bulwark our support and protection of the position of the Republic of China in the United Nations. Although certain risks are attached to all of

---

[1] Source: Department of State, Central Files, UN 6 CHICOM. Secret; No Distribution. Drafted by Sisco, UNP Director Elizabeth Ann Brown, and Betty Jane Jones of UNP. A checkmark on the source text indicates that it was seen by Rusk.

them, I believe that the best way to protect the GRC's place in the UN is for the United States not to stand still. The risks of such a position are greater than any other. The following are several principal courses of action, listed insofar as feasible at this stage in descending order of preference. Some could be used in combination.

1. *An Assembly declaratory resolution recognizing that there are now two successors to China's seat in the UN, both of which should be represented in the Assembly.*

Such a resolution would be one approach to a two-China conclusion. It would have the advantage over the study committee approach of being more manageable and less susceptible to being broadened to cover the questions of the other divided states. It would seek to preserve a seat for the Republic of China. If the Chinese Communists refused the seat offered them, as is likely, its seat would remain open and the Republic of China would continue its membership. Any subsequent pressure for a one-China solution should be manageable.

Such a declaratory resolution would seek to deal with the problem in the Assembly. Our strategy would be to defer dealing with the Security Council aspect until the situation in the Assembly had clarified. However, we can anticipate pressure and broad support for some kind of a General Assembly study of the Security Council problem in addition to the problem in its broadest aspect.

If, as we expect, both Chinas once again affirm their opposition to such a two-China approach, it is not clear whether the Assembly would decide to take formal action on it. Nevertheless, our objective of preventing the replacement of the GRC by Red China would have been achieved.

2. *GA Study Committee.*

Such a proposal would probably buy us another year. However, there are some difficulties with the study committee approach which carry risks for us. We would want the Assembly to deal only with the Assembly; the study committee would be likely to want also to deal with the Security Council aspect. There would be a real risk that the outcome of the committee study might be a one-China, one-Formosa solution or possibly even one China, and the wrong one.

Moreover, the problem of obtaining a satisfactory composition reflecting of sentiment toward both Chinas is a formidable one. We would also have to decide whether to participate in such a Committee, our tentative conclusion being that this would probably be necessary in order to protect our position.

In short, the study committee idea seems less manageable and more risky. We must recognize also that since Fanfani peddled this proposal broadly last year and it is therefore well-known, it is likely to be widely regarded as a time-buying device and less attractive than a substantive declaratory judgment by the Assembly in favor of a two-China solution.

3. *Mandate to Secretary General or GA President to explore with Taiwan and Peking the possibility of a two-China solution.*

This has a number of disadvantages. Such an approach could well be broadened into a negotiation of terms on which the Chinese Communists might be prepared to enter the UN. There might be a recommendation for the wrong China. Such an approach might be made very quickly and hence gain us little time.

4. *Resort to the International Court of Justice.*

This would obtain relatively little support in view of the general recognition that the problem is political, not juridical. Moreover, it would involve the Court in a highly contentious political matter which it is unreasonable to ask it to adjudicate. The outcome would also be uncertain.

5. *Stick with the present strategy.*

At the last Assembly the vote was 47–47 and the "important question" principle was upheld by a margin of seven votes. There have been some favorable developments in Africa and our present vote count indicates a slight edge in our favor.

We do not believe, however, that we can rely on this present vote count as the GA draws nearer. There are likely to be serious defections among our traditional supporters. The debate on China in our country has given rise to an expectation of greater flexibility in the US position. The recent Gallup Poll indicates that 56% of the American people would support Chinese Communist admission to the UN if this would improve US-Chinese relations.

Moreover, the political price that we would have to pay if we are to mount the extensive lobbying campaign required, particularly among such restive allies as Italy, Canada, Japan and Australia, would be prohibitively high. Finally, we cannot be certain that these tactics would succeed even with exhaustive lobbying.

6. *Stick with present strategy but stop lobbying.*

An important variant on the foregoing course would be for the US to maintain its previous position on the substance of Chinese representation but to desist from our traditional active lobbying. Of the courses mentioned, a passive attitude of this kind would do less damage to our relations with the GRC than taking any initiative toward a two-China approach but would give us the least control over the outcome.

Tactics

Various of our allies are prepared to work closely with us on new tactics. If we decide a new approach is desirable, there are two possible ways we can proceed:

1. We can decide to take the initiative, informing the GRC of the results of our analysis of the situation and attempting to convince it that its interests would be best served if we, in response to a number of approaches from our allies, informed our friends that we would be willing to consider a new approach to the Chirep question at the next GA. If the Chinese, contrary to our expectations, agree, or if we decide to go ahead over their objections, this would give us some control over the direction of new moves.

2. If we assume that it will not be possible to persuade the GRC of the correctness of our conclusions or that our relationship with the GRC is such as to preclude our taking the initiative, we could simply stand aside this year, making it plain to others (Canada, Japan, Italy, Australia) that they are free to submit whatever proposals they choose to produce a solution, but that the United States will maintain its present position and vote against any resolutions designed to open the way to the entrance of Communist China. In this way we would avoid any break with the GRC, and the burden would be on others to exhaust the possibilities for a solution.

The President suggested drawing on outside experts for advice on Chinese representation. I believe the IO Advisory Committee, the members of which are listed in the attachment[2] would be an excellent group to undertake such a task if we decide it would be useful. It has already expressed a desire to discuss the Chinese representation question, and it would be willing to make its views known privately if we so desire.

As you are aware, Ambassador Goldberg and I will be consulting with the Canadians in Ottawa on May 16. Since Canada has been pressing for discussion of Chinese representation and is clearly anxious to undertake some new initiative, we believe we could make good use of these consultations for a first exploratory discussion with Canada. These consultations also make more urgent the need for a decision on our part.

Recommendation[3]

That you convene an early meeting including Ambassador Goldberg, Mr. Bundy, Mr. Meeker, and myself for a preliminary discussion of Chinese representation, taking account of the analysis in this paper, with a view to arriving at a consensus which could be discussed with the President, if possible prior to our consultations in Ottawa.

---

[2] Not printed.

[3] The source text bears no indication of Rusk's reaction.

**144.   Letter From the Representative to the United Nations
(Goldberg) to President Johnson[1]**

New York, April 28, 1966.

Dear Mr. President:

I understand through Bob Komer you would like my current views on the Chinese Representation issue in the UN. You may recall that after the decision in the General Assembly last year I wrote you saying I was convinced we would have to move to a policy which would recognize the right of both the Government of the Republic of China and Communist China to UN seats.

I have discussed this again recently with Secretary Rusk and am especially anxious that we reach an early decision. We are already being unusually pressed by the Chinese and also by some of our friends such as Japan, Canada, and others about our policy.

Only you can make decisions required on this issue, and I hope you and the Secretary and I can sit down and discuss the matter before I go to Ottawa on May 17, where I will certainly be queried.

The attached memorandum[2] explains my views in detail. In essence they are as follows:

1. We run the grave and unacceptable risk of the majority vote going against the Government of the Republic of China in next Fall's General Assembly. There is even a substantial risk that we might lose two-thirds majority vote.

2. Our new basic policy, both for UN tactical reasons and for broader strategic reasons, should be (A) to assure maintenance of a Government of the Republic of China seat in UN and (B) to shift responsibility for any continued non-participation by Chinese Communists from us on to them in line with our developing concept of containment but not isolation.

3. We should therefore support a "Successor State" resolution in the next General Assembly which would recognize both the Government of the Republic of China and the Chinese Communists as having UN membership.

4. How we would get to the point is very important. I propose that as the first step I be authorized to explore with Pearson and Martin the

---

[1] Source: Department of State, Central Files, UN 6 CHICOM. Secret. Filed with an undated covering memorandum from Read to Rostow that states that a scheduled meeting on April 28 between Rusk and Goldberg to consider "the ChiRep question" had been cancelled but would be rescheduled early the following week.

[2] Not printed.

possibility of Canada taking the initiative on the successor state resolution next Fall without attribution to US: They are known to be interested in some such move. If they decide to do it we should then make an early approach to the Government of the Republic of China to assure them we will protect their seat in the UN to the hilt but also to warn them we cannot be expected to oppose Peking as strongly as in past against proposals to admit it. We would have to consider carefully how and when people like the United Kingdom and Japan would be informed.

5.   It will be much preferable, once launched, that a successor state resolution be adopted. We should therefore not oppose it and at an appropriate time, in consideration with Canadians, we might need to come out for it.

6.   It may turn out that we would have to commit ourselves to some degree also about the Security Council seat, although I would prefer not to do this at this point.

I am sending the Secretary and Joe Sisco a copy of this letter.[3]

Respectfully submitted

Arthur J. Goldberg

---

[3] The letter and memorandum were transmitted in telegram UNMIS 53 from USUN, April 27. (Department of State, Central Files, UN 6 CHICOM)

---

145.   Memorandum From the President's Special Assistant (Rostow) to President Johnson[1]

Washington, April 30, 1966, 9:45 a.m.

Mr. President:

Ambassador Goldberg proposes here[2] (and in a telephone call to me) that we:

1.   Decide soon to encourage the Canadians to propose a "successor State" position on the ChiRep issue at the next General Assembly (two-China policy).

---

[1] Source: Johnson Library, National Security File, Agency File, United Nations, Vol. 3. Secret; Exdis. A copy was sent to Bill Moyers.

[2] A copy of Goldberg's April 28 letter is attached.

2. That he be empowered to tell Foreign Minister Martin of Canada on the occasion of his meeting about May 17 that if they take the initiative we would not oppose.

3. If Canadians agree, we inform the Nationalist Chinese we shall protect their Assembly seat to the hilt but cannot oppose Peking for General Assembly as strongly as in the past.

4. He is vague on Security Council seat.

When he called me about this, I said:

—talk to Secretary Rusk;
—let President have the resultant recommendation well in advance of any meeting with him.

The meeting with Secretary Rusk may take place next Wednesday, May 4.

My first reaction is that:

—deciding now and telling the Canadians to go on this line with our support is premature;
—we must weigh carefully, before we make this historic decision:

a. The impact on an already shaky Taiwan.

b. The domestic political reaction which could go either way; but I recall General Eisenhower told President Kennedy this is the one issue on which he could take after him in public. It is possible the General's view has changed since 1961. But we ought to know.

c. I believe we have a solemn, secret commitment to Taiwan we would use our Security Council veto to keep the ChiComs out. I'm sure you know, but in any case, we have to think about how to deal with this problem.

d. The relation of any such move to Vietnam.

You may wish to have Secretary Rusk suggest to Ambassador Goldberg that we not make up our minds before the meeting with the Canadians in May, but that Goldberg join in the work of the China ideas group which is being set up as a result of your decision of April 23rd.[3]

Walt

Have Goldberg talk to Secretary Rusk and bring issue to you shortly thereafter

---

[3] An April 23 memorandum from Rostow to Rusk recording several Presidential decisions made that day states that the President "reiterated his desire that the regional Assistant Secretaries develop new constructive proposals with the assistance of the best brains that can be mobilized from outside the Government." Concerning China, it states: "Imaginative ways of handling the China problem, which would get us off the defensive, and deal with the ChiRep issue in the next General Assembly. In this connection, the views of Ambassador Goldberg should be solicited." (Johnson Library, National Security File, Rostow Files, Non-Vietnam)

Have Secretary Rusk set aside immediate decision and invite Goldberg to put views into China study group for later decision by you[4]

---

[4] The source text bears no indication of the President's reaction. A memorandum of a May 3 telephone conversation between Rusk and Rostow reads in part as follows: "R wanted Sec to know of President's response to R's memo re Goldberg's letter on going to the Canadians; R read Sec the alternative responses the Pres had checked, Sec thought the next step was that Sec should talk to Goldberg. R told of his conversation with Ben Read re setting up China study group and Goldberg having a hall in which to express his views; the Canadian thing was the Sec's problem." A copy is attached to Read's April 28 memorandum to Rostow cited in footnote 1, Document 144.

---

146. Telegram From the Department of State to the Embassy in the Republic of China[1]

Washington, May 7, 1966, 4:45 p.m.

1147. 1. We are disturbed, although not particularly surprised, by report in FCT 9218[2] that GRC may be gearing up propaganda campaign in US to "counter current trend of appeasement in US toward Communist China."

2. Judging by minimal impact of Madame Chiang's efforts to rouse American audiences, we doubt that GRC campaign here is likely to accomplish desired objectives. On contrary, it could work to GRC disadvantage by souring even present support of current US policy on China, particularly as result of concerted effort to attack personalities involved in current public discussion of China policy.

3. We are therefore anxious to quietly discourage GRC from propaganda effort at its incipience rather than having to deal with it in more public fashion at a later stage. We realize that GRC will not easily be deterred from making direct pitch to US public and that you are inhibited from using information on special group contained in TDCS report. However, we wonder whether problem cannot be discreetly discussed with key personalities in more general terms, stressing thesis pro-

---

[1] Source: Department of State, Central Files, POL 1 CHICOM–US. Secret; Exdis. Drafted by Sneider; cleared by Albert L. Seligmann of INR/RFE/NA and in draft by Deputy Assistant Secretary for Public Affairs William J. Jorden, Dean, and Fearey; and approved by Bundy.

[2] Not found.

pounded by FonMin Shen (FCT 9219)[3] that US policy not changed, but warning that climate of opinion in US nevertheless changed to extent that any concerted campaign by GRC to influence American public opinion could well prove counterproductive to its interests.[4]

Rusk

---

[3] Not found.

[4] Hummel reported in telegram 1259 from Taipei, May 11, that he had taken the matter up privately with Chiang Ching-kuo and Vice Foreign Minister Sampson Shen, both of whom had expressed agreement. (Department of State, Central Files, POL 1 CHICOM–US)

---

147. Telegram From the Embassy in the Republic of China to the Department of State[1]

Taipei, May 11, 1966, 0759Z.

1258. 1. Defense Minister Chiang Ching-kuo (CCK) called me in today to request reconsideration decision to withdraw F–104As and Bs.

2. He made it clear he was not questioning right of USG to withdraw 104s but he was questioning manner in which USG had handled this matter and wished to point out some of the problems caused to GRC.

3. He said 18 aircraft could not be crucial element in USG deployments and likewise they were not crucial to defense of Taiwan. He did not wish to make an appeal on military grounds but was more concerned about other aspects.

4. He said after 18 March notification that 104s would be temporarily retained President Chiang had approved organizational structure, selection of pilots for training, and other activities directed toward utilization these aircraft. If they now to be withdrawn "it would be very difficult to explain to President Chiang" (he said exactly this to Adm Sharp yesterday). Also would inevitably cause morale problems in CAF as well as adding to widespread uncertainty in Taiwan about future course of US policy. Some Legislative Yuan members, for instance, have appar-

---

[1] Source: Department of State, Central Files, DEF 19–8 US–CHINAT. Secret; Priority. Repeated to CINCPAC.

ently given credence to rumors that 7th Fleet mission in Taiwan Straits is to be curtailed or eliminated. CCK of course understood that such rumors have no basis but abrupt and untidy withdrawal of 104s will likely be misinterpreted along similar lines.

5. CCK asked me to convey urgently to Washington his request that decision be reviewed and reversed.

6. I said I understood his concern over way in which this had been handled and that in spite of best of intentions it would with hindsight have been much better if USG had never authorized temporary retention. None of us had any idea that "temporary" would mean only a few weeks with consequent inconvenience to GRC and possibilities for misunderstanding.

7. I suggested that imminent temporary deployment of one USAF F–100 squadron to Tainan during May and June would help relieve some local apprehensions, to which CCK agreed, saying he intended to visit the squadron as soon as it arrived, presumably in order to generate local publicity.

8. I said I knew enough from Washington communications to be sure there was virtually no chance of reversal of decision now. However I would report fully to Washington and see what could be done.

9. *Comment*: Admiral Ni made similar comments to me last night, and Adm Sharp and Adm Gentner have had separate requests from CCK. It is obvious there is genuine GRC concern, coupled with justifiable irritation over US handling of this matter. However believe deployment USAF F–100s is the best answer to GRC concern and that Department should authorize me to reply in a day or two regretting that decision on 104s cannot be changed.[2]

10. Adm Sharp has spoken to CCK of additional possibility temporary deployment USMC F–4 squadron. He has seen this message and is reporting separately today on his conversations.

Hummel

---

[2] Telegram 1183 to Taipei, May 13, authorized the Embassy to do this. (Ibid.)

148.   Memorandum From the Assistant Secretary of State for Far Eastern Affairs (Bundy) to Secretary of State Rusk[1]

Washington, May 13, 1966.

SUBJECT

ChiCom-U.S. Foreign Minister's Meeting

I attach a suggested draft letter to the Chinese Communists (Tab A) proposing a Foreign Minister's meeting to discuss means of lessening tensions in the Far East. We recommend that the letter be signed by the President. A Presidential letter will both give the proposal greater authority and prestige and, in the future, provide proof that the highest authority took positive measures to reduce the risks of a wider war in the Far East.

The letter could be delivered in Warsaw at the time of the next scheduled talks on May 25. Ambassador Gronouski might hand it to Wang without discussing its contents to avoid eavesdropping by the Polish and others. Alternatively, the letter could be delivered by Ambassador Gronouski's advisor (Dean) before or following the next meeting when he goes to the Chinese Communist Embassy to exchange texts of the opening statements. Or, thirdly, Embassy Warsaw could deliver the letter to the Chinese Communist Embassy prior to the May 25 talks.

While we are inclined to believe that the Chinese will reject the proposal, it is possible that they may believe a refusal would be interpreted by others as a further sign of Peking's intransigence. In the event they did accept and specified Warsaw as the meeting place we would hope the meeting or meetings would be held in a place (the U.S. and Chicom Embassies, perhaps) safe from eavesdropping.

We believe that the GRC should be informed beforehand that we are proposing a Foreign Minister's meeting in an effort to prevent Chicom miscalculations of our intentions. We must also tell the GRC, that, while we believe the prospects for a Chicom acceptance are remote, we believe it is essential to take all possible measures to avoid a wider war growing out of tensions or miscalculations in the Far East.

We believe that, after transmitting the letter, we should also inform the British, Australians, and South Koreans, at the highest levels only, that we have taken this step.

We would recommend that this initiative be handled with great care. In the event Peking declines the President's offer we should avoid

---

[1] Source: Department of State, Central Files, POL CHICOM–US. Top Secret; Exdis. Drafted by Dean on May 13. Bundy did not initial the memorandum, but it bears notations indicating that it was received in the Executive Secretariat, and Document 152 indicates that it was discussed with Rusk. The date is handwritten on the source text.

the temptation to make public the proposal and their refusal (unless the Chinese themselves publicize the exchange). If it is necessary, at some future time, to make known the offer the fact that we did not use it for propaganda purposes at the time will lend added weight and meaning to our move.

Tab A

Dear Mr. Prime Minister:

In the light of mounting tensions in the Far East I have considered for some time whether it would be wise to have meeting of our respective Foreign Ministers to discuss the grave issues of peace and war and to seek some means of lessening tensions in Asia.

You may recall that your representative at the Ambassadorial talks in Geneva originally raised the question of a foreign minister's meeting. Now I should like to propose such a meeting. My Secretary of State would be willing to meet with your Foreign Minister either at the next session of the Warsaw talks or at some other time or place convenient to your Foreign Minister. I would propose an open agenda. Our objective would be to provide each side an opportunity to discuss at a higher level some of the questions we have dealt with in Warsaw, to consider frankly and authoritatively our respective policies and intentions, to correct misconceptions about our respective views, and to seek means to dampen down the risks of a wider war in Asia.

In the interests of working towards peace and a better understanding between the American and Chinese people I hope your Foreign Minister will be able to meet with my Secretary of State.

Sincerely,

149. Memorandum From Secretary of State Rusk to President Johnson[1]

Washington, May 14, 1966.

SUBJECT

Need for New Tactics on Chinese Representation

Recommendation

As you requested, Ambassador Goldberg and I have reviewed the problems of Chinese Representation at the next United Nations General Assembly to see whether the onus can be shifted more clearly to the Chinese Communists for their exclusion.

There appears to be little prospect that our traditional position will be sustained by the forthcoming General Assembly. In the last Assembly there was a tie vote, and the question whether a two-thirds majority is required was sustained by a very small margin. The two principal alternatives which have been discussed in the General Assembly, as an alternative to our traditional position, have been (a) a resolution expelling Taipei and seating Peking and (b) a resolution inviting Peking to take a seat while retaining Taipei as a member. The second alternative would almost certainly not be accepted by Peking and would be far preferable from the point of view of the United States.

We recommend that you authorize us to discuss these tactical problems with the Republic of China in Taipei in an attempt to get them to stand steady, rather than withdraw from the UN, if parties other than the United States develop a "two Chinas" tactic at the 21st General Assembly along the lines indicated in the discussion below.

Similarly, we should discuss the tactics with certain other countries, in the first instance with Canada and Japan.[2]

Discussion

Both Ambassador Goldberg and I conclude that relying on our previous tactics on Chinese Representation involves an unacceptable risk of defeat and expenditure of U.S. influence. As you know, in the past our approach has consisted of obtaining Assembly agreement that any change in Chinese Representation requires a two-thirds majority and defeating resolutions calling for the replacement of Chinese Nationalists

---

[1] Source: Johnson Library, National Security File, Agency File, United Nations. Top Secret. Filed as an attachment to a May 17 memorandum from Rostow to the President (Document 150).

[2] The source text bears no indication of the President's approval or disapproval, but see Document 150.

by the Chinese Communists. A number of our friends such as the Canadians, are no longer prepared to go along with this approach. If we do not now devise new tactics, we might see the next Assembly evict the GRC and invite the Chinese Communists to occupy the Chinese seat in all UN organs. The international and domestic repercussions of such a development would be strongly adverse to us.

In canvassing the alternatives, we concluded that one course with the fewest risks involves a "two-Chinas" approach, and that we should not oppose such a course if others raise it. The objective would be to reaffirm that the GRC has a right to representation in the UN, while opening the possibility for the Chinese Communists likewise to be seated. We would seek to confine this proposition in the first instance to the General Assembly, leaving the question of China's Security Council seat in abeyance until Peking is actually in the Assembly.

If unexpectedly Peking were to make a complete reversal and decide to take a seat in the Assembly along with the Republic of China, the Chinese seat in the Security Council would be at once at issue. While there would be great difficulty in retaining Chinese Nationalist representation in the Security Council, it might be possible to avoid seating the Communists pending a study of the whole question of permanent membership in the Council.

Both Peking and the Republic of China will vigorously resist any two-Chinas solution. Our first problem, therefore, will be to convince the GRC that our shift in tactics is required to avoid total defeat and is designed to assure them continuing representation in the United Nations. We would add that if they accepted the two-Chinas outcome, there is every present prospect, although without complete certainty, that Peking would not take a seat in the Assembly.

Domestic opinion in this country would be more receptive today than formerly to such a shift in our policy. A Gallup Poll taken last month indicates that 56% of those questioned would favor Red China's admission to the UN if this would improve relations between us. The recent Congressional debate also indicates a moderation of sentiment on this subject, as does the general reaction to the steps we have taken offering the opportunity for increased contacts if the Chinese Communists desire them.

Our plan would be to have Ambassador McConaughy, shortly after he arrives, take up the question with the Chinese, inform them of our decision to shift our policy as the best way to protect the position of the Republic of China in the Assembly, and explain to the Chinese that the best way to continue to exclude Red China would be for the Republic of China to hold on to its seat in the Assembly. In addition, we would ask Governor Harriman some time in June to make a supplementary approach along the same lines. I intend to be in Taipei in early July and I could do any follow-up work necessary to tie this down.

Ambassador Goldberg and Assistant Secretary Sisco will be in Ottawa on May 16 to have a full day's discussion on UN matters. The Canadians are very anxious to be "unleashed" on this question, and the Pearson statement of the other day, for all practical purposes, puts the Canadians publicly in favor of a two-Chinas solution. Ambassador Goldberg and I are agreed that we should hold off the Canadians from launching a new tactic until we have had fuller discussions with the Chinese in Taipei. However, the indications are that the Canadian ideas are already reasonably well developed. Rather than run the risk of the Canadians developing a new tactic inconsistent with our objectives, Ambassador Goldberg and I are agreed that he should indicate great interest on our part to consult fully with the Canadians on the details of a new strategy on the understanding no new move will be launched by them pending our discussions in Taipei in June.

Congressional consultations would await further exploration with Taipei.

Dean Rusk

---

150. Memorandum From the President's Special Assistant (Rostow) to President Johnson[1]

Washington, May 17, 1966, 10 a.m.

Mr. President:

This recommendation from Secretary Rusk[2] is something of a landmark since it recommends to you that we begin to shift off our present policy toward Communist China in the UN, starting with talks in Taipei.

I have the following thoughts, aside from underlining the need for the highest degree of security:

1. On the domestic scene it would be helpful if General Eisenhower could be brought aboard at some appropriate stage. I believe he warned

---

[1] Source: Johnson Library, National Security File, Agency File, United Nations. Top Secret. Copies were sent to Moyers and to Special Assistant to the President Robert E. Kintner.

[2] Rusk's May 14 memorandum (Document 149) was attached.

President Kennedy that this was the only issue in foreign policy where he might take out after him. If the facts were laid before him by Secretary Rusk, and you put the issue to him, it seems to me possible that—as in the case of birth control—he might shift his position.

2. We are putting a heavy burden on a new ambassador to ask McConaughy to take up this question with the Chinese on Formosa immediately after his arrival. In traditional oriental style, a shadow may lie across his term as ambassador, as a bringer of bad news. It may be wise to let Averell start the conversation. At least the question ought to be put to Secretary Rusk.

3. It may be wise to caution the Canadians hard against a leak, since we plan to tell them of our Taipei probe.

4. Before approving finally the Taipei probe, you may wish to have a final session walking around the problem.

Walt

Set up a meeting[3]

Let it go

---

[3] This option is checked on the source text.

---

151. Telegram From the Mission to the United Nations to the Department of State[1]

New York, May 17, 1966, 1929Z.

4920. For the Secretary and the President from Goldberg. US-Canadian talks re ChiRep.

1. Goldberg, accompanied by Butterworth, Sisco, and Pedersen called on PriMin Pearson. FonMin Martin and Under-Secy Ritchie also present on Canadian side. One hour's conversation devoted almost exclusively to China reflected Pearson's and Martin's strong feeling there is need for movement on ChiRep issue at UN. Both stressed that they under strong pressure domestic opinion to make some change. Both

---

[1] Source: Department of State, Central Files, UN 6 CHICOM. Secret; Nodis.

feel Red China should be subjected to world opinion at UN. In responding to their views Goldberg adhered to line contained Goldberg–Rusk
memo to Pres.[2] Our impression is that over coming weeks Canadians
will develop and refine their ideas on "two Chinas" tactics for discussion
with us. Pearson and Martin gave categoric assurances, however, that no
move would be made by Canadians without further consultations with
us. Pearson seemed firm on need to protect GRC's position at UN, saying
that Canada would be "hard put not to vote in favor of a two-China res";
at same time it would be "hard put not to be against res which would
expel GRC".

2. Goldberg reviewed ChiRep experience in last GA, indicated no
change had been made in our policy but matter had been reviewed by
Secy and himself in recent days and was under active consideration. Our
assessment, based on 47–47 vote, that past traditional tactic unlikely to
hold, particularly since Africans, who will be pressing at UN on Rhodesia and SWA, cannot be relied upon in such circumstances to maintain
line on ChiRep.

3. Alluding to Pearson speech, Goldberg indicated interest on our
part in any new thoughts Canadians had developed, stressing at same
time that no new move be launched before we had opportunity for full
consultation with Taipei as well as other key Asian friends such as Japan,
Australia, Thailand, and Philippines. Said we would talk to Canadians
again after we had talked to Chinese to try to induce more realistic
understanding of situation by them. In meantime stressed US talking
only to Canada and not even to UK in this sense. Asked Canadians to
respect our confidence.

4. Pearson said if asked whether his speech indicated change in
Canadian view he would reply to effect that, yes it represented sense of
need to bring Communist China into contact with world but also that
Communist Chinese views and behavior and their conditions on UN
membership made it difficult to see how change could come. Said we
could be guaranteed of Canadian confidence and that they would give
us their views on how to proceed.

5. Goldberg stressed as he had earlier with Martin that he thought
neither US nor Canada had yet examined carefully enough what effect of
change in ChiRep policy might be on USSR. Sovs might think we were
doing it only to embarrass them in relation to Chinese. We had important
objectives with Sovs, such as nuclear treaty and non-proliferation, and
would not want to jeopardize Sov movement toward West. Pearson said
Sovs difficult to talk to at best and ChiRep would be subject almost
impossible to discuss with them. Agreed to importance of factor and said
they would give it consideration.

---

[2] Document 149.

6. Pearson said he very conscious of difficult situation ChiComs would create in UN. Thought this period we would have to ride through. Noted Molotov and Vyshinsky had been about as difficult and nasty as possible but that exposure to UN over years had ultimately moderated their behavior. Suggested exposure to counter-debate might similarly make it difficult for ChiComs to maintain outside China some of more outrageous positions they took at home.

Goldberg

---

152. Action Memorandum From the Assistant Secretary of State for Far Eastern Affairs (Bundy) to Secretary of State Rusk[1]

Washington, May 20, 1966.

SUBJECT

Draft Warsaw Instructions

1. The instructions for the next meeting between Amb Gronouski and the Chicoms on May 25 present many issues. The President has expressed his personal interest and desire to clear the instructions himself.

2. The attached draft (Tab A)[2] has been cleared in Defense and throughout the Department, except for the ACDA reservation noted in sub-paragraph e below. The following are the key points:

a. The discussion in paragraph 5 of the May 12 incident, particularly the last sentence.

b. The general language of assurance in paragraph 8. This substantially repeats prior language, but obviously takes on special importance at the present time.

c. The discussion of South Vietnam in paragraph 9. This too repeats themes previously used, but emphasizes them specifically in order to cover in detail two points raised by the President with Ambassador Gronouski: that we would cease bombing in Vietnam if there were an appropriate response, and the underscoring that our objective in Vietnam is a peaceful settlement.

d. The discussion in paragraphs 11–14 of our peaceful intentions toward Communist China. This too repeats earlier themes, but the tone is important.

---

[1] Source: Department of State, Central Files, POL CHICOM–US. Secret; Exdis.

[2] Not attached to the source text, but see Document 153.

e. The discussion in paragraph 16 of the Chicom proposal concerning non-first use. In this paragraph, ACDA has a reservation concerning the first three full sentences at the top of page 7 ("Mr. Ambassador . . . convenience.") These sentences have been cleared with Defense, but ACDA points out that they imply our willingness to accept a non-first use agreement, which as you know we have consistently rejected in Europe and which, in Asian terms, would be inconsistent with our actual military plans for the defense of Korea and Taiwan. The question is whether we wish to be this responsive when we know that in fact we could not accept a non-first use agreement which did not cover other types of forces and weapons. Defense reports that Secretary McNamara believes that this degree of forthcoming response is warranted, without significant risk. Ambassador Gronouski strongly favors it. Our own inclination is that this would not be a serious risk, but we must weigh the possibility of leak and serious concern in Seoul and Taipei.

f. The extensive discussion in paragraph 16 of our willingness to engage in disarmament discussions, and the specific communication stated in paragraph 17. The President has told Ambassador Gronouski that he wishes the message to emphasize our interest in disarmament and our wish for serious discussions. Mr. Sisco has prepared the message in paragraph 17 specifically in order to smoke out the Chicoms on the WDC exploratory group. There is general agreement that these elements of the instructions are wise, but I flag them for your attention.

3. In preparing these instructions, we have re-evaluated the proposal discussed with you last week that we give the Chicoms a message suggesting a meeting at Foreign Minister level. Such a message might be furnished in writing, and could be done at any time without regard to the specific date of the talks. In the last two days, Messrs. Ball, Johnson, and Thompson have concurred in the judgment that in the existing political circumstances in South Vietnam such a message at the present time would only be construed as a sign of weakness by Peiping, and would not have the positive effect we had envisaged a week ago. Thus, it would be our recommendation that we put this on ice for the present, while arming Ambassador Gronouski with a draft message which could be readily reviewed and authorized if the circumstances changed at any time. Ambassador Goldberg's views are discussed in the note from Joe Sisco attached at Tab B.[3]

4. In view of the President's desire to review this finally, and Ambassador Gronouski's departure Sunday, there would be advantage

---

[3] The attached memorandum from Sisco to Rusk, May 20, stated that he had had a further talk with Goldberg "with a view to getting him to go along with" the draft message to Gronouski without the proposal for a meeting at the Foreign Minister level and that Goldberg was "now agreeable" to this provided that Gronouski was given a draft message with the proposal which could be reviewed and authorized "as soon as circumstances changed."

if you could complete your review not later than Saturday.[4] For this purpose I am asking S/S to make a simultaneous immediate distribution of this memorandum, with the draft instructions, to Mr. Ball, Ambassador Thompson, Ambassador Johnson and Mr. Sisco. Ambassador Gronouski has already seen it and concurs.

5. If you approve these instructions, subject to any amendments you may make, I will prepare a Read–Rostow memorandum for submission to the President. You might wish to indicate by checks (in the margin of paragraph 2, above) which points in this memorandum you would specifically wish me to include in the memo to Rostow.

Recommendations:[5]

A. With regard to instructions at Tab A:

B. With regard to Presidential clearance:

1 Approve preparation of Read–Rostow memorandum incorporating points indicated in Paragraph 2 above.
2 No need for memo to Rostow
3 Prefer

---

[4] May 21.

[5] Rusk initialed his approval of recommendation A. Next to the line "With regard to Presidential clearance," the following notation appears in his handwriting: "Show him full text. DR."

---

153.   Telegram From the Department of State to the Embassy in Poland[1]

Washington, May 23, 1966, 11:19 a.m.

1752. Guidance for 130th Meeting, May 25, 1966.

1. Wang is scheduled to open. We anticipate that he will make bitter attack on U.S. for May 12 plane incident. Chicoms have charged that shooting down of Chinese plane over Yunnan was deliberate, planned war provocation. Wang's statement will probably echo May 13 *Liberation Army Daily* editorial which stated "While flagrantly extending the war of

---

[1] Source: Department of State, Central Files POL CHICOM–US. Confidential; Immediate; Limdis. Drafted by Dean; cleared by Jacobson, George B. Roberts, Jr., of FE/VN, Barber of Defense, Jacob D. Beam of ACDA, Assistant Legal Adviser for Far Eastern Affairs George H. Aldrich, Sisco, Bundy, and Rostow; and approved by Rusk. Repeated to Hong Kong, Taipei, and Saigon.

aggression in Vietnam, US imperialism has openly declared that China is its chief enemy and clamored that 'there exists the danger of war with China.' It was at this very moment that US air pirates intruded into China's airspace and made a surprise attack on Chinese aircraft. This was by no means an isolated or accidental case but a well planned act of the Johnson Administration—in attempt to extend further war of aggression against Vietnam to China. . . . Nefarious US imperialism is the biggest scoundrel of our times and an arch-enemy of the Chinese people."

2. Wang probably will also list U.S. acts of "aggression" against mainland China including: occupation of Taiwan, "several hundred" intrusions into China's territorial airspace and waters, and strafing attacks on Chinese fishing boats. He may repeat ChiCom allegations that U.S. intensifying war in Vietnam and bent on spreading flames of war to China. It is likely Wang will refer to recent 4 points Chou En-lai gave in interview with *Dawn* (China will not provoke war, China means what it says, China is prepared, a war will have no boundaries). See FBIS 90, May 10.[2]

3. Wang may raise air attacks on ChiCom Economic and Cultural Delegation quarters in Khang Kay on March 24. He may attempt justify ChiCom shoot-down of US A3B near Luichow Peninsula on April 12 and claim A3B's flight as additional evidence U.S. hostile intent. Considering recent nuclear test, also possible Wang may raise ChiCom's 1964 draft agreed announcement on meeting heads of states to discuss complete prohibition and destruction of nuclear weapons. (See record 123rd meeting.)[3] Similar proposal repeated in Sino-Albanian communiqué of May 14.

4. FYI: Following response has been cleared with Ambassador Gronouski. Suggest Harding prepare translation based on this text. You will be informed of any changes. End FYI.

5. Mr. Ambassador, in response to your charges concerning an intrusion of your border on May 12 by U.S. aircraft and the subsequent shooting down of one of your aircraft there appears to be considerable confusion about what actually did occur. We did have aircraft in the NW sector of NVN on that date. Our pilots claim, however, that they at all times remained south of the Red River. They state they were attacked by an unidentified aircraft and returned its fire. They saw it explode but saw no parachute. We have checked carefully with our pilots and with the

---

[2] The May 10 Foreign Broadcast Information Service report included the text of a May 9 New China News Agency release quoting Chou's four-point statement, which he had reportedly made to a Pakistani correspondent on April 10. McNaughton sent a copy to McNamara with a May 19 memorandum calling it to his attention. (Washington National Records Center, RG 330, OSD Files: FRC 70 A 4443, 092 China Reds) The full text of Chou's four-point statement is in *American Foreign Policy: Current Documents, 1966*, p. 666.

[3] See Document 69.

careful navigational equipment that was available on the American aircraft involved; these accounts concur that the U.S. aircraft were at all times over DRV territory. We repeat that American pilots have explicit instructions to avoid flying into your air space. If the evidence available to us should have been in error, we would of course have regretted this intrusion into your territory.

6. Reverting to the case of Captain Smith's flight in the Hainan area, we repeat that this was a case of mischance and navigational error.

7. As to the A3B aircraft on April 12, it too was far off course because of navigational errors when it was attacked by your pilots. Nonetheless, we understand that this plane was not over Chinese territorial waters when it was shot down. We would like to know if there were any survivors.

8. I am deeply disturbed by these incidents on both sides because misinterpretation of the motives behind these incidents by either side could lead to a further increase in tensions. I should like to repeat what I said in our last meeting. We have no hostile intent towards your government or your people. President Johnson has said that we seek the end of no regime and our Secretary of State has recently said we do not intend to provoke war. We have acted with restraint and care in the past and we are doing so today. FYI: Ambassador Gronouski is fully briefed on details May 12 air incident. End FYI.

9. Mr. Ambassador, by this time it should be clear that we intend to live up to our commitments to the Government of SVN. We are prepared to continue our present action as long as it is required to convince Hanoi and the Viet Cong that their efforts to take over SVN by force, terror and infiltration will not succeed. At the same time we are equally and sincerely prepared to seek a peaceful solution. We have stated time and again that our objective in South Vietnam is a condition of peace in which the South Vietnamese people can be free to choose their own future without outside coercion or force. We seek neither territory nor bases, economic domination nor military alliance in Vietnam. There are many roads towards a peaceful solution. We are willing at any time to engage in discussions or negotiations leading towards peace, without conditions. Alternately we are willing to undertake a reciprocal dampening down of the war. We will respond if others are prepared to reduce their use of force. Specifically, we are willing to suspend or even cease our air attacks on North Vietnam if Hanoi gives clear evidence that it is prepared to take reciprocal action, for example with respect to its infiltration of military personnel and equipment into South Vietnam and its military activity and terrorism in South Vietnam. Such evidence and suspension of the bombing could be determined by mutually acceptable observers.

10. It seems clear to me that Hanoi will eventually realize that a military victory is not possible. The DRV may hope to wait until the military

position is reversed, but this will not occur. As Hanoi continues to send more reinforcements south we will be compelled to reinforce the GVN. Over a period of time the VC and DRV forces will face further losses and defeats. The DRV, eventually, will realize that it could avoid all this bloodshed and destruction by evidencing willingness to engage in negotiations leading to a peaceful solution.

11. Mr. Ambassador, I have noted that NCNA has commented on Secretary Rusk's statement of March 16 before the House Subcommittee on the Far East. NCNA said that "all talks about 'improving relations' and 'avoidance' of a state of hostility are a sham." The *People's Daily* of April 6 said that the hints of "goodwill dropped by the U.S. are obviously part of its counter-revolutionary dual policy, an attempt to undermine the Chinese people's fighting determination and reduce their combat-readiness . . . The evidence is increasingly clear that the U.S. imperialists are preparing to impose war on the Chinese people." Similarly observer in the March 29 *People's Daily* said that "these blasts of good will set off by Washington at a time when U.S. imperialism is working more energetically than ever to concentrate its aggression on China, are indeed absurd and ridiculous . . . . All such expressions as a flexible policy, 'without isolation,' and 'more contact' are only pretenses for intensifying the U.S. containment of China."

12. Mr. Ambassador, I regret that your government seems to reject all our proposals for easing tensions. Judging from what your side says it appears that you choose to believe that U.S. does not seek a better mutual understanding. Despite our statements to contrary you say that U.S. only wants war with China. As I have tried to indicate, such a conclusion is not warranted by the facts.

13. There may be other reasons, both internal and external, why you wish to avoid a better relationship. Mr. Ambassador, we are willing to try to reach some mutual agreement on peaceful solutions of such critical problems as Vietnam but your side has rejected all such moves. We would like to work towards a reduction of tensions and a better understanding but your side rejects our efforts, We have explained our intentions towards your country but your side rejects our statements because you claim we are not sincere. You say we must prove our sincerity by actual deeds, by accepting, in fact, your own solutions. Mr. Ambassador, your side has its own convictions. So do we. In the interests of peace we are willing to search for a just solution. Are you willing to do the same? Mr. Ambassador, I intend to continue my efforts to convince you that my government seeks a just and lasting peace. We stand ready to fulfill the commitments we have made concerning travel contacts and visits, joint investigations, and discussions concerning peaceful solutions of the problems confronting us in the Far East.

14. I would like to draw your attention to the remarks I made at our 128th meeting on December 15, 1965.[4] At that time I said that "peace and stability in the Far East is as much in your interest as it is in ours . . . It would permit the withdrawal of U.S. forces. If we could be assured of peace throughout the Far East and the whole Pacific, our fleets and our bases would no longer be necessary."

15. There are a few additional matters I should like to raise. At our last meeting, I told you that I would ask for a further report on your charges that the Chinese Consulate in Phong Saly was attacked. I am informed that we have no additional information concerning this incident.

16. Mr. Ambassador, I have noted with considerable interest Premier Chou En-lai's statement of May 10 in which he said that China must conduct nuclear tests to develop nuclear weapons, because, although China had proposed a non-first use agreement to the United States, we had rejected the proposal. Mr. Ambassador, does this statement indicate that your government would consider an agreement to ban nuclear tests if it were linked to a non-first use agreement? This is an important point and I would like to ask you to seek clarification from your government. Perhaps you could let me know about this matter at your earliest convenience. While we believe that any disarmament agreement must be a rounded one which covers all types of forces and weapons, we are interested in any serious proposal that would contribute to disarmament. We are willing to explore disarmament issues with your government either here at Warsaw or elsewhere. In this connection, I would like to comment on Premier Chou En-lai's statements about the World Disarmament Conference in his April 10 interview with a Pakistani reporter for *Dawn*. He said that "a world disarmament conference in the present circumstances will yield no useful, practical results and will only provide U.S. imperialism with a smoke-screen of peace under which it will freely expand its war of aggression against Vietnam." You may recall my earlier comments about the proposed World Disarmament Conference. Last December I told you that we had our doubts about the effectiveness of a World Disarmament Conference because we believe it to be an unwieldy body that could make little positive contribution to disarmament. Nevertheless, I indicated to you that we were prepared to discuss the prospects for such a conference with you in a small exploratory group. We hope that Premier Chou's statement does not imply that your government believes that such an exploratory group for a World Disarmament Congress would not be able to make progress towards meaningful disarmament.

17. FYI. Request you send following letter to Ambassador Wang after 130th meeting:

---

[4] See Document 114.

"The Government of the United States has expressed its willingness to participate in an exploratory group to prepare a possible World Disarmament Conference. We note that your government has also called for a meeting of all heads of state to discuss disarmament. The Government of the United States would like to learn the views of the Government of the People's Republic of China with regard to its possible participation in an exploratory group to examine questions relating to convening a World Disarmament Conference or disarmament talks on some other basis." Ambassador Gronouski will sign letter. End FYI.

18. Mr. Ambassador, I have been requested by some of the families of the American prisoners in China to raise their cases with you once more. At our last meeting you informed me that it was your country's practice to grant time off for good behavior. I hope this regulation can be applied to our prisoners and I would appreciate any information you can give me concerning their cases.

19. Lately I have been receiving an increasing number of letters addressed to me from serious-minded Americans who have a great interest in establishing communication with individuals or organizations in China. They do not know the appropriate addresses or what ministry or organization they should write. Would it be possible for me to send these letters to you for the requested information?

20. It is our turn to propose date of next meeting. Suggest August 17.

Rusk

---

154. **Editorial Note**

On May 24, 1966, the President met with Acting Secretary Ball, Ambassador Goldberg, Assistant Secretary Bundy, and Walt Rostow for a discussion of China policy from 12:25 to 1:20 p.m. Prior to the meeting, he met with Goldberg from 11:37 a.m. until 12:25 p.m. The subject of that discussion is not indicated. (Johnson Library, President's Appointment Diary) No record of the meeting has been found.

According to a memorandum of a May 24 telephone conversation between Ball and U. Alexis Johnson, Ball stated that at the meeting they had "only gone over the ChiRep business" and that no decision had been made. Johnson asked "if we were going ahead with Taipei," and Ball replied that "there was no final decision even on that; the thought was that Walt would do some softening up and we would then leave it until the Secretary goes out." (Ibid., Papers of George Ball, China (Peking))

A June 14 briefing memorandum from Sisco to Rusk states that as a result of the meeting with the President, they were asked to prepare for Presidential approval an instruction for Ambassador Walter P. McConaughy, whose appointment as Ambassador to the Republic of China had been announced early in May but had not been confirmed by the Senate, on the assumption that he would raise the question when he arrived in Taipei. The memorandum states that McConaughy's approach "was essentially conceived as softening up exercise" to be followed by Rusk's conversations in Taipei in July. (Department of State, Central Files, UN 6 CHICOM)

---

155. Telegram From the Embassy in Poland to the Department of State[1]

Warsaw, May 25, 1966, 1955Z.

2066. Gronouski–Wang talks.[2]

1. Wang opened 130th meeting with prepared statement containing no surprises. He started with claim that May 12 plane shoot down over Yunnan was deliberate, systematic act of war provocation and repeated ChiCom Defense spokesman statement of May 12. Wang then handed over photographs of US fuel tanks and rocket parts and claimed these were iron-clad evidence of incident. Wang said incident definitely not accidental. He then read list of other "war provocations" against China including serious warning 399 through 402, the April 12 A3B intrusion, April 7 air attack on Chinese fishing boats. Wang claimed facts show US war provocations have been growing in frequency and intensity. He said he was authorized to lodge serious warning and protest most strongly to USG. Wang added, "You should think over carefully what grave consequences you will have to face if you go on like this."

2. Wang then commented on US China policy. Said top US officials recently have said US has changed its posture towards China from con-

---

[1] Source: Department of State, Central Files, POL CHICOM–US. Confidential; Immediate; Limdis. Repeated to Hong Kong, Taipei, and USUN. Passed to the White House and USIA.

[2] Gronouski sent a detailed record of the meeting in airgram A–877, May 30. (Ibid.)

tainment plus isolation to containment without isolation. He said these statements by bigwigs of USG indicate worn-out policy of containment plus isolation has gone bankrupt. Also said policy of containment without isolation is out and out fraud. "How can you succeed in containing China? China can never be isolated. USG says it wants to enlarge unofficial contacts with China and discuss questions of disarmament and nonproliferation of nuclear weapons with Peking and does not intend to attack China . . . US tries to cover its aggressive designs with flimsy veil, but it can never succeed."

3.   Wang said US has occupied China's territory of Taiwan by force, built strings of military bases around China, incessantly sent warships and military aircraft to intrude in China's territorial air and sea space in its "unbridled military provocations." He also claimed US opposes restoration to China of its legimate seat in UN; "US has imposed trade embargo on China; openly declared China its principal enemy; shifted its global strategy to Asia; and is feverishly planning carry its war of aggression from Viet-Nam to China."

4.   Wang read complete text Chou En-lai four points (China will take no initiative to provoke war with US, they mean what they say, China is prepared, if war breaks out it will have no boundaries, see FBIS 90, May 10). He said whatever policies of hostility US may adopt, China will never make slightest change in its solemn position.

5.   Wang switched to Viet-Nam, claimed US had further intensified its war of aggression, increased troops, stepped up air raids, used B–52s against North Viet-Nam, used poison gas, US bent on extending flames of war of aggression to whole of Indo-China, US instigating attacks by its Thai and SVN puppets on Cambodia and Laos, US planes bombed Chinese economic cultural mission in Khang on March 24. Wang claimed Mansfield's call for peace talks was swindle. Claimed defeat of US in Viet-Nam a foregone conclusion, said US had already changed 13 horses in SVN and having difficulty finding 14th horse. "Like ants in frying pan, US in very difficult position in Viet-Nam." Wang said only way out was for US to accept DRV's four points and Front's five points, withdraw all troops and recognize Front as sole representative of SVN prople.

6.   Using Department's instructions I responded by telling Wang that American pilots have explicit instructions avoid flying into ChiCom airspace. I said that if evidence concerning May 12 plane incident available to US should have been in error, we would of course have regretted incident. Said I was deeply disturbed by incidents on both sides because misinterpretation of motives by either side could lead to further increase in tensions. I repeated President's statement that we seek end of no regime. Followed up with Department's guidance on Viet-Nam, US relations with Communist China, American prisoners, and disarmament. I added that by not taking up our proposals for exchange newsmen, doctors, educators, his side was making it difficult to prevent its own isola-

tion. I defined our concept of containment—defense of non-Communist countries who are threatened by outside-directed force of subversion, and told Wang that as long as Peking seeks spread its views through force and revolution we will continue defend ourselves and allies. I said our objective was to live in peace with his and all other countries, and that I hoped in time his government will adopt same objective. Said we hopefully looking forward to day when on cultural, philosophical and other grounds there could be maximum of intercourse between all nations. I denied use of poison gas in Viet-Nam.

7. Wang, his advisor, and interpreter took special note of my question whether Chou En-lai's May 10 statement linked banning of nuclear testing to a non-first use agreement. They consulted amongst themselves for several minutes. Later Wang made no mention of this statement nor did he refer again to subject of disarmament. This is unusual since Wang almost always responds to each subject I bring up.

8. Wang responded to my statement with long commentary on US policy of containment. Said US only purpose was to carry out policy of hostility to China. "US says one thing and does another." He said, "If US does not change and completely abandon old policy of aggression against China, and refuses to withdraw all forces from Taiwan Straits and Taiwan, then China cannot believe so-called sincere desire of US to improve relations."

9. Wang denied China aggressive. Said China would strive shoulder to shoulder and hand in hand with all oppressed people for liberation, but that China has not committed aggression against any country nor engaged in terrorist action or subversion against any foreign country.

10. Wang returned to subject of Viet-Nam but offered nothing new. Wang also referred again to May 12 incident and said US explanation completely untrue. "Since US calls itself strong power why shouldn't you have courage to admit this crime?" Referred again to US air attack on Chinese Consulate at Phong Saly.

11. Wang said he had already made clear his answer concerning Captain Smith. Smith is criminal who intruded into Chinese airspace and will be dealt with according to Chinese law. As regards Walsh, he was spy and must be dealt with in accordance with Chinese law. Wang said he had nothing further to say on this matter.

12. I replied with rebuttal touching on May 12 plane incident, fishing boats, and Viet-Nam. I repeated that if we in error concerning May 12 plane shoot-down and incident occurred over Chinese territory, I would extend sincere regrets for this accidental encounter. Also said I was concerned about his claim US planes attacked Chinese fishing boats and would like to investigate them further to make sure that if incidents did take place, they do not reoccur. Told Wang I disappointed by his earlier rejection my suggestion we jointly investigate these incidents. I also told Wang again that US not hostile to his government or people. Said US

forces are in Asia in direct response to situations not of our own making. His leaders preach war and revolution and should not be surprised if other countries, particularly those in Far East, are fearful of this threat to their own peace and security. Consequently, many have asked for our assistance. I said Wang's side ought to test our willingness to negotiate to prove if we have sincere desire reach peaceful solution.

13. Wang's reply contained nothing new. I suggested next meeting convene on August 17. Wang replied he busy in August. He suggested September 7 for next meeting. Meeting lasted two hours fifty minutes.

14. At conclusion meeting I asked Wang and his staff to farewell drink for Dean on May 26. Wang regretted and said he would not have time.

15. Atmosphere of meeting was relatively mild. The Chinese did not make an emotional issue of the May 12 plane incident, attacks on fishermen, or other US "war provocations." When Wang read from his instructions his voice was low and deliberate. In some of his rebuttals, particularly when discussing US hostility to China, he abandoned his papers, raised his voice and became more excited, gesturing and sometimes groping for words. He played same line over and over, particularly on containment. He made no new points or new commitments. His statement on Viet-Nam was routine as was his statement on US relations with China. He rejected all prospect of relaxing tensions through increased contacts.

16. Department may wish to inform Captain Smith's wife and brother about Wang's comments concerning Smith since both are aware we intended raise subject this meeting.

17. Suggest delay in briefing GRC in Washington and Taipei until we submit more detailed telegram for GRC briefing. Delay could be explained by referring to fact previous briefings based only on partial, incomplete reports.

18. Dean and Harding will deliver letter on World Disarmament Conference (para 17 reftel) at 10:30 am May 26.[3]

Gronouski

---

[3] Telegram 2071 from Warsaw, May 26, reported that they had delivered the letter (see Document 153) that day, and that the Chinese had asked about the meaning of Gronouski's query about Chou's May 10 statement on nuclear testing. (Department of State, Central Files, POL CHICOM–US)

156. Memorandum From the Ambassador at Large (Harriman) to the President's Special Assistant (Moyers)[1]

Washington, June 3, 1966.

Attached is the memorandum I wrote to the President November 19, 1964.[2] Much of it is now outdated, except the fundamental truth that the image of the President abroad is the single most important factor in molding world opinion towards the United States.

It seems to me that today much can be made of the fact that the President has achieved an extraordinary victory in the Dominican election in proving his faith in the ability of people to decide their own future if given the opportunity without interference. This ties in with his objectives in Vietnam.

We discussed the profound impression which the President's speech made on the African Ambassadors. This I believe could and should be gotten across in some way to the African peoples.

It is difficult to carry the worldwide unpopularity and misunderstanding of Vietnam along with an unpopular China policy inherited primarily from Dulles. I feel the President could well gain in most parts of the world by a spectacular change in attitude towards Red China. It would then, I believe, be easier to gain better understanding of Vietnam.

Without being specific, I would suggest the President's acceptance of "containment, but not isolation" through adoption perhaps of a two-China policy. The Department has been studying this matter for five years to my knowledge. But the subject requires considerable study to bring it up to date, although a part of this has already been done. I understand there is a notion being considered to let some other nation propose this in the UN without our opposition. The US would cover up its past by abstaining. To me, this would miss a real opportunity for the President to take leadership.

I fully recognize the problem of giving full support to the war in Vietnam, while at the same time making a gesture towards Red China. But on balance I see an enormous "plus" in this move towards obtaining greater credibility and more understanding of our Vietnam policy in world opinion.

Incidentally, there might be an opportunity for a public rapprochement with Bill Fulbright as the instigator of the China hearings, without embracing Fulbright's softness on Vietnam.

---

[1] Source: Library of Congress, Manuscript Division, Harriman Papers, Kennedy–Johnson Administrations, L.B. Johnson, Jan.–July 1966. Secret; Personal.

[2] Attached but not printed.

I can only assure you of one thing, that a suggestion of the above would be opposed by the State Department for a dozen reasons, including unhappiness in Taipei.

Bob McNamara had an unusually good public reaction to his Montreal speech.[3] I am speaking of the body of his speech, not his final proposal for the two-year service. I refer particularly to his readiness to have a new look at our relations with Red China, as well as his emphasis on other policies, rather than military power, to achieve security. Of course, the latter got attention because of Bob's position. He really said nothing new, but it confirmed the newsworthiness of "man bites dog." It seems to me, however, that since Bob's speech went over well it might be worth while for the President to take some occasion to indicate his support of Bob's ideas (omitting two-year service proposal).

I mentioned to you the possibility of the President's taking leadership in advocating action by NATO to break down East/West European barriers, possibly at the conclusion of the Brussels Foreign Ministers conference. An opportunity exists prior to DeGaulle's visit to Moscow.

You asked me for suggestions. The above is all I can come up with this afternoon. I thoroughly enjoyed lunch and look forward to talking with you next week.

Averell[4]

---

[3] Reference is to an address given by McNamara on May 18 before the American Society of Newspaper Editors in Montreal. The text is printed in *American Foreign Policy: Current Documents, 1966*, pp. 14–21.

[4] Printed from a copy that indicates Harriman signed the original.

---

157. Telegram From the Embassy in the Republic of China to the Department of State[1]

Taipei, June 15, 1966, 1005Z.

1448. 1. Following observations and suggestions offered for Dept's consideration in connection with visit to Taipei of Secy Rusk.

2. Top GRC officials have carefully followed recent statements by US administration officials, Congressional leaders and private citizens

---

[1] Source: Department of State, Central Files, ORG 7 S. Top Secret; Exdis.

on subject of US policy toward mainland China. While official reactions from MOFA have been restrained, and unofficial reactions (from Chiang Ching-kuo and other GRC officials) carefully refrain from raising alarm, believe GRC fully aware of implications of implied US denial of GRC national goal of return to mainland.

3. Therefore believe we have opportunity, because ground has been prepared, for somewhat franker discussion than has been customary. There are risks in being too explicit about US disbelief in GRC ever under any circumstances returning to mainland, but believe Secy can and should be forthright in acknowledging that USG envisages possibility (perhaps remote in probability and in timing) of changes in mainland regime which could cause USG to modify present policies.

4. Believe any less forthright statement would be mistake because new Ambassador will need to begin discussions with GRC of long-term implications for Taiwan—discussions which have heretofore usually been taboo in very high level conversations. Need to open this topic is also a function of possibility US ChiRep tactics may have to be changed and USG may have to try to persuade Gimo not to walk out of UNGA if some kind of resolution with "two Chinas" implications is passed.

5. Discussions with Gimo and FonMin could include following statements volunteered by Secretary:

a. Observations on SEATO and ANZUS conferences and on situation in Vietnam.

b. Importance to the US of close relations with the GRC and the importance to the US and the free world of a strong democratic Taiwan.

c. Appreciation for economic and social progress.

d. Appreciation for GRC efforts through Vanguard program to raise food production in underdeveloped countries and extend their ties with free world. Also could indicate US desire to work out appropriate ways to assist Vanguard.

e. Thanks for allowing USG use of GRC military facilities.

f. Reaffirmation of US commitments to GRC, summarizing in succinct form: Defense Treaty, opposition to ChiCom entry into UN, US use of veto in Security Council "if it would be effective", assurances that USG will not bargain away at Warsaw any of these commitments, and any other appropriate assurances.

g. Reminder of GRC commitment to obtain joint agreement before using force against mainland.

h. Expression of concern at very high level of GRC military budget which could if further expanded hamper economic development.

6. Secretary should be prepared to deal with:

a. Request for "unequivocal" reaffirmation of US support for GRC as sole Govt of China (this is context in which US attitudes toward changes on mainland could be brought forward by Secretary).

b. Request for US public statement that if ChiComs enter UN the US will withdraw (this would be place for explanation of US concern about GA voting, hopefully including US assurance that if voting lineup continues to seem favorable then US contemplates no change in strategy).

    c. Possible but improbable ultimatum by Gimo that if UN votes any kind of entry to ChiComs then GRC must withdraw from UN or at least from UNGA.

    d. Ominous and cryptic GRC statements sometimes heard by EmbOffs that if goal of return to mainland disappears then stability on Taiwan will be threatened, presumably either by GRC military hotheads, or by Taiwanese demands for greater political power.

    e. Request for US support of an Asian anti-Communist military alliance.

    7. It is possible that in spite of GRC understanding of recent US statements Gimo will again request US logistic support for massive assault on mainland "as only means of dealing with root of Vietnam problem." Without trying to outline detailed scenario, suggest Secretary should say frankly that American traditions and present day opinions will not support such an action, and that US is committed instead to containment of aggression while strengthening chances for peaceful solutions.

    8. Believe we have passed the point where offers to study "concepts" for assault on mainland will be either useful or credible to GRC.

Hummel

---

158. Telegram From the Department of State to the Consulate General at Hong Kong[1]

Washington, June 16, 1966, 10:23 a.m.

1632. 1. UK HK Chargé Hopson's report on his conversation with Ch'en Yi prior to departure from Peiping for Hong Kong for Chiefs of Missions Conference follows:

    2. After referring to full exposition on Vietnam which he gave me last year, Ch'en Yi said there has been talk abroad of peaceful negotiations, the convening of the Geneva Conference, etc., to discuss an end to the war. But the Vietnamese (both DRV and SVNLF), the people most

---

[1] Source: Department of State, Central Files, POL 15–1 CHICOM. Confidential; Limdis. Drafted by Dean, cleared by Robert W. Drexler in INR/RFE, and approved by Jacobson. Repeated to Saigon and London.

concerned were against negotiations. Conditions were not ripe; reason was that U.S. had no intention of withdrawing from Vietnam. The Chinese Government supported this stand. The U.S. had never expressed the intention of withdrawing; on the contrary the Americans were expanding the war and in the final stage would escalate it to China. Some people thought that events would not develop in this way but China had to be prepared. Judging from their dealings with the U.S. since 1945, the Chinese could not assume that U.S. adventurous policy had "no" limit. Nothing was unlimited, but the fact was that U.S. would not withdraw from Vietnam and last stage would be U.S. escalation of war to China. He hoped this estimate would be proved wrong. The facts, however, were more likely to prove it correct. The U.S. was meeting difficulties in Vietnam and they would meet even greater difficulties in China if they attacked.

3. There were many conditions for ending the war but the following were the two principal preconditions:

(a) The U.S. must immediately withdraw from Vietnam; and
(b) They must recognize the South Vietnamese National Liberation Front as the sole representative of the Vietnamese people.

4. If these two conditions (the minimum proposed by the people on the ground) were accepted, all other problems could be solved. Stopping of American bombing of North Vietnam and reunification would present no problems if basic conditions were met. It would also be easy to implement the Geneva Agreements which stipulated that Vietnam should not take part in military alliances. The SVNLF could discuss this matter with the North Vietnamese without outside interference.

5. The British Government could help by stressing these two Vietnamese preconditions. The Chinese and the North Vietnamese would regard any proposals divorced from these conditions as being pro-American.

6. Naturally Ch'en Yi wanted to see China's rightful seat in the United Nations restored. But more important was the question of relations between China and the U.S.: If Sino-American relations were improved, then the question of the UN would be solved. The question now was that the Americans were not willing to stop their aggression in Vietnam and no matter what "His Excellency Rusk" said, they were preparing to escalate that war. There were of course other outstanding Sino-American issues but if there were no withdrawal from Vietnam there was no question of talking about the improvement in Sino-American relations. Some people said that China was not interested in acquiring her seat at the UN. The Chinese would definitely not make any concessions in a matter of inherent rights. But the main question was Vietnam and the danger of escalation of the war to China.

7. When the Americans had withdrawn from Vietnam leaving the South and the North Vietnamese to settle their problems themselves, there would be hope of improving Sino-US relations.

8. Ch'en Yi referred to the four points made by Chou En-lai on 10 April[2] (my tel No. 358) and asked that these should be conveyed to the Americans as well as to the Conference of British Heads of Mission. Chou En-lai's four points ("China will never start a war with U.S.; what China says counts; China is prepared for escalation; if Americans extend war to China there will be no boundaries to that war") all revolved around the question of Vietnam and Sino-American relations.

9. Referring to Ch'en Yi's "two preconditions," I reminded him of the English saying that "politics is the art of the possible." I said that the Americans had entered into obligations with the South Vietnamese Government which made it impossible for them to withdraw from Vietnam immediately without further ado. For those obligations to be fulfilled, the right conditions had to be created. Moreover what was the basis for calling the SVNLF the only legal representative of the Vietnamese people? The SVNLF might represent a faction—perhaps an important faction but there was nothing legal about their status. I had no doubt that if a conference were convened, ways could be found of ensuring their participation or representing their point of view. But there was no legal basis whatsoever for claiming that they were the only legal representatives. If therefore Ch'en Yi's two preconditions were rigidly applied no solution was possible.

10. Ch'en Yi said that he knew that the Americans could not accept them, but he also knew that the Vietnamese would not accept any departure from them either. The only course therefore was to be prepared for the worst.

11. Vietnam and Sino-American relations also figured to some extent in the exchanges on Sino-British relations for a summary of which please see my immediately following telegram.

Rusk

---

[2] See footnote 3, Document 153.

159. Letter From Secretary of Defense McNamara to Defense Minister of the Republic of China Chiang Ching-kuo[1]

Washington, June 16, 1966.

Dear Mr. Minister:

Thank you for your letter forwarded to me by Ambassador Chow on 25 April.[2]

Your comments on Communist aggression in the Far East were of great interest. In this respect, I particularly appreciated your assurance of continued cooperation in countering such aggression.

Following his discussions with you in March, Assistant Secretary Bundy informed me of the problems which you raised.

You commented in your letter on Communist Chinese plans to attack Taiwan in the immediate future by air. Our review of this threat has revealed no evidence of such plans nor any significant movement of units into base areas within range of Taiwan which would indicate that the Communist Chinese had such an attack in mind. I know you are appreciative, however, of Admiral Sharp's recent temporary deployments of F–100 and F–4 aircraft to Taiwan. These deployments again demonstrate US capability to respond promptly with effective force should the need arise.

I consider very important your reference to conferences with Vice Admiral Gentner and Major General Johnson on ways and means to improve your air defense capabilities. This type of high-level review is required periodically to assure a thorough understanding of the many problems of air defense and to achieve maximum capabilities with available units and equipment. In this regard, I have been informed that a Systems Training Program is now being instituted in Taiwan which will realistically simulate air defense situations for intensified training of air defense personnel. I hope that this program will provide you with a new and more effective means of evaluating and improving your air defense system.

With respect to your comments on deficiencies of your F–86F aircraft, I have learned the two crashes within the past year were attributed to structural failure, with the possibility that two other crashes may have been due to similar causes. We are expediting production and delivery of modification kits which, when installed, will insure the structural integrity of these aircraft. I know that Major General Johnson and his staff will

---

[1] Source: Washington National Records Center, RG 330, OSD Files: FRC 70 A 4443, China Nats 373.24. Secret. Drafted by T.L. Ridge of OASD/ISA/FER.

[2] Dated April 15; the letter is attached but not printed.

render every possible assistance in dealing with this problem. In the meantime, we will continue to implement our plans to replace the F–86F's with F–5 aircraft commensurate with the availability of funds and our worldwide commitments for F–5's.

You also referred to the Military Assistance Program. The degree of US concern for the security of the Republic of China and our other allies facing the Communist threat is indicated by our past and current Military Assistance Programs. As you are aware, your cumulative program for the period FY 1951 through FY 1966 amounts to more than $2.4 billion, making the Republic of China the second largest current recipient in our total worldwide program. In the proposed FY 1967 program now before the Congress, we have once again allocated approximately three-fourths of the total program, which includes over fifty countries, to the ten countries adjacent to the borders of Soviet Russia and Communist China, where our forward strategy draws the front lines of free world defense. The proposed FY 1967 program for the Republic of China is again one of the largest.

Even within this very large current program, however, certain of the items which you mentioned in the Memorandum you left with me last September,[3] and which you again discussed with Assistant Secretary Bundy, cannot be programmed. Because of this and because of our continuing mutual concern that your armed forces have adequate modern equipment, we believe that the quality rather than the size of the force should be emphasized.

I was pleased to note your reaffirmation of our understanding of military sales. As you know we have just sent a team to Taiwan to investigate the possibilities of co-production of military vehicles. This and other possible projects will represent a significant investment and should be carefully evaluated in terms of effects on your overall economy.

As you have no doubt been informed, the US Congress recently authorized the loan of a destroyer and destroyer escort to the Republic of China. These will be included within your Military Assistance Program as funds permit. We have also agreed to the sale of another APD to replace the one which was recently lost while under tow. When these ships and the recently acquired APD's have been reconditioned, and the latter type converted, to assure their maximum combat effectiveness, the naval capabilities of the Republic of China should be significantly improved.

I hope you will continue to consult freely with Vice Admiral Gentner and Major General Johnson on matters of military concern to you. I

---

[3] Dated September 16, 1965, the memorandum is attached but not printed; for Chiang's September 22 conversation with McNamara, see Document 104.

can assure you that they and Admiral Sharp are able spokesmen on programs that are of mutual interest to our countries.

Please convey to President Chiang my personal regards and sincere best wishes for every success during his new term of office.

Sincerely,

Robert S. McNamara[4]

---

[4] Printed from a copy that indicates McNamara signed the original.

---

160.   Memorandum From the Executive Secretary of the National Security Council (Smith) to President Johnson[1]

Washington, June 29, 1966, 7 p.m.

Mr. President:

Consul General Rice in Hong Kong sends in a highly interesting summary of what is apparently going on in Communist China.

Bromley Smith

Attachment

From Hong Kong (2327)

SUBJECT

Mainland China: Speculation on Recent Developments

At no time in recent years have there occurred on Mainland China developments at once so important and so clouded in obscurity as those

---

[1] Source: Johnson Library, National Security File, Country File, China, Vol. VI. No classification marking. A handwritten "L" on Smith's note indicates that it was seen by the President. The attachment is a retyped copy of telegram 2327 from Hong Kong, June 25, and is identical in substance to the telegram as received, a copy of which is ibid. Another copy is in Department of State, Central Files, POL CHICOM.

of the past few months. Part of what has been happening is on-stage drama, but the stage managers' identities have been unclear. Their purposes have been ambiguous, and the noises from the wings suggest that the most important events have been occurring offstage. I have, at least, so concluded since my return earlier this month to the vantage point provided by Hongkong. Evidently foreign observers on the Mainland enjoy no substantially better overview of events: One of them, British Chargé Hopson, remarked to me a week ago that it is impossible for those observers now to know what is really going on in China.

It may nevertheless be worthwhile at this point to draw back from reporting of daily events and speculate about what may be going on—if only to identify some of the main unanswered questions and to set up hypotheses and alternative explanations to be tested for subsequent acceptance or discard when further facts become known. Within my post there is a healthy range of opinion on which I have drawn and which should facilitate further hammering-out of conclusions on the anvil of argument.

Multiple Character of the Crisis

First of all, have we been observing an ideological purge, a dispute over policy, or a power struggle? Almost certainly all three.

In arguing over policy or in criticizing an official's performance in a Communist State, ideology provides much of the language, and ideological correctness is likely to be advanced as the main yardstick. No group of leaders could address the major problems China faces or contemplate the setbacks it has recently suffered, without arguing over policies. Even if ChiCom leaders were all selflessly devoid of individual ambition to wield power—and there is much reason to think otherwise—the outcome of policy disputes and ideological arguments will help decide who moves up, down, or out. It is the relative weight which should be assigned each of these three aspects of the present struggle which cannot be judged with any degree of accuracy.

The Internal Power Struggle

The antagonists in the power struggle must surely have in the back of their minds Mao's age (now 73) and the question of who will succeed him. And the shadow of this coming event must lend urgency to maneuverings for position among the leadership under Mao—maneuverings in which Mao may not have played a deliberate role. At the same time official statements and the atmospherics both suggest to some members of my staff that there may have been a serious challenge from within the party to the authority of Mao himself. If Mao himself unleashed the present storm, its violence—before which all China seems to be bowing down as though Mao were God—suggests his doing so was triggered by something of no mean importance. A May 4 editorial in the

Liberation Army Journal about a "life and death struggle" against elements which include "Right opportunists within the Party" may have overstated the case with typical Chinese Communist hyperbole, but such circumstances as recourse to an Army journal to contradict the Party's leading newspaper suggest a serious struggle did indeed occur. In any case, political power abhors a vacuum and there will always be those who are tempted—sometimes prematurely—to seize authority from apparently failing hands. That a hard-liner, ranking Politburo member and "close comrade in arms" of Mao like Peng Chen would fall during a "cultural" purge suggests how dangerous it can be to be called—as Peng was in the talk of some Chinese—the "Crown Prince" while the Sovereign is still alive.

The Cultural Purge

The ideological purge now being attempted in China under the current "Cultural Revolution" undoubtedly is intended to be more sweeping than any which has occurred in China since about 221 B.C. It was then that the authoritarian first Emperor of the Ch'in Dynasty ordered the burning of the Confucian books, in an effort to destroy the ideological basis of Feudalism and the authority of the scholar-official class which had served the Feudal Lords.

As Chou En-lai has put it, the present objective—and it represents an unrealistically big order—is "to liquidate completely all old ideas, all old culture, all old customs and traditions which have been created in the course of thousands of years by the exploiting classes to corrupt the people." The current cultural campaign is largely directed against what might be broadly termed today's class of scholar-officials, who are or are suspected of being the carriers of that old culture—not only scholars and educators, but also newspaper editors and other Party specialists in the field of publicity and propaganda. A topmost Communist scholar like Kuo Mo-jo may perhaps escape a worse fate by publicly asserting that everything he has ever published was "rubbish," but a Peking newspaper editor like Teng T'o will not get off so easily for having at one point written, in veiled but understandable language, that one of Mao's foreign policy assessments—that the East wind was prevailing over the West wind—was "great empty talk."

A few isolated cases of double-talk might be passed over without resulting in an ideological purge, but frequent and more explicit challenges of the Party line could not. It is the official line that the thinking of Mao Tse-tung provides the basis for solving all problems. "Mao's thought" is undoubtedly intended to serve as a gyroscope, keeping the Chinese Communist ship of state away from the shoals of revisionism and on the revolutionary course he has set—now and for the future after he is gone. This line has been questioned too often of late, while he is still alive, to instill confidence it would be generally accepted after he goes. A

Mao who attacked Peking University students for giving only lip-service to Communism could scarcely be expected to tolerate explicit challenge, and evidently he has not.

Who is in Charge?

We do not know to what extent Mao is in charge of the purge, and to what extent he has felt personally threatened by events leading up to it. Mr. Hopson, the British Chargé, reports that the atmosphere in Peking reminds him of that in Moscow during the time of the doctors' plot. I would not blame Mao, given his suspicious and obsessive character, if he did not feel safe in Peking. In any case, he appears to have stayed away from the Capital throughout the past half-year. (The last two times we have heard of his whereabouts he was, respectively, near Canton and probably in the vicinity of Shanghai: except in political terms their climate is not all that much healthier than Peking's.)

Reports of conversations held with Mao at Canton last March present the picture of a man complaining that his subordinates do not tell him everything—which is undoubtedly true—and in the grip of what we would regard as obsessions. However, the vigor of his arguments makes it clear he has not become, as one commentator had concluded, a senile vegetable. It would accordingly be logical to suppose he is well able to fight back against his adversaries. It is not likely that he is directing the campaign in detail: that was not his habit when, a far younger man, he was directing campaigns from his cave in Yenan, so it is unlikely he is doing so today. It is also unlikely that Mao's subordinates, in carrying out operations under his authority, do not utilize it in ways which serve their own interests and discredit their rivals.

It is now clear that the campaign is being spear-headed by or in the name of Minister of Defense Lin Piao. Retrospectively, one is entitled to wonder whether the opening maneuvers of this campaign did not begin long ago. For some time Lin has been building himself up as a leading exponent of "the thought of Mao Tse-tung." The abolition of military ranks and distinctions of uniform, a reversion to practices of civil war days which created so much speculation at the time, put the leaders of the Peoples Liberation Army in position to point to themselves as exemplars or pure revolutionary orthodoxy. And the extension of the commissar system from the People's Liberation Army to industrial, financial, and commercial sectors of the economy, with many Army veterans becoming its commissars, may have inserted the influence of Lin and his associates deep into the citadels of the pragmatists and revisionists who had been challenging Maoism as the solution of all China's problems.

It is also possible that Mao may have decided to back Lin as the successor to his own position of Party Leader. A number two man like Liu Shao-chi, who is almost Mao's age, might not provide a succession which is long enough to ensure its consolidation, and Mao may remember the fate of the one really revolutionary and authoritarian Chinese Dynasty—it perished in a power struggle shortly after its founder's death. Lin Piao not only has more charisma than Lin: at 59 he is a decade younger than the average among the full members of the Politburo.

The foregoing hypothesis is open to questions based, inter alia, on long-held assumptions that Lin was in chronically poor health. However, these assumptions are drawn into question by evidence of his intense if not generally publicized activity in 1960–61, as indicated in captured documents from that period. Moreover, the veterans of the long march were a tough lot: many of them endured great hardships, survived serious illnesses such as tuberculosis, and have lived to ripe age.

Mao's most recent pictures showed him meeting the Albanian Premier, who was in China in May, in company of the triumvirate of Lin Piao, Teng Hsiao-ping, and Chou En-lai—not looking moribund. The ever-supple Chou En-lai has been acting as exponent of the Cultural Revolution and has just been entrusted with an important mission abroad. Teng also was with Mao during a recent meeting with Japanese Communist leaders. And Lin has retained the greater prominence into which he stepped, with the publication last September of his article on "People's War"; it is only he who now is being cited as having "creatively applied the thought of Mao Tse-tung."

All of this may help answer the question as to what men are really in charge of China and the purge: it suggests that under Mao the party chairman there is a triumvirate: Lin, the Head of Armed Forces; Teng, the Party Secretary; and Chou, the Prime Minister. Chief of State Liu Shao-ch'i continues to perform his representational duties, but his chance for succession to Party leadership may have been hurt by close association with the career of P'eng Chen, Mayor of Peking and only Politburo member known to have been caught so far in the purge.

The Policy Struggle

China has, within the past few years, suffered two sets of great policy failures, one internal and the other external. The first, of course, was the failure of the policies of the Great Leap towards rapid industrialization and full-scale Communism. Defense Minister P'eng Te-huai objected to them and was purged in consequence; it later failed and China was so badly shaken that the third Five-Year Plan had to be postponed for three years, and may still be the subject of dispute.

The second was the great series of setbacks attending initiatives in the foreign field which, had they succeeded, might have diverted U.S. efforts from Vietnam. (The disaster in Indonesia was the most resounding: Communist China may have intended Indonesia to serve as the southern arm of a great pincers on the two sides of Southeast Asia.)

The foregoing failures would undoubtedly have brought down the elected regime in any parliamentary democracy. They undoubtedly raised serious strains within the regime in China where, given its one-party system, policy dispute would be largely contained within the Party but could hardly be excluded from it.

It may be premature to say what the final result will be, in policy terms, of the leadership struggle and ideologic purge which have been going on. However, it appears clear that the ship of state is, internally at least, on a leftward track: the pragmatists are being discredited and there is published and other evidence of plans for another Leap Forward.

The greatest issues in the external policy sphere evidently have concerned China's confrontation with the U.S. There is reason to think Mao expressed, at a meeting late last September of the Party's Central Committee, the conviction the U.S. and the USSR would attack China within the next two or three years. Mao professed that same belief to the head of the Japanese Communist Party as recently as last March. It is doubtful all within the Chinese leadership believe such an attack inevitable or that efforts to avoid it should not be made: Chen Yi on June 9 conveyed to British Chargé Hopson the impression he did not totally share Mao's apparent conviction. And even if the leadership were agreed that an early war with us were inevitable it does not follow they would be careless about precipitating it on the theory that how it comes does not greatly matter. They will greatly prefer the external and internal advantages of being the party to conflict which is the apparent victim of aggression. This undoubtedly contributes to the apparent Chinese Communist intention not to become directly embroiled with the U.S. in Vietnam provided we do not precipitate such embroilment.

To most Western minds, and undoubtedly to some Chinese Communist military and non-military minds as well, a conviction we will soon attack China—consequent to frustration in Vietnam or out of more deliberate calculations—would not be consistent with presumably reliable reports of continued Chinese Communist supply of tanks and MIG's to Pakistan. It might be assumed China would want not only to retain its present inventory of these items but also to build it to the maximum extent from current production against the day of our attack. This may leave out of account two considerations: Mao may hope Pakistan would put such matériel to good use for renewed operations against India—to the discomfiture of both the U.S. and the USSR—in case we were embroiled in a war with China. (A U.S. war on China, its leaders like to warn, would not be limited.) Moreover, Mao's defense strategy would depend primarily on the resources of manpower, space, and time rather than complex weapons—he would pit China's strengths against our weaknesses, not vice versa.

Accordingly, the ChiCom supply of tanks and planes to Pakistan is one more evidence that Mao remains in command of major decisions in China and that his strategic thinking prevails there.

Rice

161. Study Prepared by the Special State–Defense Study Group[1]

Washington, June 1966.

COMMUNIST CHINA: LONG RANGE STUDY

[Here follow a foreword, table of contents, and introduction.]

Abstract

A. The Problem

The essence of the problem which Communist China poses for the United States may be stated very simply: The Chinese regime's objectives of regional hegemony and world revolution clash with our own fundamental interests in preventing domination of Asia by any single power and in developing a peaceful and open world society of free nations.

---

[1] Source: Johnson Library, National Security File, Country File, China—Communist China Long Range Study by the Special State–Defense Study Group. Top Secret; Special Handling Required; Not Releasable to Foreign Nationals. According to the foreword, the study was undertaken on March 8, 1965, as a result of an agreement between the Deputy Secretary of Defense and the Deputy Under Secretary of State for Political Affairs. The Study Group operated under the policy guidance of those two officials and the JCS Chairman. It was directed by Joseph A. Yager of the Policy Planning Council and Brigadier General Stephen W. Henry, USAF. Its mission was to examine the politico-military position of the United States vis-à-vis "Communist China and other potentially hostile or disruptive forces in the Far East" through 1976. Before preparing the Long Range Study, the Study Group prepared a Short Range Report, dated April 30, 1965; see Document 92 and footnote 2 thereto.

On October 19 the Far East Interdepartmental Regional Group (a sub-group of the Senior Interdepartmental Group) endorsed the basic policy concepts developed in the Long Range Study, as summarized by the FE/IRG China Working Group. The minutes of the October 19 meeting and the China Working Group report are filed in Department of State, FE/IRG Files: Lot 70 D 56.

The Chinese must overcome formidable external obstacles and serious domestic deficiencies if they are ever to reach their ambitious goals. Nevertheless, the weakness of most of the nations East and South of China, China's own size and revolutionary dynamism, and her growing military power combine to make her a major source of difficulty for us in the present period.

B.   Broad Strategic Choices for the U.S.

In seeking to cope with the problem which China poses for us, we must choose among three broad national strategies; disengagement, containment and showdown.

The first and last of these possible strategies possess disadvantages which clearly exceed their advantages:

—In the absence of a stable, advantageous balance of power in Asia—or even the prospect of such a balance in the foreseeable future— disengagement would not only be a betrayal of those Asians who have relied upon our support and protection, but would in fairly short order ensure domination of much of Asia by a single hostile power.
—Seeking an early showdown is not, given the pride and intransigence of the Chinese people and their leaders, a feasible means of bringing about a desired change in Chinese policy, but would lead to a war which would impose on us uncertain, but probably large, costs in blood, treasure and prestige for highly uncertain gains.

Having excluded both extremes, we are left with a national strategy of seeking concurrently to check the spread of Chinese Communist power and influence and to induce moderation of Peking's current expansionist policies. As will be brought out later, this strategy of containment must be applied differently in the different sectors of China's periphery. In all areas, however, containment is not a negative defensive strategy, but requires the dynamic and imaginative application of a wide variety of political, military, economic and psychological measures.

Before considering how a containment strategy should be applied, it is necessary to ask how possible developments in mainland China and surrounding areas may either facilitate or interfere with that strategy's success. For purposes of this Abstract, we will concentrate on a mainstream projection of future possibilities and ignore the contingencies which are set forth in Chapters II and III.

C.   Possible Developments Within Communist China

Peking is today in the twilight of the regime's revolutionary age. How the new day which will dawn after Mao's passing will differ from the one that is now fading, no one can now say, but sooner or later important changes will occur.

All of the apparent contenders to succeed to Mao's power appear to belong to his school of hard-line, doctrinaire Communism. They were all steeled in the long struggle for power against overwhelming odds, followed by more years of stubborn effort to remake the most populous nation on earth. But even among this group of old revolutionaries, as current evidence suggests, recent failures at home and abroad may have caused differences on basic policy issues. Certainly the pressures for a policy reappraisal must already exist and may grow after Mao's death.

Outstanding among the sources of such pressures is the continued indifferent performance of the economy and the prospect that its future performance will be little, if any, better. Chinese economic growth is weighed down by the failure of the regime thus far to solve the problem of expanding agricultural output faster than population. If, as appears to be the most likely of various possibilities, the agricultural sector and population both grow by about two percent annually over the coming decade, the economy as a whole will probably not be able to expand output by more than about 3-1/2 percent annually. More rapid growth would require greater support from agriculture in the form of industrial raw materials, food for urban workers and export earnings to pay for imports of machinery and technology.

Even the modest over-all rate of growth projected above will require the recapture and investment of a substantial fraction of increases in the national product. As a consequence, per capita consumption may rise very little, if at all, and consumption levels in the country-side may actually be forced down to permit the rise in urban consumption associated with continuing industrialization. The regime may therefore be caught in a vicious circle. Increased agricultural output requires greatly expanded supplies of chemical fertilizers and probably also added material incentives. Neither can be provided in sufficient measure at existing levels of production.

This circle might be broken if industry could perform substantially better despite the constraints imposed by the slow pace of agriculture. The main difficulty here is in the heavy commitment of scarce engineering and scientific manpower to military production programs, particularly the advanced weapons program. Because military programs have top priority, non-military industry suffers and the industrial sector is unable to produce (or to pay for the import of) incentive goods and chemical fertilizer in the quantities that would give agriculture the needed boost.

Prolonged semi-failure in the economic field cannot but have adverse effects on the morale of the cadres and on the people's responsiveness to exhortations for continued effort. Nevertheless, there is no reason to expect a fatal weakening of the regime's well-organized system of control, much less the appearance of effective organized dissidence. The new generation may, as Mao fears, be lacking in revolutionary zeal, but it will also probably accept conformity to political orthodoxy as the inevitable condition of survival in a totalitarian society.

Despite serious economic constraints and a probable decline of elan among cadres at all levels, the regime should be able to carry out a limited number of military programs over the next ten years. The ground forces will probably remain at about their present size, but will be given more modern equipment. The air force will be strengthened by domestic production of substantial numbers of jet fighters, a smaller number of jet medium bombers, and possibly some jet transports. The principal additions to the navy will be in the form of fast patrol craft and submarines, probably including several capable of firing ballistic missiles with a range of about 350 nautical miles.

The most significant advance over the next decade will be in the field of nuclear weaponry. By the mid-1970s, Communist China may have deployed as many as 60 MRBMs and a few ICBMs, possibly with thermonuclear warheads. The Chinese may thus possess a significant and growing regional strategic capability and the beginnings of a counter-deterrent force targeted against the continental United States.

In external relations, Peking will continue to avoid actions involving a high risk of a direct military clash with either the U.S. or the USSR, but will probably continue to pursue policies inimical to the interests of both great powers. Even after Mao, the Chinese leaders may be expected to continue trying to subvert the USSR's leadership of the international Communist movement and to oppose "U.S. imperialism" on many fronts. Peking will also continue efforts to expand its influence beyond its borders by a combination of means emphasizing subversion, diplomatic maneuver and, when possible, support of "wars of national liberation."

However the current struggle in Vietnam comes out, Southeast Asia will continue to be an attractive area for the application of Chinese tactics and an area of prime Chinese interest. Chinese hostility toward India will probably persist and China will attempt to divert Indian energies and undermine Indian self-confidence and prestige by a combination of subversion, military threats on the disputed Sino-Indian border, and intrigue with India's enemy, Pakistan. Toward Japan, China will seek on the one hand to disrupt the U.S.–Japan alliance by arousing Japanese fears of becoming involved in a nuclear war and on the other hand to expand economic relations with Japan in the interests of her own development effort.

D.   *Possible Developments in China's Periphery*

   1. Southeast Asia

The outcome in Vietnam is of critical importance for other parts of Southeast Asia and will also have important repercussions in more distant areas. For the purpose of this study, we assume that, well before 1976, large-scale military operations will have been terminated under conditions generally favorable to the U.S. but that some Communist-inspired guerrilla warfare will continue. To guard against a renewal of Communist military activity, a substantial U.S. combat force will probably have to remain in Vietnam for some time. The Government of Vietnam will have made some progress in rehabilitating the country, but will not yet have forged strong ties with the masses of the people and will continue to be afflicted by internal factionalism.

In North Vietnam, failure of the war effort would depress the cadres and undermine the regime's credit with the people. Even with Soviet aid, the damage and disruptions of years of war could not be quickly overcome.

After failing to take over South Vietnam by force, Communist strategy in Laos might follow one of two courses. The Pathet Lao might re-enter the Vientiane government and, under cover of ostensible observance of the 1962 Geneva agreements, seek to take over the entire country by subversion. Or, with North Vietnamese support, the Pathet Lao might try to over-run non-Communist areas by military means. The former alternative appears more probable, especially if the Communists have good reason to fear a U.S.-supported Thai counteraction to any attempt they might make militarily to move up to the Mekong.

In Thailand, the problem of Communist insurgency will persist, but the projected events in Vietnam would have a tonic effect and confirm the Thais in the wisdom of their pro-U.S. alignment. The same events would probably induce Sihanouk to move Cambodia toward a more genuinely neutral position. Burma, in her self-imposed isolation, will be relatively little influenced by these or any other external events and will continue to be characterized by economic weakness and internal dissension.

2. Southwest Pacific

Indonesia will probably be ruled by a conservative government under strong military influence. Despite the persistence of highly difficult problems of economic development and political fragmentation, Indonesia's prestige in the immediate area will increase, facilitating Djakarta's efforts to take the lead in sub-regional cooperation.

Both Malaysia and Singapore will benefit from the end of Sukarno's policy of confrontation, but these two former British colonial areas will face new problems of external defense as the U.K. reduces its military presence there. Also, both will experience some economic difficulties and both may become more subject to internal communal controversy as their present leaders are succeeded by less talented men.

The Philippines may experience increasing social unrest owing to the failure of an opportunistic and often corrupt leadership to solve the country's economic problems and give its youth a sense of purpose. Leftist, pro-neutralist, nationalist, and anti-American sentiment will grow in student and intellectual circles, but the security ties with the U.S. will nevertheless be maintained.

Australia and New Zealand will continue to give us effective support and to pursue polices reflecting the broad coincidence of their national interests with our own.

3. South Asia

The chances are good that over the next ten years India will remain under reasonably effective nationalist, non-Communist and civilian leadership. Assuming that effective measures are taken to increase agricultural output and to reduce restrictions on private initiative—and that large quantities of foreign economic aid continue to be available—India should do a little better economically than Communist China. India will probably acquire a limited nuclear weapons capability within the next few years.

Pakistan should do even better economically, again assuming the continued availability of substantial foreign aid, but militarily Pakistan's ability to compete with India will probably deteriorate. Frustration over the Kashmir issue and fear of India will encourage Pakistan to continue to look to China, and possibly also to the USSR, for support and protection. Pakistan is most unlikely, however, to move into the camp of either great Communist power, and it will preserve a significant if diminishing relationship with the U.S. The present Ayub government or a similar regime based on the Army and the bureaucracy should remain in office through most of the decade.

4. East Asia

Over the next ten years, we can expect to find ourselves dealing with an increasingly strong, prosperous, confident and nationalistic Japan ruled by a pro-Western conservative government.

Japan will play an increasingly important role in Asian political and economic developments. Japan will move more cautiously in the security field, but by the mid-1970s she may alter her defense posture, become an air and naval power of regional importance and possibly assume some responsibility for the defense of South Korea. An independent Japanese nuclear weapons program is a serious possibility during the decade.

Her security and economic relations with the U.S. will remain vitally important to Japan. Termination or even renegotiation of the Mutual Defense Treaty now seems unlikely. Within the next few years, however, the U.S. may be confronted by a serious Japanese effort to regain full administrative control over the Ryukyus.

Economic relations between Japan and mainland China will probably expand greatly and Japanese recognition of Peking is likely within the decade. Japanese-Soviet relations should improve markedly, especially in the economic sphere.

The Korean peninsula will probably remain divided at the truce line, but interest in reunification may increase in both North and South Korea along with a heightened sense of political and economic competition between the two regimes. Both North and South Korea should maintain respectable rates of economic growth, but both may experience domestic political instability. The influence of Japan will be felt increasingly in both North and South Korea.

On Taiwan, the death of Chiang Kai-shek may bring power rivalries among the GRC military to the fore. A more fundamental problem will be the continued Taiwanese resentment at being excluded from political leadership. In time, however, a new and more stable balance should be struck between Taiwanese and mainlander interests, based on Taiwan's sound economy and on the fact that both groups share an interest in continued stability.

Even by 1976, the GRC will probably still proclaim recovery of the mainland as its primary objective, but will have tacitly acquiesced in a two-Chinas situation. Well before 1976, a majority of governments will have shifted recognition from Taipei to Peking and voted for Peking's admission to the United Nations.

E.   *General Lines of U.S. Action*

In light of the possible developments in Communist China and surrounding areas, how should the U.S. apply the strategy of containment over the next decade?

1. Alternative Containment Postures

a.   *In East and Southeast Asia*, three general containment postures are at least theoretically available to us:

(1) Close-in containment and forward defense, including maintaining a significant military presence on the mainland of Asia;
(2) Containment and defense primarily from the offshore island chain; and
(3) Remote containment and mid-Pacific defense behind buffer zones.

The last of these possibilities must be set aside for present purposes, since it presupposes greater strength and stability in the non-Communist periphery of China than appears attainable within a ten-year period.

In evaluating the remaining two strategic choices, we must distinguish between what is desirable and what is practicable. Maintaining sizable U.S. armed forces on the mainland of Asia is costly, restricts our strategic mobility and can lead to friction with the host governments and peoples. At the same time, abandonment of close-in containment in Southeast Asia is out of the question while we are locked in a struggle to preserve the freedom of South Vietnam. Even after the military phase of this struggle has been successfully concluded, we will find it necessary for some time to maintain a meaningful military presence in mainland Southeast Asia, in order to bolster the internal stability of South Vietnam and the non-Communist portion of Laos and deter further Communist aggression against those two areas of Thailand. Substantial U.S. forces may also have to remain in South Korea for many years to deter renewed Communist aggression, maintain public confidence there and still Korean fears that we might leave them alone to deal with a resurgent Japan.

We shall be able to move back from close-in containment to containment primarily from the offshore island chain only if:

(1) The likelihood of overt Communist aggression should have diminished as a consequence of a clear down-grading of expansionist goals in Peking, Hanoi, and Pyongyang.

(2) The ability of threatened non-Communist areas to cope with Communist insurgency and to meet the first shock of overt aggression should have increased substantially relative to the threat.

(3) The demonstrated capability of U.S. forces to redeploy rapidly into the threatened areas should have greatly increased as a consequence of improved air and sea lift, standby arrangements for the use of bases and other facilities, forward pre-positioning of stocks and improved strategic warning. Conditions in all mainland areas concerned are not likely to satisfy the above requirements for many years, and possibly not within the decade under study.

b. *In South Asia*, the option of containment primarily from an off-shore island chain is not available. Close-in containment by the U.S. is not required by the nature of the threat and is also ruled out on political grounds. We are, therefore, left in this area with no choice but remote containment behind the buffer consisting of the Indian subcontinent.

2. Major Aspects of a Containment Strategy

Successful containment, whether close-in, remote or from the off-shore island chain, has three major aspects, each of which will be taken up briefly below.

a. *Deterring or Defeating Communist Expansionist Efforts.*

(1) *Overt Aggression.* Ever since the Korean War, the Chinese Communists seem to have been deterred from overt aggression in areas where there was substantial risk of a direct clash with the U.S. The continued effectiveness of this deterrent depends on our continued ability to apply appropriate defensive or retaliatory military power when and where needed and on the continued credibility of our resolve to do so.

Our base structure will probably continue to be adequate for these deterrent purposes over the coming decade. We may, however, need to negotiate new standby arrangements with Australia, the U.K. and India covering possible contingencies in South Asia.

Even today, it is unlikely that we could cope with a full-scale Communist attack on Southeast Asia without using nuclear weapons or resorting to large-scale mobilization. [*1 line of source text not declassified*] Preservation of a conventional option in these contingencies will require increases in our ability to bring conventional military power to bear in Asia, commensurate with the present threat and the anticipated improvement in the quality of Chinese Communist conventional forces.

Credibility of our nuclear deterrent might be improved by deploying to [*less than 1 line of source text not declassified*] Guam nuclear-capable forces which would be clearly and specifically designed to cover targets in China rather than in the Soviet Union and which could reach those targets without overflying Soviet territory.

(2) *Indirect Aggression.* The current hostilities in Vietnam began as a classic case of indirect aggression, but even a US/GVN success there will not constitute a permanent cure for Communist-directed and supported insurgency. Laos, and more recently Thailand, are already victims of indirect aggression. Possible future targets include Malaysia, the Philippines, Burma and Indonesia. We must therefore carefully study the lessons of our experience in Vietnam and make necessary adjustments in techniques of propaganda, civic action and economic assistance, as well as in military doctrine and weapons development.

(3) *Subversion and Diplomatic Maneuver.* The Chinese leaders consider the underdeveloped, formerly colonial areas of Asia, Africa and Latin America as the arena in which China can best contest for world power status and influence. Subversion and disruptive diplomacy are their principal chosen instruments in these areas.

Economic aid is perhaps our major tool in dealing with this form of the Communist threat. Military aid can also play a role in helping develop forces capable of contributing to internal security. Diplomatic and psychological efforts can emphasize the lack of relevance of Chinese experience to much of the underdeveloped world, the limited ability of the Chinese to provide useful assistance, and the threat to the integrity of new and weak nations posed by Chinese-supported subversion and insurgency.

b. *Strengthening Areas Threatened by Asian Communism.*

Strengthening the free nations around Communist China is essential to the success of remote containment in South Asia and to any hope of moving back from close-in containment in East or Southeast Asia. We need urgently to acquire a better understanding of how relatively backward nations develop politically and how we can influence that development in desired directions.

The principal means available to us for strengthening nations under the Asian Communist threat are again our programs of economic and military aid. In most of Asia, agricultural development and population control are keys to sustained economic growth. Both should receive a high priority in our aid programs.

The fragmentation of the area around China increases its vulnerability to Communist pressures. Through our aid programs and otherwise we should do what we can to promote regional and subregional political, military and economic cooperation.

   c. *Additional Measures to Influence Asian Communist Behavior.*

In barring the way to expansion of Asian Communism and in strengthening the non-Communist areas around China we, of course, exert a powerful influence on the Communist leaders to moderate their policies. These generalized effects of our deterrent posture should be supplemented by timely application of a number of specific measures.

(1) We should obtain the advantages of differential treatment of Communist regimes in Asia as we have in Europe. Recognition of Outer Mongolia is probably the place to begin. The day when one of the lesser Asian Communist regimes might become an Asian Poland or Romania might be closer than is now apparent.

(2) We should try to induce present or future Communist leaders to reappraise U.S. intentions by avoiding actions which irritate the Chinese without compensating benefits, by reassuring Peking publicly, privately and by our actions that we do not intend to work for the overthrow of the regime, by showing continuing interest in discussing arms control proposals, and by modifying our export controls to permit humanitarian shipments to mainland China (i.e., food, drugs, and medical equipment).

(3) We should seek to increase Peking's interest in developing a more constructive relationship by continuing efforts to develop unofficial contacts, proposing the exchange of cultural and educational materials and exhibitions and holding out the prospect of step-by-step general relaxation of our economic controls in the context of reciprocal Chinese moves toward improved relations. Gaining access to the U.S. market should be particularly attractive to the Chinese.

(4) We should expose Chinese elite groups to a wider range of information through an expanded Voice of America Chinese language service and through indirectly feeding into information channels leading into China (e.g., Japan and overseas Chinese communities) material which might add to intellectual ferment there.

F. Longer-term Perspectives.

A strategy of containment need not result in a frozen confrontation. Successful containment in fact both facilitates and takes advantage of favorable change.

At the present time, however, the national interests of the U.S. and China clash on two fundamental points:

1. The U.S. stands for orderly, peaceful evolution toward an international system based on law and respect for diversity among national societies. The Chinese Communists stand for revolutionary change leading ultimately to a Communist world.

2. The U.S. is prepared to accept China as one of many components in a peaceful Asian balance of power. The present leadership in Peking will not settle for anything less than regional hegemony and aspires, first, to acceptance as one of three global powers and, eventually to leadership of a Communist world.

Time and a more realistic assessment of the adversary's intentions and capabilities may be expected to downgrade the practical importance of the first fundamental difference between U.S. and Chinese interests. The second difference, which concerns China's proper place in the world, may prove less easy to resolve. The Chinese desire to be recognized as the equal of the U.S. and the USSR has its psychological roots in China's long history during most of which China was the center and guiding light of its own world.

The threat which China poses for us, however, is not that she may actually achieve super-power status. Realistically appraised, China's present strength and future potentialities for many decades to come are simply inadequate for the international role to which her present leaders aspire. The danger is that merely by striving to achieve the unattainable China may seriously damage our interests in Asia or draw us into a large-scale war to protect them.

China's chances of overtaking the U.S., the USSR or Western Europe in wealth and power during the present century are negligible. Even in Asia, China will not bulk as large proportionately ten or twenty years from now as she does today. Only in the field of nuclear weapons will China's claim to great power status acquire some substance, but in this respect, too, China will continue to be outmatched by the U.S. and the USSR.

In the last quarter of the twentieth century, Japan will be the great power of Asia. By the late 1970s, Japan's per capita GNP will probably be more than ten times that of China and the economic gap between the two nations will still be widening. Japan may also have become a nuclear power and, if so, her greater wealth and technical resources will permit her quickly to surpass China in numbers of nuclear weapons and sophistication of delivery vehicles. Because of greater access to foreign aid, even India may do somewhat better than China economically, and she will probably acquire nuclear weapons in the relatively near future.

If the above picture is even a rough approximation of the shape of things to come, the gap between Chinese aspirations and Chinese capabilities must become increasingly apparent to all thoughtful Chinese. In time, the disparity between goals and reality should induce a fundamental reappraisal and change in Chinese policy.

No responsible Chinese leadership can escape the task of social, political and economic modernization. But given China's size, huge population, cultural conservatism and limited natural resources, the question of whether any leadership can succeed in this task remains open. Prolonged semi-failure is almost certain to wear down both the morale of the Communist cadres and the responsiveness of the Chinese people to exhortations for greater effort. Material incentives as a means of stimulating economic performance may become an imperative necessity. But the wherewithal for such incentives can be found only by reducing the priority accorded expenditures for military purposes or by seeking foreign economic assistance. A future Chinese leadership may be compelled to do both.

Chinese could turn for economic assistance to either the Soviet Union or to one or more non-Communist nations. Our long-term problem may well be how to ensure that, as containment succeeds, China will turn toward the free world rather than toward the Soviet Union.

The answer may lie in two directions. On the one hand, as Chinese policy moderates, we should try to draw China into activities on the broader world scene where, through exposure to outside reality and successful assumption of international responsibility, she might gain a degree of status and respect which could substitute in part for the unattainable goals of regional domination and super-power status. On the other hand, by gradually shifting as circumstances permit from a military policy of close-in containment to containment largely from offshore island positions, and by demonstrating in other ways that we are not committed to a policy of hostility or military "encirclement", we might ease the tension between China and ourselves, thereby facilitating a decision that Chinese interests were better served by normalizing relations with us rather than risking another betrayal at the hands of Russians. In any event, over the next decade and beyond, the dealings between China, the Soviet Union, and increasingly, Japan will form one of the most important sets of relationships in the world, in which our own security and position in Asia will be heavily involved.

We might over the very long run hope for a situation in which containment in China, insofar as it remains necessary, is left largely to Japan and the Soviet Union with our power and influence held in reserve to rectify any imbalances which might arise. If we achieve the advantageous regional balance of power which is among our major objectives in Asia, and if we draw China increasingly into a cooperative relationship with ourselves and other free nations, the strategy of containment will truly have succeeded.

[Here follow Chapters I–V and Appendices A–C. Volume II contains Annex I, "Economic Trends and Prospects," and Volume III, "Military and Political Factors," contains Annexes II–X.]

162. Telegram From the Embassy in the Republic of China to the Department of State[1]

Taipei, July 1, 1966, 1110Z.

22. Re: Deptel 1383.[2] Chinese Representation.

1. I saw Pres. Chiang yesterday afternoon for hour and a half discussion at tea at his Yangmingshan residence. Also present were DCM Hummel, FonMin Wei, Secy Gen Chang Chun, Vice FonMin Sampson Shen, with James Shen interpreting.

2. I opened official conversation with statement of reasoning that had led USG to bomb POL storage in North Vietnam, as contained Depcirtel 2568.[3] Chiang expressed hearty agreement with US decision and said he disagreed with Canadian and British critics who had "selfish motives" and whose views, he said, would be different if they were able to consider this problem objectively.

3. I then repeated in abbreviated form some of factors I had outlined to FonMin June 29 (Embtel 1523)[4] that led us to believe that past ChiRep tactics might not serve in upcoming GA. Chiang indicated he had already had report from FonMin on our conversation yesterday. He minimized problems of UN tactics, saying that power of decision lies with USG. If US held firm and did not waver, there would be no problem this session. He referred several times to statement he said made recently by unidentified "US Delegation spokesman at UN" in which US support for GRC seat reaffirmed, but no mention made of opposition to ChiCom entry. This conspicuous omission, he said, could only encourage countries such as Canada, which already were wavering, to become even more unpredictable.

4. He then made following points forcefully, with some reiteration:

A. On mainland, GRC had consistently refused to agree to a coalition government with ChiComs.

---

[1] Source: Department of State, Central Files, UN 6 CHICOM. Secret; Priority; Exdis. Repeated to Canberra and Manila for the Secretary and Bundy.

[2] Telegram 1383 to Taipei, June 24, reported that there had been a further high-level meeting on the Chinese representation question and that Rusk wanted to "make major pitch on this new tactic himself" when he was in Taipei. It instructed McConaughy to initiate talks on the subject promptly but to limit himself to the line taken by Bundy and Sisco in a June 15 meeting with Chow and GRC UN Representative Liu. (Ibid.) The June 15 meeting is summarized in telegram 2901 to USUN, June 16; Sisco and Bundy expressed concern that past tactics would not work and said U.S. policymakers were reviewing the problem. (Ibid.) Telegram 1384 to Taipei, June 24, approved by Rusk and Goldberg, conveyed guidelines for Rusk's use. (Ibid.)

[3] Dated June 25. (Ibid., POL 27 VIET S)

[4] Dated June 25. (Ibid., UN 6 CHICOM)

B. Any sort of "two Chinas" resolution, if passed and accepted, would amount to a kind of Chinese coalition situation in the UN, which GRC absolutely could not agree to, and which would compel GRC promptly to withdraw from UN.

C. Chinese tradition for many centuries has required that there be no truckling, surrender to or compromise with a rebel regime. This was epitomized in statement by third century statesman Chu-ko Liang who said, "the legitimate government cannot agree to coexist with a usurper". (han tsei pu liang li 3352, 6329, 0008, 9357, 4539.)[5] This typifies Chinese national spirit in time of crisis.

D. As long as GRC exists, it will seek the destruction of ChiComs as a usurper regime; it is better to go down to defeat fighting than to compromise a principle so deeply rooted in basic tradition and morality of Chinese people. This is fundamental to the honor of the GRC. With integrity preserved, the lawful government can rise again, even from the ashes of defeat.

E. Canada probably cannot understand how important this is to Chinese, but USG should be able to appreciate the principle, because of its long and close ties with China. It is up to USG to make Canadians understand that under no circumstances will GRC compromise its UN position, and that GRC will certainly walk out of UN if any adverse vote occurs.

F. GRC has suffered many insults in UN and has derived little benefit from membership. For the UN "to allow the ChiComs to enter" would be the last straw and GRC would definitely get out.

5. I said I was authorized to assure GRC that USG will continue strongly oppose entry of ChiComs into UN. I noted that he is assuming more influence on part of US over actions of other UN countries than we possess. We are determined not have a defeat on this issue but it is essential for two governments discuss and agree on tactics best calculated to keep GRC in and ChiComs out.

6. It was imperative in our view for the GRC to resolve to hold fast to its UN seat and not allow unpalatable debate or language in resolutions to cause GRC to walk out. I understood the traditions he referred to, but there was also a Chinese tradition of not abandoning the battlefield to the enemy. I hoped GRC would not act impulsively or out of any sense of outrage; if GRC would stand fast then ChiComs almost certainly would be precluded from coming into UN. In no event should GRC allow contest to go wrong way by default. If seat became vacant, danger would become great that ChiComs would move in.

---

[5] The numbers are standard telegraphic code for the Chinese characters.

7. Chiang said we could count on GRC not acting impulsively. It would not be an impulsive decision but would be an inevitable and correct one that if GA votes to allow ChiComs to enter, then regardless of whether the resolution also has a provision retaining the GRC seat, the GRC would have to walk out. GRC will never even consider doing otherwise, and would never agree to do otherwise. To stay in UN under such circumstances would not only cause disillusionment in Taiwan (both among Taiwanese and mainlanders, he said) but would also be a betrayal of the majority of the people in mainland China who look to GRC as a symbol of hope and steadfastness. Chinese representation shared with Communists could not be explained or reconciled.

8. I set forth that problem is how to deal with dangerous contingencies which USG believed likely to arise in the UN this fall. We hoped GRC would help us keep ChiComs out of UN by accepting the tactics which a changing situation might demand. Secretary Rusk would want to discuss means of dealing with this problem in upcoming GA. We had not yet come to any final conclusion as to what tactics would be best.

9. Chiang replied pointedly that FonMin Wei would be ready for a full exchange of views with Secy Rusk on matters of UN tactics.

10. Chiang closed conversation with assertion that since UN Charter was clear on GRC membership as one of principal five, it should not be difficult for USG to adopt procedural tactics, such as insisting on two-thirds important question formula, so that any hostile resolution could be defeated. He said that GRC believed in determination of USG to hold line against ChiComs, and that if USG does not waver, but demonstrates its determination, then there should be no danger. If USG wavers, then attitude of other countries would weaken, and attitude of GRC would also change (presumably attitude toward USG). If an adverse resolution were to pass, GRC would certainly withdraw. USG could convey this position to Canadian Government or any other government, if it wishes, since this was a public stand.

11. This morning during course of protocol call on Secy Gen Chang Chun (DCM present, with Protocol Director Shah interpreting) I said I was concerned that President might not understand that USG influence on other countries was limited. The days were gone when US could force others to conform to US views. Situation in the UN, therefore, was not one where simple US determination could prevail. Chang said he thought Gimo understood this, but that GRC believed necessary votes could still be maintained on old formula, and certainly on important question, if we all worked hard and if US attitude did not waver. Gimo intended, he said, first to make clear that GRC could not stay in UN if UN "voted to allow" ChiCom entry. Second, Gimo wanted to say that GRC believed no change in tactics needed, but GRC willing to discuss tactics if USG had new ones to offer, providing new tactics in line with first point.

GRC thought that important question formula should suffice. I reminded Secy Gen that on two occasions last fall UN organ had by simple majority vote overturned requirement for two-thirds vote on matters which were clearly "important questions" within meaning of Charter. We were not confident that "important question" rule would hold.

12. *Comment:* Not unexpectedly Gimo attempted take initiative in following respects: (A) he attempted rule out further discussion of new tactics at his level; (B) he was seemingly adamant in insistence on walking out of UN if any kind of "two Chinas" resolution passes; (C) he professed to believe that USG holds simple key to UN procedural problems if it will continue strongly support traditional tactics; (D) he contended USG needs only to use its influence with countries such as Canada to get them to fall in line. These positions tend to limit further discussion, and if Secy is to achieve meaningful exchange of views with Gimo he will have to deal with them quite directly. It is still unclear whether Gimo really believes USG has capability to hold traditional line; this could be genuine or it could be based on belief that USG should make a unilateral declaration that US would leave UN if ChiComs voted in. In any event best course is for us to hope, until convinced otherwise, that all these points are tactical maneuvers that will turn out in due course to be negotiable.

13. New FonMin Wei so far not very impressive figure, and it is doubtful that he has great influence on Gimo. This will make it doubly difficult to have meaningful discussions with GRC, since Gimo may not fully understand, or may not wish to understand, dangers in using old tactics in UN, and FonMin may not be able to exercise effective influence even if we can convince him.

14. One topic not touched on, which Secy should consider exploring with Gimo, is seriously adverse consequences to entire common cause if GRC walks out and gates thus opened wide to ChiCom entry. This places heavy obligation on GRC.

15. I have carefully refrained from giving any hint as to nature or language of any prospective new resolution. Hence I have not gone into the matter of the great difference between a mere left-handed invitation to ChiComs and actual entry of ChiComs into UN. Way is open for Secretary to assume that Chinese are saying they will walk out if and only if ChiComs actually appear to take UN seat. He can say that we are confident this will not happen, and ChiComs will not be able to accept any invitation so long as GRC remains in its seat. Gimo will probably try to close this off promptly by strong assertion his intention to withdraw as soon as UN "votes to allow ChiComs to come in", but argument can be pressed with some hope of progress.

16. I plan no further explorations before Secretary's arrival July 3. Believe subject these discussions being held closely to small group within GRC (as they are within Embassy). Vice Pres. Yen and DefMin

Chiang Ching-kuo have probably been filled in. Believe Secretary may wish to raise this question in preliminary way with Vice President during his call July 3.

McConaughy

---

163. Telegram From the Embassy in the Republic of China to the Department of State[1]

Taipei, July 5, 1966, 0645Z.

42. Uncleared draft résumé. Secretary's discussion of ChiRep with GRC.[2]

1. Secretary accompanied by Ambassador and Bundy July 3 and 4 discussed ChiRep situation separately with President Chiang and Fon-Min Wei Tao-ming who in one session accompanied by DefMin Chiang Ching-kuojo.

2. In first session with FonMin and other Foreign Ministry officers July 3, Wei presented in detail GRC analysis of ChiRep prospects which at this point indicates increased support for GRC position over 1965 UNGA vote. Wei counted Dahomey, CAR and Congo (Kinshasa) as sure to support GRC against background on basis first two cases of severed relations with ChiComs and in third case (Congo) of assurances recently conveyed by visiting Cabinet Minister that GOC would not permit repetition 1965 situation when delegate at UN disobeyed instructions. Wei described GRC also as encouraged by ChiCom policy reverses in Africa and in Afro-Asian world and by disadvantage to ChiComs which would result from current internal problems and Vietnam escalation. Wei also believes margin on important question may be increased as to as much as ten this year. Wei strongly and repeatedly urged US reach and announce early decision strongly support GRC ChiRep position using past tactics, said early decision would be instrumental maintain strength in GRC position while delay could cause doubt and confusion among GRC sup-

---

[1] Source: Johnson Library, National Security File, Country File, China, Vol. 6A. Secret; Exdis. Repeated to Tokyo for the Secretary and Bundy.

[2] Memoranda of Rusk's conversations in Taipei on July 3 and 4 are in Department of State, Conference Files: Lot 67 D 305, CF 60.

porters. Wei believes lateness of introduction of important question resolution at last UNGA and shortness of time between votes on important question and on substance may have cost GRC some votes and he requested the US introduce at early point in session and strongly support important question resolution.

3. Secretary told Wei that although he hopes GRC assessment correct, US much less sanguine about prospect for making past tactic again produce desired result. Said GRC need not worry about basic US policy support but instead should focus on thinking on contingency basis about possible need for new tactics and what form such new tactics might best take. Secy said neither Canada nor Italy can be depended on to continue support past tactical formula and in case of Canada, likelihood of some new initiative in direction two Chinas formula very high. Pointed out that US unable deter such development.

4. In second session July 4, Wei expressed GRC doubt that defection by Canada, which he termed not major power, and by Italy, which he said without influence in key area which is Africa, would take away other votes from GRC. Wei also argued that Canada defection would not detract from such other Commonwealth support as GRC enjoys. Wei again expressed confidence in GRC estimate of prospects, again urged US at early date announce decision support GRC on past tactics. Wei stressed belief that GRC friends in Africa, who appreciative GRC efforts help them with economic development, would not desert them in showdown or make them a scapegoat for dissatisfaction with other US or Western policies.

5. At this session Secretary again spelled out US worry and concern that past tactics may not again produce desired result, reiterated that given attitude SYG, Britain, France, etc. some of whom have greater influence in key areas such as Africa than US is able to wield, need for contingency thinking is clear.

6. Secretary asked if GRC has recent information re position Indonesia and India. Wei and Vice FonMin Shen replied that GRC has been advised India would support but not lobby for ChiComs, and that contacts with Indonesians are being restored but abstention would be the best to be hoped for.

7. Secretary told Wei that many countries would support continuation GRC membership in UN. At same time, there is considerable sentiment in favor of opening possibility of ChiCom membership. If situation developed in this direction, with ChiComs unwilling to accept while GRC remained in, would be disaster if GRC felt it had to withdraw, thus leaving field open to ChiComs. Wei did not reply directly, but reiterated GRC confidence.

8. Secretary told Wei that USG would have great difficulty in giving commitment at this stage to any particular tactics on ChiRep, without better idea of prospect for successful outcome.

9. Secretary and Wei agreed important respective representatives keep in close touch and compare assessments in detail soon so that difficulties in estimates can be examined and effective action decided.

10. Final session with Gimo devoted mostly to other matters, but Secy brought up ChiRep, saying there is no question of our policy or of objective we wish to achieve. However, he said, situation could develop where there would be danger of turbulent and undisciplined GA overturning two-thirds vote requirement on important question. Said we must not be exposed to defeat on keeping GRC seat both in GA and in SC.

11. Gimo replied he had already given his views to Amb McConaughy, and that he thought so long as US insists on legality of procedures under UN Charter, particularly Art 18, the problem would not be serious. He said he hoped Secy while in Japan would not say anything to dampen prevailing Japanese enthusiasm for supporting traditional tactics in UN.

12. Secy said trouble was that President Chiang was honorable man, but that there were so many cynics in unpredictable UN that sound legal position might not suffice.

McConaughy

---

164. **Telegram From the Embassy in the Republic of China to the Department of State**[1]

Taipei, July 5, 1966, 0815Z.

45. 1. One statement by Secretary in conversation with Pres Chiang is being reported only by this telegram, and will be omitted from airgram containing MemCon. Occasion was during last meeting with Gimo 1100 a.m. July 4.

2. Secretary said that if US becomes involved in any part of an attack on the Chinese Communist mainland then USG must see the con-

---

[1] Source: Department of State, Central Files, ORG 7 S. Top Secret; Exdis. Repeated to Tokyo for Rusk.

flict through to a conclusion and cannot be half in and half out. He said he could not imagine any general engagement between US forces and Chi-Coms being limited to conventional weapons. He reminded Pres Chiang that they had discussed this before (during Secy's visit April 1964).

McConaughy

---

165. **Telegram From the Embassy in the Republic of China to the Department of State**[1]

Taipei, July 5, 1966, 0930Z.

50. 1. This is uncleared summary of major topics in discussions during Secy's visit Taipei. ChiRep and exchange of resources under PL 480 are subjects separate messages.[2]

2. Gimo emphasized following points:

A. The major powers have a responsibility to assist in seeing that 600 million on China mainland do not remain indefinitely under Communist tyranny.

B. The GRC is determined to regain control of the mainland, but particularly in view of recent purges, and the restiveness that the purges show, GRC can afford to wait for an opportunity that will surely come.

C. Support to US in the Vietnam situation has first priority with GRC, and return to the mainland second priority.

D. In Vietnam, the ChiComs will probably not intervene in force, although they are undoubtedly now considering what to do to react to the raids on POL installations. They are in a dilemma: If they do nothing, they run a risk of losing control of Hanoi. On the other hand, they do not want to risk a frontal clash with the US.

E. If war goes on in present form US must consider what to do. It will not be advisable for US forces to go north of the 17th parallel, for if they did they would face serious guerrilla actions in North Vietnam, and

---

[1] Source: Johnson Library, National Security File, Country File, China, Vol. 6A. Secret; Exdis. Repeated to Tokyo for Rusk.

[2] See Document 163. Telegram 38 from Taipei, July 4, reported a proposal for an "exchange of resources" under PL 480 to support GRC aid programs in Africa. (Department of State, Central Files, AID (US) 15 CHINAT)

if necessary the Vietcong would retreat all the way to China and continue fighting from Chinese sanctuary.

F. The US must cut the lines of communication between North and South Vietnam, and equally important, between China and North Vietnam. In view of dissension and division within Communist China, we should think what steps, perhaps military or paramilitary, to take to achieve the results we want.

G. The ChiComs are counting on weariness and on criticisms of US policy by US Congressmen and other prominent Americans to force a US decision to withdraw eventually, after a long war of attrition.

H. The ChiComs feel fairly confident; they know they have overcome serious problems in the past and they believe they can survive anything. The ChiComs believe that US will not send its troops to North Vietnam and that the US will not support a GRC return to the mainland. They are therefore confident they will be able to wait until forces of dissatisfaction in the US cause a withdrawal.

I. The GRC still believes the ChiComs are capable of airdropping enough troops on Taiwan to seriously cripple GRC's military capability. Although the ChiCom troops would be wiped out, they would inflict enough damage so that ChiComs would not have to worry for some time about a GRC attack.

3. The Secretary made following observations:

A. US commitment in Defense Treaty is strong and well known. Even in statements by private US citizens on China policy there has been no suggestion that Taiwan should be turned over to ChiComs.

B. US determination to curb Communists is entirely firm. US has a million men overseas to do this, and has suffered 170,000 casualties since end of World War II, mostly in Asia.

C. ChiCom extremism combined with isolation has produced concern even among European Communist countries over how to curb Peiping. Soviets and Poles, among others, much worried over this. It is even possible (and the Gimo expressed agreement) that Sovs would welcome seeing Communist China split into regional Communist regimes.

D. However, the US believes that any attack on ChiComs likely to cause Sovs to bring Sino-Soviet Treaty of 1950 into force. On other hand, if ChiComs chose to enter into war on ground in Southeast Asia, Sovs possibly would not invoke that treaty.

E. The US will not allow indefinite continuation of "neither peace, nor war" situation in Vietnam; there will be "either more peace or more war." US determination is clear, and is supported by majority of Americans.

McConaughy

**166.   Telegram From the Embassy in the Republic of China to the
Department of State[1]**

Taipei, July 7, 1966, 0755Z.

70. 1. During a call by me on DefMin Chiang Ching-kuo July 6 he
raised subject of high level consultations and of Blue Lion Committee
referring to points conveyed to him by Chargé Hummel in October last
year (Deptel 396).[2]

2. He said he would like to broaden scope of Blue Lion Committee
so that I, with TDC chief and DCM, would participate with him and a
very limited number of associates, in general and wide ranging discussions in very small and secure group on problems of mutual interest. He
indicated that these discussions would probably not involve any plans
for return to mainland, but would include situation on mainland, Chi-
Com capabilities and intentions, Vietnam war, general Far East and
world strategic and political problems, etc. insofar as they affected our
joint interests here.

3. I said that I heartily agreed we should make occasions for such
discussions but that I would like a few days to think over whether Blue
Lion Committee was best framework. He said that of course we would
have other means and occasions for discussions in addition to Committee, but that he was following USG proposal (para B of Deptel 396) to use
Blue Lion framework.

4. It seems likely that Gimo has instructed him to proceed to carry
out long delayed consultations and that Gimo has decided to keep to the
letter of US proposal, notwithstanding DefMin's statement to Hummel
in October (Embtel 489)[3] that consultations would not require any formal
mechanism or committee. It is encouraging that GRC apparently does
not, at least at the present time, intend to revive request for joint contingency planning for attacking mainland.

5. On balance it seems advisable to follow original formula, and at
least for the time being accept the Blue Lion label. For one thing, GRC
seems to take it for granted that we should use this framework as we said
we would last year. For another, if these talks become known to ChiComs
it would be better to have them named "Blue Lion" which, if ChiComs
have capability to penetrate GRC military, they should know is under
strictly limited ground rules. Furthermore, Chiang Ching-kuo envisages

---

[1] Source: Department of State, Central Files, POL CHINAT–US. Secret; Priority; Limdis. Repeated to CINCPAC.

[2] See footnote 3, Document 108.

[3] Document 108.

very informal, rather personal setup, with flexible procedures, no fixed meeting dates and no set agenda or agreed minutes.

6. I shall proceed, along with Adm Gentner, to explore GRC ideas further and arrange a preliminary meeting.[4]

McConaughy

---

[4] Telegram 4843 to Taipei, July 11, reported that Chiang Ching-kuo's approach, especially his indication that plans for return to the mainland would not be among topics for discussion, seemed to be encouraging evidence the GRC was prepared for talks that could be beneficial "both substantively and psychologically." The Department did not object to the Blue Lion label for discussions but was anxious to avoid raising their visibility "from Peiping viewpoint" and favored informal, flexible procedures. (Department of State, Central Files, POL CHINAT–US)

---

167. Memorandum for the Record[1]

Washington, July 8, 1966.

SUBJECT

Minutes of the Meeting of the 303 Committee, 8 July 1966

PRESENT

Mr. Rostow, Ambassador Johnson, Mr. Vance, and Mr. Helms

Mr. Bill Moyers and Mr. Cord Meyer were present for Items 1 and 2

Mr. Leonard Marks and Mr. Robert Kintner were present for Item 1

[Here follow participants for items not printed here.]

1. *Radio China*

a. The discussion on the possibilities of creating a "Radio China"[2] opened with a statement by Ambassador Johnson to the effect that he felt

---

[1] Source: Department of State, INR Historical Files, 303 Committee Files, 303 c.41, August 5, 1966. Secret; Eyes Only. Drafted by Peter Jessup of the NSC staff on July 9.

[2] A CIA memorandum of October 7, 1965, for the 303 Committee proposing that CIA be authorized to proceed with a plan for a "gray" radio targeted at Communist China is ibid., 303 c.29, Oct. 28, 1965. Records of 303 Committee discussions and related memoranda are ibid., 303 c.37, May 5, 1966, 303 c.38, June 9, 1966, 303 c.39, June 24, 1966, and 303 c.40, July 8, 1966. A Radio Study Group, established at the direction of McGeorge Bundy in November 1965 to examine this and other issues concerning the Voice of America, Radio Liberty, and Radio Free Europe, endorsed the proposal with one member dissenting; its report, April 28, 1966, is in the Johnson Library, National Security File, Rostow Files, Special Group Memoranda.

that the United States could accomplish "most of what we want to do" through the existing framework of USIA.

b. Mr. Marks confirmed the statement in his paper dated June 30, 1966,[3] that he knew of no legal restrictions on his programming and that he anticipated no problems in finding material and/or personnel.

c. Mr. Helms reminded the committee that originally the concept had been a Chinese voice rather than a U.S. official voice.

d. Mr. Moyers stated that he had welcomed the concept of a gray radio at first, but he found that (1) all China hands with whom he was conversant were against the idea; (2) the margin of benefit by "going gray" appeared very slim; and (3) VOA should be given a try at it. Mr. Kintner interposed that at first he leaned toward an unofficial voice, but he now thought VOA could undertake the job.

e. Mr. Helms noted that the Agency was prepared to undertake the job if there was demonstrable enthusiasm but, in the absence of same, he had no intention of pressing for the project in the face of opposition.

f. Mr. Vance said he felt that undertaking such a new venture was not worth the major costs at this time.

g. Mr. Rostow summed up by saying that a private or CIA venture would be uphill work in the current atmosphere with all the recent publicity. He added, however, that he could not buy the prejudices of the China experts about their exclusive expertise in the field of broadcasting to China. Everything pointed to letting VOA beef up their broadcasts via the new Philippine transmitters, he added.

h. The Executive Secretary noted that with this consensus for USIA to shoulder the responsibility, the subject would no longer be of concern to the 303 Committee.

i. Mr. Meyer itemized three matters of contents which should not be overlooked in any programming aimed at China: (1) regular reporting on cross currents in the communist world; (2) news commentaries which included emphasis on Chinese foreign policy failures; and (3) emphasis on traditional Chinese culture.

j. Mr. Marks noted that he would need the help of various agencies, and Mr. Helms replied that the CIA was ready to cooperate in any way.

k. It was pointed out that the original CIA proposal remained extant and could be resurrected at some later date.

[Here follows discussion of unrelated subjects.]

Peter Jessup

---

[3] A copy is in Department of State, INR Files, 303 Committee Files, 303 c.40, July 8, 1966.

168.   Editorial Note

On July 12, 1966, President Johnson discussed U.S. policy in Asia in an address to the American Alumni Council broadcast on radio and television. He stated in part:

"There is a fourth essential for peace in Asia which may seem the most difficult of all: reconciliation between nations that now call themselves enemies.

"A peaceful mainland China is central to a peaceful Asia.

"A hostile China must be discouraged from aggression.

"A misguided China must be encouraged toward understanding of the outside world and toward policies of peaceful cooperation.

"For lasting peace can never come to Asia as long as the 700 million people of mainland China are isolated by their rulers from the outside world.

"We have learned in our relations with other such states that the weakness of neighbors is a temptation, and only firmness that is backed by power can really deter power that is backed by ambition. But we have also learned that the greatest force for opening closed minds and closed societies is the free flow of ideas and people and goods." (*Public Papers of the Presidents of the United States: Lyndon B. Johnson, 1966*, Book II, pages 721–722; for the complete text, see ibid., pages 718–722)

---

169.   Telegram From the Embassy in the Republic of China to the Department of State[1]

Taipei, July 19, 1966, 0900Z.

200. Subject: Reaction to President's July 12 speech. Ref: Depcirtel 9794.[2]

1. First high-level official GRC reaction (other than press) to President's speech on Far East was elicited by Ambassador from President

---

[1] Source: Department of State, Central Files, POL 15–1 US/JOHNSON. Confidential; Priority. Repeated to USUN and Hong Kong.

[2] Dated July 18. (Ibid.)

Chiang July 18 during tea the President gave for Gen. Waters. Following discussion of military situation in Vietnam and related subjects, President asked Ambassador about recent developments in general. Ambassador took occasion to mention President's speech and to reiterate that speech did not represent change in basic US China policy, but that it did reflect a somewhat different approach in line with essential US posture of not foreclosing possibility for settling any and all differences by non-military means. If ChiComs should rebuff these gestures, it would be they rather than we who would lose by such a confirmation of their intransigence.

2. President Chiang said he had studied President's speech closely, as had many others. He said it had created concern in some circles. Chiang said he was glad to hear that speech represented no basic change in policy. He would accept this and not criticise speech. Excitement and unhappiness stirred up by speech in some quarters around world were due to lack of understanding of President Johnson's situation. Chiang noted that Ambassador's assurances were in line with statements by Secretary Rusk. Chiang conjectured (without any assent from Ambassador) that motivation for speech "may have been largely domestic."

3. *Comment:* Suggestion that President's speech was designed assuage domestic critics is one of prevalent GRC rationalizations designed to minimize importance of US foreign relations developments (the other being GRC conviction that ChiComs will in any case not respond to US overtures). Fact that GRC officials so far have reacted relatively mildly should not, however, be taken to mean they are not deeply disturbed and that there is not an influential group within the GRC urging a "counterattack" against what they fear is a serious softening of US policy toward ChiComs. However so long as developments occur in limited context and without immediate practical effect, moderate reaction probably will continue to prevail, with criticism focused chiefly on "tactical" aspects (such as effect on ChiRep). Given Chiang's favorable expression of view, Embassy expects that reaction that will eventually be forthcoming from Foreign Ministry will be generally along relatively moderate lines of aide-mémoire on Secretary's testimony before Zablocki Committee. Dept's attention is called, however, to CAS report FCT–9275,[3] which illustrates view of those within GRC who would take stronger position.

McConaughy

---

[3] Not found.

170. Telegram From the Department of State to the Embassy in Canada[1]

Washington, July 25, 1966, 5:30 p.m.

14522. Subject: Secretary's conversation with Paul Martin, July 22[2]—Chinese representation.

1. Martin opened discussion by asking about the Secretary's visit to Taipei and our view of the voting situation.

2. The Secretary responded that Taipei was now well aware that we felt there was a serious tactical problem whether the important question/substitution approach could succeed in the next General Assembly. He noted that his trip had revealed how strongly several key Asian countries feel about the issue, and particularly reported that Prime Minister Sato had urged privately that we do all possible to round up the votes on the present approach. The Secretary said it would be a disaster if the Chi-Coms displaced the GRC in the GA, and that we needed the most careful possible review of the votes to see if there was a major tactical problem in preventing this result.

3. The Secretary went on to say that it was important to distinguish between the General Assembly and the Security Council. The GRC was named in the Charter as a Security Council member, and the CPR was simply not the same government. (The Secretary conceded that the British and perhaps others did not share this legal view.) The Secretary also referred to the question whether the Asian nations would really want Communist China to occupy a permanent "Asian" seat on the Security Council, and whether it might not be necessary to consider a Charter amendment to designate some other Asian country or to provide for a method of selection for the permanent seat.

4. Martin agreed on the necessity of a careful review of the votes. He thought that the ICJ decision on Southwest Africa and the Rhodesian issue—on which he saw the British not being able to come up with any answer satisfactory to African opinion—could have a serious effect on African voting patterns. On the other hand, he noted that U Thant, in a conversation held within the past 10 days, had expressed the view that there would be little change from past voting patterns.

5. On the basic Canadian attitude, Martin said that the GOC had always approached the issue with full recognition of its relationship to

---

[1] Source: Department of State, Central Files, UN 6 CHICOM. Secret; Priority; Exdis. Drafted by Bundy on July 23, cleared by Deputy Assistant Secretary for IO William B. Buffum, and approved by Rusk. Also sent to Geneva for Goldberg and repeated to Taipei, USUN, Tokyo, and London.

[2] The conversation took place over lunch at the Department of State. A memorandum of the portion of the conversation concerning Chinese representation is ibid.

the US and of all that the issue meant to the USG. Nonetheless, the GRC had to recognize that there was "overwhelming sentiment" developing in Canada, as shown by the 65% in a recent Gallup Poll in favor of Chi-Com admission. He noted in passing that there appeared to be a similar trend in the US. He said that Canada would have taken a different line before now but for its concern for the USG position. He then went on to say that the ChiComs might not come in if offered admission, but that "there may be a lot" in GOC acting to make admission possible. However, the GOC would never act to expel GRC, although it might take or join in steps that "would have the effect of ushering them out."

6.   The Secretary rejoined vigorously that the issue was not one that affected the vital interests of Canada; "You have a free ride on it." On the other hand, the Asian countries who face the militancy of Communist China would feel great pain if she were admitted. The Secretary strongly questioned whether this should be done merely to please sentiment in Canada and European countries.

7.   Martin responded that the state of public opinion in Canada and elsewhere was a fact that statesmen must take into account, and the Secretary rejoined that the French particularly simply had no further stake in Asia. Martin responded that ChiCom admission was "bound to happen" eventually.

8.   The Secretary said that it seemed to him the best thing would be for us to compare notes on the voting and to stay in close touch. Although making a mild complaint that GOC had not been informed on Secretary's discussions in Taipei (FYI: We had in fact given general description to Embassy officer, and Embassy had not otherwise approached us), Martin did not seem to differ from this conclusion. He did refer again to recent SYG opinion and returned to his argument about the African vote, contending that African attitudes on such issues as Rhodesia and the ICJ decision did in fact wash over into the Communist Chinese issue.

9.   *Comment:* In the light of the indications in Ambassador Goldberg's conversations in Ottawa in May, it seemed noteworthy that Martin did not indicate that GOC planned to take some "two Chinas" initiative in the near future. We have other information, received on an unauthorized basis from Canadian Embassy officers here, that Martin directed the Canadian Delegation in New York to submit alternative "two Chinas" resolutions, but did not find any of these acceptable. While his general remarks continue to suggest that the Canadians cannot be relied on in a pinch, and might join in an initiative from some other quarter, it appears to Department less likely that they will take any lead, at least for the present. Ottawa may wish to comment, but our general posture should be to lie low as far as direct discussions with Canadians are concerned except on voting prospects. We expect they will ask for fuller

report on Taipei discussions next week, and we will give them straight-forward account.

Rusk

---

171.   Memorandum From the President's Special Assistant (Rostow) to President Johnson[1]

Washington, July 25, 1966.

The underlying memorandum[2] summarizes the current situation in Communist China following the eight months of turmoil and confusion. The major conclusions are:

1.   Mao is now in effective control of the Chinese Communist Party and of the policies of the Peking regime.

2.   The long standing stability of the Chinese leadership has been shaken.

3.   The chance of a peaceful and orderly succession to the aging Mao appears greatly lessened.

4.   Support for the regime will weaken further as Peking tries to substitute exhortation for material incentives.

5.   Effective political leadership or economic management will be difficult in the present atmosphere of confusion and apprehension.

6.   Most observers agree that the radical turn taken in internal affairs will not spread to foreign policy.

7.   The internal crisis serves to reduce the chance of Chinese inter-vention in Vietnam.

8.   It highly unlikely that Peking will soften its anti-Soviet line.

Walt

---

[1] Source: Johnson Library, National Security File, Country File, China, Vol. VI. Secret. Filed with a covering memorandum of July 25 from Rostow to the President.

[2] The memorandum from the Office of National Estimates of the Central Intelligence Agency to the Director of Central Intelligence, July 15, on the subject "The Crisis in China," is attached but not printed.

172. **Memorandum From the President's Special Assistant (Rostow) to President Johnson**[1]

Washington, July 28, 1966, 11:10 a.m.

Mr. President:

It may be that, looking back, the crisis inside Communist China will be viewed by historians as the most significant event now taking place on the world scene. Obviously it is extremely hard to follow in detail.

The attached intelligence cable presents the crisis as a final stand of Mao and the Old Guard seeking to suppress forces for change inside the Communist party. It implies that these forces will, in time, assert themselves.

Something like this analysis would be accepted by most of those who have followed the evolution of mainland China since 1949. What no one knows—and experts argue over—is how long it will take for this strong, pragmatic opposition to assert itself and what will happen in the meantime.

The latter is what matters most to us from day to day. Nevertheless, I thought you might like to read this interesting assessment.

Walt

Attachment

TEXT OF CIA INTELLIGENCE INFORMATION CABLE
(TDCS 314/09256–66)[2]

SUBJECT

Mao's Opposition

SOURCE

Staff officers of this Organization

This is [less than 1 line of source text not declassified] appraisal of the current situation. It is not an official judgment by this Agency or any

---

[1] Source: Johnson Library, National Security File, Country File, China, Vol. VI. Confidential; No Foreign Dissem. A handwritten "L" on the source text indicates that the President saw the memorandum. Another handwritten notation reads: "Rec'd 11:45 a.m."

[2] The source text is the retyped text of the CIA cable, dated July 25.

component. It represents the observations and interpretations of staff officers and is based on information available to them at the time of its preparation. Prepared for internal use as a guide to the operational environment, this commentary is disseminated in the belief that it may be useful to other agencies in assessing the situation for their own purposes.

Summary: Mao's opposition is widespread and continuing. It is characterized by the Party as "more insidious and cunning" than any previous anti-party clique. The opposition is found in artists of all types, Politburo members, Party senior propagandists, military personnel and university presidents. However, functional non-political offices, such as Party Economic and Foreign Affairs Departments seem to be outside the purge. As Mao again attempts to force his Party and his people to accept the discipline of Maoism, the effort may be too much for both and the Chinese may quietly walk away from his leadership.

As the purge widens throughout China there is need to examine just who has been caught opposing today's Roi Soleil. It is certainly a mixed bag—historians, playwrights, movie directors, Politburo members, virtually all of the Party's senior propagandists, military personalities and university presidents. Mao and Lin have recognized the universality of the opposition, indeed, have perhaps created it in part. So many are involved that one wonders at first just who remains loyal and who is pressing the attack against the bourgeois royalists, the revisionists, and all the members of the black gang of the three-family village and the four-family store.

Certain vital Communist Party entities have as yet been above reproach: the public security apparatus, the Communist Party staff offices of Agriculture and Forestry, Finance and Trade, Industry and Communications, as well as Foreign Affairs—all appear to have escaped open criticism. It almost seems that the functional non-political offices are outside the purge and that those under censure are the offices which are involved in the ideology of Communism and the extension of Communist Party control.

The party now characterizes its opposition as "more insidious and cunning than the two previous anti-party cliques which have been crushed." These are the men who "reached out to grab at power in the party, the Army, and the government to usurp the leadership so as to restore capitalism." These charges are extremely serious; the problem lies in whether they are genuine or false. In the past the Communists have been pretty literal and we would guess that these charges should be taken seriously as a clear reflection of the intentions of the opposition.

Assuming these charges are in earnest we must answer another question: To whom do they specifically apply?

There has been an opposition faction in China since the Communist assumption of power in 1949. After Mao embarked on the communes and the Great Leap Forward and these two efforts failed badly, criticism grew to a high point in 1962. From 1959 to 1962, by Mao's own admission, the "heavy national calamities and the sabotage of the Soviet revisionists" so weakened China that a major purge to contain this criticism was not possible. Actually this is partly an excuse, since Mao forced the démarche with the Soviets leading to the removal of the technicians; still, there can be no doubt that the Soviet departure hurt China. The intellectuals now under heavy attack did use this period of party weakness to advance ideas which, when read, literally refuted Maoism. This is why Wu Han and Teng T'o were able to print their satires and why the party did not act against them.

In late 1962 Mao felt strong enough to begin the rectification he knew was necessary—the socialist education campaign. This developed throughout 1963 and led to the direct attack on Yang Hsien Chen, the leading theoretician of the higher party school, whose dialectic arguments directly opposed those of Mao and were applied by the opposition to buttress agreements for private plots, free markets, and increase in small enterprises. All of this was anathema to Mao, but not necessarily to a number of party leaders who were beginning to move away from Mao's leadership and his theories. As senior party members defied Mao, many lesser individuals used this shelter to produce anti-Maoist novels, essays and motion pictures.

By 1965 the rectification movement was faltering badly. The socialist education movement was by then being carried forward in the nationwide four clearances effort. Probably no disciplinary movement of the party was so thoroughly honored in the breach as the four clearances. By the fall of 1965 the party was no longer in direct control of the people. The opposition within the party had continued to mature and Mao found it necessary to begin a broad attack on his critics in November 1965. The first battle of the socialist cultural revolution took place in Shanghai when the municipal committee denounced the historian Wu Han and the fight with the Peking Municipal Committee began.

Therefore, we can answer our question. The opposition lay in the leadership of the Peking Municipal Committee, P'eng Chen and his subordinates, the propaganda department of the party, which allowed the development of the intellectual opposition, and the many party members who felt that the relaxation of Maoist Doctrine presaged a more adaptable Communism. This opposition is not dead despite the three months socialist cultural revolution purge. Mao is attempting a cleansing of the entire country of such anti-Maoist thought. He has not abandoned his intent to lead world Communism, but he realizes he must fully re-establish Maoism in China and regain control of the drifting party apparatus.

It is doubtful that a dynasty built on the sand of Maoist philosophy will take a century to fall; once begun, a decade would seem too long. The great socialist cultural revolution now unmasks "freaks and monsters" each week. As the list of purges grows, it is a reasonable speculation that there will be more. Mao is worried about his revolution for it is clearly failing. If there is, medically, a disease definable as political paranoia it has settled on the sometimes resident of the small but now unlovely quarters overlooking Nan Hai, Peking's most exquisite lake. "Who knows whither the golden crane went, leaving but a shrine for pilgrims?" If there is any answer for the old man, it is also found in Chinese poetry—"A cup of wine under the trees; I drink alone for no friend is near."

---

173.   Memorandum From James C. Thomson, Jr., of the National Security Council Staff to the President's Special Assistant (Rostow)[1]

Washington, August 4, 1966.

SUBJECT

Relaxation of U.S. Embargo on Trade with Communist China

I want you to know of a China initiative which has been under preparation for some months and will soon be on its way to the Secretary of State for decision. I attach an advance (and *thoroughly unofficial*) draft of the relevant State document.[2] (This comes to me because I am quoted in the annexes, as a discussion participant.)

In brief, this memorandum *recommends that Rusk authorize the Department to being certain small modifications of our total embargo on trade and transactions with Communist China* which has been in effect since 1950. Specifically, Rusk is asked to approve (a) general licensing of relevant transactions for those categories of U.S. citizens now entitled to travel to

---

[1] Source: Johnson Library, National Security File, Country File, China, Vol. VII. Secret; Eyes Only. Filed with a covering note of August 4 from Thomson to Rostow that indicates that William J. Jorden of the NSC staff had read Thomson's memorandum and concurred.

[2] A draft memorandum from Bundy and Solomon to Rusk is attached but not printed.

Communist China, (b) an end to the special bunkering controls that have been in effect for 16 years, and (c) preparation for unilateral relaxation of trade controls (subject to the President's approval) with initial focus on two-way trade in foodstuffs, non-war related pharmaceuticals, and art objects.

This recommendation to the Secretary results from *the first interagency review of the complete China trade picture since the outbreak of the Korean War.* To the casual observer, it may seem that the mountain has labored and brought forth a mouse. Yet I anticipate resistance at the top of the Department even to these minimal steps.

The *rationale for modification of our trade embargo* is familiar to you: In the short run, despite anticipated Chinese Communist denunciation of such moves, we alter a substantive element of our previously rigid and defensive posture toward China, and we demonstrate to our critical friends and allies a welcome degree of confidence and flexibility. In so doing, we give substance and meaning to the Administration's new rhetoric—"firmness and flexibility," "containment without isolation," "reconciliation," etc. Equally important, for the longer run, we communicate a new and supportive message to elements within mainland China that are pushing for policies of pragmatism and accommodation with the outside world.

I bring this matter to your attention for obvious reasons. In his July 12th speech on Asia, the President went far in words toward changing our China posture at the highest level. The response has been extraordinarily good, both in terms of the approval his words have won, at home and abroad, and in terms of the absence of strong criticism (even from Taiwan). *If we are to keep up the momentum of the past six months, we must begin to match out words with action.* There is no better place to start than the subject of trade regulations which have outlived their original rationale and usefulness.

As you know, however, there is certain *built-in resistance to any such adjustments on the 7th floor at State.* We therefore face a situation in which the President's declared hopes—"the free flow of ideas, people, and goods"—may well be obstructed, despite hearty support for those hopes within the working bureaucracy—*unless the White House can deftly intervene.*

I realize that there are a large number of complex political ramifications to this issue—among them, the Vietnam War, the elections, the idiotic furor over the German rolling mill, etc. But I would argue that as long *as we are standing firm in Vietnam, the President has far more benefit than risk to reap in maintaining momentum on China actions as well as China rhetoric.* I would add that such actions could not take place at a more important moment in Chinese political history: the more we can do to support the mainland pragmatists by our actions and to cause confusion to the theologians in Peking, the better for our national interests and the achievement of stability and peace in Asia.

Jim

174. Telegram From the Embassy in Japan to the Department of State[1]

Tokyo, August 11, 1966, 1030Z.

1126. 1. The problem of China looms large in the future of that half of the world's population which lives in East and South Asia, and it casts a shadow over the rest of the world as well. Before leaving Tokyo, I should like to address myself to this problem as it appears from Japan, the only important industrialized and modernized nation in Asia and our one great Pacific partner on whom the future of our own posture in East Asia is heavily dependent.

2. During the five years I have been here, I have seen bilateral American-Japanese problems decrease markedly in number and intensity. Short of a major depression in either country, our economic relations raise no great difficulties, though some specific irritants, such as salmon fisheries, remain. The determination of much of the Japanese left to break the security relationship with the U.S. in 1970 has all along posed the greatest threat to our bilateral relations, but the growing realism about world problems on the part of the Japanese and their increasing defense mindedness make it now seem improbable that this problem will of itself cause serious difficulties in 1970 or thereafter. One specific aspect of the defense relationship, however, does bear careful watching and a readiness for rapid and flexible action on our part. This is the growing confrontation in the Ryukyu Islands between Japanese nationalistic pride and U.S. and Japanese defense needs. The deep emotional reaction of the Japanese in 1965 to U.S. actions in the Vietnamese war also shows that so

---

[1] Source: Department of State, Central Files, POL CHICOM. Secret; Exdis. A copy was sent to the President with an August 16 covering memorandum from Komer supporting Reischauer's arguments. A note in Johnson's handwriting on Komer's memorandum reads, "Ask Rostow to contact Rusk & comment. L." An attached note in an unknown hand reads, "Call Bill Moyers before you do anything about attached." (Johnson Library, National Security File, Country File, China, Vol. VI)

long as this war continues it will have dangerously explosive possibilities for U.S.-Japanese relations. But the Ryukyu and Vietnamese situations are themselves in part reflections of the China problem. It seems safe to conclude that the continuing danger areas in U.S.-Japanese relations lie not so much in our bilateral relations as in our respective approaches to regional Asian problems. Among the latter the deep Japanese uneasiness over the China problem, and over American policies toward China presents the greatest threat.

3.   The fundamental reasons for Japanese uneasiness over our China policy have often been reported from this Embassy. While attitudes vary greatly among age and occupational groups, the Japanese for the most part have a strong sense of closeness to the Chinese, which they express in the term "same race and same culture." They look with respect and affection to China as the country from which their own civilization in early days was in large part derived. They feel that their geographic proximity to the Chinese giant makes the maintenance of friendly relations all the more imperative from them. Despite their recent great economic success, they still feel uncertainties about their economic future, and, continuing to think along channels well established over the past forty years, they look upon close economic relations with China as necessary for their own economic well being. In all these respects—racial, cultural, historical, geographic and economic—they feel that the United States stands in a very different position with regard to China and that, therefore, US policy is likely to diverge sharply from Japan's interests. They thus picture in their mind's eye a relatively small Japan which has strong reasons to be friendly to both the U.S. and China but is tragically caught between the mutual antagonisms between these two great giants. While more realistic Japanese would feel that the Chinese are more responsible than Americans for this situation, they tend to excuse the Chinese as driven by understandable psychological compulsions and in any case not open to reason. On the other hand, they tend to feel that the United States, as the stronger and more reasonable of the two nations, should make the adjustments to ease the Sino-American tensions that Japanese find so disturbing.

4.   Despite these pervasive Japanese attitudes, the GOJ, particularly under Prime Minister Sato and Foreign Minister Shiina, has given us strong support on our China policy. The men now in charge of the Japanese Government represent those Japanese who are most fully in sympathy with the US position. A large part of their own party, however, is restive about Japan's close identification with our China policy, and the public at large is decidedly unhappy about it. Except for the extreme left, there is general sympathy for Taiwan's "independence" of continental China and its continued membership in the U.N. There is also an increasing awareness of the threat inherent in Peking's dogmatism and of the

need to discourage its open aggressiveness. At the same time, the Japanese by and large believe that it is only sensible to admit that two Chinas (or one China and one Taiwan) do exist. They are not satisfied with a policy which ostensibly maintains that the GRC is the one and only representative of the great historical entity known as China. They feel that Communist China is here to stay for the foreseeable future and that the best outcome that can be realistically hoped for is that it will in time become a less cantankerous member of world society and will be satisfied to accept peaceful coexistence, at least to the extent that this term is understood by the Soviet Union. To hasten this process, they feel that it is important to increase trade and cultural contacts with Peking and to allow Peking or even encourage it to enter the U.N. (on the U.N.'s terms, of course, and not Peking's). The Japanese are fearful that as things are now going an overly inflexible U.S. will drift into conflict with a blindly intransigent China, and Japan will be caught in the resultant catastrophe. While they welcome recent efforts on our part to foster the movement of newspapermen, scholars and the like between the U.S. and China, they wonder why we cannot go further than this. They are unhappy about a ChiRep strategy that is clearly aimed at keeping Peking out of the U.N. rather than facilitating its ultimate entrance. Many of them realize that for the time being Peking no doubt will refuse to enter the U.N. if Taipei is also there, but they see no reason why the responsibility for Peking's absence from the U.N. should not fall on Peking itself rather than on a joint U.S. and Japanese blackball operation.

5. Japanese unease at being linked to a China policy which they consider is basically unrealistic and not in Japan's long-range interests is, in my judgment, the most serious problem that now exists in U.S.-Japanese relations. It places a heavy burden on our relations, which may become heavier rather than lighter the longer it lasts. Growing Japanese realism about the ChiCom menace is likely to be more than offset by mounting fears of a U.S.-ChiCom military confrontation and a rapidly rising sense of national pride, which makes Japanese increasingly desirous of asserting a position on ChiRep and other China policies more in line with basic Japanese feelings and less open to the charge of subservience to the U.S.

6. The heavy price we pay in U.S.-Japanese relations for our current stand on ChiRep policy is, of course, only one of many factors that must be taken into consideration in deciding on that policy. I am aware of the arguments for maintaining the present position or something as close to it as possible. It should be remembered, however, that Japan is not the only country in which we pay a price for our present stand. The cost may be higher here than elsewhere, but I believe that we pay something of a price in practically every other of our major industrialized allies and in many other countries throughout the world. It is also my considered

opinion that, wholly aside from the price we pay in Japan and other countries, it is to U.S. interests to modify our stand on the ChiRep issue and our whole attitude toward Peking.

7.   No sensible person would deny the great threat to world peace posed by the blind dogmatism of the Peking leaders and their tragic ignorance of the outside world. I personally am less optimistic than some observers about the rapidity with which these dangerous attitudes may change, because I feel that they are not just the product of Communist dogmatism and the very special and restricted experience of the Peking leaders. They are perhaps more fundamentally an expression of frustration on the part of the Chinese people, whose traditional pride and sense of superiority to all other nations have been gravely injured by a century of continuing humiliations. I, therefore, see no alternative to our present policies of firm containment. It would be folly on our part and a betrayal of our own basic ideals if we did not continue to give full support to the right of the people who live on Taiwan to self-determination. I have throughout given complete support to our policy of strong but measured military containment in Vietnam and neighboring areas. I believe that we just be prepared to continue to contribute to the security and stability of the Asian countries that surround China, though I would hope that in the future we could find ways to be not so much the primary actor in such defense as one of a group of outside powers that gives the necessary support to local forces of nationalism and regional efforts to maintain stability.

8.   I am thus strongly in sympathy with what we are doing with regard to the containment of the threat of Communist China, but I feel that the public definition of our attitude towards this threat and our future relation with Communist China does not contribute to the efficacy of these actions and, in fact, tends to undermine them. As I see the situation, we make a pretense of believing that the twelve million people on Taiwan, and not the seven hundred million in continental China, represent the great historical political entity known as China and that the Chinese Communist regime is not here to stay, but may be swept away almost any time by the GRC on Taiwan. We of course do not really believe either proposition, and I feel that it is highly damaging to ourselves and our policies that we make the pretense of doing so. It is confusing to the American people, it distresses almost all our major allies, including the Japanese, and it angers many of the less-developed nations, who sometimes interpret our seeming scorn for Peking as a broader scorn for all less developed nations. Some people may argue that these pretenses are necessary to bolster up our small Asian allies in the Far East and maintain morale in Taiwan. I would not deny that we would face a difficult problem, particularly in Taiwan, in persuading the leaders to accommodate themselves to a recognition of reality, but in the long run this will be

necessary in any case. In the meantime, the maintenance of our pretense permits the continuation of serious economic and political distortions of what would otherwise be a most encouraging situation in Taiwan itself; it sometimes encourages dangerous tendencies among our more committed allies, such as the Koreans; it is damaging to the development of regional solidarity in Southeast Asia; and most of all it stands in the way of the development in Japan, in Europe and throughout the world of the sort of broad international concern for peace and stability in Asia that is needed to replace the one-man policement role we are performing today.

9. I believe that most people would agree that the best we can reasonably hope for from Communist China in the foreseeable future is that it may gradually relax its present drive for immediate world revolution and that in time it will accept peaceful coexistence, at least as a temporary stratagem, and will thus wish to rejoin the world on the world's terms. Most people would also agree that, in order to work toward this one and only realistic objective, we should not only continue to frustrate ChiCom expansionist drives but should also help to develop greater communication and contact between Peking and the outside world. Our willingness to exchange newspapermen, scholars, and the like is a helpful step in this direction. The opening of trade in non-strategic goods would also be useful. Since all our major allies trade with the ChiComs, our present trade embargo is all but meaningless economically, while being psychologically disadvantageous to us. More important than these concrete steps, however, would be the redefinition of our attitude toward Peking. China presents us with what is fundamentally a psychological problem. The leaders are of course tragically misled by their own dogmatic beliefs, but even more basic is Chinese pride, made all the more fierce and unbending because of the past century of humiliation and the present frustrations growing out of China's obvious weakness and backwardness. Nothing stands more firmly in the way of a Chinese readiness to seek a rapprochement with the world than their resentment of what they regard to be the callous pretense on the part of the world's greatest power that China does not really exists or that, if it does exist, it is so depraved or so unstable or so inconsequential that it should be barred from world society. I would not claim that a more realistic and more tolerant and appreciative attitude on our part would bring any quick change in Chinese attitudes. I am sure that it would not. But at least it would remove the greatest single barrier on our side that now stands in the way of China moving in the direction we would hope to see it go, and at the same time it would remove a serious barrier to the development of a broader international approach to the problem of containing Chinese Communist expansionism.

10. It might be argued that until China shows itself more conciliatory toward the U.S., particularly at this time when we are engaged in the

war in Vietnam, we might lose face or might weaken our containment policy if we were to redefine our attitude toward Peking in this way. I would disagree strongly. I do not see how face would be involved. As by far the world's greatest nation, we lose face by pretending to believe things that most people in the world, including ourselves, realize are not true. We lose face by letting our basic policies seem to be determined by the peculiar sensitivities of a small country like Taiwan. The only sound course is for us to stand frankly on our own ideals and on our own judgments, and these do not include the concepts that the GRC will reconquer the continent or that we must approve of Communist China to admit that it exists. As to a redefinition of our attitude weakening the containment policy, I believe that the reverse is the case. The very fact that we are militarily so committed in Vietnam would prevent any serious misinterpretation of our actions. On the contrary, our clarified stand would be more understandable to our own people as well as to outsiders; we could count on increased sympathy and possibly more actual aid from the rest of the world; we would have laid the ground work for a broader international approach to the continuing ChiCom menace; and most important, by showing respect for Chinese nationalism we would help to strengthen all Asian nationalism and the possibilities for increased regional solidarity, which in the long run are the only real answers to the threat of Communist subversion.

11. In conclusion, let me outline specifically what it is that I advocate. It is merely the further clarification of the current semi-official phrase "containment with [*without*] isolation" and the sections of the President's July 12 speech[2] which call for a "peace of conciliation" and "the full participation by all nations in an international community under law." In other words, we should make clear that, however strongly we insist on the right of Taiwan to retain its membership in the United Nations, we recognize that Peking represents a great country which, according to the basic concepts of the U.N. and our own ideals of international society, should also be represented in the U.N. and other international bodies, so long as it is willing to join these on the same terms that are expected of every other nation. We should also make clear that we are ready to live peacefully with Peking and develop such friendly cooperation as it is willing to accept; that we believe that the form of government which exists in continental China is a matter for the people who live there to decide; and that we have no intention of interfering in any way in the domestic affairs of continental China. In addition, we should find ways to express our admiration for the great historic entity of China as not only the largest nation in the world today in terms of population but as one of the truly great national units throughout human history.

---

[2] See Document 168.

12. We have for some time been hinting at the sort of attitude I advocate, but I believe that we should move to a clear and unequivocal definition of this attitude as soon as possible. I realize that the delicacy of the political situation on Taiwan would require carefully coordinated steps over a certain period of time before the new positions could be reached. But we should not allow the peculiarities of one small country to continue to determine the position of the world's greatest power year after year. In view of the dangers of an adverse outcome on the ChiRep vote, in the U.N. this autumn, we need to move with considerable speed. World opinion and votes in the U.N. are likely in any case to push us step by step towards the type of redefinition of our attitude I have outlined above. If we move in this direction only out of pressing necessity and with obvious reluctance, we shall probably end up with most of the disadvantages of our present stance and few of the possible benefits of the new. I am convinced that it is overwhelmingly in our interests to move quickly and on our initiative to the new stance, which is both in keeping with the realities and with our own fundamental ideals.

Reischauer

---

175.   Memorandum of Conversation[1]

Chamcook, New Brunswick, August 21, 1966.

SUBJECT

Communist China and Admission to UN

PARTICIPANTS

United States
The President
Ambassador W. Walton Butterworth
Rufus Z. Smith, Director for Relations with Canada

Canada
Prime Minister Pearson
Ambassador A. E. Ritchie
H. Basil Robinson, Assistant Under-Secretary for External Affairs

---

[1] Source: Department of State, Central Files, UN 6 CHICOM. Secret. Drafted by Smith; approved at the White House on August 30. The source text is labeled "Part 5 of 9."

(The President met with Prime Minister Pearson on the occasion of his participation in a cornerstone laying ceremony at the Roosevelt Campobello International Park on Campobello Island, New Brunswick. He was the luncheon guest of the Prime Minister at Rossmount Inn in the little town on Chamcook, N.B. The lunch was preceded by approximately an hour and a half of serious conversation in a parlor of the Inn set aside for the purpose.)

The Prime Minister commented that there appeared to be some real problems inside Communist China. The Chinese seemed to have settled the leadership question, but it appeared that the structure of the leadership is no longer quite so monolithic.

The Prime Minister asked whether the President saw any big issue coming up at the UN General Assembly other than the Chinese representation question. He went on to say that he would like to see the Chinese Communists in the United Nations where they would have to defend their position before the world, but he did not want to sell out the Chinese Nationalists. He concluded by asking whether public opinion on the question is changing in the US.

The President responded that he thought American public opinion had moderated somewhat as a result of the Fulbright hearings and the speeches of a number of professors. He thought, however, that opinion could quickly swing back, although he was not sure that would be good if one believes the UN should include those who disagree with one's position. For that matter, he said, the Chinese Communists probably don't want to come in, although that may be a sham argument, and he admitted there was a good deal of reason to what the Prime Minister said.

The President concluded the remarks about China by saying we are still examining the situation. He thought that the two governments should keep in close touch on the issue and that with the relationship what it is between our two countries we could always work out any differences between us.

176. Memorandum From the President's Special Assistant (Rostow) to President Johnson[1]

Washington, August 30, 1966, 1:15 p.m.

Mr. President.

This Hong Kong analysis of the ChiCom political scene is a bit long-winded, but worth reading given the importance of the subject.[2]

In brief:

1. Mao has chosen Lin Piao as his successor.
2. Together they are determined to set up a power structure, via the Army, which will override the moderate opposition in the Party and the bureaucracy, as well as in intellectual life.
3. It is not certain that Lin Piao will be able to consolidate his position as Mao's successor.
4. If he does consolidate his position, he's bad news.

Walt

---

[1] Source: Johnson Library, National Security File, Country File, China, Vol. VII. No classification marking. A handwritten "L" on the source text indicates that it was seen by the President.

[2] A typed copy of telegram 1392 from Hong Kong, August 30, is attached but not printed. (Department of State, Central Files, POL 15–1 CHICOM)

---

177. Telegram From the Department of State to the Embassy in Poland[1]

Washington, August 31, 1966, 5:23 p.m.

38572. Gronouski–Wang talks: Guidance for 131st meeting, September 7, 1966.

---

[1] Source: Department of State, Central Files, POL CHICOM–US. Confidential; Limdis. Drafted by Kreisberg on August 19; cleared in draft by Vietnam Working Group Director Robert H. Miller, Aldrich, UNP Deputy Director William Gleysteen, and J. Stapleton Roy of SOV, and by SCA Deputy Administrator Barbara M. Watson, Dr. Creech of USDA, Anderson of DOD/ISA, Bundy, Harriman, and William Jorden; and approved by Rusk. Repeated to Moscow, Saigon, Taipei, and Hong Kong.

1. We are scheduled to start this session. Suggest you open along following lines:

2. Mr. Ambassador, in three meetings in this series in which I have personally participated, I have endeavored to communicate desire of my Government to see improvement in relations between our two countries. I have reiterated that we have no hostile intent toward your country or your people. I have conveyed wish of my Government to enlarge areas of contact and communication between our two peoples so that through increased knowledge may come greater understanding and possibility of gradual reduction in tensions and conflicts that presently exist between us. I have expressed my Government's interest in discussing problems of disarmament and in pursuing specific views of your side on this subject. We are under no illusion that this process would be easy or rapid one. We are all too aware of great ideological and political differences between our two countries. I deeply regret our inability in these meetings, in part because of these differences, to pursue to a fruitful conclusion any of these potential areas of agreement.

3. But we are deeply convinced that violence and war are not adequate or acceptable means for settling differences between states today. President Johnson stated in speech July 12 that "reconciliation between nations that now call themselves enemies" was one of essentials for peace in Asia. He emphasized that any "isolation" of your country in world comes not from actions by US or other countries, but by your own choice. FYI: Peking has not so far commented on the President's speech. End FYI. It is not US which blocks path toward peaceful cooperation and exchange between scientists, scholars, doctors, artists, and athletes of our two countries. We know there is active correspondence on professional matters between many of your scientists and those of US. We know of large purchases of American books and other publications made by your Government in US. You are obviously interested in exchange of knowledge and we understand this, because so are we. What we do not understand is why you are afraid of permitting such exchanges by direct, face-to-face contact? Why not openly acknowledge that such direct exchanges would be of mutual benefit. Mr. Chou En-lai was reported by New China News Agency on July 31 to have told gathering of scientists in Peking that: "We are willing to learn modestly strong points and experiences of people of other countries." This is point of view we share and is reason we have indicated our willingness to see such exchanges of knowledge between citizens of our two countries. FYI: If ChiComs reject or do not reply to invitation to attend High Energy Physics Conference in Palo Alto, you should regret such action. End FYI.

4. Even though your Government has so far not agreed to such exchanges as we have proposed, Mr. Ambassador, I would like at this point to note potential mutual benefit which would be derived from

exchange of plant and horticultural samples between interested institutions of our two countries. As you may know, exchanges of plant samples provide opportunities for cross-breeding and strengthening of plant strains and thereby provide basis for improving and increasing agricultural production.

5. Mr. Ambassador, we have noted with dismay view expressed in *People's Daily* of July 24 that "the Chinese people have always held that a conference table can never bring the oppressed nations a new world of independence and freedom, nor can an international agreement guarantee the oppressed nations a life of liberation and happiness." Overwhelming evidence of world history in last 20 years repudiates view that peaceful negotiations offers no prospect for social and political change. This position is false reflection on people and governments of dozens of countries in Africa and Asia: Burma, India, Ceylon, Pakistan, Malaysia, the Philippines, Morocco, Tunisia, Ghana, Guinea, Tanzania, Kenya, and I could go on and name many more. It is only when your Government realizes impossibility of imposing its will and its ideology upon others through force and is prepared to discuss and negotiate differences at conference table that progress can be made toward goal of peace that is, I am convinced, desire of Chinese people along with those of rest of world. We do not consider valid political and economic premises of your Government in ruling your people. But we have no intention of interfering with your internal affairs. It is not for you or for us to lay down rules and principles by which other governments and peoples should govern themselves.

6. Mr. Ambassador, we have repeatedly stressed that people of South Vietnam should be able to decide their own future and choose their own form of political, economic, and social organization, free from all outside interference. Our entire position in Vietnam can be summed up as an effort to assist the people of South Vietnam to achieve this goal. We do not want to maintain bases in Southeast Asia and we have repeatedly pledged to withdraw our troops from South Vietnam when its security and freedom of choice are assured. We do not oppose the reunification of Vietnam. We support the right of self-determination through the free choice of the Vietnamese people. Likewise, the US does not oppose the neutrality or non- alignment of all the countries of Southeast Asia if that is their desire. It is in its opposition to any resolution in Vietnam which is not achieved by violence and war that your Government has found itself isolated from overwhelming majority of people and governments in world. I am sure you are aware, Mr. Ambassador, from your own reading as well as from what I and my predecessor have said in these meetings, that US is absolutely resolved to continue its support of the Government of SVN in resisting communist aggression from north with its goal of imposing by force the political system of North

Vietnam on people of South Vietnam. I urge you not to doubt this and not to encourage others to doubt our determination. Military success by communist side in Vietnam is impossible. But we are prepared to seek honorable peace, one with honor for all sides. I have indicated before to you my Government's willingness to discuss means of achieving such an honorable peace with representatives of your or any other government directly involved. I reiterate that offer to you now. At our last meeting I suggested that one means by which movement toward an end to conflict could be found was through mutual dampening down of hostilities. My Government would be interested in any constructive proposals your side might wish to put forward. We are willing to consider all propositions but we will not accept ultimata. We do not attempt to intimidate others and we cannot ourselves be intimidated. I assure you, Mr. Ambassador, that you have only to test our sincerity by accepting our offer to discuss peaceful settlement in Vietnam. Our willingness to halt destruction and slaughter of war is clear and unequivocal.

7. Your Government, Mr. Ambassador, appears to consider that Geneva Agreements no longer exist. *People's Daily* commentary I quoted earlier alleges that Geneva Agreements have been "reduced to ashes". It scoffs at willingness of US to work toward settling conflict in Vietnam on basis of Geneva Agreements and at efforts of numerous distinguished and sincere international figures to achieve this end, one which authorities in Hanoi claim they also seek. Mr. T'ao Chu in a speech on July 22 said that "whoever still attempts to use the Geneva Agreements to tie the hands of the Vietnamese people, the Chinese people, and the revolutionary people of the world will never succeed . . . . The Geneva Agreements are already non-existent". This is position which authorities in North Vietnam have not advanced.

8. Mr. Ambassador, I would like to note that apparent position of your Government on peaceful resolution of disputes (including your rejection, as stated in the *People's Daily* of June 20, 1966 of any disarmament negotiations at the present time) and statements by your Government's officials setting forth extraordinary "conditions" under which your Government would even consider joining UN raise strong doubt that your Government has any interest whatsoever in participating in peaceful international organizations. The very foundation of UN is conviction that resolution of disputes and conflicts by peaceful means is not only possible but necessary. On this issue every member of UN is in agreement.

9. Mr. Ambassador, I regret to call your attention to unprovoked firing by vessel *Nan Hai* 155 belonging to your country on US military aircraft on July 30 at 20° 37'N, 107° 32'E. A second US military aircraft was fired upon by armed vessels of your country's flag on August 2 at 34° 35'N, 123° 05'E. Both incidents took place on open seas and in clearly

international waters. US aircraft on neither occasion returned fire directed at them but only this restraint and forebearance in face of blatant provocation averted what could have been grave incident. I strongly urge that you request your Government to take appropriate measures to avoid recurrence of such incidents which could lead to consequences I believe neither of us would wish.

10. Mr. Ambassador, at our 118th meeting on November 13, 1963 and again at 127th meeting on September 20, 1965 we requested that your side provide us with names on American dogtags (identification tags) reportedly on exhibit in War Museum in Peking. I am sure you will understand strong desire on part of parents of American soldiers missing-in-action in Korea for any information that might pertain to their sons. I hope that on humanitarian grounds you will find it possible to meet this request.

11. We anticipate that in his presentation Wang may protest press leak of last meeting. We would not plan to respond other than to reiterate regret already conveyed. (Deptel 1837)[2] Wang will probably respond to our query on non-first use agreement and WDC Preparatory Meeting along lines of *People's Daily Commentary* June 20 (FBIS June 20). *Commentary* rejects any connection between test ban and "non-first use." It implicitly replies to letter handed Wang at last meeting on WDC with flat rejection of ChiCom participation in WDC in any disarmament negotiations. Wang may also raise question of alleged US attack on ChiCom fishing boats in Tonkin Gulf May 28 and SEATO naval exercise Sea Imp and may revert to shoot-down of ChiCom plane May 12 which was discussed last meeting. He may also protest Syrian defector case or Dutch case involving attempted ChiCom defection. Kreisberg will provide you with detailed rebuttals on these and other points Wang may raise.

12. It is Wang's turn to suggest timing of next meeting. You may agree to any date within next three months—we prefer November 30 or December 7.

13. FYI: In general, we anticipate that tension on mainland and indications of continuing international CCP dispute will result in Wang's taking particularly hard line in this meeting and we do not exclude possibility of last minute postponement at their initiative. End FYI.

Rusk

---

[2] Telegram 1837 to Warsaw, June 3, transmitted the text of a brief letter of apology for the leak of the talks reflected in a *New York Times* article of June 3; telegram 1853, June 4, authorized delivery of the letter. (Ibid.) The article stated that the United States had raised the possibility of making an agreement with China that neither would be the first to use nuclear weapons if the Chinese would agree to stop nuclear testing. Information about the leak was sent to Rusk in Tosec 38 to Oslo, June 3. (Ibid.)

178.   Memorandum From Alfred Jenkins of the National Security Council Staff to the President's Special Assistant (Rostow)[1]

Washington, September 1, 1966.

SUBJECT

DOD Interest in ChiRep

Mort Halperin told me at lunch today that a *DOD memorandum* on ChiRep[2] advocating abandonment of the old formula and *pointing toward a "two China" policy* had been approved all the way through McNamara, *without any discernible opposition in Defense.*

According to Mort, *McNamara commissioned his staff to find some way of getting DOD into ChiRep policy deliberations.* The reasoning was that our present stand damages our relations with friends, and that particularly in the case of Japan such damage has defense implications.

Mort said he was talking out of school, of course, and would appreciate our treating this accordingly.

As you have observed, the issue is not appropriate for NSC deliberation but I wonder whether it would be an appropriate Tuesday luncheon topic.

Al
WJJ[3]

---

[1] Source: Johnson Library, National Security File, Country File, China, Vol. VII. Confidential.

[2] The memorandum has not been found.

[3] Jorden initialed below Jenkins' signature.

179.   Memorandum From Alfred Jenkins of the National Security Council Staff to the President's Special Assistant (Rostow)[1]

Washington, September 6, 1966.

SUBJECT

ChiRep Item at Secretary's Meeting on UN Problems

Background

1.   Prior to Red Guard excesses and Lin Piao's redeclaration of global "People's War," majority U.S. opinion—public, academic, congressional and bureaucratic—seemed to hold that effort should be made to bring Communist China into the world community. The clear trend in international opinion was similar.

2.   The effects of recent Peking extravagances on sentiment for a UN invitation is not yet known, and could go either way. (My Chirep memo of Aug. 31, para 6.)[2]

3.   Our ability to defeat an Albanian-type resolution (ejecting the GRC and seating the PRC) is at present questionable. A recent field round-up of voting predictions produced too many "uncertains" to be very meaningful, and did not take account of (a) most recent Peking belligerence, or perhaps more importantly, (b) the following lament in U Thant's resignation statement:

"I must confess to a sense of dissatisfaction with the fact that the organization has not yet achieved universality of membership."

Alternatives

4.   Of a whole spectrum of possible approaches to the problem, the following two appear to be the only ones which at this late date warrant U.S. consideration:

a.   Attempt to have a friendly member introduce a resolution along the lines of the draft at Tab A,[3] which reaffirms GRC status and also invites the PRC to occupy seats in the General Assembly.

---

[1] Source: Johnson Library, National Security File, Agency File, United Nations, Vol. 4. Secret. Filed as an attachment to a September 6 memorandum from Harold K. Saunders of the NSC staff to Rostow, which transmitted NSC staff views on the main issues to be discussed at Rusk's UNGA strategy meeting. Concerning the Jenkins memorandum, Saunders commented, "I have deliberately stayed an outsider on this one, but I am wondering whether we shouldn't soon give the President a rundown on where we stand. Time is getting very short. The ticklish aspect of this problem is that the Secretary is somewhat alone in resisting change."

[2] The memorandum reported the status of the issue. (Ibid., Name File, Jenkins Memos)

[3] The tabs are attached but not printed.

b. Attempt to defeat the Albanian-type resolution, without having any other one introduced.

The two alternative drafts at Tab B[4] may be discussed at the meeting, but have not elicited much interest so far. Either of them would probably be widely viewed as a too-patent gimmick, or overly moralistic.

Considerations

5. Alternative a) would be responsive to the President's desire that we get off the defensive.

It would surely keep the PRC out of the UN, for it would be interpreted by the Chicoms as an insult. It would provoke a blast and an indignant rejection from Peking.

It would nevertheless be interpreted by many who have considered our policies as too rigid, as welcome evidence of movement in those policies.

6. However, evidence is we would have difficulty in finding a suitable sponsor, partly because of the lateness of the shift in our tactics, and partly because many on both sides of the China issue could not support this resolution. Even we presumably would have to abstain on the second part of this two-part resolution, and hence on the later vote on the resolution as a whole—if only because the prerequisite and exceedingly difficult ground work with the GRC has not been laid (Secretary's visit to Taipei).

Furthermore, a number of our friends who have been uneasy with the "puppet" tag from their support of us in the past, have asked that we give them fair warning if we ever depart from our position, so that they may at least precede us in that shift. It is very late to give such warning now.

7. With alternative b), we would remain on the defensive, with a policy the effectiveness of which is of doubtful longevity. Although there is some indication that the voting could even be slightly more favorable than last year, the crucial uncertain vote (especially African) is more unpredictable than ever, and we could end up with the PRC in and the GRC completely out of the UN.

8. There are many other considerations, but these are the more salient. There is no course which is attractive and safe.

---

[4] Both affirmed that the Republic of China was a founding and continuing UN member. The first requested the President of the General Assembly to inquire of the PRC whether it was prepared to accept the obligations of the UN Charter; the second expressed willingness to consider General Assembly membership for the PRC on being informed that it had accepted the Charter and its obligations.

Recommendation

9. All things considered, I recommend that you take the following position:

Since requisite groundwork for a clear change in policy or tactics has not been laid, we should

a. State more unequivocally than in our last message to the field our continued opposition to an Albanian-type resolution and our expectation as of now that this is the only resolution which will be presented.

b. Keep constant tabs on likely voting on such a resolution. If the chance of losing becomes too great, consult immediately for sponsorship and support of a para 4, a) type resolution. (A last minute shift in extremis would be more acceptable to our friends—including the GRC—than a planned shift before that, at this late date.)

c. If that alternative, too, should go awry (e.g. no appropriate sponsor, too much friendly opposition, or amendment putting PRC in Security Council) attempt to shift immediately to a resolution establishing a study group to consider this complex question, and report back to the Assembly. This alternative is a poor third, since we could not predict or perhaps greatly influence the outcome. It is a stop-gap if something deemed worse should loom. Timing and mechanics are complex, but we could probably gain support for the desired priority sequence in voting, where more than one resolution is tabled.

10. Finally, we should bear in mind that the mood on the mainland is ugly, not yet fully understood, and probably not yet settled into a definitive course. U Thant was not far wrong when he said China was having a nervous breakdown—a malady requiring on the part of others patience and firmness, understanding and wariness, flexibility, and at times forceful opposition. We cannot yet predict the dominant conclusions which the UN membership will draw from China's present madness. We should therefore keep an open mind concerning resolutions which may be introduced by others than the Albanian group. Especially if we are otherwise in trouble, it is possible that such initiative might bring some of the advantages sought in a "non-defensive" approach, without the costs which would be associated with our having initiated it.

Meanwhile, as the situation permits, we can continue our quiet, carefully measured program of attempted reconciliation. It will not be reciprocated, but as a minimum it helps throw Mao and company off balance, and hopefully builds for the non-Mao future.

Alfred Jenkins[5]

---

[5] Printed from a copy that bears this typed signature.

180. **Telegram From the Embassy in Poland to the Department of State**[1]

Warsaw, September 7, 1966, 1958Z.

549. Gronouski–Wang Talks, 131st meeting.[2]

1. Wang offered no new themes, proposals, positions. Both formal presentation and rebuttal comments restricted to reiteration past public ChiCom attacks on U.S. aggression and provocation against CPR and DRV, and repudiation of U.S. indications of desire improve U.S.-CPR relations and wish for peace in Vietnam as "fraud." Indication of intention make his prepared statement public given at very end of meeting was only surprise (Warsaw 548).[3] Wang proposed January 11 for next meeting and after fruitless efforts to move date up to December or November I agreed.

2. I opened with guidance provided by State 38572,[4] as supplemented by paragraph on August 29 Tonkin Gulf incident provided by State 40808 [41808].[5] Wang's opening statement focused on following themes:

3. U.S.-CPR relations. Wang cited U.S. hostility toward CPR since 1949. He said ChiComs refused be "hoodwinked" by U.S. official talk of "building bridges" and improvement of CPR-U.S. relations. He attacked continued U.S. occupation of Taiwan and turning Taiwan into U.S. colony and military base (Secretary's visit to Taipei this summer seen as effort to "hatch criminal plots" against CPR) and reiterated determination of Peking to "liberate" Taiwan, and demand for total U.S. withdrawal from Straits area. He called recent Seoul conference of Asian States a U.S. attempt to organize a "new military alliance" against CPR and charged U.S.-Soviet-Japanese collusion in plotting against Peking. ChiComs and Asian people would never be duped by U.S. and it clear, Wang said, there no sincerity in U.S. talk of easing relations with Peking.

4. Vietnam. Wang referred to U.S. expansion of bombing of North Vietnam, increase in force level in South, and provocations against Cambodia but concluded we "foredoomed to failure." He charged U.S.-Soviet collaboration on peace initiatives and denounced U.S. "peace swindles" and talks of "de-escalation." He demanded an "immediate and complete" U.S. withdrawal from Vietnam and reiterated references

---

[1] Source: Department of State, Central Files POL CHICOM–US. Confidential; Immediate; Limdis. Repeated to Hong Kong, Moscow, Saigon, and Taipei and passed to the White House, CIA, and USIA.

[2] Gronouski sent a detailed report of the meeting in airgram A–205, September 8. (Ibid.)

[3] Dated September 7. (Ibid.)

[4] Document 177.

[5] Telegram 41808 to Warsaw, September 6. (Department of State, Central Files, POL CHICOM–US)

to the U.S. having "torn to shreds" the Geneva Accords. Wang cited Ho Chi Minh's July 17 appeal at length and pledged ChiCom support for DRV. He stated that China "reliable rear area" for Vietnamese people, that "aggression against Vietnam is aggression against China" and that U.S. would be "committing grave historical blunder and will find it too late to repent" if it "underestimates actions" which CPR will take to support Vietnamese people. (Wang reiterated this last statement verbatim again during rebuttal.)

5. In rebuttal I told Wang I would not trade threats with him on Vietnam but emphasized our determination meet challenges which might be presented. I emphasized U.S. willingness withdraw from Vietnam when aggression halted and urged CPR to test U.S. On U.S.-CPR incidents on high seas (Wang had raised both May 28 and August 29 charges of U.S. attacks on ChiCom ships), I reiterated our proposal for joint investigations, denied May 29 charge and offered further investigation of August incident if ChiComs provided more information. I rebutted remaining Wang points briefly, noting we would not discuss U.S.-Soviet relations in these talks but that differing U.S.-Soviet positions on Vietnam plain for all to see. Used very helpful Dept and Hong Kong messages on Ch'en Yi–Kosaka conversation (Wang clearly taken aback and unaware of reported Ch'en Yi remarks). I noted Ch'en appeared be making same points we had made in talks here and told Wang I hoped ChiComs might be willing open door to more fruitful exchanges of views and relaxation of tensions. I said I was surprised at contrast between Ch'en Yi's remarks and hard tone of Wang's presentation. (Wang did not respond immediately but at end of meeting repeated ChiCom determination on Vietnam and, noting this in reply to my reference to Ch'en Yi, said his statement represented view of Chinese people.)

6. In response Wang once more went through much of his opening statement argument, in abbreviated form but with few variations. He asked why U.S. "haggled" over scholars and newsmen when key issues such as Taiwan unresolved. He raised specific charge U.S. using poison gas, claiming Secy. McNamara had made Sept 1965 speech justifying use of such gas, and charged U.S. atrocities in SVN, bombing of civilians in NVN. He cited growing U.S. military strength despite "over 1000" arms control discussions to argue that U.S. talked of disarmament to cover up arms expansion. He then said Peking would not participate in WDC or any exploratory group on WDC but made no reference to our exchange of letters[6] (exchange thus remains completely private since I believe we have not mentioned exchange to anyone, including allies so far).

---

[6] For the U.S. letter of May 26, see Documents 153 and 155. Telegram 539 from Warsaw, September 7, transmitted the text of a letter rejecting the U.S. proposal, which the Embassy had received from the Chinese Embassy the day before. (Department of State, Central Files, POL CHICOM–US)

7. I responded by reviewing usefulness of people-to-people exchanges, rejected as completely false allegation on poison gas (and of McNamara justification), and emphasized we had never intentionally struck at any nonmilitary target in Vietnam. I queried why DRV unwilling allow outside neutral observers (ICC, ICRC) inspect alleged U.S. activities in North if these actually existed. I emphasized if ChiCom aim to see U.S. troops out of VN, they should use their influence to prevail on DRV to halt infiltration and end conflict. On disarmament, I regretted ChiCom rejection of exploratory group and reiterated hope they at some point would recognize usefulness of genuine exchange of views on arms control issues.

8. Wang responded that U.S.-CPR tension due to "occupation of Taiwan," "provocations" against CPR territory, and aggression against CPR's "most intimate neighbor". By leaving these issues unsettled and haggling over side issues, U.S. shows "insincerity." U.S. should show "sincerity" by withdrawing from Taiwan and halt use of force in Vietnam. He then once more went over old ground on Vietnam and I decided no point in prolonging discussion.

9. Wang suggested Jan 11, 1967 for next meeting, noting in response my attempt move date up to December 7 or 14 that this period "inconvenient" for him and that "under current circumstances," he did not think more frequent meetings were necessary. After further back and forth, I agreed to Jan 11 date.

10. Wang then expressed strong ChiCom regret at U.S. violation of confidence of talks, alluding to past leaks and referring to Bundy's Feb. 12 speech to our offer at 128th meeting in December on nonreciprocal admission of ChiCom newsmen. Said Peking had decided release opening ChiCom statement at current meeting. I expressed strong regret, noting my May letter said leaks were unintentional and unauthorized. I said we could not prevent their releasing statement but reserved right to make whatever response we believed appropriate. Wang seemed defensive, anxious to show his release not unprecedented (we do not here recall precedent for publication of full text of statement although partial revelations have taken place before) and that U.S. really responsible for ChiCom move.

11. Overall atmosphere of meeting was relaxed, even at end, and Wang did not at any time appear agitated or excited although ChiCom side exhibited considerable surprise at my reference to Ch'en Yi–Kosaka conversation.

12. I assume ChiCom opening statement intended for Soviets as well as us and that this accounts, at least in part, for its utter sterility. I am somewhat concerned at obvious ChiCom effort prolong gaps between meetings longer and longer (next gap will be four months). Wang's casual remark that "in current circumstances" more frequent meetings

not necessary was first flat indication he has given of intention continue stretch out periods between meetings. I am determined on our side to try and narrow this gap in future. ChiComs obviously apparently continue find existence of Warsaw channel useful both for facade of effort to deal with U.S. and for potential crisis communication but disinclined encourage frequent contact.

Gronouski

181.   Telegram From the Embassy in Poland to the Department of State[1]

Warsaw, September 9, 1966, 0944Z.

568. 1. I am aware of polemic aspects of ChiCom letter[2] but am reluctant go to extent of formal rejection and return of their reply. Virtually all our meetings with Chinese here in Warsaw and earlier in Geneva have been conducted in atmosphere of polemics and invective which under any normal circumstances would be grounds for U.S. representative to walk out of meetings. ChiCom opening statement in meeting Sept. 7 filled with attacks and slanders against U.S. which, if made to me by Polish Govt official would be totally unacceptable and grounds for my instant protest.

2. We have accepted this in past, however, as one aspect of dealing with ChiComs in this admittedly extraordinary, semi-diplomatic contact. So long as general purpose of contact continues useful, I am prepared to accept ChiCom polemics as part of the game.

3. ChiCom letter, it seems to me, falls within same "extraordinary" character. What we would and could not accept from country with which we have diplomatic relations does not and should not necessarily carry over into this bizarre U.S.-ChiCom link here.

---

[1] Source: Department of State, Central Files, POL CHICOM–US. Confidential; Immediate; Limdis. Repeated to Hong Kong and Taipei and passed to the White House and USIA.

[2] Reference is to the letter cited in footnote 6, Document 180. It called the U.S. proposal a "sheer swindle" aimed at covering up "crimes of aggression." Telegram 43393 to Warsaw, September 8, stated that its language was so abusive as to be unacceptable and instructed the Embassy to return it with the oral explanation that it was unacceptable because it used offensive language at variance with universally accepted diplomatic norms. (Department of State, Central Files, POL CHICOM–US)

4. I would also suggest possibility that in their strange "tit for tat" approach to diplomacy if we reject their letter, ChiComs might decide return our letter to them on Gemini shot which handed to them yesterday.[3] As you aware, they have in past accepted our notifications and with this, at least moral obligation to accept responsibility for return of astronauts in case of emergency. I would be reluctant to risk precipitating possible rejection of our letter of notification, and I have no doubt they could fabricate grounds for doing so, by returning their letter on disarmament at present time.

5. I therefore strongly urge Dept reconsider instruction to return ChiCom letter.[4]

Gronouski

---

[3] Airgram A–197 from Warsaw, September 8, reported that the Embassy had transmitted a news release with a covering letter to the Chinese Embassy. It noted that no discussion had ever been held with the Chinese on the question of what would happen if a U.S. space flight landed for any reason in Chinese Communist territory, but that the Chinese had been informed in advance of each manned space shot that had overflown mainland China. (Ibid., SP 1 US)

[4] Telegram 44217 to Warsaw, September 9, withdrew the instructions. (Ibid., POL CHICOM–US)

---

182. **Memorandum From the Assistant Secretary of State for International Organization Affairs (Sisco) to Secretary of State Rusk**[1]

Washington, September 13, 1966.

SUBJECT

Your luncheon Meeting with the President on September 13, 1966[2]

Chinese Representation—I assume you will wish to talk to the President on why you have concluded we should not make a change in our

---

[1] Source: Department of State, Central Files, UN 6 CHICOM. Secret; Exdis. A handwritten notation on the source text indicates that Bundy concurred.

[2] Rusk, McNamara, Rostow, and Moyers met with the President for their regular Tuesday luncheon meeting at 2:15 p.m. on September 13. McNamara, Rostow, and Moyers left at 3:45 p.m., Rusk at 4:01 p.m. A note in the President's Daily Diary states that according to Rostow, the agenda for the meeting was "of unusual importance—as well as rather long." (Johnson Library) No record of the discussion has been found.

position on Chinese Representation in present circumstances, leaving open the possibility of a shift if the vote count weakens when we come closer to the time this matter is considered by the Assembly. My own judgment is that we should seek to have the matter considered after, and not before, the elections in this country. In doing so, you will no doubt want to inform the President that Ambassador Goldberg strongly believes we should shift to a two-China policy, and that we announce this change in the General Debate speech. You might indicate to the President that you will be talking to Ambassador Goldberg later in the week regarding this matter.

183.   Editorial Note

The National Security Council met on September 15, 1966, to review issues concerning the pending meeting of the UN General Assembly. A brief undated memorandum of the meeting by NSC staff member Nathaniel Davis records no discussion related to China except a brief reference in the last paragraph, headed "Other Items," which reads as follows: "Ambassador Goldberg touched briefly on general disarmament questions, Chinese representation, Korea, peace-keeping, etc. The President asked Secretary McNamara if he had any comments, which he didn't, and the President closed the meeting." (Johnson Library, National Security File, NSC Meetings File, Vol. 4, Tab 46, 9/15/66)

184.   Memorandum From Alfred Jenkins of the National Security Council Staff to the President's Special Assistant (Rostow)[1]

Washington, September 16, 1966.

SUBJECT

Time for Caution on our Part?

It is possible that the present mainland upheaval is sufficiently planned and controlled so that in a couple of months Peking's affairs

---

[1] Source: Johnson Library, National Security File, Name File, Jenkins Memos. Secret. Copies were sent to William J. Jorden and Donald Ropa of the NSC staff.

might not prove to be significantly altered, except for new faces in prominent places. However, without speculating further with inadequate evidence as to just what is going on, it seems just as possible that some real watershed in the Chinese scene may be reached. There is something awesome in the spectacle of the oldest civilization on earth methodically digging up its roots to the tune of raucous, uncivilized ballyhoo and bedlam. True, this spectacle could prove to be partly busy-work to cover up and to facilitate Lin's and Mao's attacks on the CCP party structure. In the process, however, the steam has obviously built up such a head that if deadly serious plans—whatever they be—should go awry, a drastic "out" might be sought.

The Asian communist people at State believe this is a time for considerable caution on our part. They particularly believe we should take strict measures just now against the possibility of our doing anything which might be interpreted as military provocation. I am inclined to agree. The boys at State are loath to put this idea into regular bureaucratic channels lest it touch off delaying debate as to just what is happening on the mainland. Hence if there is any merit in asking that our military and public postures be cautious just now, it may be a matter which should receive treatment from the top down rather than the other way around.

You may wish to consider bringing up at the Tuesday luncheon, or through other channels, the possibility of temporarily restricting the more provocative of our forward operations along the Chinese border and of our actions against shipping in the Gulf of Tonkin, during the immediate period of understandably heightened Chinese nervousness. I recognize that insistent Vietnam military requirements must still be overriding. We can hope that the chaos on the mainland may continue a while, and may prove to be in our interest in the denouement. Meanwhile we should try not to provide a way out for a Mao in trouble, should he sooner or later require a particularly devilish devil.

AJ

185.   Circular Telegram From the Department of State to Certain Posts[1]

Washington, September 16, 1966, 8:52 p.m.

49274. Ref: CA–1799.[2] Subj: Chinese Representation at UNGA.

1. Unless representations believed unhelpful Dept requests that all posts proceed with any additional conversations they consider necessary to ensure that host governments understand that there no change in US policy on Chirep at 21st UNGA and desire to assure maximum opposition to any resolution of "Albanian" type that would expel GRC and replace it by Communist China. Specifically other governments should be fully aware that:

(a) Sponsors of traditional Albanian-type resolution are expected to table unambiguous resolution explicitly calling for expulsion of GRC and seating of Chinese Communists in GA and throughout UN structure. (FYI) Also as in past years it does not appear that any country or group of countries will present the Assembly with an alternative to this tactic. We are making effort to work out arrangements whereby Chirep debate will not occur before mid-November. End FYI.

(b) USG will strongly oppose Albanian-type resolution substituting ChiComs for GRC and requests support of maximum number of other governments.

(c) USG will in addition seek maximum support for Assembly action to reaffirm view that any proposal to change representation of China is "important question" requiring two-thirds majority.

2. In explaining USG's decision posts should draw as appropriate on following:

a. Nothing during past year has diminished our belief that Communist China's entry into UN within circumstances of its present policy would radically disrupt UN's activities. Apart from its totally unacceptable demand for the expulsion of the GRC, Peking has in no way moderated its extraordinary conditions for UN entry, i.e., cancellation UN 1950 resolution condemning ChiComs and North Koreans as aggressors, adoption UN resolution condemning US as aggressor, revision UN Charter, inclusion all "independent states", and exclusion all "imperialist puppets".

(b) ChiCom hostility to UN and to much of outer world has been highlighted in recent months by turmoil within China symbolized by

---

[1] Source: Department of State, Central Files, UN 6 CHICOM. Confidential; Priority. Drafted by Gleysteen, cleared by Berger, and approved by Sisco. Sent to 101 Embassies; repeated to 10 Embassies, Hong Kong, USUN, the U.S. Mission in Geneva, and Paris for USRO.

[2] Dated September 2. (Ibid., UN 3 GA)

emergence of "Red Guards" and related activity. Whatever final outcome of these developments, their present effect is to underscore militancy and unyielding mood of Peking's current leaders.

(c) There has been no softening and possibly some hardening of attitude toward Communist China among those Asian governments which are most directly exposed to dangers of activity advocated and supported by ChiComs as in Vietnam. (FYI—Some of these Asian leaders have expressed view that this would be inappropriate time to change present method of dealing with Chirep in UN. End FYI.) As examples these views you may wish to cite Philippine President Marcos's Sept 15 address in Washington or communiqué of Asian Parliamentary Union (Philippines, South Korea, Thailand, Republic of China, South Vietnam, Laos, Malaysia, and Japan) expressing firm opposition to ChiCom admission to UN.

(d) Our present vote estimates indicate that a distinct majority would support our position on important question formula while prospects for defeating Albanian-type resolution are about same as last year. (FYI—Several other governments including Soviets and French seem to conclude situation presently more favorable for our position than last year. Although we will as in other years determine precise moves at UNGA in light of developments during session, our present vote tally, which must be balanced against uncertainties this far in advance of vote, shows substantial margin for upholding important question resolution and bare majority against Albanian resolution. End FYI.)

3. Dept requests continuing reports of any significant developments concerning host governments' attitude on Chirep prior to GA debate. In reporting any discussions with local officials request special effort to distinguish voting prospects for Albanian-type resolution and "important question" formula. Some governments do not seem fully familiar with latter.

Rusk

186.   Telegram From the Embassy in the Republic of China to the Department of State[1]

Taipei, September 20, 1966, 0932Z.

901. Meeting with Chiang Ching-kuo.

1. DefMin Chiang Ching-kuo yesterday called on me at his request, with major purpose of discussing mainland purge developments and GRC desire to take advantage of opportunities GRC sees in present situation.

2. CCK said he was directed by his father the Gimo to present GRC views on changes in situation since Secy Rusk's conversations with Gimo July 3–4. Major elements, CCK said, are (A) Red Guard activity on mainland; (B) decreased possibility for starting Vietnam peace negotiations; (C) further deterioration in Sino-Soviet relations.

3. CCK stressed that GRC policies and actions continue to be synchronized and coordinated with USG and that GRC would, as in the past, keep firmly in mind US desires and interests. He reiterated Gimo statement to Secretary that first and most urgent thing is to solve Vietnam problem, and that return to mainland was secondary and longer range objective. However he said GRC believed that now is opportune time for action to topple Peiping regime. He said USSR would like to see US bogged down in a war with the Chinese Communists, and Peiping hopes that in the end the US and USSR will come to a nuclear exchange. The GRC did not want to see a large scale war with Peiping either by the US or by the USSR, because Peiping would have too many advantages in terms of very large population and large territory in which to maneuver. Only the GRC possesses unique advantages capable of solving the ChiCom problem without setting off larger conflagration and without running risk of bogging down as foreign invader on China mainland. Interestingly, he indicated that this should be done while Gimo still holds reins of government, since in present circumstances GRC possesses both military and political force capable of toppling Peking. (It is not entirely clear, but perfectly possible, that CCK intended the inference to be "if not used during Gimo's lifetime, US may not have this weapon at its disposal later" presumably because political drawing power would be diminished.)

4. A further reason for acting now, he said, is the grave danger, as GRC sees it, that result of dragging out of Vietnam war will be direct conflict between USG and Peking.

---

[1] Source: Department of State, Central Files, POL 2 CHICOM. Secret; Limdis. Received at 8:05 a.m. Repeated to Hong Kong.

5. He said that Red Guards on mainland are: (a) anti-capitalist and anti-imperialist, which means anti-US; (b) anti-revisionist, which means anti-USSR; and (c) against traditional Chinese culture, which means anti-GRC. CCK said that ChiComs have stated that if Cultural Revolution not successful, Chiang Kai-shek will return to take over. (This is based on paragraph in *Liberation Army Daily* June 6 and both CCK and Gimo have referred to it before.) CCK pointed out that Soviets would like to topple Mao, and this is also desire of GRC and USG, making curious identity of aim. He said that Sovs, however, hope to see establishment of pro-Soviet regime, but that Chinese people would not easily acquiesce again in Communist regime, particularly after recent excesses of Red Guards. He said that GRC should be used to advantage to ensure an anti-Communist China.

6. CCK closed his presentation by saying that this was for my reference and study, and that no immediate reply was expected. He hoped that we could have further discussions of these and other views.

7. I expressed satisfaction with his frankness, and said I would have to think over his presentation and consult Washington. I reminded him that basic US policy has been not to use force against the mainland regime, and said I knew of no change in this policy. I said USG was not sure that regime was crumbling, and that while there were obviously great convulsions occurring, Mao and his chosen lieutenants were still in apparent full control. Perhaps more repressive measures would be used to continue the control, and end result could be a regime more formidable than before. The elements being purged had been as extremely hostile to the US as are the surviving elements. We assume that present leadership will continue to be hostile in any event. I said there might be ways by which to capitalize on the present situation but it was questionable that use of force was the right way, and stated that CCK should be prepared for a negative reaction from Washington.

8. CCK also conveyed Gimo request that we keep GRC informed of any substantive US-Soviet discussions on the subject of China.

9. I asked CCK if he considered that our talk was within Blue Lion framework. His answer made it clear that he considered Blue Lion talks to be talks about particular detailed plans, and that he wished to set up briefings for me to go over some of the proposed contingency plans. He emphasized that the briefings would be for my background information only, and that no comment or policy discussion of plans would be expected from me.

10. *Comment:* GRC has recently given [*1-1/2 lines of source text not declassified*]. CCK has made strong on-the-record statements in speeches and in recent interview with US news reporter to effect that now is the time for return to the mainland. [*less than 1 line of source text not declassified*] also has been reporting strong desire of Gimo for action by GRC, and

Gimo dissatisfaction that plans presented to him are inadequate. All these signs lead to conclusion that Gimo (and perhaps others) are determined to re-open USG discussion of mainland return that was cut off in February when we refused to discuss a particular plan.

11. Our objective is to continue promised dialogue on mainland situation on useful basis, fend off mainland attack pitch without too flat a turndown, without running risk of giving ChiComs wrong signal if they learn of talks, and without lending any unwarranted hopes to GRC leadership that US attitude may change. I want to think over my next move, and will have opportunity to probe further Sept 30–Oct 1 when CCK has invited me on trip to Tsoying–Kaohsiung (this is same trip scheduled for Sept 15–16 which was canceled by typhoon).

12. Memcon being pouched.[2]

McConaughy

---

[2] Enclosed with airgram A–250, September 23. (Ibid., POL CHINAT–US)

---

187. Memorandum of Conversation[1]

SecDel/MC/#12   New York, September 20, 1966, 1 p.m.

SECRETARY'S DELEGATION TO THE TWENTY-FIRST SESSION OF
THE UNITED NATIONS GENERAL ASSEMBLY
New York, September–October 1966

SUBJECT

China

PARTICIPANTS

US	Foreign
Ambassador Llewellyn Thompson, S/AL	Anatoliy F. Dobrynin, Ambassador to the US

Dobrynin took the initiative in asking how our relations with Communist China were developing. I said that I thought the Chinese had lost

---

[1] Source: Department of State, Central Files, POL CHICOM. Secret; Limdis. Approved by Thompson on September 24. The meeting took place at the Passy Restaurant in New York. The source text is Part V of X.

their minds. Dobrynin agreed. He asked how I interpreted recent Chi-Com actions, particularly the activities of the Red Guards. I said I did not know how the State Department in general regarded this but that my own personal opinion was that one of the greatest factors was Mao's concern that his successors would not follow his policies. Also, he obviously had been concerned particularly with the problem of the Chinese youth who had not participated in the original revolution, and Mao probably thought their present activities were both good training and a means of dedicating them to his own ideas. Dobrynin said this agreed with his own appraisal.

Dobrynin asked why I thought the Chinese had published their opening statement in the talks with Ambassador Gronouski. I said I thought the Soviets were responsible for this. Dobrynin pointed out that *Pravda* had not made any comment of its own but had simply published what Ambassador Gronouski had said in an interview. He agreed, however, that others had put an interpretation on this, indicating Chinese collusion with us. He agreed that this was probably the reason for the Chinese action.

In the course of the discussion of this subject, I said I thought the action of the Red Guards and other steps, particularly with respect to education, would compound the Chinese Communist economic difficulties. Dobrynin said that their information was that the Chinese had been rather careful to keep hands off their top scientists, particularly their atomic scientists. I said we also had information to this effect, but I thought that in the last week or two there were some indications that even these people were beginning to be affected.

188. Memorandum From the President's Special Assistant (Rostow) to President Johnson[1]

Washington, September 20, 1966, 2:30 p.m.

Mr. President:

This is another in the China series.[2]

It is a recap of the Red Guards operation that makes clear the object of the exercise is an assault on the Communist Party apparatus.

What is not clear is whether the object is to yield a purged Communist Party or a kind of military takeover.

I cannot help believing that this wild trouble in China may make it easier for Hanoi to get out of the war.

Walt

---

[1] Source: Johnson Library, National Security File, Country File, China, Vol. VII. Confidential. A handwritten "L" on the source text indicates that it was seen by the President.

[2] A retyped copy of telegram 1988 from Hong Kong, September 19, on the subject "Red Guards and Party Purge," is attached. A copy of the telegram, September 17, is in Department of State, Central Files, POL 13–2 CHICOM.

---

189. Memorandum of Conversation[1]

SecDel/MC/52   New York, September 20, 1966, 5:30 p.m.

SECRETARY'S DELEGATION TO THE TWENTY-FIRST SESSION OF
THE UNITED NATIONS GENERAL ASSEMBLY
New York, September–October 1966

SUBJECT

ChiRep

PARTICIPANTS

U.S.	Canada
The Secretary	H.E. Paul Martin, Secretary of State for
Mr. Leonard Meeker, Legal	External Affairs
Adviser	H.E. A.E. Ritchie, Ambassador in
Mr. Bertus Wabeke (Notetaker)	Washington
	Mr. H. Basil Robinson, Assistant Under
	Secretary, Department of External Affairs

---

[1] Source: Department of State, Conference Files: Lot 67 D 305, CF 83. Confidential. Drafted on September 29. Approved in S on October 18. The source text is Part III of III. The meeting was held at the Barclay Hotel in New York City.

Mr. Martin raised the question of Chinese representation by asking when the Secretary expected the issue to come up and how he saw the vote. The Secretary replied that our tabulation and those of our friends show some slight improvement. He added, however, that in his opinion this improvement was not very significant. This, he said, is an "important question." He went on to say that he was bothered by the cynical attitude many UN members were taking toward the Charter on such issues as Article 19 or the importance of Chinese representation. Martin readily agreed that it was "important all right," but predicted the issue would cause us trouble.

Martin then inquired where Senegal stood on ChiRep. The Secretary stated its vote seemed in doubt, it might abstain. Martin explained that they had had Senghor in Ottawa the day before. The impression of the man had been that he was a scholar and an intellectual. Martin recalled that last year Senghor had abstained. Now, according to Martin, Senghor said he would vote for an Albanian-type resolution "without reservation." Martin confessed: "This shook me." The Secretary commented that this change in attitude on the part of Senghor was probably due to French influence.

The Secretary then invited Martin to consider what are the important countries with regard to this issue. The Secretary pointed out that the ten countries on the Pacific that are living under the gun of Chinese Communism are all firm. He cited the strong resolution which the Asian Parliamentary Union had passed on the subject. Martin agreed that one had to give weight to such considerations. But he went on to say that if the US were not so powerful and friendly, Canada, Australia, and New Zealand would long ago have taken a "positive decision." As it is, Martin said, "we do think twice. After all, I would rather be popular in Washington than in Peking."

Martin then assured the Secretary that "we have not made up our minds what we are going to do, and we shall consult first." He argued, however, that it is pretty hard not to let the ChiComs in, "provided Formosa is not thrown out." To admit the ChiComs, according to Martin, "would create a wonderful atmosphere." On the other hand, "if we go through the General Assembly, and Canada stays with the old decision, we lose a lot of respect in our country." Martin claimed that public sentiment in Canada was "overwhelmingly" in favor of ChiCom admission. At a later stage of the discussion, Martin cited the latest Gallup Poll, which reportedly showed 59% in favor of admitting Red China. The Secretary suggested that all Martin needed to do vis-à-vis his own public was simply to tell the Canadians how it would be with the ChiComs in the UN.

The Secretary went on to state that it might be possible to consider ChiCom admission if they did not constitute the major obstacle to settling the Viet-Nam war. Furthermore, the Secretary made the point that if the ChiComs were to be seated in the Security Council, the Security Council would be "dead". And he speculated that if they had been in the Council when the Kashmir conflict arose, this problem could not have been settled the way it was. Martin agreed that if the ChiComs came in, there would be confusion, but he seemed prepared to take this into the bargain. He stated he thought the U.S. had made a great mistake. He claimed that everywhere Canada was being taunted for being "just a satellite of the U.S."

The Secretary then suggested that Martin look at the question in terms of Canadian national interest. Martin countered that "if we miss this season, we create a tragic situation for the world. The ChiComs will acquire more bombs. In a few years you would not be able to do much about China. The interest of mankind is involved." Martin speculated what would happen if Canada, after consultation with the U.S., were to take the plunge and vote for ChiCom admission. At first, according to Martin, there would be "hell" in the country. As in 1955 under Eisenhower, some would worry about reprisals by the U.S. "We would go through Gethsemane." But after that things would quiet down. "The tactical picture would not have changed one bit. But we would have gotten the problem off our necks."

The Secretary made the point that this was not the time to make the ChiComs feel their policy is right. The Secretary stated that President De Gaulle had prolonged the war by his statement in Phnom Penh. The ChiComs should be allowed to find out that their policy is leading them into a dead end. Martin countered that the same could have been said about the Soviets some years ago and concluded that "if we had the ChiComs around the table, things could not be worse than they are now by having them in isolation."

The Secretary reminded Martin of the Berlin crisis and the Cuban crisis as far as the Soviets are concerned, and pointed out that those who have diplomatic relations with Communist China don't seem to have any discussion with them. Martin insisted, however, that the attempt must be made "to get the ChiComs into international society." When the Secretary argued that we should not mislead the ChiComs to think that their behavior pays off, Martin objected that the ChiComs surely do not believe that to let them into the UN could be tantamount to sanctioning their system. Sooner or later, according to Martin, the ChiComs will be in anyway. He concluded, therefore, that the "right course politically, is to get it over with now." Martin then stated that for him the crux of the matter was whether or not the issue was so important that "we can afford to disagree with the U.S."

The Secretary remarked that he would weigh Martin's views more heavily if Canada had troops in Viet-Nam. As it is, the Secretary stated, "you have no risks." Martin replied that he was not ashamed of what Canada was doing in Viet-Nam. The Secretary then assured him that he was not pressuring Canada to be in Viet-Nam. After a brief dissertation by Martin on the debate over recognition of Communist China within the U.K. Government in 1950, the Secretary concluded the conversation by urging Martin not to surprise us and asked him to keep in touch.

190. Memorandum by the Board of National Estimates, Central Intelligence Agency[1]

ONE Special Memorandum No. 14–66   Washington, September 23, 1966.

SUBJECT

The China Tangle[2]

1. The situation in China today is one of confusion, contradiction and rapid change. The more spectacular events have been widely reported: Mao has chosen a new successor, Lin Piao, re-juggled the top leadership, and most important, launched an extensive purge of the party. With the removal of Peng Chen and the demotion of Liu Shao-chi and Teng Hsiao-ping, the men who have run the party for Mao have been forced to give way to a new group. Military men, notably the old Marshals of the PLA, are prominent in the revised Politburo. Moreover, elements of the old party machine are now also under attack by the Red Guard, which has been formed primarily for this purpose by Lin and Mao, and to some degree is overseen by the PLA.

2. It seems to us that the party cannot have been subjected to such a radical upheaval merely because it had been sluggish or unresponsive to Mao's orders. More likely Mao was confronted with actual open opposition in party forums, leading him to conclude—possibly with good reason—that he could no longer trust the party as it had been constituted and led to execute his basic policies. To be sure, Mao may be simply suffering from the pathological suspiciousness of a senile autocrat, yet we

---

[1] Source: Johnson Library, National Security File, Country File, China, Vol. VII. Secret.

[2] This memorandum was produced solely by CIA. It was prepared by the Office of National Estimates and coordinated with the Directorate of Intelligence Research Staff. [Footnote in the source text.]

still do not believe he would have wrapped himself in the mantle of the PLA and unleashed the Red Guards unless he had good reason to think there was some real and potent threat to his authority.

3. There may have been specific policy issues which brought on the crisis—such as the Vietnam war, military questions, the Sino-Soviet conflict or economic problems. This cannot be demonstrated from the available evidence. It is reasonable to believe, however, that the manner and style of Mao's approach would generate opposition among those who had to run the country's affairs, and would, by its nature, have to be opposed by a more moderate line.

4. Lin Piao is still a shadowy figure. We do not know how far he is loyal to Mao or how far he is pursuing an ambitious plan of his own. We are inclined to believe that Mao deliberately turned to Lin as he lost confidence in the party, but that the proximity of power is acting as a strong stimulant in Lin. If Mao and Lin successfully purge the party and replace Liu's and Teng's men with their own, then Lin will obviously have gone a long way to consolidating his role of heir apparent. However, even with the power and prestige of Mao behind him, and perhaps allied with the wily and astute Chou En-lai, Lin's task remains difficult and dangerous. The leaders of the old party machine are not without assets. They are presumably working now to turn the tide against the Red Guard. The forces arrayed against them are formidable—Mao, Lin, the PLA—but even in defeat the former party leaders could throw the nation into great confusion.

5. Thus a basic instability could continue for some time, possibly until Mao leaves the scene and a successor regime finally consolidates its control. In any case, we expect protracted and complicated maneuvers. Some further turmoil at the top is likely, and sharp reversals of policies cannot be ruled out.

6. There are indeed some few signs that reason and sanity have not totally departed the Chinese scene. Despite the flood tide of harsh criticism against moderates and pragmatists, the regime has not yet abandoned the relatively realistic and restrained approach to economic policy of recent years. As spokesman for this policy, Chou En-lai has called on the Red Guards to leave the farms and factories alone; Lin Piao, however, has not touched on this aspect but has called for heavier blows against those within the party "who have taken the capitalist road." In attempting to curb unnecessary disruptions to the economy, Peking has shown particular apprehension over potential threats to the fall harvest. In view of the disappointing early harvest, there is valid cause for concern. But while Mao and Lin appear to have conceded Chou the need to maintain some stability in the economy, we cannot be sure that Mao will not again veer in an extremist direction and launch a campaign against the ideological impurities now being tacitly ignored. Action against the peasants

private plots would be a key indicator that such an extremist campaign was underway.

7. Caution is also being shown in foreign affairs, specifically on Vietnam. Concentration on the enemies within has resulted in a drop in press attention to Vietnam and to foreign affairs generally. China has not abandoned or even eased its stand on Vietnam, but it has pushed the matter to the back burner for at least the time being. Aside from some heavily qualified hyperbole about the Red Guards being ready to "fight a war at any time," the current upheaval has concentrated on domestic issues. We estimated recently that it was unlikely that the Chinese would intervene with their own forces in the Vietnam war. And we continue to believe this is the best judgment of Chinese policy. But the questions of who is in charge in China and what he or they are seeking to accomplish certainly bear on the matter. It would only be prudent to allow for some chance that turmoil in China will produce a radical break with the caution that has so far characterized Chinese policy in Vietnam.

8. There is one further aspect of the Chinese crisis that is of great interest for the US. This is the effect on Hanoi. Thus far, the North Vietnamese have appeared to act as if nothing has happened in China. But they must be concerned over the disruptions and uncertainties. At the very least, China is increasingly exposed as a rather uncertain and unstable ally, and the net result may be a loss of influence in Hanoi. If so, this might improve the chances for other interested parties, particularly the USSR if it was so minded, to encourage Hanoi to consider a political settlement.

9. As for the longer term, the present crisis cannot help but have a profound effect on China. It is already apparent that Mao's permanent revolution is meeting resistance. The recurrent trauma of government by exhortation as a substitute for effective policies to deal with real problems, is clearly taking its toll among the Chinese people. Despite a widespread support for Mao's objectives of building a strong and independent China, there must be growing disenchantment with his methods for reaching this goal. Attempts to modernize China by following doctrines coined in Mao's guerrilla days must appear increasingly ridiculous. Some intellectuals and even some party leaders were aware of this earlier but it has by now probably reached broader sectors of opinion.

10. No amount of glorification of the omniscient leader will dissolve the tightening constraints of the economy. Most Chinese will judge any government on its ability to help them meet their basic needs of food, clothing and shelter. The present regime has yet to come up with a reasonable plan for feeding its over 750 million people and at the same time financing an economic development program. As the growing popula-

tion pushes against the limited resources of the stagnant economy, the risk of a major economic crisis will grow.

11. In the face of these problems, only a pragmatic leadership seems likely to make any progress at all in dealing with China's immense problems. Such a leadership would also be forced to make an important reassessment of the premises of Mao's foreign policy, including, probably, relations with the USSR. If we are correct in these assumptions, the long range trends are moving inexorably against Mao's brand of socialism, and his desperate effort to reverse the tide may actually hurry his ultimate defeat. In short, his fears of "revisionism" in China are probably well grounded.

For the Board of National Estimates:
Abbot Smith
Acting Chairman

---

191. Telegram From the Department of State to the Embassy in the Republic of China[1]

Washington, September 29, 1966, 6:57 p.m.

56941. Consultations with GRC. Refs: A—Taipei's 901; B—Taipei's A–250;[2] C—Hong Kong's 2095;[3] D—Hong Kong's 2072.[4]

1. From your conversation with Chiang Ching-kuo reported refs A and B, it apparent GRC now desires resume consultation with respect to

---

[1] Source: Department of State, Central Files, POL CHINAT–US. Secret; Priority; Limdis. Drafted by Bennett; cleared in draft by Roy, Admiral Lemos of DOD/ISA, Richard H. Donald of ACA, and [text not declassified] of CIA; and approved by Berger. Repeated to Hong Kong.

[2] See Document 186 and footnote 2 thereto.

[3] Telegram 2095 from Hong Kong, September 21, warned that Ch'en Yi's recent comments to a Japanese delegation indicated that Chinese Communist policy was dominated by an extremist Mao–Lin leadership preoccupied with the possibility of war with the United States. It warned of the risk of giving the Chinese Communists the wrong signal at that time and urged rejection of any Nationalist proposals for operations against the mainland. (Department of State, Central Files, POL CHICOM–US)

[4] Telegram 2072 from Hong Kong, September 20, commented on Ch'en's comments to the Japanese delegation and urged extra precautions against any steps that might risk Chinese involvement or force greater North Vietnamese dependence on China. (Ibid., POL CHICOM)

mainland and continues hope win some form US approval, even if only on contingency basis, for military action against mainland. In present situation on mainland and in Viet-Nam it crucial we and GRC avoid actions which might give wrong signal to ChiComs. As you noted to CCK, our position against initiation use of force against mainland has not changed. In circumstances now foreseen, we could not assist GRC landings on mainland and could not agree to any unilateral GRC military action against mainland. We feel GRC tacitly accepts our position in assuring us, as both President Chiang and CCK have done, that GRC gives priority to solution Viet-Nam problem over return to mainland.

2. We believe we should welcome interest of President Chiang and CCK in exchanging views with us on Far East problems and we hope through maintenance this dialogue avoid GRC feeling isolated from US policy. This consideration especially important in view seven-nation meeting on Viet-Nam.

3. Regarding ref C para 3, assume Embassy will continue monitoring GRC activities and report immediately any GRC plans for unilateral actions which could convey wrong signal to ChiComs.

4. We see no objection to Blue Lion consultations continuing on same basis as in past and with lowest possible level visibility. Regarding briefings mentioned para 9 ref A, we believe it must be made clear to GRC that original Blue Lion ground rules remain in force. We cannot become involved in contingency military planning re mainland jointly with GRC, though joint planning for defense Taiwan and Pescadores under our treaty should of course continue.

5. CCK's separate proposal re intelligence operations, while entirely too sweeping in total, may offer way of permitting minor concession to reduce appearance of flat rejection of GRC desires and detrimental GRC reaction. We will discuss specifics with you through [*less than 1 line of source text not declassified*] channels.[5]

6. Regarding ref A para 8, you may inform CCK there have been no US-Soviet discussions on Communist China including recent Rusk–Gromyko conversations in New York. Within recent weeks low level Soviet officials have become somewhat freer in remarking on Chinese developments in conversations with US counterparts but only to extent of repeating Soviet press commentary. We will of course keep GRC informed of any significant developments in this respect.

Rusk

---

[5] A copy of a message agreed upon at a September 30 meeting between Berger and Colby is filed with an October 4 memorandum from William McAfee of the Bureau of Intelligence and Research to Hughes, recording the meeting. (Ibid., INR Files, 1966 FE Weekly Staff Meetings)

192. Telegram From the Mission to the United Nations to the Department of State[1]

New York, October 4, 1966, 0151Z.

1214. For Secretary and Sisco. Goldberg conversation with Gromyko.

1. I called on Gromyko Oct 3 at Sov Mission in accordance arrangements in reftel.[2] Gromyko opened discussion by stating he had been told of my desire call on him and said he interested to exchange views but asked me to begin. I replied that I had been informed of his interest in conversation with me.

[Here follows discussion concerning a possible treaty on outer space, Vietnam, and nonproliferation.]

5. I then brought up question of Chinese representation stating that in recent review US policy on this matter, I had been interested to note that impact of any possible shift in US posture on US–USSR relations had received little stress. I said that perhaps, in light of recent events in China and extraordinary phenomenon of Red Guards, this consideration perhaps should figure more importantly in our assessment adding that, in a personal way, I had explored this question with friends and brought it to attention of Prime Minister Pearson of Canada in recent conversation with him. Gromyko appeared taken aback by my launching of ChiRep question, and said that he could only repeat long-held Sov view that rightful occupant Chinese seat in UN was PRC. He inquired immediately whether stress on US-Sov aspect of ChiRep study was personal one on my part and I confirmed that it was. He also expressed some surprise at my frank statement that domestic public opinion which recent Gallup Poll had shown 59 percent in favor "two Chinas" policy no longer important consideration in US assessment of ChiRep matter. I added, of course, that this only one consideration anyway and decision had to be taken in context world events. He then expressed in what appeared to be somewhat confused manner Sov puzzlement over recent events in Communist China stating that they not fully informed about them or sure of their meaning. Admitted that their result was lack of satisfactory relations with PRC but observed that this should be seen against background of common basic ideology and not assessed in same way as unsatisfactory relations between states of differing ideologies. (This statement made in uncharacteristically halting and uncertain manner.)

[Here follows discussion of a possible treaty on outer space.]

Goldberg

---

[1] Source: Department of State, Central Files, POL 7 USSR. Secret; Priority; Exdis. Repeated to Moscow and the White House.

[2] Not identified.

193.   Telegram from the Embassy in the Republic of China to the Department of State[1]

Taipei, October 25, 1966, 0500Z.

1227. Ref: State 70990 (Limdis);[2] Taipei 1106 (Limdis);[3] Hong Kong 2905 (Limdis).[4]

1. [*less than 1 line of source text not declassified*] has reported all available data concerning October 15 naval incident [*less than 1 line of source text not declassified*]. Major outlines are that incident took place in area between Matsu and mainland; five small GRC boats attacked ChiCom vessels; four of GRC small craft lost together with ten of the fifteen personnel who participated in operation; ChiCom losses apparently one small boat; incident was apparently not mounted for intelligence collecting, but to attack ChiCom ships as part of new GRC response to mainland turmoil and hopefully to stage symbolic victory for psychological and morale reasons at time of President Chiang's birthday.

2. No MAP or other US supplied equipment was used in this operation. Raid was conducted by Intelligence Bureau of Ministry of National Defense (IBMND), same group which has run most small GRC incursions. The IBMND built the boats used, the two largest of which (M 5's) were 25-foot assault boats.

3. I have given serious thought to advisability of making approach of some kind to GRC concerning Matsu incident, and believe that [*less than 1 line of source text not declassified*] information concerning GRC intent in this case warrants our raising issue with GRC. I appreciate fact that such incidents, even though not wholly new, may arouse ChiCom suspicion or cause reaction particularly at time when leadership in Peking may be seriously split on policy issues including Viet-Nam. Before any decision is taken concerning form of representation to GRC, believe following factors should be considered:

A. We know from new, [*less than 1 line of source text not declassified*] reporting (being disseminated today) that this incident reflects a GRC

---

[1] Source: Department of State, Central Files, POL 27 CHICOM–CHINAT. Secret; Priority; Limdis. Repeated to Hong Kong and to Manila for Bundy.

[2] Telegram 70990 to Taipei, October 21, requested Embassy comment concerning an October 15 naval clash near Matsu, reported in the press on October 18, and an Embassy recommendation as to whether the matter should be taken up with Chiang Ching-kuo or the Ministry of Foreign Affairs to avoid repetition of such provocative actions at a time when the mainland situation was unsettled and Chinese Communist decisions on possible intervention in Vietnam might hang in the balance. It also asked whether any U.S.-supplied equipment had been used in the operation. (Ibid.)

[3] Dated October 12. (Ibid., POL CHINAT–US)

[4] Not found.

decision to have IBMND resume such maritime operations after two-year lull. We know [*less than 1 line of source text not declassified*] of some 22 small maritime incursions of various kinds conducted in 1964, most of them by IBMND. These GRC incursions continued on small scale, apparently five in 1965 and four in 1966 prior to October 15 case. Latest incident is of larger scale than 1965–66 operational level (with exception of course of 6 August 1965 GRC naval sortie), and calls to mind some six Matsu area small operations conducted in 1964, one of which (October) was very similar to subject case. In view of previous USG acceptance of such GRC incursions, GRC would wonder why we have chosen this particular time to make approach, particularly if ChiComs have made no specific response.

B. We know [*less than 1 line of source text not declassified*] that Matsu incident has been mounted in direct response to Gimo's demands that his forces undertake some positive action against ChiComs. Protest to GRC on activities it has been carrying out in response to President Chiang's orders, however, unlikely to be productive.

C. As I observed in Taipei's 1106, we stand to gain a good deal from continuing our useful relations with the GRC [*less than 1 line of source text not declassified*] and we should if possible avoid diminishing their utility.

D. If we raise Matsu affair with CCK or MOFA, Chinese may believe that we are trying to establish new ground rules to further limit their actions concerning mainland. While new limitation may be desirable or even necessary at some later stage, to try to implement them now would arouse GRC suspicions and make officials here less cooperative at very time (before ChiRep vote) we need to have most influence.

E. Past ground rules, as understood both by GRC and by US officials here, have allowed GRC clear latitude to conduct unilateral "intelligence gathering operations," but not "military raids." October 15 operation must be considered as one kind of "military raid," although we have not protested to GRC in past borderline cases of this kind. It is useful to note that these ground rules allow short duration, small scale landing operations on mainland where objective is to abduct ChiCom personnel and acquire documents for intelligence purposes. October 15 engagement, while probably outside present ground rules, was conducted entirely at sea between small boats, and may be considered by ChiComs as less dangerous, and easier to handle than "intelligence collection operation" conducted against mainland itself.

4. On balance I believe we should take this up with GRC and I wish to discuss both substance and tactics with Bundy during his visit here next week.

5. [*less than 1 line of source text not declassified*]

McConaughy

---

194. **Telegram From the Department of State to the Embassy in Thailand**[1]

Washington, October 28, 1966, 9:37 p.m.

75499. Tosec 143. For Secretary from Acting Secretary. Subject: Chi-Rep.

1. We have received three separate approaches which signify not surprising build-up of pressure from our allies over ChiRep issue.

2. First approach was from Belgian Foreign Minister Harmel yesterday to Ambassador Knight stating that Belgian Government would begin conversations with Canadian and Italian representatives at UN to introduce proposal for study committee on ChiRep leading toward tabling report at next UNGA. Harmel's vague discussion indicated he thinking of wide terms of reference for committee (including ChiCom seat in SC) and tempted by idea of abstaining on Albanian resolution if Belgian study committee proposal not adopted. After discussion with Knight, Harmel seemed inclined to vote against Albanian resolution but thought this would be easier for Belgium if study committee resolution also tabled.

3. Second approach was from Italian Ambassador to Sisco in which Ambassador said he instructed to bring to our attention statement made by Fanfani yesterday in Parliament which hinted need for establishment of UNGA study group to make recommendation on ChiRep question. Ambassador added he had impression no immediate move being contemplated by Italian Government. Sisco promised to report approach to

---

[1] Source: Department of State, Central Files, UN 6 CHICOM. Secret; Exdis. Drafted by Gleysteen, cleared by Berger, cleared in draft by Acting Secretary Katzenbach, and approved by Sisco. Repeated to USUN for Goldberg.

me, emphasized that our policy remained unchanged, and requested Italian Government take no further initiative without first consulting US. Sisco gave numerous reasons why we would have reservation about timing of any move which might be interpreted by Peking as concession to its hard-line policy. Report of his conversation being repeated separately.[2]

4. Third approach was from Canadian Ambassador who handed me letter from Paul Martin to you[3] (which I am repeating by separate telegram), stating that Canadian Cabinet had decided it would "appear most appropriate" for Canada to go on record in GA to effect that Canada considers most equitable interim solution to be representation of both ChiComs and GRC in UN, adding that this separate initiative would still enable Canada to adhere to previous position against Albanian resolution. Martin letter notes he will be leaving Ottawa for Eastern Europe and Italy beginning November 4 and does not see possibility discussion with you prior his return November 16. I stressed our desire for further discussion before Canadian position frozen and I emphasized particular importance of timing of Canadian action mentioning possibility that Canadians might better postpone such move until next session of UNGA.

5. *Comment.* On basis our latest nose count, we feel our prospect for obtaining simple majority against Albanian resolution is precarious. We particularly bothered by persistence of Chile's and Iran's willingness to part ways with us on substantive resolution despite our high-level representations. We have now analyzed carefully UNESCO voting on ChiRep, and while we sustained our position by expected margin, several countries voted contrary to firm promises.

6. In this situation, I recommend we make additional interim rejoinders to the Belgian, Italian and Canadian representatives before you return, telling them not take any step pending further consultation. We, in concert with Goldberg, will have further recommendations for you upon your return. ChiRep debate does not begin until Nov. 21 and we therefore have time.

Katzenbach

---

[2] Transmitted in telegram 7516 to USUN (sent to Bangkok as Tosec 139), October 28. (Ibid.)

[3] Ambassador Ritchie's letter to Katzenbach, October 28, conveying Martin's message of October 27 to Rusk, is ibid.

195. Memorandum From Alfred Jenkins of the National Security Council Staff to the President's Special Assistant (Rostow)[1]

Washington, November 2, 1966.

SUBJECT

ChiRep

The latest tally on probable voting is about where it was when you left town. It is possible that we could have a slightly higher margin on our side than last year for the important question vote. On the substantive vote, the best guess is that we will have perhaps two votes margin in our favor but events in Africa, mainland China, or elsewhere, could still affect this considerably. Furthermore, since the vote will not come until about December 1 (debate begins Nov. 21), mainland events could take a somewhat clearer turn with unpredictable results on the voting. The fact that the tally is close to last year's vote does not indicate stability. Several nations have shifted from *each* side of the question to the other side.

After the IRG meeting today, Sam Berger called me into his office to say that he wanted me to know of a memo being prepared as the result of a meeting held this morning with Joe Sisco, but that it was being very closely held within the Department.[2] He said that he had become finally convinced that it was too late under any circumstances for us to shift to a two-China approach at this session, even in extremis. After considerable discussion it was agreed that as a contingency position we would *not* oppose efforts on the part of friendly nations, such as Canada, Italy or Belgium, to turn to a study group. We would recommend to the Secretary, however, that we be a member of such a study group. (I am very glad to see this change in our position.)

I think this makes sense. It may make some sort of contribution on the right side of the present mainland struggle without incurring just at this unpredictable time some of the risks of a more definitive change in U.S. policy. I hope the Secretary will buy this policy. It is obviously essen-

---

[1] Source: Johnson Library, National Security File, Name File, Jenkins Memos. Secret. Copies were sent to William J. Jorden and Donald Ropa of the NSC staff.

[2] A November 3 memorandum from Sisco to Rusk sets forth three alternatives: continuing the same tactics, supporting dual representation, and supporting a Study Committee. It dismissed the first alternative as ineffective and the second as unacceptable because of the reaction of Taipei and other governments that were publicly committed to support the U.S. position and because Congress and the public were not prepared for such a sudden reversal. The memorandum stated that adoption of a passive role concerning a Study Committee proposal had been considered but that direct U.S. involvement would provide the best assurance of getting acceptable results. A copy is attached to a November 4 memorandum from Sisco to Rusk. (Department of State, Central Files, UN 6 CHICOM)

tial that our contingency position, if it becomes that, be closely held, lest it affect disastrously our initial and only overt position.

Al Jenkins

---

196. **Telegram From the Embassy in the Republic of China to the Department of State**[1]

Taipei, November 3, 1966, 1040Z.

1308. For Secretary and Berger from Bundy.[2]

1. Outstanding feature of my visit here was subtly cool, though correct, reception by Gimo himself. Every single detail of the meeting was in this direction, including transfer from residence to formal setting of office, last-minute back and forth on time resulting in delay after arrival, last-minute exclusion of Hummel so that Ambassador had to take notes, and above all fact that conversation lasted only forty minutes and was terminated politely but with unusual firmness and even abruptness by Gimo. It was certainly in total contrast in warmth and length with any previous conversation I have had here with Gimo over many years.

2. As to substance, while Gimo heard me out politely on Manila summary, and found communiqué satisfactory, he was notably curt on declaration, saying only that he "had to objection" to it. Even more significant, the main message that the Gimo wished to get across was that the ChiCom nuclear-missile test[3] meant they would be in a position within six months either to employ or to threaten use of these weapons specifically in Vietnam. I of course responded that any such use would be a madness far beyond any irrationality now discernible on the mainland, since they must be aware of massive power that we could use in this event.

---

[1] Source: Department of State, Central Files, POL 7 US/BUNDY. Secret; Priority; Exdis. Received at 6:27 a.m.

[2] Assistant Secretary Bundy visited Taiwan November 2–3 after accompanying President Johnson on a trip to Asia and the Pacific, October 17–November 2, including the Manila Summit Conference October 24–25.

[3] The Government of the People's Republic of China announced on October 27 that China had successfully tested a guided missile with a nuclear warhead. The text of the announcement as printed in the *Peking Review*, October 28, 1966, p. iii, is also printed in *American Foreign Policy: Current Documents, 1966*, pp. 676–677.

3. In marked contrast, Chiang Ching-kuo and C.K. Yen have been if anything more friendly and outgoing than in the past. CCK in particular talked most responsibly and interestingly about whole ChiCom picture and Soviet relationship. He made no attempt to tie the nuclear-missile test to Vietnam, and the only pitch I encountered on any of the other conversations was a fairly mild plea by the Foreign Minister for stepped-up mainland operations of a "commando" character.

4. Trying to put these pieces of the puzzle together, I am inclined to think that Gimo is personally more upset by our repeated references to reconciliation themes, during the trip and specifically in the Manila declaration, than others here may be. But I would be inclined to go further and to suppose that Gimo's coolness reflects to some degree sense of personal affront over our omission of Taipei from schedule, fairly perfunctory tone of President's birthday message to him,[4] and general feeling of personal neglect over long period of time.

5. To the extent that Gimo's reaction rests on substance, it is unavoidable. However, his personal state of feeling could become important if we should confront in the next month any necessity for a change of position in UN. For what it may be worth, this subject has not even been mentioned at any level in 24 hours of conversation here. They obviously do not want to get into any suggestion of change by me, although of course I shall have to indicate if asked tonight that we must and will keep situation under close review, with possibility of tactical change still present.

6. In any event, I think we must consider some personal touch that involves our President directly. A letter reporting on Manila and the whole trip, with some reference to my visit, could at least help to ease the feelings, which are not wholly incomprehensible, of a crotchety old man who still has the power to make decisions that can affect our interests seriously.

7. Ambassador concurs.

McConaughy

---

[4] Dated October 17. (Johnson Library, National Security File, Special Head of State Correspondence, China, 3/1/66–12/31/66)

197.   Memorandum of Conversation[1]

Washington, November 3, 1966, 5:30 p.m.

SUBJECT

Chinese Representation

PARTICIPANTS

Canada
A.E. Ritchie, Canadian Ambassador
Peter M. Roberts, Counselor, Canadian Embassy

US
The Under Secretary
Rufus Z. Smith, Director, Officer of Canadian Affairs, EUR
Donald Morris, Special Assistant to the Under Secretary

Ambassador Ritchie opened the conversation by saying it seemed desirable to impose on the Under Secretary's time once more in order, first, to provide the Department with the draft text on which the Canadian Government has been working as a possible early initiative on the question of Chinese representation in the UN and, secondly, to point out again that Canadian Foreign Minister Martin was scheduled to depart for Europe the following evening. His intent was to convey the Canadian thinking on this subject to the Department in as concrete a form as possible prior to Mr. Martin's departure so that if the Secretary wished to consult personally with Mr. Martin he would have a more tangible basis on which to do it.

The Under Secretary responded that he had not yet had a chance to talk with the Secretary on this subject and it was difficult for him to say just when he would be able to. He pointed out that with the President leaving the next day for Texas it would be difficult to go into the question in depth with the Secretary prior to Mr. Martin's departure. He therefore wanted to reiterate his hope that the Canadian Government would give us time to consider the matter further and an opportunity to discuss both the substance of the problem and questions of timing. He noted in this regard that the Secretary would also probably want to discuss the matter with the President.

When the Ambassador mentioned specifically that Mr. Martin would be leaving Ottawa the next day and would return on November 16, the Under Secretary remarked that he assumed of course that Mr. Martin would be totally out of touch even during the period of his jour-

---

[1] Source: Department of State, Central Files, UN 6 CHICOM. Secret; Nodis. No drafting information appears on the source text. Approved in U on November 7. The meeting was held in Under Secretary Katzenbach's office.

ney. The Ambassador responded that one of the difficult points was that the Canadian Government would obviously want to talk before November 16 with other governments. He hoped therefore it would not be necessary from the United States point of view that his Government refrain from talking with at least some other counties. He said he was not speaking of widespread consultation at this point but had in mind a few key countries. (He mentioned specifically only the UK.) He said he was not thinking of active lobbying by Canadian representatives but certainly they would want to show the text of their draft resolution to some others.

The Under Secretary asked that the GOC at least give him a chance to talk to the Secretary before approaches were made to any other government. He would try to do it that evening or perhaps the following morning.

The Ambassador then turned to the substance of the Canadian proposal. He said there were two purposes which his Government had in mind. The first was to make it possible for the GOC and other governments which felt the same way to express a point of view on the subject of Chinese representation which, by their so doing, would accomplish the second purpose, namely to be able still to oppose an Albanian-type resolution. The Canadian Government had been working for some time on a draft of a resolution which would accomplish these two purposes and has come up with a proposal which would call upon the President of the General Assembly to carry out an investigation of the possible basis for an interim solution. (The Ambassador then handed the Under Secretary the text which is attached to this memorandum.)[2] He said the word "interim" had been chosen deliberately since it was recognized that the draft dealt with the de facto situation of two Chinas and did not attempt to present a long-range definitive de jure solution.

After an initial glance at the text, the Under Secretary noted particularly the provision for Chinese Communist representation on the Security Council. He said he was of course speaking off the cuff but it certainly seemed to him that this provision was hardly necessary in order to express the point of view Canada was trying to get across. The Ambassador responded that his Government has considered the point put did not see how the resolution would be acceptable to many other governments unless such a provision were made. The document, in his view, would otherwise not be a credible document.

---

[2] The text of the proposal is not attached. A copy is attached to the November 4 memorandum from Sisco to Rusk cited in footnote 2, Document 195. The proposal included a preamble suggesting an interim arrangement in which both Chinese Governments would be seated in the General Assembly and the People's Republic of China would have China's seat in the Security Council, and it requested the President of the General Assembly to explore the possibilities outlined in the preamble as the basis for an interim solution.

The Under Secretary asked what the Canadians had in mind with regard to tactics. Would their resolution be pressed to a vote and if so, when? after consideration of the "important matter" question? after a vote on the Albanian-type resolution?

The Ambassador responded that certainly they had in mind that such a resolution would be put to a vote but as to timing he could not say at this point. The Under Secretary stressed that tactics and substance quickly become intertwined.

The Ambassador remarked that the GOC did not expect that the Chinese Communists would welcome the Canadian resolution all that warmly, but at the same time he thought the Chinese Communists would not be able to maintain that the Canadian proposal was entirely unreasonable. He argued that the real problem for Canada and for certain other governments was how to continue to oppose an Albanian-type resolution. The alternative to something like the Canadian proposal would be to abstain on the Albanian resolution.

The Ambassador reaffirmed that the Canadian proposal had been drawn up only after Cabinet-level consideration, although he could not be certain that the Cabinet had considered the detailed wording of the draft. He asserted that his Government regarded the proposal as a positive approach and as the best means of preserving the real interest of Taiwan. Throughout their consideration there had been a continuing effort to meet what they knew were the real concerns of the United States, and he wanted to reiterate that he would be available to discuss the matter at any time.

The Under Secretary reiterated that he would take the matter up as soon as possible with the Secretary. He nevertheless wanted to say now it seemed to him there were many ways of skinning a cat and that the Canadian draft was not the only way of meeting the problem. There were many other courses which ought to be considered. The Ambassador wryly remarked that there were indeed many ways to skin a cat but a cat, after all, had only nine lives.

In parting, the Ambassador stressed again the urgency of the matter and indicated his Government felt a need to begin consultation with other governments very shortly. He understood the plan was to approach the British the following Monday (November 7).

198.   Special National Intelligence Estimate[1]

SNIE 13–8–66   Washington, November 3, 1966.

COMMUNIST CHINA'S ADVANCED WEAPONS PROGRAM

The Problem

To make a preliminary evaluation of recent information bearing on Communist China's advanced weapons program.

The Estimate

1. On 27 October 1966, the Chinese announced that they had successfully launched a guided missile which carried a nuclear warhead. We have confirmed that there was a nuclear explosion, [*less than 1 line of source text not declassified*] detonated in the lower atmosphere about 100 miles east of the Lop Nor nuclear test site. As nearly as we can ascertain, the device was delivered by a ballistic missile, as the Chinese claim. Such a missile, in or near the MRBM class, may have been fired from the Shuang-ch'eng-tzu missile test range over a distance of about 400 nautical miles. At this point we are not able to judge with confidence what this event implies for China's advanced weapons capability. The Chinese may have conducted this test for propaganda and political purposes, using equipment that would not be satisfactory for a weapon system. We think it somewhat more likely that they have tested a missile-warhead combination which, while considerably below US or Soviet standards, could be used as a weapon in the short or perhaps medium range. If this is the case, the Chinese could have a few such weapons ready for deployment in 1967 or 1968.

2. We have recently received information indicating that the Chinese also have under development a much larger and more complex missile system. We believe that this is an ICBM, although a space role cannot

---

[1] Source: Department of State, INR/EAP Files: Lot 90 D 99. Top Secret; Controlled Dissem. According to a note on the cover sheet, the estimate was submitted by Director of Central Intelligence Helms and concurred in by the U.S. Intelligence Board on November 3. The Central Intelligence Agency and the intelligence organizations of the Departments of State, Defense, the Atomic Energy Commission, and the National Security Agency participated in the preparation of the estimate. All members of the U.S. Intelligence Board concurred, except the FBI Representative, who abstained on the grounds that the subject was outside his jurisdiction.

A November 1 memorandum from INR/RFE Director Fred Greene to Hughes states that the SNIE was intended to be a summary of portions of NIE 13–2–66 of the same title, sanitized for distribution to persons not cleared for access to NIE 13–2–66, but that the draft SNIE had been revised to incorporate information about the fourth Chinese nuclear test explosion. (Ibid.) NIE 13–2–66, "Communist China's Advanced Weapons Program," dated July 1, is not printed. (Central Intelligence Agency, NIE Files)

be discounted. We believe a launch facility will be completed early in 1967. No major component of an ICBM has been detected but there are indications that the Chinese might be able to begin flight testing by the latter part of 1967. If so, and if they are able to produce the missiles and other equipment necessary to sustain an active and successful test program, a few ICBMs, with fission nuclear warheads, could be operational by the early 1970's. The first generation of such missiles would probably be large, costly, and, again by US or Soviet standards, deficient in reliability and accuracy. Nevertheless, the Chinese would probably wish to have a few operational at least for political and psychological effect. The development of an ICBM booster would also give the Chinese the capacity to put a fairly large payload into orbit early in the ICBM test program.

3. An ICBM could not be fired to full range within the borders of China, and we cannot establish at this time how the Chinese would carry out full range ICBM tests. Preliminary flight testing of system components, however, could be accomplished within the borders of China.

4. At the same time, the Chinese will be working toward a high yield thermonuclear warhead. The third Chinese test device, which contained some thermonuclear material, performed quite inefficiently and apparently was heavy and bulky, indicating that the Chinese have much to learn about thermonuclear technology. It did, however, constitute an initial step toward the attainment of a thermonuclear capability. Thus, we cannot rule out the possibility that the Chinese will be able to develop a thermonuclear warhead by the early 1970's.

---

199. Memorandum From Alfred Jenkins of the National Security Council Staff to the President's Special Assistant (Rostow)[1]

Washington, November 4, 1966.

SUBJECT

Lifting Remaining Travel Restrictions on China

At the last EA (formerly FE) /IRG meeting, the Acting Chairman Sam Berger raised the only voice in dissent to the China Working

---

[1] Source: Johnson Library, National Security File, Country File, China, Vol. VII. Secret. Copies were sent to Jorden and Ropa.

Group's proposal that the few remaining restrictions on travel to China be removed (Tab A).[2] One other member, the CIA representative, had some reservations but did not oppose. It was strongly supported by Defense and AID representatives and by ACA. Sam simply feels that this is a curious time to lift the ban in view of unsettled political conditions on the mainland. He thinks we could get adverse domestic reaction for that reason.

So far, reaction to each of the several stages of liberalization of travel has met with very good public reception and most of us at the meeting felt that this would be true of this proposed final step. There is a new requirement that justification for restrictions be printed in the *Federal Register* (Tab B).[3] I think we would be more likely to incur unfavorable domestic reaction by failing to lift the negligible remaining restrictions, since I don't believe we can make a convincing case that "travel would seriously impair the conduct of United States foreign affairs." Short of that, I think the average citizen would (and should) interpret the continuation of such restrictions as overly paternalistic management of mature Americans. The academic community particularly is very vocally critical of our present remaining restrictions—on both political and "citizens' rights" considerations.

I don't think this is one the White House really needs to fight for but if the issue should come up at the weekly luncheon or otherwise, I recommend that you take a quietly favorable attitude toward the Working Group's unanimous recommendation to the IRG. Berger is doing a memo to the Secretary.[4]

Al Jenkins

---

[2] Tab A, a copy of the report of the China Working Group to the Far East Interdepartmental Regional Group proposing the removal of restrictions on travel to Communist China by U.S. citizens, undated, is attached but not printed. Another copy of the report is filed with the minutes of the November 2 meeting of the Far East Interdepartmental Regional Group in Department of State, FE/IRG Files: Lot 70 D 56. The Bureau of Far Eastern Affairs became the Bureau of East Asian and Pacific Affairs on November 1, and the Far East Interdepartmental Regional Group changed its name accordingly.

[3] Not attached to the source text.

[4] Not found.

200.   Memorandum From Secretary of State Rusk to President Johnson[1]

Washington, November 5, 1966.

SUBJECT

Chinese Representation

Recommendation[2]

That you authorize me to try to persuade the Canadians to alter their present "one China-one Taiwan" proposal to one more acceptable to us, involving a UN General Assembly Study Committee.[3]

Discussion

The Canadian Cabinet has decided to consult with friendly governments immediately on the introduction of a United Nations General Assembly resolution which would ask the President of the Assembly to explore possibilities of a solution based on a seat for both the Republic of China and Red China in the Assembly, with the Security Council seat going to Peking. The Canadians say that without this opportunity, they would be obliged this year to abstain on the Albanian resolution, which provides for replacing the Republic of China by Red China in all UN organs. The Belgians and the Italians have also informed us of their intention to make a similar new move.

The Canadian shift makes a critical difference. If we lose the support of these friends, it is probable that the Albanian resolution will obtain a simple majority for the first time. We could probably still prevent its adoption by relying on the procedural device of requiring that such a resolution receive a 2/3 majority for adoption, but we will have suffered an important defeat.

I have urged Paul Martin not to do anything further about this until I have had a chance to raise the matter with you. He is proceeding with

---

[1] Source: Johnson Library, National Security File, Memos to the President, Walt W. Rostow. Secret. The source text does not indicate the drafter, but Sisco's November 4 memorandum cited in footnote 2, Document 195, which forwarded the draft memorandum to Rusk, indicates that it was drafted by Sisco and Buffum and cleared by Berger and Meeker. Sisco's memorandum states that the proposal reflected a consensus of views reached at a meeting with Katzenbach, Berger, and Meeker and that Goldberg concurred. The source text was sent to the President with a November 5 memorandum from Rostow noting that NSC staff member Nathaniel Davis thought the proposal was probably the "best we can do" to avoid being in a minority.

[2] The source text indicates the recommendation was approved.

[3] In a telephone conversation on November 6, Rusk told the President that he would not object to setting up a study committee if it would mean defeat of the Albanian resolution. A study committee would "complicate" the issue for a year or two. Without that, the United States risked not being able to defeat the Albanian resolution. (Johnson Library, Recordings and Transcripts, Recording of a Telephone Conversation between President Johnson and Rusk, November 6, 7:10 p.m., tape F66.30, side B, PNO 1)

consultations with a few governments (UK, Italy, Belgium, Australia, New Zealand, and Japan) at once, but has agreed to defer submission of his proposal formally to the General Assembly for a short time pending consultations with us.

We could stand on our present tactics and oppose Canada's new move; we do not believe they can be dissuaded. Canada and the Belgians have told us that unless they are able to pursue a new course, they no longer will oppose the Albanian resolution; others such as Italy, whose Government is under strong Socialist pressure, are likely to take the same position. In these circumstances, the necessary majority to prevent Red China replacing the GRC would be seriously undermined.

A second option would be for us to stand aside; let the Canadians and others go ahead as they see fit on the assumption the Canadian proposal probably would not get the required 2/3 vote in the face of Peking's opposition. This has great risks since there are elements in the Canadian proposal, e.g. giving the Security Council seat to Red China, which we would not want the Assembly to endorse even by a simple majority.

We conclude, therefore, we must engage the Canadians next week with the safest countermeasure we can offer, i.e. establishment of a Study Committee to examine all facets of the Chinese representation issue and report back to the next General Assembly. There are admitted risks in pursuing this suggestion since we can not be sure of the composition of the Committee and more importantly, we can not guarantee what its recommendations will be. At a minimum, I would expect that this Committee would recommend some form of "two Chinas" solution, and that we would have to take a stand on this during the Committee's work and subsequently at next year's General Assembly.

We feel strongly that the present Canadian text prejudges the ultimate decision of the Assembly. I would like to make a major effort with the Canadians to move them from their present course to another which we could support. This would be the best protection for the GRC. The Canadians seem to have the bit in their teeth, and I am not certain how far we can get with them.

A shift to a Study Committee would be a less radical departure from past tactics than Canada's "one China-one Taiwan" proposal, it would be more palatable to our close Asian allies, and while the GRC would oppose a Study Committee, it is less offensive because the ultimate solution would not be prejudged. It offers some flexibility on how rapidly subsequent Assemblies move towards a definite substantive decision.

I would also consult quickly with the GRC to assure they understand the reasons for our efforts with the Canadians and others.

Ambassador Goldberg concurs in the recommendation.

Dean Rusk

201.   Editorial Note

Representative to the United Nations Arthur J. Goldberg met with President Johnson at the LBJ Ranch on November 7, 1966. A November 9 memorandum from Nathaniel Davis of the NSC staff to Special Assistant Walt Rostow reports that Chinese representation was among the subjects Goldberg discussed with the President. (Johnson Library, National Security File, Agency File, United Nations, Vol. 5) A statement by Goldberg, released to the press by the White House Press Secretary's office in San Antonio, Texas, on November 7, included the statement that the United States did not wish to increase the isolation of mainland China from the rest of the world but that it would not consent to "the demands of Peking that the Republic of China on Taiwan be excluded and the UN itself transformed, in order to pave the way for Peking's admission." For the text, see Department of State *Bulletin*, December 5, 1966, pages 851–855.

202.   Telegram From the Department of State to the Embassy in Canada[1]

Washington, November 9, 1966, 1:06 p.m.

81612. For Ambassador from Secretary.

1.   Please convey following message from me to Pearson[2] urgently: *[Begin] Text.*

Dear Mike:

Under Secretary Katzenbach has explained to Ambassador Ritchie the serious problems we have with the Canadian draft resolution on Chinese representation. I hope that you will be able to give this problem your personal and urgent attention.

From my conversations with Paul Martin over a period of time, and from discussions with Ambassador Ritchie, I gather that your govern-

---

[1] Source: Department of State, Central Files, UN 6 CHICOM. Secret; Immediate; Exdis. Drafted by Bundy, cleared by Sisco and Rufus Z. Smith, and approved by Rusk. Repeated to USUN for Goldberg and to London, Canberra, Wellington, Tokyo, Rome, Brussels, and Taipei.

[2] Ambassador Butterworth reported in telegram 784 from Ottawa, November 8, that he had delivered the message to Prime Minister Pearson, who was in a meeting and therefore unable to discuss its contents at that time. (Ibid.)

ment may be moved in part by the feeling that an offer of membership in the UN would have a constructive effect on Chinese Communist behavior, including the outcome of the present internal convulsion, and also by a related feeling that such an offer might have some favorable effect on the prospects for peace in Vietnam.

I must confess that, as of this particular time at least, both of these arguments seem to me to have little substance. None of us can tell where the present convulsion on the mainland is headed, but surely the dominant fact is that Mao and Lin Piao appear to be at least tenuously on top, and appear clearly to stand for a harsh line in all aspects of policy. Our own China experts are in total agreement that this is a time for watchful waiting, and not for injecting any new special factor if it can be avoided. (I may say that this applies equally to any military action that could be construed as a direct or indirect threat to Communist China, and I can assure you of our continued prudence in this regard.) As things now stand, I find it hard to avoid the conclusion that at this moment what must appear to be a naked offer of membership will if anything encourage the hard-liners and work against the possible emergence of different policies out of the present turmoil in China.

The same point applies to the prospects for peace in Vietnam. We have tried our utmost to have the UN play a useful role to this end, and the outcome to date suggests many factors other than the absence of Peking from New York. But surely, in any event, Peking will come only if the Republic of China withdraws, and in these conditions the encouragement to hard-line policies, not merely immediately, but for a long period to come, would only be compounded.

Moreover, there is the further imponderable of Sino-Soviet relations. Any major change in the pattern of presentation of the Chinese representation issue can only confront the Soviet Union with serious problems. In terms of the really serious interest the USSR and its Eastern European friends now appear to be taking toward peace in Vietnam, I doubt very much if they would feel that a new controversy on this issue would be helpful.

All in all, our own conclusion would have been that it was better for this year to put the issue to one side, and to deal with it on previous lines. And our soundings in New York, as well as widely in Europe and elsewhere, had indicated sufficient support to maintain this view, even among nations most desirous of some early change in the situation.

So much for our view of the merits of the case. Having followed closely the thrust of our policy over the past year, from the bombing pause in January to our handling of Communist China and the theme of reconciliation stressed by the President on his recent trip, I know that you recognize that our motives and objectives yield to none in our concern for peace in Vietnam and an eventual wider peace in Asia.

This brings me to the other main point that Paul Martin has stressed in the past, and Ambassador Ritchie most recently. This is that your government feels under strong political pressure to show some forward movement on the issue during this session, and to make clear and explicit the Canadian view that a new answer must be found along "two Chinas" lines. It would be presumptuous of me to contest this argument, which apparently leads you to the conclusion that you must put forward and support a new proposal of some sort.

But from a purely practical standpoint, I must then point out that your present proposal is almost bound to create maximum mischief for minimum result.

First, it is an incompatible hybrid between an action and a study resolution. While ostensibly directing the GA President to explore the issue, the preamble states the exact solution to be explored. Which is it meant to be, for only the most naive could conclude that you have not pre-judged the outcome of any exploration?

Second, your resolution states the answer for the Security Council as well as the General Assembly. Of course, this issue will have to be faced in due course if Peking should ever accept membership in the General Assembly. But surely we must all recognize that a Peking seat in the Security Council raises far more serious issues even than General Assembly membership; for the short run, any serious student would have to conclude that Peking on the Security Council would spell total ineffectiveness by the Council for a long period to come on any issue such as the recent disputes about Cyprus and Kashmir and a whole host of past examples in which Canada has often played a great part. Must we charge across that bridge in any fashion now? May we not wish to examine it at some point against the possibility of some Charter amendment providing, perhaps, for rotation of a permanent Asian seat on the Security Council among India, Japan, and China?

I mention this point because it seems very clear that most Asian nations do not welcome the thought that Peking would sit as an Asian permanent member with a veto in the Security Council. Surely those who live at great distance from the present scene in Asia should give great weight to the views of nations most directly and deeply concerned about the irrational militancy of the present Peking regime.

Moreover, inclusion of the Security Council as a specific element can only have the gravest effects on the reaction of the Republic of China. I have always taken at face value Paul Martin's assurance that your government does *not* wish to see that government out of the UN, and I need not repeat to you the depth of our convictions on this subject, convictions I believe to be shared by the great majority of the UN membership. Yet your proposal as it stands, by including the Security Council, is bound to arouse the strongest emotions—and wholly understandable ones—in the Nationalist Chinese government, including the moderates who represent its hopeful future voice. If you are trying to force the Republic of China right out of the UN, you could not choose a better course. But that can hardly be your purpose.

Thirdly, as to the choice of a party to explore the issue, the President of the General Assembly seems to us to have grave disadvantages. His mandate is limited in time, and he is a single individual not necessarily representative of the spectrum of views and interests of the membership on a complex issue.

All of the above are serious defects of substance. They lead us to the clear conclusion that we would in any event have to oppose your Resolution in its present form, if it were introduced, and indeed would have to exert every ounce of our influence to defeat it by the heaviest possible margin. I need not underscore the seriousness of such a split between our two nations.

But the difficulty is even more grave than this. Again from a purely practical standpoint, the introduction of your Resolution could only create a state of total confusion in the General Assembly as it considers the Important Question issue and the Albanian Resolution. I cannot say what votes you would be able to obtain for your Resolution, but at the very least it would throw a last-minute and unforeseen element into the situation, so that the resulting vote patterns would become the result of almost unpredictable and emotional currents in New York. I cannot believe that this is the constructive way to go about resolving the problem.

Let me now turn to our own affirmative proposal for a substitute resolution. Although we would have preferred to let the whole issue lie for this session, we have always known that the issue would have to be faced at some point, and we approach the matter in a constructive spirit. The idea of a study committee has a long history in the thinking of other members and in our own contingency planning. Under present circumstances, it seems to us to avoid virtually all the grave disadvantages of your proposal, while at the same time representing clear forward movement on the issue along the line that your government feels under political pressure to obtain.

This is most definitely not a delaying tactic on our part. Rather it faces the whole issue head-on and will require a full report on all aspects of the problem by the study committee for the next General Assembly. In the nature of things, this can hardly fail to include a serious examination of the complex issue of the Security Council, as well as an examination of the conditions under which Peiping might be offered a General Assembly seat—a matter, incidentally, on which your proposal is totally silent. In short, from a substantive standpoint, it does everything you could ask and at the same time provides the period of detailed examination that we believe is required both in terms of the complexity of the issue and in light of the present uncertainties of Communist Chinese behavior.

I might add that we would wholly support membership by Canada on the study committee.

Therefore, it is our earnest suggestion that your government not submit its Resolution and take the lead with others (such as the Italians) in sponsoring a proposal such as contained in the draft Resolution that we have given Ambassador Ritchie.[3] If you wish to make your own view of the desirable outcome clear, you will surely have ample opportunity during the debate, as will all the other nations involved.

We ourselves, while not sponsoring such a substitute proposal, would be prepared to join in its support, while we would expect—in accordance with our understanding of your position—that if such a proposal were put forward and were supported by us, you in turn would continue to support the Important Question and to vote against the Albanian Resolution. With the study committee resolution before the General Assembly, the latter would of course become in clear contradiction to it, while I hope that your government continues to appreciate the grave consequences for the whole work of the United Nations that would flow from any defeat on the Important Question.

We are already consulting with key interested nations in this sense, including the circle with which you have shared your proposed resolution.

Finally, let me make clear that the President, who is of course now resting in Texas in preparation for his operation Friday, has gone over this whole matter with the greatest care and has personally approved the position I have stated. We hope that your government will reconsider its position and be prepared to act as I have suggested. Please let me know just as soon as you possibly can.

With warm regards,

Sincerely

Dean Rusk[4]

End Text.

---

[3] The text of the U.S. alternative draft resolution was transmitted in telegram 81492, November 8. It provided that the General Assembly, noting that "the GRC is a founding member of the United Nations," that "the PRC has attached conditions to its representation," and that "the complexities involved in this question require the most searching consideration," decided to establish a committee to study all facets of the situation and make recommendations to the 22d General Assembly for an equitable and practicable solution. (Ibid.) Katzenbach gave the draft to Ritchie on November 8; their discussion is summarized in telegram 81500, November 8. (Ibid.)

[4] In a reply transmitted in telegram 801 from Ottawa, November 11, Pearson wrote that he was giving serious and urgent consideration to Rusk's letter but added that the Canadians were convinced that some forward movement on the issue was desirable and that their initiative represented a realistic and balanced approach. (Ibid.)

2. For Info Addressees (other than USUN): We also sending you State 81502[5] showing line we are taking with GRC. We are talking here today with British, Australians, New Zealanders, Belgians, and second round with Japanese, who were seen last night in Tokyo. Italians were seen last night particularly with view to their interest in study committee idea. All of our conversations here will be reported to interested posts during the day. You should take no action on basis this cable unless otherwise instructed, but should carefully study lines we have taken with Canadians and GRC, being prepared to adapt these to your local situation in any discussion that may arise with host government.

Rusk

---

[5] Telegram 81502, November 8, summarized a conversation that day between Katzenbach and Ambassador Chow, in which Katzenbach stated the U.S. view that the only feasible way to deal with the Canadian resolution was to try to persuade the Canadians to alter it and to give them a substitute proposal. (Ibid.)

---

203. Telegram From the Department of State to the Embassy in the United Kingdom[1]

Washington, November 10, 1966, 9:21 a.m.

82445. Subj: Canadian Initiative on ChiRep.

1. Assistant Secretaries Sisco and Bundy called in British Minister Stewart to talk about Canadian proposal on ChiRep (see septel). Sisco explained our very strong objections to Canadian draft resolution, especially its prejudgment of issue with drastic proposal which amounts to "one China, one Taiwan" arrangement with Peking in SC. He thought it would be hard to devise proposal better calculated to provoke GRC into walking out of UN. Apart from unacceptability Canadian scheme, we felt this no time for move which might encourage hardline tendencies in Peking, adversely affect peace prospects in Viet Nam and create problems for many allies in Asia. Our problems compounded by shortness of

---

[1] Source: Department of State, Central Files, UN 6 CHICOM. Secret, Immediate; Limdis. Drafted by Gleysteen, cleared by Bundy and Judd, and approved by Sisco. Repeated to USUN, Ottawa, and Taipei.

time to consult friendly governments, Congress and public. In addition there was effect on UN itself; if Communist China were seated in SC UN peacekeeping actions in Cyprus and Kashmir would have been inconceivable.

2. Sisco went on to say that since Canadians were under domestic pressure to give sense of movement we were prepared, on assumption of continued Canadian opposition to Albanian resolution and support for important question procedure to go along with alternative arrangement of study committee to study all facets of Chirep in both GA and SC and make recommendations to next regular session of GA. Study committee would permit us to pursue question in evolutionary and reasonable way with examination of all alternatives. It would moreover provide Canadians and other governments with ample opportunity to express views on substance of question.

3. After handing Stewart copy of illustrative resolution we could support, Sisco noted that we had made our views clear to Canadians yesterday telling them that we flatly opposed to their resolution and suggesting this alternative. We did not yet know ultimate Canadian reaction. We had also talked with Chinese, Italians and would today be seeing Japanese, Australians, New Zealanders and Belgians who we hoped would sympathize with our reaction.

4. FYI Only. Stewart (asking that it not be reported to other governments) said UK had already been consulted by Canadians in London and had told them UK did not like Canadian resolution and did not intend any policy change this year, i.e., British would continue support important question procedure, would support para one of Albanian resolution and would make explanation of vote on para two expelling GRC. British considered Canadian resolution a stall which would in any event fail. Stewart added quite frankly that if UK were to support such resolution they would expect to be thrown out of Peking. End FYI.

5. Stewart remarked that while British had refused support Canadian resolution they had agreed not to lobby against it and he assumed we wished British support for our alternative. Sisco confirmed this and said Amb Goldberg would want to discuss precise tactics after consultations with various governments over next few days. Officer accompanying Stewart thought it necessary to remind us that when the British reviewed idea of study committee in April this year they frowned on idea because it would appear too much a procedural device designed to avoid coming to grips with substance of issue. Stewart, however, preferred not to prejudge his Government's reaction.

Rusk

204. Telegram From the Department of State to the Embassy in the Republic of China[1]

Washington, November 10, 1966, 11:56 p.m.

83437. Subj: GRC Reaction to Canadian Chirep Initiative. Following uncleared record of conversation is FYI Noforn and subject to revision on review:

1. Secretary together with Asst Secretaries Sisco and Bundy saw GRC Ambassador Chou this evening at latter's request. Chou covered many of same points made in Taipei to Ambassador McConaughy[2] but at no point claimed study committee proposal would be "even worse than a two-Chinas resolution." Nor did he imply threat that GRC would consider walking out of UN if study committee established.

2. Chou told Secretary GRC profoundly distressed by Canadian move and did not understand how Canadians could contemplate such disservice to free world at this time except perhaps in terms of Paul Martin's special preoccupation with issue. GRC had found that its reaction was shared by many countries, especially Japan and Australia, and it hoped US would use this additional support to stop Canadian initiative and hold to previous tactics. GRC has been humiliated for 17 years in UN over Chirep issue and could not face additional humiliation of being held in suspense while study committee deliberated recommendations.

3) Secretary emphasized that we fully agree with GRC's strong objections to Canadian proposal which we found bad, ill-timed and mischievous. Having spilled "a lot of blood" over this issue with Paul Martin in many rough encounters over past two years, Secretary stressed that he wanted it reported very clearly to Taipei that there has never been any collusion between Canada and US. Secretary had tried to persuade Martin that Canadians should defer on this matter to countries with real responsibilities in Asia, but Martin has persisted on grounds of domestic pressures in Canada which he claimed necessitated Canadian initiative this year. Perhaps wheat sales and other factors played role but in any case GRC should understand that we have been doing battle for them

---

[1] Source: Department of State, Central Files, UN 6 CHICOM. Secret; Priority; Exdis. Drafted and approved by Gleysteen and cleared by Sisco. Repeated to USUN, Rome, Brussels, Tokyo, Wellington, Canberra, and London.

[2] Telegram 1382 from Taipei, November 10, reported discussions between McConaughy and Foreign Minister Wei, in which Wei argued that the United States should exert maximum pressure on the Canadians to abandon their proposal or any substitute, such as a study committee. He declared that in the GRC view, a study committee resolution would be "even worse than two-Chinas resolution" and that if such a resolution were adopted, the GRC would have to consider taking the step intimated by Chiang Kai-shek in his June 30 conversation with McConaughy (see Document 162), that is, withdrawal from the United Nations. (Department of State, Central Files, UN 6 CHICOM)

including very strong letter which Secy has sent Pearson yesterday after talking to President.

4. Secretary noted that Canadian move could not have come at worse time because it threw confusion into situation which could not stand confusion—i.e., number of countries such as Italy, Belgium, Chile which had been on verge of shifting position before Canadian initiative could no longer afford to resist domestic pressures and carry on with traditional approach. We had great trouble with Italians last year and could hardly expect Fanfani to drop study committee concept this year in face of Ottawa's action. Facts were that Canadians had not consulted us and we had not been able to dissuade them from initiative, including possibility they would still go ahead and table highly objectionable res.

5. Situation we now face, according to Secretary, remains essentially same as one month ago in that we must still sustain important question procedure and defeat Albanian resolution, but in view Canadian decision we now had to use counter measure to retain our support for these same purposes. Actual result of study committee, which designed to avoid pre-judgment of issue, would be to put off decision on Chirep just as we have done since 1950. Secretary urged that GRC not draw conclusion about Chirep before UN does thereby give open field to Communist China. Despite annual debate GRC remained in both GA and SC.

6. During remainder conversation Ambassador Chou engaged in repetitive but insistent request that US marshal other governments in all-out effort to deter any Canadian initiative, refrain from supporting study committee proposal, and hold to past tactics on Chirep even if this course risked defeat. Chou argued Canadian move was largely bluff which could be called by firm US response and he claimed we would have adequate votes (53–48) to hold line against Albanian res despite Canadians. Ambassador emphasized that if on contrary US were to continue support for study committee while GRC made all out efforts against, result would be deplorable division between allies.

7. In response Secretary explained that we did not expect GRC support for study committee but simply asked that GRC not prejudge situation by making prior assumption about outcome of such tactic. Study committee might not materialize and if it did group would not necessarily recommend ChiCom membership in UN. Quite possible that over next few months some move would be made to inquire about Peking's attitude and if Peking refused various schemes advanced in UN, Communist China would not be admitted. Secretary asked why, if GRC could go along with study committee in 1950, it could not do so today. Our problem was votes. Without some move which would assure support from number of particular countries we thought it very likely that Albanian resolution would achieve simple majority this year and there was also serious question whether we could hold support for important

question procedure. This was unacceptable risk for US and it was for this reason that we were prepared to support study committee.

8) Although Ambassador Chou argued GRC vote count against Albanian resolution was adequate despite impact of Canadian move, he asserted we should in any case risk be willing defeat because any change would be first crack in crumbling dike. Question involved national honor and if situation in UN had in fact deteriorated to point where study committee-type tactics necessary it would be better to face defeat now rather than be humiliated over course of next year.

9) Both Secretary and Sisco used specific examples to illustrate how Canadian initiative would erode our support against Albanian resolution unless many countries were offered some other alternative. They also disputed Chou's insistence in assuming inevitably bad consequences of study committee by showing that GRC had in past agreed to shifts in tactics without disastrous consequences. Ambassador's response was to repeat that GRC had its back to wall on this issue and preferred defeat to going along with change which would be interpreted domestically and internationally as advance acknowledgment of failure, making ultimate humiliation that much greater. Chou also pointed out that GRC considered any switch particularly regrettable because likely impact within Communist China would be to encourage militancy.

10) Secretary interjected that Ambassador was fully aware of our special concern about dangers of ChiCom militancy since we had to bear military consequences in Viet-Nam. It was our judgment, however, that defeat on Albanian resolution this year would be far more damaging in this sense than our agreement to study committee as alternative to Canadian resolution.

11) Secretary repeated that we do not expect GRC to support study committee idea and said we think it most useful for GRC to put its views strongly to Canadians. We also hoped Canadians would be made sharply aware of Australian, Japanese and other negative reactions. Even so we had to consider our tactics in light of newly confused situation in GA, and we hoped the GRC would not retreat before battle by making premature judgment about outcome of study committee.

12) In summing up Ambassador Chou stated that GRC was opposed to any change as beginning of uncontrollable process and asserted GRC had to consider matter in terms of its national honor and dignity since its leaders were answerable to history. Secretary said he could not complain about this view but could not accept it. We did not agree with Ambassador's estimate of current situation in GA and we strongly disagreed with his judgment about effects of Canadian resolution. We would, of course, continue to take account GRC's views and Secretary suggested that strategy group in New York resolve conflicting estimates of likely votes on various resolutions.

13) Secretary concluded by stating that we were in agreement with GRC on importance of reaffirming important question procedure, we were in agreement on opposition to Albanian res and we were in agreement in our common opposition to Canadian res. Insofar as study committee was concerned, however, Secretary declared that we were prepared to support this measure because we had too much at stake to accept defeat on the Albanian res in GA this year.

Rusk

---

205. Telegram From the Department of State to the Mission to the United Nations[1]

Washington, November 11, 1966, 5:40 p.m.

83599. For Goldberg.

1. We commend you for skillful manner in which you are pursuing delicate conversations on complex and difficult Chinese representation question.

2. We fully endorse your statement to Chileans that: (1) Important Question Resolution must be upheld; (2) Albanian Resolution must be rejected; and (3) we should try isolate and deflect Canadian proposal by achieving common agreement on Study Committee approach.

3. We know you appreciate fully how essential it is to get the Important Question Resolution introduced promptly as maximum protection and are glad you plan wait no later than tomorrow. Scenario along above lines might help ease concern of Japan, Australia, Philippines and GRC regarding Study Committee idea as alternate to Canadian proposal and as way to bulwark support for reaffirmation Important Question Resolution and defeat Albanian Resolution.

4. You will have noted telegram from McConaughy in which he makes some concerned suggestions regarding special efforts which may help us with GRC.[2] We confident you fully agree with these suggestions since in fact you have been proceeding along these lines. We think similar

---

[1] Source: Department of State, Central Files, UN 6 CHICOM. Secret; Limdis. Drafted by Sisco, cleared in substance by Bundy, and approved by Sisco.

[2] In telegram 1386 from Taipei, November 11, McConaughy urged the importance of convincing the GRC that it was being fully consulted and informed on the Chinese representation issue in order to prevent further deterioration of the atmosphere in Taipei. He suggested daily briefings and consultations with GRC officials in New York, Washington, and Taipei, inclusion of a GRC representative in group meetings in New York whenever possible, and a letter from Rusk to Wei. (Ibid.)

special efforts are also desirable and necessary with Japanese who are showing extreme nervousness. In particular, we would draw your attention to paragraph (c) of Taipei's 1386[3] and Secretary's comment to Chou yesterday regarding need to put together as promptly as possible current vote counts on propositions likely to be before General Assembly.

5. Regarding Study Committee, we realize that whether it will require a 2/3 vote for adoption or simple majority will be considerably influenced by what substantive material is included in the preamble. As you know, we do not want ultimate solution prejudged as Canadian preamble would do.

6. If Study Committee Resolution is devoid of substance as present Italian text,[4] we assume only simple majority vote required. We have stated our intention to support the Study Committee idea if the countries interested in pressing it are thereby willing to continue to support Important Question Resolution, oppose Albanian Resolution, and abandon unacceptable Canadian Resolution. However, given great difficulties GRC is having re Study Committee, we believe it undesirable for us to get out in front on this proposal and to lobby for it. We particularly welcome therefore the reluctant dragon posture you have adopted re Study Committee; it has struck just right balance.

7. Indeed, simplest outcome would be for Important Question Resolution to be reaffirmed and Albanian Resolution defeated in the first instance and Study Committee proposal fall by the board for lack of required majority. We would appreciate your views on this.

8. We find interesting your suggestion that perhaps this Committee might be made up of prominent statesmen rather than member government representatives. Group of past GA Presidents would be highly attractive to us. However, we doubt such proposal would prove feasible since obviously list of past Presidents loaded completely on our side. As to member government composition Study Committee, our strong preference would be to stick as close to Credentials Committee ratio of 5–3–1 as possible, though realize composition will be at least as tough a job as your finding on SW African Committee.

Rusk

---

[3] Paragraph (c) suggested giving the GRC an assessment of the effect the Canadian resolution or the U.S. study committee proposal would have on the voting on the important question or Albanian resolutions.

[4] Telegram 2210 from USUN, November 10, transmitted the text of a draft resolution that the Italian Representative gave to Goldberg on November 9. It stated that the General Assembly, conscious of the importance of the principle of universality of the United Nations to its effectiveness, bearing in mind that China was a founding member of the United Nations, and noting that the People's Republic of China had attached conditions to its participation in the United Nations, decided to establish a committee of member states to study the situation and make recommendations to the 22d General Assembly. (Department of State, Central Files, UN 6 CHICOM)

206. Memorandum From the President's Special Assistant (Rostow) to President Johnson[1]

Washington, November 14, 1966, 6:20 p.m.

SUBJECT

Chinese Representation in the UN

We introduced the Important Question Resolution at the UN this afternoon with the Belgians and others as co-sponsors.

Efforts to enlist the Italians and Canadians as co-sponsors were unsuccessful. The Italians wanted iron-clad assurances—we did not feel we could give them—that we would not drop the study committee idea if we win the votes on the Important Question and the Albanian resolutions. We are trying to make sure that the order of voting in New York is: first, the Important Question (to require a two-thirds vote for any change in Chinese representation); second, the Albanian Resolution (to substitute Red China for the Republic of China in the UN); and third, the modified Canadian or Italian Resolution (looking toward a study committee). The introduction of our Resolution today makes it likely that it will be the first to be voted on. If the study committee proposal comes up, we might have to go through a second Important Question vote.

Canadian Foreign Minister Martin and Italian Foreign Minister Fanfani met today in Rome to discuss their respective tactics on Chinese representation. Preliminary reports indicate that they did not reach any agreement. The Foreign Minister of the Republic of China is expected to arrive in Washington tomorrow.

Secretary Rusk will address himself to this issue at tomorrow's luncheon-meeting.[2]

Walt

---

[1] Source: Johnson Library, National Security File, Agency File, United Nations, Vol. 5. Secret. A handwritten "L" on the source text indicates that the President saw the memorandum.

[2] According to Johnson's Daily Diary, he had lunch on November 15 from 2:05 to 3:40 with Rusk, McNamara, Rostow, and Moyers. Chinese representation was one of several issues discussed. (Ibid.) No record of the discussion has been found.

207. Memorandum of Conversation[1]

Washington, November 15, 1966, 11 a.m.

SUBJECT

Communist China

PARTICIPANTS

Zentaro Kosaka, Former Japanese Foreign Minister
Kazuo Chiba, First Secretary, Embassy of Japan

The Secretary
Richard L. Sneider, Country Director for Japan

At the invitation of the Secretary Mr. Kosaka reviewed the impressions gained from his trip to Communist China. Mr. Kosaka first explained that his trip to Communist China was an effort to wrest contacts with Communist China from Japanese leftwing control. Kosaka said that he had told Chen Yi he was pro-American and gained more respect from Chen Yi. He also told Chinese leaders that the US had no intention of bombing Communist China to which Chen Yi agreed. He felt that the Chinese Communist top leadership wanted its views transmitted to the US and therefore he has made his trip to Washington. Basically his objective is, as a representative of the Free World, to try to make Communist China open its door to the Free World.

Mr. Kosaka then reviewed his major observations on Communist China, as follows:

(1) The "cultural revolution" has excluded rational thinking, eliminated able men, and reflects the senility of Mao.

(2) The young generation is being force-fed Mao's thoughts and there is no feedback of the popular views to the highest level. Mao's objective is to divide his friends from his enemies, i.e. those accused of being pro-American, bourgeois elements and pro-Soviet revisionists.

(3) The success of Mao's effort depends on an increase of agricultural production to meet rising population. Mao is seeking to spread his cult to agricultural areas through the Red Guard movement which is pushing for the abolition of private plots and reinstitution of communes. However, the farmers are apathetic and Kosaka felt that the abolition of private plots is not possible. He found that there are only about 120 million hectares of arable land, approximately one hectare per farm family. Farm income is low with a family of 5 to 6 earning from $208 to $416

---

[1] Source: Department of State, Central Files, POL 1 CHICOM. Secret. Drafted by Sneider and approved in S on November 29. The meeting was held in Secretary Rusk's office. The source text is "Part II of III."

annually. In comparison industrial workers earn $300 per worker annually. At the same time costs of bicycles, $50, and TV sets, $200, are out of the range of farm families. Clothing is available but coarse. The Chinese leadership to meet agricultural discontent compares farm living standards today with those of 17 years ago rather than with those of other comparable areas in the Free World at the present time.

(4) Generally, Chinese people have enough to eat, more schooling and free medical care which is an improvement over the pre-Communist period.

(5) Chinese leadership claims that agricultural production will increase this year and has offered to export cotton and rice to Japan. Kosaka mentioned that there is a discrepancy between Hong Kong estimates of Chinese Communist agricultural production of 175 million tons and Communist China's estimates of 200 million tons. Kosaka expressed doubts about production increases because the extensive movement of the Red Guard on Chinese railroads has disrupted transportation. After the crop comes in he expects this will be the basis for criticism of the Mao leadership.

(6) The Chinese recognize that they are now underdeveloped and talk in of terms [of] needing 20–30 years to become a developed economy.

(7) Chinese higher education is now undergoing significant changes. The universities and higher schools are closed until next February and there are plans to shorten the school year and eliminate entrance exams. In the future only students with clear-cut revolutionary background will be admitted to the top universities, with the result of eliminating some of the best students and a general lowering of academic standards.

Kosaka concluded by saying that the key problem of Communist China is when will the current contradictions come into the open. The Chinese leadership says that they will not but Kosaka anticipates that the farmers will be disillusioned after the harvest and maybe cause a basic showdown. He felt that it was important to let the Chinese see the progress occurring outside Communist China and open Chinese eyes. He asked whether there was anything the Secretary wished him to convey to Chinese leadership since Liao Ch'eng-chih, head of the Chinese Communist trade office, offered to convey any message in the utmost secrecy.

The Secretary then questioned Kosaka on other aspects of Chinese Communist developments. Kosaka mentioned that he had contact with the Red Guards at the Peking secondary school. He found them young and very articulate but they all talked the same language. When he asked them why the Red Guards had been formed and the Young Communist League not utilized, they replied that the YCL was "old people" while the Red Guard was more militant and class conscious. In response to the Secretary's inquiry about Kosaka's impressions on the internal leadership struggle, Kosaka said that as long as Mao is alive the opposition forces in the Communist Party will be suppressed but they are strong and the struggle will continue. He mentioned that he had tried to see Lin Piao but was advised that Lin as a military man saw no foreigners.

Kosaka mentioned that Chou had stressed Chinese Communist peaceful intentions to the U.S. but there were two differences between the countries: (1) the U.S. refused to recognize the five principles; and (2) the U.S. refused to withdraw from Taiwan and the Taiwan Straits. The Secretary said that at Warsaw the Chinese Communists had continually maintained the position that there was nothing to discuss until we surrendered Formosa which the U.S. was not prepared to do.

On Sino-Japanese relations, Kosaka said that the Chinese Communists accepted the present relationship with non-governmental trade and cultural ties and no diplomatic relations. They expressed opposition to Sato but praise for Ikeda and they are evidently trying to split the Liberal Democratic Party. In response to a question by the Secretary, Kosaka said that there were no Japanese government officials in Peking but there is a Liao–Takasaki trade office there and one official who had resigned from the government. He mentioned in passing that the Liao–Takasaki trade negotiations on the renewal of the Liao–Takasaki trade agreement had broken down recently due to the Chinese insistence that the Japanese buy more rice.

208. Telegram From the Department of State to the Embassy in Poland[1]

Washington, November 15, 1966, 1:16 p.m.

84624. (A) Warsaw's 1165;[2] (B) Bucharest's 626.[3]

1. Department has carefully considered your suggestion in Ref A that we take initiative in suggesting to ChiComs change of venue of Warsaw talks from present neutral Polish ground to alternating between US and ChiCom Embassies. Without prejudice to possibility of taking such initiative somewhat later, we have concluded it undesirable raise this issue with ChiComs at present time.

2. Primary factor this conclusion is current complexity and sensitivity of discussions and considerations affecting ChiRep. US initiative to shift venue of talks, if leaked by accident either here or intentionally by ChiComs, would lend itself so easily to misinterpretation that it could have significant and serious effect on course of ChiRep debate.

3. Furthermore, degree of uncertainty and vagueness as to actual ChiCom intentions on talks (ref B) suggests desirability of caution on our part in moving at current time. We believe it may be preferable for us to sit tight and wait to see whether ChiComs make move on change in venue rather than attempt preempt them.

4. Depending on developments in next month, however, we do not rule out suggesting possible shift in venue to ChiComs along lines your suggestions at January meeting. Our present thinking, however, is any such feeler to ChiComs should be in lowest possible key, preferably by informal, private approach after meeting rather than by raising issue in formal letter or in open session. We will, in any event, be prepared deal with this issue if ChiComs raise it at January meeting.

Rusk

---

[1] Source: Department of State, Central Files, POL CHICOM–US. Secret; Limdis. Drafted by Paul H. Kreisberg of EA/ACA; cleared by William W. Thomas of EA/ROC, Louise McNutt of EA/RA, and Jacobson; and approved by Berger.

[2] Telegram 1165 from Warsaw, November 9, referred to a report from Geneva that the Romanian Chargé had told Consul General Roger W. Tubby the Chinese Communists might be interested in moving the Ambassadorial talks to Rangoon because they thought Gronouski had given the Poles information about the talks. Gronouski noted that the Soviets or the Poles might have discussed information from their tapes of the talks with the Chinese or that the Chinese might suspect the taping and want an excuse to move the talks from Warsaw. He suggested a U.S. proposal to the Chinese to hold all subsequent talks alternating in each other's Embassies. (Ibid.) The Geneva report was in telegram 1466 from Geneva, November 4. (Ibid., POL 17 ROM–POL)

[3] Telegram 626 from Bucharest, November 11, reported that Ambassador Richard H. Davis had asked Acting Foreign Minister Macovescu the source of statements by Romanian representatives in Rangoon, Moscow, and Geneva to the effect that the Warsaw talks were to be shifted to Rangoon. Macovescu had replied that the reports had come from diplomatic sources in Rangoon and not from the Chinese. (Ibid.)

209.   Telegram From the Department of State to the Embassy in the Republic of China[1]

Washington, November 15, 1966, 9:58 p.m.

85359. ChiRep. Ref: State's 83437.[2] Following uncleared record of conversation, is FYI Noforn, and subject to revision on review:

1.   GRC Foreign Minister Wei accompanied by Vice Minister Yang, Ambassador Liu, and Ambassador Chow called on Secretary November 15 to discuss Chinese representation. Bundy and Sisco also present. Principal impressions gained from conversation were (a) moderation of GRC presentation and muting of threat to withdraw and (b) distinct willingness expressed by GRC reps to go along with simple study committee resolution without prejudicial language in preamble.

2.   Wei opened by saying that it was his purpose to convey to Secretary GRC position on recent developments in UN which have been cause for some emotion and much deliberation. GRC basic policy, Wei said, is to overthrow ChiComs and recover mainland and therefore GRC is opposed to any form of two Chinas. While GRC attaches importance to its UN seat, it attaches even more to this basic position. If anything along line of two Chinas should happen, this would seriously upset GRC basic position, GRC's raison d'etre, and GRC's role in Asia. GRC would rather keep its basic position than its UN seat. A UN seat on the other hand would be meaningless if its basic position were undermined.

3.   The Secretary said he thought the GRC's international standing was also important to its basic position. (He also later reminded Wei that it was our position that GRC's position regarding the mainland cannot be settled by force.) As he had told Ambassador Chow November 10 (reftel), he said we attach the greatest importance to passage of IQ resolution and defeat of Albanian resolution. The Canadian move had been a great surprise and it was most harmful. We have tried for many years to keep the Canadians in line on the ChiRep question, but Canada is not a US puppet and the USG does not have decisive influence in the Canadian Government. Nonetheless we think we can defeat Canadian resolution.

4.   Mr. Sisco described present tactical situation in the GA and what we know of discussions in progress between Martin and Fanfani. So far as we know, the Canadian-Italian consultations were still inconclusive. Sisco said there are two possibilities in the present situation: On one hand, a study committee resolution which contains sufficient substance

---

[1] Source: Department of State, Central Files, UN 6 CHICOM. Secret; Immediate; Exdis. Drafted and approved by Bennett and cleared by Bundy and Sisco. Repeated to USUN and Tokyo.

[2] Document 204.

in the preamble which would likely necessitate a 2/3 vote for adoption. From Chinese point of view advantage of this proposal would be that it unlikely to achieve a 2/3 vote. However, such preamble likely to have a two China formula in it. Other possibility is a study committee resolution which did not prejudge ultimate solution and probably would only necessitate a simple majority to adopt. Such resolution would have advantage of not prejudicing GRC position, although better chance for its adoption since only simple majority required.

5.   Secretary said Communists would vote against any resolution with reference to two Chinas for the same reason as GRC. Other countries such as the UK would also be opposed and for this reason Canadian resolution might not pass. The Secretary added that, while we could probably defeat the Canadian resolution, a simple resolution for a study committee without substantive language in the preamble would be more difficult.

6.   Ambassador Liu said that he had told Ambassador Goldberg that of all the texts of resolutions he had seen, he preferred the text of the US study committee resolution. He said however that it would be best to delete from it any reference to the People's Republic of China and suggested that paragraphs two and three of the preamble be dropped. He also observed that the Italian resolution is not as harmless as it looks, noting that "China" is referred to without specifying which one. He hoped that the US would intervene with the Italians to bring about a non-prejudicial text.

7.   The Secretary noted that he had already personally approached Fanfani on the IQ.[3] He mentioned the difficult tactical decisions we face and said that frankly and on most confidential basis we would be content to see the Important Question passed, the Albanian resolution defeated, and no other resolution passed.

8.   Vice Minister Yang pointed out that to introduce any resolution might confuse the GA delegates and undermine our position on the Important Question and the Albanian resolution and the Secretary agreed. The question was raised whether introduction of a third resolution should wait until after voting on the Albanian resolution. Mr. Sisco noted that if the Canadian resolution came after the other two, a substantial number of countries might favor it because of its two Chinas content,

---

[3] Telegram 83743, November 12, transmitted a message from Rusk to Italian Foreign Minister Amintore Fanfani urging him to instruct the Italian Delegation in New York to co-sponsor the important question resolution and to agree that the proposals should be voted on in the following order: important question resolution, Albanian resolution, study committee resolution. (Department of State, Central Files, UN 6 CHICOM) On November 14, 15 countries, including the United States and Italy, submitted a draft resolution reaffirming the General Assembly's 1961 resolution that any proposal to change China's representation was an important question. (U.N. Document A/L.494)

but we still do not think it would get a 2/3 vote. The Communists would be strongly opposed and he referred to the incident last year when Peking turned down an attempt to water down the standard Albanian formula.

9. The Secretary said present events on the mainland make this a particularly bad time for the international community to appear to encourage Chinese Communist militancy. However, some countries view Chinese representation as an important domestic political issue. The Government in Italy takes this view, as does Belgium. The nature of the political pressure in Canada is not so clear. The Secretary said that we would not lobby for Italian study committee proposal and we would strongly oppose the Canadian resolution. He suggested that the GRC should make its strong opposition to the Canadian resolution vigorously known in New York. Our support of study committee proposal had been made to protect 4 or 5 critical votes on the Albanian resolution. Canada, Belgium, Italy, and Chile had made it clear that they could vote against Albanian resolution only if some third proposal is put forward in the GA. Sisco added that Italians had told us that Fanfani study committee proposal made in Parliament under pressure of Socialists and that there was risk fall of Italian Government if it not put forward.

10. Ambassador Liu said that what concerns the GRC most is that if there is an untoward development, it might seriously affect the GRC's basic position. If it "met reverse" GRC might have no choice but to leave UN. Secretary said he hoped GRC did not consider passage of a study committee resolution as cause for leaving UN. He noted that with the GRC having diplomatic relations with some 60 countries, as opposed to some 46 for the PRC, study committee formed on this basis would be long way from defeat. Secretary noted that we were not married to any precise language. We want to be in touch with the GRC on which type of resolution they would prefer. Ambassador Liu said the GRC was moving toward the US line of thinking, a simple study committee resolution.

11. There was some discussion of the concept of a study committee consisting of "wise men," about which Ambassador Liu expressed doubt. Secretary suggested that some of GA past presidents might be good possibilities. It was agreed however that the more recent past presidents of the General Assembly would prove troublesome. Liu said Chinese strongly prefer committee of member states.

12. Vice Minister Yang asked whether, if the US draft resolution were tabled, we could pick up support from other countries on the Albanian resolution. Sisco replied that some countries, such as Denmark, might shift to abstention and he hoped we could get good vote on Albanian resolution as result. Yang observed stronger vote on Albanian resolution would have helpful influence on finding of study committee.

13. Before the meeting closed, the Secretary said he wished to make two points:

a. He reminded Minister that he had told Zablocki Subcommittee last March it is US policy to support position of GRC in UN and oppose membership of Chinese Communists.
b. He urged GRC to avoid rash moves which might leave it with only its basic position but without international understanding and support.

14. Following departure of Secretary and after lunch there was further brief discussion during which Ambassador Liu said he had been instructed by Taipei to tell Goldberg he authorized to cooperate with US. Since according to GRC information Canadians and Italians have been approaching other delegations, Liu urged that US approach them too, to avoid their becoming confused.

15. Sisco cautioned the Chinese that what the Secretary had said about our being content to see no third resolution passed was for their ears only. We were telling others that we prepared to support non-prejudicial study committee resolution and relations with other close friends and allies thus involved.

Rusk

---

210.   **Telegram From the Embassy in the Republic of China to the Department of State**[1]

Taipei, November 21, 1966, 1111Z.

1483. 1. Acting FonMin Sampson Shen called me to MOFA 5:30 local time this afternoon to inform me officially that a GRC decision has been taken at the highest level that if Italian resolution calling for study committee were to pass, the GRC will on the same day announce its withdrawal from the UN. He said GRC had telegraphed to FonMin Wei today, telling him to convey this decision to Secretary, if in New York, and to Goldberg.

---

[1] Source: Department of State, Central Files, UN 6 CHICOM. Secret; Flash; Exdis. Received at 6:29 a.m. Repeated to USUN. Passed to the White House.

2. Shen said that decision reached after consideration of its consequences, and was taken in light of fact that USG, after supporting position of GRC in UN for many years, now felt it necessary support study committee resolution that has effect of calling into question GRC rights as founding members of UN. GRC felt it would only encounter insults if it stayed in after study committee resolution is passed. GRC would continue to work against resolution, and felt there was some possibility it might not pass.

3. I registered vigorous adverse reaction to decision, terming it hasty, ill-advised, not consonant with position taken by FonMin Wei with Secretary last week, and not in line with our agreed policy of close advance consultation and cooperation on matters of major mutual concern. I noted that step if taken would amount to abandonment of UN field to ChiComs presenting them with a major opportunity which they might seize to detriment of all allies.

4. I deplored GRC failure to give me chance to present US position again before decision taken and said I would prefer not to take decision as definitive at this stage. I put Shen on notice that GRC might receive request from me for early appointment with Pres. Chiang after I had received instructions from Washington.

5. Full report of conversation follows septel.[2]

McConaughy

---

[2] A more detailed report was sent in telegram 1484 from Taipei, November 21. (Ibid.)

---

211. Message From Secretary of State Rusk to the President's Special Counsel (Jacobson)[1]

Washington, undated.

1. I will be calling President later in the day regarding Chinese representation issue. Situation is as follows.

---

[1] Source: Johnson Library, National Security File, Agency File, United Nations, Vol. 5. Confidential. Drafted by Sisco on November 21 and concurred in by Bundy. A handwritten note to Rostow on the source text states that the Secretary had made these points to the President by telephone at about 11:15 a.m.

2. Italians submitting this morning a draft resolution providing for the establishment of a Study Committee. This text does not prejudge the ultimate solution and we will vote for it. Resolution will be co-sponsored by Belgium, Chile, Brazil, Bolivia, Trinidad-Tobago, and possibly several others.[2]

3. At meeting late last night, Martin of Canada pressed Goldberg to include in Study Committee resolution explicit language carrying with it slight "two-China" connotation. Both Goldberg and I fully agreed that we should turn down this language since it would only cause pain not only to the GRC but to our closest Asian allies.

4. President will have seen Taipei's 1483[3] in which Acting Foreign Minister informed McConaughy that, if Italian resolution were to pass, GRC will on same day announce its withdrawal from UN. This line completely inconsistent with what GRC Foreign Minister Wei told me last Wednesday that GRC prepared, though publicly opposing, "to cooperate" with Study Committee which did not prejudge ultimate substantive solution. I can only assume that this latest GRC view represents last minute reaction by Gimo. Since Assembly will debate matter for at least another ten days before any propositions are voted upon, we will have time to work on Taipei to try to convince them to stay in the UN even if the Study Committee proposal should be adopted, which is probable but not certain at this point. In the meantime Goldberg is seeing Wei this morning to inform him we announcing publicly our support for the Study Committee, reminding him of statement Foreign Minister made to me last week of GRC willingness to cooperate, and telling GRC to sit tight.

5. I sent to you late Sunday evening[4] the text of speech Goldberg made at GA this morning. Both Goldberg and I have cut it back severely to take into account even more fully GRC's sensitivities and to try to avoid any public statement which would give major offense to them.

---

[2] The draft resolution was submitted on November 21. (U.N. Document A/L.500)
[3] Document 210.
[4] November 20.

212. Telegram From the Department of State to the Embassy in the Republic of China[1]

Washington, November 21, 1966, 9:10 p.m.

88823. To Ambassador from Secretary. Refs: A—Taipei's 1483; B—Taipei's 1484.[2]

1. Request you make appointment with President Chiang as soon as possible to discuss with him personally our surprise and dismay at sudden GRC decision to withdraw from UN if Italian study committee resolution passed. While I leave exact language to you, I desire that in speaking to Chiang you cover these points:

2. When I was in Taipei last July, I made it clear to President Chiang that there is no need for the GRC to worry about the US policy of support but that it should join with us in focusing on contingency tactics should serious danger arise that might threaten the position of the GRC in 21st General Assembly. Until recently we had reason to hope that this danger would not arise and that need for new tactics would be avoided, at least this year. Unfortunately, early this month a decision by Government of Canada to embark on drastic new initiative on the Chinese representation question suddenly endangered our common position in GA. The Under Secretary fully reviewed the situation with Ambassador Chow November 8 and told him that we had as a result been required to support tactic of a study committee resolution phrased in such a way as not to prejudice the outcome of the committee's work. I later personally explained reasons we felt these tactics necessary to both Ambassador Chow and FM Wei. Wei and other GRC reps have subsequently indicated to me willingness to go along with simple study committee resolution to head off the Canadians.

3. The principal reason that we have told Italians and others that we would support non-prejudicial study committee resolution is to keep ROC in the UN and prevent the passage of any resolution such as that sponsored by Albania.[3] We were and are convinced that without this tactical change there would be a further erosion of support for US/GRC position on both Important Question and Albanian resolution. In our minds, the supreme objective is to assure that the Important Question

---

[1] Source: Department of State, Central Files, UN 6 CHICOM. Secret; Immediate; Exdis. Drafted by Bennett; cleared by Sisco, Bundy, and Meeker; and approved and initialed by Rusk. Repeated to USUN and Tokyo.

[2] See Document 210 and footnote 2 thereto.

[3] On November 16, 11 countries including Albania submitted a draft resolution recognizing representatives of the People's Republic of China as the only lawful representatives of China to the United Nations and expelling representatives of Chiang Kai-shek. (U.N. Document A/L.496)

passes and the Albanian resolution is defeated. After having fended off an Italian initiative last year only with difficulty, we faced this year the Canadian initiative and restiveness on the part of Belgium, Chile, Italy and others. Our support for study committee resolution was to prevent support building up for Canadian resolution. Our tactic was designed to cut the ground from under the Canadian resolution, which represented a new danger this year.

4. I am sure that Ambassador Chow and FM Wei have reported to you our vigorous efforts to divert the Canadians from introducing resolution calling for one China and one Taiwan and for seating of Peiping in the Security Council. We believe our efforts are succeeding. We have also sought to eliminate from draft resolution sponsored by Italy and others references prejudicing GRC interests. Here we have succeeded.

5. Study committee resolution which has now been submitted by Italy and others does not prejudge the outcome and does not undermine GRC's basic position. I told FM Wei that we would not lobby for study committee resolution, although we will vote for it, and that we would strongly oppose a resolution like the one contemplated by Canada. This continues to be US position. There is, of course, no reason why GRC should not make its opposition to these proposals known in New York and we would understand if it did. But we ask most earnestly that GRC not take rash step of withdrawing from the UN if the study committee resolution passed. The Soviet and pro-Chinese Communist bloc will oppose the study committee resolution and Peking will refuse to cooperate with any such committee, so long as the Republic of China remains in the UN. But if the Republic of China withdraws from the UN, both Peking and its supporters will seize this opportunity to move into the vacancy. Thus withdrawal from the UN would accomplish the very results sought by the Albanian resolution.

6. Ambassador McConaughy has told me of the change in the GRC's position on the study committee and of your intention to withdraw from UN should the Italian study committee resolution pass. I am surprised and dismayed at this. You will have given Peking a major victory which would enable them to pose as the sole representative of China in the eyes of the world. Withdrawal from UN would deprive GRC of international understanding and support on which it must depend in working toward fulfillment of its own basic policies. It would deal a body blow to effectiveness of UN and make position of US and GRC allies in Asia vastly more difficult. It would encourage Peking's militancy at very time when important decisions with respect to Viet-Nam and future thrust of Peking's policies may be in balance. GRC withdrawal from the UN would in short only help our enemies.

7. I would be misleading you if I failed to make clear in advance that the US would be most deeply disturbed by a radical action on your

part which would have such far reaching consequences for the US as well as the ROC.

8.   FYI: We do not wish you to raise the matter of a veto in the Security Council. If President Chiang asks about our stand, you should respond there has been no change in our previous assurances. End FYI.

Rusk

---

213.   **Telegram From the Embassy in the Republic of China to the Department of State**[1]

Taipei, November 23, 1966, 1515Z.

1515. ChiRep. Ref: State 88823.[2]

1.   Herewith report of two-hour conversation with President Chiang four to six p.m. Nov 23. DCM Hummel accompanied me and on Chinese side were Madame Chiang, acting FonMin Shen, and interpreter Frederick Ch'ien. Conversation was relaxed and friendly throughout, even during Gimo's most pointed remarks about US policy. Location was Gimo's residence, not office, high tea was served, and absence of other top GRC officials who usually sit in on important conversations (Vice President, Secretary General, Chiang Ching-kuo) made for unusually intimate atmosphere.

2.   After brief discussion of Eugene Black's recent visit, for which Gimo expressed appreciation, I said that as GRC aware, we are now at very critical stage of ChiRep tactics in UN. Because of the possibility of divergence of views between our governments, Secretary Rusk had asked me to deliver a somewhat extended message, containing an explanation of where we now stand, how we got there, and our views of the next steps that need to be taken. I said I had been in close touch with FonMin Wei and acting FonMin Shen and we have had very helpful dialogues. My request to see Gimo therefore not any reflection on Embassy's excellent relations with MOFA. However at this critical stage we felt it

---

[1] Source: Department of State, Central Files, UN 6 CHICOM. Secret; Immediate; Exdis. Received at 11:53 a.m. Repeated to USUN. Passed to the White House.

[2] Document 212.

best to convey USG views directly to President Chiang. I said I had made an outline of points Secretary wished me to convey, as well as my own views, and I proposed to make six major points.

   a. The history of the tactical maneuvers we have undertaken since Secretary's visit to Taipei in July, in order to maintain the position of the GRC.
   b. The reasons for our reluctant acquiescence in a simple type of study committee resolution.
   c. A summary of US efforts to dissuade the Canadians, and since those efforts failed, to block the prejudicial Canadian resolution.
   d. Our position on the Italian Study Committee resolution and our attitude toward the GRC reaction to that resolution.
   e. The adverse consequences we see if the GRC decides to withdraw from the UN if that resolution is passed.
   f. The effects on the US of a GRC withdrawal from the UN.

3. I then expanded on these points one by one, saying first that when Secretary Rusk was here in July he had assured President Chiang and others that GRC had no reason to worry about US support for Chinese position in UN. These assurances are still good today. Secretary had also said at that time US and GRC should concert their efforts closely on possible contingency tactics in case GRC position should be threatened in the UN. Until early November it seemed that the Canadians, in spite of their previous intimations that they were thinking of new moves, would adhere to past position. Then suddenly they told us they would introduce a new draft resolution, very objectionable to us, setting up a study committee and pre-judging the results of that committee's deliberations in a preamble that in effect called for one China and one Taiwan. I said everything we have done since then in this study committee situation has been directed at stopping this very destructive resolution. I recalled that Under Secretary Katzenbach on Nov 8 had explained to Ambassador Chow reason why we felt obliged to go along with some kind of non-prejudicial study committee resolution in order to maintain votes on Albanian resolution. It had been our policy from the beginning, and it remained imperative, that we defeat that Communist resolution. Secretary Rusk had also explained to FonMin Wei and Ambassadors Chow and Liu on Nov 15 that we were far from enthusiastic about any study committee but that if victory were to be assured on the two most important resolutions, some kind of study committee resolution would have to be introduced. I reminded Gimo that Secretary Rusk had understood from FonMin Wei that GRC would stand firm and would be able to go along with a simple form of study committee, in order assist in preventing Canada's harmful resolution from passing.

4. I said that our reasoning in this started from the premise that it was absolutely essential to keep GRC in UN. I said we had to take into account a trend of opinion among many nations in the UN that has been

adverse to GRC interests in recent years and months, both among some ill-informed small new nations and also among some old established UN members who should know better. I said this trend was continuing, although it was illogical in view of present turmoil on mainland, excesses of Red Guards, and militant actions and statements from Peiping. In the face of this trend, and of Canadian initiative, USG no longer had power to muster a safe majority against Albanian resolution.

5. I said it was necessary, above all, to pass important question and defeat Albanian resolutions and that until destructive Canadian action we thought that there was probably a definite favorable, though narrow margin on both. After the Canadians began their maneuvering, several countries we had relied on hinted they might not be able to support US against Albanian resolution if no study committee resolution could be introduced. In order to assure enough votes on the major issues some new gesture was needed, although it should not, of course, undermine any vital GRC interest. I said we had to face the fact that we needed the cooperation of other countries in order to defeat the very bad Canadian resolution, and we have so far been successful in obtaining this cooperation. Canada has not yet introduced any counter-proposal. I emphasized that we now are reasonably confident that the order of voting will be first, important question, second the Albanian, and then a study committee. If we can get favorable votes on the first two, we will have definite protection for ourselves and for the GRC, and if we achieve this it will be because of the small concession we made in acquiescing in but not pushing, a simple study committee resolution. We had worked hard and successfully to assure that nothing in favor of two Chinas appears in the Italian resolution and we had been able to prevent other prejudicial language.

6. I said although we had failed to dissuade Canada from trying to pursue its course, we had effectively prevented other countries (Italy, Belgium, Chile) from going along with the Canadians. We believe that the simple study committee resolution now before the UN does not prejudge the issue and does not undermine any major GRC interests. We do not like it and we know that it is an annoyance to the GRC. However, we believe that all of us should be prepared to suffer some minor annoyances in order to maintain vital interests, and particularly in light of the critical situation in the Far East. We understand and sympathize with the GRC's strong views against any new procedure, and we appreciate that GRC feels it must oppose the study committee.

7. Gimo interrupted at this point with assertion that any study committee resolution implies the existence of two Chinas. He said if study committee resolution is passed this can mean nothing other than that there are two Chinas to be considered.

8. I repeated we understood that GRC must oppose any study committee and that there would be no problem caused between us by GRC efforts to defeat it. I said we are not going to lobby for it ourselves and we will not be sorry if it is defeated. However, I said, in order to win on the most important issues, which are in the first two resolutions, we were forced to commit ourselves passively to support a study committee. Secretary Rusk and I wish earnestly to appeal to you not to take your government out of the UN if study committee passes. In our view such a step would be rash and its consequences would be very adverse to all of us. Their full magnitude would perhaps not be apparent at first but must be carefully considered. I said we know Communist countries will oppose the study committee and Peiping can be counted on to object strongly. We are confident that Peiping will not cooperate with any study committee so long as the GRC remains in the UN and for this reason we believe that the formation of such a committee should be without serious risk to GRC. However, if GRC is out of UN, Peiping will move into the vacant China seat, if not this year then next year. Therefore in our view the departure of the GRC would have the same deeply hurtful effect as the passage of the Albanian resolution.

9. Secretary Rusk, I said, had received my report of my talk with Acting FonMin Shen November 21. He was surprised and dismayed at the statement that GRC would withdraw if study committee passed. Secretary Rusk believes that this would constitute a major victory for the Chinese Communists who would be able to pose as the sole representative of China. We believe that some naive countries would be impressed by ChiCom gain and would believe that ChiCom influence has been greatly increased. The departure of GRC from UN would inevitably tend to deprive it of the support, understanding, communication, and assistance which it has received from many nations and which it needs for fulfillment of its policies. The Secretary believes such a step would deal a body blow to the UN, and would cause severe problems for the US and for the Asian allies of US and GRC. It could be expected to encourage the most militant tendencies of the Chinese Communists and would come at a most inopportune time in a critical stage of the Vietnam war, when ChiCom policy decisions are believed to be hanging in the balance. In short, we are convinced that GRC withdrawal would have effect of helping our enemies and hurting us and our allies.

10. Finally, our own concern would be profound if GRC took this step which would have far-reaching adverse consequences for the US as well as for GRC.

11. I said these are Secretary's views and he of course wants to have views of GRC. I suggested Gimo might wish to think over these points and give me his reaction later. I expressed hope that we could continue

dialogue between US and GRC, concert our views, and work out a joint approach.

12. I then gave my own hope that after this difficult year in UN we might see a turn for the better. There might be more nations who would experience a revulsion against current Peiping statements and actions. I noted that Soviets were lukewarm in supporting ChiComs in UN this year and speculated that countries like Indonesia and Ghana might be able to come all the way over to our side on this issue next year. I said it is also conceivable ChiComs might take some extremely rash action that would destroy the support they presently receive from various other countries. Important thing is to get through this present year and to stand fast on the basic requirement. I said "If you can stand with us, we can win through".

Gimo said GRC had already given serious consideration to most of these points, but he thanked me for outlining them clearly. He said GRC has thought of UN as something precious, and felt the obligations and anxieties of a founding member. He said that for this reason if GRC had to make any decision damaging to UN it would be only after careful consideration of consequences. GRC does not start only today in concern for and efforts to safeguard principles and Charter of UN; it started long ago. These efforts have been not only for the UN itself, or for GRC, but for the US also, and GRC will always be mindful of sacrifices in men and treasure made by US in WWII. I said USG also treasures its long and close association with GRC in good times and in bad.

Gimo said he fully understood what I had said, and that he appreciated sincerity of Secretary's tactical efforts in the difficult problems of the UN. He said he was aware of the hard work done by USG in achieving present text of Italian resolution, and he understood the reasons for the US policy of passive acquiescence in a study committee. However, he said, whether the resolution passes or not is something the US can arrange.

I denied this emphatically, saying I wished it were true but that we simply do not have the power to ensure its defeat.

Gimo in characteristic fashion shrugged this off, saying that we are good friends, and so should not argue. Fact remains, he said, that "passive support" is in fact support, and that although USG says it is not lobbying, passive support has the same effect, as he had just seen a news report that after Amb. Johnson saw Shiina in Tokyo, the Japanese announced they would vote in favor of a study committee. This, he said, looked like lobbying to him.

I said Amb. Johnson had not asked for Japanese support of study committee but Gimo remained unconvinced, saying that although he had no report of substance of conversation he believed the events were more than coincidental.

Gimo said that while he understood what USG had tried to do to safeguard GRC position, to Chinese people in Taiwan, on mainland, and overseas, it will appear that a study committee if established shatters the GRC position, and therefore the GRC position with Chinese people cannot be safeguarded in this manner. He said it was up to the US to decide whether study committee resolution should pass or not. First two resolutions could be won, and USG has announced it will give passive support to the third. It is still in the realm of possibility, he said, for USG to maneuver to defeat the study committee and thus to reassure the GRC of the friendship and motives of the US.

I reiterated that we do not have the capability to defeat resolution, and that GRC cooperation and understanding is very important to us. I said that I thought that our friends in UN would understand quite well what we had to do in order to prevent serious reverse, and would understand we had simply chosen the lesser of evils, and had not modified our policy of full support for GRC.

Gimo said he and I were old friends, and we did not need to pursue this further, since we understood each other. He recalled that Secretary in July had emphasized the importance of upholding the UN and the UN Charter. He said the GRC was well aware of its obligations to uphold these fundamentals, and that he knew the US to be a major upholder to them. He said GRC believed that any damage to position of GRC in UN constituted damage to UN Charter and ideals because of GRC status as founding member. He said he had told Secretary that as long as any formula does not damage the legitimate position of GRC or of UN Charter, GRC will go along, but if anything damages these, GRC cannot go along.

I said we agreed with these principles, and with the importance of the Charter. I pointed out that the study committee resolution contains the phrase "in keeping with the principles and purposes of the Charter", and that we believed this to be a safeguard for the GRC. I said USG certainly did not wish to harm the interests of the GRC, and that we did not believe the resolution had that effect.

Gimo said he fully understood USG goodwill and good intentions having this inserted in the resolution as a safeguard. However he wanted to make two points: (a) the US should not take an action that would cause Chinese people everywhere to have doubt of US basic policy, or to think US has shattered the position of the GRC or has given up the GRC. He urged that US think of these effects.

I said we agreed it was very important not to mislead anyone as to our intentions, and not to cause any Chinese to misunderstand us or to believe US was abandoning GRC, since this was not the case.

Gimo expressed hope that US course would be in accordance with this idea. He went on to his second point, (b), saying that to any ordinary Chinese the passage of a study committee was tantamount to a 2-Chinas formula. Even if the first two resolutions were to pass safely, assuring one more year for the GRC, it would be widely understood that next year or the year after the ChiComs would come in. He said that rather than be expelled in disgrace later, GRC would do better to leave now. He said that if the study committee resolution is adopted, then to the general public it would mean that the US has changed to a 2-China policy, and that US is ready to give up the GRC. Even if the GRC were willing to endure for the sake of the UN and the US, the Chinese people would not stand for a government of that sort.

Gimo said that USG should understand that GRC has been in a very awkward position for a long time, particularly since the Yalta conference when GRC gave acquiescence to a damaging fait accompli, brought about without any GRC consultation or knowledge. GRC had suffered the loss of Outer Mongolia, of Manchuria, and ultimately the mainland of China. Chinese have had many bitter lessons, and now if in the face of a study committee, GRC stays in the UN the Chinese people will be disillusioned with Chinese Government as well (*Comment:* presumably as well as with GRC's allies). He said GRC can give up anything, and had even lost the mainland, but could not give up its legal position. After all, he said, "My government and to some extent myself must bear a heavy historical responsibility. If GRC stays in UN there would be no way to answer our responsibilities to our history, our people, and ourselves". He said he did not intend to force his ideas upon USG, but it was clear that GRC could not acquiesce in seeing UN principles and UN Charter being destroyed, as well as destruction of GRC position. He said he had appreciated close US cooperation in the past decade or so and that he wished once again to thank USG for its assistance in maintaining GRC in Taiwan. He said he was not trying to force us into any course and would try to refrain from doing damage to US. He recalled that GRC had for many years kept US interests closely in mind. He said even if GRC were not in UN, GRC would be willing to cooperate fully with USG to defeat ChiComs. He said he believed US still had possibility of maneuvering to keep Chinese Communists out of UN even if GRC were not in, and therefore he believed GRC would not be doing damage to US interests.

I expressed appreciation for his generous sentiments in regard to past US assistance and cooperation. I said I wondered if some way could not be found to make clear to Chinese people everywhere that a study committee does not change policy of US or position of GRC. I said perhaps the committee would come up next year with a favorable recommendation and even if this were not the case, we should not take it for granted that there must be a disastrous result. I said I believed this could be explained so as not to damage GRC standing.

Gimo said it would be almost impossible to explain this. He repeated that US tactics in the UN were of course up to the US and that

GRC without interfering would keep in close contact to discuss such tactics. However, he said, by far the best tactic would be the defeat of the study committee.

I said I would like to make a military analogy. I believed we were engaged in a very important central battle on the first two resolutions in the UN. The study committee question, while important, was somewhere off on one flank. The major cause, on the main front, was gravely in doubt, and in order to be sure of winning there we have had to take a little strength from the non-vital flank in order to bolster the main front. We have been forced to do this in order to insure against an unacceptable defeat. We earnestly hope that none of our allies would be so upset by the position on the flank that they would desert the entire battlefield.

Gimo said he understood the analogy and agreed that the issues as far as US was concerned were tactical. GRC would cooperate with allies as long as tactics were not harmful to GRC principles.

I said I also hoped for continued cooperation. I warned that it was not likely that in event of withdrawal from UN, GRC position could be maintained and protected, as Gimo seemed to think. I said I was not prepared to go into detail on consequences, magnitude could not now be predicted, but adverse effects would surely be more far-reaching than President apparently assumed.

Gimo again said that even if GRC not in UN, USG could find ways to keep ChiComs out. He observed that anyway GRC had caused many problems for UN.

I said GRC presence in UN had been invaluable in many ways. I recalled that study committee proposal in 1950 had come to nothing, and hoped that this time it could be sidetracked also.

Gimo said that things had changed greatly since 1950 and that GRC had made careful study of the problem. He closed the conversation by saying that we must try not to let this present serious issue prevent our cooperation on other issues.

Comment: Gimo gives every evidence of having thought his course through, and being determined to proceed, in sorrow rather than in anger. There are two imponderables, however: (a) precise nature and finality of walkout, and (b) possibility, rather remote, that senior GRC officials will be willing and able to persuade Gimo to change his mind. At this point I am bearish on the prospect for a reversal of decision, but not inclined to consider it entirely hopeless.

McConaughy

214.   Circular Telegram From the Department of State to Certain Posts[1]

Washington, November 23, 1966, 8:40 p.m.

90629. Subj: ChiRep. Ref: Depcirtel 88129.[2]

1. Study Committee res submitted this year by Italians and others offers opportunity to improve votes in favor IQ res and against Albanian res since this new proposition may appeal to some countries which have in past either voted affirmatively or abstained on Albanian res in absence other alternatives before Assembly. Dept considers it important that we exploit this opportunity to maximum extent that is appropriate.

2. Apart from local problems there is especially delicate aspect of any representations which posts may make to host govts. We have informed GRC that while we will vote for study committee res, we will not lobby for it. GRC is strongly opposed to proposal, and any discussions which posts undertake must in no way appear to host govts as direct or indirect effort to influence them toward favorable vote on study committee res. Our purpose is strictly limited to maximizing margin of votes in favor of IQ res and against Albanian res, in order to show that GA is opposed to extremist solutions.

3. Department strongly recommends, unless objection perceived, that representations be made urgently and at high level. Arguments given below may be drawn on selectively depending on attitude of host governments. While we desire maximum number of affirmative votes for IQ res and negative votes for Albanian res, posts authorized as final fallback in both instances to suggest possibility of abstention or absence if effect would be net improvement from our viewpoint.

4. Posts requested to report priority results of representations to Dept repeating info for USUN.

5. Following are suggested arguments:

(a) Host govt has in past supported (or abstained on) Albanian res because it favored admission of ChiComs and not because it wished to expel GRC. USG has made it clear that it has not and will not lobby for study committee res, but availability this res provides host government

---

[1] Source: Department of State, Central Files, UN 6 CHICOM. Confidential; Priority. Drafted by Gleysteen; cleared by Berger and by the advisers for United Nations affairs in NEA, ARA, AF, and EUR; and approved by Sisco. Sent to 30 Embassies and repeated to Kingston, Port-of-Spain, Santiago, Taipei, and USUN.
[2] Circular telegram 88129, November 19, sent to 79 Embassies, stated that the United States would support the study committee resolution but would not lobby for it; it instructed the recipient Embassies to explain to their host governments that the principal U.S. aim was to ensure reaffirmation of the important question resolution and defeat of the Albanian resolution. (Ibid.)

with an alternative that avoids extreme of Albanian res which would produce irrevocable decision to expel GRC contrary to host govt's policy. Thus we urge host govt not support (or abstain on) Albanian res.

(b) Where appropriate, also urge for same reasons that host govt reexamine its vote on important question res. Charter explicitly provides that important question must be decided by a two-thirds majority. Change in representation of China obviously important question. Aside from Charter provisions, however, there is also additional political consideration that failure to uphold important question procedure could at some future time result in expulsion of GRC, a situation both USG and host govt wish to avoid.

Rusk

---

215. Telegram From the Embassy in the Republic of China to the Department of State[1]

Taipei, November 24, 1966.

1517. For Assistant Secretary Bundy.

1. I want you to know of some of the GRC atmospherics here on matters other than UN items, which may or may not be further reflections of stiffening overall GRC mood. Minister Chiang Ching-kuo has been giving [less than 1 line of source text not declassified] considerable static since he was informed of USIB's wish to phase out [less than 1 line of source text not declassified] program. In addition to adverse GRC [less than 1 line of source text not declassified] reactions which you know about in general, GRC intel officials have suddenly cancelled a pre-existing joint maritime program, and Minister Chiang has been unavailable to [less than 1 line of source text not declassified] in the last three–four weeks, although topics to be discussed (including next ChiCom detonation) are of direct and particular interest to him.

2. We do not yet know whether above static is an integral part of overall starchiness we are now experiencing from President Chiang, or is

---

[1] Source: Department of State, Central Files, POL CHINAT–US. Secret; Priority; Limdis; Roger Channel. Received at 11:44 a.m. No time of transmission appears on the source text.

essentially Chiang Ching-kuo-inspired pressures on [*less than 1 line of source text not declassified*] in response [*less than 1 line of source text not declassified*] news and in possible attempt force some modification of this U.S. intent. [*less than 1 line of source text not declassified*] has not yet received an indication of Chiang Ching-kuo's reactions to the recently delivered formal written notification and exploration of [*less than 1 line of source text not declassified*] termination. Presumably when [*less than 1 line of source text not declassified*] does get such indication, and when other returns are in, we will know more about cause and effect as between the overall and the specific. A hopeful note is indication received 23 November [*less than 1 line of source text not declassified*] that GRC has consented resume special operations.

3. This cable has been prepared with the participation and concurrence [*less than 1 line of source text not declassified*].

McConaughy

216. Memorandum of Conversation[1]

Washington, November 25, 1966.

SUBJECT

Secretary's Conversation with Canadian Foreign Minister Martin: ChiRep

PARTICIPANTS

US Side	Canadian Side
The Secretary	Foreign Minister Martin
Walter J. Stoessel, Jr., Dep. Asst. Sec., EUR	Yvon Beaulne, Minister

Referring to the Canadian proposal on Chinese representation, the Secretary said he had one action recommendation to make to the Foreign Minister. The Secretary noted that some of our Allies in the Far East who rely on us have the feeling that Canada would never have put forward its proposal without consultation and agreement with the United States.

---

[1] Source: Department of State, Central Files, UN 6 CHICOM. Secret; Exdis. Drafted by Stoessel and approved in S on December 6. The source text is "Part 1 of 10 parts." The meeting was held in Secretary Rusk's dining room at the Department of State.

The Secretary hoped that Canadian Ambassadors in Taiwan, Korea, Japan, the Philippines, Australia and Thailand would make clear to their host governments that this was not the case. It was urgent that this should be done as soon as possible and before November 28, if feasible.

Martin said that Taiwan certainly knew the true situation on this matter since there had already been a discussion on the subject between Taiwan representatives and the Canadians. He would undertake to instruct other Canadian Ambassadors in the countries mentioned by the Secretary to clarify the situation to the host governments.

The Secretary said he had heard a news report that the question of Communist China's entry into the Security Council might come up in January. He did not know exactly how this might arise; whether on an issue of credentials or otherwise, but in any case he wanted the Foreign Minister to know that we would vote against. We would expect that our vote in this sense would be considered as a veto; if not—if somehow the matter were considered as a procedural one—this would be intolerable for the United States. We will not be over-run on this issue. Martin said he did not see how Communist China could be considered for membership in the Security Council unless it were a member of the UN organization, but in any case he was sure that the US vote against would be regarded as a veto.

With regard to the Canadian proposal on ChiRep, Martin commented that he had told his people there were some things the Canadians had to do which Dean Rusk would not like, but nevertheless Rusk had never threatened him.

The Secretary said that Mr. Martin had to do what he considered necessary, but it was clear that the Canadian move on ChiRep had been made without the concurrence of the United States, the United Kingdom, and the USSR, Australia and even Communist China. No one went along with it.

Martin replied that the UK wanted the Canadians to go even further than they had gone. Nevertheless he was sure that what Canada had done was right and that the US would agree to this in due course.

The Secretary said that perhaps Martin had made his point with the Canadian press—*The Toronto Globe*—but internationally the move had not been accepted.

Martin replied that *The Toronto Globe* actually did not like the Canadian proposal on ChiRep, although its view on diplomatic recognition of China was another matter. In any event, he was sure that Canada had been right. He did not feel it was useful to pursue the discussion of this subject at this time, but perhaps at some later date they could talk with the Secretary about it when things had cooled off somewhat.

On another aspect of Chinese representation, Martin noted that the Indian Ambassador to the UN was convinced that there would be no progress concerning Communist China's entry into the UN until Communist China and the United States started talking and worked out an arrangement. The UN could do nothing. The Secretary noted that we have done more talking directly with the Chinese Communists than any other member of the UN with the possible exception of the Soviet Union.

Commenting on his visit to Italy, Martin said that all of his discussions with Italian officials had been on Chinese representation. He had found Moro especially concerned to do nothing which would go counter to US views on the subject. Martin also had had a most interesting talk with Nenni. Nenni had said that he personally would like to go farther than the study resolution but he doubted the advisability of doing so, given the opposition of the United States. Nenni had noted that politics was the art of the possible and he advised against seeking more than the study resolution at this time.

217. Telegram From the White House Situation Room to President Johnson at the LBJ Ranch, in Texas[1]

Washington, November 26, 1966, 1631Z.

CAP 661063. For the President from Secretary Rusk.

1. As you know, Chiang Kai-shek has formally told us that he would withdraw immediately from the UN if the Italian draft study committee resolution passed. The vote on this may come as early as Monday night, so that any further action we take must be done at once.

2. We gave Ambassador McConaughy all the arguments, and he has laid them out brilliantly to the Gimo, but without apparently budging him. McConaughy has also been hitting every senior Chinese official he can reach. Finally, I have enlisted Walter Judd to write a personal message to the Gimo. However, it seems to me clear that the matter requires a personal message by you, in view of the disastrous effect of such a withdrawal and the very important impact that your personal intervention might have.

3. I have therefore drafted a fairly short and fundamental letter for your approval.[2] It stresses particularly holding off on any action until I

---

[1] Source: Johnson Library, National Security File, Country File, China, Vol. VII. Secret.

[2] A note from Bromley Smith to Rostow, attached to the source text, states that the President cleared the short version of the letter to Chiang and that the Rusk message to the Foreign Minister was also sent.

can visit Taipei on my forthcoming trip, probably between December 5 and December 7 (well after the UN vote).

4. At same time, I have prepared a longer message from myself to the Chinese Foreign Minister in New York. It is designed to supplement your letter by repeating the more technical arguments. If, however, upon seeing the two messages together, you thought it desirable to transfer some or all of the arguments in the second draft letter to your own letter, this could readily be done.

5. I hope that you can give me your reaction so as to permit dispatch of both letters as soon as possible. This would permit the Gimo to reflect before his final decision—which as of now appears to be for withdrawal.

Attachment

1. Please deliver urgently to President Chiang following message from President Johnson:

2. "Dear Mr. President: Ambassador McConaughy has given me a full report on his recent conversation with you about our common problem in the United Nations. I appreciate your courtesy in explaining to him so fully the Republic of China's position on the question of a General Assembly resolution calling for a study committee to consider the question of Chinese representation. In candor I must say that I was profoundly concerned to learn that your government is considering withdrawal from the United Nations should the General Assembly pass the Italian-sponsored resolution now before it. We cannot at this point predict whether the resolution will pass. But, even if it should, your withdrawal from the United Nations would in my opinion be a tragedy for both our countries. Its consequences would be far-reaching and fraught with dangers, not only for China but for the free world position in Asia.

3. "I have asked Secretary of State Rusk to make himself ready to visit Taipei to consult with you about problems of mutual concern, including especially the situation in the United Nations, when he is in Asia early next month. I hope you will be able to receive him at that time and that you will defer any final decision involving an irrevocable step on your part until you and he have had an opportunity to review the situation fully. Secretary Rusk will be prepared to go over with you in fullest detail the entire background of this matter, including our strenuous efforts over the years to maintain support in the United Nations for our traditional position on Chinese representation.

4. "I am writing you in these frank terms because of the high value I attach to your friendship and because the Republic of China is one of the

United States closest and most trusted allies. Continuing close cooperation between our governments is vital to freedom's cause in Asia; and, in
the struggle for freedom, political actions are often as important as those
fought on the field of battle. Your standing in history as one of the great
leaders of the Chinese people, already secure, will gain added luster by
your indomitable defense of your country's rights in the United Nations.
Sincerely yours, Lyndon B. Johnson."

Please deliver following personal letter to GRC Foreign Minister:

Begin text

Dear Mr. Minister:

1. As you undoubtedly know, Ambassador McConaughy has
talked at length with your President about the position of your government in connection with the Italian resolution for a study committee.
Although this conversation covered most of the critical matters, I am
sending you this personal letter to underscore certain points. At the same
time, President Johnson is sending a personal and separate letter to your
President.

2. First of all, let me assure you again that the United States decision
to vote for a non-prejudicial study committee resolution was taken only
after the most careful and thoroughgoing deliberation. As you know, we
have maintained closest consultations with the GRC in Taipei, Washington and New York from the time earlier in the year when I and other officials discussed with your government the danger which might develop
at the UNGA this autumn and the possible need for new tactics. We have
had only one objective in view: to preserve the position of the Republic of
China in the United Nations.

3. In early November, Canada, without prior consultation and
despite our strongest protests, told us that it would introduce a resolution with "one-China-one-Taiwan" overtones and calling for the seating
of Peiping in the Security Council. The situation in the General Assembly
was made even more perilous by the restiveness on the question shown
by Italy, Belgium and Chile. In this sudden emergency we had no choice
but to fall back on the tactic of a study committee in an effort to head off
Canada's dangerous initiative, which if unchecked could have lost us
their support and the support of others on the important question and
against the Albanian resolution. This step has now succeeded in
forestalling the threatened Canadian move. I hope that it will also enable
us to achieve a better vote than last year on the important question resolution and against the Albanian resolution.

4. I am sure you understand that in taking this step the United
States is in no way altering its policy of firm support of the Republic of
China. We remain determined to oppose with the full strength and influence of the United States all attempts to expel the Republic of China from
the United Nations and to seat the Communists.

5.   We have a close treaty bond with the Republic of China which is a solemn obligation. China and the United States have a history of particularly close friendship and alliance extending over many years. The cooperation and collaboration between us has had many remarkable accomplishments and successes and I am sure there will be many more. In view of this long and intimate association between our countries, I am confident that our position in this matter enjoys your understanding and that of your President.

6.   Your President has suggested to Ambassador McConaughy that it might still be possible for the United States to maneuver to defeat the Italian resolution. We have told several governments who have asked us that we would not object if they were to vote against it. We have not urged any government to vote for it. As I told you last week, the United States would in fact be content if the Italian proposal were to fail, and we entirely understand your government's efforts to defeat it. We cannot go beyond this because our vote for the Italian resolution was the price we had to pay for critically needed support on the important question and Albanian resolutions.

7.   In talking to Ambassador McConaughy, your President observed that to the public the study committee resolution appears tantamount to a two-Chinas formula. This is not, however, the view of the United States. Our representatives have exerted themselves with success to assure that no language is incorporated in the study committee resolution which prejudges the outcome of the study. The resolution's operative paragraph stipulates that the committee's findings be "in keeping with the principles and purposes of the Charter." This stipulation in our view was essential as a safeguard of the GRC position. There is moreover no means of foretelling at this time whether the committee will in fact ultimately arrive at any agreed conclusions; nor, if reached, what those conclusions might be; nor what action the General Assembly might take on them. Why leave the field of battle and thus precipitate the very situation we both have striven so long and successfully to prevent when the outcome has yet to be determined? This is the time to stay and fight and not withdraw.

8.   There is one point your President made to Ambassador McConaughy which I want particularly to mention. This is the suggestion that the United States could still find means to prevent the Chinese Communists from entering the United Nations even if the Republic of China were to withdraw. If you should withdraw, we believe the voting situation would change drastically and that Peiping would be seated. Your withdrawal from the United Nations would bring about exactly what the supporters of the Albanian resolution desire.

9.   Representatives from Communist China could with relative ease appear in the General Assembly and ask that their credentials be accepted as the only representatives from China. If you had withdrawn

from the UN, it seems to us a foregone conclusion that the Assembly would accept such credentials. As to the Security Council, I reaffirmed our position to your President in 1964. That position stands. However, the Security Council would have to act independently on credentials of any representative seeking accreditation there. If your representatives had left the UN, there would be an overwhelming sentiment to accept representatives from Peiping, and the possibility of a veto would be far less relevant than in case of a contest between competing representatives, and indeed would in all probability no longer exist.

10. I believe the consequences of a withdrawal from the United Nations by the Republic of China would be extremely serious for both our countries. By opening the United Nations door to Peiping, the Communists would be given an important victory at no cost to themselves—and at a time when the Communist forces on the mainland of China are in deep disarray. The encouragement this victory would give to the Communists could have incalculable consequences for the struggle for freedom we are now waging in Viet-nam. It would deal a blow to the effectiveness of the United Nations, and it would make more difficult the position of our countries' friends and allies in Asia.

11. Another consequence, which I consider just as serious, is the irreparable damage that withdrawal from the United Nations would do to the world position of your own government, which for the achievement of its policies must have international understanding and support. GRC withdrawal would confuse the Republic of China's friends abroad and hearten its enemies. This step would come at a moment when the US particularly needs GRC cooperation in the difficult UN situation and would be regarded as a reverse to our common cause.

12. Finally, I would like to leave this thought with you. Communist China's aim is to get the Republic of China out of the UN by one means or other, and establish itself in the UN and in the eyes of the world as the only legitimate government of China. So long as you remain in the UN, as they have repeated again only Thursday, the Communist Chinese will not accept membership. Your presence in the UN, in effect, is the surest guarantee against a Communist China presence.

Sincerely yours,

Dean Rusk

End text.

218.   Telegram From the Embassy in the Republic of China to the Department of State[1]

Taipei, November 28, 1966, 1130Z.

1568. ChiRep. Ref: State 91770 [*91771*].[2]

1. I had forty-five minute conversation with President Chiang at 11 this morning Nov 28 at his residence to deliver Pres Johnson's letter contained reftel. DCM accompanied me, and as before only Mme Chiang, Acting FonMin Shen, and interpreter Frederick Ch'ien were present. Atmosphere was somewhat more relaxed than on my previous call Nov 23 (Taipei 1515).[3]

2. I made same introductory comments about the burden I knew Gimo was carrying, and hoped he had some relaxation over weekend. I said I appreciated his making time to see me on short notice. Gimo said he always took pleasure in seeing me and DCM Hummel.

3. I handed to Gimo original and copies of President Johnson's letter, and interpreter gave immediate verbal rendering, Mme Chiang and Shen reading copies as translation proceeded. Gimo said he had listened carefully, and appreciated the letter.

4. I told Gimo that it seemed likely that Secy Rusk could come to Taipei on evening of Dec 6, staying all following day and leaving about noon Dec 8.

5. Gimo said that of course he welcomed Secretary's visit. He said that insofar as UN problems were concerned, GRC still hoped Italian resolution might not pass and then GRC would need to take no action. The situation would of course be discussed with Secy Rusk. However, he said, he understood that voting in UN will take place this week and if Italian resolution passes, GRC cannot remain silent. The timing is very important. However, he said, referring to the letter from President Johnson, which he considered to be sincere and frank, he would bring the letter to the attention of officials of his govt so that they could consult further on the problem.

6. I asked if dates for Secy's visit were convenient, and Gimo replied that they were.

7. Gimo said that the most important question to study now is how to defeat the Italian resolution. He said that once it has passed the GRC

---

[1] Source: Department of State, Central Files, UN 6 CHICOM. Secret; Immediate; Exdis. Repeated to USUN. Passed to the White House.

[2] Telegram 91771, November 26, transmitted the text of Johnson's message to Chiang. Telegram 91770, November 26, sent to USUN and repeated to Taipei, transmitted the text of Rusk's message to Wei. (Both ibid.) For texts of the messages, see Document 217.

[3] Document 213.

"would have to make its position clear to the world." He hoped this was understood by USG.

8. I replied that I understood what he had told me on this point in this conversation and in previous conversations.

9. Gimo said that of course before he took any action he would have to consult with officers of his govt. He said that he would inform the USG of his govt's decision, would get USG reaction, and would continue consult with us.

10. I said I hoped we could keep in very close contact on this matter, and that I was available at any hour of day or night for any consultations.

11. Gimo repeated that the most important task is to defeat the Italian resolution. He said that he had studied the Secretary's letter to Fon-Min Wei, and that although he fully understood that USG has adopted passive attitude, it is still most important that the resolution be defeated.

12. I said I wished to give a brief résumé of recent developments relative to the pending UN resolutions. I said there had been full exchanges on this in Washington, New York, and elsewhere with GRC officials and with representatives of many countries. I said we had also told US Embassies to make it clear to other govts that we are not lobbying for, pushing, or soliciting votes for the resolution. Our representatives are also making it explicit that we would not object to or hold it against any country wishing to oppose the resolution.

13. I noted that our intention to vote affirmatively on Italian resolution was based on the commitment we were compelled to give in order to obtain the very crucial votes of certain countries that were wavering on the Albanian resolution. We are now bound to honor our word but Gimo could rest assured that our vote is not an enthusiastic one. We believe that our tactical decision has safeguarded from 6 to 8 votes which are essential in order to assure defeat of Albanian proposal. It could be seen that our move would have a successful result.

14. I said we had given careful and sympathetic consideration to the diplomatic note sent to us November 26 asking us not to vote for the Italian proposal.[4] In view of commitment we have already made to other nations in order to assure defeat of the Albanian resolution, we cannot change our vote now. However, I was confident other nations understood our position and clearly realized we are not pressing any other country to vote for the Italian proposal.

15. Gimo asked if US position could be made clear to Japanese Govt. He said similar diplomatic note had also been sent to Japanese Embassy here requesting GOJ abstain. He said that what I had told him of US instructions should be made clear to GOJ and he made a direct request that we accomplish this.

---

[4] Not found.

16. I said I was sure that this had already been done, but would send a special message (see septel) asking that US position be explained once again to GOJ.[5]

17. Gimo expressed his thanks. He said that my approach today, the letter from President Johnson, and Secretary Rusk's letter to FonMin Wei would all be discussed with GRC officials. He said that I would be informed of decision when it is reached.

18. I said we had carefully studied the voting prospects on all three resolutions, and that on the essential ones, which were the important question and the Albanian, we were confident of favorable outcome. We do not yet know, however, what will be the result of voting on Italian proposal. The position of many countries appeared uncertain, and we do not know whether it will be defeated or passed.

19 Gimo repeated that if USG were to support GRC in working on this, Italian resolution could be defeated. He said GRC is fully aware of the very important implications of the Italian resolution and would have to take a position based on GRC's own interests, and also those of US, UN and allies. He said all these interests will be taken into account in GRC deliberations.

20. I said we had been thinking of contingency planning in the event that the Italian resolution were to pass and of appropriate action GRC might take to make its position clear. I said I would like to suggest in rough form some language GRC might wish to consider for use in a declaration in UN in that event, along following lines: "GRC has every confidence that any objective study of ChiRep must have the result of reaffirmation of the status of the GRC as the only qualified, lawful and representative Government of China. Therefore, GRC has nothing to fear from a study of the question, although it is unnecessary. However, in the event of any objectionable recommendation by the study committee, the GRC reserves its full rights to take any action it considers necessary and appropriate under the circumstances." I said it was our belief that such a statement would be dignified, appropriate, and sufficient to safeguard GRC interests and prestige.

21. Gimo replied that my suggestion would be of value for GRC reference and discussion, but Chinese people would never understand if such a statement were made. However, he said, he would have to consult with other govt officials on this as well as other points.

---

[5] McConaughy sent this message in telegram 1565 from Taipei, November 28. Telegram 92145, November 28, conveyed the request to Tokyo, and telegram 3998 from Tokyo, November 29, reported that Ambassador Johnson had spoken to Vice Foreign Minister Shimoda, who stated that he would instruct the Japanese Ambassador in Taipei to make it clear to the GRC that the U.S. Government had never asked the Japanese Government to support the Italian resolution. (All in Department of State, Central Files, UN 6 CHICOM)

22. I said I hoped the public would be enabled to understand the US position. I noted that Chinese press seems to be giving the erroneous impression that USG has been proceeding in the direction of a "two-Chinas" policy in the UN. This could be damaging to our joint interests if it should become widespread. I hoped the impression could be corrected.

23. Gimo assured me he would do what could be done to see that Chinese people understood and do not get wrong impression of US intentions. However, the Chinese people would not understand if GRC were to take any action that does not conform to its present foreign policies. He said he would carefully consider this matter. Alloted time for interview was clearly up at this point.

24. As we left Presidential residence, I told Acting FonMin Shen that I had a few additional points I wished to make and we adjourned to Shen's office for further discussion.

25. I told Shen that I wished to reaffirm the contingency assurance given by Secretary Rusk in 1964 that USG intended veto any attempt at ChiCom admission to Security Council, if veto would be effective. However, if the GRC had already left the UN, our parliamentary position in trying to keep Chinese Communists out would be vastly more difficult. We have grave doubt that veto in the Security Council would be effective under those circumstances. Most Security Council members would probably think that in absence of GRC from UN, filling of vacant China seat would be purely procedural matter of credentials, and that veto would be inapplicable on those grounds. I told Shen GRC should not assume that it would be possible to keep ChiComs out of UN if GRC withdrew. We anticipated that once GRC left, ChiComs would have relatively easy sailing. If GRC stayed firmly in UN, however, chances of keeping ChiComs out would be very good. GRC should be under no delusion that walkout could be only a temporary maneuver. Both from the viewpoint of psychological effect on vote of countries that are already wavering, and in terms of parliamentary procedures open to the opposition, walkout would likely be final, however GRC intended.

26. I noted that recent ChiCom public statements reveal a somewhat softer position on conditions for ChiCom entry into UN. I referred to November 25 column in *Peoples Daily*, signed "Observer" which strongly attacked Canadian proposition but which omitted any reference to the preposterous conditions that ChiComs laid down last year as prerequisites to their entry into UN. This article also carefully avoided usual intemperate language which might alienate the uncommitted. It is possible that ChiComs are now actively interested in obtaining UN entry. In any event, it is evident to us that there would be great rejoicing in Peiping if GRC walked out. GRC should give most sober and skeptical consideration to any prospective course that would play into hands of ChiComs and harm US, UN, and allies.

27. I said it was our considered view that US security position in Southeast Asia could be seriously prejudiced by GRC walkout. I asked Shen to give this his solemn consideration. Chinese Communists would be emboldened by apparent success their tough stance, and might be tempted to intervene more openly in SEA. I reminded Shen that Gimo had assured Secretary Rusk on July 3 that GRC policy was first and foremost to give help to US position in Vietnam, ahead of any other GRC obligation. If GRC did not hold fast in UN, US position in Vietnam would be affected adversely. Secretary Rusk said in letter to FonMin Wei, GRC departure would confuse GRC's friends and help its enemies. It would be interpreted as a grave setback for the US and allies, exposing allied position in Vietnam and undermining allied influence in UN.

28. I said that if GRC persisted in withdrawal move, it would almost seem that GRC was not interested in maintaining the traditional posture of a great national government, aware of its international ties and responsibilities. In self-imposed isolation from international life, GRC would have more the posture of a local regime of some kind. A GRC with no UN status would give impetus to the unfriendly argument in the UN that government here was acting as a local regime and should be considered as under the authority of Peiping. USG of course did not share such unwarranted opinion but its widespread existence in UN might make it difficult to uphold the juridical position of GRC.

29. I repeated my view expressed to Chang Chun on Nov. 26 that GRC could not really be humiliated by resolutely staying in UN and defending its principles. I said that abusive tactics of unworthy persons or nations cannot humilate those who are worthy. By remaining in UN, GRC status would by no means be demeaned, but rather would be enhanced by exhibition of GRC courage and resolve in standing up to contemptible efforts of its enemies.

30. Shen promised to convey all the foregoing representations to President immediately. He said would give final answer after further deliberations had been undertaken.

31. Shen then said with considerable asperity that the GRC had just about reached its limit in enduring insults at UN. He said GRC position in Security Council had been eroded, the GRC had been "kicked out of" ECOSOC, and with the departure of Wellington Koo for the first time there was no representative on the ICJ of a permanent member of SC. He said that most recently in course of tactical deliberation on Israel–Jordan situation, USG had not consulted GRC, that GRC was not included in any of consultative groups, and that the US officials "walked right by GRC representatives in UN lounge, without greeting or comment." He said GRC is not in fact highly regarded by UN members or even by some US officials. However, calming down considerably, he said GRC would give all these US representations very serious consideration. He said he

did not know how the decision would come out, but he thought it would be reached and would be conveyed to me in a very short time.

32. In closing the conversation I urged again that no final walkout decision if Italian resolution were to pass should be taken before Secretary Rusk's visit.

33. *Comment:* Failure of Gimo and Shen to reiterate previous assertion that decision is final is of course hopeful sign. However, I believe crisis is far from over and it is entirely conceivable that Gimo has been somewhat stung by our references to rash and precipitous decision and is merely demonstrating to us the soberness with which GRC will consider all aspects of situation. It is also possible that representations made by me and by Embassy officers to substantial number of GRC figures may have resulted in some voices being raised against Gimo's proposed course of action. If there have been such voices, however, they have probably not been very loud and Gimo clearly has capability to override them if he remains determined to walk out. GRC mind seems a little less closed today than yesterday but situation remains precarious.

McConaughy

219. Telegram From the Embassy in the Republic of China to the Department of State[1]

Taipei, November 29, 1966, 1110Z.

1589. ChiRep. Reference: Taipei's 1587.[2]

1. Shen called me to MOFA at 4 pm Nov 29. Also present were DCM and MOFA officer Wang Meng-hsien.

2. Shen said he had been instructed to tell me that the original GRC position on what the GRC would have to do in the event of passage of Italian resolution had been changed. He said this was the result of letters GRC had received from President Johnson and Secretary Rusk and of my representations. He said that GRC had decided it could not take a position that USG considers detrimental of US interests.

---

[1] Source: Department of State, Central Files, UN 6 CHICOM. Secret; Immediate; Exdis. Sent also to USUN and passed to the White House.

[2] Telegram 1587 from Taipei, November 29, reported on McConaughy's conversation with Shen. (Ibid.)

3. He then read the text of declaration (now canceled) which Fon-Min Wei would have been instructed to make in UN after passage of Italian resolution, if GRC position had not been changed. That statement included the phrases: "This leaves GRC no alternative but to withdraw from the UN. This does not mean any loss of face for the GRC, but it does not mean GRC cannot allow itself to be sacrificed on the altar of appeasement."

4. Shen then said present instructions to FonMin Wei were to proceed with a kind of walkout, and to be absent from the GA for a time. He said that GRC position was that if nothing at all were done, Chinese people would think GRC under the thumb of USG. If GRC were to stay with no reaction, there would be no way to explain to Chinese people.

5. He then read at dictation speed full text of new declaration which FonMin Wei now instructed to make (reported septel).[3] Shen explained that GRC intended effect of this statement to be temporary withdrawal from GA only and not from other organizations. He said GRC might even return to current session GA at any time to join debate if delegation so instructed. I pointed out that unfriendly elements in UN could still seize on GRC declaration of withdrawal and assert that Chinese seat in UN was vacant. I suggested that clearer language might be used so as to avoid misunderstanding.

6. Shen said Chinese text only of text of this declaration had been sent to ChiDel, which would make its own English translation.

7. I suggested ChiDel should consult with USDel parliamentary experts so as to minimize possibility that language of declaration might be used to bar GRC. I said USG is fearful that hostile elements could seize on any walkout and through parliamentary tactics try to declare China's seat to be vacant. I recalled that present GA President is not sympathetic on this issue. I urged that great caution be used in wording of declaration so that no bridges could be burned. After some discussion with DCM of wording of Chinese text, it appeared that better and more accurate translation for ChiDel phrase "withdraw its presence" might be "absent itself." Shen agreed to telegraph ChiDel to consult with USDel on this point.

8. I expressed my own gratification, and that of my govt. with GRC decision. I said I appreciated that it could not have been easy and that grave and sober consideration had produced this result.

9. Shen said he had conveyed to President Chiang "every word" I said to Shen yesterday after meeting with Chiang (Taipei 1568).[4] Shen said Gimo had called a meeting this morning at which present decision had been taken.

---

[3] The text was sent in telegram 1587.

[4] Document 218.

10. MOFA official Wang Meng-hsien seemed quite confident that Italian resolution would be defeated, on basis of his examination of reports of statements made during last few days in GA. I expressed hope that no walkout problem of any sort would be created. Meeting ended with mutual compliments and congratulations as I expressed happiness with statesmanlike GRC basic decision.

McConaughy

---

220. **Information Memorandum From the Deputy Assistant Secretary of State for International Organization Affairs (Popper) to Secretary of State Rusk**[1]

Washington, November 29, 1966.

SUBJECT

The Vote on Chinese Representation

Today's votes on Chinese representation were even better than we had anticipated, doubtless due in large part to the existence of the study committee alternative to the Albanian resolution. The important question resolution was carried 66–48–7 as opposed to last year's vote of 56–49–11. The Albanian resolution was defeated 46–57–17, in contrast to last year's tie vote of 47–47–20.

By a surprisingly large vote of 51–37–30 the Assembly decided that the study committee resolution fell under the important question procedure. Syria's unexpected initiative, which produced this vote, undoubtedly contributed substantially to the overwhelming defeat of the study committee resolution, 34–62–25.

The voting on the procedural question and the Italian resolution reflected the strong desire of the Communist countries and their non-aligned supporters to ensure defeat of the study committee resolution. Ironically, the Syrian move also served the interest of the GRC—to bury the study committee idea. The absence of a roll call on the Syrian motion was helpful to us in not highlighting our negative vote.

---

[1] Source: Department of State, Central Files, UN 6 CHICOM. Confidential. Drafted by Gleysteen and Popper. A handwritten note on the source text reads: "Secretary Saw."

You might be interested in a few significant points which we have noted in our first reading of the results. The most striking was Canada's decision to abstain on the Albanian resolution while voting in favor of the important question and the Italian resolution. Other interesting results were:

1) Japan voted in the same manner as the U.S. on all three resolutions;

2) The U.K. abstained on the study committee resolution;

3) Indonesia acted in accordance with its assurances by voting in favor of the IQ resolution, in favor of the Albanian resolution and abstaining on the study committee;

4) Disappointingly, Ghana voted "no" on the important question and "yes" on the Albanian resolution;

5) Sierra Leone managed to keep its delegate in line; he voted "no" on the Albanian resolution;

6) Senegal, in spite of our efforts, voted against us on both the IQ and Albanian resolutions;

7) Iran proved obdurate to the end by abstaining on all resolutions;

8) Saudi Arabia shifted from their threatened abstention to a negative vote on the Albanian resolution as we urged;

9) Australia, the Philippines and Thailand all voted against the Italian resolution; and

10) Chile voted along with us on all three resolutions.

The effect of today's decisions is for the time being to strengthen the GRC's position in the UN and to increase the difficulty of either replacing the GRC by Communist China or of moving toward a two-China alternative. In this context our handling of the events precipitated by the Canadian initiative has been successful. The GRC, too, dealt with the situation skillfully.

221.   Action Memorandum From the Assistant Secretary of State for East Asian and Pacific Affairs (Bundy), the Legal Adviser, and the Acting Administrator of the Bureau of Security and Consular Affairs (Heymann) to Secretary of State Rusk[1]

Washington, December 1, 1966.

SUBJECT

Removal of Passport Restrictions for Travel to Communist China

Discussion:

A. *The Requirements of the New Regulations*

1.   We have carefully considered the language of Section 51.72 of the Department's new passport regulations (Tab A)[2] in terms of its relevance to Communist China. The regulations authorize us to impose area restrictions on travel of American citizens only in the event of hostilities or in cases where we find that unrestricted "travel would seriously impair the conduct of United States foreign affairs". This rather strict standard for restricting travel paraphrases the even more limiting language of the Supreme Court's decision in *Zemel v. Rusk*, 381 U.S. 1, authorizing restrictions only "when it can be demonstrated that unlimited travel to the area would directly and materially interfere with the safety and welfare of . . . the nation as a whole". Under the terms of the regulations, if we are to maintain travel restrictions, we must publish by December 19th the names of the areas which meet this standard "along with a statement of the circumstances requiring the restriction".

2.   We have strong doubts that a persuasive case can be maintained that removal of the current restrictions on travel to Communist China would "seriously impair the conduct of United States foreign affairs". In a very real sense, we have already taken the position that the travel of American citizens to Communist China does not in fact "seriously impair" the conduct of our foreign policy toward that country. The categories of American citizens whom we are prepared to allow to visit mainland China have, over the past year, been expanded to the point where

---

[1] Source: Department of State, Conference Files: Lot 67 D 586, CF 104. Secret. Drafted by Heymann and Kreisberg, and cleared by Stoessel, McCloskey, Coordinator of Cuban Affairs Robert A. Stevenson, and MacArthur, who added the following handwritten note: "I concur in the substance but believe that we should inform the Democratic and Republican leadership of what we intend to do and why before we make a public announcement. This would help avoid misunderstanding on the 'Hill'. DMacA."

[2] Attached but not printed. On October 20 the Department of State published revised regulations on nationality, passports, and travel controls; for text, see 31 *Federal Register* 13537.

literally tens of thousands of individuals can qualify[3] (although only about 300 have applied and been granted passport validations). Moreover, our general position, as formulated by the President on July 12, 1966, that "the greatest force for opening closed minds and closed societies is the free flow of ideas and people and goods" also makes it difficult for us to argue in public that restrictions on travel to Communist China are necessary or desirable.

B. *Foreign Policy Considerations* (for additional memo from "L" on this subject, see Tab B)[4]

3. The benefits and risks of removing the present restriction on travel to Communist China depend (a) upon how Peking responds to our action and (b) upon the timing of our actions.

4. We have little doubt that our national interests would be served in an important way by the travel of some thousands of Americans to Communist China each year. As is indicated by the President's statement referred to above, the gradual expansion of the categories of American citizens whom we are prepared to allow to visit mainland China, and our efforts at Warsaw, our interest in increasing the number and scope of our peaceful relationships with Communist China is as much a part of our long-range policy for China as is our firm commitment to resist that country's aggressive actions vigorously. Opening a wide and mutually profitable range of peaceful contacts is a necessary complement to resistance to Communist Chinese aggression. Both have the same end of eventually persuading mainland China to turn its energies into nonaggressive, responsible channels.

5. There are, we believe, several risks of unrestricted travel to China which should be considered.

(a) First, there may be significant effects on the flow of intelligence. For example, China might attempt to make use of ethnic Chinese in the United States to obtain classified information which is not now available to them. We believe that the prospective gains to the U.S. in intelligence about China, a closed society, would be greater than those which would be realized by China. Much of the information we lack about China would be filled in by ordinary observation. The information they lack cannot be obtained without a security clearance.

(b) Second, unrestricted travel would, to a small extent, increase Peking's power to harass the United States by imprisoning Americans, if this were its desire. The increase in power would, however, be small. It has ample opportunity for harassment today in the form of the excep-

---

[3] For texts of statements issued by the Department of State on March 10 and on July 11, see Department of State *Bulletin*, March 28, 1966, pp. 491–492, and August 15, 1966, pp. 234–235.

[4] The memorandum from Meeker to Rusk, December 1, is attached but not printed.

tions for newsmen, doctors, scientists, scholars, and people prominent in commercial, cultural, athletic and other fields. The experience of other nations whose citizens travel to China suggests that this risk is not excessive, despite such recent events as the detention of the Dutch Chargé and the excesses of the Red Guards. On balance, we believe that Peking will accept responsibility for any Americans that it permits to enter. More important, its opportunities for harassment are almost as great today as they would be after restrictions were removed. We would, of course, issue a written warning of the risks to any American indicating an intention to travel to Communist China and could review at any time the desirability of a reimposition of travel restrictions if this seemed warranted.

(c) The complete removal of travel restrictions to Communist China would enable the Chinese to selectively invite individuals and their invitations might focus on persons who have extreme political views. This could well create a flow of traffic which might not only increase the ability of the Chinese to influence "left wing" political groups in the United States but also create a body of one-sided propaganda advocates for Peking in the U.S. who could boast they "had been there". We believe that Peking would quickly find itself on untenable propaganda grounds if it pursued a policy of admitting only advocates of the "far left". Their policy toward other countries has been to allow a reasonable cross-section of public opinion to visit the mainland even though they have attempted to channel visitors from the "left". In any event it is now and will continue to be possible for American communists or other sympathizers with the Peking regime to clandestinely visit Communist China and return to the U.S. It is probably in the U.S. national interest to try and surface such visitors in public by permitting or even encouraging them to apply for passports.

(d) A total dropping of the present travel restrictions might be interpreted as a far more significant political move than the earlier partial relaxation of our travel restrictions and as indicating a qualitative shift in the U.S. attitude toward Communist China. We believe, however, that the present palpable strength of our posture in Vietnam provides us with an ideal opportunity to take this step without undue risk of misinterpretation that we are changing our fundamental position on communist aggression. The Republic of China has expressed its misgivings about the relaxation in U.S. travel restrictions in the past but in a very low key. In the immediate context of the ChiRep debate in the 21st UN General Assembly, however, this reaction would probably be considerably stronger to the presently proposed move.

6. In contrast to the limited risks we believe there is a real foreign policy gain to be realized by removing the restriction on travel to China. In much of the world the U.S. is regarded as blind to the need of an

eventual accommodation with the most populous country of the world and one that will soon be a nuclear power. Our policy of resisting Chinese aggression is confused with an alleged policy of unwillingness to face the realities of the future power of China. We can eliminate this confusion and make clear our desire to reach an eventual accommodation with a non-belligerent Communist China by opening every avenue of peaceful relations that is consistent with our national security and our opposition to Chinese belligerence. Removing all prohibitions on travel of Americans to China—and thus assuming the same posture in this regard as the great majority of our NATO and SEATO allies—would be an important step in that direction.

7. Despite our liberal exceptions to the travel ban, at present in the eyes of much of the world we share with China the responsibility for preventing informal contacts. For example, Peking is reportedly telling foreign visitors that, by validating passports for travel to mainland China in a discriminatory manner, the United States is attempting to dictate to the Chinese whom they may invite to their country, and that the Chinese will not accept such dictation. This is obviously a subterfuge but, considering the breadth of our present exceptions to the travel restrictions, there would be very little cost in calling Peking's bluff by eliminating all restrictions on travel to that country. Only in this way can we make it wholly clear that mainland China's isolation is of its own making.

C. Domestic Political Considerations

8. To a surprising extent the American people and the Congress regard travel restrictions, not as a barometer of our feeling toward a country, but as an interference with an inherent right and freedom of American citizens. This has become apparent in the surprising Congressional opposition to the Willis and Eastland bills which were intended to impose penalties for violation of our travel restrictions. An explanation by the Department of State that we are recognizing and respecting the freedom of American citizens to travel abroad wherever they wish except where our foreign policy absolutely requires travel restrictions may very well prove to be entirely acceptable to a substantial majority of the public, the press and the Congress. Certainly there is reason to suspect resentment of the present situation where we authorize chosen categories of Americans to travel to China but forbid everyone else.

9. This public justification for removing the restrictions ties in perfectly with the occasion presented by our new regulations. For the first time in these regulations we formally recognize significant limitations on our power to restrict travel in the interests of respecting the freedoms of American citizens. We could and would explain that, like Albania, Communist China was dropped from the restricted list simply because we could not meet the new strict criteria—i.e., we could not justify a con-

tinuing imposition on the freedom of American citizens. This may well be an extremely popular approach.

10. In addition, we would propose to explain it simply as a logical extension of the wide exceptions to the restrictions on travel to Communist China already in force and to emphasize that the dropping of these restrictions was completely consistent with the views already expressed by the President and yourself on the desirability of the freer exchange of ideas among nations and the U.S. hope that the Chinese will agree eventually to respond to these U.S. initiatives.

D. *The Problem of Timing* (for additional memo from "L" on this subject, see Tab B)

11. There are advantages and disadvantages to dropping the remaining restrictions on travel to Communist China at this time. The most serious problem is presented by the close juxtaposition of our action to the debate on Chinese representation in the United Nations General Assembly. In view of recent misunderstandings with the GRC, our action might be over-interpreted and could possibly result in an exacerbation of U.S./GRC relations.

12. On the other hand, the overwhelming GRC success in the General Assembly appears to have secured the GRC position in the United Nations for some time to come and should enormously strengthen GRC self-confidence. Under these circumstances it may be that the U.S. move to drop travel restrictions will be no more of a problem for the GRC than it has been on the occasion of our previous relaxations of travel restrictions. We recommend, therefore, that you assess the climate of U.S.-GRC relations in the light of your forthcoming visit to Taipei, and that our final decision on timing depend upon your on-the-spot instructions.

Recommendation:[5]

That depending upon your instructions after visiting Taipei, the Department either

A. Publish the names of the restricted areas on December 19 omitting Communist China as well as Albania, or

B. Publish an announcement in the *Federal Register* stating that the Department has not yet completed its review of the areas for which travel should be restricted and extending currently existing travel restrictions for a further 90-day period.

---

[5] The source text bears no indication of approval or disapproval. On December 16 the Department of State amended the passport regulations by extending all area restrictions until March 15, 1967. For text, see 31 *Federal Register* 16143. For text of the Department's statement concerning this, issued on December 23, see Department of State *Bulletin,* January 16, 1967, pp. 102–103.

222.   Memorandum for Secretary of State Rusk Prepared in the Central Intelligence Agency[1]

Washington, undated.

This memorandum describes the current state of CIA–GRC relations in the context of their historical development, and cites the critical CIA–GRC intelligence activities that deserve special attention.

1. In the early 1950s the fundamental CIA–GRC relationship was established under circumstances in which CIA appeared to be the only U.S. agency in a position to assist the GRC in their ambitions, among other things, to conduct operations against the Mainland. After the Korean War, this assistance shifted from unproductive paramilitary operations to the development of highly productive and valuable technical operations involving communications intelligence and low and high overhead reconnaissance aircraft flights. The development of these very useful programs was facilitated by the position of Chiang Ching-kuo as the chief of all GRC intelligence activities, by CIA's support to media operations of great interest to the GRC, and by the apparently stable international position of the GRC. Chinese Communist reverses, particularly economic, and the GRC's belief that the Vietnam war might make possible their involvement in some sort of counterattack, also contributed to the GRC's motivation in cooperating with CIA in consolidating and expanding the productive comint and overhead reconnaissance activities.

2. In 1964 the growth of CIA–GRC relationships began to level off and then deteriorated slightly as CIA minimized its support to unproductive, infeasible GRC Mainland operations, particularly paramilitary, and reduced the size of its Taipei Station. While both actions were taken essentially for reasons of marginal productivity, tight budgets, and security, the GRC apparently chose to believe that these actions were somehow connected with a larger U.S. intent to "disengage", which they seem to read as being reinforced by, among other events, reductions in the Military Aid Program, and by the U.S. efforts to prevent Chinese Communist involvement in the Vietnam war. Nevertheless, the GRC maintained good fundamental relationships with CIA by continuing to give full support to the critical comint and high overhead reconnaissance programs

---

[1] Source: Department of State, INR Files, 1966 FE Weekly Staff Meetings. Secret. The memorandum, unsigned and undated, is attached to an unsigned covering December 1 memorandum to Bundy. Both are attached to a December 5 memorandum from McAfee to Hughes recording a December 1 meeting between Bundy and Colby, at which the memorandum was given to Bundy for his use in briefing the Secretary for his forthcoming trip to Asia.

and by facilitating the establishment of an over-the-horizon radar site on Taiwan designed to monitor Chinese Communist missile firings.

3. In late 1965, CIA determined that the commercial passenger activities of the Civil Air Transport (CAT) airline should be terminated because CAT was no longer essential to the support of CIA clandestine activities and was not intended to compete commercially with other airlines. Although the intent to terminate CAT was conveyed to the GRC through the CAT organization and was accompanied by reassurances of assistance in establishing the GRC's own national flag air carrier, the GRC has prolonged the phase-out negotiations partly because they are aware of CIA's equity in CAT and consider termination of CAT, again, as part of "disengagement."

4. In mid-1966, the United States Intelligence Board decided the Grosbeak program would be terminated because the product did not justify the risk of crew losses and the men, money, and equipment involved could be better used elsewhere in the context of the Vietnam war. This decision was made after an extensive analysis of the program's value and was conditioned by the fact that in the preceding two years only two Grosbeak flights had been made. The two flights reflected CIA and GRC concern over crew losses versus the flight's product. Therefore, it was calculated that, while the GRC might challenge the termination decision as a further example of U.S. "disengagement", they would eventually accept it because they privately and fundamentally did not want to make any more flights.

5. Contrarily, however, the GRC's reaction, expressed by Chiang Ching-kuo, was to challenge directly CIA's right to terminate an established joint project and to demand a letter of termination intent before any phase-out negotiations could be begun. This letter was delivered to the GRC on 17 November and has not been answered. Subsequent unilateral GRC actions have terminated a joint maritime collection team and the Joint Operations Office without explanation. Neither activity is important to CIA–GRC collection interests. To date, the three critical collection activities—comint, high-level reconnaissance, and over-the-horizon radar—have not been seriously threatened by the GRC. At one point, however, the GRC did suggest that the high-level reconnaissance program might be canceled but they have since flown one mission.

6. An analysis of the reasons for the GRC's adverse reaction to the Grosbeak termination strongly suggests that their reaction was not motivated solely by the Grosbeak decision. Rather their reaction is motivated partly by their strong pique at the U.S., particularly for CIA's very lukewarm response to their resurrected ambitious paramilitary schemes directed at the Mainland's turmoil, and partly by their distrust of U.S. intentions in the recent UN Chirep action. The GRC's adverse reaction has been further conditioned by their recognition that the special rela-

tionship with CIA, which they believed existed as a means of facilitating ambitions with or without reference to U.S. policies, was in reality a relationship fully and officially governed on the U.S. side by U.S. interests and needs as determined by the policy-making levels of the government.

7. A forecast of the GRC's likely further action bearing on its joint activities with CIA is difficult to make because of the variety of the governing factors. It is anticipated, though, that the GRC's action will be less adverse than might have been expected prior to the UN Chirep vote. On the other hand, should CIA for budgetary reasons have to reduce further its support to non-critical joint operations, particularly the media operations, the GRC may actually respond by moving against one of the three critical activities. In any case, it is unlikely that the GRC will move adversely against any of the three critical activities except as a desperation measure, since they also receive highly useful intelligence benefits from these activities.

8. CIA does not intend to challenge any further adverse GRC unilateral action against non-critical joint activities. The critical programs will continue to receive essential CIA support for their own value and, should the GRC unilaterally act against any of them, CIA will seek to ameliorate the GRC's action. CIA does not wish to continue non-critical activities solely as the GRC's price for the critical programs.

9. During your visit to Taipei we suggest that you not raise the subject of CIA–GRC relations with the GRC leaders. Should the GRC raise the topic however, we suggest that you restate U.S. interest in continuing the three critical activities of comint, high-level overhead reconnaissance, and over-the-horizon radar.

10. Mr. [*less than 1 line of source text not declassified*], CIA Taipei Station Chief, has kept the Ambassador fully informed of the current CIA–GRC relationship.

223. National Intelligence Estimate[1]

NIE 11–12–66   Washington, December 1, 1966.

THE OUTLOOK FOR SINO-SOVIET RELATIONS

The Problem

To examine current developments in the Sino-Soviet dispute and their possible significance for the future relations of the two Communist states.

Conclusions

A. We believe that Sino-Soviet relations will continue to deteriorate so long as the Mao Tse-tung–Lin Piao leadership group retains authority. But we do not foresee a deliberate break in state relations; the Soviets are apprehensive about the costs of such a development within the Communist movement and the Chinese probably fear its possible impact on Hanoi.

B. Even so, we cannot completely exclude a sudden explosion of the dispute into a new and more virulent form in the near term. The Vietnamese war has added to the uncertainties and the urgency of the dispute, the emotions of the principals involved could come to have greater relevance, and unplanned incidents could provoke greater hostility and more forceful retaliations. Moreover, the situation in China is fluid; it is possible that domestic requirements or pressures might cause the leadership to force a severance of all remaining vestiges of contact with the USSR.

C. In the longer term, prospects for major changes leading either to a further deterioration or an easing of the dispute appear to rest mainly on what happens in China after Mao. The emergence of a Chinese regime even more anti-Soviet than its predecessor is certainly one of the possibilities. In this event, hostility could reach new levels of intensity. All forms of cooperation, including even the transit across China of Soviet supplies for North Vietnam's war effort might cease. Though serious military incidents along the Sino-Soviet border are also possible, both sides would almost certainly seek to avoid war.

---

[1] Source: Department of State, INR/EAP Files: Lot 90 D 110. Secret; Controlled Dissem. According to a note on the cover sheet, the estimate was submitted by Helms and prepared by the Central Intelligence Agency and the intelligence organizations of the Departments of State and Defense and the National Security Agency. All members of the U.S. Intelligence Board concurred on December 1 except the AEC Representative and the Assistant FBI Director, who abstained because the subject was outside their jurisdiction.

D. The emergence of a more flexible leadership in Peking could lead to some easing of tensions. We do not believe that any Chinese regime would offer the Soviets substantial concessions, but in exchange for certain benefits, such as renewed economic and military assistance, new Chinese leaders might be willing to damp down the dispute. Even a limited Sino-Soviet rapprochement would be likely to have some important effects on the international scene since world opinion has come to expect active discord between the two. An easing of the dispute could also lead to greater Sino-Soviet harmony vis-à-vis the Vietnamese war, assuming its continuation.

E. Nevertheless, any Sino-Soviet rapprochement in either the short or longer term is likely to have definite limits. We expect little or no positive cooperation at the party level and a continuing general atmosphere of barely suppressed suspicion and mistrust. Moreover, the Sino-Soviet relationship would remain highly vulnerable to clashes of national interests over a broad range of issues, and if China's power began to give punch to its national assertiveness, serious trouble could develop, particularly over the frontiers.

Discussion

I. *Introduction*

1. The Sino-Soviet dispute has greatly intensified in recent months. Peking has stepped up the frequency and fury of its attacks on the USSR. Moscow, which for almost two years sought to convey an image of reason and restraint in the dispute, has since August begun to reply forcefully in kind. China accuses the USSR of acting in collusion with the US, and Moscow charges that Peking serves the imperialist cause by refusing to cooperate with the rest of the Communist world. China claims that the Soviet leadership is deliberately transforming the USSR into a bourgeois society, Moscow asserts that current developments and policies in China have "nothing in common with Marxism-Leninism." And each side now publicly contends that the other is beyond redemption so long as its present leaders are in control.

2. Hostility between the USSR and Communist China has, of course, existed for many years. Serious, though concealed, differences arose even during periods of relative harmony in Stalin's time, and open antagonism dates back at least to 1960. The reasons for Sino-Soviet friction and for the long decline in the relationship are complex, and over the years a substantial number of issues have been involved in the dispute. Underlying everything have been conflicts of national interest and ambition, some of a largely traditional nature, such as Sino-Russian competition in Mongolia and Korea, and others which have assumed a largely Communist character, such as the rivalry for political and ideological preeminence within the "socialist world." Different stages of internal

development and great disparities in wealth and power have helped to create conflicting attitudes and a general feeling of ill will between the two countries. Doctrinal disagreements and quarrels over Communist strategy, cultural antipathies, and even personal enmities (as between Khrushchev and Mao) have all played important roles. Certain key moves made in the dispute have also stimulated discord and helped to give the contest a momentum of its own: for example, the USSR's refusal in the late 1950's to satisfy China's demands for the wherewithal to achieve a nuclear weapons capability, and Peking's decision in the same period to challenge Moscow's dominance in the Bloc.

3.   Three developments appear to have contributed the most to the current sharpening of the dispute. First, China's internal quarrels have been accompanied by the mounting violence in polemical attacks on the USSR and its adherents in the movement. The campaign against domestic revisionists and anti-Maoists, part of an apparent struggle within the Chinese leadership, has evidently encouraged comparable attacks on Mao's principal enemies abroad as well. Secondly, China's growing isolation within the Communist movement—it is now virtually without significant allies—has frustrated and embittered Peking, and this seems to have reinforced its determination to remain arrogant and intransigent vis-à-vis the USSR. Finally, the war in Vietnam has become a key area of dissension, since it involves the most fundamental differences over Communist strategy and tactics.

II.   Recent Background

4.   The present Soviet leaders decided late in 1964, shortly after their assumption of power, that Soviet policy toward China was sorely in need of repair. They apparently believed that Khrushchev had caused unnecessary damage to Soviet prestige and leadership of the Communist movement by his insistence on engaging polemically with Peking and his efforts to commit other parties to a formal repudiation of Chinese views. They did not wish to compromise the USSR's basic political and ideological position in the dispute, and probably had no strong expectation that relations with China could be significantly improved. But they did hope that a new approach could reverse growing support for the Chinese within the movement and eventually help to isolate Peking from the rest of the Communist world.

5.   To this end, Khrushchev's successors acted with calculated restraint, avoiding polemics, retreating from demands for an anti-Chinese international Communist conference, and, in general, seeking to shift the blame for the continuing dispute onto Peking. At the same time, partly to disprove Chinese charges of Soviet unreliability and softness, and partly to contest actively with Peking for influence in Hanoi, they also sought to reestablish the USSR's credentials as a major Asian power and publicly committed themselves to increase their support of North

Vietnam. And, in support of this general line, they placed stricter limits on negotiations with the West and reintroduced a number of cold-war themes into their propaganda.

6. The Chinese Communists seem initially to have misread Khrushchev's fall from power as a blow against revisionism and as a further vindication of their own harsh revolutionary line. They soon rebuffed the efforts of the new Soviet leadership to mute polemics, and were apparently unprepared for the effectiveness of the new Soviet tactics. They were also unprepared for the series of setbacks they encountered abroad: for example, the failure of their efforts to form an Afro-Asian front in 1965 without Soviet participation, highlighted by the fiasco over the Algiers conference; the loss of their position in Indonesia; the characterization of their trade policies by the previously friendly Castro as political blackmail; and, in general, their growing unpopularity among Afro-Asian neutralists.

7. The Chinese became aware that things were going against them and that some of their early supporters, such as the Japanese Communists and the North Koreans, were beginning to drift away from their camp. But rather than change course, they persisted in unyielding policies and insisted that "temporary set-backs" could not deflect them from long-term objectives. Even their growing vulnerability to Soviet allegations that only China stood in the way of unified Communist support for North Vietnam did not persuade them to modify policies. Last spring, in fact, Peking adopted a domestic line which could hardly have been fashioned to do it more harm in the movement or render it more susceptible to Soviet ridicule and cries of alarm. Indeed, all of the world's Communist Parties have been mystified by the course of events in China, and virtually all have been alienated by the antiparty aspects of Red Guard rampages, the appearances of Maoist megalomania and Chinese chauvinism, and the general turmoil which seems to have swept over China.

III. Current Problems and Developments

8. The USSR and Communist China today find it difficult to maintain even the pretense of a meaningful political and military alliance. Party contacts practically do not exist. State relations are minimal, formal, and often not polite. Cultural contacts are kept up, but on a very small scale. Trade, which reached a peak of over $2 billion in 1959, sank to about $400 million last year and will probably decline even further this year. Only negligible quantities of military supplies are still shipped from the USSR, principally certain spare parts contracted for earlier and items of equipment which the Chinese could produce themselves or obtain elsewhere. The 1950 Treaty of Friendship, Alliance, and Mutual Assistance has not been formally renounced, but both sides have expressed doubt as to its continuing validity; Peking has indicated that it does not count on—or even necessarily want—Soviet military assist-

ance, and the USSR has clearly implied that in many circumstances it would not feel at all bound to extend such assistance. The two countries do not even cooperate easily or well on problems associated with the provision of military assistance to North Vietnam. Peking has in various ways hampered the delivery of Soviet equipment to North Vietnam.

9. *The Situation on the Border.* Tension has existed along the Sino-Soviet frontier since at least 1962 (when some 50,000 border tribesmen in Sinkiang, apparently stirred up by the Soviets, emigrated en masse to the USSR). Since 1963, Moscow has undertaken some modest reinforcement of its military and security forces in regions near China, especially opposite Sinkiang and eastern Manchuria. It has also stepped up its military assistance to Mongolia and this year began the construction of an air defense system in that country. The Chinese have apparently begun to give some attention to air defenses in areas of Sinkiang bordering the USSR. They have also sought to impose stiff new regulations governing the use of border rivers and have apparently harassed the Soviets along the land frontiers as well.

10. *Condition of the Communist Movement.* Sino-Soviet rivalry within the world Communist movement is still bitter and intense. The Chinese glorify Mao, vilify the USSR, and define their views as "universal truth;" the Soviets allow the Chinese to discredit themselves in this way and try, for the most part successfully, to block Peking's maneuvers. The character of this competition, however, has changed greatly over the past two years. The USSR must still reckon with the split, partly because of the maneuverability it gives parties which are anxious to avoid Soviet domination, and partly because a number of parties maintain a neutral posture in the dispute, including, most notably, the North Vietnamese. But while Moscow was confronted only two years ago with a serious challenge to its leadership, today it faces a China which can count on full support only from Albania, the Communist Party of New Zealand, a handful of tiny splinter groups, and a small number of front groups which are obviously Chinese controlled.

11. *Impact of the Vietnamese War.* The Soviets have increasingly sought to use the Vietnamese war as an issue against China. They have charged, for example, that Peking's failure to cooperate had prolonged the war by preventing a "quick end" to US "outrages." And they have employed their aid to North Vietnam as a means to increase their influence in Hanoi at Chinese expense, and in this they have apparently had some success. But while thus offering the Soviets an effective tool to use against the Chinese, the war also tends to limit the USSR's maneuverability in the dispute. Moscow must contend with Hanoi's refusal to choose sides, which means also that North Vietnam is unwilling to accept Soviet political guidance on the conduct of the war. Moreover, Chinese control

over direct land and air supply routes to North Vietnam is a factor limiting Soviet influence in Hanoi.

12. The eventual outcome of the war will clearly have a major bearing on the further course of the Sino-Soviet quarrel. The Soviet attitude toward the war appears to be mixed. The effect it has had in imposing strains on American resources and burdens on American relations with Europe and friendly countries elsewhere must be seen as advantageous. On the other hand, the Soviets are aware also that the situation carries some risk of direct confrontation which, in that area and under present circumstances, they must wish to avoid. For them, the optimum outcome would be one which, by a political process perhaps including a negotiation, gave Hanoi a good prospect of achieving its aims in South Vietnam and thus inflicted a major reverse on US policy. Evidently the Soviets do not think that the moment has yet come when they can set in motion a scenario which would end in this way. But should they be able to, in the face of continuing Chinese opposition to a political solution, they would strike a major blow at Peking's influence among the Asian Communists which would also go far to reestablish Moscow's ascendancy throughout the Communist movement.

13. For their part, the Chinese apparently wish for the present to see the Vietnam struggle continue. They see it as a prime example of a "people's war" waged against their main enemy, US imperialism. They hope for an outcome which would support their claim that this Maoist strategy is essential to revolutionary advance and at the same time diminish Soviet claims to give authoritative guidance to the revolutionary struggle.

IV.   Short-term Prospects

14. No clear pattern emerges from the most recent developments in the dispute: the mutual expulsions of the few remaining students, the Chinese demonstrations against the Soviet Embassy in Peking, the exchanges of diplomatic protest notes, the rising pitch of invective, and the hints from both capitals of growing difficulties over the transshipment of Soviet supplies to North Vietnam. Ordinarily, an accelerating deterioration of relations such as this might be expected to lead to a complete and final break. Neither China nor the USSR, however, has allowed matters to get completely out of hand.

15. Peking seems willing to run the risk of provoking a formal break in diplomatic relations, but seems reluctant to take the final step itself. It almost certainly wants to avoid the onus for doing so. It may, in addition, wish to avoid a total rupture because of a concern that this would complicate the Vietnamese war and relations with Hanoi, and, perhaps, because of a fear that Hanoi, if forced to choose, might align itself with the USSR.

16. The Soviets probably hope to avoid a formal break in state relations. They probably find their presence in Peking useful for a number of very practical reasons, including the maintenance of a listening post. They may also feel that the continued show of the Soviet flag provides some encouragement to any elements in the Chinese Party which oppose present Maoist policies and some opportunity for contacts with such elements if future conditions permit. More important, they continue to be impressed with the probable costs of initiating a break in terms of their relations with other Communist parties.

17. A further deterioration of relations appears to be the most likely near-term prospect in Sino-Soviet relations. The Soviets for their part will wish to exploit what they perceive to be growing Chinese weaknesses. They may, for example, state publicly what they have already suggested privately: the Mao–Lin Piao regime is abandoning communism and becoming, in essence, a Fascist dictatorship. Some rise in the frequency, though probably not the magnitude, of incidents along the Sino-Soviet border also seems likely. Continued difficulties associated with the transit across China of Soviet supplies for Vietnam seem almost certain. Forced reductions in the size of diplomatic missions are possible. But we do not foresee a deliberate formal rupture in state relations between the two countries; the Soviets will probably remain generally apprehensive about its possible costs in the movement, and the Chinese will probably continue to fear its possible impact in Hanoi.

18. The Soviets are genuinely concerned about the trend of events in China. They also wish to capitalize on the apprehensions of others and to insure China's isolation in the Communist movement. For these reasons, Moscow will probably continue to seek some form of international Communist condemnation of Chinese extremism and obstructionism. But the Soviets know that many parties, though hostile to Peking, would not favor an international conference explicitly called for that purpose, or any enterprise which threatened to expel the Chinese from the movement.

19. A further intensification of the dispute is not itself likely to alter China's bellicose international stance or its foreign policies generally. It might, however, have some effects on the USSR's foreign policies. We do not believe that growing Sino-Soviet friction automatically assures a commensurate Soviet effort to improve relations with the West. But, as China has become more and more isolated and discredited, the Soviets have become less sensitive to Chinese accusations and perhaps less responsive to Chinese pressures for militancy. Since August, for example, there have been a number of signs that the USSR has become more interested in some movement in its relations with the US. In any case, as a simple matter of prudence, Moscow's inclination to avoid crises in the

West would probably be reinforced by a fear of possible major difficulties in the East.

20. We cannot completely exclude a sudden explosion of the dispute into a new and even more virulent form, even in the near term. The Vietnamese war has added to the uncertainties and has no doubt increased the sense of urgency associated with the contest. The emotions of the chief actors in the dispute could come to have even greater relevance, and unplanned incidents could provoke even greater hostility and lead to new forms of mutual retaliation. Moreover, the internal situation in China is fluid; it is possible that domestic requirements or pressures might cause the leadership to force a severance of all remaining vestiges of contact.

V.   The Outlook After Mao

21. Prospects for significant changes in the Sino-Soviet relationship—either a further, radical deterioration or an easing of the dispute—appear to rest in the main on what happens in China. We cannot foresee, however, what is most likely to emerge from the present turmoil in Peking, nor can we estimate the timing of possible developments.

A Radical Deterioration of Relations

22. The emergence after Mao of a Chinese regime even less flexible and more nationalistic than its predecessor is certainly one of the possibilities. Such a regime, either for its own purposes or because of miscalculation, might bring matters to a head with the USSR. The ways in which this could be done, and the consequences of such an act, are beyond counting. Hostility so intense as to lead to a severance of all forms of cooperation concerning Vietnam is certainly one possibility. Serious military incidents along the Sino-Soviet frontier are also possible, but both sides would almost certainly seek to avoid war. China probably would be constrained by its military inferiority and the USSR by its anxieties over the military and political costs.

Prospects for an Easing of the Dispute

23. The present Soviet leaders—and any likely successors to them—would look to Peking for improvements in the Sino-Soviet relationship. They are not of a mind, and see no need, for any substantial changes in their own position. While thus convinced that most of the movement toward compromise must come from China, they surely do not expect this from the existing Chinese leadership. They may calculate, however, that the successor regime will be dominated by men less anti-Soviet than Mao. The Soviet leaders may even believe that the present radical course of Chinese policy will hasten the day when there will be a reaction against the radical Maoist line.

24. Should such a reaction occur, Moscow might then hope for some kind of grand Communist unity under Soviet sponsorship, but it almost

certainly would not count on a restoration of the close relations it enjoyed with Peking in the early and middle 1950's. The Soviet leaders probably would try, however, to encourage a new leadership in Peking to end China's overt anti-Soviet campaign and its competition with the USSR in the Third World, in Vietnam, and in the international movement. As part of this program, they almost certainly would offer the Chinese economic aid.

25. A successor leadership in Peking might be interested in an improvement of relations, but we do not believe that any Chinese regime would be likely to offer substantial concessions to this end. Mao's personality certainly played an important role in setting the tone of the Sino-Soviet polemic and his views also contributed to the substance of the dispute, as did Khrushchev's. But Mao's departure from the scene and his replacement by a more flexible leadership would not heal all the wounds or remove basic issues. The Chinese leadership as a whole—not just Mao—seems genuinely to feel that it is the aggrieved party in the dispute and that it has been the victim of a double-cross, specifically, the USSR's failure to fulfill promises to give China extensive technical, economic, and especially military assistance. More important, any conceivable new leadership in Peking is likely to retain strong feelings about Chinese national independence, cultural and ideological superiority, and perhaps racial superiority as well. Divergent Chinese and Soviet national interests are likely to remain a source of friction and distrust for many years to come.

Consequences of an Improvement

26. Nevertheless, we believe that a future Chinese leadership might see advantages in a damping down of the dispute and in a resumption of some forms of cooperation with the Soviets. It might see benefits, for example, in a resumption of Soviet economic, technical, and military aid programs. It might see some virtue in attempting to revive the credibility of past Soviet commitments to defend China. And it might be willing, in exchange for such benefits, to reduce polemics and to agree to cooperate with the USSR in Vietnam if the war was still in progress.

27. Such an agreement might even include harmony among Moscow, Peking, and Hanoi concerning overall strategy and the question of the war's continuation or settlement. If, in these circumstances, the decision were made to continue the fighting, Hanoi would benefit from the establishment of Sino-Soviet cooperation in a number of ways. It would probably receive military supplies somewhat faster and perhaps in greater quantity; the establishment in China of supply bases for Soviet matériel, for example, would expedite shipment and perhaps allow an improvement in the mix of weapons delivered. Finally, a greater degree of unity would give Hanoi's political statements and warnings somewhat more force than in the past.

28. Even a very limited rapprochement between the USSR and Communist China would be likely to have an effect on the international scene as a whole. World opinion has come to expect active discord between the two, and world politics rests in part on the assumption of its continuation. The changes in opinion and politics which would probably flow from any such adjustment in the Sino-Soviet relationship, however, are not easily foreseen. They might be subtle and very gradual: a slow renewal of confidence within the Communist movement, for example, or a growth of anxiety in Europe about the USSR's intentions in the West, now that its frontiers in the East were more "secure." Or they could be more substantial, as in Vietnam, and perhaps as in India, which might fear that any trend toward Sino-Soviet harmony would seriously threaten its security interests. Some of these effects would probably be present even though, as we believe likely, a limited rapprochement failed to hide all evidence of continuing basic differences and clashes of interests.

The Long Term View

29. Over the long term, to the extent that China proved successful in realizing economic, technical, and military progress, Soviet fears of a strong China on its borders are likely to grow. The prospect of a powerful China is probably some way off in Soviet calculations, and would not, in any case, necessarily prevent Moscow from seeking to normalize relations. But it would serve, we think, to limit the USSR's inclination to consider China as an ally and to reinforce other alternatives in Soviet foreign policy. These alternatives will probably include continuing interest in good relations with Japan and India, as potential checkmates to Chinese influence in Asia, and, over time, a more urgent interest in a European settlement.

30. On the Chinese side, while changes in the regime and its policies may produce an interest in normalizing relations with the USSR in order to obtain economic and military assistance, Peking is not likely to be willing to pay much of a political price for such aid. It almost certainly would not accept Soviet leadership in the world Communist movement, renounce its traditional interests in border areas, or forgo its claims to a leading role in both Asian and world affairs. China's requirements, political and economic, are likely to cause any non-Maoist successor regime to look to Japan and the West as the major source of the necessary capital and technology for China's development.

31. Thus, while we believe that the Sino-Soviet relationship could come to be characterized by improved state-to-state relationships and a relaxation in the bitter ideological struggle, we expect little or no positive cooperation at the party level and a continuing general atmosphere of barely suppressed suspicion and mistrust. Moreover, the relationship would remain highly vulnerable to clashes of national interest over a

broad range of issues, and if China's power began to give punch to its national assertiveness, serious trouble could develop, particularly over the frontiers.

---

224. Telegram From Secretary of State Rusk to the Department of State[1]

Saigon, December 10, 1966.

13023. Secto 35. Eyes only for the President and the Acting Secretary. There was no major surprise in my brief visit in Taipei. It was clear that spirits had been greatly boosted by the good vote in the United Nations. I encountered no complaints or recriminations from any officials, including President Chiang, about our handling of the matters or about our vote for the Italian resolution.

Before my arrival the South Vietnamese had put in some requests for additional assistance from the Republic of China and I found a generally sympathetic attitude on the part of officials in Taipei. It seems to me that this is now a matter of expediting specific arrangements and getting Chinese technical personnel in position to go to work.

President Chiang spoke at considerable length about the mainland, details of which will be furnished through memorandum of conversation. He expressed concern to see the problem of Taipei become involved in the problem of Viet-Nam. Apparently, he had in mind the possibility that if the two were intermingled, concessions would be made to Peking with respect to Taipei in exchange for peace in Viet-Nam. This led him to indicate that it would be a mistake for Chinese combat troops to be in Viet-Nam but I was not completely clear that he might not have been fishing for a request for such troops from me.

More interestingly, he developed at some length the thesis that he, his government and his armed forces are considered by Peking to be their no. 1 enemy. He said that in the "past few days" he had become concerned about the possibility that Peking would launch a nuclear strike on

---

[1] Source: Department of State, Central Files, ORG 7 S. Secret; Immediate; Nodis. The source text does not indicate the time of transmission; the telegram was received at 2:09 a.m. Passed to the White House. Rusk was in Taipei December 7–9. Memoranda of his conversations with Chiang Kai-shek, Chiang Ching-kuo, Foreign Minister Wei, Vice President Yen, and Economic Minister K.T. Li are ibid., Conference Files: Lot 67 D 586, CF 103.

Formosa with "ten or twelve weapons" and reduce that island to ashes. He said that Peking would probably feel that the Americans might not retaliate because world opinion would consider that Peking has a perfect right to bomb a part of its own territory but that, in any event, Peking would expect to survive any such retaliation and its main enemy on Formosa would be gone. I told him that I would not wish to comment offhand on such a serious and far-reaching matter, that I did not believe the contingency he had in mind would in fact occur although no one can guarantee what the future might hold, that such developments seemed to me to lie in the realm of the insane and irrational, but that the U.S. considered its Mutual Security Treaty with the Republic of China fully in effect. I did not draw him out on what conclusions he drew from his fears because I rather thought that he would immediately recommend a first strike against mainland Chinese nuclear installations.

President Chiang rather expects that Mao Tse-tung and Lin Piao will establish their full control on the mainland and will follow a militant policy dangerous to all of us.

I was once again tremendously impressed with the performance of the Republic of China on Formosa and I am bringing back some quite exciting material about their technical assistance to other countries which will be useful for Congressional briefings as a good sample of how a successful aid program can multiply itself in many directions.

225. Letter From the Chargé in the Republic of China (Hummel) to the Executive Secretary of the Department of State (Read)[1]

Taipei, December 16, 1966.

Dear Ben:

Prior to leaving Taipei on December 9 the Secretary requested that the record of his remarks concerning Gromyko's views on mainland China be recorded in two copies only, one for him and one for the Embassy. In accordance with his instructions, we forward this separate record of the Secretary's remarks, which have been deleted from our air-

---

[1] Source: Department of State, Central Files, POL CHINAT–US. Top Secret; Nodis; Official–Informal.

grams A–406 and A–409, both dated December 14.[2] The Embassy has retained the only other copy of this separate record.

One of the Secretary's references to Gromyko's views was included by error in Taipei's A–405, dated December 14 (conversation with Foreign Minister Wei).[3] This was on page 3 of the enclosure, second paragraph, fourth sentence which begins "He had merely said that irrationality had entered the scene . . .". We have sent you a telegram today requesting deletion of this sentence. It is included on the attached record.

Sincerely,

Art

Attachment

The following remarks have, at the Secretary's request, been deleted from the Memcons of the Secretary's conversations in Taipei, December 7–8, 1966.

The Secretary and the Gimo, December 8, 1966

The Gimo asked if the Soviets ever interpret to US officials events in Communist China. The Secretary said Gromyko is always unwilling to talk about the Chicoms. On one occasion the Secretary had asked Gromyko what is happening on the China mainland. Gromyko had replied that to tell the truth he did not know. Gromyko said that there is now an element of irrationality in Peiping, and this irrationality makes it difficult to interpret events.

The Secretary said that he wished to tell the Gimo in great confidence that Gromyko had once observed with regret that there is no provision in the Test Ban Treaty to enforce its provisions on non-signer nations. The Secretary said that the US would follow up this remark, and it is a very important development that the Soviets should worry about the Chicoms in this connection.

The Secretary said he had once asked Gromyko whether, in the event that Hanoi did come to the conference table, the Chicoms would intervene with military force to prevent Hanoi from making peace. Gromyko had replied that that would be inconceivable.

---

[2] Not printed. (Ibid.)
[3] Not printed. (Ibid., POL CAN–CHICOM)

The Secretary and DefMin Chiang Ching-kuo, December 8, 1966

The Secretary said he had recently asked Gromyko what is happening on the China mainland. Gromyko had replied that he simply did not know. Gromyko said that the irrational quality of present activities prevents any rational analysis.

The Secretary and Foreign Minister Wei, December 7, 1966

He (Gromyko) had said that irrationality had entered the scene in mainland China, making analysis very difficult.

---

226.   Action Memorandum From the Assistant Secretary of State for East Asian and Pacific Affairs (Bundy) to Secretary of State Rusk[1]

Washington, December 30, 1966.

SUBJECT

Instructions for 132nd Warsaw Talks

Discussion

1. Attached at Tab A[2] are the draft instructions we have prepared for the 132nd Warsaw meeting with the Chinese Communists scheduled to take place January 11, 1967.

2. We have broached no major new themes in the current instructions. Paras 2–4 reiterate general US policy in Asia and toward Peking. Paras 5–7 discuss our policy in Southeast Asia and the Manila Conference. Para 8 expresses the hope that Peking will subscribe to the Treaty on the Peaceful Uses of Outer Space. Paras 9–10 discuss communication with and travel to Communist China. Paras 11–17 include a major review of our position on the Americans still being held by Peking. Paras 18–24 respond to anticipated ChiCom accusations against the US for provocations and alleged incidents against ChiCom territory and ships. In Para 26 we suggest that the next meeting take place between March 22 and April 12.

---

[1] Source: Department of State, Central Files, POL CHICOM–US. Confidential; Limdis. Drafted by Kreisberg.

[2] Attached at Tab A is a copy of telegram 111764, January 3, 1967 (Document 228).

3. The major contingency we have allowed for is that Peking will take the initiative to move the talks or to suspend them. Paras 27–34 provide guidance for Ambassador Gronouski in dealing with several alternative actions the Chinese might take. I call your attention particularly to the proposal in Para 32 that we offer to hold a higher-level meeting (at the Under-Secretary level) with the Chinese in the event they move to suspend or break the talks. A memorandum on this proposal is attached at Tab B.

Recommendation

A) That you approve the draft instructions except for Para 32 on an Under-Secretary level meeting. (This would permit dispatch of the instructions without delay, in the event you wish to deliberate further on the desirability of Para 32.)[3]

or

B) That you approve the draft instructions to Amb. Gronouski, including paragraph 32. (The instructions in either case would be cleared with the White House.)[4]

Tab B[5]

IMPLICATIONS OF A HIGHER LEVEL SINO-US MEETING

1. The basic purpose of suggesting a higher-level (Deputy Under Secretary, Under Secretary or Secretary) meeting with the Chinese Communists, in the event of a move by the latter to suspend the Ambassadorial level talks, is to further assure that world public opinion unequivocally understands that the breakdown in communications is the responsibility of the Chinese. We strongly doubt Peking would agree (they publicly denounced a suggestion by Senator Mansfield earlier this year for a US-ChiCom Foreign Minister conference). Acceptance by the Chinese would strengthen the impression Peking may be most anxious to avoid, that the ChiComs are acting in collusion with the US.

2. In the unlikely event that the Chinese would agree, the talks would serve to provide a mechanism capable of restoring the suspended

---

[3] Rusk approved this recommendation on January 2 with the handwritten note, "W/o par 32 at this point. DR."

[4] Under "Recommendation" all the text in parentheses was written in by hand as was all except the first two words in recommendation B.

[5] Secret; Exdis. Drafted by Richard H. Donald of EA/ACA on December 21.

lines of communication between the Chinese and ourselves. In addition, there is the possibility—however slight—that the talks, on their own merits, could further our communications with the Chinese in terms of peace in Southeast Asia and increased understanding of the basic premises of our China policy.

3. The announcement that the US had proposed such a meeting, and in greater degree the holding of such a meeting if it in fact took place, would have important repercussions in a number of areas of primary concern to the United States.

(a) *US Domestic*—Such a move would probably be favored by a majority of Americans, as reflecting the Administration's efforts to increase contacts with Communist China and to seek a peaceful settlement in Vietnam.

(b) *World Public Opinion*—It should increase the credibility of our China Policy and our desire for a peaceful settlement in Vietnam, and effectively place the onus on Communist China for not only the suspension of the Warsaw talks but for China's overall isolation as well.

(c) *The Soviet Union*—The US initiative to "up-grade" our communications with China would probably increase the uncertainty of the USSR over what the US is up to with China. This would be true even if Peking rejects the proposal.

(d) *The Republic of China*—The US move would tend to be interpreted by the GRC as containing the seeds of a US deal with Peking at the cost of Taipei and as further evidence to support their suspicions that the US is prepared to "accommodate" the communists. A great deal of this potential damage to GRC confidence can, however, be avoided by frank discussions in advance of our motives and by disclosure of the bulk of the substance of the meeting if it takes place. This formula has worked well in respect to the Warsaw talks.

(e) *Other East Asian Governments such as the GVN, Thailand, etc.*—Same as (d) above, only to a lesser degree.

227.   Memorandum From William McAfee of the Bureau of Intelligence and Research to the Bureau's Director (Hughes)[1]

Washington, January 3, 1967.

SUBJECT

Regular CIA–EA Meeting, 29 December 1966

PARTICIPANTS

EA—Messrs. Bundy, Berger, Lakeland, Hamilton (Laos), and Pickering (Thailand)
CIA—Messrs. Colby and Smith
INR—Mr. Gardner

Nationalist China

Mr. Colby said that during his recent trip to the Far East he had spent some time in Taipei and while there had had a two hour talk with Chiang Ching-kuo, the Generalissimo's son.[2] Most of the talk had had to do with the suspension/cancellation of the Grosbeak operation and Chiang, Mr. Colby said, had given it to him with "both barrels."

Mr. Bundy noted that during his own recent visit he too had been put under fire by Chiang, on the same cause.

Mr. Colby went on to recount some of the details of his own experience. Chiang had asserted that cessation of the operation was "unacceptable", and he rejected flatly as unnecessary Mr. Colby's thought that perhaps representatives of the GRC and the US might conduct a joint review of the matter and the effectiveness of the Grosbeak operation. The decision to end the exercise, Chiang said, was his reward for having relied upon the United States and particularly on CIA. The GRC had lost some 120 men in the Grosbeak incursions and he simply could not see how, with that investment in human lives, he could confront his Air Force with the decision to end the program. It was with extreme difficulty that he had succeeded in establishing tenuous authority over the older army generals; he had achieved this only by pointing to Air Force support, and the decision to suspend thus would cost him not only Air Force fealty but also would thereby gravely endanger his position with the Army.

Mr. Bundy here interjected that this was a pretty serious comment on the solidity of Chiang Ching-kuo's authority, and Mr. Colby agreed.

[*1 paragraph (5 lines of source text) not declassified*]

Further, the Grosbeak decision had come on top of a number of other depressants. There had been a turn-down of General Yeh's list of propos-

---

[1] Source: Department of State, INR Files, 1966 FE Weekly Staff Meetings. Secret. Also sent to Denney and Evans. Drafted by James R. Gardner of INR/DDC.

[2] An unsigned December 15 memorandum to Bundy conveyed the text of a cable report from Colby, who met with Chiang Ching-kuo on December 12. (Ibid., China, 1966)

als for operations against the mainland, there had been the abrasions of the Chirep issue in the UN this year, there had been the withdrawal of F–104's from Taiwan, etc. The effects were becoming noticeable. The Nationalists were no longer pushing the idea of a joint GRC–US intelligence office, or of a joint planning group to consider actions against the mainland. Nationalist cooling on these, Mr. Colby said, was some cause for relief. A slow-down in U–2 operations could be considered as slightly more serious, but only if there were a choking off the SI operations on the island would we suffer palpable damage to our intelligence interests. Mr. Bundy agreed.

Mr. Colby went on to say that from Chiang Ching-kuo's point of view recent developments had been unfortunate, but that it was time he faced up to issues. It was important that his thinking be brought back to the realm of the real world and off the level of fantasy, and that ideas of invading the mainland and reassuming control there be abandoned. Bringing the Nationalists to face reality was bound to be a laborious and difficult process, but it was necessary.

[Here follows discussion of other subjects.]

---

228.   Telegram From the Department of State to the Embassy in Poland[1]

Washington, January 3, 1967, 7:07 p.m.

111764. Gronouski–Wang Talks: Guidance for 132nd Meeting, January 11, 1967.

1. It is Wang's turn to open. We anticipate rigid and hard presentation from him focusing on allegations of US provocations against Chinese territory, ships, and ChiCom Embassy in Hanoi. Wang will almost certainly refer to Vietnam and the increase in US forces and may refer to US alleged intention to further "escalate" war by sending B–52s to Thailand. He will probably repeat ChiCom intentions to "fight side by side" with Vietnamese but we doubt he will make more specific ChiCom threat of intervention. Wang may also return to point made at last meeting that

---

[1] Source: Department of State, Central Files, POL CHICOM–US. Confidential; Limdis. Drafted by Kreisberg on December 28; cleared by Vietnam Working Group Director Robert H. Miller, Assistant Legal Adviser for East Asian and Pacific Affairs George H. Aldrich, Bundy, J. Stapleton Roy of EUR/SOV, Holland and Anderson of DOD/ISA, Jacobson, and Jenkins; and approved by Rusk. Repeated to Moscow, Saigon, Taipei, and Hong Kong.

US-Soviets colluding on Vietnam and against ChiComs. We believe we must respond to some but not all these allegations. Wang may refer to US press reports of our offer at last meeting to exchange seed samples and again charge US violation of integrity of talks in effort to forestall comment by us on his unilateral publication of opening statement at last meeting. It possible that Wang may again move to release text of his opening statement after present meeting in order to further degrade significance of meetings and provide ChiComs with defense against Soviet innuendos at US-ChiCom collusion. We also do not exclude possibility that the Chinese side may take an initiative to propose a shift in the talks to another site. Even more seriously, they could take some action to suspend the talks although current evidence continues suggest they still find these meetings of some value. We have, however, included specific contingency guidance for such developments. Following is approved guidance for your opening presentation.

[Here follow paragraphs 2–26.]

27. FYI. In view rumors circulating over last few months of ChiCom desire move talks to Rangoon or elsewhere from Warsaw, believe we should be prepared respond to any ChiCom initiative this regard but should not ourselves at present time take initiative to suggest change in venue if ChiComs do not raise subject. Following is contingent guidance in event issue arises:

28. If ChiComs suggest move in acceptable manner either during regular meeting or in private discussions afterwards, you should probe as far as possible for their motivations in suggesting change and their suggested alternatives for meeting site and agree take subject under advisement without indicating US reaction. Our present thinking is that we would be willing move talks in order obtain greater security of contact if agreement could be reached on mutually acceptable site. We will want, however, to consider our specific response to ChiComs in context their approach.

29. We do not exclude possibility ChiComs may wish find some way to suspend present series of meetings without accepting public responsibility for breaking contact. One approach could be direct move to suspend talks on pretext that they unable talk with us in Warsaw while we "bombing" their Embassy in Hanoi. Alternative might be to launch ad hominem attack on you (as suggested by Geneva's 1466 rptd Warsaw Deptel 80795)[2] and refuse further discussions while you US representative.

30. Basic US objective is to maintain Ambassadorial contact with ChiComs if this at all possible but, if talks suspended, to endeavor place responsibility for suspension clearly on ChiComs. If ChiComs express

---

[2] See footnote 2, Document 208.

intention suspend talks on basis US bombing their Embassy in Hanoi, you should first reject their charges along lines para 22 above, refuse accept such charges as pretext for suspending talks, emphasize US willingness and desire continue meetings, and continue with presentation of guidance. If ChiComs indicate intention walk out of meeting or refuse agree to set date for next meeting, you should emphasize seriousness of move, emphasize importance of maintaining communication in times of stress citing 1958 and 1962 Taiwan Strait crises as examples, urge them reconsider, and, if they persist in their position, express deep US regret and your intention make statement to press on subject. Press statement should follow line outlined in this para. Specific language left to your discretion in particular context of ChiCom action.

31. If ChiComs lodge personal attack on you, we would expect you strongly repudiate charges, emphasize unprecedented nature of accusation, and demand an explanation for ChiCom action. We believe you should then complete delivery of prepared guidance but move immediately thereafter to end meeting and suggest date for next meeting if ChiComs in rebuttal return to their allegations against you. We would propose two week interval on this occasion and emphasize that purpose of this to provide opportunity for ChiComs to reconsider allegations they have made. Emphasize as in para 29 above US desire continue talks and willingness do so in Warsaw or elsewhere if there genuine and reasonable grounds for shifting site but that such discussions cannot take place in context unjustifiable accusations made by Wang.

32. We anticipate that if the ChiComs have decided to suspend the talks there is little we can do to affect their decision other than maximize their embarrassment. We would assume such a ChiCom decision would be based on their desire be relieved of political embarrassment of dealing with US in confidential talks at same time that they attack Soviets for doing same thing and warn Hanoi against negotiating with US.

33. If ChiComs choose break or suspend talks, approaches outlined above obviously do not exhaust possibilities. We cannot provide you with exhaustive responses to all possible ChiCom gambits but believe line outlined above provides sufficient general guidance handle other situations which may arise.

Rusk

229. Memorandum From the President's Special Assistant (Rostow) to President Johnson[1]

Washington, January 9, 1967.

SUBJECT

China's Vaulting Chaos

Mao's regime is in serious difficulty, to a degree that civil war has become a distinct possibility.

Months of growing chaos in the top leadership are now followed by widespread resistance to pro-Mao elements in Central, South and East China, as Mao's Red Guards and other "rebel" groups have attempted to move the Cultural Revolution to farms and factories. You have noted reports of violent clashes in Canton, Foochow, Shanghai, Nanking, the Chusan Islands and Peking itself, and of the breakdown of rail service in several sectors. In Nanking large-scale arrests (apparently of pro-Mao elements!) *by Army and public security forces* have been reported.

The source of most of our information on this highly confused situation remains press reports of "wall newspapers" in Peking. However, both Peking and Shanghai broadcasts have now confirmed serious resistance, and have warned of adverse effects on production. At the same time the Peking broadcast insists "It is an erroneous point of view that the Great Cultural Revolution antagonizes the development of production!" Mao forces are evidently determined to go through with their attempted "proletarianization" of the nation despite mounting costs now threatening the regime itself.

Most of the clashes have occurred in areas where Propaganda Chief T'ao Chu, number four in the Peking hierarchy, retains strong support of the party machinery. Much of this resistance has doubtless been triggered by recent official attacks on T'ao, principally on the part of Mao's wife. Attacks on T'ao were probably in turn prompted by his attempts to protect provincial party cadre who are opposing the Mao–Lin line.

The battle is clearly drawn. On Mao and Lin's side appear to be:

—a small and seemingly dwindling minority in the party;
—probably the bulk of the seriously divided Red Guards; and
—an indeterminate percentage of the armed forces.

Ranged against these are, apparently:

—the bulk of both the leadership and the lesser party apparatus;
—a goodly portion of the worker groups so far tested by Red Guard revolutionary activity; and
—an unknown portion of the Army.

---

[1] Source: Johnson Library, National Security File, Country File, China, Vol. VIII. Secret.

Much more resistance from workers and peasants seems sure to come, as Mao's revolution is carried further into the provinces.

The big question mark is the direction in which the Army will finally lend its predominant support. It cannot stand aside much longer, if present chaos continues. If it proves to be as divided as other major elements of the nation have been, the "Mao dynasty" is in for more bloody convulsions, and almost certain demise.

Premier Chou remains the best hope of achieving a compromise in the interest of preserving the nation and the regime's hard-won, limited accomplishments. However, Mao has made his war one of veritable "religious" fervor, and compromise now appears highly unlikely. We must expect one side or the other to win out. As of now the anti-Mao forces appear the stronger, and gaining. It is curious that Mao's heir apparent, Lin Piao, has not appeared since November 26. Mao–Lin interests in Peking appear to have been left primarily in Madame Mao's hands, and the precarious condition of those interests is underlined today by wall posters announcing the dissolution of the capital's anti-Mao public security forces, and—perhaps the most significant straw in today's East wind—other posters accusing National Defense Council Member, General Liu Chih-chien, of siding with the anti-Maoists.

Walt

---

230.   Telegram From the Department of State to the Embassy in Poland[1]

Washington, January 11, 1967, 5:48 p.m.

116572. Ref: Deptel 111764.[2] Gronouski–Wang Talks.[3]

1. In event Wang takes harsh line hypothesized in para 29 of reftel, you are authorized, in addition to guidance provided paras 30 and 31 to make following statement:

---

[1] Source: Department of State, Central Files, POL CHICOM–US. Confidential; Limdis. Drafted by Kreisberg on January 5; cleared by Bundy, Jacobson, and Jorden; and approved by Rusk. Repeated to Moscow, Saigon, Taipei, and Hong Kong.

[2] Document 228.

[3] The meeting scheduled for January 11 was postponed to January 25 at Chinese request made by telephone to the U.S. Embassy on January 7. (Telegram 1652 from Warsaw, January 7; ibid.)

2.   "In view of seriousness of accusation and actions contemplated by your side, Mr. Ambassador, and the threat which these pose to the continuation of our talks here, talks which regardless of the differences and sharp controversy which has frequently marked them have been of value in enabling our two Governments to communicate with each other, I request that you convey to your Government the following proposal. Our two sides should agree to a meeting at a higher level through special representatives to review the results and basis of these meetings in the overall context of the relations between our two countries. In the event your side agrees to such a meeting, I would propose that the time and place of meeting should be determined in further meetings between us."

3.   You should inform Wang you intend make comment to press on his position on continuation of talks following current meeting and that you will at that time inform press of our proposal.

Rusk

---

231.   Memorandum From the President's Special Assistant (Rostow) to President Johnson[1]

Washington, January 13, 1967, 6:30 p.m.

SUBJECT

A Look at the Past Week in China

The stubborn stalemate between Mao and his opponents persists after the struggle's most convulsive week yet:

1.   While reports of breakdown in public order involving violence in a dozen major cities may be exaggerated, both Peking and provincial radios have confirmed widespread disorder. Peking is urging striking workers to return to their jobs, and fear is expressed of potentially serious damage to the economy.

2.   Peking editorials calling for the Army's backing and soliciting its loyalty, poster attacks against three top military leaders, and a reorganization of the military's Cultural Revolution Committee give clearest indication yet that Army support of Mao is problematical. The test may

---

[1] Source: Johnson Library, National Security File, Country File, China, Vol. VIII. Secret. A handwritten "L" on the source text indicates that President Johnson saw the memorandum.

come if Mao's young activists go to the farms as planned, and there meet widespread opposition similar to that met in many factories. (Some 90% of Army personnel come from farm families.)

3. The week saw the first really earnest attempt by Premier Chou En-lai to moderate activities of the Red Guards and to protect several top leaders from their wrath. Significantly, Madame Mao has backed Chou in these efforts and for the first time Chou has claimed Mao's support in them as well. I read the new forthrightness of Chou's moderation efforts as further indication of the strength of Mao's opponents. Throughout his career Chou has had the instinctive knack of nicely timed gravitation to the winning side.

4. The provincial party apparatus, believed overwhelmingly to support Mao's chief opponents, apparently remains intact (with only Shanghai in doubt) after the most determined attacks to date against it.

5. The continued silence (since November 26) of Mao's heir apparent, Defense Minister Lin Piao, is an increasingly intriguing puzzle.

It is true that in all the confusion of the week, Mao and his supporters have retained the initiative. The opposition has only reacted. Still, no significant victories can yet be chalked up for Mao, and there is no evidence that the opposition is buckling.

The Cultural Revolution has had a pulsating character throughout. The pattern has been:

1. Attacks on those "following the capitalist line" by Mao–Lin and their supporters;
2. Determined and predominantly successful resistance from the opposition;
3. Mao–Lin appraisal of the opposition's strength, resulting in brief tactical withdrawal;
4. Renewed attack, usually through a new avenue.

Chou's moderation efforts may signify entry once again into a phase three situation.

The basic fact of the matter is that all of the problems undermining Mao's position remain

—fragmented and embittered leaders,
—revisionist and indolent cadre,
—policy and personal differences in every major element of the society,
—a long list of failures in domestic and foreign policies, and
—a populace as a whole which must by now be bone weary of 17 years of incessant ideological floggings.

Finally, and very importantly, Mao's own prestige has been seriously, perhaps irretrievably, tarnished in this as yet unavailing fracas.

Walt

232. **Memorandum From the President's Special Assistant (Rostow) to President Johnson**[1]

Washington, January 25, 1967.

Mr. President:

This is the best single reconstruction I have read of the inner politics of mainland China in this crisis.

It is written by Bill Wells, an imaginative, scholarly, bold CIA man in Hong Kong.

Walt

Attachment

Following is the text of a CIA report [*less than 1 line of source text not declassified*] dated January 19, 1967

SUBJECT

China—The Three Kingdoms Revisited

[*1 paragraph (3 lines of source text) not declassified*]

Today's events in China have a dynastic rather than communistic flavor. Politically, the period is that of the first great Chinese dynasty— the Han, but it is not clear whether we are watching its formation and the death agonies of the Ch'in or are seeing the end of the Han when the empire was swept with the rebellion of the Yellow Turbans, a rebellion which was in turn suppressed, but left the nation divided among a number of regional chieftains. A novel of this latter epoch begins, "Empires wax and wane, states fall apart and then reunite." After seventeen years of unity China is beginning to feel again the shudders which foretell political change.

Between mid-December and mid-January the political turmoil spread by the cultural revolution churned in dozens of areas, leaving the onlooker dazed. Nevertheless the basic divisions become much clearer.

---

[1] Source: Johnson Library, National Security File, Country File, China, Vol. VIII. Confidential. A handwritten note on the source text indicates it was received at 10:55 a.m.

[*1-1/2 lines of source text not declassified*] there is no longer doubt of the power struggle between Mao and Lin Piao on one hand and Liu Shao Ch'i and Teng Hsiao-P'ing on the other; we have learned of the Central Committee Meeting in October (which lasted 17 days) and to which Mao and Lin made two remarkable speeches. We have heard Lin compare Mao's struggle to keep control of the Central Committee to Stalin's struggle for power, and admit that the bourgeois advocates in the Central Committee remain in the dominant position in a number of fields. Mao in turn admits to great loss of control in the party, but makes it clear that he intends to grasp full power again whatever the cost. We heard that at Christmas time Lin Piao tried finally to crush the opposition and intrigued with T'Ao Chu to bring the great regional satraps, Li Ching-Ch'uan from the southwest, Liu Lan-T'ao from the northwest, and Sung Jen-Ch'iung from Manchuria to Peking, supposedly to reach a compromise. Accepting Tao's pledge of safety they came. But Lin's proposals were not accepted, and he then ordered their arrest. T'ao Chu then made his choice. Standing behind his word, T'ao arranged the departure of the three from Peking secretly by air and Lin's plot failed. T'ao, then ranked fourth in the party hierarchy, was excommunicated and immediately attacked. By mid-January he had apparently lost all his positions in the party.

Throughout early January the Mao–Lin position was increasingly attacked. To counter this, new "revolutionary rebel headquarters" have appeared in Shanghai, Foochow, Tsinan and Peking—all areas dominated by Army-controlled subordinates of Lin Piao from the days when he commanded the Fourth Field Army and its predecessor forces. These new rebel headquarters are set up to seize control of vital communication links, the post and telegraph services, the railways, radio and the newspapers. The magic name of Mao Tse-Tung still holds great strength, and in Shanghai two newspapers become the voice for these new cultural revolution vanguards. Hasty attempts were made to remove the party command of the all China Federation of Trade Unions and pack it with supporters of Mao and Lin. Liu Ning-I, long China's No. 1 labor man (after Liu Shao-Ch'i) came under attack, and open clashes broke out in Shanghai between laborers and the new revolutionary rebels.

The new rebels are now added to the wandering, destructive Red Guards and to the organized workers teams of the Liu–Teng party apparat. Yet nothing seems to stay Mao's drive to complete his revolution. On 9 December Chou En-Lai, who may yet become the mediator but who now seems clearly identified with Mao and Lin, announced in a speech before thousands at the Peking Workers' Stadium that after 20 December the Red Guards would be given military training. In mid-January Chou reiterated his belief in the ultimate success of Mao's cultural revolution.

Whether Mao will succeed in fully restoring his control will depend a great deal on whether or not he and Lin Piao can reestablish their control of the party apparatus. Gaining this control may rest in part on seizing and using the information in the work team personnel dossiers. On 8 September the Central Committee of the party and the State Council published a regulation concerning the handling of state and party secret documents generated during the cultural revolution. We have not seen this regulation, but it was obviously not obeyed, for it was supplemented by a directive on 5 October on the same subject issued by the Central Committee and a similar directive on 6 October issued by the Military Affairs Committee. By 16 November Party Central felt that a supplementary directive was required. The full purpose of these directives has simply been to force the party apparat to place the cultural revolution documents and probably the party personnel records in the hands of Mao and Lin Piao.

We have pondered in earlier studies why Lin Piao has not used the Army to force the party apparat to bend to his will. Since the capture of the famous "work papers" in 1961 it has been clear that he does not fully control the command officer corps, for many of these officers owe allegiance to senior marshals who do not accept Lin as their leader. It is now clear that Lin never even gained full control of the political department of the army. Cleverly opposed by the organizational elements of the party, probably through appointments made by Teng Hsiao-P'ing, the Secretary General, and Yang Shang-K'um, the Chief of the Party's Administrative Office, the army political department remained under the direction of the party. Lin may have counted heavily on General Liu Chih-Chien, long a mainstay of the political department and until three weeks ago the principal army officer on Mao's cultural revolution subcommittee of the Central Committee, who turned against Lin and Mao in late December and may now be under arrest. Liu's defection, like that of T'Ao Chu, must have been a hard pill for Mao to accept, and cannot help but have set back the time schedule of the GPCR. Liu must have participated in the preparations for the third wave of the struggle against the party apparat—that is, the training of the Peoples Army (PLA) cadres to be Mao's GPCR activists in establishing the revolutionary rebel headquarters now appearing in China. Although it is by no means clear, we believe this training has been conducted in many of the military regions and districts for some weeks.

On 26 November the Shanghai *Wen Hui Pao*, so often Mao's GPCR mouthpiece, described the closing ceremonies at Tsinan of the 2nd Congress of activists of the Tsinan armed forces. This "Congress" for the study of the works of Mao was attended by 1,127 delegates. We speculate that from this group and many such others being trained throughout

China, have come the hard core activists now seizing the newspapers and labor unions in many cities.

China at mid-January appeared to be two circles of political power. One circle is dominated by loyal subordinates of Lin Piao and the army, although there is great confusion at every level. In the other circle the party apparat reigns but barely rules. The strategy of the apparat is purely defensive. Like the Chinese heroes of the three kingdoms, each official is now thinking of alliance and of regional defense until the legitimate rule of the Communist Party is reestablished under Mao or any other leader who will reaffirm his predominance in his region. They have not reached the point in political time where separate states are thought possible. This spring, however, may bring a consideration of this possibility.

Historic parallels are never exact although this time events insist on historic comparison. Some things have changed forever. The grim fact of China's huge contemporary population guarantees little time for the fun of political misadventure. Food prices are rising in Canton. We have no way of estimating how badly the transport of food within China has suffered under the vast movement of Red Guards, the forced transport stoppages of the recalcitrant work teams or their battles with the municipal Red Guards, and now through the onslaught of rebel revolutionaries. The tie-ups, however, must have been and must be massive. Today only one passenger train runs north from Canton City to Wuhan and the north. Without transport China would not merely suffer the ravages of 1961's malnutrition, but the hell of starvation. Moreover, China at mid-month is bitterly cold. Hong Kong shivers in the worst cold of a decade. Human dislocation, rising prices, short rations and cold are Mao's new enemies. The party apparat knows this. Throughout China local party units have been offering raises in wages and individual incentives to inspire loyalty; indeed a labor bureaucracy may have developed such incentives for years. Over and over they are accused by the Mao–Lin adherents of tempting the masses with sugar coated bullets.

It is, moreover, difficult to assess how long Mao and Lin can travel the same road. Lin must know that so many of the vital managers of the party have been arrested, insulted and ridiculed, that his power position is in jeopardy.

Modern China may deprecate "face" as a feudal characteristic, but self-confession has its limits and these have probably been reached. Mao's recent accusations flick like a snake's tongue; no one is immune— the reorganized propaganda department, the newspapers, his fellows on the cultural revolution subcommittee, even his most old and trusted ministers. Lin will have an increasingly difficult time organizing the cultural revolution while his mentor purges follower after follower.

In Chinese history the era of the three kingdoms is an interregnum, a period of warring anarchy despised by the classical Chinese historian, who prefers the established dynasty with its cultural grace. In our last analysis we suggested that China's anarchical period would not last long for historic reasons. We still believe this. Nevertheless it is worthwhile to look back 1600 years to the time when China divided into the three great states of Shu, Wu and Wei, and when the art of political intrigue reached its height. As short-lived as the modern divisions may be, they will be with us in 1967 when a series of Chinese bravos will pass across the face of the nation until one, shrewder than the rest, assumes command.

---

233. Telegram From the Embassy in the Republic of China to the Department of State[1]

Taipei, January 23, 1967, 1016Z.

2162. 1. Following is Embassy assessment present GRC posture on military initiative against mainland:

2. Military: There continue to be no overt signs of preparation for any major military action against the mainland, and no detectable increases in planning, training, or accumulation of supplies or shipping. The GRC has made no special requests for US military assistance to take advantage of events on the mainland. We have reliable reports that President Chiang has ordered that no actions be taken to provoke ChiComs.

3. Authoritative public statements of government policy: GRC decided in October 1966 that traditional "counterattack" theme would no longer be pushed because of low credibility among overseas Chinese, those on the mainland, and elsewhere. Ambassador Liu's UNGA speech, and President Chiang's Double Ten, New Years Day and Freedom Day (January 23) messages all muted military aspect of GRC policy of "national recovery."

4. The word filters down: GRC has apparently found it difficult to switch smoothly from time-honored "counterattack" propaganda line to new approach which emphasizes cultural, moral and historical aspects

---

[1] Source: Department of State, Central Files, POL CHICOM–CHINAT. Secret. Repeated to Hong Kong, Tokyo, New Delhi, Seoul, Saigon, Manila, Bangkok, London, Vientiane, and Warsaw and to CINCPAC for POLAD.

of GRC aspirations for fellow-countrymen on mainland. Ambassador Chou Shu-k'ai's recent embarrassment is good example of this. He attracted considerable attention when on January 10 he reportedly said in Washington that GRC was preparing for "counterattack." By January 19, however, he was using instead President Chiang's New Years Day thesis that GRC's return to mainland was primarily a political, not military matter. GRC Ambassador to Manila apparently made similar shift in public statements at about the same time. Our expressions of concern January 12 and 14 to GRC (Taipei's 2083)[2] may have helped achieve these shifts.

5.   Press and public opinion on Taiwan: GRC maintains the claim that it is sole legitimate government of all China. Legal basis for national government apparatus, with mainlanders making all important decisions, and for international status in UN, rests on this claim. Given these present day realities as well as historical background and past public utterances about "counterattack" or "mainland recovery" it would be strange indeed if all comments on these subjects suddenly ceased, and they have not. Traditional "re-take the mainland" slogans still appear painted on walls in Taipei, and are shouted in unison at military parades and anti-Communist rallies. Polemicists in KMT and Legislative Yuan continue to urge prompt action against mainland to take advantage of current disarray. However, until there is some evidence in form of official approaches, statements, or military preparations, these ritualistic warcries should not be construed as presaging a GRC intention to launch an invasion of the mainland at this time.

6.   Future GRC actions: If situation on mainland changes markedly, calls for counterattack from certain old guard KMT elements could become louder and more frequent. Some officials could seek to persuade President Chiang that large scale military action is feasible. In this event we anticipate that the GRC would initiate official consultations as required under the 1954 Mutual Security Treaty and that US logistic assistance would be requested. In the unlikely event that GRC decided to take unilateral military action on any large scale we believe that such preparations would be detected by us in advance. GRC could initiate small scale activity without our prior knowledge.

7.   Embassy and other US agencies will maintain close watch for signs of unilateral military action.

Hummel

---

[2] Telegram 2083 from Taipei, January 16, reported that the Chargé had delivered a message to Vice Foreign Minister Shen as instructed in telegram 118633, January 13. (Both ibid.)

234. Telegram From the Embassy in Poland to the Department of State[1]

Warsaw, January 25, 1967, 1929Z.

1822. Gronouski–Wang Talks: 132nd meeting.[2]

1. Meeting lasted 3 hours 15 minutes. Wang opened with refutation of Pres. Johnson's expression of U.S. hopes for reconciliation and development cooperation with Chinese people. Described this position as "big lie" and reviewed at length recent "serious warnings" and series of alleged U.S. violations of ChiCom territory and attacks on ChiCom fishing boats and Embassy in Hanoi to demonstrate U.S. intensifying provocative acts. (Wang also raised incident of GRC–ChiCom air clash last week with accusation that this U.S. instigated.) Conveyed "serious warning and strongest protest" against these incidents but in routine language. Wang handed over five photos including damaged CPR Embassy Hanoi and equipment said to have been jettisoned from U.S. plane over Kwangsi Sept. 9.

2. Wang then moved to Viet-Nam on which no new themes raised. Emphasized that total withdrawal only way out for U.S. Accused U.S. of working together with Soviets for peace talks.

3. These only two subjects covered in opening statement which short and routine. Only conspicuous aspects were repeated references to Mao and his thought and to Lin Piao call for Chinese people to support people of Viet-Nam. (Lin identified as Vice-Premier and Minister of Defense.)

4. I responded using guidance Deptel 111764.[3] It evident at this point that Wang well briefed and that most of his material kept in reserve for rebuttal (which also salted with quotes from Mao). Wang raised Taiwan issue, reiterating old line that key to U.S.–ChiCom dispute not over mutual visits and exchanges of seed samples or meteorological information but U.S. "occupation" of Taiwan and interference ChiCom internal affairs. If this unresolved, "absolutely impossible to improve U.S.-Chinese relations." Wang charged U.S. trying "deceive" Chinese people and "lull their fighting spirit" with proposals for contacts so that it can "impose war on Chinese people at appropriate time."

5. Wang then rejected my description of incident involving rescued Chinese fishermen. He lodged strong protest against U.S. treatment of

---

[1] Source: Department of State, Geneva Talks Files: Lot 72 D 415. Confidential; Limdis. Repeated to Hong Kong, London, Moscow, and Taipei. Passed to the White House.

[2] Gronouski reported in telegram 1821 from Warsaw, sent 3 hours earlier, that the meeting had been without incident. He sent a detailed record of the meeting in airgram A–465, January 26. (Both ibid.)

[3] Document 228.

fishermen, claiming they had told ChiCom authorities of being imprisoned, interrogated about ChiCom military and economic intelligence, maltreated, and that attempts made recruit them as spies or defectors to Taiwan. Claimed Chinese had irrefutable evidence that U.S. had not rescued but forced fishermen into Vietnamese ports against their will.

6. Wang rejected as unacceptable suggestion that U.S. forces would withdraw from VN in six months after conflict subsided, demanded immediate U.S. withdrawal now, charged U.S. had attacked ChiCom Embassy Hanoi in effort intimidate Peking. (Later in meeting he reiterated this, noting no other Embassy in Hanoi damaged but Chinese.) Wang continued at length on subject Viet-Nam including quotations from Harrison Salisbury articles on U.S. bombing of civilian areas in Viet-Nam and warning to U.S. not to "misjudge opponents and make miscalculations."

7. In prepared text comment on outer-space treaty Wang charged treaty had nothing to do with peace or disarmament, another fraud "like the test-ban," and that treaty would not prevent U.S. and Soviets from launching military payloads "such as spy in the sky."

8. Wang repeated stock position on U.S. prisoners on mainland, emphasizing this internal ChiCom matter, that Captain Smith a criminal and that visit of Smith family members to Peking not proper matter for Ambassadorial talks but for Red Cross. In counter-rebuttal I emphasized propriety of discussing prisoners and failure of Chinese to live up to 1955 agreement. Wang acknowledged U.S. right to express its views on subject in meetings.

9. Wang defended his release of opening statement after last meeting on grounds need clarify U.S. distortions through repeated disclosures of contents. I responded, reemphasizing desirability maintenance of confidence in meetings.

10. In counter-rebuttal I focused on uselessness of dwelling on issues on which both sides knew our views at variance, such as Taiwan but emphasized need to attempt create climate better understanding within which larger problems might become easier to resolve. Emphasized absurdity of allegation that U.S. intention in proposing private cultural, journalistic contacts was to lull ChiCom into euphoria in order attack them. Said our purpose precisely the opposite—to diminish fear of attack and war by both sides. I reviewed at length U.S. position on Viet-Nam peace negotiations and urged ChiComs if they feared U.S. presence in Viet-Nam posed threat to them to join in move toward peace. On fishermen, I quoted at length from fishermen's statements in Saigon's A–327[4] in refutation Wang's allegations.

---

[4] Dated December 22, 1966. (Department of State, Central Files, POL 27–7 VIET)

11. Wang responded by going over old ground on prisoners, Chinese fishermen and Viet-Nam. He launched into prolonged, extemporaneous excursion on "hundreds of years of U.S. oppression, slaughter" of Chinese people, emphasizing inconsistency between U.S. actions and words and insisting U.S. words could not be believed. As meeting already in course three hours, I limited my response to reiteration U.S. position on prisoners and expression of incredulity that simple humanitarian gesture in helping fishermen in distress should be interpreted as U.S. plot.

12. I then proposed April 5 for next meeting. Wang said all of April and May inconvenient for him and refused move from this position. He proposed June 14 and "retreated" to June 7 but prolonged discussion unavailing in moving him from what apparently firm instructions hold to June date. Wang repeated position he first advanced at last meeting that more frequent sessions unnecessary and that there no need adhere to past practice of 3–4 month intervals. I finally agreed after emphasizing my belief more frequent contacts desirable, and told him I would inform press we had suggested earlier meeting but that this not agreeable to Chinese side. He interposed no objection and I so informed press.

13. Atmospherics. ChiComs all appeared in identical dark blue Chungshan uniforms with Mao Tse-tung buttons on left chest. Wang brought along new "advisor", Chang Chu-hsuan (Commercial Counselor in diplomatic list), but gave no hint of reason for change or whereabouts of previous advisor, Li Lien-pi. Repeated references to "great leader of Chinese people," Mao, and to thought of Mao an unusual feature in talks although this had begun appear (on much less noticeable scale) at last meeting. Chinese side immediately caught reference to unidentified quote from Mao used in my presentation and laughed in acknowledgement. No significant change in general atmosphere of meeting from others this year. At end of meeting he took initiative to come to me to insist I look at photos he had handed over to me and to insist these "proved" U.S. provocations and hostile acts against them. He said "These should be sent directly to President Johnson." I agreed transmit them back to Dept. In response my question whether he planning return shortly to Peking, he said it was not certain.

14. Kreisberg and Anderson will go to ChiCom Embassy tomorrow, as usual, to exchange opening statements with ChiCom interpreter.

15. *Comment:* While more explosive contingencies for which we prepared fortunately did not arise, ChiComs clearly operating under extremely tight limitations from Peking. They obviously do not want to have to meet with us any more frequently than absolutely necessary at least under present circumstances (both internal and foreign). Four and half month interval between talks probably represents even more frequent meeting period than they wish. At same time, I am encouraged to

believe that their present intention is to avoid any break or suspension of Warsaw channel to U.S.

16. Unusually large press turnout for meeting. Wang apparently declined agree permit newsmen or photographers in conference room before meeting. I issued routine press statement after talks.

Gronouski

---

235.   **Memorandum From Peter Jessup of the National Security Council Staff to the President's Special Assistant (Rostow)**[1]

Washington, January 27, 1967.

SUBJECT

Roche Request on Chinese Nuclear Facilities[2]

It can be safely stated that the Lop Nor test site and Shuang Cheng Tzu missile test centers in China cannot be "played with" if overrun by Red Guards. They are complexes sophisticated enough so that only the very few qualified Chinese technical personnel can cope with them.

It can be further stated that the USSR has no particular need to seize such facilities; they are of no use to the Russians who are a dozen years ahead of the Chinese in systems and guidance. Their only interest would be the same as ours in case of war, to utterly destroy them for purposes of denial.

It is probable that Soviet planners are well aware of the potential unifying factor in the Chinese picture should there be foreign intervention. After a tradition of many decades of "foreign devils," the Russians would be most unlikely to intervene short of all-out war.

---

[1] Source: Johnson Library, National Security File, Country File, China, Nuclear Factories. Secret.

[2] The President's Special Consultant John P. Roche stated in a January 26 memorandum to Rostow that he suspected the Soviet Union was making contingency plans "to seize the Sinkiang nuclear factories if the roof goes up." He added that the Soviets were "not going to leave that stuff lying around loose for Red Guards to play with." Noting that such action would presumably involve an airborne task force, he concluded: "I trust our intelligence services will keep an eye out for any indications of preparations for such an operation." (Ibid.)

The intelligence community has a daily watch on the order of battle and military buildup on the Sino-Soviet frontier. A recent study was completed analyzing its growth over a 24-month period. The increase is gradual and logical in the light of tensions and is not believed to indicate sudden action at this time. These matters are under constant review by the United States Intelligence Board.

It might be pointed out at this time that whereas the average reader perhaps considers that the Russians are chortling with joy at the apparent chaos overtaking China, serious Soviet thinkers, government officials, and Communist Party hierarchy are deeply concerned by the events since this is a failure of the system and may have distinct repercussions in other parts of the communist world.[3]

PJ

[3] Jenkins also commented in a January 27 memorandum to Rostow that Roche's scenario seemed highly improbable. (Ibid.)

236. Memorandum From Alfred Jenkins of the National Security Council Staff to the President's Special Assistant (Rostow)[1]

Washington, February 3, 1967.

SUBJECT

Highlights of China Panel Meetings, February 1–2[2]

1. *No one foresaw a year ago* the breakdown of the Chinese Communist regime's authority and the resulting *chaos*. There was also agreement that *no one could foresee* what *China* would be *like a year from now.*

[1] Source: Johnson Library, National Security File, Country File, China, Vol. VIII. Confidential.

[2] On December 7, 1966, the Department of State announced the formation of a panel of advisers on China comprised of A. Doak Barnett, Alexander Eckstein, John K. Fairbank, Julius C. Holmes, Ralph L. Powell, Lucian W. Pye, Robert A. Scalapino, Philip D. Sprouse, George E. Taylor, and Paul A. Varg. The text of the press release was sent to Taipei in telegram 98530 the same day. (Department of State, Central Files, POL 1 CHICOM–US) Records pertaining to the panel, including records of its discussions, are ibid., EA Files: Lot 73 D 8.

2. It was comforting to note the degree of agreement among the outside experts and government personnel as to the broad outlines of what is now going on in China and the probable antecedent developments (i.e., general confirmation of INR and Agency studies).

3. There was general agreement that while failures in domestic and foreign policy, Mao's fear of revisionism, resulting policy differences and opposition to the excesses of the Cultural Revolution all contributed to the present situation, it has *now* become basically *a struggle over who is to run China* and other considerations have become blurred in the confusion.

4. Basic problems running through present difficulties include:

   a. China's thin resources margin;
   b. the difficulty of preserving elan in times of failure;
   c. deep ideological wrenchings of the Sino-Soviet disagreement; and
   d. disagreement as to what measures work best, considering the magnitude of the problem of governing and modernizing such a vast country with limited resources.

5. For purposes of discussion, the spectrum of *possible outcomes* was broken down into four categories:

   a. *Mao–Lin reconsolidation of power.* There was agreement that this was hard to envisage unless the military holds together and is willing to play a more active role. There seemed to be about an even split of opinion as to the likelihood of this. In any event, there was agreement that such a solution would be short-range and that we will surely be dealing with a different China of some sort in the fairly near future.
   b. *A compromise, probably under Chou En-lai's aegis.* This would be likely only if 1) a successful attempt is made to moderate the Cultural Revolution and 2) the desire for nationhood is given an opportunity to assert itself because of the prospect of the country's falling apart.
   c. *The Party apparatus wins predominant support of the Army and prevails.* Many participants considered this to be the most likely of the four possibilities, but some felt that the Mao–Lin faction might still win the first round. Several believed that in this event, Mao would be kicked up rather than out, in order to borrow the umbrella of his prestige and charisma. Some thought that Mao's prestige may now be sinking to the point where, if the trend continues much longer, he could actually be a liability.
   d. *The country breaks up into regional units, probably under predominantly military control.* (Also considered in this category was emergence of a "Nasser" with broad control. Another variant would be loss of peripheral regions under Soviet domination, but set up as "autonomous.")

6. The group not only *differed* in judgment *as to which* of these outcomes was the *most likely* but *also as to which* would be *most desirable* from the U.S. standpoint. There was agreement, however, that we probably could not appreciably affect the outcome, and that attempts to do so would be counterproductive at best and dangerously foolhardy at worst.

7. The distinction was drawn between a "posture" and a "policy" toward Communist China. Agreement was unanimous that *our present "posture" of quiet reasonableness and hope for ultimate reconciliation is about right.* Several participants *questioned whether we had a full-fledged "policy" toward Communist China* at the present time, and some maintained that we could not or should not have, insofar as "policy" implies a series of actions. Several participants argued strongly that we should take policy steps even now. It was conceded that any attempted steps toward reconciliation now would be rebuffed and would not appreciably affect China. The purpose would be to prepare for the future, to tidy up present "anachronisms" and to gain in the eyes of third countries. It was pointed out by others that in doing so we might well lose substantially in the eyes of Asian friends, who, after all, are the ones most concerned. It was strongly felt by some that even though it might not seem to make sense to attempt conciliatory gestures when they would not meet with response, the U.S. could only take these steps with grace at a time when China is weak—i.e., when they would not be interpreted as a knuckling under to pressure from a strong China.

8. The *discussion of possible policy steps* (trade, contacts and travel, UN membership and Taiwan considerations) was felt to be *too brief,* because of time, and the suggestion was made that these items be taken up in greater degree at the next meeting (probably early June).

9. There was a *division of opinion* as to whether in posture and policy we should in the U.S. interests:

a. try to *drive the mainland into deeper chaos*—or at least passively witness such chaos with satisfaction, or

b. even now *adopt policies which would look toward* a time of more reasonable and pragmatic government in China and its *articulation with the world community.*

10. There were three "special appearances" during the conference:

a. Walter McConaughy spoke on the policies, attitudes, and likely plans of the GRC. About one-third of the group around the coffee table, during the break, expressed the opinion that this was "a good try" but actually was a waste of conference time, since everyone was already aware of what was said.

b. Foy Kohler spoke interestingly on Sino-Soviet differences and their implications. In brief, he saw no prospect of a very meaningful reconciliation but believed that if a faction came to power in China which sought Soviet help, a limited price in such help might be paid for "the psychological asset of papering over differences between the two Communist giants." He thought the Soviets were and would continue to be active in trying to bring about such a regime.

c. The Secretary, after a brief opening statement concerning the problem of organizing a durable peace, fielded questions on a variety of subjects with his usual skill and contagious conviction. Most of the time was spent on Vietnam.

Comment: The conference went well and was mutually advantageous. Nothing really new emerged but there was general agreement that thinking about some issues had been usefully sharpened. I should say that the conference was a distinct success from the standpoint of government-academic relationships.

I found especially notable the relative *lack of disagreement with our policies in Vietnam* and total lack of tendentiousness in discussing them. This contrasts markedly with much of my experience of last summer's academic swing—especially at Harvard.

In thinking back over the conference, I am left with one outstanding disappointment. It seems to me that our academic friends are concentrating in their policy probings on some possibly useful but peripheral measures. As you know, *before the present chaos* on the mainland set in, *I saw* some *utility* in trying to go a bit further than we had *in "bridge-building."* Considering the state of the mainland *since, however,* the *real question* concerning these relatively minor and peripheral issues becomes *one of timing.* As I restated recently I now believe that, having not taken some of these steps in more normal times, we should *postpone them* until we can make a much better judgment as to the course of events in China. (Recognition of Mongolia is in a different category.) I do not believe that our Asian friends, particularly, would understand our motivations and there is some merit in *saving our limited leverage* for a time when some reason returns to the mainland. Meanwhile it seems to me that an occasional high-level reference to the desire for ultimate reconciliation is still in order.

We should marshall our planning resources not so much on matters of travel, limited trade and a new UN approach at this time, but *concentrate* on the central issues: those having to do with *China in the balance of power* in the Asia–Pacific region. We have, of course, been making a tremendous—and I believe eminently correct—effort in filling the power vacuum left by the demise of Japanese militarism, pre-empting it from communist militarism. As a result, we are beginning to have an Asia of real hope. If we are beginning to approach success in the knottiest of Asian problems, the Sino-Vietnam one, we are entering a broad watershed period which will require some changes for its other side. Very little was said in the conference about *how China of whatever future complexion relates to* the future role of Japan, the future status of Taiwan, the sort of Southeast Asia we want to see post-Vietnam and how much it will require, what sort of presence from us, the possible future pull on China from successful Asian regional ventures, the desirability and degree of Soviet presence and investment in some of these ventures, the composition of probable future regional military coalescences (probably first involving parts of Southeast Asia and Southwest Pacific), the likelihood and desirability of Japanese participation and the need for U.S. balancing of Japan in that event, the effects if Japan and/or India go nuclear, etc. Some of these were mentioned, but hardly more than en passant. I hope that in the next meeting we can gain the benefit of more discussion in these areas from this impressive group of outsiders.

Al Jenkins

---

237. Memorandum From Alfred Jenkins of the National Security Council Staff to the President's Special Assistant (Rostow)[1]

Washington, February 15, 1967.

SUBJECT

Is Mao Engaged in Tactical Backtracking?

Events of the last couple of days have the smell of something rather big having happened in Peking. Unquestionably an effort is being made to curb the excesses of the Cultural Revolution, at least for the present:

—Red Guards have again been urged to return home and this time appear to be complying;
—primary and secondary education are to be resumed;
—widespread humiliation of errant leaders and cadre is to cease and reliable elements in the party apparatus are to be won over rather than attacked;
—the military, having for the most part not responded to the plea to support revolutionary rebel take-over, is now moving in on the side of simply maintaining public order;
—spring planting in the countryside is to be emphasized at the expense of political activity;
—the xenophobic spree has been turned off like a faucet, at least for the present.

These developments follow a brief period wherein the Army was tested with far less than satisfactory results from the Maoist viewpoint. I believe this to have been only the last in a series of surprises for Mao con-

---

[1] Source: Johnson Library, National Security File, Country File, China, Vol. VIII. Confidential. Copies were sent to Jorden and Ropa. Rostow sent a copy to the President with a covering note of the same date. A handwritten "L" on the covering note indicates that it was seen by the President.

cerning the magnitude of his opposition, as he has successively turned during the Cultural Revolution to the several major elements in the society. He has increasingly suffered from a classical phenomenon of a regime of this sort: the difficulty of receiving accurate reports, either from the home or the foreign front, which would often be unflattering to one who has been deified.

If because of the test results of the Cultural Revolution Mao is now forced to face reality and curb that Revolution far short of its goals, his prestige will again have suffered severely. Having built revolutionary fires, he may even find it difficult to lower the temperature of the Revolution to the desired degree. Animosity has obviously been greatly heightened among the split leadership and Mao's methods in conducting the Revolution have contributed to sharpening the large opposition which he has progressively uncovered in each phase of the Revolution.

As Lin Piao's activity and perhaps even prestige has sunk, Chou Enlai's has risen. However, while Lin is less obviously heir apparent, Chou is not yet in that role. Chou may be smart enough not to aspire to being heir apparent, when it is not now apparent what he would be inheriting! He is emerging stronger, but I still look upon him as a first class "DCM" to a "political appointee"—which may yet turn out to be a *military self-*appointee.

What can be said is that the forces of moderation (in *domestic* policy) are on the march and are not likely to be stopped. If those forces should coalesce and become articulate, I believe the peasants, the most important element not yet appreciably tested, may support them. For never have so many worked so hard for so little—after having been promised so much for so long.

Alfred Jenkins

238. Memorandum From the President's Special Consultant (Roche) to President Johnson[1]

Washington, February 15, 1967.

The press today carried a story from Tokyo that Ambassador Alexis Johnson had made a speech suggesting that the United States wanted the anti-Mao faction in China to win.[2]

I believe this is a serious mistake for three reasons:

1) In my judgment we should want Mao to win. A victory for the anti-Mao forces would probably lead to some sort of Sino-Soviet reconciliation—a development which I do not consider to be in the American national interest.

2) If *in fact* we do want the anti-Mao forces to win, a speech like Johnson's works to Mao's advantage.

3) If *in fact* we want Mao to win and Johnson's speech is an attempt to *hurt* the anti-Mao faction by giving it "imperialist support," we are getting too clever for our own good. Machiavelli died broke.

I would suggest that the Secretary of State issue firm instructions to our missions not to dabble in the religious wars of the Communist world.[3]

JR

---

[1] Source: Johnson Library, National Security File, Country File, China, Vol. XIII. Secret. A note on the source text in Johnson's handwriting reads: "To Walt for report soon. L." A note in Rostow's handwriting reads: "W.J. Check and report, please. W.R."

[2] For text of Johnson's speech before the Asian Affairs Research Council in Tokyo on February 13, see the Department of State *Bulletin*, March 13, 1967, pp. 420–424.

[3] A February 17 memorandum from William Jorden to Rostow states that Johnson's speech reviewed U.S. relations with China since 1784 and that his references to current policy were totally consistent with U.S. policy as expressed by the President and Secretary. Jorden commented that given the current situation in China, almost anything said in favor of pragmatism or reason would be interpreted by some as taking a stand in the internal conflict. He concluded: "I don't think we should stop talking about China and the hope for reconciliation, or the hope that reason will prevail." (Johnson Library, National Security File, Name File, Jorden Memos)

239. Telegram From the Embassy in the Republic of China to the Department of State[1]

Taipei, February 17, 1967, 0758Z.

2460. Ref Taipei 2351.[2]

1. During call by Joe Yager and myself on DefMin Chiang Ching-kuo today latter raised subject of my approach to MOFA Feb 8 on GRC irregulars in tri-border area.

2. He indicated mild surprise that I had gone to MOFA since, he said, MOFA was not conversant with the problem. I refrained from replying that that was one reason I had gone through MOFA, to be sure they would be informed.

3. He said flatly and directly that GRC was not supplying arms or funds to irregular units in Thailand. He said Thai Govt had repeatedly requested that GRC exercise better control over the units to prevent loss of civil control in northern Thailand. He said neither Tuan Hsi-wen nor Li Wen-huan was amenable to much control, and that they had until recently refused to come to Taiwan for discussions. Tuan had finally visited Taiwan a few months ago, but conversations had not been satisfactory. Gen Hsu Ju-ch'i had just been sent to the area by the GRC to look into present conditions, and when Hsu returned DefMin would be in touch with Embassy again. DefMin said he thought USG had not understood the situation correctly, possibly because of statement Tuan Hsi-wen might have made on return to Thailand, in order to bolster his prestige asserting that GRC would send assistance.

4. DefMin repeated that GRC aware of delicacy of situation and had no intention of augmenting or supplying the units. He said that he was referring, as I had earlier, only to the organized units, and not to certain intelligence collection efforts in the border area, which would of course continue.

5. I thanked him for the information, and asked about the reported plans for an air lift through Laos. He said that the irregular units in Thailand had requested that the GRC arrange an air shipment through Laos, but that the GRC had refused.

---

[1] Source: Department of State, Central Files, DEF 6–5 CHINAT. Secret; Limdis. Repeated to Bangkok, Rangoon, and Vientiane.

[2] Telegram 2351 from Taipei, February 7, reported that in a meeting with Sampson Shen that day, Hummel expressed U.S. concern about reports that increasing GRC planning and activity seemed to be leading toward an enlarged and more active paramilitary force in the Thai–Laos–Burma border area and stated the U.S. view that such increased activity would backfire. Hummel was carrying out instructions conveyed in telegram 131645, February 4. (Both ibid.)

6. *Comment:* Lack of candor on this subject is par for the course and was to be expected. However believe we have made some headway on this problem in that: (a) DefMin has assured us that GRC is not going to augment or supply the units (and even if this turns out to be untrue we have additional leverage because of the assertion); (b) He has promised to be in touch with us again when Gen Hsu returns and we may be able to glean more information and obtain more assurances at that time; (c) He has denied any intention to establish an air supply route through Laos, (although at same time apparently misrepresenting the GRC's reported recent use of the route).

Hummel

---

240. **Memorandum From the President's Special Assistant (Rostow) to President Johnson**[1]

Washington, February 20, 1967, 6:30 p.m.

SUBJECT

Opposition to Mao

The situation in China is so confused as to defy brief description. The accompanying map[2] is the best that can be done by way of indicating the province-by-province situation as of today, but it does not reflect the magnitude of the confusion. It shows that most of China is still in dispute, but the significant fact is that not a single province or municipality shown as in either the pro- or anti-Mao camp is without elements of significant opposition.

I strongly suspect that the Soviets have been instigating and aiding anti-Mao resistance in Sinkiang, Manchuria and possibly Inner Mongolia.

Ever since Mao's call to "seize power" throughout the country, there have been numerous phony power seizures, so that it has been difficult

---

[1] Source: Johnson Library, National Security File, Country File, China, Vol. VIII. Secret. A handwritten "L" on the source text indicates that the President saw the memorandum.

[2] Not attached to the source text.

for anyone to tell who are the "genuine revolutionaries" and who the "enemy." Even local military units have difficulty in identifying which of competing rival groups actually have Mao's sanction, and which authority in the confused military chain of command to respond to.

Much of this confusion arises from the fact that the revolution itself was artificial in its inception, inasmuch as Mao imposed it from the top. Its stated objectives have been too generalized and too vacillating to afford practical guidance for consistent action, even if major elements of the society desired to further its objectives.

Mao's opposition has eagerly added to the confusion by promoting dissention, by offering economic incentives to workers and peasants, by walking off the job, and at times by feigning support. Peking complains that many groups have "used the name of revolutionary rebel organizations falsely." Furthermore, there is continued resistance to the few "revolutionary" organizations which have received Peking's blessing as genuine. It is possible that their control does not extend much beyond provincial capitals.

Mao still retains the initiative, and the opposition is not broadly organized except perhaps in Tibet, Szechuan and Inner Mongolia. The atmosphere of suspicion, mistrust, and—perhaps most of all—uncertainty, now pervades the entire unhappy country. Mao has unleashed forces which are not yet ready to listen to exhortations for moderation. The Minister of Security has called on genuine revolutionaries to "put an end to armed struggle" and to "stop using loudspeakers to insult their enemies." However, typical provincial radio comment continues to say to all "demons and monsters" that the revolutionary rebels will "resolutely suppress you and smash your dogs' heads."

Mao's grand design in foreign policy of two years ago has failed completely, and it now appears that his domestic economy may well be disrupted by the Cultural Revolution as seriously as it was by the Great Leap of 1958–59.

Walt

241. Memorandum From Alfred Jenkins of the National Security Council Staff to the President's Special Assistant (Rostow)[1]

Washington, February 24, 1967.

SUBJECT

Ascendancy of Premier Chou and His Policies

Strenuous attempts in the past ten days to reverse the alarming trend toward anarchy in China can only be interpreted as an ignominious failure of Mao's Cultural Revolution—at least temporarily, and almost certainly for the long run as well. However, this tactical backtracking, if it can be accomplished, may save the nation from literally breaking apart.

Mao appears consistently, at each stage of his grand design to restore purity and elan to the revolution, to have underestimated the strength of his opposition. The final blow was the relative unresponsiveness of the armed forces when they were called upon some three weeks ago to support the seizure of power by "revolutionary rebels." (No significant Maoist successes have been reported for over two weeks.) For the most part the Army has stepped in merely in attempts to restore order, and not to further the fortunes of the Maoist revolutionaries.

Not surprisingly, there has been a steady decline in the prestige of Defense Minister Lin Piao, identified with the more extreme measures of the Cultural Revolution along with Madame Mao and Cultural Revolution head Chen Po-ta.

As usual, Premier Chou En-lai, a moderate at least in domestic policies, has timed his moves with consummate skill. In the past week he has appeared to be virtually in charge in Peking, with important directives being issued in the names of Mao and Chou—even those which ex officio Lin Piao would be expected to sign. Chou's recent confidence, and the reinstitution of moderate policies he has advocated for the Cultural Revolution, almost certainly mean that he believes he and his pragmatic policies now have strong, and perhaps predominant, support in the armed forces.

Increasingly demonstrable damage to China's marginal economy, stemming from the excesses of the Cultural Revolution, was doubtless foremost among other factors enabling Chou and his supporters to bring about the present attempted shift away from the Mao–Lin romantically

---

[1] Source: Johnson Library, National Security File, Country File, China, Vol. VIII. Secret. Copies were sent to Jorden and Ropa. The source text was sent to President Johnson with a February 24 covering note from Bromley Smith; a handwritten "L" on the covering note indicates that it was seen by the President.

unrealistic program to remake Chinese society. The inexorable demands of spring planting are a staunch support to Chou in his efforts to restore reason.

No one can say whether he can be successful. The very respect for the central government has been seriously damaged, and regional interests have become both more insistent and more confident.

The tremendous amount of resentment engendered in all segments of society in this turbulence may be long in abating. The chief disadvantaged group in Chinese society is the emerging younger generation who have a secondary or higher education. They were first flattered and drummed up to revolutionary ferver, and now are told that they have acted immaturely and should go home and keep quiet. They are not likely to do the latter.

Basically underlying the party dissention which exploded last year has been the choice between technological growth and restoring revolutionary elan. The Cultural Revolution may have insured that neither choice will be available for a time: the likely prospect is for a period of political weakness in which policies will be contradictory and indecisive.

Alfred Jenkins

---

242. Telegram From the Embassy in the Republic of China to the Department of State[1]

Taipei, February 25, 1967, 0417Z.

2547. Ref State 135828.[2] Subj: Country Team assessment of GRC intentions.

1. Conclusion: There are no signs that the GRC intends to make any significant military or paramilitary moves against Communist China in the near future; on the contrary, the GRCs current stance is marked by its cautious, wait-and-see character.

---

[1] Source: Department of State, Central Files, POL CHICOM–CHINAT. Secret; Limdis.

[2] Telegram 135828, February 13, suggested that the Embassy consider reinstituting its former period telegrams summarizing indications of possible GRC actions against the mainland. It suggested reporting on a biweekly basis while the current mainland turmoil continued at a significant level. (Ibid.)

2. Discussion: During the latter half of 1966, the GRC groped for a proper response to the upset of Mao's Cultural Revolution. Various intelligence and paramilitary schemes for possible exploitation of the situation were drawn up, but they consisted in the main of operations beyond GRC capabilities, or possible only with sizeable US support. The GRC apparently understands that such US support will not be forthcoming.

3. GRC intelligence units continue to formulate plans for sabotage and other small-scale operations against the mainland, but these units lack the capabilities to carry out these plans to any significant extent. Results are unlikely to be any better than in the past.

4. Since last fall there has been some shift of emphasis in the GRC's approach to the problem of mainland turmoil. President Chiang has ruled specifically against any precipitate action at this time. This decision was made explicit in the President's New Year's message, in which he called for political rather than military action. Subsequently, we have received reliable intelligence reports documenting the GRC's disinclination to take military action at this time.

5. This wait-and-see stance is largely a product of the GRC's limited capabilities for unilateral action, but it is reinforced now by real conviction that outside pressures might retard rather than accelerate disintegrative trends on the mainland. This position may shift if a real break-down of Communist authority on the mainland occurs, or if the GRC concludes that it has occurred. Even then, however, we would expect the response of the GRC to be conditioned by the amount of US support it thought it could muster.

McConaughy

243. Action Memorandum From the Deputy Assistant Secretary of State for East Asian and Pacific Affairs (Berger) to Secretary of State Rusk[1]

Washington, March 1, 1967.

SUBJECT

Letter from Ambassador Thompson to Mr. Bundy[2]

1. Ambassador Thompson, in the attached letter, would like authority to offer to pass some of our reports on developments in Communist China to a top Soviet leader. He would do it orally and informally, and has in mind Gromyko, Firubin, or Lapin, in the course of a call. The particular report he has in mind to pass would be the first twelve paragraphs of Hong Kong's 5773, also attached.[3] Alternately, or additionally, he thinks it would be useful to show Gromyko the reporting telegram of Gronouski's next talk with the Chinese.

2. Ambassador Thompson thinks this might help allay Soviet suspicions of our relations with the Chinese, and perhaps lead to an exchange.

3. He wanted these ideas tried out with you. He asked this be kept very close, since the Soviets would be concerned if there was any leak that we were exchanging information on China, and he wants to be able to say only two people know about it in the Department.

4. I see no difficulty in offering to give the Soviets the first twelve paragraphs of the Hong Kong telegram. It reports what may be happening in various provinces in China. If the Soviets show any interest in our reports we can then provide others, including Gronouski's report of his next talks.

5. If you agree, I will send a letter to Ambassador Thompson along these lines.[4]

---

[1] Source: Department of State, Central Files, POL CHICOM–US. Secret; Exdis.

[2] Dated February 21; attached but not printed.

[3] Telegram 5773 from Hong Kong, dated February 17, is attached but not printed.

[4] Rusk initialed his approval on March 5.

244. Memorandum From Alfred Jenkins of the National Security Council Staff to the President's Special Assistant (Rostow)[1]

Washington, March 6, 1967.

SUBJECT

The Next Chinese Dynasty and U.S. Policy

A. Failure of Mao's Supreme (and Last?) Effort at Purification

The turning point in the Cultural Revolution in the past three weeks has probably been a decisive one. There are still many imponderables, but the following seems fairly certain:

1. Insofar as the Cultural Revolution was to be an ideological remolding campaign, it has failed. Even as a purge device it appears to have failed far short of Mao's extravagant objectives, but it may well have succeeded for Chou En-lai's.

2. The prestige and authority of the Party have been damaged, but dissolution has stopped short of wrecking the Party's machinery; the concept of revolutionary communes, which Mao seems earlier to have envisaged as supplanting the Party, has been shelved. "Three-way alliances" are a far cry from "Paris communes," and are consonant with Chou's policies of stability and reason.

3. The damage to industry and agriculture is doubtless considerable, but will probably not be ruinous if present efforts to restore order are successful. Much depends upon peasant—and Army—reaction to increased Army participation in production. We should know more about the extent of damage in another month or so.

4. As expected, the Army is playing the crucial role in the Revolution's apparent denouement. The Army earlier would not back Mao's revolutionary rebels' take-overs, but is now backing Chou's efforts at preservation of nationhood and attention to the economy.

5. "Regionalism" is not a likelihood: the Army wouldn't have it.

6. The Army's crucial loyalty proved to be not to Mao and Lin, but to stability—to the status quo. Most elements of the society seem to be preponderantly of like mind—and the status quo is "creeping revisionism."

---

[1] Source: Johnson Library, National Security File, Country File, China, Vol. IX. Secret. Copies were sent to Jorden and Ropa. Rostow sent this memorandum to the President with a March 7 covering memorandum noting that he was inclined to agree that "in their own peculiar way the Chinese have turned the corner towards a 'moderate' domestic and foreign policy," although he thought its emergence might be slow and tortuous. He concluded: "But they started at the possibility of famine and drew back; and that's a beginning at least."

7. However, the battle is far from over. The prestige of Mao himself is probably still high; support for Maoism is obviously less, but of unknown proportions. Clearly, however, the actions of Chou are currently eclipsing the thought of Mao, even while the two leaders are professing to be in league—an accommodation which Mao had to make, not Chou. Chou's great problem is that the state of the nation is such that even his policies will require Army insurance for their implementation. This is dangerous. He may not succeed.

B.   Has the Succession, in Effect, Taken Place?

There are those who believe that Mao is still fully in charge, and that he now purposefully desires to halt at the present "Half-way House" with Chou as its major domo. I doubt the validity of both assumptions. Mao has simply been unable to carry out his announced policies, and reports of ill health are increasingly convincing. The recent Albanian report of Mao's partial incapacitation is more credible than the Mauritanian one that he is in good health. The Mauritanians, who had never seen Mao previously, could have met a double. This would not have been possible with the Albanians. Furthermore, the Albanians have no reason to invent ill-health for Mao—quite the contrary. True, Maoism, under whatever—doubtless complex—auspices, ran the Cultural Revolution as long as it ran, but it has about run down. Some elements will surely continue to push for reforms in line with Mao's doctrinal purity, but their cause has received an impressive rebuff and we may have seen the last determined effort.

Prior to the sudden ascendancy of Lin Piao, the only three contenders other than Chou for Mao's mantle were Liu Shao-ch'i, Teng Hsiao-p'ing and P'eng Chen. The latter three seem to be no longer in the running, and Liu's status is at least problematical. Furthermore, the policies which Chou has long advocated now appear to have military backing. Mao may be able to weather this embarrassment, but Lin may not.

So long as Mao's extreme policies were in command, the Army did not assist in the purging of provincial leaders. (The Army's role in the Peking purges is not clear.) Reports from the recent trouble spots of Inner Mongolia, Sinkiang, Szechwan and Kwangtung now suggest compromises, with strong hints that some of the top leadership have been replaced, with Army acquiescence or connivance. Those involved are mostly Liu and Teng men, whose political demise *both* Mao *and* Chou would probably applaud. It will be interesting to see whether Chou men take their places. The top men in running the economy now appear to be Li Hsien-nien and T'ao Chen-lin, both of whom are long-time associates of Chou. Certainly they have not secured or retained influence because of adherence to a particular policy line, for Li is far to the right within the lop-sided Chinese Communist spectrum, while T'ao was one of the most zealous of the Great Leapers. Chou himself appears lately to have a strong hand in running the military establishment.

C.   *Policy Implications*

It is too early to decide that Chou is comfortably in the saddle and likely to remain there. The power struggle could continue for some time. Furthermore, we cannot be sure that Chou wants the top job. However, at the moment he is more in the saddle than anyone else and there is no one yet visible who is likely to challenge him successfully. Even if Chou does not want the top job he may have to rule, in fact if not in name, during a "holding in trust" period.

It is not too early to try to divine what sort of China we might have if Chou is to dominate the scene. This is a murky area in which to prophesy, for Chou has been an executor rather than an initiator, but it is worth the effort. The transition to some new course, which is now bound to come under whatever leadership, is likely to take quite a few more months. The outlines of the new course may be apparent by about May, however, and it is conceivable that we may be faced with some hard decisions by summer.

It seems to me that if Chou is running things we may expect something like the following:

1.   Pragmatic, somewhat "revisionist," and increasingly effective economic policies, with heavy emphasis on agriculture.

2.   An emphasis on "expertness" over "redress," with favorable effect on the economy and defense, after the effects of the Cultural Revolution can be overcome.

3.   A China tending more to look to its own needs, possibly to the extent of being predominantly isolationist for a time, except for considerations of 4. and 5. below.

4.   A foreign policy less ambitious, more realistic and rational, and therefore at the same time more effective. Something of the "Bandung spirit" could return.

5.   Attempts to capitalize on rationality and moderation to gain international acceptance, prestige and legitimatization.

6.   Continued, but less frenetic, anti-Americanism. Post-Vietnam, chance greater for some accommodation.

7.   Possibly a slow papering over of Sino-Soviet differences, but short of fraternal alliance. Chou has never loved the Russians.

8.   Continued support for North Vietnam, but less obduracy in the event Hanoi should want to call a halt.

9.   If the Gimo should die, a wooing of the GRC toward a "deal"—in the expectation it will be softened up for such by its bleak future qua GRC resulting from Peking's successes in 5. above at Taipei's correlative expense.

If something like the above is in the offing, we have some hard policy decisions to make at some as yet unpredictable point. They all relate to two very basic decisions:

1. What sort of Taiwan (among the likely viable varieties) is it in the U.S. interest to have eventuate? How can we contribute to bringing it about?

Can the GRC, as such, survive the prospect of a "moderate" mainland regime which may be virtually universally accepted? Will it even attempt to, or will it make a deal with a moderate Peking giving promise of progress, thus yielding not only to "inevitability" but to deep Sinocentric urges—especially if it seems to be a case of faute de mieux? Would the Taiwanese permit this? Should the UN interest itself in the status of the Island if such a conceivably bloody test appeared likely?

2. What should be our posture toward a more moderate mainland China?

Since the post-Maoist regime (with or without Mao as "Chairman Emeritus") is likely, at least for a time, to continue to be anti-American and to rebuff advances from us, should we fight its acceptance by others? Should we read this putative regime's near-universal acceptance as being inevitable and make a try for the supposed advantages of early overtures, in the hope of a new day in Sino-American relations? Even if ultimate near-universal acceptance appears inevitable, is there merit in our delaying overtures until we appear to be swept along (because of GRC or other considerations)? Has the combination of China's "madness" and its growing power reached the point where we should seize upon the first good excuse to get China better articulated with international problems?

To what extent should we discuss these vital questions with certain allies before the time of decision? This applies especially, perhaps, to our Asian allies, and among them most particularly Japan. Since in the quest for a stable Asia the overriding desideratum is a reasonably promising balance of power, where does the Soviet Union, as a Pacific power, fit into the scheme?

These are some of the questions to which, it seems to me, the Government Community should now be addressing itself, and concerning which I hope to have something to say in future memoranda.

Alfred Jenkins

245. Memorandum From the Representative to the United Nations (Goldberg) to President Johnson[1]

Washington, March 9, 1967.

SUBJECT

Report on First Leg of Asian Trip

Because of my responsibilities in connection with the Outer Space Treaty, I was able to visit only five countries on the first leg of the trip to Asia and to spend a shorter time in each one than I would have desired: one day each in Korea, Taiwan and the Philippines, two and a half days in Japan, and three days in South Vietnam.

[Here follows discussion of South Vietnam and Japan.]

III. Republic of China (Taiwan)

I found it interesting that the Generalissimo, with whom I spent half a day,[2] expressed fears similar to those of Sato, namely: that the Soviets would choose to take advantage of the disorder on the mainland to fulfill long harbored expansionist designs. In this very limited sense, he seemed to have something in common with the mainland regime.

At the same time he has clearly not renounced hopes of overthrowing that regime. Indeed, the major portion of his discussion with me consisted of the following analysis and request, which he asked specifically be conveyed to you. Given the serious split between Moscow and Peking, the drain of Vietnam on Peking's resources, and the serious turmoil on the mainland itself, now is the golden opportunity to rid the mainland of the Communist regime and destroy the Chinese nuclear threat. Unless this is done, the war in Vietnam cannot be ended and will in fact be extended to a wider area. The people on the mainland, while not able to overthrow the Communist regime from within, have now become anti-Mao (in addition to being anti-Communist) and would rally to his cause if he were to return to the mainland with force. All that is needed to set this process in motion is the approval and logistic support—but not manpower—of the US.

I, of course, undertook to convey this analysis and request to you and avoided any substantive reply. Nevertheless, feeling it advisable to

---

[1] Source: Johnson Library, National Security File, Agency File, United Nations. Secret. Goldberg sent the memorandum with a covering note to the President stating that it supplemented his oral report the previous day. It is filed with a covering note of March 10 from Rostow. A handwritten "L" on Rostow's covering note indicates that it was seen by the President.

[2] On March 1. Telegram 2623 from Taipei, March 2, reported the conversation; a detailed memorandum of conversation was transmitted with airgram A–595, March 4. (Both ibid., and in Department of State, Central Files, POL 7 US/GOLDBERG)

prepare the way for a rejection of the Generalissimo's request, I did note that US commitments elsewhere were onerous, that the American people were in no mood to increase their involvement in potentially dangerous situations, and that the general American mood was one wanting to reduce rather than create new tension in Asia. I need scarcely add that my own conviction is that the Generalissimo's request should be politely but categorically rejected.

As requested by the Secretary of State, I raised the question of our recognition of Outer Mongolia leaving further discussion to our Ambassador.

[Here follows discussion of Korea and the Philippines.]

246.   Telegram From the Embassy in Laos to the Department of State[1]

Vientiane, March 10, 1967, 0216Z.

5546. 1. During wide-ranging critique of U.S. policy which it was my function to present at recent Baguio meeting, I made certain suggestions on medium and long range policies for Taiwan and the Pescadores. These suggestions were tabled "for further staffing."

2. In order provide framework for those who wish examine these suggestions further, I will spell out in this message the rather sketchy oral statement which I made at Baguio. As I said in that presentation, it is a proposal which I believe ought to be examined in further detail.

3. Moreover, it is based on two premises. The first is the assumption that Communist China's internal problems will keep it occupied for a long time and that our function is to prepare the framework into which we would like to see China fitted when and if it decides to rejoin polite society. The second assumption is that we will achieve a successful and satisfactory stabilization of the military problem in Southeast Asia which will permit us to withdraw a large portion of our armed forces from Vietnam, but which will leave us the necessity of remaining alert for possible ready reintroduction. Flowing from these two premises, would be the probability that we could thin out our U.S. troop commitments in both Korea and Vietnam to more or less "trip-wire" proportions.

---

[1] Source: Department of State, Central Files, POL 1 CHINAT–US. Secret; Limdis. Repeated to Hong Kong, Taipei, Tokyo, CINCPAC, JCS, and USUN.

4. From this base, I predicated the idea that our interests and those of Japan lay in seeing Taiwan and the Pescadores permanently divorced from Mainland China, even a Mainland China which converted to a considerable benevolence. In short, both we and the Japanese have a vested interest in a "Two China" situation.

5. My proposal, therefore, was that we move, with appropriate associates, to define the sovereignty of the GRC as limited to Taiwan and the Pescadores, in accordance with the administrative sphere assigned the GRC by the Supreme Commander for the Allied Powers, under whose authority the GRC ultimately occupies and administers these islands. There is a sound legal case for this, well preserved in our diplomatic acts and in treaties affecting this territory.

6. This, in turn, would lead to a definition of territorial representatives in the United Nations and establish a "Two China" situation there, providing the framework into which an ultimate, reformed, Mainland China might one day be fitted.

7. It would also require the GRC abandonment of the Offshore Islands and a clear stipulation by the U.S. Government (as distinct from our current deliberate vagueness) that the so-called "Formosa Resolution" applies to Taiwan and the Pescadores only.

8. In order to give some enforcement to these measures, I further recommended the deployment of a forward ready reserve of U.S. ground forces to Taiwan. This would doubtless have to be accomplished before we went to the mat with the GRC on such matters as the Offshore Islands and the Formosa resolution. The troops would be some of those withdrawn from Korea and Vietnam.

9. In part, this deployment would have a military and psychological purpose, to give positive evidence, in the area, of our readiness to renew our presence in either Vietnam or Korea should conditions warrant. In larger part, it would have a political purpose, directly associated with China policy.

10. Its first political purpose would be to prevent a deal behind our backs and against our interest. To borrow Ed Rice's phrase "When the empire unites, it tends to divide; when the empire divides, it tends to unite". A deliberate "Two China" policy would please the Taiwanese and perhaps many of the second generation Mainlanders: but there would be many of the old Mainlanders who would rather make a deal with Peking than be subjected to permanent divorce from the Mainland. Our troop presence would be designed to inhibit this.

11. Moreover, our troop presence would be designed as a blue chip for eventual negotiations with Peking. As matters now stand, even a regenerate Mainland regime could be expected to demand the return of Taiwan before agreeing to any sort of normal relations with the U.S. In the event, there would be a great popular pressure, at home and abroad,

to make this sacrifice, especially if Peking appeared less and less bloody minded. In the current circumstances, the only things we could bargain against Peking's demand would be the Offshore Islands. Now, these the ChiComs could take in any event unless we were willing to fight for them (highly dubious prospect).

12. Hence, if, when faced with Peking's demand, we have a lot of U.S. troops whose presence we can trade away against an international agreement guaranteeing the independence of Taiwan and the Pescadores, we are in a far better bargaining position. As Admiral Sharp points out, Guam is good a place as any for our ready reserve, and we would really not deprive ourselves of much military advantage if we withdrew there, especially if we could do this in return for an agreed independence for Taipei.

13. Finally, it can be argued that U.S. troops in Taiwan would obviate the GRC requirement for a large, costly standing army. If this argument is accepted, we would have less MAP costs, less effective opposition to "Two Chinas" and more resources, both financial and human, for Taiwan's economic development.

14. These, then, are the elements for a staff study. I hope it can be presented in final form for debate at next year's Baguio Conference.

Sullivan

247. Telegram From the Consulate General at Hong Kong to the Department of State[1]

Hong Kong, March 15, 1967, 0428Z.

6436. Ref: Vientiane 5546.[2] Subject: Staffing out Ambassador Sullivan's China policy suggestions.[3]

1. It is rare that anybody attacks an old problem with a brand new plan which is wholly feasible and I think this is no exception. Sometimes

---

[1] Source: Department of State, Central Files, POL 1 CHINAT–US. Secret; Limdis. Repeated to Vientiane, Taipei, Tokyo, CINCPAC, JCS, and USUN.

[2] Document 246.

[3] Telegram 3404 from Taipei, May 3, reported that McConaughy intended to discuss Document 246 and telegram 6436 during his upcoming consultations in Washington, and that he believed an oral exchange would be more useful than further telegraphic discussion. (Department of State, Central Files, POL 1 CHINAT–US)

however the plan does contain new ideas which, perhaps with slight modifications, serve to advance such problems towards solutions. I think both these remarks apply to Ambassador Sullivan's imaginative and ingenious proposal.

2.   Central to this new plan is a proposal for the future stationing of U.S. troops on Taiwan, ostensibly for the primary purpose of serving as ready reserve for reintroduction if necessary into Southeast Asia but actually to inhibit a GRC–Mainland deal behind our backs, eventually to force the GRC to evacuate the Offshore Islands, and ultimately to trade withdrawal of our troops for ChiCom acceptance of an international agreement guaranteeing independence of Taiwan and the Pescadores.

3.   For reasons set forth in subsequent paragraphs I think this plan infeasible. Against background of estimates of present military balance in Offshore Islands–Taiwan Straits area, however, it does suggest means whereby U.S. forces could perhaps be used to achieve one of Ambassador Sullivan's objectives—bringing about evacuation of Offshores and consequent de facto separation of Taiwan from Mainland. If the increased ChiCom inventories of supersonic all-weather aircraft and of naval units means GRC could not successfully handle another Taiwan Straits crisis without U.S. help, then we have improved chance of successfully pressing for evacuation of Offshores. This result might be obtained prior to emergence such crisis when and if President Chiang becomes convinced military return to Mainland not possible or after he is succeeded by more realistic leadership. It might be obtained in event of such crisis by making our lending necessary military assistance conditional on GRC agreement to evacuation of the Offshores. (A case, and perhaps a better one, could be made for further modernization GRC defense establishment to give it qualitative air and naval superiority so that we would not need become directly involved in such a crisis, and I submit this too deserves staffing out.)

4.   Main defect of Sullivan plan is its deviousness, which is open to objection on purely pragmatic grounds that we would not be able convincingly to mask our purposes and thereby accomplish them. The Chinese are past masters and we mere children when it comes to dissembling innocence and carrying on devious games. I do not believe we could propose bringing to Taiwan the forces Ambassador Sullivan has in mind, for the ends he contemplates, without the ever-suspicious Chinese seeing through our purposes. If their agreement were forthcoming it would be because of Chinese confidence that our designs could be thwarted, and the presence of our troops used instead to serve GRC interests.

5.   Most of us who have worked full-time on Chinese affairs would disagree with assumption contained paragraph 11 reftel that evacuation Offshores is something we now could use in bargaining with Peking.

(The presence on the Offshores of GRC forces suits the ChiComs because it may some day give Peking the chance to deal the GRC a devastating blow; meanwhile they like it because it helps prevent a so-called Two-Chinas solution.) It also is far from sure that ChiComs would bargain for the evacuation of U.S. forces from Taiwan. Instead they might bank on stirring up Chinese xenophobia on Taiwan against the U.S. occupation of the island and U.S. efforts to control its government. Finding that the ChiComs would not bargain for the evacuation of bases we had built up to accommodate our forces—doubtless at considerable expense—we would be tempted to retain the bases and keep our forces on Taiwan.

6. In that event we would find ourselves more deeply and perhaps inextricably involved with the two Chinese sides. As I pointed out in Baguio, our experience with past involvements in China has been anything but happy or profitable, and pursuing them is likely to prove no more fortunate and to leave us deeper in the red. If the GRC ever gives us an honorable means of ending the involvement, we should not lightly pass it up.

7. At a time well before we had a treaty with the GRC, and when we were considering what attitude we should adopt toward a possible ChiCom invasion of Taiwan, I felt that Mainland control of Taiwan was contrary to U.S. interests, and said so. I still feel that way today and believe we must stand by our obligations under the defense treaty we subsequently negotiated. However I am not convinced that the real estate the treaty is designed to protect is worth the ultimate risks for us which the treaty—which represented intervention in an unfinished civil war—may entail. Hence, if the GRC wishes to nullify the treaty by making a deal with the Mainland, we would be relieved of our moral obligation to it and should not, I think, go so far as to use force or the threat of force against the GRC in order to hold it to that treaty.

8. I doubt any regime likely to emerge on the Chinese Mainland in the near future is going to become party to an international agreement whereby it formally accedes to the permanent separation of Taiwan from the Mainland. There is a better chance it will learn to live with such a separation. It seems to me that a situation in which it did so would represent the optimum practicable goal of relevant U.S. policy for the foreseeable future.

Rice

248. Telegram From the Embassy in the Republic of China to the
      Department of State[1]

Taipei, March 15, 1967, 1004Z.

2798. 1. DefMin Chiang Ching-kuo called on me at my residence at
his own request March 14 principally to suggest regular exchanges of
views on China Mainland, and policies and actions directed thereto. He
thought meetings should be held at least once a month.

2. He began by giving categorical assurance that GRC major policies are "fully coordinated" with those of the US, that they have been in
the past and will continue to be so in future. He said that as Gimo had told
Amb Goldberg, it is important that we achieve close coordination of
views and actions, and asked for my assessment of present Mainland situation.

3. I thanked him for assurance of close coordination and welcomed
regular exchange of views. I outlined for him the US view that Mainland
tensions were being damped down, probably for tactical and pragmatic
reasons, and as at least a temporary measure to prevent economic chaos.
I covered, inter alia, role Chou En-lai seemed to be playing, our puzzlement at the virtual disappearance of Lin and Liu from the stage, our feeling that Mao's views were unlikely to have undergone fundamental
change, and the probability that both the power struggle and the ideological controversy are far from over. I said I would like to obtain latest
assessments from Washington and Hong Kong and to continue the discussion next week.

4. CCK said he agreed with my analysis, that the Mainland situation is "highly abnormal" and that we will all need more time to observe
events before we can come to firm conclusions. In response to my question, CCK said the ChiComs would not change their views on the Vietnam war, and would do their best to block any peace settlement. A
settlement would not only be a sharp reverse for ChiCom foreign policy,
but would have serious internal consequences as well. He said he
thought the ChiComs could get through the spring planting season without too much trouble, but that there would be a critical period at the time
of the fall harvest.

5. I asked for any indications of ChiCom intentions in the Taiwan
Straits, referring to the recent incidents of ChiCom boat incursions near
the Offshore Islands. He said that aside from these incidents there were
no particular indications. Some ChiCom troops in the Fukien area had

---

[1] Source: Department of State, Central Files, POL CHINAT–US. Secret; Limdis.
Repeated to Hong Kong.

been rotated, but overall numbers remained the same. Psywar activities, however, had been stepped up, especially those aimed at Taiwanese soldiers, with Fukienese dialect replacing Mandarin as the language used in broadcasts and over loudspeakers. There had been a doubling of the number of balloon-bearing propaganda leaflets (to 380 in the past month) over the similar period last year, when prevailing winds permit such ChiCom operations. He was somewhat concerned that rumors are being spread on Taiwan that the leaflets are released here by a strong Communist underground, and to counter this, the GRC is making known that they are carried to Taiwan by balloon. The leaflets and other materials, which include books on Mao's thought and on the Cultural Revolution, are more specifically targeted toward GRC armed forces, although they use familiar themes that the US is disengaging from and will eventually abandon the GRC, that GRC troops should assist in efforts to liberate Taiwan, and exhorting troops to stage a coup and overthrow the government.

6. CCK said he was getting questions from the Legislative Yuan on the level of US military assistance, and mentioned a newspaper report that a sum of US$200 million had been earmarked for division between Korea and the GRC. I said this could not be true, since Congress had not acted on the appropriation request, and since in any case they do not earmark MAP funds by country in this manner. I assured him that the GRC's needs were put forward vigorously, but I cautioned him that Vietnam needs had priority, and that there seemed to be strong Congressional sentiment for economy elsewhere. I said that some other countries (including Korea, Thailand and the Philippines) had special requirements, and that it could be impossible to divide up a reduced appropriation among the recipients to the satisfaction of all.

7. CCK said he was sure I understood the GRC need. He said the ChiComs watch carefully all news of US military assistance, and there is a political impact caused by any change in level. I said I would try to get additional information from Washington on current prospects for MAP, although there could be no positive estimate at this stage.

8. CCK invited me to go with him on a brief visit to Matsu Island early next month, travelling by sea, without any publicity for the trip. I said I would of course like to go, but I would need to seek Washington authorization, and they might feel that Matsu was a somewhat more exposed position than Quemoy.

9. *Comment:* Believe we have enough information in Embassy derived from Hong Kong reports and Baguio discussions so that I can continue substantive discussions of Mainland situation next week. However would appreciate any new information or assessments that are available.

10. Re paras 6 and 7 above on MAP levels, realize there is little that can be said now, except to continue give warning of possible reductions. However would appreciate any additional guidance available.

11. Re Matsu trip (para 8), I will make recommendation at later time. Response to invitation can be deferred.

McConaughy

249. Telegram From the Department of State to the Embassy in the Republic of China[1]

Washington, March 16, 1967, 3:43 p.m.

156346. For Ambassador McConaughy. Ref: Taipei 2623.[2]

1. Please take early suitable opportunity to convey to President Chiang Kai-shek following oral message from the President:[3]

2. Ambassador Goldberg has personally given the President a full report of his March 1 conversation with President Chiang. The President very much appreciates the forthrightness with which President Chiang expressed to Goldberg his views on Viet-Nam, Mainland China, and other aspects of the situation in Asia. He highly values these exchanges of views between our Governments.

3. As President Chiang had requested, Ambassador Goldberg told the President of President Chiang's belief that now is the time for the Republic of China to attack and overthrow the Chinese Communist regime on the Mainland and of the reasoning which led President Chiang to this view.

---

[1] Source: Department of State, Central Files, POL 7 US/GOLDBERG. Secret; Nodis. Drafted by Bennett and Berger, cleared by Sisco and Jenkins, and approved and initialed by Rusk. Repeated to USUN for Goldberg. A March 13 memorandum from Sisco and Berger to Rusk transmitting the draft telegram is attached to the source text. Although the telegram lists Jenkins as the person who cleared for the White House, it was cleared by President Johnson. A March 15 memorandum from Rostow to the President summarizing the proposed message, with a copy attached, has the President's check mark on the approval line. (Johnson Library, National Security File, Country File, China, Vol. VIII)

[2] See footnote 2, Document 245.

[3] McConaughy reported in telegram 2839 from Taipei, March 18, that he had delivered the oral message to President Chiang, who did not comment. (Department of State, Central Files, POL CHINAT–US 1)

4. The President wishes to say that he has given the most serious thought to what President Chiang has said. On this subject the U.S. Government's views are known to President Chiang, and there has been no change in our position. The U.S. has long sought to bring about peace in the Taiwan Strait and to this end has for many years urged the Chinese Communists to renounce the use of force there. The U.S. agrees with the Republic of China's position that its mission of restoring freedom to the population on the Mainland is to be achieved mainly by political means, not military force, and was pleased to see this theme stressed in President Chiang's New Year's message to the Chinese people.

5. In the situation in which we now find ourselves in Viet-Nam, we do not seek or advocate any extension of the war. From the outset we have carefully defined our objective in Viet-Nam as limited to stopping the aggression. We have refrained from using our full military power, and we have sought to limit the war and terminate it by negotiations.

6. The course which President Chiang advocated to Ambassador Goldberg would run counter to the policies we are pursuing in Viet-Nam. Such a course would involve the Republic of China in risks and hazards and would give rise to the danger of a wider war with incalculable consequences for the peoples of Asia, the United States, and the world. The American Government and people would not only disapprove such an action but would oppose it.

7. The President wants President Chiang to know how deeply grateful he is personally for the generous cooperation President Chiang's Government has extended to the United States in connection with the Viet-Nam war, for its economic and other contributions in Viet-Nam, and for the airbase facilities granted U.S. forces in Taiwan. The President is also very conscious of the threat from the Mainland to which Taiwan is exposed and he wishes to assure President Chiang once again that the United States stands squarely behind the commitments made in its Mutual Defense Treaty with the Republic of China.[4]

---

[4] Printed from an unsigned copy.

250. **Action Memorandum From the Assistant Secretary of State for East Asian and Pacific Affairs (Bundy) to Secretary of State Rusk**[1]

Washington, March 29, 1967.

SUBJECT

A New Approach to Our Trade and Transaction Controls Against Communist China

Background:

1. On October 4 we advanced for your approval a memorandum recommending certain changes in our trade and transaction controls against Communist China. Briefly, these recommendations concerned changes in Foreign Assets Control and other regulations to provide for the rescission of special bunkering controls, to establish a general license for travel and related expenses of Americans travelling legally to Communist China, and to place under general license all tourist purchases of Chinese-type goods valued at $100.00 or less. These changes were directed not at China itself but at removing points of irritation in the enforcement of our regulations with third countries and with United States citizens. However, the changes were envisaged as a first step in a relaxation of our embargo on trade with China in the light of our exploration of possible ways to pierce mainland China's isolation. (Memorandum attached at Tab A)[2]

2. That memorandum has been held in abeyance at the request of the Under Secretary.

3. Changes in our foreign assets control regulations already approved by you and now under inter-departmental consideration would accomplish two things so far as China is concerned: (a) allow U.S. subsidiaries abroad, with certain exceptions, to engage in non-strategic trade with China, and (b) make FAC regulations inapplicable to U.S. dollar transactions between China and third parties. These proposed changes are designed to strengthen our relations with third countries by eliminating points of friction over extraterritorial application of FAC regulations. They will have practically no influence on our trade policy toward China.

4. Developments since October have added a note of urgency to the need for certain changes in our controls on trade with Communist China.

---

[1] Source: Department of State, ACA Files: Lot 72 D 175, U.S. Trade with Communist China, I. Secret. Drafted by Richard H. Donald and Frank O. McCord of ACA. The memorandum was sent by Bundy and his counterpart in the Bureau of Economic Affairs, but the source text does not indicate whether it was signed by Assistant Secretary Solomon or an Acting Assistant Secretary. The memorandum was sent through Katzenbach.

[2] The October 4 memorandum (Tab A) from Bundy and Solomon to Rusk, attached but not printed, bears a handwritten note from Katzenbach: "Bill—I think we should hold this awhile. NdK."

We are therefore now submitting our original recommendation that imports and exports of foodstuffs be placed under general export-import license, and, separately, that medical supplies usable in combatting epidemics be placed under general license for export.

5. These recommendations are based on the following considerations:

a. The breakdown of order and authority in mainland China associated with the Cultural Revolution has brought with it the strong possibility that food supplies will be very short later in 1967, conceivably reaching famine proportions. The extreme concern of the Peking regime regarding the belated organization of spring planting argues for this possibility.

b. Meningitis has already reached epidemic proportions in China. The arrival of warm weather brings with it the threat of other diseases, endemic to China, reaching epidemic proportions. A copy of your letter to the Secretary of the Treasury (Tab B)[3] proposes separately that pharmaceuticals and medical supplies be exempted from the applicability of the Foreign Assets Control regulations during this period of epidemics.

c. In the American humanitarian tradition we are concerned with famine or disease, wherever they may exist. Neither U.S. public opinion, that of China, or that of the rest of the world should be presented with a picture of total U.S. indifference to prospect of famine in China. As the only country in the world pursuing a public national policy of an embargo on food to China, it would be hard to rebut charges of callousness and of lack of concern for and friendship with the people of China.

d. The effects of famine and disease cannot necessarily be contained within the borders of China, and we should prepare in advance to be free to take what measures may be appropriate and required in our interests and those of friendly nations.

6. Trade with China has been dealt with in recent discussions of our China policy. The China Advisory Panel, which met at the beginning of February, recommended easing controls, with some members believing that paving the way for limited trade now was the most promising way for giving credibility to the U.S. stance of hoping for long term reconciliation with the people of Communist China. The members of the Panel were all highly interested in your remarks at the concluding session on the possibility that food would represent a major lever in affecting the direction that China moves.

7. Although not a major subject of discussion, there was a unanimous view among the Chiefs of Mission at Baguio earlier this month that our trade controls should be relaxed, particularly those that would "have the effect of removing certain unnecessary irritations for Americans in their dealings involving China" such as the elimination of bunkering controls and removing requirements for certificates of origin on purchases in Hong Kong up to $100 in value of Chinese-type products.

---

[3] A copy of the draft letter is attached but not printed.

8. On timing, the same two groups believed that while the Cultural Revolution was raging, no major policy initiatives towards China were advisable. At the same time both groups believed that the Cultural Revolution offered us the opportunity for further action in removing barriers on our side to eventual reconciliation. Relaxation of trade controls was specifically cited by both groups as falling within this latter category. The possibility of food shortages later this year adds urgency.

9. Changes in our regulations would not, we believe, lend material support through China to North Viet-Nam's war effort. Permitted exports include no "strategic" goods. China supplies rice to North Viet-Nam, but if cereals are sold to Communist China we do not envisage shipments of rice; 1967–68 world demand for U.S. rice already exceeds our capacity to meet it; and Peking's 1966–67 grain imports from Western sources are entirely wheat.

10. A general licensing of trade in items of artistic value is recommended on the two grounds that (1) this would contribute to reestablishment of some cultural interchange between the peoples of China and the United States, and (2) would eliminate a long-standing complaint against the U.S. Government lodged by museum curators across the country that FAC regulations deprive the United States of treasures whose value far outweighed any foreign exchange gain to Peking.

11. Fuller justification for our recommendations is contained in the original memorandum.

Recommendations:[4]

That you authorize E and EA to work out with Defense, Treasury, Commerce and Agriculture, as appropriate:

1. Changes in the special bunkering controls which would rescind those controls as applied to ships in the Chinese Communist and North Korean trade.
2. Changes in the Foreign Assets Control regulations to allow for general licensing for costs of trips to Communist China, North Korea, and North Viet-Nam for American citizens who hold passports validated for travel to those areas.
3. Changes in the Foreign Assets Control regulations to allow general licensing for Chinese-type goods up to the value of $100 per American tourist per trip abroad.
4. Changes in the Foreign Assets Control regulations to allow general licensing for art objects.
5. Procedures for placing food commodities under general license for import and export with Communist China.

These recommendations, if approved, would be put into effect at such time as you and the President direct.

---

[4] The recommendations bear no indication of approval or disapproval, but see Document 280.

251. Memorandum From the President's Special Assistant (Rostow) to President Johnson[1]

Washington, April 8, 1967.

SUBJECT

PL–480 Agreement with the Republic of China

Agriculture (Secretary Freeman) and AID (Administrator Gaud) request your authorization to negotiate a two-year, local currency agreement with the Republic of China (GRC) under PL–480 (Title I).[2] We would sell the GRC cotton, tobacco and tallow (all in surplus supply) for $37.5 million. Half the proceeds will be for our use and will help meet increasing costs in Taiwan related to our Vietnam effort. The other half would go to the GRC as a grant to be used in expanding its Project Vanguard (technical assistance to increase food production) in 23 less developed countries, mostly in Africa.

State (Acting Secretary Katzenbach) and Budget (Director Schultze) both strongly endorse this proposal (see attached memos).[3] I concur.

GRC help to other countries in boosting food output is highly useful in:

—impeding Peking's efforts to gain political and economic footholds in Africa;
—boosting GRC prestige and strengthening its position in the UN and with other nations;
—providing a good example of success for our own foreign aid programs by dramatizing Taiwan's progress;
—increasing Taiwan's involvement and interest in the rest of the world and thereby moving it away from preoccupation with the Mainland.

The proposal has clear benefits for us;

—helps the War on Hunger;
—helps our balance of payments through the use of local currency in Taiwan.

State and Agriculture have already taken soundings with Fulbright, Ellender, Morgan and Poage, none of whom raised any objection.

If you approve this proposal, Secretary Freeman will notify the two agriculture committees of the proposed agreement. It must then lie

---

[1] Source: Johnson Library, National Security File, Country File, China, Vol. IX. Secret.

[2] The memorandum from Freeman and Gaud to Johnson, undated, is attached but not printed.

[3] Katzenbach's April 7 memorandum to Johnson and Schultze's April 8 memorandum are attached but not printed.

before them for 30 days before execution. We will also have to waive the statutory requirement that all foreign currency grants in non-excess currency countries be subject to appropriations.

We hope the 30-day waiting period will expire in time to announce the agreement when GRC Vice President Yen is in Washington (May 9–10).

Upon your approval, other key Congressional members will be consulted (leadership and Appropriations chairmen).

Walt

Authorization granted[4]

Denied

See me

_____

[4] This option is checked on the source text.

---

252.   Memorandum From the President's Special Assistant (Rostow) to President Johnson[1]

Washington, April 20, 1967, 8:10 p.m.

Mr. President:

A North African herewith reports, in a quite credible way, on a visit to Communist China. We know so little about how they think that I thought you might like to read it.

Walt

_____

[1] Source: Johnson Library, National Security File, Agency File, United Nations, Vol. 7. Secret; Exdis. A handwritten "L" on the source text indicates that it was seen by the President.

Attachment[2]

SUBJECT

Malley Visit to China

Malley freely spoke to Pedersen and Thacher yesterday for over an hour about his recent visit to Communist China and said he would be willing to answer further questions. Detailed report pouched Department (Sisco–IO, Bundy–Fe and S–Walsh). Highlights as follows:

The visit lasted 18 days. The highlight was a 2-1/2 hour discussion with Chou En-lai on March 28.

Chou and other leaders constantly spoke of U.S.–USSR collusion and spoke more about USSR than U.S. They traced collusion back to Khrushchev's 1958 refusal to reaffirm that an attack on China would be considered an attack on the USSR.

Chou thought U.S. would move to attack China when we were sure it would not affect the stability of the Soviet Government. U.S. action against China would involve Chinese reaction against all bases of attack, specifically mentioning Japan, Philippines, Laos, and Thailand.

Chou said he was considering the termination of Warsaw talks because they were being exploited by the USSR.

Malley thought the Chinese wanted to enter the Vietnamese War. Chou had reiterated China prepared to send volunteers to North Vietnam a day after North Vietnam requests them.

North Vietnam representative in Peking confirmed the offer and said North Vietnam (a) Did not want Chinese and (b) Would have to accept Eastern Europe volunteers if they took the Chinese with consequent political problems for themselves.

North Vietnam representative said, however, Chinese and North Vietnamese were then discussing, on contingency basis, terms and conditions under which volunteers would be accepted if a decision was made.

Chou said North Vietnam's proposal to talk to U.S. if we stopped bombing had been cleared with him by Pham Van Dong. Said he had warned him U.S. would then stiffen its position, and that Hanoi would be stuck with its offer. Said he had been right.

Chou identified Liu Shao Chi with Soviets from time of his assumption of office. Said Central Committee had voted against Liu on March 26, but Malley had the impression that legal quorum was not present.

---

[2] The attachment is a paraphrase of telegram 4921 from USUN, April 17, which reported a conversation with Simon Malley, a correspondent with the Tunisian-owned journal *Jeune Afrique*.

Malley concluded that Mao Forces would clearly win and said Chou is confident of this also. Chou said the Government fully controlled 8 provinces. Army Chief of Staff admitted there had been revisionists in the army but denied any split.

In chance meeting with North Vietnamese Colonel Van Lau, who had gone to Burma to talk to U Thant, Van Lau heaped abuse on U Thant and said he had rejected U Thant's ceasefire idea in Burma. He expected U.S. to exploit Thant's proposal.

Van Lau said North Vietnam expected U.S. invasion for purposes of seizing and holding enclaves (which it could probably do) and for purpose of holding them to trade against withdrawal of North Vietnam's presence in South Vietnam.

Van Lau said North Vietnam had released an exchange between President Johnson and Ho Chi Minh because U.S. constantly was implying it in meaningful contact with Hanoi and they wished to make clear no meaningful discussion is going on.

Malley concluded Mao was deified in China to the extent that groups rallying around his name are certain to be successful. But thought he was far removed from day-to-day conduct of government. He also felt adulation attached to him could not be transferred to others and that if he died succession would be difficult question. He thought Chou En-lai had no power base and could be easily removed at will by those now holding the power.

Chou told Malley, in context Soviet untrustworthiness, that he had received a message from the Embassy in Cairo reporting Nasser's anger at finding Gromyko had come to Cairo to urge United Arabic Republic to go slowly in Saudi Arabia.

253. Memorandum From Alfred Jenkins of the National Security Council Staff to the President's Special Assistant (Rostow)[1]

Washington, April 21, 1967.

SUBJECT

Mao's Power and the Waiting Game

The costly game of power measurement continues in China with no clearly discernible and significant shift in power realities so far as pro- and anti-Mao elements are concerned. Recently exacerbated differences within the Maoist camp, however, may presage a further drop in Mao's fortunes. The most noteworthy fact in the top leadership struggle is that not a single person of prominence in the opposition has defected to the Maoists. The opposition is serving by standing remarkably firm and waiting long.

Almost three-fourths of the members of the Central Committee has come under serious attack during various phases of the Cultural Revolution. For all practical purposes the Party in the capital has become Mao and a small group of his subordinates.

The most significant change in the scene during the past month has been the rapid growth of power in the hands of the Army. The Army has not yet clearly indicated its support of either major faction. Mao's immediate coterie, however, clearly regards the Army as having contributed to the "adverse current" in the Cultural Revolution.

The vaunted "three way alliance" (Army, revolutionary rebels and good cadres) are an attempt to cover up the fact that the Army controls the country. The not very successful attempt ever since January 23 to use the Army against the opposition causes the Revolution to take on more of the aspect of an attempted military coup by a minority in the Party against the majority rather than of a manifestation of the revolutionary militancy of the masses in attacking the bourgeoisie, which is the way the regime has attempted to portray the Revolution.

Meanwhile the Army has its own problems. Two of its most powerful and respected old-timers are in disrepute. Hsu Hsiang-chien, Vice Chairman of the Military Affairs Committee and head of the Army's Cultural Revolution Committee, has apparently been relieved of both posts, and Yeh Chien-ying, also a member of the Military Affairs Committee, has been excoriated in a poster reporting that a recent meeting of the

---

[1] Source: Johnson Library, National Security File, Country File, China, Vol. IX. Secret. Copies were sent to Jorden and Ropa. Rostow sent the memorandum to the President with a covering note dated May 1. A handwritten "L" on the source text indicates that the President saw the memorandum.

Committee broke up without deciding issues it meant to deal with. Even Madame Mao's perceptivity was equal to observing "the situation in the Army is hardly understandable."

There has been a recent upsurge of Red Guard sanctimonious hooliganism in Peking, along with reports of serious dissension within their ranks. Military control in Peking, however, is much tighter than when the Red Guards ran riot in January and there have been expressions of resentment that the Army's curbing of them is interfering with the Revolution.

Chou En-lai's prestige has again risen with reports that he heads a six-man "presidium" of the Communist Party. The role of this organization is not yet clear but it probably will be charged with continuing efforts to eliminate Chief of State Liu Shao-chi, Party Secretary Teng Hsiao-ping, and former Propaganda Chief Tao Chu. Lin Piao remains technically the heir apparent, but his chances are still not very apparent to me.

Barring a palace coup or sudden crumbling of the support of either faction, Mao's great struggle to retain power will primarily be determined by the manner and success of the Army's application of power and the performance of the economy, particularly in the agriculture realm. The former will be chiefly affected by a reading of Peking power realities and the reaction of the masses of Chinese citizens to the Army's exercise of power. The latter, of course, depends largely upon weather (so far better than average) and peasant-worker application, about which we simply know too little as yet. At the moment all we can say is that Mao's opposition has little cause to believe that they are losing by playing the waiting game.

Alfred Jenkins

254.   Memorandum for the Record[1]

Washington, April 28, 1967.

SUBJECT

Minutes of the Meeting of the 303 Committee, 28 April 1967

PRESENT

Mr. Rostow, Mr. Thomas Hughes, Mr. Vance, and Mr. Helms
Mr. William Colby was present for Items 3 and 4

[Here follows discussion of unrelated subjects.]

3.   *Communist China—Covert Action Program*

a. Mr. Colby presented the group with a briefing[2] of the expectations and accomplishments of the covert action program against China. He made no claims of major successes but was able to indicate specific results and improvement in [*less than 1 line of source text not declassified*] broadcasts at a time when Chinese on the mainland were more open to alternatives than at any time in their recent history.

b. One instance was the statement by the Chinese musician defector which showed that one of a series of [*less than 1 line of source text not declassified*] broadcasts of which he was aware was actually believed by him and some of his circle to emanate from within China.

c. In this connection, Mr. Colby pointed to the requested approval of an enlargement of this thrust by the addition of [*less than 1 line of source text not declassified*] broadcasts [*less than 1 line of source text not declassified*] from a 50 kilowatt transmitter which would have the advantage of being independent of GRC and would reach a larger audience. This was expected to constitute less than $300,000 of the total $1,084,700 requested.

d. There was further discussion of coordinating themes and endeavouring to strike a suitable chord in such a fluid situation. The members approved the proposal in total although reserving some skepticism as to the measurability of its effect.

e. In answer to a question from Mr. Vance, Mr. Colby briefly summarized collection problems [*2 lines of source text not declassified*] since the last presentation on 12 November 1964.

[Here follows discussion of unrelated subjects.]

Peter Jessup

---

[1] Source: Department of State, INR Historical Files, 303 Committee Files, 303 c.49, April 28, 1967. Secret; Eyes Only. Copies were sent to Kohler, Vance, and Helms. Prepared by Jessup on May 1.

[2] A copy of a CIA memorandum to the 303 Committee, April 14, on the subject "Covert Action Program Against Communist China," is attached but not printed.

255. Editorial Note

An April 29, 1967, memorandum from Senate Majority Leader Mike Mansfield to President Johnson put forward several proposals pertaining to the Vietnam conflict. The first proposal, headed "An Approach Via China," argued that because U.S. bombing of North Vietnam would make it ever more heavily dependent on China, "The road to settlement with Hanoi, now, very likely runs by way of Peking rather than Moscow." Mansfield proposed making a "quiet and clearly conciliatory approach to China." He suggested that he might try to arrange a trip to Peking. He thought such a trip, to be effective, would need at least tacit Presidential approval and should be designed to get from Chou En-lai "the Chinese view of what is needed for a settlement in Viet Nam and for the restoration of more normal relations throughout the Western Pacific."

An April 30 memorandum from the President's Special Assistant Walt Rostow to Johnson stated that, after reading and considering Mansfield's proposals, Secretary of State Rusk was "strongly opposed" to a visit by Mansfield to Communist China, which would be "a major intervention in a troubled situation," would make the Soviet Union upset and suspicious, and would cause great confusion among "our friends in free Asia." Rusk believed, Rostow stated, "the proper way to proceed with respect to Communist China was to elevate the Warsaw talks to the Foreign Ministers level," but he was "hesitant to propose this until the situation within Communist China has somewhat settled down." Rostow noted that he was in general agreement with Rusk. (Filed with a covering memorandum of May 2 from Rostow to Johnson; Johnson Library, National Security File, Name File, Senator Mansfield)

256. Telegram From the Embassy in the Republic of China to the Department of State[1]

Taipei, May 2, 1967, 0445Z.

3385. 1. Yesterday afternoon Gimo and Madame Chiang hosted large party in honor of US military, commemorating establishment of MAAG 16 years ago. This annual event was unusually large this year, with over 1,000 Americans invited.

2. Gimo asked me to arrive early so we could have half hour of private discussion just before party. Madame Chiang was present, also Fon-Min Wei and DCM Hummel. Fred Chien interpreted.

3. In somewhat emotional, and clearly sincere presentation,[2] Gimo made the following points, directed at me as an old friend. Whether or not I wished to pass them on would, he said, be up to me.

4. (A) Gimo said USG has not always immediately understood the steadfastness and seriousness with which GRC views its responsibilities as ally of US. He stated his actions have always been based on moral principle, and will always be so based. Gimo repeatedly assured me that GRC will never do anything contrary to its commitments, or contrary to interest of US, which Gimo views as inseparable from interest of GRC.

5. (B) Gimo said he has often stated that the return to the mainland will be 70 percent political and 30 percent military. Up until recently GRC has had the view that the 30 percent of military action should precede political action, but now, Gimo explicitly stated, he intends to utilize political means first, after which at later time some military action may be necessary "to clean up the mess."

6. (C) Breakdown and fragmentation of authority on the mainland, and general disillusionment with communism, has created a situation where GRC political efforts can be successful, and will be welcomed, Gimo said. He intends to take seriously his responsibilities as an ally of the US to do what he can to assure the peace and security of the area, primarily through political means.

7. *Comment:* Because interview was terminated by Gimo immediately after his long presentation, in order to join reception, I had no opportunity to probe for explanation of what sort of political means GRC has in mind. However, I doubt that any major political démarche toward mainland is imminent and I take the Gimo's remarks to be intended pri-

---

[1] Source: Department of State, Central Files, POL CHINAT–US. Confidential; Limdis. Repeated to Hong Kong and CINCPAC for POLAD.

[2] A memorandum of the conversation was sent with airgram A–740 from Taipei, dated May 3. (Ibid, POL 15–1 CHINAT)

marily as a plea for greater trust and understanding on the part of USG, as well as an appeal for the US to refrain from taking any action that will damage GRC interests.

8. We have from time to time heard this sort of earnest appeal from Gimo before. A conversation I had with DefMin Chiang Ching-kuo on April 20 along similar lines (being reported by septel)[3] was obviously intended to lay the groundwork for the Gimo's presentation. Neither the Gimo nor Chiang Ching-kuo gave any indication that their remarks were related to current problems surrounding preparations for visit to Washington of Vice President Yen. However, I am sure that these problems (particularly wording of joint statement) which were aired in GRC Cabinet meeting April 27, comprise one of the stimuli that have caused the Gimo's appeal.

9. Putting political action before military was clearly foreshadowed in Gimo's New Years Day message, and the Gimo undoubtedly considers his explicit statements to me (and Chiang Ching-kuo's also) as a major concession to US views as well as realistic response to current mainland situation.

McConaughy

---

[3] Reference is apparently to a conversation on April 28 with Chiang Ching-kuo, reported in telegram 3390 from Taipei, May 2. (Ibid., POL CHINAT–US)

---

257. Telegram From the President's Special Assistant (Rostow) to President Johnson in Texas[1]

Washington, May 5, 1967, 1223Z.

CAP 67379. Herewith a summary of a major USIB appraisal of Communist China's military policy and non-nuclear forces.

I thought you would wish to read it over the weekend.[2]

Communist China's military policy and its general purpose and air defense forces.

---

[1] Source: Johnson Library, National Security File, Country File, China, Vol. IX. Top Secret; Sensitive. Received at the LBJ Ranch at 8:30 a.m. A handwritten "L" on the source text indicates that President Johnson saw it.

[2] The remainder of the telegram quotes in full the opening section of NIE 13–3–67, "Communist China's Military Policy and Its General Purpose and Air Defense Forces," May 3. A copy of the complete estimate is in the Central Intelligence Agency, NIE Files.

The problem.

To assess Communist China's general military policy and to estimate the strength and capabilities of the Chinese Communist general purpose and air defense forces through 1969.

Conclusions.

A. Whatever the outcome of the current political crisis, any Chinese leadership will probably continue to work towards a dominant position in Asia and great power status on the world scene. It will probably continue to be concerned by the danger of conflict with the US, and possibly with the USSR. Thus China will almost certainly continue to give high priority to improving its military capabilities.

B. Although the threat of force and its actual use beyond China's borders are significant elements in Peking's outlook, Chinese military strategy places primary emphasis on defense. With the possible exception of their nuclear/missile activities, we do not see in train the general programs, the development or deployment of forces, or the doctrinal discussions which would suggest a more forward strategy. At least for the short term, the high priority nuclear program is probably viewed by the Chinese as primarily for deterrence, though Peking's successes in this field bring substantial prestige and political influence, particularly in Asia.

C. In our view, Chinese forces are capable of providing a strong defense of the Mainland and launching significant offensive operations in neighboring areas. Thus far the political turmoil does not seem to have affected these Chinese capabilities or military production programs in any significant way.

D. Under a broad policy of modernization, Peking is pursuing the following programs and objectives:

1. The Army. Improvement of firepower, mainly by supplying new tanks and heavier artillery. The Army's organization and size has remained static: about 2.4 million men in 118 combat divisions of uneven quality and strength.
2. Air Defense. A growing inventory of fighters (MIG–19's), addition of better radars, and preparations for production of the SA–2, probably as part of a point defense system for key target areas. Production of the MIG–19 continues (20–25 a month) and production of the MIG–21 is expected.
3. The Navy. Five R–class submarines have been produced and about 10 more will probably be built by 1970. A construction program for guided missile patrol boats began in 1966 and is proceeding at an estimated rate of 10 per year. The South China Fleet is being strengthened by deployment of patrol and torpedo boats and by expansion of shipbuilding and shore installations in South China.

E. Nevertheless, the limitations and demands on China's economic and technological capacities are such that conventional forces will remain deficient in modern equipment at least into the early 1970's. There is little prospect for a significant increase in the mobility of Chinese ground forces; the air defense system will still be unable to cope with a major air attack; fighters will be at least a generation behind the US and USSR. Naval capabilities will still be mainly limited to offshore patrol and escort.

E. The current modernization programs for conventional forces plus even a modest effort to produce and deploy advanced weapons systems will, in our view, put pressures on an already strained economy. Thus China will face an increasingly difficult problem in allocating scarce economic resources between civilian and military needs and with the military sector. Resolution of these problems may be a cause of continued dispute, both within the military and at the top level of national decision-making.

---

258. Memorandum From the President's Special Assistant (Rostow) to President Johnson[1]

Washington, May 8, 1967, 7:10 p.m.

Mr. President:

Herewith State's essentially negative response to the possibility of introducing more GRC personnel into South Viet Nam.[2]

On the economic side, the Vietnamese don't really want more Chinese around, although we are willing. On the military side, neither the Vietnamese nor our people want Chinese forces in South Viet Nam.

Behind all this is the basic negative attitude of the Vietnamese toward Chinese, heightened by the large relatively wealthy Chinese population in Saigon.

Walt

---

[1] Source: Johnson Library, National Security File, Country File, China, Vol. IX. Secret. Filed with a note dictated by the President: "Walt: Looks like I can't get there from here. See if I can't find some way to bring other people into it. LBJ/mjdr. May 19, 1967. 12:30 p.m."

[2] Attached but not printed is an April 20 memorandum from Bundy to Rusk, with the subject heading: "Interest at Highest Levels in Expanding GRC Assistance to Viet-Nam."

259.   Memorandum of Conversation[1]

Washington, May 9, 1967, 12–12:55 p.m.

SUBJECT

Meeting of Chinese Vice President C.K. Yen with the President: Review of Events on Mainland China; Sino-Soviet Relations; Viet-Nam

PARTICIPANTS

Chinese
His Excellency Yen Chia-kan, Vice President/Prime Minister of Republic of China
Chow Shu-kai, Ambassador, Chinese Embassy
Li Kwoh-ting, Minister of Economic Affairs, Republic of China
Liu Chieh, Ambassador to the United Nations
Sampson C. Shen, Vice Minister of Foreign Affairs, Republic of China
Lai Chia-chiu, Director of the Information Department, Republic of China

Americans
The President
Secretary of State Dean Rusk
Walter P. McConaughy, Ambassador, American Embassy Taipei
James W. Symington, Chief of Protocol
William P. Bundy, Assistant Secretary for East Asian and Pacific Affairs

Vice President Yen delivered the warm greetings and good wishes of President Chiang to President Johnson and handed President Johnson a letter (attached) which President Chiang had entrusted to him for delivery.[2]

Vice President Yen opened the conversation by recalling the assurances which President Chiang had given to Ambassador McConaughy on May 1, to the effect that the GRC would always be faithful to its commitments and obligations to the United States as a close ally.[3] Vice President Yen mentioned his President's statement that his Government would never do anything which was inimical to U.S. interests and would continue to regard basic U.S. interests as being in line with the basic interests of his own Government. The Vice President said President Chiang hoped that the U.S. Government felt the same way.

The Vice President then turned to the situation on mainland China. He said it was the assessment of his Government that the conflict on the

---

[1] Source: Department of State, Central Files, POL CHINAT–US. Secret; Exdis. Drafted by McConaughy on May 12. Approved in S on May 17 and in the White House by Jenkins on May 17. The meeting took place at the White House.

[2] Vice President Yen visited Washington May 9–10. Records of his meetings with Secretary Rusk and Vice President Humphrey on May 10 are ibid., Visit Files: Lot 67 D 587, V–31. Briefing memoranda and other related material are ibid., V–30, and in the Johnson Library, National Security File, Country File, China, Visit of C.K. Yen.

A copy of President Chiang's letter is attached but not printed.

[3] See Document 256.

mainland would continue. There had been no physical liquidation by Mao of the opposition leaders so far, but this did not mean that the struggle was not intense. Mao had refrained from moving toward the full liquidation of his opponents only because he feared a widespread adverse reaction to such an extreme measure—a reaction which he could not control at this time.

The Vice President identified three stages in the cultural upheaval on the mainland as follows: (1) the public denunciation in Shanghai in 1965 of certain writings identified with Liu Shao-chi; (2) the development of the full fury of the Cultural Revolution, May–August 1966; (3) the emergence of the full-fledged open "power struggle," beginning in Shansi in January 1967.

The Vice President said the origins of the conflict go back seven years to about 1960 when the former Defense Minister, predecessor of Lin Piao, was liquidated. The Vice President thought that no one leader or faction is in effective control on the mainland now. Mao is now branding all of his opponents indiscriminately as "Revisionists." The word is being used very loosely without any precise meaning, other than that it means anti-Mao. Liu Shao-chi actually does not have a historical record of being pro-Soviet; nor does the Governor and military commander of Sinkiang Province, Wang En-mao, have a pro-Soviet record either. Wang helped to defeat the Soviet effort some years ago to set up an "East Turkestan Autonomous Republic."

The tactic of Mao is to vilify his opponents in every way he can. The revolution has become something distasteful to almost everybody except the pro-Mao group and Mao seems to take satisfaction in openly characterizing his revolution as something which is violent and something to be feared. He openly uses the Chinese phrase "tsao fan" (to make rebellion) in describing his own movement. The Vice President estimates the opposition to Mao is still very strong. Liu and other elements still have a considerable following and this limits Mao's freedom of action. The Vice President's conclusion is that the fight will go on. Mao cannot quell the dissenters, not all of whom are pro-Liu. There is a large anti-Mao group of Communists who now have something in common with the majority of the people, who are not identified with the Communist Party but who have been fairly neutral so far. As the economic situation deteriorates further, the continuing struggle will produce a steady growth in anti-Communist sentiment.

The Vice President said the GRC considered that the efforts against the Chinese Communists should be "70 per cent political" and only 30 per cent military. The GRC has "many agents" working on the mainland. The tactics being used by the agents are different from what they were before 1959. They are now instructed to mingle openly with the people, posing as fanatical pro-Communists. Some pretend that they are pro-

Mao, and some pro-Liu. They are trying to broaden and deepen the conflict. The GRC predicts that the turmoil will lead to disastrous results, especially as to production of basic food requirements. It is believed that spring planting is down at least 11 per cent. The grain loss will be seriously felt in the fall. With the further deterioration of the food situation, the GRC believes that anti-Communist sentiment will grow and the discontent will lead to an expansion of the fighting.

Answering a question of Secretary Rusk's about Chou En-lai, the Vice President doubted that Chou could ever become a "third force" in the Communist hierarchy. He was well-known to many GRC leaders, and he was clearly identified as a man who always tried to side with the winner. He had once been close to Teng Hsiao-ping, the No. 2 man in the Liu group. Then he had wavered when he thought the Liu group was losing ground and had gone over to the Mao side. He had then tried to exercise a mediating influence between the Red Guards and the Communist Party elements. He had then been subjected to some censure. He did not have the strength to emerge as a third force. Yen thought Chou would be used by Mao as long as the struggle continued, and that he would lose favor with Mao after the eventual purge of Liu. He would have a place of some importance during the struggle.

Yen thought that the regime and the entire country were in a state of confusion. The regime was not capable of effective control. Both the Army and the Party were split and disorganized. How can a regime which cannot control Army or Party control the country? There was a probability of further dissension and eventual purges. In this situation the chances for a reunified China under a different leadership were greater than ever before. In this connection, Vice President Yen said, "We have our aspirations."

The Vice President referred to the urgent efforts of the ChiComs to develop nuclear weapons. He thought that the GRC information on ChiCom nuclear weapons progress tallied closely with U.S. information. He mentioned our close consultation and effective exchange of information on this subject. Yen thought that the ChiComs had hoped to have their sixth nuclear test on the Red Holiday, May 1. They had missed this date, but Yen thought the next explosion would come soon.

Yen spoke of the feverish preparations of the Communists for war. Despite the economic failures and the poverty of the people, a population of 700 million has a high productive capacity. By ruthlessly lowering the living standard of the people still further, the Communists can accumulate large resources for production of nuclear weapons. Even though the regime had immense troubles, these troubles themselves make the regime more aggressive and not less so.

Yen thought that Sino-Soviet relations would not change essentially. The rift between the Soviets and the Mao faction is getting worse, but some sort of agreement apparently has been reached permitting the freer transit of Soviet war material overland to North Viet-Nam. Yen thought that the agreement was only "technical" and did not signify any real improvement of relations. It was a renewal of a 1965 transit agreement.

Secretary Rusk said there were some reports that the transit agreement provided for the delivery of the arms supplies to North Vietnamese personnel at the Sino-Soviet border.

Assistant Secretary Bundy said he agreed with Yen and noted that he did not believe that the Soviet transit traffic across China to North Viet-Nam had ever been significantly interfered with.

In response to a query as to the relative influence of the ChiComs and the Soviets in North Viet-Nam, Yen said he thought the Chinese Communists have more influence and are pulling most of the strings. The Chinese Communists have the advantage of proximity and can control the land supply route. They can give a green light or a red light. The sea route of supply is difficult at best and places the Soviets under a handicap. Yen thought that the Liberation Front in South Viet-Nam did not listen entirely to Ho Chi-minh's orders. The Liberation Front were mostly trained in Communist China and they are responsive to Chinese Communist direction. This gives the Chinese Communists as much influence over the Viet Cong as anyone. In other remarks Yen also suggested that Peking had some control over Hanoi.

Yen thought that the number of Chinese Communist personnel in North Viet-Nam might run as high as 60,000 to 80,000, although he could not be sure. The Chinese Communist disposition of personnel in North Viet-Nam is ostensibly for defense of the Chinese border, but the ChiCom elements in North Viet-Nam watch Hanoi very closely.

Yen said that the Generalissimo points out that the "root of the evil" is on the mainland. Of 10 Chinese Communist Army Field Marshals, one, Marshal Lo, has been purged. All the others, except Lin Piao, have been censured. 16 Communist deputy prime ministers had been disgraced in one form or another. At the provincial level, thousands and thousands of officials have been removed. There is dissension on a big scale. An immense effort is being made against Mao, and Mao is heavily burdened by external problems as well as his major internal challenge. President Chiang is convinced of the necessity for the allies to think ahead and plan for the long pull as well as the immediate crises. The Generalissimo believes we should think in terms of 20 to 30 years.

In response to a query from the President as to the GRC view of the likely course of the war in Viet-Nam, Vice President Yen noted that the United States and allied forces in Viet-Nam are far superior. But control of much of the countryside by the enemy poses a difficult problem which must be dealt with by political as well as military means. Pacification is a difficult task but is an indispensable part of the over-all effort to counter the Liberation Front. Rural development work is of prime importance. Communist control of "the surface" between the urban centers gives the Communists a big advantage. The Vice President said his Government considers that the emphasis which the United States, since the Honolulu Conference, has accorded to pacification and effective civil government is correct. The Vice President mentioned the technical assistance which the GRC is contributing in Viet-Nam, which he termed of modest proportions.

In response to another question from the President, Vice President Yen said that his Government held the view that the Soviet Union would not come to the assistance of the Chinese Communists in any foreseeable international situation, and he thought they would not directly intervene in the Chinese Communist internal struggle, although they were naturally hoping for the downfall of Mao.

In response to a question from Secretary Rusk as to what outcome of the struggle in Communist China would be best from the standpoint of U.S. interests, the Vice President said he thought the conflict would go on for a long time in any event, and that a victory by either side could not be beneficial in any way. He felt that a victorious Liu Shao-chi might in the long run pose an even greater threat than Mao to the Free World, despite Mao's violent and ruthless extremism. Liu has never actually been pro-Soviet, but he could be forced into a pro-Soviet position. A united front of the two large Communist powers which would then emerge would be the greatest threat to the Free World.

Vice President Yen thought that a continuation of the present factional struggle on the mainland would be the best situation from the standpoint of Free World interests. He thought that continued conflict would encourage the now submerged anti-Communist elements. The Vice President thought that the ordinary man on the mainland is not interested in ideologies. The ordinary Chinese will not like the sufferings that will come from economic failure. The people of the mainland will see the great contrast between the breakdown on the mainland and the success of the Republic of China on Taiwan. Hence, they will become more and more anti-Communist. "This is what we are aspiring for," the Vice President said.

Responding to a question from the President as to whether the mainland turmoil would probably tend to bring the Chinese Communists more directly into the Vietnamese war or keep them out, the Vice President said the Chinese Communist policy would be to keep the trouble going in Viet-Nam on more or less its present scale. He thought that they would try to maintain indefinitely about the present degree of U.S. involvement.

In answer to a further question from the President as to the circumstances under which the Chinese Communists might be tempted to intervene openly in Viet-Nam as they did in Korea, the Vice President thought that the Chinese Communists would deliberately avoid the sort of direct involvement which they chose in Korea. He thought they would try to "fight by proxy," avoiding a direct Sino-U.S. confrontation, and at the same time preventing the North Vietnamese from making a settlement of the war. The Vice President thought that the Chinese Communists would use all necessary means to "sabotage" any peace talks.

Speaking to another question from the President as to what sort of solution might be envisaged in such circumstances, Vice President Yen felt that a solution could come about only through the end of Communist control of mainland China, and he thought this would eventually happen. The President interjected parenthetically that he didn't see how this was to be done.

Vice President Yen said that President Chiang had instructed him to reiterate that his Government wishes to maintain close contact and frequent consultation with the United States Government. The Vice President repeated his opening remarks, saying that the Republic of China considered the interests of the two countries should be identical. "We will do nothing contrary to United States interests and we hope the United States will do nothing contrary to ours." The Vice President pointed out that the unpredictability of the mainland situation made alertness and close consultation all the more essential, adding "We will be building the Republic of China more and more."

The Vice President noted that the outbreak of a Cultural Revolution on the mainland would have been unthinkable 10 years ago. Liu's No. 2 position in the secession then seemed clear. The emergence of the Red Guards could not have been imagined.

The Vice President noted that currently the 4th Field Army in Kwangtung Province has shown some pro-Liu tendencies, and Lin Piao has been compelled to move some other army units into that area. The loyalty to Mao of many units in the Communist Army is doubtful. In Fukien Province, Mao has removed General Yeh Fei, an active political commissar. These are examples of widespread current troubles facing the Communists.

The Vice President predicted that the situation will gradually change in the Free World's favor. At the same time he cautioned that there is no room for complacency and his Government clearly understands the necessity to work hard to accelerate and intensify the changes which are causing such trouble to the Communist regime.

At this point it was time for the White House luncheon, and the meeting was terminated with the thanks of the President for the helpful presentation by the Vice President of the views of his Government on these questions.

260.   Memorandum of Conversation[1]

Washington, May 10, 1967, 10–11 a.m.

SUBJECT

Chinese Representation in the United Nations

PARTICIPANTS

Chinese

His Excellency Yen Chia-kan, Vice President/Prime Minister of the Republic of
China
Chow Shu-kai, Ambassador, Chinese Embassy
Li Kwoh-ting, Minister of Economic Affairs, Republic of China
Liu Chieh, Ambassador to the United Nations
Sampson C. Shen, Vice Minister of Foreign Affairs, Republic of China
Lai Chia-chiu, Director of the Information Department, Republic of China

Americans

Secretary of State Dean Rusk
Walter P. McConaughy, Ambassador, American Embassy Taipei
James W. Symington, Chief of Protocol
William P. Bundy, Assistant Secretary for East Asian and Pacific Affairs
Joseph J. Sisco, Assistant Secretary for International Organization Affairs
Robert W. Barnett, Deputy Assistant Secretary for East Asian and Pacific Affairs
Josiah W. Bennett, Country Director, Republic of China Affairs

During his call on the Secretary May 10, Vice President Yen, after a
discussion of recent mainland developments, told the Secretary he
hoped the United States would continue to support the GRC in the
United Nations. He said that since the days of President Kennedy, the
United States had assured the GRC of support. The Secretary interjected
humorously to say that United States support for the GRC in the United
Nations dated back to the days of Assistant Secretary of State Dean Rusk.
The Secretary went on to say that there may be some difference on tactics
between us but our purpose has not changed. The voting situation in the
General Assembly has changed from what it was years ago and we also
have many nervous friends. In the last General Assembly, for example,
Canada could have shaken many apples off the tree and we might as a
result have lost five or six essential votes. The Secretary noted that events
on the mainland have probably helped rather than harmed our position
on Chinese representation in the United Nations. He thought that the
events of the Cultural Revolution must have caused great revulsion
among intellectuals on the mainland. He said we would like to talk with
the GRC about ways of stimulating this revulsion and giving it a push.

---

[1] Source: Department of State, Central Files, UN 6 CHINAT. Secret; Exdis. Drafted by
Bennett on May 12. The meeting took place at the Department of State. Although not indicated on the source text, this was part 3 of a 4-part conversation. Memoranda of the other
portions of the conversion are ibid., Visit Files: Lot 67 D 587, V–31.

Yen told the Secretary that he would visit Expo 67 at the invitation of the Canadian Government on China's National Day next October. Ambassador Chow commented that, in regard to the previously expressed Canadian intention to recognize Red China, the Chinese Communists were taking a very rigid position which helped the GRC in Canada. The Secretary said that he wanted to make it clear that there had been no U.S. collusion with the Canadian initiative in the General Assembly last year, and he described in some detail our problems in dealing with the GOC on Chinese representation.

Ambassador Liu said he would like to take advantage of this unusual summit meeting to consult together on Chinese representation tactics. He said that the Ministry of Foreign Affairs in Taipei was reverting to the "Dean Rusk tactic" of a moratorium formula. He has already exchanged views with Mr. Sisco on this and Ambassador Liu realized that there were difficulties in seeking a moratorium. Liu then went on to say that GRC attaches great importance to President Kennedy's assurance, contained in a letter, with respect to the Security Council.

The Secretary said that it is not 100% clear that there could be a veto on the credentials question. We think so, but it is not certain that we would find agreement on this. The Secretary also pointed out that, if we were to say we will veto admission of Communist China in the Security Council, others would be able to get a free ride, confident that the United States would prevent Communist China from being admitted. On the other hand, if we plan our tactics carefully, we should be able to get a sufficient number of abstentions for the vote to fail without ever needing to veto.

Ambassador Liu noted that of the Security Council's fifteen votes, only nine were in our favor. Liu added that the Security Council has not met since January and that this month the GRC is the President.

In response to a question from the Secretary, Ambassador Liu said that he had no reason to think the Soviets are planning an initiative and Fedorenko had given it as his personal view that the Soviets would not take an initiative on Chinese representation in the Security Council. Ambassador Chow interposed that the Soviets in Geneva recently had used a new formula containing the clause that "Formosa does not represent China." He thought this might foreshadow some new Soviet attitude. Ambassador Liu observed that there is no evidence of a change in the Soviet attitude in the United Nations itself.

Ambassador Liu then said that, from the point of view of his Government domestically, President Kennedy's assurance has importance as showing that the United States proposed to use the veto if necessary. The Secretary commented that domestic political needs in Taiwan may sometimes cut across the subtle needs of winning international support for our position on Chinese representation in the United Nations.

Returning to the question of a moratorium, Ambassador Liu said he thought that having discussed Chinese representation now for five sessions, the General Assembly might this year want to put the subject aside. The Secretary replied that he thought we ought to look at this together. We had not expected the moratorium to last as many years as it did. We were not sure that a moratorium would, in fact, be possible this year.

Mr. Sisco, invited to comment by the Secretary, said it was necessary that we look at the situation in the United Nations very carefully before deciding as to tactics. The events on the mainland were two-edged, he thought; in some respects helpful to our position but, in other respects, working against it. Mr. Sisco thought Soviet statements in the specialized agencies, such as the one referred to by Ambassador Chow, were "record" statements. It was necessary to watch the Soviets in the United Nations itself in judging their attitude. Mr. Sisco went on to say that we have reservations as the possibilities of a moratorium being agreed to in the next General Assembly. The only safe thing, he thought, is to assume that the Albanian resolution will be proposed again this year. Mr. Sisco said that we had done a good job in educating many new members how to deal with the Chinese representation issue substantively, and that reversion to the moratorium tactic would be both confusing and ineffective. Vice President Yen commented at the close of this portion of the conversation that we must have close cooperation between us in Chinese representation.

---

261.   Memorandum of Conversation[1]

Washington, May 11, 1967.

SUBJECT

Informal Discussion of Ambassador Sullivan's Comments on the Taiwan Question

PARTICIPANTS

Walter P. McConaughy, Ambassador, American Embassy Taipei
Robert W. Barnett, Deputy Assistant Secretary, EA
Ralph N. Clough, S/P
Harald Jacobson, EA/ACA
Josiah W. Bennett, EA/ROC
Thomas P. Shoesmith, EA/ROC

---

[1] Source: Department of State, Central Files, POL CHINAT–US. Secret. Drafted by Shoesmith on May 26.

1. It was generally agreed that Ambassador Sullivan's specific suggestions as to courses of action by which Taiwan might be kept separate from the mainland are not realistic, although it was recognized that these were offered only as possible starting points for a consideration of the problem. Specifically, it was felt that the notion of positioning a ready reserve division in Taiwan as a means of persuading the GRC to reduce its force levels and, perhaps, as a bargaining counter vis-à-vis the Chinese Communists was entirely infeasible. Mr. Barnett pointed out that such a move would be exploited by the Chinese Communists as proof of the U.S. "occupation" of Taiwan, would be suspect by the GRC and most unlikely to persuade the GRC to reduce its military strength.

2. There also was general agreement with Mr. Jacobson's view that U.S. policies and actions should not be directed to precluding either the permanent separation of Taiwan from the mainland or eventual unification of Taiwan with the mainland should the people so desire; rather our position should remain flexible so that we can respond, in a manner which will best serve our national interests, to changes likely to take place both on the mainland and in Taiwan. The discussion did not focus specifically on the question of whether U.S. national interests will best be served by maintaining Taiwan separate from the mainland, although it was agreed that this is the practical thrust of our present policies.

3. It was agreed that no basic change in the position of Taiwan as defined by the GRC is likely during the lifetime of President Chiang. There was a difference of opinion, however, concerning the degree of support within Taiwan for remaining separate from the mainland which might be present should such change become possible. On the one hand, it was pointed out that as the island continues to develop economically, and as younger mainlanders come into position of responsibility, many mainlanders, as well as Taiwanese, will become increasingly reluctant to have Taiwan rejoined with the mainland, to which there will be a gradually declining sense of commitment and identification. On the other hand, Mr. Barnett noted that with the passage of time and changes in leadership, those in control on the mainland may find it in their interests to reach some compromise with the GRC and be willing to make substantial concessions to that end. He suggested as one possibility an arrangement under which the government on Taiwan would retain independent control of domestic affairs, including major economic and trade policies, but would have a single Foreign Office with the mainland. (Others, however, pointed out that this would be wholly inconsistent with policies adapted by the Communist regime to date—such as their relations with so-called "autonomous areas.")

4. Mr. Barnett suggested that the "Taiwan problem" should be approached from the question of the significance and implications of the GRC occupation of the Offshore Islands. In this connection, there was

considerable discussion as to the probable effect of a U.S. decision not to assist the GRC in retaining control of the Offshores. Mr. Barnett thought it quite likely that even if the Chinese Communists were reasonably confident that the United States would not assist the GRC in defending the Offshore Islands, they would not necessarily attempt to seize them. He suggested that for the Chinese Communists the GRC occupation of the Offshores not only symbolizes the continuation of the civil war but the direct association of Taiwan with the mainland. To drive the GRC from the Offshores would be to confirm its separation from the mainland. Mr. Clough, however, thought that the Chinese Communists might consider it to their advantage to administer a decisive military and political defeat to the GRC, since this could seriously weaken morale on Taiwan to the extent that the Chinese Communists might be able to force a political settlement. Mr. Bennett also noted that in view of Chiang's determination to hold the Offshores alone, if necessary, any indication that the United States would not come to the GRC's assistance even should its forces on the Offshores face certain defeat could only be regarded by the GRC as tantamount to the abandonment by the United States of its commitments under the Mutual Defense Treaty. This could have a serious adverse impact across the entire range of our relations with the GRC.

5. It was agreed that no useful purpose would be served by undertaking a staff study along the lines proposed by Ambassador Sullivan. Mr. Barnett suggested that it would be useful, prior to the next Chiefs of Mission Conference, to prepare a brief memorandum addressed to the general problem as a reference paper for the conference. Mr. Bennett noted that in commenting on Ambassador Sullivan's views, EA/ROC had recommended that a study be undertaken by EA/ROC, together with S/P, addressed to the question of whether it is in the long-range U.S. interest that Taiwan be kept separate from or rejoined to the mainland. He stated that he continued to believe that, apart from the merits of Ambassador Sullivan's specific proposals, such a study would be worthwhile. No conclusion was reached on this point, however.

262. **Memorandum From the Assistant Legal Adviser for East Asian and Pacific Affairs (Aldrich) to the Department of State Legal Adviser (Meeker)[1]**

Washington, May 16, 1967.

SUBJECT

Hong Kong Defense Commitments

The USG has no firm commitments to act in defense of Hong Kong, so far as we can determine. The NATO Treaty area is limited to Europe, North America and the North Atlantic, and the SEATO Treaty area appears to have been specifically delineated to exclude Hong Kong.

However, Mr. Livingston Merchant, on December 1, 1960, advised British Ambassador Caccia that "it went without saying that were the British to be threatened or attacked there [at Hong Kong],[2] we would give them such support as seemed appropriate at the time." Subsequently, Admiral Felt was authorized to discuss defense plans with Lord Mountbatten, but Mountbatten "made no attempt to find out what Cincpac might be able to do" and Felt did not volunteer information. British staff officers did advise their U.S. counterparts in March 1961 that they had done all they could "to convince the ChiComs that if they attacked Hong Kong, that U.S. would respond with nuclear weapons." According to Admiral Felt, his staff listened.

A working group has been recently constituted to update the 1962 Hong Kong policy paper,[3] which now contemplates the use of U.S. forces for emergency evacuation. It further provides that we would, "In the event of an actual Chinese Communist attack on Hong Kong or an outbreak of major civil disorders there having the direct support of the Chinese Communists, undertake to provide such military assistance as may be judged appropriate in the light of the conditions at the time, including the British response, the extent of hostilities (i.e., whether limited to Hong Kong or of a wider scope), and actions which might be proposed by the United Nations."

---

[1] Source: Department of State, Central Files, DEF 15 HK. Top Secret. Drafted by Mark B. Feldman of L/EA. The source text is stamped "Mr. Bundy has seen."

[2] Brackets in the source text.

[3] Reference is to a paper entitled "Hong Kong: Guidelines for Policy and Operations," prepared by the Department of State in consultation with other interested departments and agencies and issued in November 1962. The portion quoted is subparagraph 2.c.(iii) in Section IV, "Lines of Action." (Ibid., Policy Guidelines: Lot 67 D 396, Hong Kong)

263.   Telegram From the Department of State to the Consulate General in Hong Kong[1]

Washington, May 18, 1967, 6:40 p.m.

197313. Ref: Hong Kong 7983.[2] Eyes Only for Rice and Bruce from Secretary.

1. You should consider problem of Hong Kong in following context:

a. We do not know whether Peking will press the British out of Hong Kong; we are inclined to doubt it because of substantial economic losses which would occur but they are fully capable of acting irrationally.

b. We do not believe that British themselves would make a major effort to defend Hong Kong against any major Chinese Communist military assault.

c. United States would not expect to defend Hong Kong for British, nor do we expect British to ask for this support.

2. You should not intimate in any way readiness to discuss joint military planning.

3. None of above means we should not be as cooperative with and amenable as possible to British and Hong Kong government suggestions as how we can be helpful, short of involving us in moves that could lead to US military involvement in defense of Hong Kong.

Rusk

---

[1] Source: Department of State, Central Files, POL 23–8 HK. Top Secret; Nodis. Drafted and approved by Rusk; cleared by Bundy, Jacobson, Barnett, Eugene Rostow, Jenkins, and McNamara. Repeated to London. Walt Rostow sent a copy to the President with a May 19 covering note: "Mr. President: You should be aware of Sec. Rusk's formulation of our posture toward Hong Kong in the wake of the brief discussion at Tuesday's lunch." The note is initialed with an "L" in Johnson's handwriting. According to Johnson's Appointment Diary, he had lunch on Tuesday, May 16, with Rusk, McNamara, Humphrey, Helms, Rostow, Press Secretary George Christian, and General Wheeler. (Johnson Library) No record of the discussion has been found.

[2] Reference should be to telegram 7938 from Hong Kong, May 16, in which Rice stated that the question of approval of a visit to Hong Kong by Admiral Sharp, which had been left to the Consulate General, was one that should be answered in the context of general U.S. policy concerning Hong Kong and he did not know what the thinking was on this subject in Washington or whether people at a sufficiently high level had focused on it. (Department of State, Central Files, POL 23–8 HK)

264.   Telegram From the Department of State to the Embassy in Thailand[1]

Washington, May 19, 1967, 7:52 p.m.

198345. Ref: A. Bangkok 15006.[2] Following is Department's appraisal of situation in Soviet-Chinese border areas requested in reftel:

1. In general, we have no information to indicate that any serious shooting incidents have occurred in recent months between Soviet and Chinese Communist forces in border areas. However, there have been several probably true reports of local small-scale "incidents," including along Amur River, and both sides have probably stepped up their security precautions all along the border. In February and March, Red Guard newspapers in Peking mentioned border incidents, and February 22 speech by the Soviet Deputy Defense Minister confirmed that shooting incident had taken place at Blagoveshchensk earlier that month. We expect border tensions to continue but doubt that any large-scale outbreaks will occur.

2. The Soviets clearly have increased their propaganda directed at the ethnic minorities in Chinese border areas such as Sinkiang and Inner Mongolia. Small numbers of Kazakhs and Uighurs apparently have fled from Sinkiang across the border, and Soviets have used some of them to broadcast horrendous details about Red Guards' treatment ethnic minority groups under Cultural Revolution. Red Guard newspaper article in March claimed Soviets also sending subversive agents to penetrate into Communist China, but whether or not significant volume such activities actually occurring has not been confirmed.

3. In two Chinese border areas, Inner Mongolia and Sinkiang, period of uneasy relative calm apparently prevails now. Serious violence was instigated in those regions by Red Guards last January and earlier February, but then modus vivendi between Peking and local authorities was reached. Last month, Peking apparently upset this arrangement in Inner Mongolia, and there have been reports of removal Ulanfu (Party boss of Mongol ethnic derivation who had served there for fifteen years) and of reorganization military leadership there. In Sinkiang, long-time Party-military leadership headed by Wang En-mao still holds on although there is danger of resurgent Red Guard conflict and increased opposition from ethnic minority groups.

---

[1] Source: Department of States, Central Files, POL 32–1 CHICOM–USSR. Secret; Priority. Drafted by Robert P. Stephens of INR/REA; cleared by Weaver Gim of EA/THAI, INR/REA Deputy Director John H. Holdridge, John P. Sontag of INR/RSB, J. Stapleton Roy, and Donald M. Anderson of EA/ACA; and approved by John Sylvester, Jr., of EA/THAI. Repeated to Hong Kong.

[2] Dated May 18. (Ibid.)

4. In "Mongolian People's Republic" (MPR) there some evidence that Soviet military presence may have been increased recently. Soviet construction troops have been stationed in MPR for many years. Possibly because of Soviet desires, MPR has been leveling much blunt propaganda at Communist China for several months, and relations between two countries are at low point.

Rusk

265. Memorandum From the President's Special Assistant (Rostow) to President Johnson[1]

Washington, May 20, 1967.

SUBJECT

China Mainland Situation

The political situation throughout the Chinese mainland today is complex and uncertain.

While there is no good evidence that any area is not reasonably well controlled by the central government, Peking press and radio have praised the leadership of only four provinces (Heilungkiang, Shansi, Shantung and Kweichow) and two municipalities (Shanghai and Peking). Peking is pointedly silent about the remaining 22 provinces. Since May 1, Red Guards have reported disorder in five provinces (Szechwan, Tibet, Kansu, Sinkiang and Honan). As a minimum, this suggests that Peking leaders are in serious conflict over the selection of leaders there.

Lurid reports of violence in the provinces, circulated by Red Guards and picked up by the world press, are largely, though by no means entirely, discounted by the intelligence community. Fairly widespread disorder has occurred, but it is suspected that exaggerated reports are issued in order to discredit local officials slated for purge. Communications and transportation services, including those involving the Army,

---

[1] Source: Johnson Library, National Security File, Country File, China, Vol. IX. Secret. A handwritten "L" on the source text indicates that it was seen by the President.

have functioned normally since February, without anomalies attributable to unrest.

The Army has generally responded to central orders since late January, although it has tended to act more in the interest of stability than in support of the Maoists as such.

Mao's "extensive democracy" (turning to the masses for support) has been fairly effective as a weapon of destruction. However, it is at a loss when the time comes to construct a meaningful alternative to the destroyed structure. Unity fostered by targeting conservative "demons" then dissolves into bickering among the leftists over the share of the spoils. Peking has aptly termed this phenomenon "unprincipled 'civil wars.'" The regime has had to resort to increased reliance on the Army and renewed policy emphasis on law and order—at the expense of Mao's revolutionary objectives. The revolution is in a highly nervous stalemate.

Walt

---

266.   Telegram From the Embassy in the Republic of China to the Department of State[1]

Taipei, May 24, 1967, 0830Z.

3662. Subj: Country Team assessment of GRC intentions. Ref State 135828 Limdis.[2]

1.   Continuing disorders in widespread areas of Communist China have not stirred the GRC into more militant activities against the mainland. We know of no GRC plans or preparations for any major military, paramilitary, or intelligence operations against Communist China. The more modest programs of which we are aware emphasize political rather than military action; they follow the general line set by President Chiang early this year.

2.   We have reported earlier on the small increase in the number of GRC troops on Matsu, the current movement of the 1st Marine Division

---

[1] Source: Department of State, Central Files, POL 27 CHICOM–CHINAT. Secret; Limdis. Repeated to Hong Kong and to CINCPAC for POLAD.

[2] See footnote 2, Document 242.

to the Penghus, and various other military redeployments.[3] We continue to view these as part of GRC efforts to disperse its forces for defense against ChiCom attack and not to improve its offensive capabilities against the mainland.

3. An attempted GRC intelligence/incursion operation against the Fukien coast on 6 May ended in disaster, with a small boat and at least seven men lost as a result of Chinese Communist attack. Operations of this kind continue to be attempted sporadically, but steady improvements in ChiCom surveillance and coastal defense capabilities make them extremely hazardous and unproductive. Maritime raids are not a significant part of current GRC planning concerning the mainland, and we have reason to believe that certain responsible GRC officials doubt the efficacy of such incursion attempts.

4. [less than 1 line of source text not declassified] report [less than 1 line of source text not declassified] of a "program for strengthening operations behind enemy lines" is a good illustration of the content of current GRC plans concerning Communist China. The "program", which was approved by Defense Minister Chiang Ching-kuo on 3 March, specifically rejects a military "counter-attack" because of the "international situation" and because it would reunify the Communists. It calls for political and psychological warfare measures, and in doing so makes clear that GRC plans rest almost entirely on a hope, however ill-defined, that events on the mainland will develop in such a way that GRC influence will be revived.

Hummel

---

[3] Hummel discussed the movement of troops to the Penghus and to Matsu in a March 4 letter to Bennett. (Department of State, Central Files, DEF 19–8 US–CHINAT) He commented further in telegram 2656 from Taipei, March 6. (Ibid., POL CHICOM–CHINAT)

267. National Intelligence Estimate[1]

NIE 13–7–67   Washington, May 25, 1967.

THE CHINESE CULTURAL REVOLUTION

Conclusions

A. The political crisis in China continues. No end is in sight. Among the several possible outcomes, no one is distinctly more likely than others. But whatever its ultimate resolution, the Great Proletarian Cultural Revolution has already done immense damage to the top leadership and the party, has profoundly altered the internal power structure, has greatly unsettled all levels of Chinese society, has unleashed new forces of instability, and has contributed to China's growing isolation in the world.

B. We have no evidence that the Cultural Revolution has yet had any significant effects on the military capabilities of the PLA or on China's advanced weapons programs. But the PLA is assuming more and more noncombat tasks and if this trend long continues it would almost certainly affect its combat capabilities.

C. Instability and confusion are likely to persist so long as Mao retains sufficient power and vigor to push his designs for remoulding the party and combating real and imagined threats to his doctrines and policies. Mao could misjudge his power position and go too far. He is now heavily dependent on the military for support; too vigorous efforts to bridle the armed forces could produce a coup against Mao or even fragmentation of the country and civil war. But these are extreme cases and we think it more likely that a basic tendency toward preservation of national unity will persist, despite the divisive impact of the Cultural Revolution.

D. Looking beyond Mao, the Cultural Revolution has made it more likely that the succession will be a disorderly and contentious struggle. The military may play a decisive role, but Lin Piao would not necessarily be their candidate. A collective including Chou En-lai, some of the military leaders, and even some of the now disgraced party figures, might emerge. In any event we believe that many of Mao's dogmas and prac-

---

[1] Source: Department of State, S/S Files: Lot 90 D 110. Secret; Controlled Dissem. According to a note on the cover sheet, the estimate was submitted by Helms and prepared by the Central Intelligence Agency and the intelligence organizations of the Departments of State and Defense and the National Security Agency. All members of the U.S. Intelligence Board concurred on May 25 except the AEC Representative and the Assistant Director of the Federal Bureau of Investigation, who abstained because the subject was out of their jurisdiction.

tices are likely to be set aside. This might be a gradual process, though it could come more rapidly if unresolved internal and external problems have been aggravated during the last months or years of Mao's rule.

E. The political crisis has already focused the leadership's energies and attention on internal affairs and has at least temporarily damaged Chinese prestige abroad. Within this context, however, China has maintained a relatively active foreign policy, though it has become more rigid in international Communist affairs. For the most part Peking has maintained policy positions which were well established before the Cultural Revolution began. As long as the Maoists retain control, Peking is unlikely to make any important changes in the general line of its foreign policy. At any rate, in the short term, an unremitting hostility to the US and USSR is likely to remain the predominant feature of Chinese foreign policy. It is possible, however, that over the longer term, internal changes in the direction of moderation, if they do occur, will create more favorable conditions for reappraising foreign policy and perhaps for introducing elements of greater moderation.

[Here follows the Discussion portion of the estimate.]

---

268. Telegram From the Department of State to Embassy in Poland[1]

Washington, May 29, 1967, 12:24 p.m.

204093. Gronouski–Wang talks: Guidance for 133rd meeting, June 7, 1967.

1. It is our turn to open. In general we anticipate that atmosphere in which this meeting takes place likely to be cooler than for some time. Current meeting considered from our standpoint primarily as "holding operation" in which our minimum objective is to keep open some dialogue with ChiComs. Our opening statement is considerably briefer than at last meeting and we would hope this would set framework for general brief, uncomplicated session. We anticipate, however, ChiComs

---

[1] Source: Department of State, Central Files, POL CHICOM–US. Confidential; Limdis. Drafted by Kreisberg on May 22, and cleared by Bundy, Jacobson, Robert H. Miller, Bennett, Aldrich, Dr. Oswald H. Ganley of SCI, Holland of DOD/ISA, and Ambassador Gronouski. Approved by Rusk. Repeated to Moscow, Saigon, Taipei, and Hong Kong.

will focus very hard on Vietnam, question of US use of Thai bases, alleged violations of ChiCom territorial air and water and other incidents, and US-Soviet and US–GRC collusion against Peking. Your opening statement deals with some of these points in effort blunt ChiCom attack in advance. In general, we believe that in rebuttal you should not become involved in detailed comments on US military actions in Vietnam other than to emphasize that US actions not aimed at Peking and general comments on US purposes in undertaking military involvement in Vietnam. Kreisberg will provide you with additional material on specific anticipated ChiCom allegations, including possibly Hong Kong. FYI. We do not wish Hong Kong to become involved in Warsaw talks, at this point at least, other than in our replying in low key to ChiCom comments on calls by US vessels and personnel at port. End FYI. Main contingency current guidance provides for is effort by ChiComs to end or suspend talks.

2. Suggest you open as follows: "Mr. Ambassador, I would first like to reiterate a point I made at our last meeting in January: that my Government believes it is useful for these meetings, even though they may be brief, to take place at more frequent intervals than every 4-1/2 months, particularly in a period such as the present. I realize this anticipates our consideration later today of the time for our next meeting, but I wish to underline the importance which my Government attaches to the opportunity which these meetings present for our two sides to frankly and openly exchange views on matters of mutual concern and interest.

3. Mr. Ambassador, I have set forth in previous meetings my Government's position on the conflict in Vietnam. I have emphasized our willingness and fervent hope to find some means of ending the conflict and enabling the people of South Vietnam to resolve their own political problems peacefully and in their own way so that they may get about the urgent tasks of improving their lives and those of their children. I have indicated to you here in these meetings, and more importantly, my Government has made clear to the Government of North Vietnam, that we are ready at any time to discuss with them how this can best and most rapidly be achieved.

4. Mr. Ambassador, the US is prepared at this very moment to discuss arrangements for a general stand-still truce, to enter into preliminary talks with the Government of North Vietnam, and to participate in a reconvened Geneva Conference. We are prepared to halt the bombing of North Vietnam as a first step in a general effort to achieve a de-escalation of the violence and a start on meaningful negotiations, provided we receive the kind of assurances indicated in Amb. Goldberg's speech last September at the UN. We do not intend to invade North Vietnam; we do not seek to overthrow the Government of North Vietnam; we are not trying to change the political system in the North. We have taken the actions

that we have with deliberation and care to see that the area of the conflict not be expanded. All our actions are directed at demonstrating to the GNVN that its efforts to impose an arbitrary and unilateral political solution on the people of SVN will not succeed. We believe that the interests of North Vietnam lie in seeking, through confidential negotiations, an equitable peaceful settlement rather than replying entirely on the use of force by NVN directed forces in the South.

5. Mr. Ambassador, I shall not recapitulate all our efforts during the last few years or during the most recent 4 months to find a means of peacefully resolving this conflict. I am aware that your Government is thus far not a direct party to this situation and there is no need for me to go into detail on this subject. The GNVN, however, is well aware of our efforts and my Government continues to be hopeful that these will ultimately bear some fruit. I would only hope, Mr. Ambassador, that your Government will lend its moral support and encouragement to those efforts which men of good will of virtually all political persuasions throughout the world are making to bring this conflict to an end. I would further hope that your Government's firm support for 'the people of Vietnam', of which you spoke at our last meeting, will be exerted with equal firmness to any efforts by the GNVN to achieve an honorable and just settlement of the conflict through negotiations.

6. Mr. Ambassador, repeatedly during the last 4-1/2 months, radio broadcasts and official announcements by your Government have alleged US harassment and firing on vessels of your country, intrusions into your territorial air and water, and, in April and May, the shooting down of a number of US aircraft. We have examined these allegations as they have appeared. I continue to regret your Government's refusal to engage in joint investigations of such incidents when this might be useful and productive. We have ascertained one or two occasions when US aircraft may have unintentionally and briefly intruded into your airspace. At these times we have publicly acknowledged the facts. Our investigations also revealed several occasions, including individual incidents on February 25, April 7, and April 26, when vessels apparently belonging to your country fired on US aircraft in the Gulf of Tonkin area without provocation but without, I may add, eliciting counter-fire. We have found, however, no basis whatsoever for the overwhelming preponderance of your allegations. I am at a loss to understand the reasons for their being made unless your authorities are simply misinformed by the sources originating these stories.

7. It should be clear to you that we have had no hesitation in acknowledging intrusions into your territory when we are able to confirm that such intrusions may accidentally and unintentionally have taken place. This is because, as I have repeatedly told you, US Air Force

and Naval pilots are specifically instructed and cautioned to fully respect the territorial air and sea of your country.

8. But, Mr. Ambassador, we find most puzzling the claims that your Government has put forth relating to the shooting down of US fighter aircraft on April 24 and May 1. As your Government must be aware, no US aircraft intruded into your territorial air, none were shot down over your territory, and no US aircraft were missing anywhere near your frontiers during this period. If you have any further details on these allegations. I should welcome them.

9. I must point out that allegations of incidents which have never taken place not only create a needless atmosphere of tension; they also will make more difficult the ascertaining of facts and their assessment should such incidents actually occur.

10. Mr. Ambassador, my Government has repeatedly assured your Government, both publicly and through these meetings, that we intend no hostile actions against your country, have no intention of interfering in the internal affairs of the territory under your control, and that our actions and military activities in Vietnam are not directed in any way against your country. You have on a number of occasions chosen to express your disbelief in these assurances. You are mistaken to do so, and I would regret if I have been unable to convince you of this. I can only reiterate what I have said before: our intentions are indeed as I have stated them. We consider this forum as one in which each side must be able to communicate to the other, in full frankness, matters relating to policy and purpose. The dangers and risks of a misunderstanding are too great for us to attempt to deceive or mislead your Government, as you alleged at our last meeting.

11. Our objectives in Vietnam are, as I have said, limited. We have exercised great restraint and intend to continue to do so to avoid widening the scope or area of the conflict beyond Vietnam. We hope you will understand this restraint and understand the limitations we have imposed on ourselves. We are under no misapprehensions as to the degree to which we differ over the reasons for the current conflict in Vietnam and in our respective positions toward this conflict. But we strongly hope that your Government can accept what we see as an irrefutable premise: that an enlargement of the conflict beyond Vietnam and the entry of new, outside elements into the Vietnam situation will create grave and serious dangers which neither of our countries should wish to see.

12. Mr. Ambassador, it is my understanding that in recent years, scientists and medical personnel of your country have experimented with and successfully developed many traditional herbal cures for diseases. The scientific and medical community of my country would welcome an opportunity to share in the achievements made by the people and scien-

tists of your country in this area of herbal medicine and also in the treatment of certain diseases, common to your country and mine, that I understand you have effectively developed in recent years.

13. We have for the last 18 months hoped that your Government would agree to permit American doctors and public health personnel visit China to exchange experiences and knowledge with their opposite numbers on your side. We regret that your Government has thus far declined to facilitate such exchanges. I would like to suggest at this point that scientists and doctors in your country might make available samples of herbs and herbal medicines and their experience in using these to interested and qualified American scientists. In exchange, if this were desired by your Government, I am sure arrangements could be made for recent American developments in similar areas of research to be made available to scientists and doctors of your country.

14. I hope your Government will consider this proposal seriously and not reject it out of hand as a propaganda or political move. Its purpose is genuinely to enable the people of our two countries, regardless of political differences, to benefit from the achievements of science, where it may be practiced.

15. Mr. Ambassador, I was disappointed at our last meeting to hear your flat and immediate rejection of my remarks on the Americans presently being held in prison in your country. I was glad that you agreed that we have a perfect right to raise this issue in these meetings. But it is more than merely the right to 'express my views', as I believe you put it. This right I have in any event. It is a question rather of the failure of your Government to fulfill a commitment into which we entered, and had hoped you did as well, in good faith.

16. It is furthermore a question of compassion, particularly in the cases of Bishop Walsh and Captain Smith. The fact that the Red Cross Societies of our two countries may have had an exchange of correspondence on a visit by members of Captain Smith's family to Peking does not exclude this subject from our discussions here. I urge again that you transmit my request to your Government that Captain Smith be released expeditiously and that, pending his release, his wife and brother be allowed to visit him. In any event, after the passage of 21 months, I would hope that we might be given some indication of how long your authorities intend to continue to hold him. The pain and grief of continued uncertainty should not be imposed on his wife and family.

17. I hope, in addition, Mr. Ambassador, that your Government will give me a carefully considered reply to my appeal for the release of Bishop Walsh in view of his age and health. It is certainly not 'interference in your internal affairs' to raise this matter of obvious humanity. I, of course, must emphasize again that Mr. Downey, Mr. Fecteau, and Mr. Redmond should have been released 12 years ago, in accordance with

our agreement in September 1955 and urge that, however belatedly, your Government carry out this agreement now."

18. The guidance in Deptel 111764[2] for the 132nd meeting relating to possible break or suspension of talks (paras 28–33) continues to be applicable and should be drawn on by you in the event of necessity. We have given further consideration to possibility noted in reftel para 30 that Wang, whose turn it is to suggest date for next meeting, may decline to do so either on administrative grounds or in context alleged US hostile actions against Peking. You should strongly object to failure to set new meeting date but obviously if Chinese refuse agree we cannot force them to do so. Only precedent for this was at 73rd meeting on December 12, 1957, when, as result our decision designate new US representative below Ambassador-level, it was agreed that announcement concerning next meeting would be made subsequently. This led to nine-month gap in meetings. You should, however, reemphasize points now included in paras 2 and 10 in present guidance (which included in part in anticipation of such a contingency) and fact that past precedent except on one occasion noted above has been to set firm date for next meeting. You should indicate we prepared hold next meeting September 13, 1967, and that we will make statement to this effect following meeting, noting US willingness continue meet with Chinese, regretting ChiCom position, and emphasizing we hope for change in ChiCom position. We should not anticipate calling for meeting of Special Representatives (Deptel 116572)[3] unless ChiComs tie failure set date for next meeting directly to harsh public denunciation of US hostile actions against them and/or of you personally. Precise wording of public statement which would be issued by you following meeting left to your discretion in context of actual ChiCom approach in event of this contingency.

19. In event meeting proceeds normally, you should press for September meeting. ChiComs would probably prefer one considerably later but we would hope compromise on date not later than last half of October.

Rusk

---

[2] Document 228.
[3] Document 230.

269.   Memorandum From Alfred Jenkins of the National Security Council Staff to the President's Special Assistant (Rostow)[1]

Washington, June 9, 1967.

SUBJECT

The Cultural Revolution

Recent Developments:

1.   The Army's influence has grown rapidly. In an increasing list of areas Army control has become evident in public security work, press and radio, basic community services, and in the organization of both agricultural and industrial production.

2.   The extension of Army control has been generally unpopular, especially with "revolutionary rebels" whom the Army has frequently suppressed, but also with the average citizen.

3.   Despite increased Army control, public order has suffered further setbacks during the past week. Sufficient trouble has broken out both north of Shanghai and south of that city to cause transportation difficulties. Letter intercepts speak of growing lawlessness.

4.   A thinly veiled, sharp personal attack on Mao, recently published in a North Vietnamese Party journal, suggests the probability of new friction between Peking and Hanoi. Even if the Vietnamese were severely provoked by some recent Chinese action, this article is still a remarkable affront coming from a small nation so dependent upon Chinese largesse. It is also another index of the low state of Mao's prestige out of the country.

The course of the Cultural Revolution has made attempted time tables hazardous. However, it seems to me there are a number of indicators which point to a likely crucial stage within a very few months. It is possible that by September there will have been fairly significant developments. As of now, the fortunes of Maoism continue slowly to sink.

Al Jenkins

---

[1] Source: Johnson Library, National Security File, Country File, China, Vol. IX. Secret. A copy was sent to Jorden. Rostow sent the memorandum to the President on June 9 with a covering note stating that it suggested "friction between Peiping and Hanoi, which might conceivably help set the stage for a negotiation."

270. Telegram From the Embassy in Poland to the Department of State[1]

Warsaw, June 14, 1967, 1815Z.

2985. Wang–Gronouski Talks.[2] Ref: State 204093.[3]

1. Meeting lasted three hours but produced absolutely nothing new from ChiComs. Wang insisted next meeting take place no earlier than November and Nov. 8 agreed upon. I issued press statement regretting extension of meetings to 4–5 month intervals after meeting concluded.

2. I opened with statement in reftel. Wang, labeling his opening remarks as pre-statement comments, attacked U.S., U.K. and Sovs for colluding with Israel against Arabs and stated CPR firmly support Arab people. He returned to this theme later in meeting alleging U.S. and Sovs working in league to control destiny of Arabs and that U.S. support for Israel another grave war provocation.

3. Wang devoted substantial portion of opening statement, as well as later rebuttal remarks, to Taiwan. Occasion apparently 17th anniversary (June 27) of U.S. 7th Fleet separation of Taiwan mainland. He repeated usual charges of U.S. occupation, oppression of people on Taiwan, collusion with Chiang Kai-shek. Emphasized ChiComs would eventually liberate Taiwan and that U.S. sooner or later would be forced withdraw. Later in meeting he repeated there no possibility of improving U.S.–ChiCom relations or resolving any concrete problems unless U.S. withdraws from Taiwan and Taiwan Straits. He said all U.S. initiatives would be rebuffed until this problem dealt with. He raised visits by U.S. officials to Taiwan and C.K. Yen visit to Washington, charging this preparatory to new U.S.–GRC moves against mainland. I rebutted Wang's arguments and asked whether ChiComs wished reconsider "renunciation of force" agreement discussed in early years of talks. Wang did not respond.

4. Wang reiterated in completely standard language ChiCom positions on incidents involving ChiCom territorial air and water, alleged U.S. attack, and on Vietnam. No new warnings of ChiCom intervention or involvement in Vietnam. During latter part of meeting in context of re-

---

[1] Source: Department of State, Central Files, POL CHICOM–US. Confidential; Immediate; Limdis. Repeated to Hong Kong, London, Moscow, Taipei, USUN, and to Luxembourg for the Secretary. Passed to the White House and USIA.

[2] The 133d meeting, scheduled for June 7, was postponed to June 14 at Chinese request, made by a telephone call to the U.S. Embassy on June 6. (Telegram 2950 from Warsaw, June 6; ibid.) A detailed report of the meeting was sent in airgram A–800 from Warsaw, dated June 15. (Ibid.)

[3] Document 268.

ferral to possible U.S. extension of war to include territory of DRV, Wang simply said ChiComs had made preparations in event U.S. "imposes war on Chinese people."

5. He emphasized in rebuttal that at Warsaw talks "which have dragged on for 11 years," U.S. had refused settle basic differences between U.S. and ChiComs, i.e., Taiwan. He reiterated rejection of joint investigations of incidents as unnecessary and intended by U.S. to cover up "crimes" and "deceive people."

6. Wang attacked U.S. use of Thailand as base aimed at CPR as well as NVN and rejected my retort that ChiComs themselves were threatening Thailand through subversive organizations based on ChiCom territory.

7. I repeatedly pressed ChiComs on whether they would support DRV in seeking negotiated settlement if latter decided to do so, noting that ChiComs seemed more anxious than DRV to see war continue. Wang's only reply was that ChiComs believed DRV agreed with them and that U.S. should not try to sow discord between Chinese and DRV.

8. No mention of Hong Kong or suggestion that talks be ended other than Wang's insistence that no point in more frequent meetings than every 4–5 months.

9. General atmosphere about as at previous meetings. Wang, as at last meeting, appeared to labor intentionally to drag meeting out to [apparent omission] hours. He seemed to lose his temper only at one point, in referring to U.S. expansion of war. He referred to me as "liar" and "gangster" at one point and I responded by rejecting such epithets as unworthy our roles in Warsaw talks. He did not repeat them. ChiCom opening statement such propaganda potboiler I was sure Wang intended it for public release and must admit to surprise he made no mention of intention to do so. As was anticipated, meeting essentially served merely to keep line of communication open and this about all that could have been hoped for at this point.

Gronouski

---

271. **Editorial Note**

On June 26, 1967, President Johnson met with Romanian Prime Minister Ion Gheorghe Maurer, who was visiting Washington and was about to visit Peking. According to a memorandum of the conversation prepared in the Department of State, Johnson told Maurer the United States did not want war with China, did not seek to change China's system of government, had no designs on Chinese territory, and wanted only to trade with China and get along to the extent that China would permit. He stated that he would like to talk to the Chinese about a non-proliferation treaty and to "work out ground rules so that we can avoid nuclear war." He stated also that it would be "the height of folly" for the United States to want to go to war with China; nothing could be further from his mind. Noting that Maurer was about to visit other countries, Johnson stated that he was at liberty to describe their conversation and to quote anything Johnson had said, if it would be useful. For text of the memorandum of conversation, see *Foreign Relations,* 1964–1968, volume XVII, pages 430–435.

The Embassy in Bucharest reported on July 15 that Maurer had told visiting Austrian Chancellor Josef Klaus that he had found the Chinese preoccupied with the idea the United States was preparing to attack the China mainland and had told them what Johnson had said to him, but that they were not convinced. (Telegrams 61 and 62 from Bucharest, both July 15; Department of State, Central Files, POL 7 ROM)

---

272. National Intelligence Estimate[1]

NIE 13–5–67   Washington, June 29, 1967.

ECONOMIC OUTLOOK FOR COMMUNIST CHINA

Conclusions

A. Economic activity in China, especially in the industrial sector, is being slowed by the Cultural Revolution. Nevertheless, military production and development continue to enjoy a high priority, and have been considerably aided by imports from the Free World.

---

[1] Source: Department of State, S/S Files: Lot 90 D 110. Secret; Controlled Dissem. According to a note on the cover sheet, the estimate was submitted by Deputy Director of Central Intelligence Rufus Taylor and prepared by the Central Intelligence Agency and the intelligence organizations of the Departments of State and Defense and the National Security Agency. All members of the U.S. Intelligence Board concurred on June 29, except the Assistant Director of the Federal Bureau of Investigation, who abstained because the subject was outside his jurisdiction.

B. Foreign trade has grown, and the non-Communist world now accounts for three-fourths of China's trade. China's balance of payments position has improved over the past two years. Support of North Vietnam has been substantially increased during the past year, but imposes no undue strain on the Chinese economy.

C. The economic outlook depends heavily upon the development of the political situation. During the next year or two, assuming a continuation of the present level of political turmoil, the economy seems likely to deteriorate somewhat, though probably not to the point of causing a sharp decline in industrial production, widespread unemployment, or acute food shortages. The weapons programs could be continued, though some stretch out in particular items might be necessary.

D. We think it unlikely that Mao will achieve sufficient political success in the Cultural Revolution to permit him to embark upon a new economic initiative similar to the Leap Forward. When Mao disappears from the scene, there will probably be a period of confused contesting for power during which economic recovery will be neither rapid nor sure.

E. The unfavorable food-population ratio, the economic costs and imbalances inherent in the military program, and the shortcomings of the educational system are problems likely to persist for at least a decade. A pragmatic regime could probably surmount them, but any successor to the present regime will also inherit some of the ambitious political goals of its predecessor. These will strongly affect the allocation of resources, probably at the expense of laying foundations for self-sustaining economic growth.

[Here follows the Discussion portion of the estimate.]

273. Memorandum From the Republic of China Country Director (Bennett) to the Deputy Assistant Secretary of State for East Asian and Pacific Affairs (Berger)[1]

Washington, July 11, 1967.

SUBJECT

U.S. Presence on the Offshore Islands

Recalling your interest in having the facts about the U.S. presence on the offshore islands, I took the opportunity while in Taipei to ask Art Hummel to have the Embassy put together an inventory for our reference. The attached letter from Art and its inclosure[2] is the result.

To me the striking thing in this report is the extent to which the GRC has committed its effective forces to the offshore islands, including six of the GRC's fourteen forward-look divisions plus supporting armor and artillery. According to the report this constitutes nearly half of the best ground forces available to the GRC.

While in Taipei and at CINCPAC, I asked the military their assessment of the defensibility of the offshores. The general consensus was that except for one small island held by irregular forces (Wu-ch'iu Hsu), the other large islands would be very difficult and costly for the Communists to take. However, those with whom I spoke acknowledged that the Communists, were they willing to pay the cost, would probably be able to establish air superiority over the islands, thus putting themselves in a position to interdict resupply operations. The garrisons under these circumstances would be unable to hold out indefinitely, the effect on their morale would be severe, and pressures for U.S. military involvement would be very high. On the other hand, there was general agreement that any frontal assault on the islands would be almost prohibitively costly and that in any air battle over the Strait the kill ratio would probably be heavily in favor of the CAF. There was also general agreement that there is no sign of increased ChiCom activity in the offshore island area.

Attachment

U.S. ACTIVITIES ON THE OFFSHORE ISLANDS[3]

The most visible relationship of the U.S. with the Offshore islands is the MAP support given almost all GRC troops stationed there. A small

---

[1] Source: Department of State, ROC Files: Lot 74 D 25, POL 27 Offshore Islands, 1968–1969. Secret.

[2] The letter from Hummel to Bennett, July 3, is not printed.

[3] The report, not dated, was drafted by John A. Froebe, Jr., on June 30.

but significant economic aid program has also been carried on in the Off-shores, and USIS loans books and tapes to a GRC military reading room on Kinmen. In addition, the U.S. and the GRC participate in joint (secret) contingency planning for possible U.S. participation in the defense of the islands. The GRC has actively sought to enliven the interest of individual Americans in and out of government in the islands, especially Kinmen, by encouraging their visits there. Top GRC officials may hope that these visits together with the present (small-scale) U.S. involvement on the Offshore islands will influence the U.S. to assist in their defense in the event of another Communist attack.

1955 Conditional Commitment

The Congressional Resolution of January 1955 authorized the President to use U.S. forces for the defense of Taiwan and the Penghus and for "the securing and protection of such related positions and territories of that area now in friendly hands and the taking of such other measures as he judges to be required or appropriate in assuring the defense of Formosa and the Pescadores." The Executive view of defense of related positions and territories was outlined in President Eisenhower's message to Congress asking the authority conveyed in the Resolution. Eisenhower said he would act "only in situations which are recognizable as parts of, or definite preliminaries to, an attack against the main positions of Formosa and the Pescadores."

The U.S. intent has since been publicly reaffirmed in high level statements at least seven times during both the Eisenhower and Kennedy Administrations, most notably during the 1958 Kinmen crisis and most recently by President Kennedy in June 1962. In each instance we have made clear that a U.S. defense of the Offshores would depend on our evaluation of the Chicom attack at hand. Of significance, nonetheless, was the public development of the doctrine in the 1958 crisis. Secretary Dulles, with the intensive bombardment of Kinmen two weeks underway, warned Communist China in a statement September 4 that the defense of the two island groups had "increasingly become related to the defense of Taiwan." President Eisenhower in a radio–TV address a week later was more explicit: "If the present bombardment and harassment of Quemoy should be converted into a major assault, with which the local defenders could not cope, then we would be compelled to face precisely the situation that Congress visualized in 1955."

U.S. Military Assistance and US–GRC Planning for Joint Defense of the Off-shores

The most important U.S. relationship with the Offshores is the MAP support extended to most of the GRC forces stationed in the Offshores and U.S. participation in secret, joint contingency planning for US–GRC defense of the islands. MAP support was originally not given to GRC forces in Kinmen and Matsu, but was gradually extended as a result of MAP supported units on Taiwan being rotated to the islands. Military assistance for these forces can also be viewed as preparation for the contingency in which the U.S. might undertake to defend the islands.

All 64,500 troops in the Kinmen complex (including five Forward Look infantry divisions and supporting units and one Air Force anti-aircraft regiment) are MAP supported. Of the 24,800 GRC troops in the Matsu complex, 21,800 (including one Forward Look and one light infantry division and their supporting units along with one Air Force anti-aircraft regiment) are MAP supported. The remaining 3,000 non-MAP supported troops in Matsu are the para-military Anti-Communist National Salvation Corps. Thus, about one-sixth of the 544,000 MAP supported GRC forces are deployed on the Offshores. Altogether six of the 14 Forward Look divisions plus supporting armor and artillery, the GRC's most modernized and combat ready ground forces, are in the Offshores. The GRC's allocation of nearly half of its best ground forces to these islands is perhaps the clearest manifestation of the importance it attaches to the Offshores. The figures in this paragraph are those compiled by MAAG, which frequently differ somewhat from those compiled by the Ministry of National Defense, the source of the Embassy's quarterly troop strength reports.

Advising the GRC commands in the Offshores is a MAAG team of five officers and one enlisted man on Kinmen and a MAAG team of three officers and one enlisted man on Matsu, although additional MAAG advisers are frequently brought in temporarily to assist in more specialized problems. (One MAAG adviser on Kinmen [*less than 1 line of source text not declassified*].) The U.S. presence at both locations is made somewhat more prominent by the MAAG teams' flying the American flag.

Contingency U.S. participation in the defense of the two island groups is provided for in Plan Rochester, the comprehensive plan for the joint US–GRC defense of Taiwan and the Penghus pursuant to the 1954 Mutual Defense Treaty. The U.S. Taiwan Defense Command first drafted the plan with the Ministry of National Defense in 1955 and together with the Ministry has kept it updated. The current plan's premise for contingency employment of U.S. forces in the defense of the Offshores envisages possible provision of U.S. naval and air forces to supplement those of the GRC with the objective of gaining air and naval superiority in the Strait. No deployment of U.S. ground forces to the islands is contemplated by the contingency plan, the land defense being left to GRC ground forces then in place.

Officers of the U.S. Taiwan Defense Command who are engaged in joint planning find their Chinese counterparts well aware of the conditional nature of the 1955 Congressional Resolution. Many Chinese officers seem convinced, however, that the Presidential determination has already been made for a number of hypothecated contingencies, and they frequently try to sound out U.S. officers concerning these assumed decisions. Some Chinese military officers also argue that a future contingency would not be materially different from the 1958 crisis, and that the U.S. response would therefore be the same.

U.S. Economic Assistance in the Offshore Islands

U.S. economic assistance in the Offshores constitutes a small but still significant part of the current U.S. involvement in the islands. Total direct assistance has amounted over the years to about US$2.3 million, which while comprising only a fractional 0.15% of the total US$1.5 billion of U.S. economic aid given the GRC, is on a per capita basis higher than that for Taiwan proper. Direct U.S. aid for FY67 amounted to about US$133,000, the bulk of which went to Kinmen. Almost half the islands' population is estimated to have been reached by these programs. Assistance now is divided between two projects: first, PL480 agricultural surplus commodities channeled through voluntary agencies, which came to about US$70,000 in the current fiscal year but which is scheduled to be terminated after FY68; and second, the school lunch program totalling about US$63,000 for the current school year. (Financed from SAFED GRC owned SAFED funds, and administered by the GRC, the JCRR program in FY67 funnelled better than US$400,000 into irrigation, reforestation, crop improvement, livestock, fishing and sanitation.)

Miscellaneous Activities in the Offshores

Two other minor items round out U.S. activities on Kinmen and Matsu. USIS about a year ago began loaning to a small Chinese military reading room on Kinmen a limited quantity of books (about 300), records, and films along with a tape recorder and projector. Secondly, TOEFEL tests (the English language test required of Chinese students headed for study in the States) have since last year been administered several times a year by a consular officer who visits the islands for this purpose. Only a small number of students have taken the tests there.

Visits to the Offshores

For a number of years the GRC has actively encouraged a wide range of Americans, official and unofficial, to visit Kinmen (similar visits to Matsu, to which access is more difficult, are infrequent). The GRC's probable purpose is to try to enliven U.S. interest in the Offshores and create an identification with them which would strengthen the sense of U.S. commitment to their defense. The Kinmen visits are intended to impress Americans in the short space of a day with the formidable defense works and the economic development program the GRC has brought into being on Communist China's doorstep. News coverage which frequently follows the visits tends to add to the impression of U.S. identification with the Offshores.

274. Memorandum of Conversation[1]

Washington, July 27, 1967, 12:30 p.m.

SUBJECT

Communist China

PARTICIPANTS

The Secretary   Amb. Anatoliy Dobrynin, USSR
Deputy Under Secretary Kohler

During luncheon today Ambassador Dobrynin asked the Secretary's opinion about the evolution of events in China. The Secretary replied that we had the impression that Mao Tse-tung had not been able to establish the unity he was apparently seeking. The Ambassador replied that he quite agreed. The Secretary then said that he realized this might still present problems on the Soviet side, but that he felt that it would be useful if the two of us could before long exchange views and have discussions about China. He would think that the Soviets would not be too comfortable about this neighbor of theirs with its teeming population and food problems, with the longest common frontier in the world between the two countries, with Chinese development of thermo-nuclear weapons and MRBMs. Dobrynin's attitude seemed to indicate some agreement with these remarks, but he was noncommittal. He commented only that Viet-Nam made impossible meaningful discussions between us on a great many subjects.

There then ensued a certain amount of inconclusive discussion of Viet-Nam along familiar lines during which Dobrynin said that the United States had not been very helpful to the Soviet Union in this connection and that it was the impression in Moscow that Secretary McNamara's trip to Viet-Nam and new proposals for increasing our force strength there followed directly on the termination of the Glassboro talks between the President and Chairman Kosygin.

---

[1] Source: Department of State, Central Files, POL CHICOM. Confidential; Limdis. Drafted by Kohler and approved in S on July 25. The source text is labeled Part II of V.

275.   Memorandum From Alfred Jenkins of the National Security Council Staff to the President's Special Assistant (Rostow)[1]

Washington, July 26, 1967.

SUBJECT

Defiance of Peking

Our Consul General in Hong Kong reports his doubt "that the writ of any particular group in Peking necessarily extends beyond the handful of cities where so-called power seizures occurred last winter."[2] The reported detention of Vice Premier and Minister of Interior Hsieh Fu-chih in Wuhan from where he has just made his dramatic return after the personal intercession of Premier Chou En-lai, is the most open defiance yet against central authority.

Both the *People's Daily* and Peking Radio earlier today warned local authorities in Wuhan to surrender or face destruction by the Chinese Army. The interesting thing is that none of our sophisticated intelligence gathering means have given any indication that the Army is planning to do anything of the sort. Wuhan's defiance has gone on long enough now for there to be evidence of planned military action against the city, if the threat to Peking's authority is to be met with force. It is very possible that the Mao–Lin faction is unsure whether the Army would act.

This is the first clear test case of serious defiance on the part of top local authorities, prompting a threat of military action by Peking. There are at least seven other Yangtze Valley provinces which will surely watch the outcome of this test. If Peking is unable to bring this situation under control, other local authorities will decide that it is safe to be defiant, and that could mean the beginning of the end for the Mao–Lin combine.

Meanwhile, there is a rising tide of reports from all over the country indicating that the disorder is getting worse. One is tempted, in fact, to believe that Peking's indignant listing of Liu Shao-chi's erroneous policies has helped increasing numbers of the populace to realize that they prefer Liu's policies to Mao's, and are prepared actively to support anti-Mao forces.

The battle is by no means over but the downward trend in Mao–Lin fortunes, which I believe has been steady if slow since last summer, has in the past week accelerated markedly.

Al Jenkins

---

[1] Source: Johnson Library, National Security File, Country File, China, Vol. X. Top Secret. A copy was sent to Jorden. Rostow sent the memorandum to the President with a covering note of the same date; a handwritten "L" on the note indicates that it was seen by the President.

[2] Telegram 554 from Hong Kong, July 26. (Department of State, Central Files, POL CHICOM)

276.   Telegram From the Embassy in the Republic of China to the Department of State[1]

Taipei, July 31, 1967, 0915Z.

229. Subj: Country Team assessment of GRC intentions. Ref: State 135828; Taipei 3662.[2]

1. This message discusses the problem of the GRC's maritime incursions, and indicates briefly what they are and what they are not.

2. The incursions are small-scale. We know of no GRC plans to mount any large-scale military or paramilitary operations now or in the near future, such operations are unlikely and beyond GRC capabilities. The last incursion of any size was the disastrous one of August 1965 in which the GRC lost two ships near Tungshan Island. Since that time there have been seven known incursions—in rubber rafts, M–5 class fiberglass speedboats, and an outboard-powered catamaran. These have generally comprised 6–10 people, the largest being a team of about 15 men in two speedboats used in the Shuntung raid on 29 May 1967.

3. GRC intentions are small-scale. These relate to military intelligence, small-scale sabotage, occasional interdiction of fishing boats, infiltration of agents into mainland China, at least, psychological impact.

4. Various GRC entities conduct incursions, including units from the Chinese Navy, Chinese Army, the Intelligence Bureau of the Ministry of National Defense and irregular forces from the anti-Communist National Salvation Army, (an aging group of some 5,000 irregulars primarily stationed on Tung Yin Island). The particular units used do not use MAP equipment in raids and are not MAAG-supported. There is however, some occasional U.S. support to certain GRC intelligence collecting efforts.

5. There is no effective central GRC direction and coordination of these incursions. These incursions are often run without the coordination or foreknowledge of other GRC offices. There have even been cases where Defense Minister Chiang Ching-kuo has been unaware of the actual operation before the fact. We know that his present position remains somewhat ambivalent between the traditional GRC interest in "back to the mainland, "and the recent general GRC emphasis on political actions. Recently, the GRC has been attempting to make NSB and J/E MND responsible for coordinating small-scale maritime operations but it remains to be seen whether this coordination will be effective. In any case,

---

[1] Source: Department of State, Central Files, POL 27 CHICOM–CHINAT. Secret; Limdis; Noforn. Repeated to Hong Kong and to CINCPAC for POLAD.

[2] See footnote 2, Document 242, and Document 266.

in the main the incursions remain poorly coordinated and poorly executed.

6.   We know that there is a slightly heightened high-level GRC military interest of late in continuing various incursion attempts, and we must assume that they will so continue. We estimate that they will continue to use the available types of boats in incursion attempts. In addition, the GRC will have two midget submarines, each capable of landing up to six people, in operation at some future time and will probably commit them occasionally to such activities.

7.   Although GRC maritime incursions over the years have for the most part been unsuccessful, GRC leadership views them as psychologically necessary both for morale and propaganda purposes within Taiwan, and to give hope to remaining GRC adherents on the mainland.

8.   GRC news treatment of these incursions is for the most part misleading, in that public GRC accounts picture the operations as being large and more successful than they are in fact.

9.   Appropriate U.S. authority has had foreknowledge, but not control, of certain of these incursions; the GRC, nevertheless, has capability to launch such incursions without prior U.S. knowledge. Our knowledge after the fact is generally quite good, from special intelligence sources in particular.

10. Such incursions are in part understandable not in empirical result, but because they are one of the few avenues of independent capability actually open to the GRC, a GRC dedicated to the return to the mainland which tries to prove to itself and to its subjects that its goal can be achieved. This situation exists notwithstanding the fact that the top GRC military knows full well that the military balance is constantly shifting, to the disadvantage of GRC, with reference not only to advanced weapons, but to the respective ChiCom and ChiNat conventional military potentials in Taiwan Strait area.

McConaughy

277. National Intelligence Estimate[1]

NIE 13–8–67   Washington, August 3, 1967.

COMMUNIST CHINA'S STRATEGIC WEAPONS PROGRAM

The Problem

To assess China's strategic weapons policy and programs and to estimate the nature, size, and progress of these programs through the early 1970's.

Conclusions

A. It is clear that China aspires to great power status and that its present leaders have given high priority to developing a substantial strategic capability as essential to such status. With wise management of their limited resources, the Chinese could continue to make steady progress toward the achievement of these goals over the next decade.

B. The probable extent of actual progress will remain in doubt, however, so long as fanaticism and disorder continue to infect China. Some adverse effects on the advanced weapons program are probable in any event; serious disruptions could result from pressures to do too much too soon or from a general breakdown in central authority.

C. China probably now has a few fission weapons in stockpile deliverable by bomber, and has demonstrated the capability to produce thermonuclear weapons with megaton (mt) yields. It will soon have the plutonium available to aid in reducing such weapons to missile warhead size as well as to facilitate the development of more compact, light weight fission devices. For the next year or two, the limited availability of fissionable material will place significant restraints on warhead production, but this will ease significantly in the following years as the Yumen plutonium production reactor reaches full output.

D. We believe that limited deployment of an MRBM with fission warheads is likely to begin in the next six months or so. After 1968 when increasing numbers of warheads could be made available, deployment will probably proceed at a higher rate. This deployment would be designed to threaten US bases, and major cities from Japan through the Philippines, Southeast Asia, and northern India.

---

[1] Source: Department of State, S/S Files: Lot 90 D 99. Top Secret; Controlled Dissem. According to a note on the cover sheet, the estimate was submitted by Deputy Director of Central Intelligence Rufus Taylor and concurred in by the U.S. Intelligence Board on August 3. An April 4, 1968, memorandum to holders of NIE 13–8–67 is in the Johnson Library, National Security File, Intelligence File, Miscellaneous CIA Intelligence Memoranda.

E.   We estimate that the Chinese can have an ICBM system ready for deployment in the early 1970's. Conceivably, it could be ready as early as 1970–1971. But this would be a tight schedule, and should the Chinese encounter major problems, the IOC would be later. In any event, we will almost certainly detect extended range firings once they begin, and monitoring of these tests will probably provide about one year's advance warning of IOC.

F.   We have no basis at this time for estimating how far or how fast the Chinese will carry deployment of their first-generation ICBM. Assuming political and economic stability, China will probably have the resources to support a moderate and growing ICBM deployment through 1975. Beyond that time frame, there is the possibility of significant improvements to this first system.

G.   Other strategic delivery means have received less priority but China may begin production of some TU–16 medium bombers this year in the plant at Sian.

H.   China will probably not push ahead vigorously with the now semidormant diesel-powered missile-firing submarine program. The one G-class submarine launched in 1964 does not yet have a missile. It would probably be at least 1970 before additional missile launching submarines could be available. China has shown some interest in nuclear propulsion technology, but even if design on a nuclear submarine is already underway, the first unit probably could not be operational until the late 1970's.

I.   For political effect, China will probably attempt to launch an earth-satellite as soon as possible. This might be accomplished this year using an MRBM with an added stage or a heavier payload might be orbited using an early test vehicle from the ICBM program.

[Here follows the Discussion portion of the estimate.]

278.   Memorandum From Donald S. Macdonald of the Bureau of Intelligence and Research to the Director of the Bureau (Hughes)[1]

Washington, August 18, 1967.

SUBJECT

Mr. Bundy's Meeting with Mr. Colby, August 17, 1967[2]

PARTICIPANTS

Messrs. Bundy, Berger, and Habib for EA; Messrs. Colby and Ford for CIA; Mr. Stuart for INR/DDC; and Mr. Hamilton of EA for Laos item

China

Mr. Ford [*less than 1 line of source text not declassified*] reported that the current mood of the GRC leadership is one of pessimism growing out of frustration. The GRC prediction of a divided leadership on the mainland has come true—by chance—and the US is not interested in taking advantage of it. The uncertainty of status within the UN is continual. Communist China's nuclear power is growing and the Gimo feels strongly that the Communists intend using it against Taiwan. Because of the Vietnam war, the US is paying less attention to the defense of the Taiwan Strait. Yet the GRC has no alternative to the US for support.

While the fact of dependence on the US is accepted by the Gimo and other GRC leaders, the resultant pessimistic and somewhat resentful atmosphere is not an easy one in which to work. The [*less than 1 line of source text not declassified*] is effectively closed out of planning for maritime excursions and agent operations against the mainland. Nevertheless, knowledge of these activities comes to the [*less than 1 line of source text not declassified*] through a number of sources.

The fact that unilateral GRC collection against the mainland is ineffective makes the GRC dependent [*less than 1 line of source text not declassified*]. A number of highly sophisticated operations are being carried on with full GRC cooperation. At the same time, however, the GRC shows its independence whenever it can. Recent operations in cooperation with Koreans, renewed interest in the Yunnan border areas, and intelligence liaison with the South Vietnamese are illustrations of this attempt to assert independence.

In reply to Mr. Bundy's question concerning Taiwanese nationalist sentiment, Mr. Ford characterized Taiwanese nationalism as insignifi-

---

[1] Source: Department of State, INR Historical Files, 1967 FE Weekly Meetings. Secret; Eyes Only. Drafted by Stuart.

[2] Agenda at Tab A. [Footnote in the source text. Tab A is not attached.]

cant politically because there is no organized movement—nor is there likely to be, because of close GRC surveillance of prospective leaders. Mr. Ford characterized GRC control methods as an astute combination of force and shrewd political moves.

Mr. Stuart asked Mr. Ford if, in view of difficulties with the GRC over phasing out of a joint collection operation last year, he could forecast how the GRC would react to withdrawal of an additional project in which the GRC played the major role. Mr. Ford said that he would regard the closing down of an additional operation as politically unwise and a threat to some of the more sophisticated—and more useful—joint operations unless the withdrawn project were to be replaced immediately by another in which the GRC would participate actively. The GRC otherwise would seize upon the withdrawal as an indication of a change in US policy toward Taiwan, and probably as a move in the direction of coming to terms with Communist China.

[Here follows discussion of unrelated subjects.]

---

279.   Memorandum From William J. Jorden of the National Security Council Staff to President Johnson[1]

Washington, August 24, 1967, 6:30 p.m.

SUBJECT

Will China Go Back to Warlordism?

There has been much speculation that the current chaos in China will result in the collapse of central authority and the rebirth of regional warlords. Attached is a cable from Ed Rice, our Consul General in Hong Kong, on this possibility.[2] Briefly, Rice believes that the current disorders have already put regional military commanders under pressure to behave in a more autonomous way. However, he does not expect the relapse of the country into the warlord system of the 1920's because:

—The regional military commanders are not, generally speaking, local figures, but men with a strong sense of the army as a national institution.

---

[1] Source: Johnson Library, National Security File, Country File, China, Vol. X. Secret.
[2] The attachment, August 24, is a paraphrase of telegram 1126 from Hong Kong. Telegram 1126, August 23, is ibid. and in Department of State, Central Files, POL CHICOM.

—China's modern military is dependent for its existence on the national industrial sector, and the continued flow of material requires each regional commander to recognize interdependence with other regions.

In short, the regional army commanders are not potential warlords, and warlordism is not likely unless the army dissolves into the general chaos.

Bill

---

280. **Action Memorandum From the Assistant Secretary of State for East Asian and Pacific Affairs (Bundy) to Acting Secretary of State Katzenbach**[1]

Washington, September 18, 1967.

SUBJECT

Licensing of Pharmaceuticals for Sale to Communist China

1. On April 6, 1967 you spoke to the President about the licensing of certain pharmaceuticals and related medical equipment to Communist China for use in the treatment or prevention of spinal meningitis, cholera, and infectious hepatitis, diseases that were in or threatening to reach epidemic stage in mainland China at the time. The President authorized the licensing of these items but only for the duration of the epidemics.

2. Our information is that these diseases have run their course as epidemics. However, no American firm was ever approached by the Chinese Communists for the sale of any drugs during the period of the epidemics. I believe a publicized action to rescind the move to permit licensing would be viewed by an articulate segment of the American public as a step backward and contrary to the President's stated policy of concern for the people of mainland China. I believe, therefore, that no public statement and no approach to American pharmaceutical firms should be made at this time but rather, in the unlikely event that an American firm should receive a request from the Chinese Communists,

---

[1] Source: Department of State, ACA Files: Lot 72 D 175, Foreign Trade—Drugs & Pharmaceuticals, China 1968. Confidential. Drafted by Jacobson.

we act on each request in the context of the general situation obtaining at the time.

Recommendation:

3.   That you inform the President that the epidemics that caused us to act on this matter have run their course and recommend that, despite this fact, we take no action to announce the termination of the temporary relaxation of our embargo on trade with China to permit the licensing of drugs and medical equipment useful in treating or preventing those epidemics and will, as a practical matter, deal with cases, if they arise, on their merits.[2]

---

[2] Katzenbach initialed his approval on September 22.

---

281.   Memorandum From the President's Special Assistant (Rostow) to President Johnson[1]

Washington, September 25, 1967.

SUBJECT

Chinese Chaos and U.S. Interests

Ed Rice, our outgoing Consul General in Hong Kong, states in his "swan song" cable[2] that he remains convinced that Mao cannot win and consolidate power. He reasons:

—the Cultural Revolution has been pushed in ways which generate widening opposition;
—the opposition lacks the structure which might make it susceptible to identification, attack and destruction;
—prominent Maoists in Peking are primarily propagandists and agitators;
—therefore, their proposals for building a governmental structure to replace that which they have been destroying are vague and deficient.

---

[1] Source: Johnson Library, National Security File, Country File, China, Vol. XI. Secret. A handwritten "L" on the source text indicates that it was seen by the President.

[2] A paraphrase of telegram 1786 from Hong Kong, September 21, is attached but not printed. A copy of the telegram is in Department of State, Central Files, POL CHICOM.

Rice raises the question whether the chaos produced in China by the Maoists is in our interest. He concludes that while we may hope for some benefit from this chaos, the Maoists' spirit of unreason and violence make China not only a bad neighbor but also the source of an infection which cannot be confined to China itself. At any rate, Rice believes it is against our interests to speak in public of any benefits to us from Maoist chaos.

Walt

282. Telegram From the Embassy in the Republic of China to the Department of State[1]

Taipei, October 12, 1967, 1040Z.

1052. 1. Defense Minister Chiang Ching-kuo called on me Oct 11 at his request. His principal theme was that thorough USG–GRC exchange of views on mainland situation particularly necessary now because of recent changes there.

2. After brief analysis current ChiCom attempts to restore order, CCK stated that Mao may regain control for short period but this would not last. Minister said he anticipated long term struggle. He believed Communist regime now in greater difficulty than ever in past. He said ROC should look problem squarely in eye and try to see how enemy could be weakened.

3. Minister said he felt US and ROC should have even closer contact and share each other's thinking more completely. Specifically he said ChiComs are greatest enemy and greatest threat to both US and ROC. This gives both countries a basic common interest. He stressed that ROC believes political action against mainland is most important, as President Chiang made clear in his Double Ten speech. He termed this speech as significant statement of current GRC policy and thinking. CCK said that within framework of not taking military action, US and ROC should see how best to stir up changes on mainland and unrest in Communist armed forces which might accelerate collapse of regime. Minister said he

---

[1] Source: Department of State, Central Files, POL CHICOM. Secret; Exdis.

felt political warfare and other possible steps "not so much military as political actions and in fact primarily political actions" were required. He said he had no specific proposals to offer now, but we both should look into it. CCK added that if we allow things to remain as they are, Mao will have short periods of stability and will be able to increase his power. CCK then reiterated hope both sides could look into possibilities offered by political warfare. Later CCK added once again, that in undertaking any political warfare actions against mainland, ROC principle was to assume responsibility and not involve US in the political struggle against the Chinese Communists.

4.   CCK said GRC not satisfied with its current inadequate information on mainland events. ROC realizes there many more significant changes occurring than those of which it aware. ROC must secure more information before being able to obtain complete understanding of conditions on mainland. Therefore, CCK said, ROC wishes to pay great attention to improved cooperation with us in the intelligence sphere so that we can unite and make effective our efforts. He recognized that additional efforts were called for on ROC's part. He said ROC had not undertaken any major intelligence operations on the mainland and it wishes to consult with us before it takes any such operations. CCK reiterated his hope that we could continue our efforts to obtain more information.

5.   CCK told me that ROC hoped to join up with some anti-Maoist elements on mainland to increase ROC's effectiveness. He noted that Chinese were traditionally anti-Soviet but that Chinese people in general were favorably disposed to us and that this factor should be exploited and use made of it with anti-Maoist elements which were also anti-Russian.

6.   I concurred that both our countries should pay even closer attention to mainland developments. Said I would report Minister's conversation and suggested another meeting be held when Washington's reply received. I put in caveat that while I felt joint US–GRC analysis of political situation on mainland extremely important, USG position was that any actions which would needlessly be provocative towards Communist China should be avoided. US wanted to prevent escalation war in Vietnam. Therefore avoidance provocation towards ChiComs was important factor in US policy considerations. On other hand if war in Vietnam were to expand through direct ChiCom intervention then new situation would be created which would require full assessment. But as long as Communist China did not intervene massively and overtly, USG position and attitude of US people would not agree to any action on mainland which looked like adventurism.

7.   Minister replied that he fully understood this position and this was why he had stressed avoidance of any US military actions and he

said GRC guiding principle was not to contradict US policy. He added that his statements were of course only preliminary at this stage.

8. Embassy comments on Chiang Ching-kuo's statements being forwarded by septel.[2] Memcon will be forwarded by air pouch.[3]

McConaughy

***

[2] McConaughy commented in telegram 1053 from Taipei, October 12. (Ibid.)

[3] A memorandum of conversation was enclosed with airgram A–274, October 14. (Ibid., POL CHINAT–US)

---

283.   Telegram From the Department of State to the Embassy in the Republic of China[1]

Washington, October 27, 1967, 2244Z.

61104. Refs: A. Taipei 1052; B. Taipei 1053; C. Taipei A–274.[2]

1. We agree with your assessment of CCK's motives in his suggestion that US–GRC intelligence cooperation be improved. Specifically, we agree that CCK's likely fundamental motive is President Chiang's concern that apparent lessening of mainland disorders means lessening GRC opportunities. We do not overlook or minimize, however, that another likely motive of Chiang and CCK is to probe US policy and operational interests.

2. Whatever CCK's motive, we agree that his approach offers a useful opportunity for follow-up conversations and do not wish to give flat negative. We suggest, therefore, that at your next meeting you confirm our interest in closer consultation and in meaningful joint intelligence gathering activities with a view to meeting our mutual need for more complete grasp of mainland situation. You may wish to solicit CCK's views as to what specific proposals he would like us to consider and ask him how he wishes to proceed. FYI. We refer of course to desirability of CCK agreeing that consultations on clandestine intelligence operations

***

[1] Source: Department of State, Central Files, POL CHINAT–US. Secret; Exdis. Drafted by Republic of China Country Director Thomas P. Shoesmith; cleared by Jacobson and Holdridge; and approved by Berger.

[2] See Document 282 and footnotes 2 and 3 thereto.

would best be conducted [*less than 1 line of source text not declassified*]. End FYI.

3. We suggest you also confirm our interest in improving our respective analyses of mainland situation and in continuing to exchange views on this subject. In that connection, you may wish to mention current plan to have several of our mainland experts visit Taipei this December for informal exchange of views with GRC and fact that Department now providing Chinese Embassy on regular basis with our current appraisals of mainland situation. FYI. Possibilities for providing GRC greater volume intelligence documents appear extremely limited, but we prepared review situation if CCK indicates specific areas of interest. End FYI.

4. It is possible that in your next and subsequent exchanges a clearer picture of CCK's objectives may emerge. His conversation with you as reported Refs A and C suggest that he may be seeking some expression of US support for an expanded GRC program of "political warfare" action on mainland, including sabotage, guerrilla drops and clandestine political activities. He also may wish to involve us in joint planning of such activity. Should he make such purpose clear, it would be necessary specifically to inform CCK that our established consultations groundrule applies to political warfare (as distinct from intelligence gathering) as well as military action against mainland. It might also then be necessary to reiterate your entirely appropriate definition of US attitude toward provocative actions (Ref B, para 6[3] and Ref C, page 6, para 3).

Rusk

---

[3] Reference is apparently to paragraph 6 of telegram 1052, Document 282.

---

284.   Telegram From the Department of State to the Embassy in Italy[1]

Washington, November 3, 1967, 0126Z.

64101. 1. Italian Chargé Terruzzi called on Under Secretary Rostow today to request US support for Italian initiative to sponsor study com-

---

[1] Source: Department of State, Central Files, UN 6 CHICOM. Confidential; Priority. Drafted by Gleysteen; cleared by Berger, Italy Country Director Wells Stabler, and Eugene Rostow's Special Assistant Thomas O. Enders; and approved by Deputy Assistant Secretary for IO Ward P. Allen. Sent also to Santiago, Brussels, Tokyo, Canberra, Bangkok, and Wellington. Repeated to USUN and Taipei.

mittee resolution on Chirep. Although he said he was acting on Fanfani's instruction, Terruzzi was quite fuzzy as to whether Italians were consulting us about wisdom of such move or informing us of decision already made.

2. After indicating Italy would again oppose Albanian resolution and possibly co-sponsor Important Question resolution Terruzzi explained Italian desire to "do something more" and their wish to obtain our support for submission of study committee resolution which would link Chirep problem to question of universality of membership. In response Rostow's question Terruzzi added, after search of his instructions, that he thought Italian Government had already decided to go ahead but was still most interested in US reaction.

3. Rostow commented that while we publicly supported study committee resolution last year and still recognized potential utility of this approach, we believed it would be a mistake to submit resolution this year. Our soundings showed that most countries hoped Chirep debate would be as routine as possible primarily because of conditions on China mainland. Also clear that study committee resolution would be overwhelmingly defeated, possibly by even larger margin than last year. Thus we failed to see advantage of advancing resolution at this time and saw no point to jeopardizing future utility of study committee concept by subjecting it to sure defeat for second year.

4. Terruzzi argued study committee might be useful as way to test Chicom attitude—i.e. were Chinese prepared to accept certain conditions which might be formulated and presented to them? Rostow noted there would be no testing of Chicoms in this fashion if resolution were not adopted, which we sure would be the case.

5. When asked what US would do if Italians proceeded to table study committee resolution, Rostow said matter had not been decided and would have to be considered by President. He personally assumed that in view of our unchanged underlying support we would probably vote in favor. He cautioned, however, that he did not wish to deal with this question at this stage.

6. Since Chargé did not seem grasp point Rostow concluded conversation by explicitly asking Terruzzi to convey following response to Rome: Our judgment is that it would be mistake for Italians to undertake Chirep initiative this year because we considered it politically inopportune in light of Assembly attitudes, conditions in China, and certainty that resolution would be badly defeated. Second and overwhelming defeat of this measure would be unhelpful to our interests since study committee resolution could prove feasible and desirable at later time. If Italian Government were to insist on pursuing matter, we would of course give it further careful consideration. Rostow added, however,

that he was quite certain that we would not be in position to co-sponsor such resolution.

7. Terruzzi left informal translation of illustrative resolution (see SepTel) which Italians have in mind.

8. *Comment:* Although we believe Belgians and some other co-sponsors of Italian initiative last year are cool to reintroduction this year, we are by no means certain we will be able to head off Italians at this late stage. Moreover, Chileans have never dropped idea and may well conclude that Italian position is sufficient to justify their precipitating issue.

9. Embassy Rome requested to ensure that Rostow's comments accurately conveyed to Fanfani.

Embassies Santiago and Brussels requested to bring US reaction to attention of Chilean and Belgian Governments so that there no misunderstanding of our position.

Embassies Tokyo, Wellington, Bangkok, and Canberra authorized to inform Governments confidentially of our reaction.

10. GRC informed directly in Washington and New York.

Rusk

---

285.   Telegram From the Embassy in the Republic of China to the Department of State[1]

Taipei, November 7, 1967, 0645Z.

1318. Ref A. State 61104;[2] B. State 34987.[3]

1. I called on Defense Minister Chiang Ching-kuo (CCK) Nov 6 at my request as follow-up to our conversation of Oct 11, with special view to further exploration of his views of "political warfare" against mainland, in light of Ref A. I was accompanied by DCM Hummel [*less than 1 line of source text not declassified*].

2. I said that within the framework, which he understood, of avoiding provocative actions against the mainland, Washington had given a

---

[1] Source: Department of State, Central Files, POL CHICOM–CHINAT. Secret; Exdis.

[2] Document 283.

[3] Dated September 9. (Department of State, Central Files, POL CHICOM)

basically affirmative response to his suggestions of Oct 11, and that we did want to improve our joint intelligence collection and analysis. I spoke of the opportunities for identifying potential defectors and agents, and for building channels to them. I reminded him that a team of US intelligence specialists would be arriving from Washington next month to discuss mainland conditions (Ref B) and said that we wanted to expand our exchange of information with GRC and think of ways to improve intelligence cooperation and analysis. I said we were not certain just what CCK had meant by intensified political warfare operations. If he was thinking of getting in touch with anti-Mao elements, I said, then we were favorably disposed toward consideration of such efforts, but we would have to be mindful of the need to avoid provocations and offensive actions.

3. CCK replied that as he had said in our previous conversation of Oct 11, he wanted to intensify joint US–GRC efforts directed at the mainland, and wanted to adhere to the principle of close exchange of info. He had not yet considered what specific actions should be taken, but he meant by political warfare (1) to do what can be done to impede Mao's efforts to form internal "alliances" that include dissident elements, and (2) to make efforts to see that the internal struggles on the mainland do not stop. He said the GRC wanted to get into contact with elements that are anti-Mao and with those that have failed to make accommodations to Mao's policies. He said the GRC has been in contact with some of these elements in deep interior areas far from Taiwan where little could be done to assist them. What is now needed, he said, is contact with new elements nearer the coast, and when these contacts are achieved he would be talking with the USG about what to do.

4. In an effort to draw CCK out further, I mentioned influential elements in several areas (Sinkiang, Tibet, Kwangtung and Kwangsi) that seem still to oppose Mao, but it was obvious that he had said all he wanted to say at that time. [*less than 1 line of source text not declassified*] offered [*less than 1 line of source text not declassified*] knowledge and resources on mainland contact operations, stating that he would be glad to work with NSB head, Gen. Chou Chung-feng, or any other officer CCK might designate, to discuss possible further steps. CCK replied in polite but non-committal terms to statements of Ambassador [*less than 1 line of source text not declassified*] and then changed the subject.

5. *Comment:* It is conceivable that GRC has indeed made new contacts with dissident elements in the interior of China, but the absence of evidence, and past experience, points against the possibility. In fact it occurs to us here that the embarrassing paucity of GRC contacts may be additional factor in probable overall GRC political disinclination to see us involved in GRC–ChiCom contacts. [*less than 1 line of source text not de-*

classified] will nevertheless proceed get into contact with Gen. Chou to test whether any further intelligence liaison is contemplated.

6. It seems to me that CCK in raising this subject last month was following instructions, probably from the Gimo, to sound us out in general terms without making any specific proposals for action at this time. CCK's rather general response to further probing has narrowed the field of subject matter apparently to exclude sabotage and the dropping of large action teams. What he apparently wanted was a general expression of interest, or at least lack of discouragement, from the USG on the subject of making contact with dissident elements on the mainland for essentially political purposes. He now has had this expression of USG interest, hedged with appropriate caveats about avoiding provocative actions. He seems not to want to go further in detailed discussions at this time, and I do not think we should press him.

7. In summary, it now appears that CCK was on a very general fishing expedition rather than on a mission to achieve closer cooperation in intelligence planning and operations.

8. [less than 1 line of source text not declassified] concurs in this cable.

9. Memcon follows by airgram.[4]

McConaughy

---

[4] Airgram A–312, November 11. (Ibid., POL CHICOM)

---

286.   Memorandum From Alfred Jenkins of the National Security Council Staff to the President's Special Assistant (Rostow)[1]

Washington, November 8, 1967.

SUBJECT

Comments on Professor Rowe's ChiRep Study[2]

My reactions to this paper are definite and simple. It does the job it starts out to do well, but in my opinion does the wrong job:

---

[1] Source: Johnson Library, National Security File, Country File, China, Vol. XI. Secret. Copies were sent to Jorden and Davis.

[2] The attached undated paper, entitled "The Status of China in the United Nations," was prepared by a study group under the Scholarly Studies Program of the American-Asian Educational Exchange. It is filed with an undated covering memorandum from the group's chairman, Professor David N. Rowe of Yale University. Eugene V. Rostow sent the package with a November 4 covering note to Walt Rostow, who gave it to Jenkins with a handwritten notation requesting his comments.

1.   The study attempts to gear our presumed inflexible rectitude to a supposedly safe mechanical automaticity. It is dangerous to do that in this matter, for it prejudices "for all time" judgment as to the U.S. interest.

2.   The United States' position on ChiRep has changed already with changing circumstances, and the time could come when it should change again. For years we simply opposed Chinese Communist entry, and that was that. More recently we have left our policy open-ended. We insist that the position of the GRC be maintained, but we are (or were last year) silent on some other implications. Furthermore, we are on record now as having favored a study group, and if the question arises again this year we may have trouble voting against the resolution—although we wish the issue would not come up.

3.   I think we have placed things about right. This issue is too important for us to lose our flexibility on it. We may be faced with a markedly different situation next year.

4.   I do not think we should show any "forward movement" on Chi-Rep this year. Last year, up until fall, a fairly good case could be made for cautious forward movement, provided we still supported the GRC's position. Communist China was certainly no rose even then, but since the 1959 excesses of the Great Leap, creeping revisionism *had* brought from 1961 visions of a maturing of the Revolution on a vaguely Soviet pattern. That still does not produce a rose, but Brezhnevism is better than Stalinism. Last year there was increasing discomfort at ponderous China's being unarticulated with the world. A case could be made up to last summer for attempting to further Peking's processes of inching toward reasonableness in internal policies by hinting at alternatives externally— in the hopes that external policies too might "mature." This especially made sense when it appeared that an alternative road could be dangled at Peking in a serious and instructive yet academic experiment—academic because we could almost certainly test reactions while ensuring that the political outcome of the problem would not be altered for at least a year or so. The following year, if we should want the practical outcome still not to be changed, this would doubtless be for reasons (primarily trends in the nature of the regime) which would strike others similarly, and we would not be taking an unreasonable calculated risk. (After all, in extremis, we could have our way with the veto.)

5.   Since resumption of Maoism with a vengeance this fall, however, attempts to "further the process of reasonableness in Peking," through major steps, would be doomed to failure and inexplicable to the public at home or abroad. The timing would be fatuous.

6.   This does not mean that the dignified, general stand of (a) hostility only by provocation and not by definition, and (b) hope for eventual reconciliation should not be reiterated. It should be, sparingly.

7. As you know, it is my belief that the combination of our Vietnam stand and our stand of reasonableness vis-à-vis Communist China have helped crystalize China's deep policy problems and differences, contributing to an indeterminate but real degree to hastening and exacerbating the troubles associated with the Cultural Revolution.

8. But no big gifts should be dangled now, such as involving the United Nations, freer trade invitations, etc.—not while the regime is weakened by bitter dissension, with change amounting to its virtual dissolution not completely unthinkable! Taking steps to further the maturation of the Revolution only makes sense when its maturation is proceeding along revisionist lines.

9. We should meticulously keep our UN position *flexible* within the basic judgment of what is good, at a given time, for U.S. interests and the health of the UN. We shall occasionally have to reach into the gimmick bag as we have in the past—and this paper is a creditable recitation of possibilities for gimmickry—but we should reach in sparingly.

10. This is the tread water year, in any event.

AJ

---

287. Telegram From the Department of State to the Embassy in the Republic of China[1]

Washington, November 18, 1967, 0113Z.

71292. Ref: State 70661.[2] Following summary FYI only and Noforn. It is uncleared and subject to revision upon review.

1. GRC FonMin Wei and Ambassador Chow called on Secretary November 17 to request reconsideration of our decision to vote for, but not lobby for, Chirep study committee resolution if text tabled same as last year. At outset Wei asked whether we had any confirmation of over-

---

[1] Source: Department of State, Central Files, UN 6 CHICOM. Confidential; Priority. Drafted by Gleysteen and approved by Popper. Also sent to USUN and repeated to Rome, The Hague, Brussels, Santiago, Tokyo, Canberra, Bangkok, Manila, and Seoul.

[2] Telegram 70661, November 17, informed the Embassy in Taipei that Popper had called in Ambassador Chow on November 16 to inform him of a U.S. decision to vote for a study committee resolution that was expected to be the same as the 1966 resolution. (Ibid.)

night GRC report from Rome that Italians would not table resolution unless assured in advance of at least 20 favorable votes. Secretary said we did not.

2.   FonMin and Ambassador in rather discursive presentation explained GRC did not like being put in situation where trouble came from its friends rather than its enemies. GRC had been working this year, particularly among Latin Americans, to reduce potential support for study committee resolution and, partly as result of US efforts to dissuade Italian and Chilean initiatives, had been able to shift number of Latin Americans to opposition. US decision to vote for resolution would undercut GRC efforts. Greatest problem, however, was how GRC could explain US vote in Taiwan. US vote last year had caused serious difficulties but GRC had been able to weather crisis on understanding that US vote was tactic adopted out of necessity whereas situation this year clearly did not require study committee. GRC recognized negative US vote might jeopardize Italian votes on Important Question and Albanian resolutions but did not believe this too important.

3.   Secretary commented that Italians had reached their decision after big controversy in Cabinet. Nenni had used his role in political coalition so that he was in essence conditioning his support of Italian position vis-à-vis Important Question and Albanian resolutions to re-submission of study committee proposal. Originally Italians had in mind far worse text which we had indicated we would have to vote against. Even though US position had to take into account problems of several "soft sisters" on this question (Italy, Chile and others) GRC should be able to relax because it could be certain that study committee resolution would not be adopted by Assembly. After reminding Wei that Taipei ultimately seemed quite satisfied with outcome of last year's Chirep debate, Secretary emphasized that we should concentrate on main issues which were to maximize our support for IQ resolution and against Albanian resolution; study committee issue was sideshow which GRC could brush off.

4.   Wei reiterated that US vote in favor of study committee could not be explained adequately to President Chiang and GRC and that it would create doubt among people because concept clearly implied two Chinas. FonMin added that he couldn't understand why Italians and others persisted in this approach when it was so obvious that two-Chinas arrangements were completely unacceptable to Chinese. Given the lack of necessity this year, Wei urged US reverse its position and vote against Italian resolution.

5.   Secretary stated that US could not be so casual about reversing decision. Since study committee device did not appear necessary this year, US had tried strenuously to dissuade Italians from pursuing matter, but once sponsors decide to go ahead we had to keep in mind our future position when we might very well need study committee to hold line

against Albanian resolution. Moreover, US had other problems to be considered. Nenni, for example, could create grave difficulties if he were to throw Italian Government into real crisis, and there were similar problems in other countries.

6.   Referring to a previous conversation in which Secretary had cautioned GRC not to see ghosts where there were none, Chow stressed that he wanted to avoid another crisis of confidence between US and GRC. It was possible overcome crisis last year because GRC recognized US had moved under duress; this was not the case this year and GRC found US support for study committee incomprehensible.

7.   Secretary said that while FonMin and Ambassador could feel free to tell Gimo they had pressed us very hard, he urged that they not push him too far on this matter. He said he would give thought to their request and would, of course, be most pleased if the Italians were at last minute to stop short of tabling resolution. However, while US understood GRC's position, we had broad and long-range considerations to keep in mind not only in terms of our relations with certain other countries but possible future need for device of study committee which might develop in later Assemblies. In any case, US support of study committee would be passive and we would not seek to influence votes of others.

8.   At conclusion of meeting Wei and Chow referred again to GRC efforts with Latin American governments saying they feared Italians would deliberately misconstrue US position and thus counteract GRC campaign against study committee. Secretary assured them US certainly would do nothing to shift votes wrong way.

Rusk

288. **Information Memorandum From the Assistant Secretary of State for International Organization Affairs (Sisco) to Secretary of State Rusk**[1]

Washington, November 28, 1967.

SUBJECT

Vote on Chinese Representation

The General Assembly again adopted the Important Question, and rejected the Albanian and Study Committee resolutions by a slightly larger margin than last year. A comparison of the voting is as follows:

	1966	1967
Important Question	66–48–7	69–48–4
Albanian resolution	46–57–17	45–58–17
Study Committee	34–62–25	32–57–30

The voting closely paralleled our earlier estimates. However, a notable defection on the Albanian resolution was Ecuador, which shifted from no to an abstention. Saudi Arabia, which was expected to vote no, was absent, but we gained a no vote from Cameroon, which had abstained in 1966.

A motion by Australia to give priority in the voting to the Important Question resolution was adopted 67–41 with 12 abstentions. A separate move by Syria to require a two-thirds majority on the Study Committee proposal was adopted 36–31 (US) with 53 abstentions. This vote was substantially different from last year (51–37–30) because some countries, such as the USSR and East Europeans, shifted from yes to abstain. The rollcall vote this year perhaps made it more difficult for them to maintain a position inconsistent with their opposition to the IQ resolution.

---

[1] Source: Department of State, Central Files, UN 6 CHICOM. Unclassified. Drafted by John W. Kimball of IO/UNP.

289. Telegram From the Embassy in the Republic of China to the Department of State[1]

Taipei, December 1, 1967, 0930Z.

1551. Ref: State 75479.[2]

1. Further [*less than 1 line of source text not declassified*] information concerning Kwangtung raid gives added support to conclusion that press story was fabrication planted by pro-GRC newsman in three Hong Kong Chinese language newspapers on November 22.

2. Department's observation (para 2 reftel) that GRC seems to feel obliged present image of being actively engaged in hastening downfall of Chinese Communists in order maintain credibility of mainland recovery goal, is entirely accurate. Even if President Chiang and top Chinese officials feel this goal is not presently achievable, GRC believes it must maintain claim to be government of all China and keep alive, at least publicly, its goal of mainland recovery, in order to justify its rule on Taiwan and protect its legitimacy. Consequently, GRC pronouncements about mainland recovery are still relatively frequent, even though major emphasis is now on political rather than military action to achieve this end. Latest statement in mainland recovery was made by Defense Minister Chiang Ching-kuo (CCK) Nov 27 in Tokyo. CCK said he believed that "in the not too distant future we will certainly overthrow the Communist regime." Such statements disturb and concern Japanese, ourselves and other governments. On the other hand, this concern should be tempered by fact that GRC has been making similar and sometimes even more militant statements intermittently for the past 18 years, during which time GRC has undertaken no major military action against mainland.

3. Peking must also be well aware that GRC's bellicose public utterances and its cautious actual military posture are far apart. GRC statements about mainland recovery are probably analyzed correctly by Peking as propaganda rather than as evidence of firm GRC plans.

4. At the same time we should bear in mind President Chiang's occasional earnest requests to high ranking visitors for assistance in persuading USG that Peking is major enemy and must be destroyed. It is

---

[1] Source: Department of State, Central Files, DEF 15 CHINAT. Secret; Exdis. Repeated to Tokyo and Hong Kong.

[2] Telegram 75479, November 28, referred to a story in the Hong Kong press that GRC commandos had destroyed 8 MIG–19 jets in a raid on a mainland airbase, noting that a Hong Kong report seemed to confirm the Embassy's suspicion that the press story was a fabrication. Considering that during Japanese Prime Minister Sato's recent visit to Washington, he had expressed concern about Chiang Kai-shek's intentions, the telegram requested Embassy views of GRC intentions and of the advisability of reminding the GRC of the U.S. position with respect to the use of force against the mainland. (Ibid.)

possible that Sato's apparent concern about GRC intentions grew out of his conversation with President Chiang during September visit reported Taipei's 906.[3] Chiang reportedly asked Sato for GOJ assistance in persuading USG to support a military counterattack.

5. It is worth noting that our contacts with Japanese Embassy Taipei have consistently given evidence that the latter usually are not very well informed of high level GRC deliberations. Their contacts are, perhaps understandably, chiefly with Japanese-speaking Taiwanese, and the views manifested to us by GOJ officers here often reflect their lack of contact with inner circles of GRC. We note, also, that Amb Johnson's probing in Tokyo (Tokyo's 3662)[4] does not reveal any great GOJ concern about GRC attacks on mainland. (See also Tokyo's 3701.)[5] Soundings by Embassy Taipei (reported septel) also fail to indicate Japanese Embassy concern on this point.

6. President Chiang has repeatedly been informed that US does not want wider war in Far East and can not agree to counterattack. A cogent expression of this view was contained in President's message to Gimo on March 1967 (see Deptel 156346).[6] GRC officials have been frequently reminded of US views in previous and subsequent conversations by Ambassador, and by Secretary and by Bundy on visits in 1966. GRC's full awareness of US opposition to military action against mainland clearly indicated by CCK in October conversation with Ambassador (Taipei's 1052).[7]

7. We have firm evidence that GRC is not seriously considering any major unilateral action in Taiwan Straits area at this time and that GRC military intentions confirm closely with GRC recent public posture of watching and waiting for conditions on the mainland to develop (without GRC intervention). Although President Chiang and some of his top advisors are probably concerned about future implications of apparent abatement of Cultural Revolution activity and partial restoration of order on mainland, we believe it highly unlikely that fear of losing any supposed last opportunity would prompt Gimo to launch rash military attack against mainland. GRC analysts believe Mao has recently regained control of mainland situation. They also believe, however, that Mao's future policies will again plunge mainland into chaos. This longer range view may be of some comfort to Gimo and others who realize GRC by itself does not have sufficient military strength, logistic capability, or air cover to launch successful large scale attack.

---

[3] Dated September 27. (Ibid., POL CHICOM–CHINAT)
[4] Dated May 24. (Ibid., POL 27 CHICOM–CHINAT)
[5] Dated December 1. (Ibid., POL CHICOM–CHINAT)
[6] Document 249.
[7] Document 282.

8. We know [*less than 1 line of source text not declassified*] that just concluded KMT Central Committee Plenum did not discuss or develop any new policy or plan indicating a change in GRC's present cautious wait and see approach to mainland events. We also know [*less than 1 line of source text not declassified*] that GRC is sharply reducing number of officers engaged in contingency planning of unilateral major operations against mainland.

9. A sharp distinction also must be made between GRC propaganda statements concerning mainland recovery and GRC intelligence activities against mainland. While we believe GRC intends no major military action against mainland at this time we know, [*less than 1 line of source text not declassified*] that GRC has definite intention continue very small scale incursions by Marine operations along coast and/or intelligence forays along Yunnan border areas. GRC motive in continuing small scale incursions is not only for intelligence gain but more importantly (since most of previous attempts have been unsuccessful) for internal psychological purposes—to demonstrate they are showing the flag and to prove they are continuing offensive against enemy. This determination to show the flag in the mainland may continue to cause some anxiety in Tokyo and other capitals, which may not be fully informed about actual GRC intentions and motivations, and may judge import of GRC actions and assertions to be more ambitious and potentially dangerous than they actually are. CCK, for example, reportedly started at Tokyo press conference Nov 29 that guerrilla raids against mainland would be increased. In recent GRC statements it has been implicit that anti-Mao forces on mainland (not forces sent from Taiwan) were carrying out guerrilla activity. CCK's statement reported in local press leaves source of guerrilla raids deliberately vague. GRC, as part of its psychological warfare effort, may continue to take credit for anti-Maoist activities on mainland, even though GRC lacks real control over reported events. Our ability to dissuade GRC from this type of propaganda is very limited because these statements stem from very fundamental GRC policies and aspirations, and do not violate GRC commitments to US related to Mutual Defense Treaty.

10. Ambassador has agreement with CCK that they will meet shortly after CCK's return from Japan. At that time Ambassador intends to reiterate position that US continues to be strongly opposed to provocative actions launched at mainland by GRC other than small scale intelligence collection forays which we have countenanced in the past.

11. We believe that visit here of either Secretary or Assistant Secretary Bundy, as part of tour of the area, would be very useful primarily to reassure GRC of continued closeness of our alliance relationship and our recognition of importance of conservation of GRC economic and defense capabilities as essential elements of free world assets in East Asia during

present critical period. This particularly important in light of proposed drastic slash in MAP funds. However, GRC is completely cognizant of US position against use of force against mainland and of GRC obligations under 1954 Defense Treaty and exchange of notes, and we believe special high level visit for sole purpose reinforcing this view would not be necessary or productive.

12. Para 5 reftel requests Country Team assessment of possible GRC reaction to extremely deep cut in MAP. Specifically it is asked if the GRC might attempt to pressure USG to restore the funds by creating serious incident in Straits area to provoke strong ChiCom reaction, which then could be portrayed by GRC as threat to Offshores and Taiwan. Although there is no available evidence pointing to any such intention, the GRC does have the capability launch unilateral actions such as an air strike or raid from Chinmen which might possibly provoke serious consequences—possibly without prior US knowledge. We do know [*less than 1 line of source text not declassified*] that the GRC does have unilateral contingency plans (though no present intention) for unilateral operations.

13. GRC has been sharply warned by US at least twice in recent years that in the event that GRC actions needlessly provoke a ChiCom attack on Taiwan, US might not consider defensive commitments under terms of 1954 Mutual Security Treaty to be applicable. While a deep cut in MAP will somewhat adversely affect US–GRC relations and cause GRC to have further fears of some measure of US "disengagement", we believe it unlikely that GRC would respond to MAP cut by deliberately staging provocative incident against mainland. Such an action would call for improbable supposition that President Chiang, casting his usual caution aside, would be willing to risk everything on a rash and vengeful act. [*less than 1 line of source text not declassified*] report of recent medical exam by competent physicians and observation of his activities, President Chiang is in exceptionally good health. He is mentally active and alert and is in full control of his faculties. Although in future years, as with any person of advanced age, his mental condition could deteriorate to point where he might make irrational decisions, there is no sign at present of any such deterioration or lessening of his sense of responsibility. Country Team concurs.

McConaughy

290. Telegram From the Embassy in the Republic of China to the Department of State[1]

Taipei, December 5, 1967, 0855Z.

1569. Ref State 78711.[2]

1. When DefMin Chiang Ching-kuo (CCK) came to my residence yesterday (Dec 4) at his own request to brief me on his recent trip to Japan (reported septel), I took opportunity to prepare him for prospective substantial MAP cut and to suggest possibility of reducing size of GRC ground forces as one means of reducing military expenditures.

2. I reminded CCK that I and US military representatives here had already told him of probable sizeable reduction in MAP funds for the current fiscal year. I said that while the final appropriation has not yet been passed, it now appeared highly likely that the world-wide MAP program would be significantly reduced. I said that the GRC would have to take its essentially proportionate share of a rather drastic reduction along with most other recipients. It appeared that military assistance to Korea and Thailand, for compelling reasons, would not be affected as much as the GRC. I told him that COMUSTDC VAdm Chew and MAAG Chief MGen Cicolella had been for some time discussing with me ways to cushion the adverse effects and offset part of the program losses that seemed almost certain. I hoped that Gen Cicolella's constructive ideas for economies and greater combat efficiency within the GRC military establishment would help, and I thought his suggestions for enabling the GRC armed forces to earn revenues for military purchases by rebuilding and overhauling US combat equipment used in Vietnam might also hold considerable promise. I said we all hoped that the reduction would be instituted for a single year only, but we could not be sure of this, because once Congress makes deep cuts it is possible they will be inclined to follow the newly established level as a precedent in future years. I emphasized that the impending cut did not represent any change in US policy, and that the defense needs of the GRC were well appreciated in Washington and at CINCPAC. I pointed out that the cutbacks of major investment items including F–5 aircraft would not be felt for two years or more because the procurement pipeline was very long. If the cuts are not restored in future years, I said, there could eventually be a heavy adverse impact in the essential categories of modern weapons unless we plan carefully,

---

[1] Source: Department of State, Central Files, DEF 19 US–CHINAT. Secret; Priority. Repeated to CINCPAC.

[2] Telegram 78711, December 2, reported that Congressional reductions in military assistance programs made it almost certain that FY 68 military assistance to the GRC would be reduced to the $50 million grant level, and requested the Embassy's views as to the impact of this. (Ibid.)

and coordinate closely to make the best use of the resources that are available. I said there would of course be an immediate impact on operating funds. I knew that his officers had been in close contact with Gen Cicolella, and I believed that I had kept Washington well informed of the GRC needs and of the effects of the proposed reductions.

3. CCK said that any deep cuts would be a very serious and important matter to the GRC. He intended for his senior MND and service officers to keep in close touch with Gen Cicolella on this problem. He said that as a matter of policy it was necessary to keep up the combat effectiveness of GRC forces at a time when ChiCom military effectiveness is increasing steadily. He asked that USG pay close attention to the pressing need for implementation of this basic policy.

4. CCK observed that in past years the significance, although not the magnitude, of military assistance to Korea and to the GRC has been very similar since the role of the two countries as vital parts of the system of deterrence of ChiCom aggression was comparable. He said that although he realized Korea was making a troop contribution in Vietnam he hoped that "in principle" MAP for Korea and for the GRC would be considered together, although the amounts furnished the two countries would of course differ. I said I understood his point and I would make sure that Washington understood also.

5. I then said that the question has been raised as to whether the GRC should not consider reducing its ground forces, while at same time upgrading their effectiveness and firepower. I asked for his reaction to this thought, which might have effect of saving needed funds during a period of stringency resulting from MAP reduction.

6. CCK paused, considering his reply and said carefully that it would of course be necessary to confer closely with MAAG about the best means of maintaining the combat effectiveness of GRC forces. However, he said, "any reduction in the size of our ground forces is something we cannot consider (pu neng k'ao lu)." He said any such move would be essentially a political one, with grave political repercussions. He pointed out that while the reduction in MAP would have some adverse impact in the GRC, if it did not affect the status of capability of the armed forces, it would not be misunderstood by "the average person" on the GRC as signifying any change in basic US–China policy, especially since it was a Congressional rather than an administration action, and would be of general and impartial worldwide application. On the other hand, any reduction of the force levels in the GRC would lead people to think there had been a change in policy, attributable to US action and affecting the security of the GRC. Anyway, he said, reducing the ground forces would not result in much saving. He said he realized and understood the difficulties the USG is having with MAP, but that the GRC also has its difficulties. Any reduction of forces would have misleading implications and

would also have a bad effect on morale of GRC forces. Even raising the subject for general discussion would have adverse repercussions. Since any saving would be small, and the repercussions great, it would be very much better not to pursue this proposal at all. He again said he would discuss carefully with MAAG the best means of maintaining and improving the combat effectiveness of existing GRC forces with available resources.

7. I observed that we on the US side all hope that the GRC can ensure that the impending MAP cut will not have an adverse effect on the economic development of the country. We are deeply impressed with the remarkable progress made in the economic field in Taiwan, and we earnestly hope that the GRC can avoid any diversion of resources from economic development to defense that would impede economic growth. I realized it would not be easy to meet essential requirements in both sectors, but it was important that a major effort be made to do so, and we hoped we could help.

8. CCK replied that he understood my point very well. He wanted to state that what he had said earlier was put forward in the light not only of GRC interests but also the security interests of the US. He said that approaches other than reduction of forces would have to be found. He said he and his government believed that us problems are also those of the GRC, and those of the GRC are also US problems. We would consult closely in seeking solutions. We felt that basically money is a secondary factor, the most important element being the underlying spirit and attitude of the cooperating countries.

McConaughy

---

291. **Telegram From the Embassy in the Republic of China to the Department of State**[1]

Taipei, December 14, 1967, 0310Z.

1634. Ref: State 82115; Taipei 1594.[2]

1. Tight security precautions and continued state of martial law have long been considered by ROC as absolutely essential to its protec-

---

[1] Source: Department of State, Central Files, POL 29 CHINAT. Secret. Repeated to Tokyo.

[2] Telegram 82115, December 9, requested information for a follow-up report to Senator Fulbright about the early fall security sweep mentioned in telegram 1594 from Taipei, December 7. (Both ibid.)

tion against the threat posed by Communist China. Legalistically, GRC looks upon Taiwanese independence movements as secessionist in nature, and like all other such threats to political status quo, as merely variant forms of "rebellion", designed to weaken it in the face of the Communist threat. Practically speaking, GRC probably estimates that without strict security controls a mainlander government could not effectively control a population which is over 80 percent Taiwanese.

2.   Police sweeps of various types are a periodic exercise on Taiwan. For example, prior to Chinese New Year's there are local sweeps directed against petty criminals. A more general sweep is also an annual occurrence. Such a sweep was conducted June 8, 1965. On May 14 and 18, 1966, there were two sweeps in anticipation of Chiang's inauguration for fourth term. This fall there seems to have been two sweeps: a small one in late August directed at Taiwanese independence advocates or their associates, and a general sweep on October 5, timed to catch potential security risks by double ten.

3.   Only the pattern for the general police sweep seems at all established. Reportedly, the garrison command sets a quota of persons to be picked up for each municipality or county and mobilizes all available regular military police, and special security forces. Curfew is put in effect about 1:00 a.m. on an unannounced day, and no one except police is allowed to move until 6:00 a.m. Trains are stopped at their nearest station. During this period everyone, at home or in public places, has his household registration and identity card checked for irregularities and against lists of wanted criminals. In this year's general sweep, the press reported the next day that about 100 were arrested in Taipei. According to one Embassy source in the garrison command, 80 out of the 100 detained in Taipei in October were picked up from the wanted list of habitual bad check passers. Only part of the remaining 20 (a "handful" according to garrison command source) were detained as "threats to social stability". The exact number detained in the two sweeps late this year is unknown: 230 is the largest island-wide estimate the Embassy has heard. Presumably this excludes temporary detention.

4.   One reason that the exact number detained in such sweeps is not particularly significant is that certain police subdivisions, finding it hard to meet their assigned detention quotas, apparently detain a few of the local social misfits (petty racketeers, vagrants, etc.) for a few days just to fill out their list. The percentage of Taiwanese detained in this year's sweeps is not accurately known. The Embassy has, however, heard complaints from Taiwanese in the past that police sweeps pick up an even larger percentage of Taiwanese than their proportion in the general population would make likely.

5.   Martial law on Taiwan is justified by GRC as necessary consequence of existence of a state of hostilities with the Chinese Communists. It covers a wide variety of threats to public safety and public order. Any

case considered to involve either rebellion or sedition would fall under its provisions. Article 5 of the rules regarding the punishing of rebellion and sedition provides for ten years to life imprisonment for "participation in a rebel organization or meeting." Article 6 provides for 7 years to life for "spreading a rumor or disseminating untrue information which might endanger public peace or order or disturb the mind of the people". Article 7 provides 7 years to life imprisonment for a person who "uses written articles, pictures, books or speeches for publicity purposes for the benefit of a rebellious organization." Article 4 provides for the death penalty, life or imprisonment for not less than ten years for a series of actions such as sabotage, espionage, etc., but also including the "collecting of funds or supplies for or furnishing money or properties to a rebel", "providing protection to or hiding a rebel", "instigating a labor, student or market strike or disturbing public peace and order . . . under the instruction or for the benefit of a rebel".

6. Despite stringent nature of law, very few of those picked up in this year's sweeps are likely to be tried under its provisions. For example, those passing bad checks probably were forced to pay up or their family made to provide guarantees for release. To Embassy's knowledge, there have been no trials or political grounds of any of the persons picked up during either August or October sweeps; but under martial law, trial need not be public.

7. Embassy strongly doubts that large number of Taiwanese active in independence movement or other anti-KMT activities were picked up during August and October police sweeps. Story of sweeps has been common topic of discussion among U.S. students studying here and among Taipei correspondents. It has also been heard in Hong Kong and in Tokyo, where it has been covered in Taiwanese independence movement periodicals. However, only seven names have come to attention of Embassy from all these sources as persons who may have been arrested on political grounds and two of these names appear to refer to same person. As a result, Embassy is inclined to believe that only a handful of those arrested in general sweep were arrested on political grounds.

8. Taiwan's security system is closely related to maintenance of minority government rule over Taiwanese population, ramifications of this issue are very great, and totally beyond purview of MOFA or any other Ministry. Long established U.S. policy of encouraging broader Taiwanese participation in government has produced little effect, since policy is established by top leadership which firmly believes strong centralized control is absolutely essential, especially during period of national emergency. If United States representations were to be made on this subject, they would have to be made to President Chiang himself. What we know as to recent sweeps would not justify any démarche to him based on conduct of those sweeps.

9 Case of Kuo Hsi-lin, recent deportee from Japan, appears to be one that would give Japanese some opportunity to make representations if GOJ should feel warranted. Iijima, First Secretary Japanese Embassy, called on Embassy Taipei on Dec. 12 to ask what U.S. knows of Kuo's probable future. Stated that Japanese immigration service was given assurances Kuo would not be tried for political crimes and that GRC Embassy Tokyo also gave Kuo a written statement to that effect. Kuo case could easily fall under martial law as interpreted here. In such an event, prosecution of his case would probably follow lines of Huang Chi-ming case. (A–193[3] and previous.) Exit from and entry into Taiwan are responsiblity of a department of the garrison command. (There is no separate immigration service.) Violation of immigration laws might be treated as security offense. Even without such a decision, if maximum penalties sought for all laws broken by Kuo in his illegal entry into and exit from Taiwan, sentence could probably be as severe as if membership in Taiwanese independence movement were charged.

10. Several specific details in this report come from very sensitive sources and should not be released in any public manner. Embassy hopes, however, that background will be of some value for briefing interested parties in U.S.

11. FYI. Embassy is preparing a series of airgrams on internal security and political stability situation on Taiwan that should begin appearing next month.[4]

McConaughy

---

[3] Airgram A–193 from Taipei, September 13. (Ibid.)
[4] A series of six airgrams on this subject, sent between March 1 and May 17, is ibid., POL 2 CHINAT.

---

292. Telegram From the Department of State to the Embassy in the Republic of China[1]

Washington, December 15, 1967, 0059Z.

84908. 1. Chinese Ambassador Chow at his request called on Bundy December 14 to discuss grant MAP prospects. Bundy noted agreement

---

[1] Source: Department of State, Central Files, DEF 19 US–CHINAT. Secret Drafted by Shoesmith and approved by Bundy. Repeated to CINCPAC for POLAD, CHIEF MAAG CHINA, and COMUSTDC.

of House/Senate conferees December 13 setting overall grant military assistance total at $400 million ($220 million below Administration request), and commented that, given relative fixity other MAP programs, this figure will mean major reduction in grant MAP for GRC. He also observed that in view overall Congressional climate on spending, it probably will be difficult to avoid similar lower grant levels in FY 69. Bundy noted, however, that Congressional action on military sales would not have significant impact this year on possibility such sales to GRC.

2. Chow indicated understanding of situation and special considerations involved in Korean MAP, but expressed hope that reduction in grant MAP for GRC would not be proportionately larger than cut in overall total. He also inquired as to possibility recent events in Greece might increase availability grant funds for GRC. Referring again to difficulty of making substantial reduction in a number of programs, Bundy stated that cut in China MAP probably will be greater than approximate 37 percent reduction in Administration's original request. He acknowledged that Greek situation might release some funds, but stated that amount not likely be large.

3. Bundy emphasized urgent importance we and GRC together consider frankly how to weather these hard facts of life. He noted our concern to maintain GRC defense capabilities and suggested that GRC consider usefulness to visit by U.S. team to consult on how make best use of resources available for this purpose. Bundy indicated that we must first obtain clearer picture of FY 68 and FY 69 situation, but we should soon be in position work together with GRC on problem. Chow indicated agreement with this suggestion but offered no specific comment.

4. Chow did not appear under instructions to make specific representation on this subject. Throughout conversation, he evidenced realistic appreciation of situation and did not urge that GRC be given preferential treatment; nor did he refer to possible adverse political and economic impact of major reduction in grant MAP.

Katzenbach

293.   Telegram From the Department of State to the Consulate General in Hong Kong[1]

Washington, December 27, 1967, 0115Z.

89597. Subject: KC–135 Deployment to Ching Chuan Kang Air Base. Joint State/Defense Message.

1.   Increase in B–52 sortie rates in SEA, which has been approved at high level, has necessitated relocation of KC–135's which provide PACAF fighter support. We are considering a proposal to base ten PACAF support tankers (five from Takhil and five from Kadena) and five U-Tapao based radio relay aircraft at Ching Chuan Kang by approximately February 1, 1968. It is necessary to redeploy these KC–135's in order to permit increased B–52 operations at U-Tapao and F–111 deployment at Takhli. U-Tapao and Takhli are extremely crowded and could not accommodate new deployments without reduction in number of KC–135's. Move of KC–135's from Kadena to Ching Chuan Kang will increase their effectiveness since they will be based nearer to SEA refueling areas. Operation from Ching Chuan Kang will require 432 additional US personnel. No new construction would be needed. As you know, GRC has previously approved KC–135's use of Ching Chuan Kang as weather alternate, and it has been so used.

2.   For Taipei: We would like the Ambassador's comments on the proposal and assessment as to what the GRC's reaction would be if we approach them with a request to deploy 15 KC–135's (10 tankers and 5 radio relay) and approximately 430 personnel to CCK. The aircraft would be utilized for fighter refueling and radio relay operations at rate of approximately one sortie per day per aircraft.[2]

3.   For AMConsul HK: Request your comments on above proposal, particularly regarding likely Chicom reaction to specific deployment under consideration and increasing Taiwan role in Viet Nam.[3]

Rusk

---

[1] Source: Department of State, Central Files, DEF 15 CHINAT–US. Secret; Limdis. Drafted by T.L. Ridge of OSD/ISA; cleared by Shoesmith, Richard H. Donald of ACA, Steadman of OSD/ISA, Captain Alldredge of the Joint Staff, and Lieutenant Colonel Lively of the Air Force; approved by Berger. Also sent to Taipei. Repeated to JCS, CINCPAC, Bangkok, PACAF, SAC, and COMUSMACV.

[2] The Embassy commented in telegram 1743 from Taipei, December 28. (Ibid.)

[3] The Consulate General commented in telegram 3676, December 29, that any reaction beyond a propaganda blast was unlikely. (Ibid.) Telegram 96329 to Taipei, January 10, authorized the Embassy to request GRC approval to base 15 KC–135's plus approximately 450 additional personnel at Ching Chuan Kang. Telegram 1945 from Taipei, January 22, reported GRC approval. (Ibid., DEF 15 CHINAT–US)

294. Telegram From the Department of State to the Embassy in Poland[1]

Washington, January 4, 1968, 0105Z.

92930. Subj: 134th Ambassadorial-level US–ChiCom Meeting.

1. Assuming the meeting materializes as scheduled on January 8,[2] we anticipate another sterile tirade from Ch'en Tung[3] focussing primarily on Vietnam, air incidents, possibly disarmament, and again Taiwan. We believe it unlikely Ch'en will break any fresh ground. We do not ourselves present any new initiative other than to suggest the possibility of bilateral discussions on Astronaut Assistance and Return but will reiterate our existing offers on contacts, etc. Text of proposed guidance as follows:

2. "Mr. Chargé d'Affaires. This meeting marks the end of the second year in which I have been participating in these discussions. During this period, I have attempted to the best of my ability to communicate to you my Government's views and attitudes on a variety of issues. I have particularly emphasized the willingness of the United States to proceed constructively to discuss a variety of matters which I had hoped were of mutual interest to the Govts and peoples of both of our countries. These have included, as I am sure you recall, Mr. Chargé d'Affaires, proposals to facilitate

—the travel by doctors, scholars, scientists, newspapermen, and other persons of our two countries;
—the exchange of scientific and other types of data, information, and material;
—the exchange of types of agricultural samples which would benefit the development of scientific research and agronomy in your country and mine;
—joint investigation of incidents on the high seas;
—disarmament and the control of nuclear weapons.

---

[1] Source; Department of State, Central Files, POL CHICOM–US. Confidential; Priority; Limdis. Drafted by Kreisberg on December 27. Cleared by Bundy, Aldrich, Alan F. Neidle of ACDA/IR, Herman I. Chinn of SCI, Harriman's Special Assistant Frank A. Sieverts, SCA Deputy Administrator Nathan Lewin, and Morton Halperin of DOD/ISA, and approved and initialed by Rusk. Repeated to Taipei, London, Saigon, Moscow, Hong Kong, and CINCPAC.

[2] The meeting, originally scheduled for November 8, was postponed to January 8 at Chinese request. (Telegram 1268 from Warsaw and telegram 61850 to Warsaw, both October 30; ibid.)

[3] A telephone message from the Chinese Embassy in Warsaw on January 1 stated that since Ambassador Wang could not return to Warsaw for the January 8 meeting, the Chinese Government proposed as a temporary measure that Chargé Ch'en Tung take part in the meeting; the United States agreed to the arrangement. (Telegram 1704 from Warsaw and telegram 91928 to Warsaw, January 1 and 2, respectively; both ibid.)

3. I have on other occasions expressed my regret that your Government has rejected these suggestions, all of which I take this opportunity to reiterate in their entirety. Some of these we had believed, from the past record of our meetings, at one time had been of interest to your Government but to date I am sorry to see no indication that your Government has considered the benefits and advantages they might bring to both our countries.

4. Mr. Chargé d'Affaires, it might be useful for me to review for you my Government's views on the purpose of our meetings. Our objectives are threefold: First and foremost, we view them as a forum through which our two Governments can work gradually toward greater mutual understanding and begin to break down the barriers and antagonisms which have stood between us. Secondly, we see in them a point of contact where urgent and critical matters relating to the national interests of our two countries and to world peace can be communicated in private and with full frankness. Thirdly, we see in them an opportunity to exchange views on other problems and issues which either of us may feel it useful to raise with the other.

5. We succeeded, in the opening meetings in this series in 1955, in reaching agreement on the return of civilians to their own countries. In retrospect and even in spite of our many disagreements over the implementation of that initial agreement, it represented a significant step forward toward the resolution of specific problems. As I have noted before, we have never seen why, after gradually releasing so many of the American citizens being detained in your country, you drew the line at the handful who still remain.

6. To date, however, that has been our only agreed understanding in this forum. And in recent years, Mr. Chargé d'Affaires, despite the efforts of my Government to pose various means of improving relations between the peoples of our two countries, your Government has limited itself more and more to repetition of editorials, commentaries, and general statements on international affairs already given wide publicity by your radio and news media.

7. Mr. Chargé d'Affaires, I and my Government are indeed interested in the views of your Government on matters of general international concern. But let us also get on with the substantive, and we would hope productive, business of our meetings.

8. Mr. Chargé d'Affaires, your Government is aware, I am sure, of the existence of the International Telecommunications Satellite Corporation (INTELSAT) established in 1964. I would at this point like to call your Government's attention to a message addressed by President Johnson to the US Congress on August 14, 1967 on membership in INTELSAT. The President stated: 'We support a global system of commercial satellite communications which is available to all nations—large and small, de-

veloped and developing—on a non-discriminatory basis . . . We seek no domination of satellite communications to the exclusion of any other nation—or group of nations.'

9. Mr. Chargé d'Affaires, the scientists of your country have demonstrated their skill, ingenuity, and competence in many fields. Conceivably, one day in the not too distant future astronauts of your country will join those of other nations in venturing into the exciting and enormously important exploration of space. In this connection, my Government believes that it would be in the interest of both our countries for us to reach an understanding on the question of rescue and return of astronauts and space vehicles. I would be interested in the views of your Government on this subject.

10. Mr. Chargé d'Affaires, as your country continues to carry out nuclear tests, I am sure that the enormous power and destructive potential of nuclear weapons is becoming increasingly clear to the political, military, and scientific leaders of your country. The need to control these weapons, to avert their use, and to move gradually toward disarmament can hardly be open to doubt by anyone today. We have sought repeatedly, Mr. Chargé d'Affaires, to have your Government clarify and spell out in detail its views on controlling nuclear weapons and on constructive moves toward disarmament which would preserve the security of all states. Unilateral declarations on the use of nuclear weapons and calls for uncontrolled and uninspected disarmament obviously do not answer the real problems of security and assurance in a world in which mutual trust and confidence are imperfect.

11. Mr. Chargé d'Affaires, my Government, together with other nations, has been engaged in serious negotiations designed to conclude an agreement barring the further spread of nuclear weapons. On July 31, 1963 your Government issued a statement on disarmament, part (2) C of which specifically called for 'the prohibition of the export and import of nuclear weapons and technical data on their manufacture.' As I understand your language, its spirit is precisely in keeping with the purpose of the Non-Proliferation Treaty to which I just referred. I would hope your Government will be willing to look at the Treaty in this light and join with many other states in seeking by practical and progressive steps to deal with this and other problems of disarmament.

12. FYI: If Ch'en raises ABM question, you should make statement below, but not otherwise. Mr. Chargé d'Affaires, I am sure your Government has noted the various public statements in recent months about the United States decision to deploy an anti-ballistic missile system, but I would like to underscore one or two points. In the first place, it is clear that it is purely defensive. It employs components which cannot conceivably in themselves present a threat to any nation. In the absence of mutual assurances that offer hope for an end to the arms race and the spread of

nuclear weapons, we reluctantly felt that prudence demanded we make the deployment. Our interest in putting an end to the arms race and the huge expenditures of human and material resources that it entails remains undiminished. We would much prefer ourselves to devote our resources to the enormous tasks that remain unfinished, both in our own country and in others, in housing, education, transportation, health and welfare. Is this not a common goal we both share and toward which we should both be able to work and cooperate?

13. Mr. Chargé d'Affaires, I mentioned earlier the achievements of your country's scientists in many fields. I would like to take particular note of your achievements in the field of insulin chemistry. Such progress, like that in heart surgery recently achieved in South Africa, and that in synthesizing a protein virus in my country, should be shared with all scientists without regard to politics. We regret that, at the present time, the PRC is the only major scientific country in the world which is unwilling to permit open, widespread exchange of scientists and scientific, unclassified research and information with the US. We would like to see such exchanges and I am prepared to discuss with you now or at a subsequent meeting means of remedying this situation, and assure you of the USG's desire to encourage exchanges of visits between your scientists and ours.

14. Mr. Chargé d'Affaires, I have discussed with you at length on previous occasions my Government's views on the Vietnam conflict, our reasons for involvement in that conflict, and our limited objectives and willingness to withdraw our forces from Vietnam when the threat to the security of SVN has ended. I have made it clear that we do not seek to invade North Vietnam or to destroy or change the Government in NVN and, in the same context, made clear we do not seek a wider war, that we do not intend to attack your country, and do not have any territorial aspirations in that entire area. We sincerely hope your Government understands this. (FYI: If in his opening statement, Ch'en includes direct threat against US, you should note that this is a matter of gravest consequence you can only report to your Govt and follow with remainder of para 14. End FYI.) We also hope your Government has considered—as we have—the grave consequences which a war between our two countries would have. To wish to avert such a conflict is not cowardice or a sign of being what your Chairman calls a 'paper tiger'. Secretary Rusk responded on October 12 to a question whether the main US objective in Asia was the so-called 'containment' of your country with an emphatic 'No. The central objective is an organized and reliable peace.' But we will assist those countries that feel themselves threatened and to whom we have pledged our support and friendship. There should be not the faintest germ of doubt in your Government's appreciation of that fact.

15. It is sometimes difficult for one country to understand the psychology, the 'style' of another. And because the American system permits all views to be expressed openly, allows all kinds of dissent and debate, it is sometimes possible for other countries with different patterns and traditions of political and social behavior and action to mistake the workings of the democratic process and the free expression of diverse opinions in the US for weakness or lack of determination.

16. It is true, Mr Chargé d'Affaires, that we are periodically confronted by incidents involving ships or aircraft of our two countries. We are convinced that you know these are not purposefully and intentionally precipitated. But despite our most persistent efforts, it occasionally happens that as a result of malfunction or navigational error, US aircraft do intrude briefly and shallowly into your territorial airspace. We will continue to take every practicable measure to prevent such occurrences.

17. The serious warnings your Government issues with such regularity, I have noted before and reiterate today, with rare exception, cannot be verified. Many, of course, relate to the Paracel Islands—what you call the Hsisha Islands. As you know, sovereignty over this island group is in dispute. On your claims of US naval violations of your waters, our records consistently show that US Navy ships have not entered your territorial waters, even if measured by the 12-mile sea limit your Government claims rather than a 3-mile sea limit.

18. Conceivably, there may be some genuine misunderstanding on our part of the charting of your coastal waters. We would welcome receiving more up-to-date cartographic charts of your offshore waters, if you believe our plots are inaccurate, or your marking off your territorial water claims on generally available older charts for our information.

19. If it would be of interest to you, I would also at our next meeting be prepared to provide you with more detailed information on the actual positions of specific US naval vessels to clarify any question relating to their entry into your territorial waters. My Government would welcome similar information from your side including the name or hull number of the ship, time, and coordinates of the position involved. Perhaps this might clarify our respective positions and possibly resolve some of our differences. FYI: Following para to be used only if this specific subject is raised by Wang. End FYI.

20. On your figure of 125 air intrusions by US aircraft over a one-year period, I am unable to accept your figures without specific documentation. I would, however, be interested in receiving any specific plottings by your authorities of specific air intrusions you believe have occurred (excluding, of course, those of whose existence we have already publicly indicated our awareness).

21. Mr. Chargé d'Affaires, I would like to express my appreciation for the release of Mr. David J. Steele, whose sailboat apparently crossed

into your territorial waters near Hainan, at the HK border on September 19, 1967. I also note that your authorities on June 17, 1967 released to HK an American citizen named Leon James, otherwise known as Holden Johnson, who had crossed over into your territory without permission. I regret, however, that your Government has not as yet responded to my letters dated August 27, 1967 and September 12, 1967[4] requesting information on Lt. Robert Flynn (USN) and other crewmen of two US Navy aircraft shot down over your territory on August 21, 1967. (FYI: If Wang deals with this question in his opening statement, but rejects requests for return of Flynn, change preceding sentence to regret rejection.) These planes, we acknowledge, crossed into your territory but with no hostile intent and inadvertently. We note that Lt. Flynn has thus far not been permitted to write his family. Major (formerly Captain) Philip Smith, on the other hand, was permitted to write his family almost immediately and to receive mail and packages. While, as in the case of Major Smith, we continue to hope your authorities will release Lt. Flynn, we strongly urge that he be permitted to write and receive letters and packages while he is under detention by your authorities. I also reiterate my request that you facilitate arrangements for the return of the bodies of the dead crewmen for burial in the US."

22. FYI: We assume Ch'en Tung will again try to postpone the next meeting for 4–5 months or even longer. You should propose a date in mid-April and see how much you can whittle down Ch'en Tung's reluctance. We are, however, if need be, prepared to delay until June.

23. Response to contingencies authorized for 132nd and 133rd meetings on break or suspension of talks remain in effect.

24. Para 8 should be used only if subsequent specific authorization received.[5] End FYI.

Rusk

---

[4] The texts of the letters were transmitted in telegrams 25858 and 34505, dated August 23 and September 8, respectively; both ibid., POL 31–1 CHICOM–US. A similar letter was delivered to the Chinese Embassy in Warsaw on November 7. (Telegram 65293 to Warsaw and telegram 1340 from Warsaw, November 6 and 7, respectively; both ibid.)

[5] No such authorization was sent.

295. Telegram From the Embassy in Poland to the Department of State[1]

Warsaw, January 8, 1968, 1725Z.

1763. Subj: 134th Gronouski–Wang meeting.[2]

1. Meeting lasted 2 hours 15 minutes. ChiComs had no new points to make. Atmosphere of meeting clearly an improvement over last session in June when Wang may have been intent on making good record for himself before returning for "cultural revolutionizing" to Peking.

2. Chargé Ch'en Tung's opening statement (which very brief, however) devoted to subject of US–CPR relations centering on Taiwan as key obstacle to improvement in US–CPR relations. (This in itself represented major relaxation from height of cultural revolution when ChiCom public statements appeared reject idea that Taiwan overriding issue dividing US and CPR in favor of thesis that Viet-Nam and whole question of US opposition to world revolution more important than Taiwan alone.) Ch'en referred to President's statement Dec. 19[3] and Secretary's press conference remarks Oct. 12[4] on living in harmony with ChiComs and peaceful coexistence, but characterized them as baseless. Said "peaceful coexistence" between US and Peking out of question while US "occupying" Taiwan. ChiComs during 12 years of talks with US had repeatedly sought get US to withdraw all its armed forces from Taiwan and stop aggression against mainland so that "peaceful coexistence" on basis "five principles" (panchshila) could be established between US and CPR. China had exhibited much patience and made many efforts but nothing had been achieved. Ch'en referred to GRC claims to fight back to mainland "with US support" and noted it was particularly grave that US directed GRC to send [garble] over mainland. Said GRC had been launching military provocations against mainland with US cooperation.

---

[1] Source: Department of State, Central Files, POL CHICOM–US. Confidential; Immediate; Limdis. Repeated to Hong Kong, London, Moscow, Saigon, Taipei, and CINCPAC for POLAD.

[2] Gronouski sent a detailed report of the meeting in airgram A–417 from Warsaw, January 11. (Ibid.) Rostow sent a brief telegram to the President at the LBJ Ranch on January 9 stating that the meeting was "clearly better in tone and atmosphere than the previous session" and commenting: "It appears that the professional diplomats have recaptured the Foreign Office from the Red Guards." (Johnson Library, National Security File, Country File, Poland, Gronouski–Wang Talks)

[3] Reference is to remarks made by President Johnson in a television interview on December 19. For the transcript, see *Public Papers of the Presidents of the United States: Lyndon B. Johnson, 1967*, Book II, pp. 1158–1173.

[4] For the transcript of Secretary Rusk's October 12 news conference, see Department of State *Bulletin*, October 30, 1967, pp. 555–564.

3. I made statement on basis Departmental guidance (Deptel 92930)[5] and added language on attacks on Chinese ships along lines that used in US reply to Soviets on bombing "non-hostile" vessels. Rejected ChiCom charges on Taiwan and urged we bypass this issue and [move?] on to other matters of interest to our two governments. In rebuttal, Ch'en took up numerous other issues, restating standard ChiCom positions on Viet-Nam, disarmament, including Non-Proliferation Treaty, prisoners. He described Lt. Flynn (USN), who shot down in incident over south China Aug. 21 this year, as criminal to be dealt with as ChiComs decided and refused reply to my requests for further information on him or other prisoners. (I rejected Ch'en's contention in response. Ch'en said US clamoring to invade Cambodia and to send troops to Laos. Did not, however, mention ChiCom support for Cambodia. Soviets mentioned only once in passing reference to US-Soviet "collusion" on the Non-Proliferation Treaty. No reference to ABMs or Secy McNamara speech on this subject.[6] Recent freighter incident covered as part of long recital of all incidents involving US aircraft intrusions and ChiCom shipping since last June but not singled out for particular emphasis or made object of particular warning.

4. General tone of ChiCom presentati⟨   ⟩as sharp but polite and not especially belligerent or provocative. Repeated "grave and serious warnings" were included in referring to past incidents and possibility of expansion of war but all in highly generalized and formalized language identical with that used by Chinese in public statements. Ch'en did note US "clamoring" for "hot pursuit" into China but did not add any specific warning in this context other than that we would meet with "thorough and ignominious defeat" if we should expand the war.

5. Current meeting conspicuously lacking in repeated references to Mao and quotes from Mao that dominated June meeting. Mao mentioned only once, and sole reference to 700 million Chinese omitted June's routine (and repeated) addition that these "armed with thought of Mao Tse-tung". General language used less pejorative than at last meeting and more in keeping with pre-cultural revolution Warsaw meetings.

6. Obvious that Chargé Ch'en somewhat ill at ease on his first venture into "dangerous" area of US–ChiCom contacts. There unusual amounts of paper shuffling and confusion as to what documents to use and in what order on Chinese side. On several occasions, Ch'en clearly used guidance prepared for his use without regard to whether it applica-

---

[5] Document 294.

[6] McNamara stated in an address before a convention of United Press International editors and publishers at San Francisco on September 18 that a decision had been made to proceed with a "Chinese-oriented" deployment of anti-ballistic missiles. For text of the address, see Department of State *Bulletin*, October 9, 1967, pp. 443–451.

ble in context of our comments. For example, he belabored me for lodging unjustified charges against Chinese in my opening statement (I had made no charges at all), referred to US call for "disarmament conference" (I had made no such reference), and said it was false for me to allege there no US troops on Taiwan (I had made no such claim). On several occasions, Chinese interpreter Ch'ien clearly had to bail Chargé out of confusion he found himself in.

7. Next meeting date set for May 29, seven weeks after date I had suggested but earlier than I had thought they would agree to. They continued be vague about when Ambassador Wang returning but I made it clear we saw these meetings taking place at Ambassadorial level and I expected next meeting would be at that level.

Gronouski

296. Letter From the Ambassador to Poland (Gronouski) to Secretary of State Rusk[1]

Warsaw, January 11, 1968.

Dear Dean:

It has been some time since I felt it worthwhile to bother you with a separate personal reaction to one of our meetings with the Chinese. As you know from the formal reporting of the last two or three meetings, the Chinese posture of sterility and rigidity did not encourage me to believe that a new initiative on our part would have any significant impact.

The atmosphere and substance of the January 8 meeting, however, was enough improved over the preceding two or three sessions to raise my hopes a small notch. The "signals" that intrigue me include the following: (a) By holding this meeting, despite the absence of Ambassador Wang, by volunteering that the Chargé contact is a temporary exigency, and by readily agreeing to a reasonable date for the next meeting, the Chinese made clear their desire to maintain their contact with us; (b) They reverted to their pre-cultural revolution position that Taiwan is

---

[1] Source: Johnson Library, National Security File, Country File, China, Vol. XII. Confidential; Official–Informal.

the sole issue poisoning relations between China and the U.S., as against their position over the past couple of years that their conflict with us involved differences encompassing the whole world revolutionary movement; (c) They devoted their entire opening statement to strictly bilateral issues—Taiwan and an itemized listing of air intrusions, attacks on ships, etc.—and during rebuttal made only perfunctory references to Viet-Nam, avoiding the several issues which I expected them to vigorously exploit, including the current Cambodian troubles and McNamara's ABM speech; (d) There was a sharp downturn in invective as compared to each of the other meetings in which I have participated, and a complete absence of reference to the cultural revolution and the sayings of Chairman Mao; (e) The routine follow-up meeting the next morning between Kreisberg and Anderson (my counselor and interpreter) with their Chinese counterparts[2] was pervaded by a surprising atmosphere of relaxation. There was an unusual engagement by the Chinese in conversation on general interest subjects such as American balance of payment problems, the source of our oil supply, and details of their interpreter's vacation in China (including his labor experience on farm and in factory), all in a tone of genuine interest rather than criticism.

Lord knows, one swallow does not make a summer, and tone and atmosphere are no substitute for action. Yet I cannot help but think that the items catalogued in the last paragraph add up to a significant departure from the past performance. Why I do not know, although one can hypothesize that this has something to do with the improved position of Ch'en Yi and the Chinese Foreign Ministry professionals and a corresponding downgrading of the influence on foreign policy of hard-nosed Cultural Revolution types.

I believe, therefore, that this would be the appropriate time for the President or you to again make a major speech designed to appeal to and encourage the moderate element in Communist China. If the Chinese posture at this meeting was designed to signal a positive change in China's policy toward us, and I do not believe we can lightly discard this hypothesis, it is important for us to quickly respond. Such a response would implicitly let them know that we recognize and appreciate this change, and could emphasize the clear benefits that would accrue to them were relations between China and the United States improved. Aside from a general reiteration of the theme of your statement to the Zablocki Committee in 1966 and the President's State of the Union message last year, I would hope that the speech I am suggesting could offer some

---

[2] At these follow-up meetings, both sides exchanged the texts of their opening statements. A memorandum of the conversation at the January 9 meeting was transmitted in airgram A–421, January 11. (Ibid.)

additional areas in which we could move without serious political risk or weakening significant U.S. interests.[3]

Best regards.

Sincerely yours,

John

---

[3] The source text is filed with a January 18 covering memorandum from Jenkins to Rostow stating that Jenkins agreed with Gronouski's basic thesis but did not think the timing was right for a top-level speech. He suggested that a speech by William Bundy scheduled for February 16 might be "a good vehicle to satisfy Gronouski's desire to probe a little." He concluded: "It seems to me that affairs on the mainland are still much too messy for us to use our bluest chips in the game. Let's save 'em a while longer."

---

297. Memorandum for the Record[1]

Washington, February 2, 1968.

SUBJECT

China Experts Meeting with the President, February 2, 1968 (Sponsored by the National Committee on United States–China Relations)

PARTICIPANTS

The President, Professors Edwin O. Reischauer, Harvard, Robert A. Scalapino, Univ. of California, Alexander Eckstein, Univ. of Michigan, Lucian W. Pye, MIT, A. Doak Barnett, Columbia, and George Taylor, Univ. of Washington; Messrs. Carl F. Stover, National Institute of Public Affairs, Cecil Thomas, Executive Director of the National Committee, Walt Rostow and Alfred Jenkins

Mr. Rostow said that the visiting China specialists had examined three subjects for discussion with the President: (1) the situation in China; (2) alternative future directions of the evolving situation; and (3) policy considerations for the United States. They expected to concentrate on the last of these.

The President welcomed the participants, saying that he valued the opportunity to hear their recommendations on policy alternatives con-

---

[1] Source: Johnson Library, National Security File, Meeting Notes File, February 2, 1968, Meeting with China Experts. No classification marking. Prepared by Jenkins on February 2. Copies were sent to the President, Rostow, Roche, and Jorden.

cerning China. He said that we had been following two channels in our China policy: bridge-building on the one hand and necessary deterrents on the other. The President invited comment from the participants in turn around the table.

Ambassador Reischauer said that he was especially heartened by the President's reference to China in his July 12, 1966 speech. He felt that this time of disorder in China might be a good time to show our flexibility. In doing so, we would look beyond present crises. We should lay out our reconciliation approach now.

The President observed that we do not, in fact, hold to a rigid course of action. We are keeping our options open.

Professor Eckstein said he thought it encouraging that we had offered an exchange of agricultural expertise, of seeds, etc., and that in recent times we had broadened considerably our efforts at contact. He thought we should go further and relax our embargo against Chinese goods. This would not be of much economic importance, but would have political value in indicating more flexibility. He thought it would entail no serious risks concerning China's war-making potential.

Mr. Thomas said that he was not a China specialist, but he would like to direct to the President's attention what he thought to be public concern about China. Recently, under National Committee on U.S.–China Relations sponsorship, a Norwegian journalist, Mr. Munthe-Kaas, had spoken in 22 cities throughout the country. Without exception, audiences were anxious to hear and talk about China. the predominant opinion seemed to be in favor of a more flexible approach to that country, including trade.

The President observed that we have to keep hammering away at this. He said that he would like to get a "Presidential commission" to keep at it. East-West trade was only one thing the public was interested in, however. It was also interested in Vietnam. That is the great cost of Vietnam—because of it we do not get the chance to do some of the other things which would be desirable.

Professor Pye said that we must look beyond Vietnam to China, the really big problem. The reporters may be provocative, but we must not let that affect our perspective. We should approach China at the big-problem level. We should discuss with China such issues as non-proliferation of nuclear weapons, disarmament, etc. There should be a dialogue on that sort of thing at Warsaw. We should try to get China to see the nature of the world to come. It is true that we cannot negotiate with China today, but we should engage in this kind of discussion just as we did with the Soviets.

Professor Barnett said that the group held differing views as to the need for considering initiatives just at this time. China is going through a period of great change and is very disrupted. Even now, however, he himself felt we should look beyond Vietnam. He, too, liked the flavor of the President's July 1966 speech. We should even now be working out the steps implied in that speech. He agreed with Professor Eckstein that we should keep going beyond consideration of Vietnam. We should remove trade restrictions except for the basic COCOM list. We should get China into the international community. We should work actively toward achieving dual Chinese representation in the United Nations. Professor Barnett said he was impressed by the value of an advisor like Bohlen on the Soviet Union. He felt that we needed a man of similar seniority to advise on China.

The President asked the group to submit nominations. He said he needed at his elbow an advisor on the Soviet Union, and he had had both Thompson and Bohlen in that role. He needed the same for China. There has been a failure to communicate with the Chinese. The President said he had asked Gronouski to go to Warsaw to carry on the talks because he thought he had the qualifications which would make it possible to communicate. Unfortunately, however, the Chinese have continued to insist that they are interested in discussing nothing except Taiwan. The President said he had tried hard to bring about communication but he had failed. He said that he was, of course, ultimately responsible for such a failure, just as President Kennedy took the responsibility for failure in the Bay of Pigs. We have made a truly major effort to communicate and to keep our policy flexible. We are not hidebound. Since there has been no response to our efforts, we must be doing something wrong.

Professor Barnett maintained that we had not failed, because as long as Mao was there we simply could not expect any response. He thought it important, however, to keep making attempts.

The President thought perhaps we were not searching enough. Competent men were needed to put on assignments of this kind. Also needed just now were a dozen men for ambassadorships and for some other posts throughout the government. Actually, we need Reischauer in a dozen places.

Professor Eckstein said we need people, for instance, at the deputy assistant secretary level, who know a great deal about China. As for China, there is more hope of change than there has been for a long time. There is transition to something quite dissimilar—perhaps in time to be compared to the changes in the Soviet Union. The dialogue which is possible now may be minimal, but our policy of reconciliation should go right along (sic). It is very important that we focus a great deal of attention on China because that situation could get quite messy, and later China may contain a third of the population of the world. We should get China into the United Nations. Public discussion is one way to get around present pressures. The Charter should be revised. Professor Eckstein further expressed the belief that every country calling itself a state should accept the responsibility of a state and should automatically be in the United Nations. That would mean North Korea, North and South Vietnam and all other entities acting as countries. If such a position were taken, it might even lead to the acceptance by both Peking and Taiwan of the presence of the other in the UN. He said that he detected a changing mood in the country; in the business community, in labor circles, in civic groups and in churches. He said the Committee represented by this group constituted an answer to the rigidities represented in the Committee of One Million. The time has come to engage in more open discussions.

The President said we were going through a dangerous period in this respect. It is hard to wage a major war against one communist group without having the public oppose all communists. It is amazing, however, that we can go through the Vietnam experience and not have more clamor against the Soviet Union. The President said he thought Professor Eckstein was right in his evaluation of the openmindedness found among various groups in the country. This is surprising when we look at the contributions of the McCarthy period. We would expect emotions now to be even higher in view of the *Pueblo* capture, and talk of cutting off the head of President Park and of killing the American Ambassador. Perhaps people are too busy wanting to stop the bombing to think of these things. We must carry on an endurance contest in Vietnam in such a way as not to lead to inflexibility on other issues.

Professor Scalapino cautioned that in the case of China we are dealing with exceedingly complex issues. If we are to count on moderation in the American people's viewpoint, we will have to keep reiterating that these questions are indeed complex and not subject to simple formulae for resolution. The American people today can grasp a high level of complexities if they are led to do so. They can, for instance, understand the import of so-called "people's wars" if they are explained. The real problem is that so long as the Maoists are in control they will try to cause trouble such as in Burma, other parts of Asia (the President interjected "and the Dominican Republic").

The President said he fully agreed that the American people were ready to understand complexities and that complex issues did not have to be put in simple terms which might be misleading.

In concluding, the President said that, firstly, he very much appreciated the fact that the group had come to talk with him. Secondly, he had profited from the discussion and, thirdly, he wanted to ask of the group two things:

—that two or three members of the group write for him a directive as though addressed to the Secretary of State, asking him to take steps "A through F"—things which ought to be done concerning China;
—recommend someone who could serve as a counterpart to Bohlen.

The President also said that he would welcome hearing from any member of the group at any time on suggestions concerning the Warsaw talks, or any other suggestions concerning China. The President then briefly reviewed recent events leading up to an atmosphere of crisis, which built up all through January. In closing, the President invited the professors to "play President" in preparing for him the memo, and also to write him their full thoughts in letters within the next six weeks or so.

Alfred Jenkins

---

298.   Telegram From the Department of State to the Embassy in the Republic of China[1]

Washington, February 13, 1968, 0250Z.

114300. From Bundy for Ambassador.

1. I am scheduled to address Cincinnati Council on World Affairs February 16 on subject US policy toward Communist China. I regret final draft not completed in time provide you with full text but believe you should be aware of general thrust and particularly those portions dealing specifically with our policy toward GRC.

2. Principal objectives this speech are to clarify certain misconceptions and misunderstandings regarding US policy toward Chinese Communist regime on mainland and GRC, to relate both these aspects of our China policy and attempt to remove some of ambiguities which have arisen in this area, and to reiterate our willingness to continue to seek reconciliation with mainland China. Speech does not announce any new departures in specific courses of action which would alter actual substance of our relations with GRC or Communist China. It details at some length record of Chinese Communist self-isolation, persistent hostility toward US, and threat posed by its aggressive posture toward outside world. It also reiterates fact that US commitment to GRC not open to negotiation and that US cannot accept Chinese Communist demand for participation in any international body to exclusion of GRC.

---

[1] Source: Department of State, Central Files, POL 1 CHICOM–US. Secret; Priority; Exdis. Drafted by Shoesmith, cleared by Kreisberg, and approved by Bundy.

3. However, although noting that Peking's refusal to expand and improve contacts between US and Communist China makes unrealistic any suggestion that US recognize Peking, speech acknowledges possibility for movement in that direction at some point if Peking's attitudes change. In addition, speech makes clear that US has been treating, and is prepared to continue to treat, separately with government of mainland China and GRC. In so doing speech employs somewhat more restrictive definition of substance of our relations with GRC than has been used in past. Portions of draft which bear on these points and others which we anticipate will be especially sensitive with GRC are as follows:

4. US recognition of Chinese Communist control of mainland: "... it must be perfectly clear to anyone who has looked at this history of last 18 years that USG does not doubt existence of Communist China. We fought against its soldiers in Korea. We have negotiated with its representatives in international conferences in Geneva twice. We have maintained regular bilateral contact with it on an Ambassadorial level for 14 years, first in Geneva and now in Warsaw. Territory controlled and administered by Peking is well known to Government of US and when matters arise which pertain to this area and involve interests of US or American citizens, obviously our approach is to Chinese Communist authorities. This is reality and it fully acknowledged by this Government."

5. Relations between US and GRC: "What is this relationship? It is one of friendship going back many years, of mutual respect, and of common security interests in present circumstances in Asia. The United States recognizes the Government of Republic of China and deals with that Government on matters which, for most part, relate to areas over which it exercises actual control. Demands of Chicoms, accompanied by threats of force and use of force, for control of Taiwan are, of course, totally unacceptable. There can be no bargaining with lives of more than 13 million people who have made clear their rejection of Chinese Communist control. Under our treaty of 1954 with the Republic of China, we have a commitment to help it defend itself against an armed attack.

6. Whatever final resolution there may ultimately be to question of Taiwan, it should, in all events, meet with approval of GRC and its people, whose interests are most directly affected. Given present posture of Peking, including its totally unfounded allegation that island is under US occupation, there is at present no means of resolving this issue. Therefore, our best hope is to see whether progress can be made on other issues and problems creating strain between the United States and Communist China."

7. Trade embargo: "I noted earlier situation in Korean war under which our present restrictions on trade and remittance of funds to Communist China were put into effect. Certainly while Korean war continued there could have been no question of trade with a country with

whose soldiers we were engaged in fierce conflict. In years since then, admittedly situation has changed very considerably. Peking itself has grown increasingly able to produce many industrial materials which it needs. And gradually more and more states, including many such as Japan, Australia, and West Germany which do not recognize the Peking regime, have in fact entered into active trade with mainland China in non-strategic goods and commodities. Peking has consistently, however, for many years given no hint whatsoever of any interest in trading with the United States. Rather it has rejected even the vaguest hints that such trade might be possible. . . . In recent months USG has been reviewing this trade policy to determine if it would be feasible and in our interest to remove barriers on our side to mutually beneficial trade in non-strategic goods with mainland. We are doing this in belief that such peaceful trade should be possible without harming our strategic interests in area."

8. US-Chinese confrontation: "We are convinced that no war is inevitable. Seen in terms of national interests of our two countries, there no fundamental reason why United States and Communist China should come into conflict and every reason for us both to exert every effort to avert such a disaster. . . . US hopes for better relations with mainland China. It recognizes as I have said earlier that major differences exist in our political, social, and economic systems as well as on many concrete issues. Their resolution will be difficult and probably slow. Interests not only of US but of many other states deeply concerned over security, economic development, and political and social progress in Asia are involved. US recognizes that major interests of Chinese both on mainland of China and on Taiwan are also involved. There is need for all concerned to work toward lessening of tensions without abandoning or surrendering values and interests. United States intends to continue to strive toward this goal. We hope that Peking will alter its absolute opposition and resistance to these efforts on our part. We hope also that it will change its dedication to violent revolutionary overthrow of governments and social structures which do not match its image of society. We recognize that our abilities to influence rate at which this occurs are limited and that such changes will fundamentally be result of changed perceptions derived from within Chinese society and leadership itself. But we convinced that these changes will occur. When they do, United States will be prepared to respond positively to them."

9. We recognize likelihood that statement of US policy along above lines may provoke strong negative reaction by GRC and could make our working relations more difficult. In our judgment, however, such reaction will not damage basic structure of our relationship with GRC. We also feel that such statement, in addition to providing clearer basis for and greater flexibility in our China policy, might possibly open way for more frank and realistic dialogue with GRC concerning possibilities for

long-range accommodation to its position on Taiwan in manner which will meet both our national interests. Please comment urgently.

10. Full text will be forwarded ASAP.

Rusk

---

299. Editorial Note

At 2146 EST on February 13, 1968, a U.S. Navy A–1H was shot down by a Chinese MIG about 5 miles off the coast of Hainan. The plane was one of two unarmed aircraft that had strayed into Chinese air space while en route from the Philippines to Danang. The pilot of the other plane reported that he had seen a parachute and heard a beeper after the plane was shot down. (Memoranda for the record by Brigadier General James A. Shannon, USAF, and Rear Admiral S.D. Cramer, Jr., USN, of the National Military Command Center, both February 14; Johnson Library, National Security File, Country File, China, Vol. XII)

Secretary of Defense McNamara called President Johnson the next morning to inform him that the plane had been shot down. (Ibid., Recordings and Transcripts, recording of a telephone conversation between Johnson and McNamara, February 14, 1968, 7:53 a.m., tape F68.02, side A, PNO 5) The President's Special Assistant Walt W. Rostow reported in a February 14, noon, memorandum to the President, that the Seventh Fleet wanted to launch a rescue helicopter from the USS *Kearsarge* at 0400 Vietnam time, with fighter aircraft from the carrier *Coral Sea* providing protection. Rostow's memorandum states that Secretary of State Rusk opposed the operation, arguing that the risk to the helicopter crew was too great and that the man was in Chinese territorial waters, and that Secretary of Defense McNamara also opposed it. JCS Chairman General Wheeler and Secretary of Defense-designate Clark M. Clifford advocated making a rescue attempt. (Ibid., Intelligence File, Plane Downed in Hainan Territorial Waters, Feb. 1968) A second Rostow memorandum of 12:40 p.m. states that the fighter aircraft were to remain 25 miles off shore unless the helicopter was attacked and that the entire rescue party was under strict instruction to initiate no hostile action. (Ibid.)

President Johnson met with his advisers at 1:14 p.m. to discuss whether or not to undertake the rescue attempt. At this time, Rusk, McNamara, Wheeler, and Clifford all recommended against it. Rusk,

McNamara, and Clifford expressed concern about the risk of conflict with the Chinese as well as the risk to the helicopter crew. Wheeler proposed launching an electronic aircraft outside the 12-mile limit to determine if beeps from the pilot's beeper were drifting out to sea, and the President approved this action. (Notes of Meeting; ibid., Tom Johnson's Notes of Meetings, February 14, 1968—1:14 p.m., Foreign Policy Advisors on Violation of Chinese Airspace) A brief memorandum of February 15 from Rostow to the President stated that no beeper had been heard. (Ibid., Intelligence File, Plane Downed in Hainan Territorial Waters, Feb. 1968)

A February 14 memorandum from Rostow to McNamara states that the President wanted a full but very prompt investigation of the reasons for violation of Chinese Communist air space during the previous year, including a complete report concerning the latest incident; it had been reported to him that there had been nine such violations. He wanted the Joint Chiefs of Staff, as a matter of high and urgent priority, to undertake steps to eliminate, if possible, the likelihood of further such violations. (Washington National Records Center, OSD Files: FRC 73 A 1250, China Reds 360) A February 19 memorandum from McNamara to the President states that there had been eight confirmed violations since January 1, 1967, but that there might have been other unconfirmed violations. He forwarded a February 17 memorandum from General Wheeler summarizing the reasons for the violations and steps that had been and were being taken to avoid such incidents, including efforts to keep aircraft away from Chinese territory and improvements in radar and communications. (Filed with a February 20 covering note from Rostow; Johnson Library, National Security File, Country File, China, Vol. XII)

A February 15 letter from Ambassador Gronouski to Chinese Chargé Ch'en stated that the aircraft had inadvertently strayed into the "territorial airspace claimed by your country," requested information pertaining to the pilot's welfare, and urged his release at the earliest possible time. (Telegram 115499 to Warsaw and telegram 2106 from Warsaw, February 15; Department of State, Central Files, POL 31–1 CHICOM–US) A March 5 letter from Ch'en to Gronouski called the violation of Chinese air space in this incident a "ferocious war provocation" by the United States and stated that he had been instructed to issue a "serious warning and firm protest." It gave no information concerning the pilot, nor did several subsequent efforts elicit any information. (Telegram 2284 from Warsaw, March 5; memorandum from Deputy Assistant Secretary of State for East Asian and Pacific Affairs Winthrop G. Brown to Under Secretary of State for Political Affairs U. Alexis Johnson, February 13, 1969; ibid.)

300. Telegram From the Embassy in the Republic of China to the Department of State[1]

Taipei, February 14, 1968, 1045Z.

2154. For Bundy from McConaughy. Subject: China Policy Speech February 16. Ref: State 114300.[2]

1. From standpoint of our relations here it is regrettable that speech along lines reftel is to be made. It will be construed as accepting and enhancing the Communists on the mainland and relegating GRC to status of small island regime and even obliquely raising some question as to legitimacy of GRC presence on Taiwan. Chinese here will be dismayed, discouraged and puzzled as to reasons for what they will interpret as a notable policy shift at a time when ChiCom record and prospects more dismal than ever, and GRC record more impressive than ever before.

2. My immediate appraisal is that adverse effects will somewhat exceed even the strong negative reaction anticipated by you. I do not anticipate a violent explosive reaction, but the suspicions and resentments engendered by assumed policy change striking at the foundations of GRC position will continuously inject a corrosive element into our relationship. There are enough variables and unknowns in the equation to make me hesitant to attempt to evaluate at this stage the precise extent of the probable damage, but it will be cumulative and substantial.

3. Speech may have adverse effect on ChiRep issue. UN member countries may be influenced by fact that speech as drafted indicates that US is treating GRC and mainland China as separate political entities, each controlling certain territory.

4. The GRC's present leadership does not have sufficient flexibility to accept what it will consider a major change in US policy and then engage in constructive dialogue with US concerning long range accommodation to a position confined to Taiwan.

5. There should be ways to ameliorate the adverse effects, and we here of course will be using all of our resources to this end. We would be helped if you could change two passages which would have particularly grievous effect here, as follows:

(A) In paragraph 5, change third sentence to read: "The Government of the Republic of China is the only Chinese Government which the

---

[1] Source: Department of State, Central Files, POL 1 CHICOM–US. Secret; Priority; Exdis.

[2] Document 298.

United States recognizes, and the United States deals with the government on all matters of common interest."[3]

(B) Delete first sentence of paragraph 6, which would provoke strongest adverse reaction.[4]

McConaughy

---

[3] In the text of Bundy's speech as delivered, this sentence reads as follows: "The United States recognizes the Republic of China and deals with that Government on all matters of common interest." The text is in Department of State, ACA Files: Lot 71 D 144, EA/ACA Drafted Speeches, 1967–1968.

[4] In the text of Bundy's speech as delivered, this sentence reads as follows: "Any final resolution concerning Taiwan should in all events meet with the approval of the Government of the Republic of China and its people whose interests are most directly affected."

---

301. Editorial Note

The *Weekly Review* of February 16, 1968, prepared in the Central Intelligence Agency's Directorate of Intelligence, included a section entitled "Soviets Continue To Expand Forces on Chinese Border." It stated that Soviet ground forces had been augmented in the last half of 1967 in regions bordering China in the Far East and Transbaykal Military Districts. Before the reinforcement began, about 21 ground divisions were deployed in regions along the Chinese border, whereas only 15 divisions were maintained in those areas prior to 1965, when significant Soviet reinforcement began.

Special Assistant Walt Rostow sent a copy to President Johnson with a covering memorandum of February 16 noting: "The undramatic but not trivial Soviet military build-up along the Chinese Communist border during 1967 may interest you." (Johnson Library, National Security File, Country File, China, Codeword, Vol. II)

302. Memorandum From Secretary of State Rusk to President Johnson[1]

Washington, February 22, 1968.

SUBJECT

Policy Toward Communist China

You have asked for our views on the situation in Communist China, Sino-Soviet relations, and Communist Chinese foreign policies—and on the resulting possibilities for change in our own policies. Tab A, attached, is a thoughtful and sound discussion of these matters, looking predominantly to the longer term.

For immediate purposes, I believe we can take only very limited steps, since our firm posture in Asia generally remains crucial and any significant "concessions" to Communist China would be seriously misunderstood in key quarters, not to mention the Congress. Specifically:

1. I do *not* believe we should change our posture toward the UN. Even the UN's technical organs are, as a practical matter, inseparable for now from the wider question of the General Assembly.

2. On private contacts, we have the option of quiet action to extend our passport policy for travel to Communist China so that we grant passports to anyone who applies. This could be done in the near future, since it has become customary to define our travel policy for publication in the *Federal Register* on March 15 of each year. A routine announcement at that time should attract no major notice, and would ratify what we have in fact been doing on individual applications for some time. If this commends itself to you, I will put a precise paper before you for decision. The practical effect will almost certainly be nil, since Peking has not admitted any American for some time.

3. On trade, there are certain minimal steps we could also take in the near future. These would affect (a) our attempt to apply US trade controls to US subsidiaries abroad (a major source of friction with friendly countries, and one we have frequently waived under pressure); (b) certain outmoded controls on bunkering of ships; and (c) removal of the requirement of Certificates of Origin on Chinese-type goods, for purchases

---

[1] Source: Johnson Library, National Security File, Country File, China, Vol. XII. Secret. Filed with a covering note of the same date from Rostow to the President. No drafting information is indicated on the source text. The Department of State copy cites Bundy as the drafter of the memorandum but does not indicate the drafter of the attachment. That copy is filed with a February 22 covering note from Bundy to Rusk, which says the paper had been requested by the President through Walt Rostow the previous night. (Department of State, Central Files, POL 1 CHICOM–US)

up to $100 (largely an annoyance, but with some balance-of-payments implications in the current situation). A broader possibility would be (d) a change in export license policy to permit export to Communist China of foodstuffs, fertilizer, insecticides, and farm machinery. All of these relate directly to food only, and the mere act of relaxing would be widely noted and I think more applauded than condemned. Again, if this possibility commends itself to you, I will put a precise paper before you for individual decision in the near future.

I conclude with the basic thought that we must keep Communist China always in mind in our choice of military actions in Viet-Nam and elsewhere. I do not think we are running any significant risks on present lines, but any proposal for new or increased action must take full account of this factor.

Dean Rusk

Attachment

SITUATION IN COMMUNIST CHINA AND
UNITED STATES POLICY ALTERNATIVES

Situation in Communist China

After a year and a half of turmoil, Peking's major emphasis is on channeling the Cultural Revolution into non-disruptive channels, restoring order, and seeking to restore its controls over the country as a whole and to re-establish a system of administration. This emphasis is articulated largely by the military—which has assumed an increasing role—and by the remnants of the governmental administrative apparatus.

The Cultural Revolution appears, at the present stage, to have had two major objectives—to enhance Mao Tse-tung's own power through the removal of his prime political opponents, and to carry through Mao's revolutionary and Utopian ideas of destroying the old society, remolding the individual, and establishing an idealized Communist society.

The results have been the crushing of organized opposition to Mao, but at immense cost: first, to leadership cohesion and Party and government institutions; secondly, a near-total failure of Mao's aims of social and political changes; thirdly, mounting national disillusionment and cynicism, and loss of confidence in Mao and Maoism; and fourthly, incalculable economic and social dislocation.

Today, rather than pressing on with the Cultural Revolution, the leadership is seeking to control the forces they themselves unleashed and to recreate institutional controls and a basic structure of power to replace the one they themselves have weakened.

Outlook

The Peking regime faces staggering problems as it seeks to hold China together and restore order. Mao and his more dedicated followers have not given up their dream of creating a new social order, and will seek opportunities to restore the momentum of the Cultural Revolution. Factionalism at all levels remains high, and steps taken to recreate the administrative structure inevitably feed the factionalism by restoring to power many of those only recently under attack. The People's Liberation Army has been given the task of policing the country in addition to national defense. Yet it is both inhibited by the Maoists from exerting the force necessary to restore order and reluctant to do so for fear of exacerbating the severe tensions the PLA is already under.

Looking somewhat further into the future, whatever success the present uneasy power equilibrium achieves in controlling disorders, reknitting the social and economic fabric and rebuilding the administrative structure of the country is apt to be set back by the death of Mao. Mao's health is not good, and it is unlikely he will survive for long. His death (or total incapacitation) would remove an important, if now somewhat tarnished, symbol of national unity, and would immediately sharpen the struggle for power.

In summary, China appears to face a period of some years of instability and internal preoccupation. The Cultural Revolution has set loose forces that will make most difficult the task of restoring order and momentum to China's society and economy by any new leadership that may emerge.

Opportunities for U.S. Initiatives

While this situation contains obvious elements of uncertainty and danger for the stability of East Asia, it also contains elements of opportunity for the United States. These elements revolve around the possibility that the disillusionment over Maoism and the increasingly pressing nature of China's internal problems will bring with them, on the part of a new leadership, a re-examination of the premises and priorities of China's foreign policy.

Likely Developments in Peking's Foreign Policies

The close relations existing between Peking and Moscow from 1949–58 represent an exceptional interlude in the much longer historical pattern of mutual suspicion and hostility between China and Russia. This history, the long common border populated by ethnic minorities which have been politically restive under both Chinese and Russian rule, and conflicting ideological and national objectives make it unlikely that a long-term relationship of friendship and cooperation between the two can be re-established.

The death of Mao would remove certain personal obstacles to improvement in Sino-Soviet relations, but unless accompanied by a break-down of order in China, this would not fundamentally change the strategic relationship between China, the Soviets, and ourselves. Moscow will be alert for opportunities to improve its relations with Peking without sacrificing basic Soviet interests, but any such improvement would in all likelihood be based on a relationship of full independence, with each clearly conscious of the dividing line between areas of common and competitive interest.

One evident common interest is their mutual desire to weaken the international position of the U.S. This could provide a basis for tactical collaboration on some specific issues which would be damaging to U.S. interests.

We do not rule out the possibility that either in conjunction with or independent of a lessening of overt Sino-Soviet tensions, the Chinese could move to lessen tensions with the U.S. We should certainly seek, within the context of our other Asian interests, to make this alternative as attractive as possible to Peking.

Peking's policy objectives with respect to its other Asian neighbors, particularly in Southeast Asia, will probably continue to focus on drawing these states into Peking's orbit of political and economic influence and detaching them from close relationships with the U.S. After a very harsh period last spring and summer, in which major threats were laid out against several countries in the area, Peking has now moderated its tactics, although it may be launching a significant subversive effort against Burma. In general, if the situation in Southeast Asia were to soften through adverse developments in Viet-Nam, we might expect to see some increase in pressure and subversion from Peking, notably in Thailand, but the degree to which this was pressed would depend heavily on conditions in the area. Moreover, we can reckon that Peking's internal problems will somewhat reduce the degree of pressure from what would have been foreseen prior to the Cultural Revolution, and specifically in the 1965 period when the U.S. made its major decision on Viet-Nam.

More broadly, and looking into the future, our best forecast would be that the over-all goal of major influence, and when possible control, in key parts of Southeast Asia will probably be shared by Mao's successors whoever they may be. Specific tactical approaches used toward this end will vary, as they have since 1949. Should Mao's successors, however, become less rigidly committed to the concept of a Maoist revolutionary development in the world—as we strongly suggest they eventually will—the insurrectionary-subversionary element in Peking's foreign policy may be gradually de-emphasized.

In dealing with the rest of the world, Peking will continue to be handicapped by its limited resources and will probably gradually begin to accept the limitations on its abilities to influence or control the actions of other states. The problems of an internal leadership transition will also hamper the formulation and implementation of foreign policy. The general outlines of Peking's policies, however, will probably continue: emphasis on developing relations with Afro-Asian states, willingness to deal on a practical basis on economic and trade matters with even certain states it does not recognize, and avoidance of war, if at all possible, with major powers.

Peking's Attitude Toward the U.S.

The likelihood of a change in Peking's policies toward the United States is minimal in the next few years, and probably nil while Mao is alive. Nevertheless, Peking has been willing, at some political cost, to keep open the Ambassadorial-level contact in Warsaw and clearly sees an advantage in having a communication point with the United States.

Especially given the current fluid state of Peking's politics, we believe it is in the interest of the U.S. to present to a potential or emerging Chinese leadership a variety of options and alternatives to their present policies.

Alternatives to U.S. Policies

We have, in the past few years, made initial moves in this direction by offering increasing contact through travel and limited types of trade and by attempting to institute a dialogue with Peking on disarmament. Further moves in respect to travel and trade can probably be taken without damage to U.S. security interests. We should also act to minimize potential points of irritation and direct conflict with Peking, and this applies particularly to self-restraint in U.S. military air and naval operations close to Chinese borders.

There is nothing that can presently be done directly to resolve the problem of Taiwan. We are committed to its defense but for all practical purposes deal with Peking and Taipei as if they were separate states. This is a direction toward which our policies have been taking us for 15 years and it is probably in our interest to work gradually toward at least a tacit acknowledgement of this reality by both.

So long as Peking's policies remain militant and hostile, there is no net U.S. advantage to be gained from Chinese Communist participation in the UN's political organizations. If Peking were to moderate its policies even to a limited degree, we would almost certainly be confronted by growing pressure from UN members to bring Communist China into the

UN, even if this resulted in withdrawal from the UN by the GRC. There are, even at present, significant advantages which might be derived from Peking's membership in a number of the UN's technical organizations (WMO, ITU, WHO, UPU). It is politically difficult to accomplish this, however, without bringing Peking into the General Assembly or the Security Council.

In general, we anticipate in the middle-long run that China's attitude toward the United States will be subject not only to changes in Peking's leadership, which could result in some moderation of Peking's hostility towards us permitting progress towards placing our relations on a more pragmatic basis, but also to the future U.S. posture in East Asia and in particular to the pattern of activities by the United States affecting Chinese security interests. We do find it possible to envisage the gradual development of practical cultural and economic relationships in somewhat the same way as our relations have developed with the USSR, even while our political relationship remains a hostile one

At some point, it may be desirable to consider the advantage of attempting to draw Peking more into Asian regional ventures such as the Asian Development Bank, ECAFE, or the Mekong Valley Project. We suspect Peking's initial reactions would be negative but the attempt might usefully serve to underline that the U.S. does not oppose Peking's taking part in peaceful economic development programs with its Asian neighbors.

---

303. Paper Prepared by Alfred Jenkins of the National Security Council Staff[1]

Washington, February 22, 1968.

THOUGHTS ON CHINA

Prologue to the Present
The Present Predicament
The Most Probable Future
Relations with Others

The term "madness" has been applied to the present climate in Peking. In some ways it is not inappropriate. But to a Chinese, because of

---

[1] Source: Johnson Library, National Security File, Country File, China, Vol. XII. Secret. Rostow sent the paper to the President with a covering note of the same date.

the historical prologue to the present and because of the Chinese way of viewing China and the world, much of the "madness" is explained as inescapable logic and reason.

A Burning in the Belly: The "Hundred Years of Ignominy"

There is something awesome about the world's oldest continuous civilization relentlessly rending itself. Since a quarter of humanity is directly involved, and the rest indirectly, China's current writhings are as important as they are spectacular. The ancient Confucian way of life—for so long the very cement of the Chinese race—has cracked and crumbled, and it is not yet clear what will lastingly take its place. The nature of the transformation could fundamentally affect not only the shape of Asia, but in no small measure the character of world civilization itself.

China's self-conscious, embarrassed, but inevitable attack on its own past actually has been going on for a century and a quarter—ever since the Opium War of 1842 proved that an outrage, and then a long stream of outrages, could be forced upon a great civilization which had neglected to develop the gunboat prerequisite to self-determination.

China's struggle to destroy its persistent Confucian past and to come into the modern world has been waged in varying manner and degree, but—at least for the first hundred years—always against humiliating odds imposed by the foreigners. "The imperialists" enjoyed extra-territorial rights, owned most of China's large-scale production, regulated much of its trade, and even managed its customs receipts! Through this bitter "hundred years of ignominy" the Chinese developed a veritable burning in the belly for renewed national dignity. And fantasies of sheer revenge—sweet revenge against the white man's exploitation and presumption—often crowded out even those fantasies of regained grandeur. The wounds of humiliation were all the deeper because for over 3,000 years the Han people had considered that they were only truly civilized people. Their "Middle Kingdom" was in their eyes the center of the universe—in all literalness—and even by religious sanction.

Especially since the turn of the century, China has made increasingly urgent—almost frenzied—efforts to modernize into viability as a great power. The republicanism of Sun Yat-sen and Chiang Kai-shek made some progress, and gave promise of more until the Japanese war. The tragedy depleted the nation's energies, furthered the disintegration of traditional ethics and mores, encouraged corruption in officialdom, and led the Kuomintang's ruling circles to commit political suicide by leaning ruinously on the hated foreigner.

During the war, the Chinese Communists won the peasants' loyalty in the large agrarian pockets between the Japanese-held cities and lines of communication. And at Mao's cave headquarters in Yenan, the degree of self-sacrifice, patriotism, honesty and fraternity evident in that temporary and unreal community won the praises of unbiased observers and the allegiance of increasing numbers of Chinese of a whole spectrum of political and economic persuasions.

The result was that in the Civil War the all-vital intelligence on troop movements in the countryside was given to the Communists and not to the Nationalists. In the cities not only many workers, but many students, professional people and even some government officials worked clandestinely for the Communists in the interest of China's new day.

And so China was "lost." The enormity of that event was apparent, and the United States entered on an orgy of self-flagellation.

For some seven years the Chinese Communists in many ways performed impressively in bringing about a new China. The costs were high (e.g., up to twenty million persons liquidated in the land reform period) but the nation was united, at peace, and expectant. It forged ahead economically so that it was widely spoken of as a model for other developing nations. It had purposeful, cohered leadership which made a fetish of taking no guff from foreigners. And soon, it must be admitted, the *masses* of Chinese were a little better off—at least materially—than they had ever been. Mao, success-crowned, began to be deified, and his works canonized.

(If more people, Chinese and others, had read his works earlier, the story might have been different. The *Mein Kampf*-like candor of his writings would have shown up the war-time "democratic, peace-loving, agrarian reformer" era for what Mao intended it to be: a temporary show-case period to gain support—a tactical way-station on the road to communism. But not many of his writings at that time were in English. I remember my feeble, worried efforts to spread what I had read in Chinese and heard, but then I was just a Vice Consul from Georgia—and South Georgia at that. The "agrarian reformer" thesis was widely believed for a long time.)

The regime became overconfident, and Mao (against significant opposition, it now appears) in 1957 launched the so-called Great Leap Forward. This attempt to force production by rapid transition to extreme forms of social and economic organization was a colossal failure. The Russians had strongly advised against the Great Leap. Its economic dislocations disgusted them, its go-it-alone atmosphere affronted them, and its ideological implications alarmed them. Relations festered until in 1960 Russian aid and aiders were withdrawn, and the communist giants split.

The God Who Failed: The Cultural Revolution

The failure of the Great Leap Forward was not only of domestic import; the failure was on the international front, too, and that front was desperately important to the Chinese view of China's place in the sun—and to Mao's in history. China was no longer the economic model for the Afro-Asian-Latin American world, and this fact began to register itself.

That double failure, domestic and foreign, ironically made inevitable Mao's second supreme effort to enforce his "truth" on China—a truth which, being demonstrated in practice, was eventually expected to be embraced by the world—with an assist, of course, from "peoples' wars of liberation."

In order to get back on its feet after the Great Leap, China had to shelve Mao's extreme policies and adopt the road of "revisionism," skirting close to the heresy of private incentive and reward. Not only was Mao*ism* for a time quietly shelved, so was *Mao*—at least as much as his associates dared *and desired*. Mao later complained of being treated like a deceased parent. He was trotted out at times, for he had become the symbol of the *new* China's *ancient uniqueness and centrality*—a concept of womb-like balm to the Chinese psyche. After all, he was billed as the greatest living communist theoretician, in the direct Marx–Lenin–Stalin–Mao lineage and the perfecter of "peoples' wars"—and this, with luck, meant that the Chinese, appropriately, would in time inherit the earth by proxy.

But Mao is not practiced in the art of hiding his light under a bushel. He did not like being semi-shelved, nor did he like what he saw of the bureaucratization of his revolution, the growing apathy of the fattening cadres, and what he considered the recent compromises throughout the nation with "spontaneous capitalistic tendencies." Accordingly he launched the Great Proletarian Cultural Revolution, in the attempt to re-solidify his own power, and revive and purify the revolution into something of its pristine vigor, to restore the visionary romance of the Yenan cave days as a needed propellant to the lagging revolution, and to temper the younger generation (who for the most part had not experienced battle, Yenan austerity, or even, adequately, class hatred) for its post-Mao revolutionary responsibilities.

Mao had become disillusioned with the Party apparatus. Being charged with implementing policy at the local level, the Party bureaucracy had learned to temper doctrinal purity with practical realities, *but to report the results, falsely, as constant with the expectations of doctrinal purity.* It was professionally healthier to do so. This ruse was cumulative in its errors, and the day of reckoning had to come. Mao proceeded to wreck the wayward Party with the Great Cultural Revolution.

Mao's greatest opposition is human nature itself, which he is trying to remake. This is one reason why he has met instinctive opposition as he has successfully turned to each major segment of Chinese society for support during the tortuous two years of his Cultural Revolution. (His belief in the right thinking of the masses has been naively total.) Yet his utility as the national father image makes him almost indispensable at this time in Chinese history—which partly explains why the opposition, so far, has not solidified. The extremes of Mao*ism* are instinctively opposed, while *Mao* is instinctively clung to.

This genuine and terribly serious dilemma exacerbates already weighty, political, economic and military policy differences in Peking. And a suspicious, perhaps somewhat senile Mao has so reduced his trusted circle of cronies during the testiness of the Cultural Revolution that his prestigious minority has barely been able to balance the fighting-for-their-lives bureaucratic majority. This tug-of-war has insured that Peking speaks to the provinces with vacillation, indecision and even contradiction. Such confusion has generally resulted in inaction by the local agents of the central government and has given opportunistic groups, from policy opponents to plain hooligans, a breezy field day.

Forces long denied expression by Central Government unanimity and confidence have now been unleashed by Peking's division and indecision, and all sorts of repressed "bourgeois tendencies" are bursting out. These are furthered by the bureaucratic opposition, by patriotic elements which feel they were early deluded into support of a regime, the nature of which was misrepresented, by disgruntled youth, by opportunistic workers and peasantry, and by underprivileged elements of society who see advancement only through lawless acts in a time of increasing disrespect for authority.

The Party organization is discredited and its recently respected leadership largely unseated—throughout the countryside, save for the one important region of Sinkiang (nuclear installations and oil). Lower echelons are uncertain of their mandate, confused by contradictory exhortations from Peking, and affronted (earlier) by the license of the Red Guards and (more lately) by encroachments of the military. Factional fighting (for both ideological and pure power-grab reasons) and lawlessness are rampant. Industrial productivity has been curtailed, agricultural productivity will be seriously hampered for the coming year, and foreign trade jeopardized through economic dislocations and political pig-headedness. The military establishment is assigned jobs for which it is ill fitted: overseeing factories, farms and railroads. But Mao apparently is reluctant to have the military intervene to stop the factional fighting because it is one of his axioms that the people and the army love and support each other, and always act in unison. To admit that the country can only be ruled by the use of military force would be to admit what increasingly seems to be the fact: things have gone too far for Mao to reconsolidate his power. Mao The Symbol may be kept at least as long as he lives, but Maoism, as he conceives it in his domestic policies, is not likely to prevail.

The Watershed's Nether Slope: Something of a New Dynasty

While Mao's "mandate of heaven" is clearly slipping, it is too early to tell what will take its place. It may take some time yet in coming, or the military may decide almost any time that they have had enough of their country's coming apart, and impose a crisper solution. Regional break-downs could prevail for a time, but are not likely to be the pattern for long, because of the universal Chinese thirst for reconstituted nationhood, and because China's economy is now sufficiently sophisticated so that it depends upon a network of specialized contributions from all parts of the country.

It is impossible to know the true thinking of the Chinese people, because for 18 years there has not only been lack of freedom of speech, there has not even been freedom to remain silent. All have had to be vocal in support of the regime. It is just possible that the confusion and contradiction in Peking is viewed by a great many Chinese as a welcome sign of collapse, and that they want something quite different to follow. Surely many must be disillusioned with unfulfilled promises of a decade ago; must be bone tired of 18 years of overlapping mass campaigns—ideological flogging to increase production at little or no personal gain; and must be wearied by receding promises of restored Chinese primacy in the world. Too, the ridiculous lengths to which Mao has been made an infallible god could at some point trigger the most destructive of weapons: ridicule. A non-communist successor regime could thus become conceivable, but it is unlikely. Most Chinese consider capitalism as the only real alternative to communism, and the "capitalism" they knew in China was most unattractive except for the few; it was highly exploitive, with semi-colonial associations. The pragmatic communism of less Maoist periods is probably viewed as not too bad in contrast.

Much more likely, therefore, is a military-bureaucratic collegium of "communist" continuity, but less doctrinaire, increasingly adopting private incentive methods, along with the trend in several other communist countries. Domestically, the likely new management would be termed relatively moderate. In time this may also apply to foreign relations, but at first I should expect disappointingly little change there. *Much will depend upon the Chinese assessment of the future utility and promise of the "peoples' war" concept.* Much, that is, depends upon the outcome in Vietnam. If later it should appear that the "imperialists" may be on the run through even partial successes of several simultaneous peoples' wars (if they can be ginned up) there may well be a temptation for China in a post-Mao situation to paper over its differences with the Soviet Union and cooperate somewhat more fully against common enemies.

It is inconceivable, however, that the Sino-Soviet relationship will again be anything like as close as in the early 50's. Several of the people purged in the Cultural Revolution are believed to have been ousted because they favored rapprochement with the Soviet Union. If Mao loses out, these may return to favor. *I am not sure that a China in league with the Soviet Union would necessarily be mellowed thereby.* I think it might be that the Soviet Union instead would be hardened. The Soviet Union seems to harden when it feels strong, and to mellow only as a tactic of prudence when necessary. Formerly, with a fast strengthening China on the loose, the Soviets even came a bit closer to us. It may not be accidental that they have hardened somewhat toward us, now that an estranged China has been weakened by the Cultural Revolution. They might harden the more if China should become again an ally, even a tenuous and uncomfortable one.

China under almost any auspices, if it is united and growing in strength, will continue to present us, and its neighbors, with problems. It will probably not rest until it has carved out in some fashion what it considers to be its legitimate sphere of influence in Asia. Under a successor regime to Mao, and in a situation of something like power balance in Asia, that sphere might well be defined within limits tolerable to us, depending upon how the "influence" were exercised. But not as long as Mao has his way. He is too committed to world revolution as a fundamental article of faith, and too convinced that peoples' wars are the infallible way to reach that objective.

China and the United States: The Mao Dynasty and After

One of Mao's biggest problems has been to activate the traditionally politically lethargic Chinese people. The peasants have long purred: "Heaven is high, and the emperor is far away." Intrusive central government is not the Chinese norm.

Both the communist dialectic and, seemingly, Mao's own psychological make-up dictated that he use the hate-object technique, to ensure political engagement of the populace. He set about, from the very inception of his regime, to make the United States serve the indispensable purpose of the hated devil. He has tried to forge with us, paradoxically, even a sort of "inimical partnership" in the interest of his revolution! This is not just a catch phrase. I believe it accurately describes his conception of our utility to him, for both domestic and foreign policy purposes, and that he and his regime (so long as it is "his") will not respond to any *un*devilish overtures on our part. In dealing with the Chinese Communists in Tientsin for nine months after they came to power, in carrying on the negotiations in Geneva before they went to the ambassadorial level, and in four years of advising in the Warsaw talks I have seen scarcely a shred of evidence to the contrary.

So long as the true Maoists are in control, then I think we can take it for granted that we will get no response from any bridge-building efforts. Such a response would undermine Mao's basic philosophy. He believes that he can keep his revolution pure, and wound up, only through class hatred at home and devil hatred abroad.

Our occasional statements in the "ultimate reconciliation" vein, as distinguished from tangible bridge-building offers, however, should be continued—not too frequently, and in very measured tones. These are almost certainly carefully registered in various Peking circles. For just as in many ways China is our biggest headache, so we are certainly China's; it follows that what we do or do not do, and say or do not say, is carefully noted. Primarily our stand in Vietnam, but also our un-devilish statements have surely helped sharpen policy debates in Peking, and it seems certain that potential successor leadership is well aware of its policy options in our regard, if it should wish to test them.

It would not seem to be the time quite yet for new bilateral initiatives with China, or even for unilateral gestures toward China of the tangible bridge-building sort. Not only would we be rebuffed, *but China would have to go on record to that effect, and a successor regime may well feel sufficient continuity with the present one so as to make renunciation of that record awkward*, though it might otherwise be tempted to test us through response.

A better case, at least, could have been made for new initiatives prior to, say, August 1966. Prior to that time Peking's leadership seemed unified and the dislocations of the Cultural Revolution had not threatened the integrity of the nation. Big global issues such as disarmament, nonproliferation and the like seemed to call for efforts before very long to get China better articulated into the world community, for the sake of ultimate world stability. While these considerations as such are still valid, a China weakened through turmoil lends somewhat less urgency, and the prospect of a different China to come, possibly readier to respond, recommends the waiting game. We can sympathize with the Chinese people in their turmoil and strife, but from the standpoint of stark U.S. interests, and so long as China is under present auspices, situations of less advantage to us than the present one easily come to mind.

Our East Asian policies must in general be of a piece. Gestures of magnanimity or friendship toward China in the face of the presently necessary stand in Vietnam and Laos might be applauded in some European capitals and on some American campuses, but not by our friends around the periphery of China. Nor does the degree of promise in overtures to Peking at present seem to warrant creating enormous problems for us on Taiwan.

It seems to me, in short, that we have kept our future options open *better*, rather than otherwise, by keeping relatively quiet while mainland China is trying to sort itself out.

Finally, there is something to be said for keeping our own ideological skirts clean. The evils of the present Peking regime are sufficiently discernible and documentable so that an attempt to cozy up to it—while possibly serving other honorable purposes if it worked—would be widely interpreted as a compromise of those things we stand for, as well as the ditching of a rather satisfactory ally on Taiwan. The Great Problem of Taiwan must mature further before it can be solved, and an altered mainland may make it easier.

Meanwhile, we are doing other sorts of things which are very much a part of China policy. We are attempting to thwart Chinese abetted and supported aggression, and we are doing what we can to strengthen noncommunist Asia—very successfully in many instances. And we have made clear that we would not be unresponsive to a China ready to deal on other than paranoically one-sided terms.

Beyond that, it seems to me that the steps we can profitably take are limited, until we can see the color of the China which is to emerge from the present "curious, costly general election" on the mainland. Among those limited steps, we might consider the following:

1. Perhaps we could afford to twist arms in New York with less ferocity and anxiety on the Chinese Representation issue. We spend a lot of blue chips on this issue. This is certainly no time to bring China into the UN, but I think there is no danger of it. On his present tack of all-out peoples' wars, I cannot imagine that Mao would accept the limiting implications of UN membership if it were offered, and it is not likely to be offered to a Peking when everyone knows it is hard to define just what constitutes Peking today—along with other reasons which have been advanced all along against entry. Peking has said that the UN is controlled by the imperialists, especially the United States, and before it would be interested in membership the organization must be reconstituted, and must withdraw the aggressor label (re Korea) unjustly placed on China and place it where it belongs, on the United States. I think we could put the monkey on Peking's back for its self-imposed isolation, and get a lot of Europeans and Afro-Asians off ours. We could not advocate Peking's entry, of course, but we could relax more, in safety.

2. We might keep adequate China trade controls while removing the opprobrious "trading with the enemy" label, and demonstrate readiness for *future* flexibility by moving slightly from the total embargo wicket. The "working level" at State is preparing a very modest package which should be scrutinized when it is finished. Even though it is modest, it may go a bit far for now. It seems to me we should quietly move away from the *principle* of total embargo, both because it is ineffective and because it smacks of former black-and-white days in China policy, but we should not move to a degree which may make any *practical* difference so long as the Vietnam war goes on.

3. We should use the Warsaw talks more as an educational platform. The record of the talks is read in a Peking leadership circle of some indeterminate size. One of the dangerous things about present Pe-

king leadership is the almost unbelievable degree of its provincialism. We should find excuses to weave into our prepared materials at Warsaw small discourses about the nature of the open world partly already arrived, partly just around the corner: the overlapping, global patterns of social, economic and cultural organization constantly spawned by continuing revolutions in communication, travel and electronic wizardry; *the impossibility, today, of curtaining off a society if it expects to keep up with the advanced nations*—reciprocal contributions to knowledge and growth enable advancement in geometrical ratio, while even partially isolated societies will grow in more nearly arithmetic ratio; the total fund of human knowledge is now such that computer centers must specialize more and more, and a country not geared into other centers of learning is at an increasing disadvantage; etc., etc. We cannot negotiate anything meaningful at Warsaw under present conditions, but perhaps we can help worry the semi-mad Maoists into an earlier cracking up, and give the potential successors something to think about.

4.   We have done well to refrain from public appraisal of the Cultural Revolution. Its reality is embarrassing enough to the Chinese, without advertisement. At some point when the watershed in China has been passed long enough for the other side to show its character a bit, a Presidential speech on China will probably be advisable. Almost anything we say now will be turned against us by the present regime, and the *record of rejection will have grown.* We should wait until the present regime may be so discredited that its record in its dying days will not really be pertinent.

Basically, (and at the risk of speaking in broader terms than my assignment) it seems to me we will help shape the new China as much by what we *are* as what we do or do not do. Prestige kept carefully intact; quiet, abundant power in the larger sense; credibility and integrity; and fidelity to those fundamentals of the American heritage which made us strong in the first place and in turn have guided, goaded, shamed and inspired people of many other lands to revolutionary progress—these are the things which will be negotiable assets, when the time comes, with that Chinese quarter of humanity seeking a new national purpose and a new station in the world. It is we who are associated with the *real* revolution going on in Asia, and that, by and large, is the very best China policy open to us for this transitional period. We need not be lacking in initiatives when the time comes for them to pay off. That could be fairly soon, but no one can yet tell.

Alfred Jenkins

304.   Memorandum Prepared in the Central Intelligence Agency[1]

Washington, February 23, 1968.

[3 paragraphs (15-1/2 lines of source text) and subject line not declassified]

Attachment

[document number not declassified]

SUBJECT

Memorandum of Conversation Between Ambassador McConaughy and Chiang Ching-kuo on 12 February 1968

1.   Chiang Ching-kuo (CCK) said the situation in Tibet caused him particular concern. He said he had received from GRC Intelligence Agents in Tibet reports of serious internal difficulties, which would very likely be compounded by serious food shortages. He believed the USG should watch this situation closely, since in his judgment there was a possibility that some dissident elements in Tibet might ask for assistance from India, in the event that the Maoists tighten the pressures on Tibet even further. If they do not get help, then the dissident elements would likely be wiped out.

2.   The Ambassador pointed out that the Indians with all their current internal difficulties would probably be very loath to take any step that might provoke the ChiComs. CCK agreed that the Indians would be reluctant. However, he felt that an opportunity might be presented which should be exploited. He said he thought that British Intelligence might have additional information about the situation in Tibet. He suggested that the U.S. should intensify intelligence operations in Tibet, "In order to see how best to help the Tibetans attain independence."

3.   CCK moved to the present serious situation in Kwangtung province. He said this province seems to contain more military elements that are anti-Mao than most other areas, and it is also the province in which the GRC has the most underground agents. He said the GRC plans to in-

---

[1] Source: Department of State, INR Historical Files, China, 1968. Secret. A copy is attached to a memorandum of February 27 from INR Deputy Director for Coordination William C. Trueheart to Hughes, Denney, and Evans, [text not declassified]. (Ibid., EA Weekly Meetings, 1968)

tensify its clandestine work there, and to stage extensive anti-Mao activities in April and May, with particular emphasis on the Swatow area. The Ambassador asked if the GRC in fact had the capability to do this, and CCK replied he felt they did. CCK said the GRC's efforts in Kwangtung are now scattered, with one major area of activity at Nan-Hsiung (25–10N; 114–20E), near Ch'U-Chiang in the far north of the province. He said he planned to "activate our people there." He said he would keep the Ambassador [*less than one line of source text not declassified*] posted about progress and developments.

4.   The Ambassador asked if CCK foresaw any possibility that the activities would be so successful that the ChiComs might consider them to constitute a provocative act by the GRC. CCK said he had perhaps not made himself clear; the activities would not be staged in any way that could involve attribution to the GRC and they would not be aimed at any take-over of local power. His agents would simply stimulate and participate in prevailing cultural revolution activities on the anti-Mao side.

5.   The Ambassador asked if the ChiComs might not still blame the GRC for instigating the troubles. CCK replied that he did not believe this would happen. CCK said these activities would not be aimed at wresting political power for the GRC in the area, but rather at increasing political instability and chaos. Kwangtung province had been chosen simply because of a combination of agent assets and an unstable situation. The objective would be to achieve increased political instability in the area. He said Swatow appeared to be an unstable area, and that Amoy had similar serious instabilities also. He said that he wished to inform the Ambassador of the above "For the Ambassador's reference." CCK then said that he knew the Ambassador was aware that last year the GRC had conducted some small boat intelligence collection raids against the Mainland. He said that, in line with his already expressed intention to avoid provocative action in the present tense Far Eastern situation, "We are suspending these raids now, and should we want to start them again we will consult with you."

6.   CCK referred to reports that IL–28's were moving to the Nanning and North Vietnam areas, and wondered whether these aircraft were the same ones that apparently assembled in Hsuchow last fall, or whether they are new aircraft recently delivered by the Soviets.

7.   CCK referred to his conversation with DCM Hummel on January 29 in which CCK had announced the intention of his government, and the instructions by the Gimo, to refrain from provocative acts against the Mainland, during the new tensions in Vietnam and Korea. CCK reiterated that this was GRC policy and would be carried out, and he added that if there is anything the U.S. Government wants the GRC to do to help, the GRC would certainly cooperate.

8. CCK said he was watching closely the reports of a new ChiCom missile installation at Lung-Chi near Amoy, to try to discover whether they are ground-to-air missiles, or whether they are ground-to-ground missiles that could be a serious new threat to Quemoy.

9. CCK turned to the subject of internal security, in the light of the Communist attacks on the U.S. Embassy in Saigon and on President Park's residence in Seoul. He thought that the GRC had the situation well under control in Taiwan, although the GRC has recently taken new actions to prevent ChiCom infiltration. He said that last year (presumably during calendar 1967) the GRC had discovered a total of 93 "cases" of attempted espionage. He said that this had been a reduction from the previous year, but that it is obvious that the ChiComs are still making espionage attempts. During the past year, for instance, the ChiComs had been trying to use Mainland People who have sons in the GRC Armed Forces by sending wives and other female relatives from the Mainland to Hong Kong, and from there to Taiwan for espionage purposes. The Ambassador suggested that the ChiComs might also try to land small groups of infiltrators along the Taiwan coast, as the North Koreans have been doing in South Korea. CCK said he thought this would be difficult but not impossible; he thought the infiltration of dependents more likely.

---

305. Memorandum From the President's Special Assistant (Rostow) to President Johnson[1]

Washington, February 24, 1968.

SUBJECT

Comparison of Four Memoranda on China

Four memoranda recently sent you on the situation, prospects and policy recommendations with regard to China are compared below. The memoranda are attached, as follows:

Secretary Rusk's "Policy Toward Communist China" of February 22 (Tab A)[2]

CIA's "Communist China's Troubles and Prospects" of February 22 (Tab B)[3]

---

[1] Source: Johnson Library, National Security File, Country File, China, Codeword, Vol. II. Secret.

[2] Document 302.

[3] Attached but not printed.

Al Jenkins' "Thoughts on China" of February 22 (Tab C)[4]

Academic specialists' majority report, "Memorandum on China Policy" of February 12 (Tab D)[5]

Situation and Prospects

I find no disagreement whatever among the first three papers in their attempts to analyze the situation and the likely prospects for China. (Tab D is almost entirely on policy.) It is natural in addressing a subject of this extensiveness and complexity that the elements in the situation chosen to be covered vary somewhat, but there is a surprising—and comforting—degree of agreement among the three papers as to what is going on in China. The CIA paper is the most complete in this area, but of course appropriately stops short of policy discussion. I think it safe to say that there is general agreement that:

—China is in a mess, with widespread but mostly small-scale factional fighting, with lawlessness, transportation stoppages, and growing disrespect for authority resulting in significant damage to industrial production and a threat to agricultural production ;

—dissension at the top causes vacillation and contradiction to emanate from central authority;

—the Party apparatus is all but destroyed, and it will be difficult to reconstitute it;

—the military, so far generally intact, is increasingly running the country;

—despite all of this, China has not yet really come apart, and the sophisticated weapons program, including the nuclear component, so far does not seem to have been badly hurt;

—while Mao may be retained as a symbol at least as long as he lives, his extreme domestic policies almost certainly will not prevail;

—limited accommodation with the Soviet Union and/or the United States could come, post-Mao.

Policy Recommendations

All three papers dealing in policy considerations (Tabs A, C and D) believe that we are unlikely to get appreciable reciprocation during the Maoist era from any attempted rapproachment, although the academicians' paper appears to be somewhat more hopeful than the other two in this regard. All three papers, however, recommend certain steps to be taken unilaterally, where reciprocation is not expected, designed to increase contact and to signal to potential successors to the Maoists that they will have policy options in our regard.

---

[4] Document 303.

[5] Attached but not printed. The memorandum, unsigned and undated, from the group that met with Johnson on February 2 (see Document 297) is filed with a covering letter of February 12 from Reischauer, stating that the points in the memorandum represented a general consensus and that all had at least majority support within the group.

Trade

All three suggest liberalization of present trade regulations, but the academicians would go farther than the other two papers. This rather complex subject can perhaps best be reviewed after we receive State's more detailed proposals. It may be useful to invite the academicians' comments, and Congressional soundings will be important.

Travel

Both the academicians and Jenkins would favor the Secretary's proposal on travel liberalization.

Other Efforts at Contact

For some time we have been making efforts to no avail along the line advocated by the academicians. There appears to be no quarrel with our continuing these efforts, within reason.

One China, One Taiwan

In the attachment to the Secretary's memorandum the proposition is stated that we should work gradually toward at least tacit acknowledgment that we consider Peking and Taipei to represent two separate states. The other two papers do not deal quite so explicitly with this subject, but this concept seems to be implicit in both.

Offshore Islands

The academicians would have us make "determined efforts . . . to induce the Republic of China to withdraw from the offshore islands (Quemoy and Matsu)." The other two papers do not address this question. I feel that:

—for a while yet our efforts would be unavailing, and would deeply trouble Taipei;

—with Chiang's lessened emphasis on military conquest of the mainland, this withdrawal is less important (although still desirable) from our standpoint;

—it may be easier post-Mao and/or post-Chiang;

—meanwhile the status quo is crucially important to the legitimacy of Chiang's government at the national level: without the islands the national and Taiwan provincial de facto jurisdictions would be geographically coterminous.

Regional Projects

The Secretary's attachment points out the ultimate desirability of getting China associated in regional developmental projects. This was not mentioned in the other two papers—perhaps because all would agree it is not conceivable under present conditions—but is consonant with the general approach of the other papers.

Broaden Discussion

The academicians would have us engage in a broad bilateral discussion of all the fundamental problems that lie between our two nations.

This is congenial to the two government papers, not belabored in them doubtless because the authors knew we have tried to do just that, and Peking is not interested.

Warsaw as an Educational Forum

As long as preachment is avoided, I see merit in Jenkins' suggestion that we use Warsaw more to whittle away at the Chinese Communists' hardshell view of the world. The academicians imply much the same thing. If the world is being gradually but willy-nilly knit together both by the acids and the building blocks of modernity, this surely brings both new dangers and new promise. Ignorance of the process itself will increase the dangers, and the Chinese seem to be long on that sort of ignorance. This will not be a bilateral discussion, but our own stated observations which we hope would be usefully provocative.

A Bohlen Counterpart

You have already reacted favorably to this proposal of the academicians.[6]

United Nations Entry

This is one important subject on which there is a categorical difference of opinion. The academicians would have us support Peking's seating in the United Nations if it wishes to enter on the same terms as other countries. The Secretary is emphatic in his opposition to Peking entry. Jenkins agrees that it is not in our interest to have Peking under its present auspices in the UN, but does not believe it would come in on the same terms as other countries anyway—hence it is safe and seemly for us to be somewhat more relaxed. Perhaps the trend is in that direction, considering our stand on the study committee proposition.

General Comment

Except for the UN issue, there is a very large area of general agreement in the memoranda. Of the three papers, the academicians would have us go farthest toward attempted accommodation, and rather promptly. Jenkins emphasizes the importance of timing with regard to the assumed change-of-dynasty cycle, especially in those steps wherein reciprocation would be at issue. I see merit in our readying the Secretary's proposals—for another reading against events on the trade package, which will take a bit of work around town. You will presumably wish to get the views, too, of Defense, Commerce and Agriculture.

Walt

---

[6] See Document 297. The memorandum cited in footnote 4 above recommended creation of an Office of Ambassador at Large for Asia, or comparable area, at the top policy level of the Department.

306.   Action Memorandum From the Assistant Secretary of State for East Asian and Pacific Affairs (Bundy) to Secretary of State Rusk[1]

Washington, March 6, 1968.

SUBJECT

Removal of travel restriction to Mainland China

Problem

Under the applicable passport regulations the restrictions now in force against travel by American citizens to Communist China, Cuba, North Korea, and North Viet-Nam will expire on March 15, 1968. They may, of course, be renewed by appropriate announcement.

This memorandum is directed to the question whether the restriction on travel to Communist China should be continued. For the reasons stated below, we believe that it should not. A separate memorandum is being forwarded recommending renewal of the restrictions on Cuba, North Korea, and North Viet-Nam.

Discussion

I.

Last March we recommended to you that restrictions on travel to mainland China be continued in view of the unsettled political condition inside China and the xenophobic behavior of the mobs of Red Guards which were at the time committing excesses or threatening foreigners then resident in Peking and elsewhere. The official announcement stated that travel was being restricted "in view of the present unsettled conditions within mainland China and the risks and dangers which might ensue from the inadvertent involvement of American citizens in domestic disturbances."

In the course of the last six months, the general political malaise in Communist China has not eased; and its violent manifestations have

---

[1] Source: Department of State, ACA Files: Lot 72 D 175, Travel Controls (Gen.), Jan–Dec. 1968. Secret. Also sent by Deputy Legal Adviser Murray J. Belman and Acting Administrator for Security and Consular Affairs Barbara M. Watson. Drafted by Kreisberg and SCA Deputy Administrator Nathan Lewin. Cleared by Assistant Legal Adviser for SCA Frederick Smith, Jr., Jacobson, Shoesmith, and INR/REA Deputy Director John Holdridge. Macomber did not concur. He stated in a March 8 memorandum to Rusk that the proposed policy change would meet conservative opposition without gaining liberal support for the administration's Vietnam policy. (Ibid.) A handwritten note from Katzenbach attached to the source text reads: "Dean—I do not think this is the time for new initiatives on China. NdBK."

been widely evident in many provinces. At the same time, (1) the regime has given evidence of an ability to maintain order in the main cities to which foreigners have been permitted to travel; (2) it has successfully managed a large trade fair in Canton in November–December 1967 which was attended by thousands of foreigners; (3) it has resumed admitting foreigners, such as the recent groups of Australian and New Zealand students, who were conducted to a limited number of cities with virtually no untoward incidents; and (4) it has exerted strong and successful efforts to prevent a recurrence of the overt anti-foreign demonstrations which marked the January–August period last year.

Peking continues to be sensitive, as do other communist states, to activities by visitors, including technicians working in Communist China, which in other countries might be considered totally innocent. Several of these, including British and Japanese, have been detained under house arrest in the last six to eight months. Peking also continues to exert pressure on the British by holding a British newspaperman under house arrest and denying members of the British mission in Peking permission to leave the country. Individual British and other diplomats as well as most other foreign residents in Peking, however, are in general being treated politely and are free from serious harassment. We have no reason to believe that if American citizens were issued visas they would be treated any differently in the cities to which they would be permitted to go. The possibility can obviously not be excluded that the Chinese might detain or arrest an American visitor for innocent activities such as photographing in unauthorized areas or an unintentional "insult." While these hazards are, in certain respects, similar to those confronting American travelers in the Soviet Union and Eastern Europe, we recognize that they differ in degree. In the USSR and in Eastern Europe (apart from Albania and Eastern Germany), the United States has diplomatic and consular establishments able to attempt to protect such travelers, and the citizens of those countries also travel in the United States.

II.

On balance, however, we cannot say today—as we did a year ago—that there are unusual "risks and dangers of inadvertent involvement of American citizens in domestic disturbances." Moreover, the standard set down in the only major travel-control case we have won in recent years (*Zemel* v. *Rusk*) authorizes restriction of travel "when it can be demonstrated that unlimited travel to the area would directly and materially interfere with the safety and welfare of . . . the nation as a whole." We cannot fairly claim today that removal of restrictions to mainland China would have the serious consequences contemplated by the *Zemel* rule.

Our policy regarding passport validations for travel to Communist China is now so liberal as to enable virtually any individual who has some reason other than simple tourism for traveling to qualify. This gradual and progressive liberalization of our China travel restrictions (which contrasts sharply with the strict limitations imposed on travel to Cuba, North Korea and North Viet-Nam) has met with general approbation from the public and has been challenged by virtually no one. It demonstrates that we do not really consider the risks of American travel serious enough to outweigh the benefits of opening a wide and mutually profitable range of peaceful contacts between the U.S. and Communist China.

III.

There are two additional considerations relating to our general travel-restriction policy which weigh in favor of removing the restriction on travel to China:

1. The recent court decision in the Straughton Lynd case—which the Department of Justice has refused to take to the Supreme Court— virtually eliminates all our enforcement power in the travel-control area. American citizens are now free to go to North Viet-Nam, North Korea, Cuba and China, if they can get in, so long as they do not use their passports in doing so. All that stands behind our passport limitation is moral and patriotic suasion, and the effect of that obviously diminishes the more thinly it is spread. We would be best advised, therefore, to concentrate our exhortation to American citizens on countries or areas such as North Viet-Nam or North Korea—where we have vital interests in restraining travel—and not fritter it away on China.

2. The same considerations affect the travel-control legislation we have sent to Congress. We have heard from the Hill that Congressmen and Senators are concerned that the proposed bill grants excessively broad authority to the Secretary of State. The best refutation of that claim is to demonstrate that even when our authority is entirely unlimited by statute—as it is now—we have exercised great self-discipline in imposing travel restrictions.

IV.

The practical consequences of removing the restriction will probably be minimal. Peking has generally refused to permit American citizens with validated passports to visit its territory, and we do not anticipate that it will immediately change its position. It has, of course, allowed in those American citizens—such as Robert Williams and other extremists—whom it favors. Eliminating the restriction will not, we believe, substantially increase this traffic because all those who were invited were able and usually willing to visit China without State Department authorization. And in light of the *Lynd* case, they all now have the legal right to go.

A disadvantage of dropping restrictions altogether is that we will no longer have a clear record of those individuals who have indicated their interest in travel to mainland China. We doubt that this is a serious problem, however, and believe that any individual who would have applied for a validated passport will let it be known he is going to the mainland if he actually receives a Chinese visa. Those individuals, on the other hand, who would earlier not have wished their passage to the mainland to become known and would have traveled clandestinely may continue to do so.

V.

Our justification for limiting travel last year was couched in terms which should have given the GRC warning that our policy might well be changed in the future if the specific circumstances we cited were subject to change. We would plan to inform the GRC, South Viet-Nam, South Korea and the Japanese Government, as well as the UK—which will be responsible for protecting American citizens, in advance of our announcement dropping travel restrictions to mainland China.

We believe appropriate members of Congress should be informed in advance of our plans if you approve our recommended course of action.

Recommendation

That you authorize the omission of Communist China from the list to be published in March of countries to which travel restrictions will be renewed.[2]

---

[2] Rusk disapproved on March 11.

307. Telegram From the Department of State to the Embassy in the Republic of China[1]

Washington, March 9, 1968, 2340Z.

127768. Refs: [2 *document numbers not declassified*];[2] C. State 61104.[3]

1. Although our knowledge of mainland situation and of GRC resources limited, we seriously doubt GRC could take type of action CCK had indicated without exposing its involvement and thus giving rise to provocation in which US almost certainly would be implicated. At same time, we agree on inadvisability of totally negative response. Thus, we believe our response should re-emphasize primacy our interest in developing more complete information on mainland situation and should avoid appearance of approving CCK's specific plan.

2. With respect your recommendations ref B, para 7: a) we agree to informing CCK of US interest in any information GRC may develop concerning conditions in Kwangtung; b) we not in position provide any intelligence material on Kwangtung in addition to that which Embassy already passing through Dean–Wang channel and otherwise [*less than 1 line of source text not declassified*]; we would not want encourage GRC to expect special papers or appraisals on this subject; c) no objection [*less than 1 line of source text not declassified*] with GRC intelligence agencies responsible for political action indicated by CCK, but such liaison and consultation should be limited to intelligence function and, as noted in ref C, para 4, should not involve us in joint planning of such operations.

4. From CCK's description of operations he has in mind, we assume they would not involve providing arms to opposition groups, a course of action we would wish to discourage.

5. We were interested in CCK's apparent endorsement of Tibetan independence and wonder whether this is official GRC position. If so, might GRC be receptive to suggestion that it make some public statement to this effect?

Rusk

---

[1] Source: Department of State, Central Files, POL CHINA–US. Secret; Exdis. Drafted by Shoesmith, cleared in draft by Jacobson and Holdridge, and approved by Bundy.

[2] One of these messages is paraphrased in the attachment to Document 304.

[3] Document 283.

308. Telegram From the Department of State to the Embassy in the Republic of China[1]

Washington, April 11, 1968, 0034Z.

144916. Joint State/Defense message. Subject: Use of Ching Chuan Kang (CCK) as B–52 Weather Refuge Base.

1. We are considering request for subject use in event adverse weather factors require concurrent evacuation B–52 aircraft from Guam and Okinawa. The request is for safe haven purpose only and excludes B–52 aircraft launches in connection with combat operations.

2. Background:

a. Increase in B–52 sortie rates in SEA has required significant increase in forward deployment of B–52s in Guam and Okinawa as well as Thailand. The critical factor is that B–52s can be operated only at bases which have stabilized runway and taxi shoulders to support wing outriggers. Bases so constructed include those listed above and CCK and Yokota AB, Japan. Planning for evacuation KC–135s is not so limited since they do not have outrigger problem.

b. It is considered impractical to use Japanese base for political reasons. U-Tapao, Thailand, even with expanded ramps, can handle only very limited number extra B–52s. Hence, SAC cannot plan for coordinated evacuation of its total force when both Guam and Okinawa are covered by severe weather. On these occasions, which expected be infrequent, only alternative is return to Hawaii and CONUS with ensuing delays in mounting subsequent operations.

c. Temporary deployment this purpose would not require increase in personnel stationed at CCK.

3. For Taipei: Request country team comments on the proposal and assessment of probable GRC reaction to request.[2]

4. For AmConsul Hong Kong: Request your comments on proposal, particularly regarding likely Chicom reaction to deployment. Also, request any suggestions as to advisability and pitch of public announce-

---

[1] Source: Department of State, Central Files, DEF 15 CHINAT–US. Secret; Exdis. Drafted by Ridge; cleared by Steadman, Colonel Cavender of the Joint Staff, Colonel Miller of USAF, in draft by Shoesmith and Donald, and in substance by EA Deputy Assistant Secretary Philip C. Habib, Oscar V. Armstrong of EA/P, and Daniel N. Arzac of P; approved by EA Deputy Assistant Secretary G. McMurtrie Godley. Also sent to Hong Kong and repeated to JCS, CINCPAC, PACAF, USAF, SAC, COMUSTDC, and COMUSMACV.
[2] The Embassy commented in telegram 2869 from Taipei, April 20. (Ibid.)

ment, if such temporary deployments actually made, to off-set possible Chicom reaction.[3]

Rusk

---

[3] The Consulate General commented in telegram 5626 from Hong Kong, April 11. (Ibid.) Telegram 3047 from Taipei, May 10, reported the receipt of a May 7 letter from Wei stating GRC agreement to the proposed occasional use by B–52's of Ching Chuan Kang as a weather refuge. (Ibid.)

---

309. Memorandum From Alfred Jenkins of the National Security Council Staff to the President's Special Assistant (Rostow)[1]

Washington, April 30, 1968.

SUBJECT

U.S. Policy Toward the GRC

Attached is the most thoughtful paper on the vexing Taiwan problem which I have seen in some time.[2] It was prepared by Tom Shoesmith to serve as the basis for the discussion of Taiwan which consumed most of the second day of the two-day China Panel sessions. I recommend it in toto.

Shoesmith's basic thesis is that the "Taiwanization" of Taiwan is proceeding slowly but surely, and that this trend is in the U.S. interest. We need not indicate *overtly* that the U.S. foresees the possibility of an eventually independent Taiwan, and certainly our defense commitments should remain intact. At the same time, we should take steps 1) to encourage a reduced military burden for the Island, 2) to further its economic progress, and 3) to prompt an increased role in regional economic and political affairs. He advocates a more relaxed acceptance of ChiRep trends in the United Nations, although for the foreseeable future our own policy should not change. (He believes that most of the consider-

---

[1] Source: Johnson Library, National Security File, Country File, China, Vol. XII. Secret. A copy was sent to Jorden.
[2] The paper, entitled "U.S. Policy Toward the Republic of China: A New Perspective," drafted by Shoesmith on March 27, is not printed.

ations arguing for no change in our own ChiRep policy are likely to figure in the decisions of the majority of UN members—at least pending
changes on the mainland and in Taiwan which might then, in fact, cause
us to accept with equanimity some form of a "two Chinas" or "one China, one Taiwan" proposal.)

I am in general agreement with this paper, as were practically all of
the participants in the Panel, with the notable exception of George Taylor.
Lucian Pye and Paul Varg expressed some relatively minor reservations.

I mentioned in staff meeting that there was overwhelming belief in
the Panel that Taiwan was inexorably becoming more Taiwanized and
many, most notably John Fairbank, believed that ultimate independence
was the most likely prospect as trends could now be judged. (I have
asked CIA for a modest study of this trend.) In addition, there are increasing indications that Chiang Kai-shek has reassessed his own role in
history, that he has possibly accepted the unlikelihood of his return to the
mainland (although he can never say so), and that he is turning his energies toward showing how Chinese can come to grips with the 20th Century in a way in which he realized he could not have shown on the
mainland.

While I believe most of the thinking in this paper to be realistic, I
hope the "liberals" on this subject will not seize upon its long-term implications in order to "erase the GRC fiction" prematurely. In any event,
we certainly should not take any moves with respect to Taiwan in the
hopes of improving thereby our relations with the mainland. Present Peking leadership clearly does not consider that it is in Peking's interest to
improve relations with the United States. When the time comes for a
mainland leadership's advocacy of, or acquiescence in, improved relations, it is my contention that Taiwan and our commitments there may
well not stand seriously in the way.

Taiwan is growing in its own strength in almost every way, but it is
not yet strong enough or independent enough to weather safely an overt
shift in U.S. policy. The death of Chiang or an economic setback, for
instance, could cause to emerge power rivalries, policy differences and
mainlander-Taiwanese animosities which could seriously weaken the
polity, which will be fairly vulnerable for some time to come. We can perhaps keep long-term probabilities for Taiwan better in mind than we
have so far. And we can take certain practical steps, such as the tailoring
of MAP in the hopes of shaping the military establishment to accord with
its likely future role. (It is interesting to speculate on the possibly increased utility for purposes of regional reserve forces of an ultimate *Taiwan* military establishment as distinguished from a *GRC* military
establishment.)

Above all we should remember that the whole mainland–Taiwan
China tangle is not just a U.S. problem, but is one for the world, and par-

ticularly for our Asian friends. Our past policies, basically justifiable as you know I have considered them, have rather tended to convince the world that the China problem is pretty much a U.S. problem. The ultimate fate of Taiwan will depend not so much on what we do or do not do (short of scrapping our defense commitment) although our policy will certainly remain a major factor. Taiwan's fate will at least as much depend on what happens on the mainland and what course is taken on Taiwan—primarily by Chiang Ching-kuo—after the Gimo's death. Whether Ching-kuo then opts for a relatively popular base for government or looks to military support for a "tight little island" will in turn have considerable effect upon U.S. policy toward Taiwan.

AJ

310. Telegram From the Embassy in the Republic of China to the Department of State[1]

Taipei, May 14, 1968, 0757Z.

3071. Subj: Country Team Assessment of GRC Intentions. Ref: State 135828;[2] Taipei 2420.[3]

1. There have been no recent indications that the GRC intends to mount any major unilateral military operations against the mainland in the near future, though small-scale para-military or air operations could be launched without prior U.S. knowledge. Desultory planning for mainland recovery continues, but recent emphasis appears to have been rather on exploitation of propaganda windfall inherent in latest Maoist attacks on opposition figures as "KMT reactionaries".

2. GRC actions in the Taiwan Strait have continued to be defensive. As promised by Defense Minister Chiang Ching-kuo at the time of the *Pueblo* incident,[4] the GRC has taken no action that could be construed as

---

[1] Source: Department of State, Central Files, POL CHICOM–CHINAT. Secret; Noforn. Repeated to Hong Kong and CINCPAC for POLAD.

[2] See footnote 2, Document 242.

[3] Telegram 2420 from Taipei, March 12, stated that the previous 2 months had yielded no indications of GRC plans for unilateral actions against the mainland. (Ibid.)

[4] Telegram 2015 from Taipei, January 29, reported the promise made by Chiang that afternoon. (Ibid.)

provocative, and CAF patrols have only recently resumed previous practice of flying within the ChiCom-claimed twelve-mile territorial limit, with no unusual ChiCom reaction. In late February and early March GRC shore batteries on the Offshore Islands on several occasions fired on a number of small high-speed targets, with no hits reported. In view of the fact that none of these "targets" was visually sighted, it is likely that they were radar "ghosts" or clutter. The MND later admitted that they (MND) considered them to be products of "seasonal meteorological anomalies", since much the same type of activity occurred during the same period in 1967. The GRC has shown some concern over, but so far has not reacted to, apparent ChiCom augmentation of naval forces in the Fuchou–Matsu area, which could in time pose a threat to GRC resupply of Matsu.

3. After more than a year of quiescence, the problem of the KMT irregulars in the tri-border area has taken a new tack. Recent offers by the Thais and Burmese to the irregulars to serve against Communist insurgents have spurred the GRC into action. We know privately that GRC planning is underway to unify the various irregular groups to form an effective anti-Communist force in Burma under GRC control. Initially, only money and equipment would be supplied by the GRC, but the planners envisage a time when men would be sent to help the irregulars, at least during some operations. GRC officials feel that this plan would offer least political difficulty for the present and would be flexible enough for future contingency use of the irregulars. Actual GRC implementation of these plans would represent a marked shift from assurances previously given the USG on the KMT irregular question, but such implementation would in any event prove difficult, in our opinion, in view of the resistance irregular leaders have shown previous efforts to increase GRC control over them.

4. Contingency military plans for unilateral mainland recovery efforts are now continuing, but we know privately that top GRC leadership acknowledges the general unfeasibility of existing plans and is aware of GRC inability to take much major unilateral military initiative against the mainland.

5. We know that the drastic MAP cut is causing unease among the leaders of the GRC, but Defense Minister Chiang Ching-kuo and his subordinates have thus far outwardly taken the news calmly and have apparently moved to absorb cuts through reductions and careful budgeting. The GRC is taking measures to earn foreign exchange for procurement of military equipment through repair of battle-damaged U.S. equipment. Privately, we know that there are GRC plans to siphon off for military spending at least part of a $30 million amount supposedly allotted for scientific development.

6. The GRC has seized on recent Maoist attacks against opposition figures as being Kuomintang agents and supporters to try to breathe new life into the GRC's mainland recovery theme. This propaganda windfall has received heavy coverage in the local press, where Maoist denunciation of alleged association with the KMT has been played as proof of the vitality of KMT clandestine organizations on the mainland and as support for a GRC prognosis that Mao will be toppled by anti-Communists (stimulated by KMT agents), first linking up with anti-Maoists in the Chinese Communist Party, and finally with GRC forces from Taiwan. GRC press coverage has been drawn almost entirely from ChiCom propaganda output, however, with few claims of specific GRC agent activities. We have no reliable evidence supporting any significant increase of the GRC's modest clandestine activities on the China mainland.

McConaughy

---

311. Editorial Note

On May 18, 1968, the Chinese Embassy in Warsaw invited an officer from the U.S. Embassy to the Chinese Embassy and handed him a letter from Chargé Ch'en Tung to Ambassador Gronouski stating that since Ambassador Wang would not be able to return to Warsaw by May 29, the scheduled time of the next meeting, and "as there is nothing to discuss at present," the Chinese Government suggested that the 135th meeting be postponed until mid or late November. (Telegram 3219 from Warsaw, May 18; Department of State, Central Files, POL CHICOM–US) Telegram 167426 to Warsaw, May 20, transmitted the text of a letter to be conveyed to Ch'en in reply. The letter stated that the U.S. side continued to feel the talks were of value, that it was prepared to meet again with Ch'en on May 29 as an interim measure until Ambassador Wang was able to return, and that there were "several pressing matters we would wish to take up on this occasion." It urged adhering to the originally scheduled date. Telegram 3241 from Warsaw, May 21, reported that the letter had been delivered that morning. (Ibid.)

On May 24, at another meeting at the Chinese Embassy, Chinese Attaché Lo returned the U.S. letter of May 21. He read a prepared statement declaring that it could not be accepted because it addressed Ch'en Tung as the Chargé d'Affaires of the Office of the Chinese Representative to the U.S.-Chinese Ambassadorial Talks rather than as the Chargé d'Affaires of the Chinese People's Republic in Poland. Gronouski, who had been absent at the time the May 21 letter was sent, suggested to the Department that the letter should be addressed to Ch'en Tung, Chargé d'Affaires, Embassy of the People's Republic of China, Warsaw, the form of address used in a letter of March 6. (Telegram 3293 from Warsaw, May 24; ibid.) Telegram 170093 to Warsaw, May 24, concurred, and telegram 3309 from Warsaw of the same date reported that the letter had been handed to Lo that day, along with another stating that Gronouski would soon be leaving Warsaw, leaving Deputy Chief of Mission Walter E. Jenkins, Jr., as Chargé d'Affaires. (Ibid.)

On May 28, at the Chinese Embassy, Lo conveyed a letter from Ch'en Tung to Jenkins stating that U.S. arguments for holding the meeting as scheduled were "untenable." It stated that the U.S. Government had recently "stepped up its military provocations and war threats against the Chinese people" while making "various gestures of sham relaxation to hoodwink the people of the world" and that under the circumstances, there was no point in holding the meeting. (Telegram 3335 from Warsaw, May 28; ibid.) Telegram 171995 to Warsaw, May 28, 1968, instructed the Embassy to express orally strong regret at the tone of the Chinese letter and to reject as baseless the allegations made in it, emphasizing that the meetings were not a "gesture" nor were they designed to "produce a good effect" but to deal privately with problems between the two countries. In addition, the Embassy was to convey a written response proposing a meeting on June 26 or July 10. (Ibid.) Jenkins reported in telegram 3364 from Warsaw, May 28, that the Embassy had done so. (Ibid.)

On June 27, at the Chinese Embassy, Lo transmitted a letter from Ch'en to Jenkins insisting that the meeting be postponed until mid or late November. (Telegram 3745 from Warsaw, June 28; ibid.)

312. National Intelligence Estimate[1]

NIE 13–9–68   Washington, May 23, 1968.

THE SHORT-TERM OUTLOOK IN COMMUNIST CHINA

The Problem

To estimate the main trends and outlook in China over the next year or so.

Conclusions

A. The situation inside Communist China is still highly fluid and the outlook uncertain. Disorder, confusion, and unrest continue but have been reduced since the high water mark last summer. Nevertheless, the ranks of those alienated by the Greater Proletarian Cultural Revolution have grown; the costs in political control, social discipline, and economic progress have far outweighed the gains. Though Mao was successful in breaking high-level opposition in the old party apparatus, in its broader aspects his Cultural Revolution has been a failure and we believe it will be gradually phased out.

B. Mao still appears to be the central figure and source of basic policy. Mao and the regime are officially committed to the reconstruction of a new framework for administrative and political control. On balance, we believe that the trend will be toward regaining some stability, in part because of the increased influence of the moderate elements in Peking. But there still will be sharp twists and turns, occasional crises, and disorder and turmoil at various levels which will reflect strong differences among factions and leaders over policies and tactics.

C. The military will remain Peking's most reliable instrument over the coming year. As the only cohesive force with a nationwide system of command and control, the military will have to serve a variety of admin-

---

[1] Source: Department of State, S/S Files: Lot 90 D 110. Secret; Controlled Dissem. A note on the cover sheet states that it was submitted by Helms and prepared by the Central Intelligence Agency, the intelligence organizations of the Departments of State and Defense, and the National Security Agency. All members of the U.S. Intelligence Board concurred in the estimate on May 23 except the AEC and FBI representatives, who abstained because the subject was outside their jurisdiction. A May 22 memorandum from INR/REA Director Fred Greene to Hughes, filed with the source text, states that the estimate was the product of very lengthy discussions reflecting a long-standing disagreement within the Intelligence Community over the nature of the relationships among the top Chinese leaders. The key question, according to Greene, was whether Mao Tse-tung remained the architect of basic Chinese Communist policy and the prime mover in the regime or whether the underlying political dynamic was a factional struggle with Mao playing a relatively restricted role.

istrative and control functions. The scope of the rebuilding effort—political, economic, and social—may require the heavy support of the People's Liberation Army (PLA) for some years to come. Military dominance in political life may become institutionalized, particularly if political reconstruction bogs down in violence and disarray requiring the repressive force of the PLA. The corollary to this increased political role is the diversion of the PLA from normal military routine and a consequent reduction in its military readiness.

D. The damage to the economy as a direct result of the Cultural Revolution includes depressed industrial production, a delay in modernization and economic growth, aggravated labor problems, setbacks in the training of technical specialists, and a general hiatus in the formulation of new economic policies and plans. The cumulative damage to the economy of prolonged political turmoil will not be easily or quickly repaired. Whatever the political course for 1968, agricultural output is not likely to repeat last year's very good harvests, which benefited from exceptionally good weather. At best, China can hope only to restore stability and balance to the economy in 1968, foregoing any prospect of expansion. Indeed, there is a possibility that a reduction in food output, combined with problems of collection and distribution, could cause a serious food shortage by 1969, which in turn could have serious political repercussions.

E. "Red Guard diplomacy" cost Peking last year in relations with Communist as well as non-Communist regimes. Since last summer, however, the regime has taken steps to reduce the violent and provocative influence of internal affairs on foreign relations. In the main, the Cultural Revolution has not altered the general line of Chinese policy abroad; it still remains revolutionary in tone but cautious and prudent in deeds. Preoccupation with internal affairs is likely to relegate foreign concerns to a secondary role.

F. A major uncertainty in any estimate of China's future is the problem of Mao's passing. The events of the past two years have made it more likely that Mao's departure will usher in a stormy and possibly protracted period in which policy differences and power aspirations will continue to fuel a leadership struggle. Mao's legacy is likely to be an enfeebled party, a confused bureaucracy, and a divided and harried leadership. In our view the ultimate result will be to accelerate the rejection of Mao's doctrines and policies.

[Here follows the Discussion portion of the estimate.]

313.   Memorandum From Alfred Jenkins of the National Security Council Staff to the President's Special Assistant (Rostow)[1]

Washington, June 7, 1968.

SUBJECT

China Items of Interest

1.   I have learned confidentially and informally that the proposal for the recognition of Mongolia[2] has been signed off by Ambassador Bohlen and the Under Secretary and is now on the Secretary's desk. You may be hearing from him on it. I should think he will want the President's views on it, and it may be a fit subject for a Tuesday luncheon meeting. The attached Tokyo telegram (Tab A)[3] reports recent conversations by UPI correspondent Axelbank with Tsedenbal and the Mongolian People's Republic Deputy Foreign Minister in Ulan Bator, in which both indicated that the MPR would welcome recognition by the United States.

2.   A trade package, concerning which I have talked at length with Bob Barnett for many months, is in abeyance largely because of reaction of peripheral friendly countries to the President's March 31 statement and the Paris talks (i.e., fears that we are becoming soft on communism). As you know, I believe there are a few limited steps in the trade field which we could and should take any time now—especially with the Paris developments. If there should come a Vietnam settlement and either one of the two likely outcomes of the Cultural Revolution, I think we might want to attempt a bit more. Doing so must assume prior groundwork. Dana Robinson (correspondence at Tab B) has been doing some useful work with the academic community, the business community and to some extent the Hill with respect to China trade, largely in the post-Vietnam context. I think he has used very good judgment and has been working in our long-term interest. He has kept me well informed. I am sorry to hear that he has met with such negative response that he is giving up his efforts. We are effectively denying the Chinese Communists almost nothing because of our trade restrictions. Of course we should continue to make it hard for them to get certain things, but Western Europe and Japan as well as European communist countries are in general all too ready to fill the breach. I am convinced that Japan especially will increase its lenient ways.

---

[1] Source: Johnson Library, National Security File, Country File, China, Vol. XII. Confidential.

[2] Document 347.

[3] Telegram 8714 from Tokyo, May 28. None of the tabs is printed.

There have been several signs that the Chinese Communists are regularizing their international relations and attempting to repair the damage of Red Guard diplomacy. It is too soon to speak in terms of a revival of the "Bandung spirit" in Chinese Communist politics, but something of the sort could well come and make it very hard for us to deal with others' lessened restrictions on China whether it be concerning trade or ChiRep. Meanwhile, it is difficult in most people's view, I believe, to square the extreme restrictions in our trade policy with our desire for more contact and a freer flow of people, ideas and goods. We would, of course, get no response from Peking as yet, but I do believe that the limited steps proposed in Barnett's package might well hasten the day when we would be able to take bigger steps in safety and with profit.

3. At Tab C is Peking's shameless exploitation of the Kennedy assassination.

Al

---

314. Telegram From the Department of State to the Embassy in Canada[1]

Washington, June 10, 1968, 1538Z.

179549. Subj: Approach to Canadian Ambassador Regarding Canadian Policy Initiatives Toward Communist China.

1. Assistant Secretary Bundy called in Amb. Ritchie June 7 to discuss with him US concern over implications of possible Canadian initiatives toward Communist China.

2. Mr. Bundy said that the Secretary had asked him in low-key way to run through points of concern to the United States and proposed therefore to mention the various problems we see as Canada moves to possible recognition Communist China, as suggested by Prime Minister's policy statement on Canadian foreign policy and other remarks by Prime Minister and Mr. Sharp. We have noted, of course, Mr. Sharp's references

---

[1] Source: Department of State, Central Files, POL CAN–CHICOM. Secret. Drafted by Donald on June 7, cleared by Straus in EUR/CAN, and Thayer in EA/ROC, and approved by William Bundy. Repeated to 12 posts, CINCPAC, US NATO (Brussels), USUN, and CINCPAC for POLAD.

to taking into account the Government of Taiwan in pursuing recognition of Peking.

3. Mr. Bundy said that the first problem that we see is the pattern exemplified in French experience with recognition of Peking. At that time Peking made it totally clear to Paris that a continued relationship with Taipei was out of the question. Taipei, primarily for reasons of face, actually broke relations with France but did this only after being informed by French that with the arrival of Chinese Communist Mission their Embassy in Paris would lose its "raison d'etre." Mr. Bundy gave the Ambassador copy of a chronology encompassing US understanding of what transpired in course of French recognition of Peking.

4. Primary concern to US is the status of Taipei. It is doing a very good job, Mr. Bundy said, and juridically, morally, and in regional terms it is a going concern and important to Free World position.

5. Mr. Bundy said that it might be of interest to Canadian Government that we have been confidentially informed by French that in view of recent anti-French statements by Communist China, they are seriously considering not returning their Ambassador to Peking. He mentioned this, Mr. Bundy said, to indicate roller coaster nature of relationship with Chinese Communists.

6. A secondary but important point involved the timing of possible Canadian initiatives. This was involved with the Viet-Nam situation and Paris talks. Such an initiative by the Canadians would give encouragement to hard liners, both within Communist China itself and in Hanoi, and this might well rub off on North Vietnamese position in the Paris talks. The degree of damage to be anticipated here obviously depended on the terms on which the Canadians dealt with the ChiComs.

7. Bundy said that another important factor which again depended on these terms was the blow which Taipei would suffer and which might be increased if other countries were tempted to follow the Canadian example. There would be concern, particularly in East Asia, both over the blow to Taipei and over the increased prestige which Peking would gain from Canadian action.

8. In conclusion, Mr. Bundy said he wanted to indicate to Canadian Government our sense of concern, a concern based in large part on what happened when the French began a similar initiative. Mr. Bundy referred to Mr. Sharp's conversation with the Secretary and reiterated our hope that the Canadians would talk to us before they took any action vis-á-vis Communist China.

9. In response, Ambassador Ritchie said that he would report points made by Mr. Bundy and the concern which he expressed. He would like to say, however, that he did not believe that the parallel with France was necessarily applicable to Canada. In a very real sense, he believed that Mr. Sharp felt that Canada could only find out what the Chi-

Coms would have in mind by trying. He questioned the effect such an initiative would have on the Paris talks, but agreed that extent this influence would be governed by terms of Canadian initiative. He concluded by stating it goes without saying that Canadian Government would talk to us before taking any action.

Rusk

---

315. **Telegram From the Embassy in the Republic of China to the Department of State**[1]

Taipei, June 26, 1968, 1110Z.

3513. Subject: Conversation with Gimo on U.S. attitudes toward China issues.

1. At President Chiang's request I called on him at his Yangmingshan residence June 25. Gimo's purpose was to convey his deep concern about implications June 22 *New York Times* editorial on China policy, and developing trend as he saw it of U.S. thinking on China issues. In particular he was disturbed about editorial's assertion that USG considering urging President Chiang to withdraw GRC forces from Offshore Islands. Gimo said this type of statement, together with Anderson article, could encourage Chinese Communists to attack Offshores. He urged USG to issue statement repudiating editorial's insinuation that USG is considering urging a withdrawal of GRC from Quemoy and Matsu.

2. In conversation which lasted nearly two hours Gimo dwelt on what he interpreted as alarming trends U.S. policy and public attitudes towards China. He cited editorial's mention of Leonard Marks speech in early May and Katzenbach May 22 speech[2] and referred to Jack Anderson articles of last February on alleged high level USG discussions of China policy matters. He said he was particularly incensed by last para *NY Times* editorial which advocated withdrawal U.S. opposition to Chi-

---

[1] Source: Department of State, Central Files, POL CHINAT–US. Secret; Priority; Limdis.

[2] Reference is to a speech on China by Under Secretary Katzenbach before the National Press Club on May 21. For text, see the Department of State *Bulletin,* June 10, 1968, pp. 737–740.

Com entry to UN and initiation of steps to recognize Peking as seat of government for mainland China. Editorial stated: "This does not mean abandoning Taiwan, but does involve recognizing Taipei for what it is—and what it is not." Gimo said editorial is insulting and has aroused strongest resentment among Chinese people. He reasoned some of contents NY Times editorial also reflected views some influential USG officials. He said editorials such as this make Chinese have serious doubts about U.S. policy towards China and Chinese cannot help but resent what U.S. is doing. He bluntly asked what was more in interests of USG—encouragement of ChiCom regime or friendly relations with GRC?

3. President stressed repeatedly that Quemoy and Matsu were integral part of China and could not be separated from territory of China. He said retention of Quemoy and Matsu were absolutely imperative for defense of Taiwan and Pescadores and GRC would fight to last man to defend Offshores. If Quemoy and Matsu were lost, he thought it was questionable whether Taiwan and Pescadores could be successfully defended even with U.S. air and naval power. Gimo said if U.S. should adopt views attributed to U.S. officials in Anderson article and give up defense of the Offshores, this would have extremely bad effect on morale, would incite ChiCom attack on Offshores, would give ChiComs momentum required for successful attack on Taiwan, and would have lasting effects even more serious than Vietnam war. In addition, hardliners in NVN would be encouraged to stiffen position at Paris Peace Talks and to intensify war.

4. President Chiang urged U.S. to clarify once and for all its basic position towards status of Offshores. Gimo repeatedly returned to this theme and urged that USG for its own interests and for interests security in Asia should openly state that NY Times editorial has no foundation in fact and is completely groundless. He stated "for the sake of China and the U.S. and our mutual interests the insinuations contained in the NY Times editorial must be denied by USG. Only by doing this can damage already caused by editorial and Anderson articles be minimized." Gimo added that not only had NY Times editorial caused considerable concern here but many leading members of U.S. Congress had made appeasing statements concerning Communist China. This was why he thought it important for USG to make concise, resolute statement clarifying U.S. position toward Offshores along lines that Offshores are integral part of territory of Republic of China and U.S. Government has no right to determine their disposition. He referred with warm approbation to Secretary Rusk's statement concerning Taiwan[3] which was along similar lines and

---

[3] Reference is to Secretary Rusk's remarks at a press conference on June 21; for text, see ibid., July 8, 1968, pp. 33–38.

said there was even more reason for U.S. to make such a statement about Offshores since they were undisputed Chinese territory long before Taiwan was retroceded at end of World War II.

5. President warned that if USG did not come out with such a statement he seriously estimated that Communist China would be likely to launch an attack on the Offshore Islands between now and inauguration new U.S. President. He felt Peking would misinterpret *NY Times* editorial, Anderson articles, and other official statements. Partly for internal reasons—to draw dissident factions together, and partly because apparent weakness or at least uncertainty U.S. posture—ChiComs would think they had golden opportunity to attach Offshores. Gimo then added that speaking as a friend, present U.S. attitude towards Viet Cong, NVN, and Communist China appeared to Asian people as reminiscent of the attitude Chamberlain had adopted toward Nazi Germany prior WW II. He dwelt on this point at some length. He then said he believed if U.S. continues with present irresolute attitudes it would lead to World War Three, since Communist China will be encouraged to pursue more aggressive designs.

6. I told the President I appreciated his willingness to give frank expression to his views and I respected the depth of his convictions. I then said that I felt he was giving too much weight to both the *NY Times* editorial and the Anderson articles, that neither had any standing as far as U.S. Government is concerned. Repeated that *NY Times* editorials, like all other expressions of our free press, represented private views of newspaper and not official USG policy or positions. I said that I felt editorial was regrettable but it was nothing new for him and many others to read unpalatable views in *NY Times* or indeed in other papers. I told Pres that as he knew there were various shades of opinion in U.S. concerning China but, the administration supported by the Congress, was steadfast on basic policy as it now stands.

7. I then mentioned that Gimo knew we had not approached his government to suggest evacuation Quemoy or Matsu. I told him that there were officials at lower levels in the U.S. Government who constantly write background papers and think pieces embodying a great variety of views on various contingency situations, but these papers do not constitute policy. I said that there should be no concern because at the policy making levels of the government our policy towards China was well established. The expressions of editorial opinion published in our leading newspapers may have some influence but they do not necessarily represent any majority opinion. I told the President that in his own experience through the years he has been able to put up with a great deal of press commentary of this type. I expressed hope that President could continue to live with expressed views that were contrary to ROC's policy. I said that Washington was inclined to believe it was not useful in general

for USG to refute or even take cognizance of questionable editorials on foreign policy issues. It would be a confusing and unprofitable business and would draw added attention to these editorials. I said I doubted if it would be possible to have a rebuttal statement issued such as the President desired, but I would transmit his request to Washington without delay.

8. I referred to his remarks on appeasement and stated that it pained me very much, with our very high casualty rate in Vietnam and with our heavy additional defense burdens in Korea, in Western Europe and elsewhere in the world, to hear the President intimate that the United States is pursuing a Chamberlain type appeasement policy. I told the President that when we are making such heavy sacrifices in the cause of freedom and standing firm on all the cardinal principles of freedom we are defending, any characterization of "appeasement" was inappropriate and could not be justified.

9. I then referred to various speeches that have been made by top-level U.S. officials holding out the possibility of additional contacts with mainland China. I told the President that those who were advocating seeking limited contacts are not thinking in terms of formal diplomatic relations or enhancement of the international position of Communist China. Rather they were thinking in terms of establishing a better understanding with the Chinese people on the mainland, his people. I said there is a fairly widespread desire in the U.S. for cultural, intellectual, medical and press contacts with the people of the mainland. This however was not equivalent to the advocacy of formal recognition of the Chi-Com Government nor the acceptance or condoning of the Chinese Communist regime or its policies. I suggested that over the long run such people-to-people contacts, if they could be brought about, might provide some means of offsetting the dangerous spread of poisonous anti-U.S. feeling and misunderstanding fomented by the Communists in a whole new generation on the mainland.

10. Memcon will be forwarded by airgram.[4] Insights and recommendations about Gimo's position and request will be subject of septel.[5]

McConaughy

---

[4] The memorandum of conversation was enclosed with airgram A–742 from Taipei, July 2. (Department of State, Central Files, POL 1 CHINAT–US) Airgram A–807 from Taipei, July 26, forwarded a summary record of the conversation prepared by the Foreign Ministry. (Ibid., POL CHINAT–US)

[5] McConaughy sent a message to Rusk and Bundy in telegram 3554 from Taipei, June 28, calling their attention to Chiang's request. He commented further in telegram 3594, July 2. (Both ibid.)

316.   Memorandum From Alfred Jenkins of the National Security Council Staff to the President's Special Assistant (Rostow)[1]

Washington, July 2, 1968.

SUBJECT

China Mainland Situation

Since the Wuhan episode of last summer, the conservatives in general have had their way more—often with Army collusion or acquiescence. This has concerned the Maoists, and Mao on June 2 issued one of his infrequent delphic "instructions" to the effect that the masses were to be given their rein at all costs. This has resulted, not unexpectedly, in a rise in fighting throughout June. The level has not yet reached that of last summer, but it is well on the way, and we have again a situation which could deteriorate fairly rapidly.

Perhaps the chief difference between last summer and now is that Cultural Revolution dislocations have begun to bring suffering to larger and larger numbers of citizens. Illegal immigrants into Hong Kong give most frequently as reasons for fleeing, unemployment and food shortages. Lack of raw materials, labor troubles and not infrequently sabotage have reduced production in many enterprises to the point where salaries cannot be met. We have reports of both grave robberies (especially in rural areas, valuables are still often buried with the dead) and the sale of children—both typical phenomena in times of crisis in China. (One woman spoke of being offered the equivalent of about $45.00 for her son, but she was holding out for more.) Vehicles, even public buses, are being stolen for use in factional fighting, and bicycles are at such a premium in some places where public transportation has ceased to function, that they are being wrested out from under the riders.

Serious floods are reported from six provinces in Southeast China. The early rice crop in Kwangtung may be off as much as 10–15%, and planting of late rice will be delayed.

All three North-South rail lines have had interruptions for considerable periods in June from floods, landslides and fighting around the stations. (We are not sure whether military-manned priority trains are getting through, where "acts of God" are not the cause of the interruptions.) Many letters mention that the writer is stranded away from home or work because of lack of transportation.

---

[1] Source: Johnson Library, National Security File, Country File, China, Vol. XIII. Secret. A copy was sent to Jorden. Rostow sent the memorandum, along with some intelligence reports, to the President with a covering memorandum of the same date, noting that the disarray in China might help explain "the Soviet willingness to proceed with arms control measures with the U.S. and to interject itself so deeply in the Vietnam affair." (Ibid.)

No one knows what all this will ultimately mean, of course. However, one is now tempted to alter the British witticism of last fall to the effect "the situation is excellent, but not hopeless." Things must be beginning to look pretty hopeless to the average Chinese. If the regime could bring itself to give the conservatives their way, things could quiet down, but there are no signs that the regime will do that. Almost anything could happen in coming months, but the best bet still is that a portion of the military will get fed up and take matters into their own hands. If the Maoists' opposition should begin to jell, we should see radio stations taken over. So far, this has happened in only a couple of places very temporarily some months ago. It was premature.

AJ

---

317. Telegram From the Embassy in the Republic of China to the Department of State[1]

Taipei, July 9, 1968, 1046Z.

3656. Subject: Rising GRC concern over Offshore Islands. Ref: Taipei 3641.[2]

1. Heightened concern was expressed by Defense Minister Chiang Ching-kuo (CCK) July 8 in conversation with Major General R.G. Ciccolella about possible ChiCom attack on Offshore Islands (reftel). There have been similar recent expressions of concern about Offshores by President Chiang to retiring CINCPAC, Admiral Sharp, on June 20 (Taipei 3467[3] and 3612[4]) and to me on June 25 (Taipei 3513 and 3554).[5] In addition, FonMin's conversation with me on July 2 (Taipei 3592)[6] and July 8 conversation of Defense Minister with Vice Admiral John L. Chew, Commander United States–Taiwan Defense Command, focused on aspects of

---

[1] Source: Department of State, Central Files, POL CHICOM–CHINAT. Secret; Limdis. Repeated to CINCPAC.

[2] Telegram 3641 from Taipei, July 8, reported a conversation between MAAG Chief Major General R.G. Ciccolella and Chiang Ching-kuo. (Ibid.)

[3] Dated June 22. (Ibid.)

[4] Not found.

[5] Document 315 and footnote 5 thereto.

[6] Dated July 2. (Department of State, Central Files, POL CHINAT–US)

the same subject. CCK's conversation with Admiral Chew, expressing Defense Minister's anxiety about possible new ChiCom aggressive moves, included suggestion that revision of Plan Rochester should have an annex to cover contingency of possible combined defense of Offshore Islands, in event U.S. should find such defense related to defense of Taiwan and Penghu.

2. This high level worry about possible ChiCom attack on Offshores is by GRC's own admission not based on any hard evidence of ChiCom plans or preparations but only on GRC leadership's understanding of Chinese Communist leadership's tactics, motivations and psychology, as applied to current international situation. This anxiety has thus far been evidenced only by private statements of President Chiang, CCK and ForMin to top U.S. officials. There has been no evidence of general concern on this topic at lower levels in the GRC.

3. President Chiang has probably himself initiated a great deal of this concern by his reaction to the Jack Anderson series of articles last February–March, and by the *New York Times* editorial of June 22. His analysis is that the Communists may be emboldened to strike by absence of any U.S. refutation of *NY Times* editorial or Anderson stories, combined with what he interprets as other signs of U.S. reluctance to take a firm stand vis-à-vis the Chinese Communists.

4. There can be no question but that President Chiang would like very much to take this opportunity to solicit from the U.S. some type of public statement of acceptance or recognition of the GRC presence on the Offshore Islands. Subsequent follow-up consultations sought by Defense Minister and Minister of Foreign Affairs are designed to continue the pressure in this direction.

5. I continue to regard it as desirable from standpoint most effective conduct of our relations here that low-key statement be made by the Department's spokesman that would help to assuage GRC fears about the Anderson articles and the *NY Times* editorial statement about Offshores. Such a statement could easily avoid any confusion of our clear position as to exclusion of Offshores from treaty area. To be effective for these purposes, I believe a statement would need to be public. It could take the form of a simple response to an arranged question that those islands are Chinese territory and their fate is not ours to dictate.

McConaughy

318. Telegram From the Department of State to the Embassy in the Republic of China[1]

Washington, July 12, 1968, 2114Z.

201378. Ref: A. Taipei 3513.[2] B. Taipei 3554.[3] C. Taipei 3592 and 3594.[4]

1.   We have considered carefully your suggestion Ref B for some statement which would be responsive to President Chiang's request as outlined Ref A. As you made clear to Chiang, we continue to believe it would not be useful for Department to take issue with such speculative articles as Anderson series or editorials taking various positions on China policy. At time Anderson articles appeared, Department spokesman set forth our position as clearly as possible (State 133316 and 135413).[5] We believe it would be unwise and misleading to amplify that position in any way which suggests we regard GRC position on offshores in same light as its position on Taiwan. Further, to raise such issue at this time or to go beyond Secretary's June 21 statement with respect to our overtures toward Communist China would risk making Offshore Islands and China policy issues subject of partisan controversy with consequences that might be even more disturbing to GRC than events which have prompted Chiang's current concern.

2.   We concur with general thrust your response to Chiang and particularly appreciate your entirely appropriate rebuttal of Chiang's unwarranted remarks concerning our posture toward North Vietnam and Communist China. Although we unable comply with Chiang's request, we wish encourage him to engage in frank discussions with you, since it may provide opportunity to exercise some leavening influence on his views and reactions to current developments bearing on US–GRC relations. For that purpose, you requested convey orally following message from Secretary to President Chiang.

3.   *Begin message.* Ambassador McConaughy has reported in detail the observations which you were good enough to make to him on June 25. I appreciate, as always, a frank exposition of your views and I have given them the most careful thought and attention. I hope that you will continue to meet with our Ambassador from time to time for such frank discussions on matters of mutual interest and concern.

---

[1] Source: Department of State, Central Files, POL CHINAT–US. Secret; Priority; Limdis. Drafted by Shoesmith; cleared by Brown and Walt Rostow, and in draft by Donald, Kreisberg, Armstrong, Walt Rostow, Steadman, and Deputy Assistant Secretary for Public Affairs Robert J. McCloskey; and approved and initialed by Rusk.

[2] Document 315.

[3] See footnote 5, Document 315.

[4] See footnote 6, Document 317 and footnote 5, Document 315.

[5] Telegrams 133316 and 135413 to Taipei, March 20 and 23. (Department of State, Central Files, POL CHINAT–US)

4. I have noted your anxiety concerning certain speculative articles and editorials concerning U.S. policy and wish to share with you my own thoughts on the questions you raised about their significance and impact. The Department of State has for many years indicated that the position of the United States Government concerning the offshore islands is that expressed specifically and solely in the Mutual Defense Treaty of 1954 and the Joint Congressional Resolution of 1955. That remains our position. With respect to the limited conversations which we have had with the authorities of Mainland China, we have repeatedly made clear that such conversations in no way imply any change in our commitments to or any diminution of our concern for the Republic of China and Taiwan.

5. The speculative articles and editorials which you brought to the Ambassador's attention in no way qualify the position of the United States Government. They attracted no significant attention in the United States and I have seen no public discussion here arising from them. I do not believe, therefore, that any useful purpose would be served by taking public issue with such press comments, beyond that which has already occurred. Quite frankly, it would not be in the interest of either of our countries to contribute to a controversial discussion on a matter which is not being actively debated at the present time.

6. I also have noted your concern that such speculation may encourage Chinese Communists to launch an attack on offshores and your estimate that such an attack may be imminent. We are of course alert to possibility that Chinese Communists may attempt to renew tensions in Taiwan Strait, and we are especially appreciative of GRC care to avoid provoking such action. We have no indications from other sources, however, that Chinese Communists intend provoke incident in Strait or are planning such moves. We will continue to keep this matter under closest scrutiny and would appreciate any intelligence information GRC may develop.

7. Since we are very anxious that you always feel free to be frank with us, I hope that you will understand frankness on our part as well. I found it difficult to understand your assessment of the reaction of people in Asia to U.S. policies in Vietnam and toward Communist China. The American people have accepted almost 300,000 casualties since the end of World War II in trying to assist our friends in maintaining their independence against aggression. In this very year of 1968, more than 9,000 of our young men have been killed and more than 60,000 have been wounded. If these sacrifices cannot assure our friends and allies as to both our attitude and our determination, I do not see how the achievement of a sense of assurance is possible. Certainly between such close allies as the United States and the Republic of China there should be no doubt on this score. The expression of such doubts, in the face of the

extraordinary sacrifices we are being called upon to make, would not be received well by the American people and would give a powerful stimulation to those voices among us who are urging isolation and withdrawal from our responsibilities in other parts of the world. *End message.*

8. Please express to the President the Secretary's highest esteem and personal regards.

9. If you think desirable, you may leave the above text with President Chiang as an oral memorandum.

Rusk

---

319. Telegram From the Embassy in the Republic of China to the Department of State[1]

Taipei, July 17, 1968, 1030Z.

3761. Subject: MAP aspects of Gimos's July 15 conversation with Ambassador. Ref: A) State 201378;[2] B) Taipei 3730.[3]

1. During latter part of conversation reported Ref B, President Chiang turned to discussion of U.S. military assistance to GRC generally. After referring to the imminent ChiCom threat he considered to be posed to the Offshores, the Gimo observed that the defense capability of the GRC was "far from adequate" and needed to be expeditiously improved.

2. Stating that he was not making any formal request for increased military aid from the United States, he added that he hoped that all defense items, the supply of which had already been agreed upon by the two governments, could be delivered as soon as possible. He thought it

---

[1] Source: Department of State, Central Files, POL CHINAT–US. Secret; Priority; Limdis.

[2] Document 318.

[3] McConaughy reported in telegram 3730 from Taipei, July 15, that he had delivered Rusk's message to Chiang, who had accepted the decision but urged that some of the reassurance reflected in the message be incorporated in some forthcoming high-level official speech. Chiang expressed continuing concern about a possible attack on the Offshore Islands and stated that the people of Asia did not doubt U.S. policy in Vietnam but were "haunted" by the memory of the 1946 Marshall mission to China. (Department of State, Central Files, POL CHINAT–US)

urgent that Nike–Hercules and Hawk ground-to-air missiles be expeditiously supplied in increased numbers in order to help face the ChiCom threat.

3. Speaking of the MAP program in general, the President observed that U.S. military aid to the Republic of China during the next fiscal year was expected to fall below the U.S. fifty million dollar level. This, he said, was "too little". Even with the favorable U.S. policy on credit sales, the total available would be "not adequate". He expressed his hope that I would pass on these statements as "a casual remark".

4. I promised to do so, but took the opportunity to review briefly the recent Congressional mood on military aid generally and to mention the other programs of the U.S. Government—such as expediting credit sales, aiding the GRC in its own military production capabilities, and transferring some used equipment from Vietnam and elsewhere—all of which should help to meet GRC needs.

5. When discussing the danger of imminent ChiCom attack on the Offshore Islands, President Chiang emphasized at several points the urgent need to revise Plan Rochester. I noted that TDC and MAAG, and CINCPAC were presently working with the Ministry of National Defense and other interested GRC agencies on the first draft of a prospective revision.

6. Mentioning the growing Chinese Communist Air Force capability, the President expressed his hope that by next year the GRC would have at least one squadron of the latest model high capability fighter planes—such as recently supplied Korea. (Later discussion revealed that the plane in question was the F4C Phantom.) I remarked that the F5 planes now in use and programmed in larger numbers, appear to be very appropriate, efficient and relatively economical for the GRC's requirements. The Gimo responded that the F5 was good, and he appreciated our current efforts to make it available to the GRC but he wished to reiterate that he still felt that one squadron of the higher capacity fighters to lead the Chinese Air Force would greatly help the morale in his armed forces and the ability of the CAF to repel a Communist attack. He suggested that perhaps there should be some reallocation of resources, if necessary, to make this possible.

7. The President noted that while the GRC had not contributed troops to Vietnam, it was shouldering a major responsibility by tying down Communist troops on the South China coast. The level of military aid, he hoped, would be determined with this consideration in mind.

8. *Comment:* President Chiang's remarks at this meeting were among the most direct that the GRC has thus far made about recent MAP cuts. For the first time, the GRC at a high level has officially labeled our anticipated Military Assistance Program as "not adequate". By inference, the Gimo was apparently drawing a comparison between the level

of U.S. military assistance to his own government and that being provided to Korea. The Gimo apparently was seeking by this means to underscore the significance he felt the U.S. should give GRC efforts in the Far East, including in particular its contribution in reducing pressures or potential pressures on the U.S. position in Vietnam by immobilizing large numbers of ChiCom troops opposite Taiwan Strait.

McConaughy

320. Memorandum From Marshall Wright of the National Security Council Staff to the President's Special Assistant (Rostow)[1]

Washington, July 25, 1968.

Walt:

Attached is the study you wanted of the political implications of China's deteriorating economy.[2]

In sum, your instincts were pretty sound. It is State's judgment that the economic disruption is "approaching crisis proportions."

—Agriculture—The 1967 crop was the best in years, and served to insulate the regime from the effects of the Cultural Revolution. This year, however, the weather is bad. There is a drought in north China and serious floods in widespread areas in the south. The Yangtze may be on a rampage.

Domestic fertilizer production is way down, perhaps as much as 50%. Record fertilizer purchases from Japan and Europe will arrive too late to help the 1968 crop much.

—Industry—Production dropped about 15% in 1967. Production is way down in coal, the major energy source. The transportation system and the major industrial centers have been particularly hard hit by Cultural Revolution disorders.

—Foreign trade—The troubles with the industrial sector are strongly reflected in foreign trade figures. There was a 12% drop in exports in 1967, and in the first half of 1968 exports to Japan were down 32%.

---

[1] Source: Johnson Library, National Security File, Country File, China, Vol. XIII. Secret.

[2] The attachment, entitled "Political Implications of Communist China's Deteriorating Economy," unsigned and undated, is not printed.

—Political implications—The political impact of the declining economy will be magnified by the breakdown of Communist China's effective control. The prospects are for an economic mess approaching that which followed the Great Leap Forward, but without the strong central control which enabled the regime to diffuse the problem evenly throughout the country. Local famine—perhaps widespread famine—is possible. This should lead to a strengthening of pragmatic elements both in Peking and in the provinces. If widespread famine becomes a reality, there will probably be cause for international assistance. Without a major reorientation of policies, however, Peking is not likely to be responsive to offers of assistance from the United States.

Marshall

---

321.   National Intelligence Estimate[1]

NIE 13–3–68   Washington, August 1, 1968.

COMMUNIST CHINA'S GENERAL PURPOSE AND AIR DEFENSE FORCES

The Problem

To assess the impact of Communist China's political turmoil on its military establishment and to estimate the capabilities of the general purpose and air defense forces.

Conclusions

A. Communist China's armed forces (known collectively as the Peoples Liberation Army (PLA)) have been drawn deeply into the political turmoil that has afflicted China for the past two and a half years. The PLA has taken on heavy responsibilities for police and public security

---

[1] Source: Department of State, S/S Files: Lot 90 D 110. Secret; Controlled Dissem. A note on the cover sheet states that it was submitted by Helms and prepared by the Central Intelligence Agency, the intelligence organizations of the Departments of State and Defense, and the National Security Agency. All members of the U.S. Intelligence Board concurred in the estimate on August 1 except the FBI representative, who abstained because the subject was outside his jurisdiction.

work and has acquired a wide variety of administrative and control functions in the economy and government.

B. The PLA has also undergone a heavy purge, especially of its top echelons. Line combat units have so far largely escaped the purges. The PLA itself has been divided at various levels and buffeted by the politics of the Cultural Revolution. Thus far the PLA has taken its cue from the political leaders of the country, but in general it has emerged as a moderate force loosely aligned with the government bureaucracy and others whose primary concern is with order, stability, and national security.

C. Political factionalism, the general deterioration of social order in China, and the many extra duties that have been imposed on the PLA have degraded Chinese military capabilities largely in terms of readiness, morale, and discipline. But in situations where China's vital interests were at stake, many of the ill effects of the Cultural Revolution could probably be fairly quickly overcome. Units, equipment, and the command structure remain intact, and defensive dispositions are largely unimpaired. Thus the PLA could provide a strong defense of the mainland and would be capable of effective military operations should the existence of the Communist regimes in North Vietnam and North Korea be threatened.

D. Conceivably the political, social, and economic situation could deteriorate to the point where the PLA's combat effectiveness would suffer severe damage. On the other hand, a consistent trend toward moderation could enable it to regain full effectiveness within a fairly short time. On balance, we believe that the situation will not get so bad that the PLA would be unable to maintain a capability to function as a fighting force; nevertheless, much of its time and energy will continue to be diverted by nonmilitary activity and political stress. For the coming year at least, the power and authority of the PLA are likely to increase. Peking will be dependent on the PLA as the only effective instrument of control, and the military will probably play a significant role in the political reorganization currently in process.

E. Except for the disruption caused by the Cultural Revolution, there have been few developments in China's general purpose and air defense forces of great significance during the past year. Positioning of Chinese forces has changed little and continues to reflect concern with defense. The Chinese have not given a high priority to equipment programs that would improve China's ability to project its power over long distances outside its borders. The limitations of China's economic and technical capacities are such that conventional forces will remain deficient in modern equipment at least until well into the 1970's.

F. Nevertheless, the modernization program for the air defense and general purpose forces is moving ahead gradually on a fairly broad front along the following lines:

1. *The Army.* Chinese combat units vary considerably in quality and strength, but their firepower is increasing with the addition of more medium tanks and artillery. The levels of equipment the Chinese seem to be aiming at cannot be reached throughout the army much before 1975. No significant increase in the number of combat units is anticipated, although some increase in manpower might occur in response to the army's assumption of widened civil responsibilities.

2. *Air.* A growing inventory of Mig–19 fighters, addition of better radar, and a slow deployment program for surface-to-air missiles are improving China's air defense. We continue to believe that the Chinese will produce a new fighter, and we now believe that the chances are about even that it will be the Mig–21. If the Chinese do not intend to produce this aircraft, it would be four or five years before a fighter significantly more advanced than the Mig–19 could be available. There has been no significant change in the tactical strike and air support capabilities of the Chinese Air Force and Naval Air Force.

3. *The Navy.* Production of R-class submarines and guided missile patrol boats continues, but at a slower rate than had been anticipated. Other types of patrol and torpedo boats are being turned out in considerable numbers and deployment of a coastal defense cruise-missile system seems to be picking up pace.

[Here follows the Discussion portion of the estimate.]

---

322. **Telegram From the Embassy in the Republic of China to the Department of State**[1]

Taipei, August 3, 1968, 0910Z.

3967. Subject: Conversation with President Chiang on MAP matters. Ref: Taipei 3963.[2]

1. During call General R.H. Warren, Director Military Assistance ISA, on President Chiang on August 2, to my disappointment President

---

[1] Source: Department of State, Central Files, DEF 1 CHINAT. Secret; Priority. Repeated to CINCPAC for POLAD and to the Department of Defense.

[2] In telegram 3963 from Taipei, August 2, McConaughy reported a conversation that day with Chiang Ching-kuo, who for the first time had intimated willingness to discuss the possibility of reduction of GRC military forces. Chiang stated that he had been holding important discussions with General Ciccolella in which he had recognized the need to review the strength of GRC armed forces; he thought modernization of military equipment might make it possible to maintain a high state of combat capability while decreasing force levels. (Ibid.)

did not take up matter of reduction level of GRC armed forces. Instead he concentrated exclusively on major pitch for one squadron F4C planes, following up original request made to me on July 15 (Taipei 3761).[3] Gimo asked that decision be made by U.S. "within few weeks", terming matter one of highest priority and great urgency.

2. Gimo asserted repeatedly that maintenance of GRC air superiority over ChiComs in Taiwan Strait area was an imperative necessity. He was convinced that air superiority once lost could almost certainly never be regained, even with later U.S. assistance. He recalled that air superiority had enabled GRC to emerge victorious in Taiwan Strait crisis of 1958. Loss of air superiority now would have serious psychological and morale repercussions, apart from purely military considerations. Communists would be emboldened if they no longer feared GRC Air Force and almost certainly would embark on new aggressions, most likely against Offshore Islands or main island of Taiwan itself. If the Communists should achieve the capability of interdicting the supply lines between Taiwan and Offshores, consequences would be highly prejudicial to GRC defense.

3. Gimo observed that ChiComs already have three very disturbing capabilities which they are reserving mainly for use against Taiwan, viz.: short range missiles, submarines capable of operating effectively in Taiwan Strait, and MIG–21s. He asserted that ChiComs are now building MIG–21s in increasing numbers and balance of air power will soon be shifted in their favor if GRC Air Force not strengthened with some high capability ultra-modern planes, namely F4Cs. Gimo noted that while F5 remains principal reliance Chinese Air Force, it cannot match the MIG–21, and he feels a few higher performance planes are essential to spearhead CAF capability to counter MIG–21, threat and maintain deterrent posture toward ChiComs.

4. Gimo emphasized favorable geographical situation of Taiwan as central point along China periphery. Strength based on Taiwan can be readily redeployed either to S.E. Asia or to Korea. He would think of F4Cs on Taiwan as being an asset for overall allied position, and not solely for benefit or GRC.

5. Gimo said that GRC forces on Kinmen, Matsu and Taiwan itself directly tie down 500,000 ChiCom troops along coastal areas opposite Taiwan Strait and indirectly one million additional forces farther inland. The neutralization of this large Chinese Communist force could not be maintained if air superiority is lost. Also CCK and other air bases on Taiwan which would be essential for use of U.S. Air Force in event of general

---

[3] Document 319.

area hostilities could be readily knocked out by ChiComs if they obtained air superiority.

6. Gimo concluded that all these considerations added up to compelling need at earliest possible date for supplying GRC Air Force with squadron of F4Cs and he pleaded for an expeditious decision by Departments of Defense and State.

7. General Warren expressed sympathetic understanding of President Chiang's interest in highly modern aircraft as a means of maintaining needed air superiority. At same time he pointed out difficulties related to funds, availability of planes, Congressional attitudes and undeferrable requirements of S.E. Asia and other high priority exposed areas. All of this made it unlikely that planes so costly and scarce as F4Cs could be allocated to GRC in present circumstances. However he promised to relay President's request to Washington and see that it was carefully examined in Defense.

8. General Ciccolella in response to query from the President said he agreed with the President's analysis of military situation and need for maintaining GRC air superiority. (He did not have opportunity to spell out his reasons for believing that delivery of F4Cs to GRC is not a realistic possibility at this stage. But he intends to elaborate his views fully to Defense Minister Chiang Ching-kuo next week.)

9. I told President Chiang that without debating merits of F4C request at this time, I felt compelled to express my strong misgivings at the development of a requirement so appallingly expensive that if filled it would leave little or no GRC resources for agreed high priority items of military matériel—many of which have already been programmed after careful planning. I felt there was need for maintenance of a balanced defense structure and that one exceedingly expensive new item should not be allowed to exclude many other high priority items which were essential to a balanced defense force structure. I said the pressing problem before us was to determine how to cover the most essential defense requirements for all services within the strict limits of U.S. and Chinese resources available for defense purposes.

10. The President replied that according to an old Chinese proverb, "First things first." He considered that air superiority took priority over everything else and he would not himself go into the matter of priorities for competing items which in his view would not have the same urgency as the F4C.

11. At close of meeting, President made formal request that as an interim measure while F4C request is being considered, U.S. station one squadron of USAF F4Cs on Taiwan as a deterrent to ChiComs. While he would want these planes based on Taiwan, they would of course be available from this central point for use wherever needed in the East Asian area. (N.B., later in evening Minister Chiang Ching-kuo sent word

to Gens. Warren and Ciccolella that Pres. Chiang had not meant to insist that any USAF squadron stationed on Taiwan must consist of F4Cs. Any type of plane chosen by USAF would be welcome.)

12. General Warren is telegraphing to Sec Def a supplementary report of this conversation, with a fuller summary of his remarks to President Chiang.

13. Embassy will submit analysis, comments and recommendations next week after I have seen Chiang Ching-kuo again and endeavored to get force reduction back on the tracks.

McConaughy

---

323. **Memorandum From the Deputy Assistant Secretary of State for East Asian Affairs (Barnett) to Harry E.T. Thayer of the Office of Republic of China Affairs[1]**

Washington, August 7, 1968.

SUBJECT

Study in Anticipation of Foreign Crises: Taiwan Straits[2]

1. Tom Shoesmith has put together an excellent first draft on the Offshore Islands.

2. Tom's assumptions stated on page 7 serve his purpose. I believe, however, that the Offshore Islands present awkward and even dangerous problems under some contrary assumptions. I mention, illustratively:

a. A GRC attack; or,
b. A Taiwan in which the Generalissimo's control of the GRC is challenged by effective opposition.

Under these and still other assumptions, we would not, I think, be deflected from the conclusions to which Tom's general analysis leads.

---

[1] Source: Department of State, Central Files, DEF 1 CHINAT. Top Secret.

[2] An undated paper entitled "Studies in Anticipation of Foreign Crises: Taiwan Strait Crisis," drafted by ROC Country Director Thomas P. Shoesmith, was sent to the East Asia and Pacific Interdepartmental Regional Group on November 9 and discussed by the group on November 20. The discussion reached no conclusions except that further studies on the subject were needed. The paper and the record of discussion are ibid., FE/IRG Files: Lot 70 D 56. The memorandum printed here comments on a draft that has not been found. Memoranda by Brown, Barnett, Clough, Kreisberg, Greene, and Oscar V. Armstrong of EA/P, dated between August 2 and 13, commenting on the same draft are ibid., Central Files, DEF 1 CHINAT and DEF 6 CHINAT.

3. As to one of Tom's recommended courses of action, I doubt the wisdom of a U.S. attempt, under any circumstances, to persuade the GRC to remove its forces on Quemoy and Matsu. If this is done, the GRC should do it itself and for its own reasons. United States pressure would invite a process of bargaining in which the United States could be trapped into paying a price to the GRC, financially, politically, and in degree of strategic involvement, that might not be desirable or necessary to pay.

4. I do not believe that to establish, credibly, *United States* indifference to the future of the Offshore Islands would stimulate Peking to take them over. Peking and Taipei view the Offshores in an identical historical and strategic context, seeing them as the linchpin that locks the future of Taiwan into the future of the China Mainland. Both capitals know that a change of status of the Offshores—limiting effective jurisdiction of the GRC at Taiwan and the Pescadores alone and putting 100 miles of ocean between that area and the Chinese Communist territories on the Mainland—would become powerful justification for the people of Formosa— and advocates of peace everywhere in the world—to proceed, in terms of both recognition and UN representation, from the present de facto "One China"/"One Taiwan" situation towards de jure arrangements which would make notion of a "One China", including Taiwan, appear even more fanciful than now. Neither Peking nor followers of Generalissimo Chiang Kai-shek in the GRC could welcome that development.[3]

---

[3] The following paragraph is handwritten on the source text following the typewritten text: "While I remain somewhat skeptical about this argument, it is difficult to discount entirely. It certainly is relevant to the question of whether a sign of U.S. unwillingness to defend OSI would encourage CC to attempt to seize islands by force." This paragraph and other marginal notations on the source text and some of the memoranda cited in footnote 2 were apparently written by Shoesmith.

---

324. Telegram From the President's Special Assistant (Rostow) to President Johnson in Texas[1]

Washington, August 26, 1968, 1305Z.

CAP 82146. Herewith summary of an analysis by Al Jenkins of the swing to the right in China.[2]

---

[1] Source: Johnson Library, National Security File, Country File, China, Vol. XIII. Secret.

[2] Reference is to an August 21 memorandum from Jenkins to Rostow. (Ibid).

For the past six weeks or so, and most clearly in the past ten days, there has been the most country-wide shift toward the conservatives yet seen in the past two years. Matters have, in fact, gone so far in the provinces in the direction of the old-liners and under military auspices that one must wonder what is happening to the position of Lin Piao himself. Current policy is certainly different from what he has espoused since 1964.

Revolutionary committees have been set up in the last few days in both Yunnan and Fukien Provinces. Both are completely dominated by the military and each of the chairmen have in the past been under Red Guard criticism.

The Red Guards, on the other hand, have fallen on lean days indeed.

These moves have been accompanied by the strongest measures taken to date by the Army to stop factional fighting. Summary executions have been resorted to in a number of instances. A back-to-work movement appears to have met with limited but perhaps slowly growing success.

Increased army patrol activity has been noted in Peking in recent days, and an important army unit long stationed on the Korean border has been moved into Peking.

There is nothing new on the harvest, except that Peking has entered into urgent negotiations with Australia for wheat deliveries after December. Peking is expected also to negotiate with Canada for further purchases.

There has been speculation that the heavy rains and the natural peak (from melted snows far to the west) might cause devastating floods.

325. **Memorandum From Alfred Jenkins of the National Security Council Staff to the President's Special Assistant (Rostow)[1]**

Washington, August 28, 1968.

SUBJECT

The Gimo's Latest Worries

There was a paragraph in Monday's evening reading for the President putting Ambassador Chow's call on the Secretary, in which he asked urgently for a squadron of F4C's,[2] in the context of the Gimo's worries as set forth in the two attached cables.[3] I think that was adequate under present circumstances for the President, but I believe I owe you a bit more comment.

You were probably shown these two cables. The gist of Chiang's reasoning is:

—Mao will construe the Soviet occupation of Czechoslovakia as a warning and threat to him; i.e., the Soviets will now be likely, in Mao's mind, to install anti-Mao leaders as administrators of border areas of China, laying the groundwork for the downfall of Mao;

—Mao will attempt to consolidate a strong position in South China, hence will need control of flanking areas in Southeast Asia and in the Taiwan Straits area;

—accordingly, Mao will get more deeply involved in the Vietnam war, and apply pressure to the Offshore Islands—with the possibility of at least air attacks on Taiwan.

Chiang reminded McConaughy of his belief that the five southern provinces should be subtracted from Mao's control and that the Soviet Union would permit this gladly, but he said he did not wish to raise this again officially with Washington. He merely reiterated his conviction that he must have air superiority over the Chinese Communists. Ambassador Chow's call on the Secretary Monday morning, asking for a squadron of F4C's or, failing that, the stationing of U.S. sophisticated planes on Taiwan, is part of his present ploy.

As you know, we have no evidence of Chinese Communist preparation for action against the Offshore Islands or for increased participation in the Vietnam war. While under circumstances of both the Soviets and Chinese Communists being in very difficult straits may raise the possi-

---

[1] Source: Johnson Library, National Security File, Country File, China, Vol. XIII. Secret. A copy was sent to Jorden.

[2] Ambassador Chow's August 26 meeting on the Secretary is summarized in telegram 228356, August 27. (Department of State, Central Files, POL 17 CHINAT–US)

[3] The attachments, telegram 4233 from Taipei, August 23, and CINCPAC telegram 241143Z to CJCS, reported conversations on August 22 between McConaughy and Chiang Kai-shek and Admiral McCain, Admiral Sharp's successor as CINCPAC, and Chiang.

bility of completely irrational action, Chiang's reasoning as to likely developments still appears to be very far out indeed.

One is tempted, in fact, to wonder whether Chiang is losing his grip on reality. I do *not* think that this is the correct interpretation. All reports indicate that he is both mentally alert and well informed. I think the explanation for the remarkable line of reasoning outlined in the attached cables lies in his anxious grasping at straws at this particular juncture, and that he fully recognizes that they are straws. I believe that basically his request for highly sophisticated aircraft (a squadron would cost about $50 million) and the tortuous justification is a result of his very deep concern at the prospect of:

—President Johnson's retirement from office and uncertainty as to the degree of our continued presence in East Asia;
—the likely retirement of Secretary Rusk, whom Chiang considers an exceptionally staunch supporter of the GRC position;
—indications from several Presidential aspirants of a desire for further movement toward contact with Peking;
—our sharp cut in MAP support;
—talk of disturbing initiatives in the UN by Canada, Belgium and Italy, etc.

In other words, there is considerable sanity in the Gimo's "madness" if what he is doing is trying to get a new, high-silhouetted U.S. commitment of support in the later days of the Johnson Administration, which would be difficult to overlook by the new administration. He probably reasons that a new administration may well attempt new initiatives in East Asian policy before the career bureaucracy is given a chance to help with the new administration's homework. He probably wants to make it awkward for new departures to be taken hastily before the "lessons," which he believes might emerge from that homework, can be applied.

It makes no sense to give Chiang a squadron of F4C's and they are committed for many months ahead in any event. Nor would it be wise to "station" a squadron of our own sophisticated aircraft on Taiwan. We should avoid anything which could be called "bases" as such on Taiwan. We might, however, "deploy" to Taiwan a few planes from the area, briefly and intermittently. State and Defense will look into this.

In short, if we can find a way of reaffirming our present commitments to the GRC without escalating them, but possibly with the added increment of a new gesture, it is probably in our interests to do so—partly for some of the reasons which I suppose to be in Chiang's own mind. We should not, however, humor his present needs beyond the confines of U.S. interests per se. His true needs are not that great—at least as we can now see them.

326.   Telegram From the Department of State to the Embassy in the Republic of China[1]

Washington, September 13, 1968, 2338Z.

238678. Subj: US-Canadian Talks on UNGA.

1. Following FYI are excerpts concerning China from Embassy Ottawa report of Ball–Sisco talks with Canadian officials Sept.10.

2. ExtAff Min Sharp said Canadian Government's objective was mutual recognition between Ottawa and Peking. Road would not be easy, and Canada did not want to jeopardize interests of others and was troubled about contribution to world peace. It would be a little while before contacts were made, and in meantime contacts would be made with friends around world.

3. Sharp said that his Government was not intending to make any direct contacts with Peking at present time and procedure for pursuing objective was not yet firm. He said he saw no reason to change Canadian posture on China at this GA. Canadians recognize that if they do achieve mutual recognition between Peking and Ottawa, they would have to show consistency in UN. But matter would not arise this session. Amb. Ball stated that US policy remained same as at previous sessions: Viet-Nam figured importantly in this matter for us. Sharp then said that Can-Del at UN would support Important Question resolution, would abstain on Albanian-type resolution, and would give no encouragement to any Italian Study Committee proposal. Ultimate intention was to change position, but it would not happen at this session. Ambassador Ball estimated that Italy could well be expected to put up again its Study Committee resolution in view of former Moro government's having done no less. He thought voting pattern would remain about same. He said that if mutual recognition should transpire, Canadian Ambassador ought to be provided with file and loaf of bread. Sharp responded by saying that Canadians would also have to provide more police to follow Chinese Representatives in Canada. But he went on more seriously to say that Canada hoped it could promote communications with Peking, which would make effort worthwhile. Canadian public supported Government's position.

4. Dept officers briefed GRC Embassy Sept. 13 concerning talks, noting that while Canadians made no commitments, we conclude they do not intend change their ChiRep policy during GA this year.

Rusk

---

[1] Source: Department of State, Central Files, POL 16 CHICOM. Confidential. Drafted by Thomas H. Walsh of IO/UNP; cleared by Gleysteen, Shoesmith, and Rufus Z. Smith of EUR/CAN; approved by Sisco. Repeated to USUN and Ottawa.

327.   Telegram From the Department of State to the Embassy in the Republic of China[1]

Washington, September 20, 1968, 1903Z.

242120. Joint State/Defense message. Refs: (A) Taipei 4374;[2] (B) Taipei 4363;[3] (C) Taipei 4130;[4] (D) Taipei 4047;[5] (E) Taipei 4044;[6] (F) State 228356;[7] (G) CINCPAC 250955Z Aug 68 (NOTAL), (H) CINCPAC 082315Z Sept 68.[8]

1.   Reftels and other reports of USG officials' conversations with President Chiang and MinDef Chiang Ching-kuo make clear importance GRC leadership has placed on obtaining at least a minimum USG gesture of concern for strengthening air defense capabilities in Taiwan Strait area. Defense Minister Chiang's Sept. 3 remarks to Ambassador (ref B) pinned rationale for request for F–4's on GRC's assessment of increased threat to Offshores, with CCK estimate that threat would begin lessening in November. Other conversations, however, have not limited rationale exclusively to Offshores situation.

2.   We concur entirely in Country Team and CINCPAC (ref H) judgment that GRC concern for possibility Chicom attack on Offshores is unsubstantiated by any hard intelligence. At same time, we agree with Embassy recommendation (ref C) on desirability of some minimal positive response to GRC démarche, particularly in view actual and psychological effect of reduced MAP on maintenance GRC air defense capability.

---

[1] Source: Department of State, Central Files, POL CHINAT–US. Secret; Limdis. Drafted by Shoesmith; cleared by Kreisberg, Dennis F. Aughavin of G/PM–MASP, Barnett, Godley, Steadman, Lieutenant General Warren in DOD/ISA/OMA, Colonel Ridge in DOD/ISA, Major General Orwat in Joint Staff/J–5, and Brigadier General Banning in Joint Staff/J–3; and approved by Brown. Also sent to CHMAAG, USTDC, and Hong Kong, and repeated to CINCPAC for POLAD, CSAF, CNO, CMC, CSA, 327 AD, and 5th AF.

[2] Telegram 4374 from Taipei, September 5, reported that despite the concern manifested by Chiang Kai-shek and Chiang Ching-kuo of a possible Communist attack on Quemoy and Matsu, there was little hard intelligence confirming any basis for this fear. (Ibid., POL CHICOM–CHINAT)

[3] Telegram 4363 from Taipei, erroneously dated August 5, reported a September 3 conversation between McConaughy and Chiang Ching-kuo. (Ibid., POL CHINAT–US)

[4] Telegram 4130 from Taipei, August 16, reported receipt of a message from President Chiang asking if there had been any response to his August 2 request for a squadron of F4C's. (Ibid., DEF 1 CHINAT)

[5] Telegram 4047 from Taipei, August 10, reported an August 8 conversation between General Ciccolella and Chiang Chiang-kuo. (Ibid.)

[6] Telegram 4044 from Taipei, August 10, was a summary report of the August 8 conversation between Ciccolella and Chiang Ching-kuo. (Ibid.)

[7] See footnote 2, Document 325.

[8] Neither found.

3. We concur therefore in responding to GRC along lines of Country Team and CINCPAC's recommendation (ref G). We believe that intermittent and temporary rotation of limited number of high performance fighters during remainder of 1968 should be sufficient to meet situation created by GRC representations in recent months. In any event, it is maximum possibility in view other requirements.

4. In making this gesture, it is essential that we ensure that GRC does not misconstrue our response as implying either (a) agreement with its estimate of the likelihood of a Chicom attack or (b) any commitment to defend the Offshore Islands. Rather, our response must be within context of our intention and ability to meet our treaty commitment to defense of Taiwan and Pescadores. We also wish continue to avoid any increase in US military presence which suggests we regard Taiwan as permanent base.

5. We believe it appropriate that our response to President Chiang's personal concern for this matter be conveyed to MinDef Chiang. In absence Amb. McConaughy, we leave to your discretion choice of channel for that purpose. Subject to Amcon Hong Kong's comments (para 6 below), you requested make following presentation of US position, with details to be coordinated directly with CINCPAC:

a) USG has given close attention to assessments of current situation provided us by President Chiang and Minister of Defense. As we have previously stated, we would welcome receiving any indications GRC may obtain of increased Communist threat in Strait area, but on basis of evidence available to us, we cannot conclude that any significant increased threat now exists. We will, of course, keep this situation under closest scrutiny.

b) We appreciate, however, problems posed by reduction grant MAP, particularly for CAF, and wish to continue to work closely with GRC to make most efficient possible use of resources available to both sides. We have, therefore, carefully considered President Chiang's requests in light of our mutual concern to maintain and strengthen air defense of Taiwan and Pescadores.

c) As already indicated by CHMAAG and Ambassador McConaughy, as well as by Secretary Rusk, we unable to provide squadron of F–4C's to CAF as requested, not only because of high cost this aircraft in relation to limited MAP funds and already heavy burden GRC defense budget, but in view fact that existing undeferrable requirements for this aircraft already exceed availability of F–4C's.

d) It also not feasible to provide US rotational F–4C squadron in Taiwan. We are prepared, however, to provide temporary and intermittent presence in Taiwan of high performance fighters at less than squadron strength during the remainder of 1968. We would anticipate that during this three-month period from four to eight such aircraft would be present for approximately six days a month for training with the 327th Air Division subject to agreement with the GRC for utilization of GRC missile, gunnery and bombing ranges and other related facilities such as emergency jettison area and air space for GCI training. We are prepared to discuss necessary arrangements for such deployment at earliest GRC convenience.

e) We would not wish to give any publicity to this temporary and intermittent deployment and believe that it should be treated in low key as routine procedure with GRC agreement that US respond to any public inquiries concerning this matter.

6. *For Hong Kong*—We do not believe that limited action we have in mind will evoke any significant Chinese Communist reaction, recalling that similar and somewhat more visible action in 1966 created no problem in this regard. Would appreciate your comments soonest, however.[9]

Rusk

---

[9] Telegram 8800 from Hong Kong, September 21, agreed that the proposed deployment was not likely to provoke any significant Chinese Communist reaction. It noted, however, that this and other steps could have a cumulative effect and observed that the U.S. interest "in preserving status quo Taiwan problem" would be best served by avoiding any suggestion that, in the absence of indications of Communist preparations for hostile action, the United States was developing Taiwan into a U.S. operational base. (Department of State, Central Files, POL CHINAT–US)

328. **Paper Prepared by Alfred Jenkins of the National Security Council Staff[1]**

Washington, October 9, 1968.

FURTHER THOUGHTS ON CHINA

A Rebalance of Power
The U.S. Dilemma
The Timing of Policy Departures
The Dog-eared Shopping Lists
The Dubious Case for Movement

China is our central problem in Asia, and in some ways the knottiest on earth. Under present circumstances, however, progress in solving that problem cannot be made by direct approach, as some would have us try. Any approach must be in the context of Asia-wide revolutionary pressures, and with attention to the persistent Asian power imbalances which make the region unstable.

A Rebalance of Power

The last three wars in which the United States has been directly involved began for us as Asian wars. While the origins of all three were complex, a major factor in each instance was a neglected imbalance of power in the area which made for fundamental instability. In each case the United States finally had to fill the vacuum. Many argue that we did so belatedly each time—after war was inevitable. It is true that we gave signals prior to each conflict which could be, and doubtless were, interpreted by the adversaries as indicating that we did not plan to provide a counterbalance, and therefore that expansionist moves could be made with impunity. Then when aggression took place, we found it necessary to oppose it, at great cost.

Some of this cost may be laid at the door of our relative ignorance—at least until fairly recently—of the nature and importance to us and to the rest of the world of the various revolutions in Asia, peaceful and otherwise. New political institutions, forced economic modernization, and rapidly shifting social patterns have been superimposed on the old ways, and power centers have shifted, with the creation of explosive ten-

---

[1] Source: Johnson Library, National Security File, Country File, China, Vol. XIII. Secret. Jenkins sent the paper to Rostow with a covering memorandum of the same date, stating that it was the sequel to Document 303 that Rostow had requested and that its delay was primarily due to "agonizing over its basic theme and pondering contrary advice from some whom I respect."

sions. Americans have not been very familiar with the old ways, which has complicated the job of understanding the reasons behind present-day actions and reactions.

Still, in recent years our understanding of these intrusive Asian developments has grown rapidly. It is ironic that just at the time when we have achieved fuller appreciation of what must be done in Asia, both the willingness and the capacity of the United States to continue to carry the major burden there has come into question (quite apart from the correctness of our having carried it thus far).

We cannot allow another Asian power vacuum to arise. The fact remains that the next war in which our forces will be directly involved, if it comes, is more likely to come in Asia than anywhere else. Berlin, Hungary and Czechoslovakia underline the reluctance of the superpowers for a test of force in Europe, and another Near East conflagration would stand a good chance of being a proxy war. Not so in Asia. There we are intricately engaged, and must continue to be, though at a reduced level as soon as this is possible. The present balance of power, by courtesy of very heavy American presence, is unnatural to the area. If it persists for much longer, we will be asking for cumulative trouble. We must contrive a rebalance, with China principally in mind.

Japan and China, the key countries of East Asia proper (excluding the two superpowers whose interests in Asia are great) are both in an unnatural state of affairs, which cannot last.

Japan, though the third largest industrial power on earth, is all but unarmed. It is unthinkable that, considering the enormous bulge of its economic muscles, Japan will for many more years accept a situation where others can say "No!" and Japan cannot say "But, yes!" When the psychological and constitutional blocks to the inevitable transformation in Japanese defense doctrine start to give, they may dissolve more rapidly than now seems likely. Japan is bound increasingly to resent our filling its defense needs, even if we do so by insistent invitation while Japan is gleefully obsessed with the economic advantage which our defense affords. Despite the present easily documentable demands of efficiency and economy for bases in meeting our commitments in the area, we will do well in our long-term interest to insure that we act a bit harder to get: that we are sought, rather than tolerated until we are not tolerated. Until Japan rearms, as it will, we must use our leverage to press for very sizeable economic *and indirect military* contribution to the non-communist Asian balance. This is not only necessary in the overall East Asian context, it is also the very essence of a sensible China policy—especially so long as the China problem is not subject to direct approach.

The second of the great Asian nations, too, is in a highly unnatural and unstable state. China has already become powerful in Asian terms, but it is "contained." That containment has been necessary, given China's advertised intentions and demonstrable actions in line with the Maoist prescription for world revolution. However, China when strong has always had a sphere of influence on its periphery not unlike that which other strong nations throughout history have insisted upon. In China's case this natural penchant is strengthened both by its historical "center-of-the-universe" syndrome and by its determination to over-compensate, if possible, for the "century of ignominy" which it suffered at the hands of western predators. A century ago China failed to provide itself with gunboats, so it had to take alien semi-masters, both theological and secular—and both bearing a monopoly on truth to a Kingdom which had considered itself the source of truth and righteousness for at least four thousand years! Unmistakable paranoia understandably results.

Post-World War II events have decreed that this weary problem—China and the attendant regional power imbalance—is excessively ours. However, even if Asian self-interest should demand it, and even if both our will and our resources were abundant to the task, a long-term over-weening American presence would become an affront to Asian sensibilities of perhaps irreparable severity.

The U.S. Dilemma

We cannot afford to lessen our support prematurely; likewise we cannot afford to project present clear requirements very far into the future. We must reduce the problem (principally China) or further share the burden of coping with it—or both.

We are making progress—too slowly to dissolve the dilemma, but not without success—in sharing the burden. The positive aspects of our Asian policies post-World War II have been directed to this end. We have successfully bought time for non-communist Asia, and more has been made of that time than we had any right to expect from the tatterdemalion array of weak, inexperienced, mostly newly-independent nations scattered around China in the wake of World War II. Regional strength and cooperation are growing, but not fast enough to ease the faster growing insistence of our dilemma.

Diminishing the problem itself is the more attractive tack. But our would-be leverage with China remains unfeared. So long as the Maoists are in control, there is no meshing of gears to be had. In the Maoists we are confronted by secular religionists, who have insistently cast us in the devil's role for their own purposes. No compromise is possible with a set of absolutes; and logic is irrelevant in negotiating with a faith. Taiwan is a major practical issue between us, but if we could hand it over gratis the Maoists would still lock us in their "inimical embrace," because of the ideological demands of their continuing revolution and their simplistic faith.

The Timing of Policy Departures

The immediate question with respect to United States policy toward China is whether the supposedly inevitable, definitive failure of Maoist policies has now set in, to the extent of presaging a "change of dynasty." The answer, unfortunately, is that we do not know, and may not know for months to come.

What we do know is that the two great erstwhile strengths of the Maoists—Mao's prestige and the loyalty of the masses—have suffered deep erosion during the past two years of lunacy. We know from the reports of individuals from the mainland and from the cries of the regime's press and radio that cynicism, despair and simple exhaustion are left in the trail of Mao's second major attempt to remake Chinese man and reinvigorate his revolution. We know that the intellectuals and many students are fed up, and that vast numbers of cadres who worked hard to make Mao's kind of China work are angered at being bitterly struggled against. We know that Mao was virtually deified in the anxious attempt to make failure impossible, yet he has not succeeded. And when a god fails, business as usual thereafter is improbable.

On the other side of the coin, the vast country has not come apart. Economic and social damages have been serious but not catastrophic, and could be recouped if order and authority are restored. Most of the Army seems responsive to central direction. And most importantly for our purposes, there is no sign yet of meaningful change in either domestic or foreign policies—only in tactics, which have become less frenetic.

China is desperately trying to re-establish its old position and stature in a nuclear world. In a sense it is trying to do what the rest of the world is so anxious about its not having done: become a part of the modern world. The tragedy is that it is not doing so cooperatively. So far it has been unwilling to join the world except on its own terms, which are absurd. It wants literally to become the "center of the universe" again, and to refashion the rest of the world in its own image. Its efforts to regain its central position have produced crazily compressed time schedules, costly disruptions, and superhuman requirements for discipline and austerity.

An original purpose of the Cultural Revolution was to frighten, goad and inspire the populace into meeting these rigorous requirements. The movement got out of hand, policy differences and power struggles intensified, and a crisis of authority resulted. The Army was reluctantly brought into play and hundreds of thousands of fractious Red Guards packed off to work in the countryside. The biggest casualty to date is the self-confidence of the cadres and officials. The regime now intends to rebuild the party, chastened and cleansed, with the Army maintaining discipline meanwhile. That is where we are today, and it is still premature to attempt judgment on the future.

Such is the recognized importance of China in our scheme of things, however, that Americans have tended not to forgive those who later prove not to have been prophetic, even prescient, about developments in Chinese affairs. A number of Foreign Service Officers put out to pasture can attest to this fact. We cannot well weather another orgy of national self-flagellation at having seemed to guess wrongly as to the likely course of a quarter of mankind, or as to the appropriate United States response.

We have long said that at the propitious time we should insure that Peking is aware that it has policy options other than continued rabid anti-Americanism and anxious self-isolation from world currents. We have rightly attempted some steps toward that assurance. But it is not yet time energetically to woo China into the world.

The satisfactory articulation of China with the rest of the world is conceivable only on terms consonant with the sort of world envisaged in the United Nations Charter: one of cooperative diversity. That sort of world cannot be created in safe durability *without* the participation of the quarter of mankind which is Chinese, but *Maoist* China will not join that sort of world.

In recent years, as our policy toward China has become less rigid, there have been three circumstances in which it would make sense for the United States seriously to seek accommodation with the mainland regime.

1. A *"matured"* communist China, post-Maoist whether post-Mao or not, without pretentions of leading global revolution, and sufficiently "revisionist" in its dogma to permit of greater articulation with the rest of the world.
2. A true *"change of dynasty"* wherein the successor regime would follow policies consonant with the sort of world we seek to build.
3. A China still Maoist-Stalinist but so *militarily powerful* that extraordinary efforts must be made to bring about those restraints which greater articulation with the rest of the world might afford.

None of these situations has yet come about, although the first may be slowly developing, and the second is, for the first time, barely conceivable for the future.

As for the third, it is true that the Chinese Communist armed forces remain a formidable force, despite Cultural Revolution preoccupations. They pose a potential threat to other Asian nations, but not directly to us. If China's nuclear potential develops as expected, its world status and its blackmail potential toward some may be enhanced, but it is not likely to pose a significant threat directly to the United States until it develops a strong naval tradition. This may come, but it will take a long time. We have a fairly comfortable grace period in which we do not, for instance, have to allow Peking to "shoot its way into the United Nations" or make other comparable forced accommodation, come what may.

Nor is there any reason compelling us to wink at the true nature of this regime:

—By any measure it is tyrannical. It has made little pretense of developing a legal system of any sort. Both truth and justice have been what the vagaries of central doctrine have dictated at any given time.

—While in some ways the "common man" has seemed to be remembered in favorable contrast to earlier times, there has been in fact little human dignity and virtually no freedom. Not only has there been no freedom of expression, there has been no freedom of silence. All have had to be vocal in worshiping the "thoughts" and the person of a deified leader bent on sinocentric world revolution.

—In the so-called land reform movement of 1951–52 the regime put to death, or allowed "the masses" to put to death untold millions (best estimate 12–15 millions) of its own people; and a great many have lost their lives in Mao's self-serving Cultural Revolution.

—The regime massively supported North Korean aggression and materially backs North Vietnamese aggression. It raped Tibet with near-genocidal thoroughness, and attacked India.

—It has done all within its limited power to further communist revolution in Asia, Africa and Latin America. It continues to train guerrillas for "people's wars," particularly in Southeast Asia.

—Like the Soviet Union, as we have recently been reminded, Peking puts the "laws" of global "class struggle" above the tenets of the United Nations and of international law. Any act which is "anti-imperialist," such as the seizure of the *Pueblo* in international waters, is by simple definition "correct."

It is understandable that there is a wringing of the hands that China is not yet brought into the family of nations. But how is it to be done? China, under present management, is the first to say that such is inconceivable—except on terms so provincial and anachronistic, so hostile to all that has been built toward world order since World War II, so antithetical to the true revolution in human freedom of the past two centuries, that the very resignation of these positive traditions would seem to be involved in the acceptance of Chinese terms.

There are sincere and able people in the United States Government and in the academic community who say that we must try harder. Some seem to think that if we would only turn the other cheek we would get kissed. Unlikely. Others do not expect early response, but believe we should go the extra mile as a test.

I, myself, favored more attempted movement in our China policy up to the summer of 1966. But that was:

—before the Cultural Revolution *reversed* the earlier trend in China toward more rationality;
—before acute policy differences surfaced within China—differences which greater U.S. policy flexibility might have helped induce, had such been necessary;
—before Mao began to destroy Maoism (it now seems) more effectively than the rest of us could contrive;

—before China was weakened at least temporarily, giving the rest of the world a chance to watch its writhings in relative safety for a time, and hope with some realism for a change;

—before Czechoslovakia; and the simple reaction of home-spun wisdom: "You can't trust those communists!" That sentiment reaches to China in today's climate, and must be heeded by policy makers.

The Dog-eared Shopping Lists

The deal-with-China shopping lists of those of us who are Sino-philes, or those who are simply very worried about China's isolation, have been passed around town and the academic community for years. It seems that each time serious thought has been given to some of the more meaningful of the proposed steps, Peking has comported itself in such a way as to make the steps appear not to be in the U.S. interest. The present period of extreme Maoism would seem to be an especially unpromising time for forward movement. The situation is fluid, however, and could change fairly rapidly, or it could simmer along for some while.

The shopping lists vary with advocates, but they variously include:

Recognition? Peking would not recognize Washington. It would cheerfully accept our compliment, but keep us cooling our heels outside the Gate of Heavenly Peace.

Entry into the United Nations? Under present Peking management, this as a minimum would be at the cost of the seat of a well-behaved member and ally, and as a maximum at the cost of warping the United Nations out of recognition.

Unrestricted travel? This should probably be accepted now in any case, but especially since the Supreme Court has taken the teeth out of this sort of travel restriction. It could be done at any time, if there were sufficient excuse through some particular turn of events. It probably should be done quietly next March, when the annual listing of restricted countries automatically comes up. It will not enhance our relations, since Peking fears an exchange of people. It is in the category of harmless tidiness, with an eye for the future.

More contact between newsmen, scholars, scientists, etc.? On balance, this could only be to our advantage, for we are the stronger society with the more viable ideology. We pushed contact belatedly, not in the post-Bandung period when it might have worked (or if not, might have proved an interesting embarrassment to Peking) but prior to and during the Cultural Revolution, when it had no chance. We will have another chance, but the time is not yet here.

Trade on the level of that with European communist countries? This deserves more thought. Some of the arguments in favor, with comment:

—The Cultural Revolution is wearing itself out, and more practical people are coming to the fore in China. They should be encouraged by tangible moves such as lowered trade restrictions. (It is premature to make the judgment concerning the emergence of more practical leadership. U.S. top-level statements expressing hope for eventual reconciliation and our conduct at Warsaw should be adequate signaling to "the more practical people.")

—We should bring our treatment of Asian communist nations in line with our treatment of European ones. (But the communist-fed war we are now fighting is in Asia.)

—The majority of State's China Panel members believe that timing is not important; there seems never to be a "good" time to alter our policy on trade, but it must be done in the long-term U.S. interest. (To do it now would be ill received in America and most of Asia.)

—President Johnson is well known for standing firmly against communist advance in Asia, and he could take this step without being accused of being soft on communism. (During Vietnam? and post-Czech occupation?)

—We would not be announcing the resumption of trade, but simply removing impediments, to influence the "good guys" in China. (So long as the Maoists are in control, it could actually discourage the good guys.)

—This step would reassure Hanoi that the rigidities of our stand do not flow from any doctrine of blanket hostility to Asian communism, but relate to North Vietnamese aggression against South Vietnam. (We are not hostile to Asians, but we need not apologize for being hostile to the policies of Asian communist nations.)

—China gets everything it needs anyway from Japan and Western Europe; American business is at a disadvantage. (There is considerable truth in this, but there is little clamor in American business circles for trade with China—presumably because of recognition of the larger issues involved.)

—It is important, through contact, to make inroads into the dangerous provincialism of China's leaders. (So it is, but we have tried in other ways, and been rebuffed.)

We should keep clearly in mind that the very degree of success of our present policies toward China recommends caution in altering them, until the nature of China itself is more clearly altered:

—So far we have "contained" Chinese expansionist tendencies remarkably well, thereby buying valuable time for non-communist Asia.

—Although not subject to documentary proof, we can be sure that our firm stand in Vietnam and our reasonable posture of desiring contact and eventual reconciliation with mainland China have combined to exacerbate policy differences in Peking, contributing to the disunity and weakness of our self-proclaimed adversary.

—In its 19-year history the regime has never had such fundamental troubles at home, or stood so low in international esteem. It is no longer a model for developing countries.

—We have prevented Peking from ousting the Republic of China from the United Nations, and from entering itself, where, particularly in its recent mood, it would have been a disrupting influence of serious and perhaps disastrous proportions.

—For the first time there is a better than fair prospect that the very nature of the regime, because of its failures, will have to change.

Until the nature of the change is more evident, it is a time for close scrutiny rather than overtures.

The Dubious Case for Movement

Nevertheless, those who advocate movement in China policy now have a case which should not be lightly shrugged off. Essentially, they argue that we are already very late in being more forthcoming, and we take insupportable risks in not seeking accommodation more actively.

Many of Communist China's leaders who oppose Mao (including house-arrested President Liu Shao-ch'i), if not exactly pro-Soviet are at least pro-Soviet aid, which they view as the only hope of a rapid regaining of China's position in the world. While even after Mao a return to the fraternal Sino-Soviet collusion of the 1950's is unlikely, a papering over of differences involving some Soviet aid in return for an acceptable degree of political docility on China's part would have its attraction to both parties, and is not inconceivable. If this should happen, we would be accused because of our "rigid" policies of missing the chance to influence at the right moment the supposed "good guys," or even of "blind dedication to the fortunes of Chiang Kai-shek."

So long as China is unarticulated with the world mainstream, the problems posed in the areas of disarmament, non-proliferation and a more workable security mechanism, in or outside the United Nations, are obvious. Sooner or later the weight of these considerations is bound to increase.

The argument that we lose the respect of important friends through our "rigidity" is less cogent than it was before Peking scandalized itself at home and abroad in the Cultural Revolution. Post-Vietnam, and further away from the Czech crisis, if Peking should become appreciably more reasonable we should take stock again.

The death of either Mao or Chiang would also call for careful weighing of possible developments and appropriate responses, depending on the timing and the context.

In sum, our policy toward Communist China in recent years has accomplished in good measure about all that could be expected, short of bilateral accommodations which are just not yet in the cards. Our policy has been consistent but not static. It has steadfastly opposed Chinese meddling and aggression; but it has moved toward seeking contact. The ground is well laid to move further when China is ready, if it seems in our interest.

Meanwhile, the best policy toward communist Asia, beyond containment, is concentration on strengthening non-communist Asia, with a view to ultimate reduction of the U.S. component in the balance of power in the region.

The other side of China policy is Taiwan and its ramifications. I should like to address those tangles, including the offshore islands problem, in another paper.[2]

Alfred Jenkins

---

[2] No such paper has been found.

---

329.   **Telegram From the Department of State to the Embassy in the Republic of China[1]**

Washington, November 2, 1968, 1908Z.

266124. Joint State/Defense. Ref: A. State 242120;[2] B. Taipei 4806;[3] C. Taipei 4822;[4] D. CINCPAC 191150Z, Oct. 68 (NOTAL).[5]

1. Despite President Chiang's personal involvement in GRC request for F–4C squadron, we do not think Country Team recommenda-

---

[1] Source: Department of State, Central Files, DEF 19–8 US–CHINAT. Secret; Limdis. Drafted by Shoesmith; cleared by Admiral Shepard, Colonel Ridge, and Lieutenant General Warren of DOD/ISA, Brigadier General Glick and Colonel Mayland of the Joint Staff; and approved by Winthrop Brown. Repeated to CINCPAC for POLAD, CHMAAG Taiwan, COMUSTDC, and Hong Kong.

[2] Document 327.

[3] In telegram 4806 from Taipei, October 11, Chargé Dean reported that Chiang Ching-kuo had reiterated the GRC request for a squadron of F–4C's and for the stationing of a U.S. squadron of F–4C's on Taiwan as an interim measure. (Department of State, Central Files, DEF 19–8 US–CHINAT)

[4] Telegram 4822 from Taipei, October 14, conveyed the Country Team's recommendation that President Johnson send a letter to President Chiang reiterating the U.S. commitment to the defense of Taiwan but explaining that other requirements made it impossible to provide a squadron of F–4C's to the GRC or to station one on Taiwan. (Ibid.)

[5] Not found.

tion Para 3 Ref C advisable. We agree with Country Team observation that Chiang's interest may be motivated more by reasons of prestige and desire to obtain some reaffirmation of US defense commitment, than by anticipated military needs. We do not believe, however, that present circumstances or specific issue Chiang has chosen make it advisable or appropriate for President to be responsive to such interest.

2. You are requested therefore to convey to MinDef Chiang following USG response to President Chiang's specific requests:

(a) USG has given most careful and high-level consideration to President Chiang's request that F–4C squadron be provided GRC. USG fully shares President Chiang's desire maintain and improve air defense of Taiwan and Pescadores and wishes to continue consult closely with GRC on best means of meeting that priority requirement within resources available to both sides. In view strict limitation on grant MAP funds, USG unable on that basis provide F–4C squadron to CAF. Moreover, the USG cannot advise purchase by GRC in view of exceedingly high costs of F–4C aircraft and the resultant impact such purchase would have on GRC defense budget. Further, other less costly additions to the air defense system are more readily available in the near term, e.g., F–5's and package of 34 F–100's.

(b) With respect to President Chiang's request that USAF station F–4C squadron on Taiwan on permanent basis, USG does not consider that at this time the situation relating to air defense of Taiwan and Pescadores would justify such deployment, particularly in view of current operational requirements. Proposal to provide temporary and intermittent presence in Taiwan of high performance fighters through remainder of 1968 was made after careful study in an effort to be as responsive as possible to GRC's concern. If GRC does not believe this would serve our mutual defense purposes, USG would of course not wish proceed further with plans for such deployment.

3. At time you convey our response to MinDef Chiang, we believe it would be useful to provide him opportunity for detailed review of points previously made to him and President Chiang by Ambassador and CHMAAG. For that purpose, suggest you consider a joint representation to include CHMAAG and COMUSTDC. Additionally, based on General Warren's conversation with the President, it appears that he may not be fully informed on aircraft characteristics and performance. In your conversation with the MinDef, it is suggested that you invite his attention to the fact that the US has provided three squadrons of F–104G interceptor aircraft, and in June of this year provided seven additional F–104G's to maintain the air defense capability which President Chiang discussed as the basis for his F–4 request. In this regard, these have a

MACH 2 speed and are designed to support the very air defense mission which apparently constituted the basis of the President's concern.[6]

Rusk

---

[6] Dean reported in telegram 5093 from Taipei, November 8, that he, accompanied by COMUSTDC Admiral Chew and General Ciccolella, had delivered the U.S. response to Chiang Ching-kuo on November 8. (Department of State, Central Files, DEF 19–8 US–CHINAT)

---

330. Memorandum From Alfred Jenkins of the National Security Council Staff to the President's Special Assistant (Rostow)[1]

Washington, November 19, 1968.

SUBJECT

Developments Behind the Reinforced Bamboo Curtain

For several weeks developments have moved very slowly on the Chinese mainland—or so it has seemed. We cannot be sure, because many of our sources have dried up. Wall posters are fewer and are uninformative (the Red Guard authors have been packed off to the countryside), Red Guard newspapers have disappeared, and foreigners are no longer allowed to receive provincial newspapers. Mail is being more carefully censored, and the populace is shunning travelers (Tab A).[2] We used to receive through the British 500–600 local newspapers per month. We now receive none, and only two papers from the Capital.

The October Central Committee Plenum was obviously designed to be a watershed between the destructive and constructive periods in the Cultural Revolution. (Both periods were promised when the movement began.) The Party is to be rebuilt under Army supervision, with "new blood" from the workers and peasants joining the revolutionary cadres. A completely revamped educational system under control of workers and peasants is to keep the revolution pure.

---

[1] Source: Johnson Library, National Security File, Country File, China, Vol. XIII. Secret.

[2] Tab A is intelligence report [text not declassified], November 18.

The forced dispatch of swarms of school age youth to the country-side for "worker experience," however, has produced resistance from the students, their families, and the hapless peasant hosts, who complain of extra mouths to feed without compensatory work input.

Meanwhile, there are signs that some sort of Great Leap Forward may be in the offing. We are receiving a growing number of reports of the curbing of private plots and other types of private sideline production, of the increase in size and authority of production brigades, and of changes in the work point system in the direction of income equalization (Tab B).[3] Spiritual elan is again to be the substitute for material reward. The Cultural Revolution was designed to make this possible, but resistance to a new leap is likely to be intense.

Mao's basic problem is fairly obvious. While there are times when ideological motivation may serve as the prime mover of a country seeking modernization, no predetermined, fixed view of an environment can hope to cope with the galloping modern world, which is so variable in so many of its elements.

China's immense social forces moved chiefly through Mao for about a decade. But constant stimulation is proving to be no substitute for pragmatism, and the basic eclecticism of Chinese society is bound to assert itself. Mao is anti-urban (he speaks rapturously of "the quality of village life," much like a Taoist sage) at a time when urbanization is inevitable. He is anti-intellectual at a time when "knowledge is power" to a degree unique in history. China's leader is now largely in confrontation with the social forces of his country, which have striven uncertainly for a century toward modernization.

So far Mao has sufficient power, however, to make another try. In doing so he is now manifesting in extreme form a classical trait of the visionary with a corner on ersatz truth: pathological secrecy, coupled with fear of contamination from the outside. This will give us added problems in following developments.

Al

---

[3] Tab B is telegram 9971 from Hong Kong, November 15.

331. Telegram From the Embassy in Poland to the Department of State[1]

Warsaw, November 25, 1968, 1514Z.

5244. Ref: Warsaw 5167.[2] Subject: 135th meeting US–ChiCom talks.

1. Morning November 25, Attaché Lo invited EmbOff to ChiCom Embassy and handed following letter (unofficial ChiCom translation): "Mr. Ambassador.

I have received your letters of September 12 and November 15. I am now instructed to reply as follows:

1. The Chinese Government was serious in suggesting on May 18 that the 135th meeting of the Sino-U.S. Ambassadorial talks be held in the middle of November or late November. The Chinese Government has not indicated that it will change its view. It is most absurd for you to 'assume' groundlessly that China has changed its intention, and this is obviously a pretext.

2. You have now asked for a postponement of the meeting until February next year. To put it bluntly, this is because the United States is going to change its President and the U.S. Government is now in a stage wherein the incoming is superseding the outgoing, and you want to drag on until the present period is over.

3. Over the past 13 years, the Chinese Government has consistently adhered to the following two principles in the Sino-U.S. Ambassadorial talks: First—The U.S. Government undertakes to immediately withdraw all its armed forces from China's territory Taiwan Province and the Taiwan Straits area and dismantle all its military installations in Taiwan Province; second—The U.S. Government agrees that China and the United States conclude an agreement on the five principles of peaceful coexistence. But in the past 13 years, while refusing all along to reach an agreement with the Chinese Government on these two principles, the U.S. Government, putting the cart before the horse, has kept on haggling over side issues. We once again tell you in explicit terms that the Chinese

---

[1] Source: Department of State, Central Files, POL CHICOM–US. Confidential; Limdis.

[2] Telegram 5167 from Warsaw, November 15, reported delivery of a letter from Stoessel to Ch'en, the text of which was transmitted in telegram 271668 to Warsaw, November 14. The letter stated that since Ch'en's government had not confirmed the U.S.-proposed meeting date of November 20, "we must regretfully assume" that it did not intend to act on its original proposal for a November meeting; the U.S. Government remained willing to consider an alternative date in 1968 for the next meeting but suggested a meeting on February 5 or 11, 1969. (Ibid.) The U.S. proposal to meet on November 20 was made in a September 12 letter from Stoessel to Ch'en. (Telegram 236054 to Warsaw, September 10, and telegram 4490 from Warsaw, September 12; ibid.)

Government will never barter away principles. If you continue your current practice, no result whatsoever will come of the Sino-U.S. Ambassadorial talks no matter which administration of yours assumes office.

4. Since your side has found it necessary to ask for a postponement of the meeting, we can agree. We hereby make the specific suggestion that the meeting might as well be held on February 20 next year. By that time your new President will have been in office for a month and you will probably be able to make up your mind.

5. Since your side has already made public statements on the further postponement of the 135th meeting of the Sino-U.S. Ambassadorial talks, our side will issue a statement to refute them.

Chen Tung

Chargé d'Affaires A.I. of the Embassy of the People's Republic of China in Poland"

2. Original Chinese text being pouched.

Stoessel

---

332. Telegram From the Department of State to the Embassy in Poland[1]

Washington, November 29, 1968, 2338Z.

279906. Ref: Warsaw 5156.[2] Subject: US–ChiCom Ambassadorial Talks.

1. Department accepting ChiCom proposal February 20 meeting, but suggesting change in venue to embassies. Suggestion for change

---

[1] Source: Department of State, Central Files, POL CHICOM–US. Secret; Limdis. Drafted by Kreisberg and Nicholas Platt of EA/ACA; cleared by Brown, Doyle V. Martin of EUR/EE, Shoesmith, and EUR Acting Assistant Secretary Alfred Puhan; and approved and initialed by Rusk. Repeated to London, Moscow, Paris, Taipei, Tokyo, and Hong Kong.

[2] Telegram 5156 from Warsaw, November 15, transmitted the texts of two letters from Ch'en to Stoessel. (Ibid.) They replied to two June 19 letters from Jenkins that proposed a settlement of outstanding postal and telecommunications accounts and requested information about missing U.S. servicemen and U.S. prisoners in China and requested the prisoners' release. (Airgrams 8610 and 8609 to Warsaw, June 11; ibid., POL CHICOM–US and POL 27–7 CHICOM–US, respectively; telegram 3640 from Warsaw, June 19; ibid.) The Chinese letters rejected efforts to settle such issues as postal and telecommunication accounts while the Taiwan issue remained unsettled and rejected the requests concerning missing servicemen and prisoners.

based on our desire move talks to more secure surroundings, and ascertain whether ChiComs genuinely interested in private, productive exchange of views.

2. Please transmit following written message from Ambassador to ChiCom Embassy ASAP:

"Dear Mr. Chargé d'Affaires:

I have received your letter of November 25 in which you propose that the 135th Sino-US Ambassadorial meeting be held on February 20, 1969. I accept your proposal, and I shall look forward to meeting with your side at 2:00 p.m. on that date.

It is my belief that the purposes of the Sino-United States Ambassadorial talks would be furthered at this juncture by a change of venue. Therefore, I propose that henceforth our meetings alternate between our respective embassies in accordance with the proposal by Ambassador Wang Ping-nan presented at a meeting between the representatives of our two countries on September 13, 1958. If this suggestion meets with your approval, we would be prepared to discuss with you at which of our respective embassies the February 20, 1969 meeting should take place.

If the suggested change in venue is not acceptable, I shall expect to meet you at the agreed date and time at our usual meeting place.

Sincerely yours,

Walter J. Stoessel, Jr."[3]

Rusk

---

[3] Telegram 5293 from Warsaw, November 30, reported that the letter had been delivered that day. (Ibid.)

333.   Memorandum From Alfred Jenkins of the National Security
       Council Staff to the President's Special Assistant (Rostow)[1]

Washington, December 5, 1968.

SUBJECT

The Revolutionary Committee and Its Conservative Influence

The attack on the institutions of provincial administration and control during the early phases of the Cultural Revolution left Peking with an enormous task of reconstructing party and government authority. Considerable progress has been made in building a formal framework, but effective government still eludes Peking in many areas.

In theory, the Revolutionary Committees inherited the functions and authority of the former governing bodies, but in practice authority in most provinces rests overwhelmingly with the military. Earlier political struggles have left a legacy of factionalism in the body politic which in some provinces, notably in Western China, results in persistent disruptive activity. The new committees are especially weak in the instruments of control—police, propaganda media, etc. Lawlessness continues to pose serious problems although less so as time goes by. In most of Eastern China at least the Army's new get tough mandate has led to widespread arrests, mass trials, and often summary executions.

It took 20 months of wrangling to reach agreement on the selection of officials to run all 29 Revolutionary Committees. The first six committees were dominated by Maoist militants, but these have all given trouble and members have already been purged in four of them. With one or two exceptions, the 23 committees later formed have been headed by conservatives—military officers or "rehabilitated" old-line party officials. Military officers head 19 of the 29 provincial committees, and in 13 their first vice chairmen are also military men.

Although the Revolutionary Committee as an institution was originally created as a "provisional authority," official pronouncements indicate a general consensus that something built around the Revolutionary Committee will take on permanence as an institution of government. The committees are viewed as a core of a new structural form for the party and their conservative influence is likely to be strong in the revitalization of the party life.

The struggle between those who were on opposing sides during the Cultural Revolution is likely to be bitter and will pose a major obstacle to

---

[1] Source: Johnson Library, National Security File, Country File, China, Vol. XIII. Secret.

rebuilding the power structure. Recent reports of investigation into the "class backgrounds" of party cadres being considered for key posts reflect the intensive political infighting which can be expected over the personnel issue.

Almost every day that passes, however, brings added indication that something like pre-Cultural Revolution "normalcy" is returning to at least Peking's style. In other words, conservative provincial power realities are being reflected in Peking. Attached is one of the more interesting of these indicators.[2] The contrast between Chou En-lai's speech on the observation of Albania's Liberation Day and the Albanian presentation is interesting. The latter appears anachronistic—more suited to the Cultural Revolution climate of some months ago. In Chou's remarks, he all but ignores Mao's thought and the Cultural Revolution, and completely ignores Vietnam.

I am beginning to think that the time may be near when we might profitably give another signal (a minor but clear one) to Peking that it has policy alternatives in our regard, when and if it is seriously ready to meet some of the prerequisites. I think the presentation at the February 20 meeting must be prepared with special care. It may be, too, that we could quietly tidy up the FAC regulations. The somewhat larger but still modest economic package contemplated some weeks ago, died with the added burden of the Czechoslovak invasion. I plan to discuss FAC again at State, unless you see fit to deflect me.

Al

---

[2] The attachment, telegram 10358 from Hong Kong, is not printed.

---

334.   Memorandum of Conversation[1]

Washington, December 21, 1968, 7–10 p.m.

SUBJECT

U.S.–Soviet–Chinese Relations

PARTICIPANTS

Boris Davydov, Second Secretary, Embassy of the U.S.S.R.
Daniel I. Davidson, Special Assistant to Governor Harriman

Shortly before the end of an otherwise social evening, Mr. Davydov asked me if I had read the January issue of *Foreign Affairs*. Assuming that

---

[1] Source: Department of State, Central Files, POL CHICOM–US. Confidential. Drafted by Davidson. The meeting took place in Davidson's apartment in Washington.

he was referring to the Kissinger article, I replied "Yes", and asked what he thought of that article. He said that it was the clearest exposition he had seen, but that the article which interested him most was Anatole Shub's, which while primarily discussing Czechoslovakia, concluded by advocating a U.S.-Chinese rapprochement. I told him that I had only read half of that article and had not reached the portion about China.

Davydov said that it was no secret that the Soviet Union was greatly concerned over the possibility of a U.S.-Chinese alliance. He said he could understand our desire to react to Czechoslovakia and he appreciated the ineffectiveness of any possible U.S. counter-move in Europe. Nonetheless, he stated, an attempt to form a U.S.-Chinese alliance would be extremely dangerous and he expressed the hope that I could make this point to anyone of influence I knew in the next Administration. (Davydov is aware of my current connection with Henry Kissinger.)

Davydov stated that any attempt by us to greatly improve our relations with the Chinese and move them towards an alliance with us against the Soviet Union would, of necessity, even if successful, take four to six years. During this period, any hope of progress in U.S.-Soviet relations would be completely impossible. Furthermore, Davydov claimed that we should not be as confident as Shub was—that the eventual victors in the struggle for power in China would be willing to enter an anti-Soviet alliance. He said that while Mao was capable of entering into an anti-Soviet alliance, he would not think that someone like Chou En-lai would be willing to do so.

In Asia, Davydov thought the Soviet Union would attempt to counter a U.S. move towards China by increased efforts to induce Japan to give up its American alliance. In Europe, he could not rule out the possibility of Soviet use of military force. I asked him where military force could be used and he replied, Germany. I stated that I found it hard to take this seriously since military moves in Germany would at the least bring us to the edge of nuclear war. He replied that Western analysts were not the only ones who were impressed with the efficiency of the Soviet move in Czechoslovakia—that the Soviet military was also feeling confident as a result of their success.

Davydov again told me how distressed he was at Shub's recommendation. He said he was aware that some American officials had wanted the USG to bluff a reconciliation with China in order to scare the Soviet Union, but that Shub was recommending not a bluff but a real reconciliation. While he described Shub as a brash young man, he gave weight to the fact that his article had been printed in *Foreign Affairs*. Davydov implied that Shub might be expelled from Moscow in retaliation for his extremely provocative article.

Davydov said that the Soviet Union had been confident that the Johnson Administration would not try to play the dangerous game of

U.S.-Chinese reconciliation. He asked whether I could give him any indication of my estimate of the policy that the Nixon Administration was likely to follow. I told him that I was unable to even hazard a guess. He asked if we could discuss the matter further in the near future. (The conversation ended abruptly as it became obvious that Davydov's seven-year-old son was over-tired.)

---

335.   Memorandum From Alfred Jenkins of the National Security Council Staff to the President's Special Assistant (Rostow)[1]

Washington, December 30, 1968.

SUBJECT

Peking's Foreign Policy

The attached Research Memorandum[2] concerning Peking's foreign policy and especially regarding its attitude toward the United States is a very competent elaboration of the obvious—resulting in entirely appropriate inconclusiveness. In other words, it is obvious that very little indeed is obvious about the policy debate concerning Sino-U.S. relations which must be going on in Peking.

I cannot bring myself to believe that Peking's communications with us concerning the February 20 meeting constitute much of an invitation for rapprochement. It probably is something of a signal of readiness to listen to any interesting change in our own policy, which the new administration may see fit to bring forth. I am knitting brows with EA on this, but I suppose no one can go very far just now. I think our object should be to work out some sort of modest trial balloon with safety devices. With so little yet resolved in Peking, I do not think we can expect any constructive moves toward us from that quarter. All we can do is, at a minimum, somewhat exacerbate the policy struggle, and, at a maximum, provide a bit of ammunition for those who may be somewhat less inimical to us than the full-fledged Maoists.

Al

---

[1] Source: Johnson Library, National Security File, Country File—Addendum, China. Secret.

[2] The attachment, a December 23 memorandum from Hughes to Rusk (Research Memorandum REA–39), is not printed.

336. Memorandum From the President's Special Assistant
(Rostow) to President Johnson[1]

Washington, January 6, 1969, 5 p.m.

SUBJECT

Recommended Change in Treasury Regulations on the Trade of U.S. Subsidiaries Abroad with China

Attached is Secretary Rusk's memorandum[2] recommending you approve a change in Treasury regulations to permit U.S. subsidiaries abroad to sell a limited range of non-strategic goods to China. The change would enable these subsidiaries to engage in non-strategic trade with China as do other firms in the countries in which they are located—but on a more restricted basis.

The change would be made subject to soundings with the incoming Administration and with Congressional leaders. It can be put into effect administratively—without Congressional action—through publication of licensing authority in the *Federal Register*.

Secretaries Clifford, Barr, and Smith concur in the recommendation.

Under current Treasury regulations a U.S. subsidiary abroad is prohibited from selling *any* product it manufactures abroad to China without specific Treasury approval. This is part of our complete embargo on exports to China. The host countries in which these subsidiaries are located have long charged that this regulation is an inappropriate extension of U.S. jurisdiction and therefore an infringement of their sovereignty. Their position is that a U.S. subsidiary in their country, since it is subject to their jurisdiction, should operate under the same regulations as any other firm doing business in their country. They object to the "extraterritorial" aspect of our trade controls, which prohibit companies under their jurisdiction from trading with China without the express approval, on a case-by-case basis, of the U.S. Treasury.

The recommended change in our regulations would go part way toward meeting their objections. It would permit U.S. subsidiaries to sell to China those non-strategic products that can be shipped freely from the U.S. to the USSR and Eastern Europe. For all other products, the U.S. subsidiaries abroad would still have to obtain specific Treasury authorization.

---

[1] Source: Johnson Library, National Security File, Country File—Addendum, China. Secret; Nodis. A notation in unidentified handwriting at the bottom of the page reads as follows: "Walt—I don't want to rush these and do them in the last two weeks." Another handwritten notation states that Rostow had informed NSC staff member Edward Fried of the above.

[2] Rusk's January 4 memorandum is not printed.

The proposed change would serve two purposes:

—It would reduce an irritant in our relations with friendly countries—principally Canada, the UK, and France.
—It might serve as a modest response to the faint signals from Peking suggesting possible changes in their position. Although we would describe the change as merely a technical adjustment in our regulations designed to remove frictions with our Allies, Peking might interpret it as a sign of flexibility in our own position.

Secretary Rusk believes that it makes good sense to act on this now—as a useful move prior to our scheduled meeting with the Chinese Communists in Warsaw on February 20.

In addition, there is a tactical reason for making the change at this time. It would set a modest precedent which your successor could either follow up by extending the list of commodities or ignore. On the other hand, if he initiated the change at the outset of his Administration, too much significance would be read into it.

The main issue here is not substantive but psychological. Everyone agrees that this change has no strategic significance since:

—It does not apply to strategic goods; and
—The Chinese can and do buy these non-strategic products from other companies in the countries concerned.

Therefore, the change could in no way improve China's strategic position. Furthermore, the embargo on shipments to China from the U.S. would remain unchanged. Nevertheless there will be some in Congress who will ignore these facts and argue against *any* change in our regulations affecting China on the grounds that it could lead to a deterioration of the system of strategic trade controls and help China.

On the other hand there is sentiment on the Hill in favor of probing Chinese intentions. (If you approve this action, Secretary Rusk asks your advice on which Members of Congress to consult from the list he attaches at Tab C of his memo.)

This is a modest move which I believe is worth making at this time. It does not commit your successor but it could give him additional room to maneuver should opportunities present themselves.

Walt

Approve

Disapprove

Call me[3]

---

[3] This option is checked on the source text.

Questions Pertaining to Tibet

337. Memorandum for the Special Group[1]

Washington, January 9, 1964.

SUBJECT

Review of Tibetan Operations

1. *Summary*—The CIA Tibetan Activity consists of political action, propaganda, and paramilitary activity. The purpose of the program at this stage is to keep the political concept of an autonomous Tibet alive within Tibet and among foreign nations, principally India, and to build a capability for resistance against possible political developments inside Communist China.

2. *Problem*—To explain Agency expenditures in support of the Tibetan program.

3. *Background and Objectives*—At a 13 December 1963 meeting "The Special Group approved the continuation of CIA controlled Tibetan Operations [*1 line of source text not declassified*]." Previous operations had gone to support isolated Tibetan resistance groups within Tibet and to the creation of a paramilitary force on the Nepal/Tibet border of approximately 2,000 men, 800 of whom were armed by [*less than 1 line of source text not declassified*] airdrop in January 1961. In 1963, as a result of the [*2 lines of source text not declassified*] and as a result of the cited Special Group meeting, the Agency began a more broadly based political program with the exiled Tibetans. This included bringing 133 Tibetans to the United States for training in political, propaganda and paramilitary techniques; continuing the support subsidy to the Dalai Lama's entourage at Dharmsala, India; continuing support to the Nepal based Tibetan guerrillas; the reassignment of a part of the unarmed guerrillas to India for further training; and the [*6 lines of source text not declassified*]. Operational plans call for the establishment of approximately 20 singleton resident agents in Tibet [*less than 1 line of source text not declassified*] two road watch teams in Tibet to report possible Chinese Communist build-ups, and six border watch communications teams [*1 line of source text not declassified*]. The

---

[1] Source: Department of State, INR Historical Files, Special Group Files, S.G. 112, February 20, 1964. Secret; Eyes Only. The source text bears no drafting information. Memoranda for the record by Peter Jessup of February 14 and 24 state that the paper was considered at a Special Group meeting on February 13 and approved by the Special Group on February 20. (Central Intelligence Agency, DCI (McCone) Files, Job 80–B01285A, Box 1, 303 Committee Meetings (1964))

[*less than 1 line of source text not declassified*] will stay in direct touch with Dharmsala and will conduct political correspondence with Tibetan refugee groups [*less than 1 line of source text not declassified*] to create an increased Tibetan national political consciousness among these refugees. The [*less than 1 line of source text not declassified*] was established in October 1963, and the communications center serving it, [*1 line of source text not declassified*] is presently being built with a completion date scheduled in February 1964.

One of the most serious problems facing the Tibetans is a lack of trained officials equipped with linguistic and administrative abilities. The Agency is undertaking the education of some 20 selected Tibetan junior officers to meet this need. A United States advisory committee composed of prominent United States citizens has been established to sponsor the education of these Tibetans. Cornell University has tentatively agreed to provide facilities for their education.

The Agency is supporting the establishment of Tibet Houses in [*less than 1 line of source text not declassified*] Geneva, and New York City. The Tibet Houses are intended to serve as unofficial representation for the Dalai Lama to maintain the concept of a separate Tibetan political identity. The Tibet House in New York City will work closely with Tibetan supporters in the United Nations, particularly the Malayan, Irish, and Thai delegations.

The cost of the Tibetan Program for FY 1964 can be summarized in approximate figures as follows:

    a. Support of 2100 Tibetan guerrillas based in Nepal—$ 500,000
    b. Subsidy to the Dalai Lama—$ 180,000
    c. [*1 line of source text not declassified*] (equipment, transportation, installation, and operator training costs)—$ 225,000
    d. Expenses of covert training site in Colorado—$ 400,000
    e. Tibet Houses in New York, Geneva, and [*less than 1 line of source text not declassified*] (1/2 year)—$ 75,000
    f. Black air transportation of Tibetan trainees from Colorado to India—$ 185,000
    g. Miscellaneous (operating expenses of [*less than 1 line of source text not declassified*] equipment and supplies to reconnaissance teams, caching program, air resupply—not overflights, preparation stages for agent network in Tibet, agent salaries, etc.)—$ 125,000
    h. Educational program for 20 selected junior Tibetan officers— $ 45,000
    Total—$ 1,735,000

4. *Coordination*—This Tibetan operational program has been coordinated with the Department of State for a number of years. Specific operational activity has been coordinated with the Department of Defense and the [*less than 1 line of source text not declassified*] as necessary.

5. *Recommendations*—Barring sudden developments inside Communist China and Tibet, expenses for this long-range, politically-ori-

ented Tibet program are not expected to exceed this amount in the foreseeable future. In fact, there are a number of probable economics, [1-1/2 lines of source text not declassified] for example. Nonetheless, this program will continue to require fairly large expenditures over a long period of time to keep the possibility of a non-Communist government alive to the Tibetan people. We recommend continuance of this program.

338. Telegram From the Department of State to the Embassy in India[1]

Washington, December 29, 1964, 1 p.m.

1292. Please convey following message from President Johnson to Dalai Lama in reply to Dalai Lama's letter of November 18.[2]

Begin text

Your Holiness:

I thank you for your gracious letter of November 18, 1964.

As you point out, the United States Government is deeply concerned with the abrogation of the basic human rights of the Tibetan people and the progressive elimination of their distinctive cultural and religious heritage by the Communist Chinese.

The United States welcomed the opportunities in previous years to assist in bringing the plight of the Tibetan people to the attention of world opinion through the United Nations. As Your Holiness is aware, the United States has also assisted directly in programs to alleviate the material hardships of the Tibetans who have been forced to leave their homeland.

Your Holiness may be assured that the deep and abiding interest of the United States in the welfare of the Tibetan people will continue. My Government welcomes the initiative of the Governments of El Salvador, Nicaragua, and the Philippines to place the Tibetan question on the agen-

---

[1] Source: Department of State, Central Files, POL 19 TIBET/US. Confidential; Limdis. Drafted by John W. Kimball of IO/UNP; cleared by Sisco, Officer in Charge of Indian Affairs David T. Schneider, Louise McNutt of FE/RA, Henry W. Allen of SCA/ORM, Bundy, Komer, and the President; and approved by Marshall Green. Repeated to USUN.

[2] Not printed. (Johnson Library, National Security File, Special Head of State Correspondence File, Tibet—Dalai Lama)

da of the Nineteenth Session of the United Nations General Assembly. We wish, of course, to see the Tibetan item succeed in the United Nations, and we will do everything appropriate to support it.

With assurances of my highest esteem.

Sincerely yours,

Lyndon B. Johnson. *End text.*

Embassy should indicate to Tibetans that Dept expects no publicity on exchange of correspondence. Embassy may at its discretion inform appropriate GOI officials of substance President's letter.

Rusk

339. Telegram From the Mission to the United Nations to the Department of State[1]

New York, November 30, 1965, 0229Z.

2354. Tibet. Gyalo Thondup called on Goldberg and Congressman O'Hara Nov. 29. Thondup said Dalai Lama is anxious keep Tibetan issue alive and to forefront of world opinion; sees no better way accomplish this than through GA debate, though he recognizes GA debates and reses unlikely produce concrete results. Thondup said Tibetans are, however, in somewhat of quandary as to how they best proceed this year. On one hand, Tibetans own convictions re status of Tibet, plus desire give hope and encouragement to people within Tibet, lead them to prefer GA debate which would end with res recognizing political aspects of Tibetan problem through references to self-determination and independence.

On other hand, Tibetans well aware of attitude of GOI which, for two years, has assured Tibetans it willing give full and active support to res emphasizing human rights aspects of Tibetan problem. However, GOI has been very hesitant, and is more so than ever at present moment, to support res touching on political side of Tibetan problem. Would, therefore, appreciate US advice.

Goldberg assured Thondup (and asked that this be conveyed to Dalai Lama) that US Govt and people deeply concerned re plight of Tibetan

---

[1] Source: Department of State, Central Files, POL 19 TIBET/UN. Confidential. Repeated to New Delhi, Manila, Managua, and San Salvador.

people, recognize Tibetan problem has both human rights and political aspects, and prepared support appropriate res touching on both. Nevertheless, must recognize that Afro-Asian attitude has been disappointing this year in many respects (e.g. ChiRep vote and inscription of Tibetan item); Africans are unusually preoccupied with problems of own continent; and many AAs seem anxious avoid taking stand on issues which entail degree of confrontation with Communist China.

In planning strategy, therefore, Goldberg said care must be exercised not to seek res which would fail to carry or carry with only weak vote. Attitude of Asian states with sizeable Buddhist populations of central importance. This particularly true of India, partly because of its positions in AA world, partly because it is closest to and has most intimate knowledge of Tibetan problem. It is unlikely that at present time many AAs willing go much further on Tibetan res than Indians prepared to lead.

Thondup said US support and help with other delegations will be essential for any res. Goldberg said US, of course, would render appropriate help but reiterated view that essential thing for Tibetans is to get active support of Indians and other Asians. MisOff added that US help, if too obvious, would tend damage rather than improve prospects for good vote because it would lend credence to those who contend Tibetan item is essentially US-inspired "cold-war" item.[2]

Thondup then presented us with text of draft res which, he said, was drafted by Tibetans in New Delhi and approved by GOI (text which Thondup has not yet discussed with Phils and other co-sponsors, sent septel). Thondup expressed concern that res might be interpreted as retreat from 1961 res. Goldberg said it did not appear to be retreat since it reaffirmed both previous reses in preamble, and spoke of "denial of the fundamental freedom" which Tibetans have always enjoyed in operative section.

After leaving Goldberg, Thondup told MisOff he was assured in New Delhi that GOI would instruct its UN del to give "full and active support" to this res, including speech in debate and promoting support among other dels. Thondup said Indian Mission confirmed receipt of such instructions earlier in day.

Goldberg

---

[2] Telegram 1412 to USUN, December 6, stated that while the Department had been concerned that "too active" lobbying on the Tibet item might be disadvantageous, additional effort might be desirable to overcome "apparent apathy enveloping item in GA." It instructed USUN to broaden its approaches to Western European and African delegations and to include such delegations as Jordan and Iran. (Ibid.)

340.   Memorandum of Conversation[1]

Washington, December 17, 1965.

SUBJECT

Tibet

PARTICIPANTS

Mr. Gyalo Thondup
Dep. Under Secretary U Alexis Johnson
Amb. H. L. T. Koren, INR

Mr. Thondup said that the Indian attitude regarding the Tibetan question had changed, and, largely because of India's new situation vis-à-vis Communist China, India was now being more forthcoming and helpful. However, the difficulty was that India was weak militarily and hard-pressed, and therefore, reluctant to be truly forthcoming. They were supporting, although not sponsoring, the human rights resolution on Tibet now before the General Assembly. What the Tibetans wanted was support in a political sense and to have a case made for their political freedom. For instance, when approached for support, the Afro-Asians asked what the Tibetans really gained from a resolution on human rights. The Afro-Asians felt that a political resolution looking to independence was what was needed, a resolution dealing with fundamental freedom for Tibet. However, the Indians were unwilling to take this step and the current resolution, which was first aimed at fundamental freedom, was watered down at their insistence to fundamental freedoms. Prime Minister Shastri and the majority of his ministers as well as the Indian people were for the Tibetan cause. But in their present situation, they were not ready to take a position of leadership. They needed to be urged by the U.S.

Therefore, Mr. Thondup wished to pass on to Mr. Johnson the Dalai Lama's request that the U.S. re-examine its position and encourage India to take a political, rather than a purely humanitarian position regarding Tibet. Mr. Thondup went on to say that for Communist China Tibet was a weak spot militarily, spiritually, and morally. He felt that the U.S. had a right to ask for a stronger Indian position and hoped that Ambassador Bowles might take this up with Prime Minister Shastri. The near-term objective was to establish a government-in-exile under the Dalai Lama in India.

Mr. Johnson said that Taiwan posed something of a problem for us. It was not a question that Taiwan's influence with us was strong, but it

---

[1] Source: Department of State, Central Files, POL 19 TIBET. Confidential. Drafted by Koren.

was a factor that we must consider. Mr. Thondup felt that the Nationalist Chinese should take a more progressive attitude, but in talking to them he found them difficult and hampered by a hundred years of tradition and the present dominance of the conservative group. The younger officials were not so hidebound, but the present Chi-Nat stance was that once they were back on the Mainland, they would support self-determination for Tibet. There followed a brief discussion of the status of Tibet in recent history, whether it had been, in fact really independent.

Mr. Thondup said, in summary, that in future efforts it was best to avoid the question of past independence and to rally support for the Dalai Lama and the Tibetan people *in their independence struggle*. He made a strong plea for U.S. help as well as advice on how to pursue their goals. Mr. Johnson noted that the question of government-in-exile was somewhat difficult for us at the present time, because we had resisted all pressure for a Cuban Government-in-exile in this country. He promised to discuss Mr. Thondup's plea with his colleagues who had been following Tibetan matters much more closely recently than he and we would pass our considered view to him, most likely through Ambassador Bowles.

---

341. Telegram From the Department of State to the Embassy in India[1]

Washington, March 22, 1966, 1:53 p.m.

1766. For Ambassador.

1. In conversation with Deputy Under Secretary Johnson December 17, Gyalo Thondup conveyed Dalai Lama's request that USG re-examine its position and encourage India to take a political rather than a humanitarian position regarding Tibet. In this connection, Thondup said Dalai Lama's near-term aim is to establish government-in-exile in India. Mr. Johnson commented that Dept would pass USG views to Thondup most likely through you.

---

[1] Source: Department of State, Central Files, POL 30–2 TIBET. Confidential. Drafted by Arthur Dornheim of FE/ACA and Herbert G. Hagerty of NEA/SOA; cleared by NEA Deputy Assistant Secretary William J. Handley, Richard K. Stuart of INR/DDC, and in draft by Officer in Charge of Republic of China Affairs Norman B. Getsinger, Kimball of IO/UNP, and NEA/SOA Deputy Director David T. Schneider; cleared by U. Alexis Johnson. Repeated to USUN, Taipei, Hong Kong, and Kathmandu.

2. We have re-examined our position and have concluded that from our point of view, there would be little to be gained from such a change in status of the Dalai Lama, that in fact there might be some losses in supporting any change his status, that in terms our current bilateral relations with India we are unenthusiastic about adding this sensitive item to agenda of things we are pressing GOI on, and that in any event, we do not wish to become involved in the Dalai Lama's government-in-exile moves.

3. At your convenience, you are requested to call in Thondup and say you have been instructed to reply to his remarks to Deputy Under Secretary Johnson on December 17 last.

4. Your comments should be in following vein:

A. USG has given careful consideration to Dalai Lama's views. We are particularly mindful of special attention which GOI has already devoted to problems of Tibetan refugees, when the needs of its own people are so very pressing. In these circumstances USG would be most reluctant to be the first to approach GOI, the host government, to ask it to adopt a new attitude toward Dalai Lama.

B. Beyond this, as a practical matter, we feel that Dalai Lama should weigh all aspects of question before making any move this direction. Trying to look at it not only from our own angle but also from that of Indians and of Tibetans themselves, we see very little if any practical advantage deriving to anyone from such a change in status of Dalai Lama. either in terms of his dealings with UN, with his friends, with GRC, or in terms Chicoms. If anything, we see some distinct disadvantage in terms of possible jeopardy such status would place existence of present Offices of Tibet in other countries which now formally recognize Communist China, e.g. UK, Switzerland, and possible establishment of future such offices.

5. In general you should assure Thondup that USG is determined to persevere in its efforts achieve a just and peaceful solution of Tibetan problem.[2]

Rusk

---

[2] Telegram 2614 from New Delhi, March 29, reported that on March 28 the Chargé had orally conveyed the Department's response to Gyalo Thondup. (Ibid.)

342.   Memorandum for the 303 Committee[1]

Washington, January 26, 1968.

SUBJECT

Status Report on Tibetan Operations

1. *Summary*—The CIA Tibetan program, parts of which were initiated in 1956 with the cognizance of the Committee, is based on U.S. Government commitments made to the Dalai Lama in 1951 and 1956. The program consists of political action, propaganda, paramilitary and intelligence operations, appropriately coordinated with and supported by [*less than 1 line of source text not declassified*]. This program was last reviewed and endorsed by the Committee on 20 February 1964. Current activities have been coordinated with and have the approval of [*1 line of source text not declassified*], Mr. William Bundy, Assistant Secretary of State for East Asian and Pacific Affairs, and Mr. Lucius Battle, Assistant Secretary of State for Near East and South Asian Affairs.

2. *Program Objectives*—In the political action and propaganda field, Tibetan program objectives are aimed toward lessening the influence and capabilities of the Chinese regime through support, among Tibetans and among foreign nations, of the concept of an autonomous Tibet under the leadership of the Dalai Lama; toward the creation of a capability for resistance against possible political developments inside Tibet; and the containment of Chinese Communist expansion—in pursuance of U.S. policy objectives stated initially in NSC 5913/1.[2] [*6 lines of source text not declassified*]

3. *Appraisal of Current Programs*—The cultural revolution in China expanded into Tibet bringing with it tremendous disturbances including the disruption of internal transportation, communication, travel and, to a significant extent, peace and order. Unfortunately there are no apparent signs that the Tibetan people are capitalizing upon this internal chaos to seek further autonomy. Chinese security has shown no signs of deteri-

---

[1] Source: Department of State, INR Historical Files, Tibet, 1967–1968. Secret; Eyes Only. The source text bears no drafting information. A March 4 memorandum from Battle to Bohlen describes it as a CIA memorandum. (Ibid.) It was discussed at a March 19 meeting of the 303 Committee. According to Peter Jessup's memorandum for the record of the meeting, CIA representative James Critchfield stated that "achievements inside Tibet were minimal—outside more substantial." He observed that "the Tibetans by nature did not appear to be congenitally inclined toward conspiratorial proficiency." Jessup records no action by the 303 Committee at the meeting. (Johnson Library, National Security File, Intelligence File, 303 Committee)

[2] The text of NSC 5913/1, approved September 25, 1959, is printed in *Foreign Relations, 1958–1960*, vol. XVI, pp. 133–144. Also see the record of the NSC discussion of NSC 5913 on September 17, 1959, ibid., pp. 116–127.

oration and their control over Tibet, both political and military, remains as pervasive as ever. Tibetan leadership has been purged, leaving the Chinese in direct control of the local administration, and a large number of underground assets have been uncovered and neutralized.

The Tibetan program has a potential for operational success based on a reservoir of trained agent material, the location in a safe-haven of the Dalai Lama together with the nucleus of new young leaders, widespread sympathy for the Tibetan cause, indications of a more positive Indian attitude toward the political aspirations of the Tibetan government, and evidence of considerable disarray among the Chinese stationed in Tibet.

a.   At present there are no radio teams remaining inside Tibet. Radio teams continue to function [*less than 1 line of source text not declassified*] although much of their information comes from the debriefing of traders and refugees. Singleton resident agent operations in Tibet, regarded as being the long-range replacement of the black radio teams, have not progressed as planned due to continued tightening of Chinese security in the border areas. Intelligence reporting from all sources deals primarily with military, political and construction activities along the Tibetan border.

b.   The Tibetan paramilitary unit, a remnant of the 1959 resistance force, is dispersed in 15 camps [*less than 1 line of source text not declassified*]. The Tibetan leadership views the force as the paramilitary arm of its "government-in-exile" [*2 lines of source text not declassified*]. Because of the diplomatic sensitivity occasioned by the presence of the Tibetan force [*less than 1 line of source text not declassified*] it has been enjoined from offensive action which might invite Chinese [*less than 1 line of source text not declassified*] retaliation. Joint efforts to disperse the force to other uninhabited areas [*less than 1 line of source text not declassified*] have not been successful because of Chinese [*less than 1 line of source text not declassified*] reaction or of difficulties in resupply.

c.   [*1 line of source text not declassified*] responsible for radio contact with and operational direction of the radio teams, the paramilitary resistance force, and the support mechanism [*less than 1 line of source text not declassified*] continue to serve their intended purpose with a minimum of problems.

d.   Bi-lateral CIA-Tibetan intelligence collection operations into Tibet, [*less than 1 line of source text not declassified*] have increased significantly, both in number and in value during the past few years.

e.   Activities designed to develop a dynamic political program [*less than 1 line of source text not declassified*] to weld the refugee communities into a cohesive whole under the leadership of the Dalai Lama and his brother, Gyalo Thondup, continue. These include:

(1) The Geneva, New York and [*less than 1 line of source text not declassified*] "Tibet houses" continue in operation. The Geneva office serves as

the coordinating point for the resettlement of some 500 Tibetan refugees in Switzerland and other European countries and maintains contact with the international agencies concerned with Tibetan relief. Although time has dimmed some of the effectiveness of its pleas, the New York office continues to lobby among the U.N. delegations for legal and moral support for the Tibetan cause, guided in their efforts by a sitting former U.S. delegate to the U.N. who is also a well-known international lawyer. [2 *lines of source text not declassified*]

(2) The covert training program conducted in the U.S. under which some 250 Tibetans were trained, ended in November 1964.

(3) Twenty selected Tibetan junior officers studied at Cornell University, over a three year period. Due to the Katzenbach strictures, this program was concluded in July 1967; CIA is considering a continuation of the program, on a limited scale, [*less than 1 line of source text not declassified*].

(4) The Tibetan organizational party, the Cho Kha Sum, (i.e. the Defense of Religion by the Three Regions: Kham, Amdo and U-Tsang), which was established in India in April 1964 by Gyalo Thondup, now has an active press and publications arm. While the future potential of the party is still in question, the Tibetans are making an effort to mold it into an effective organization, aimed at halting a drift towards disunity among the refugees, developing a political consciousness and a political program with which to challenge the Communist efforts inside Tibet.

4. *Significant Previous 303 Committee Approvals—*

a. September 1958—initial endorsement of CIA covert support to Tibetan resistance;

b. 20 May 1959—initial approval of covert support to the Dalai Lama;

c. 14 February 1961—endorsed continuation of the covert program;

d. 13 December 1962—approved training of Tibetan guerrilla force;

e. 20 February 1964—reviewed and endorsed continuation of covert program;

f. 9 April 1965—approved relocation of Tibetan paramilitary force;

g. 8 July and 25 November 1966—endorsed the covert paramilitary program [*1 line of source text not declassified*].

These landmark reviews were interspersed with status reports and briefings of the Committee, in one period at monthly intervals. The basic decisions listed above in several instances were reviewed with Higher Authority.

5. *Coordination—*

a. *Department of State*—Since the project's inception, appropriate officials of the Department have approved various elements of the program. Department officers who have been briefed on aspects of this project include Elmer Falk and Clement J. Sobotka, Director and Deputy Director, respectively, of the Office of Refugee and Migration Affairs; Harald Jacobson, Director, Office of Asian Communist Affairs; William Gleysteen, Deputy Director, Office of U.N. Political Affairs; William Bundy, Assistant Secretary of State for East Asian and Pacific Affairs; and Lucius Battle, Assistant Secretary of State for Near East and South Asian Affairs.

b. *Ambassadors*—The past and present Ambassadors to Nepal and India have approved the Tibetan program, [*1 line of source text not declassified*].

c. [*2-1/2 lines of source text not declassified*]

6. *Projected and Planned Programs—*

a. On the political front during 1967, the Dalai Lama began what is hoped will be a long-range program of projecting himself and Tibetan affairs on an international basis. He is contemplating visits to Ceylon, Burma and Cambodia, having visited Japan and Thailand in late 1967. Invitations have also been extended from several European countries having active Tibetan refugee programs or interests.

b. Gyalo Thondup, acting for the Tibetan partnership in our liaison with the Indians, has proposed the establishment of a Tibetan Operations Center to represent Tibetan interests [*less than 1 line of source text not declassified*]. This Tibetan center would conceivably provide greater efficiency in the Tibetan handling of existing operations and in the relegation of operational tasks to Tibetan assets. [*1 line of source text not declassified*]

c. Some elements of the basic covert program remain to be implemented. They include: the deployment of landline wiretap teams to selected priority targets within Tibet; the activation of special refugee debriefing teams; a census of some 70,000 Tibetan refugees spread throughout India and its neighboring countries which may locate additional operational assets; and the resupply of arms and ammunition to the Mustang force.

7. *Costs*—At the time of the February 1964 review by the Committee, the projected annual cost for all Tibetan operations was $1,735,000. With the discontinuation of the training programs in the U.S., [*1 line of source text not declassified*] a reduction of $570,000 in this estimate for FY68 has been achieved. The remainder of $1,165,000 has been programmed in the CIA budget for FY68 for the activities described in this paper. Of this amount $650,000 was approved by the 303 Committee on 25 November 1966 in its review of the [*less than 1 line of source text not declassified*].

343.   Memorandum of Conversation[1]

Washington, December 6, 1968.

SUBJECT

Call on Mr. Rostow by Mr. Gyalo Thondup, Brother of His Holiness the Dalai Lama

PARTICIPANTS

Mr. Eugene V. Rostow, Under Secretary for Political Affairs
Mr. Gyalo Thondup
Mr. Reynold A. Riemer—M
Mrs. Kathleen C. Dougall, EA/ACA

1.   Mr. Thondup stated that he had been instructed by His Holiness the Dalai Lama to express His Holiness' gratitude to the United States Government for its assistance to Tibetan refugees—specifically the surplus food and the monetary assistance. Mr. Rostow replied that we appreciate this message deeply, and that Mr. Thondup can assure His Holiness that we will not forget the plight of the Tibetans.

2.   Mr. Thondup said he had another matter to take up. He said it would be very essential and useful if India would take the initiative in the United Nations on a resolution concerning Tibet. He said he has been trying to convince India that it is in its own interest, as well as in the interest of the people of Tibet, to do this. The Indians, he said, are afraid of the Chinese Communists. His Holiness, he said, feels that US indirect encouragement to India to take the initiative on a resolution would be helpful and His Holiness asks the advice and help of the United States on this subject. Mr. Thondup said that the Tibetan people still want to fight the Chinese Communists and that Tibet, "a small nation," is very dependent on large nations to keep the issue alive. Whatever the United States can do would help a small people's struggle for independence.

3.   Mr. Rostow said that he had talked about Tibetan matters with a high ranking member of the Indian Foreign Office in New Delhi earlier this year. He said that he will ask the views of the Indian Ambassador here in regard to a UN resolution but that India has its own policy and may not respond to suggestions.

4.   Mr. Thondup said that he is afraid of the Soviet Union's position on a UN resolution, also. In 1959 the Soviet Union was bitterly opposed to the resolution and has voted against such resolutions all along, but since last year he thinks the Soviet Union has shown a slight change. He

---

[1] Source: Department of State, Central Files, POL 19 TIBET. Confidential. Drafted by Dougall.

has had private meetings with Soviet officials and was told that "Tibet and Sinkiang are not the interest of India but of the Soviet Union."

5. In response to the fear expressed by Mr. Thondup as to the effect on Tibet of an accommodation the United States might make with the Chinese Communists, Mr. Rostow stated that we seek to bring the Chinese Communists into the family of nations but that we would not make any accommodation with the Chinese Communists at the expense of Tibet.

6. Mr. Thondup stated that there are nearly 900 Tibetan students in Europe and that a visit of His Holiness to Europe is being planned. American friends, he said, always ask why he does not come to the United States. Mr. Thondup said he did not know the reaction of the United States to a private visit of His Holiness to this country. Mr. Rostow said he would have to inquire and added that this would be a matter for the new Administration. Mr. Thondup commented that His Holiness is not an ordinary visitor and would have to make a courtesy call on the President. He expressed his gratitude to Mr. Rostow for inquiring on this subject.

7. Mr. Thondup commented at some length on events in Tibet. He said the situation now is "quite quiet" since the establishment of the Revolutionary Committee for Tibet in September. Two rival organizations are fighting each other and pressing Tibetans to join. The Tibetans, however, are taking a neutral position. There are many killings of Chinese by other Chinese. The Cultural Revolution has affected many military leaders in Tibet. Many have been dismissed; many are new. There is new leadership among the military and in the Party. The Chinese have purged all Tibetan collaborators. Some were killed, some were imprisoned, and some were tortured and released. The elderly people hate the Chinese, and the younger people are now bitter because all important posts are occupied by Chinese, not Tibetans. The Tibetans want to fight, but this is a very wrong position. Events of 1959 are an example. It is only suicide to fight the Chinese.

8. Mr. Thondup said the Chinese system in Tibet is a complete failure. The six million (sic) people in Tibet are not convinced the Chinese are doing anything for them. It is very hard for the Chinese to get used to the altitude and the type of food available in Tibet. There are food shortages because of the difficulty of bringing food long distances to Tibet. The Chinese bring in military and other supplies instead. The Chinese troops do not want to stay in Tibet.

Mongolia

344. Action Memorandum From the Assistant Secretary of State for Far Eastern Affairs (Bundy) to Secretary of State Rusk[1]

Washington, June 3, 1965.

SUBJECT

Diplomatic Recognition of the Mongolian People's Republic

Discussion:

This memorandum concerning the recognition of Outer Mongolia is submitted at the request of S/S. We continue to receive indications that the Mongols are still interested in exchanging missions (Tab A).[2] Ambassador Kohler favors recognition (Tabs B and C)[3] as does Ambassador Bohlen (Tab D).[4]

Ambassador Kohler suggests that, once a policy decision is taken, he be authorized to take quiet soundings with the Outer Mongolian Ambassador in Moscow to avoid any possibility of a rebuff to a public approach on the pretext of popular revulsion because of our behavior in Viet-Nam (Tab C).

We continue to believe that our 1961 negotiations should be resumed. (Tab E summarizes the pros and cons.)[5] If the Outer Mongolians should prove unresponsive to an approach by Ambassador Kohler, we would inform them privately that we are prepared to consider recognition again whenever they are ready. Aside from Soviet and Outer Mongolian attitudes, the problem of the GRC reaction remains, as always, the principal deterrent. In our most recent conversation with the GRC Embassy concerning Outer Mongolia we repeated to Minister Shen on May 19 that, while we were not actively contemplating recognition at that time, any U.S. commitment made with respect to the non-recognition of Outer Mongolia was not an unending one (Tab F).[6] A precis of US-GRC

---

[1] Source: Department of State, Central Files, POL 16 MONG. Secret. Sent through Ambassador at Large Llewellyn E. Thompson. Drafted by Lindsey Grant, Arthur R. Dornheim of ACA, David Dean, and Bennett, and concurred in by Deputy Assistant Secretary for EUR Richard H. Davis, SOV Deputy Director David H. Henry, MacArthur, and Assistant Legal Adviser for Far Eastern Affairs Carl F. Salans. The source text bears the handwritten notation "S saw."

[2] Airgram A–1490 from Moscow, May 17, and a March 1 letter from Ambassador Kohler to EUR Assistant Secretary Tyler. None of the tabs is printed.

[3] Telegram 2683 from Moscow, March 13; letter of June 12 from Kohler to Tyler; and telegram 3594 from Moscow, May 29.

[4] Telegram 4993 from Paris, March 4.

[5] Unsigned and undated paper entitled "Advantages and Disadvantages of Resuming Recognition Negotiations With the Mongols."

[6] No record of the conversation with Shen is attached to the source text.

exchanges on the Mongolian recognition issue is also included in Tab F.[7] Steps we might take to mitigate the expected adverse GRC reaction to our decision are discussed at Tab G.[8]

As to timing, it is extremely important that the step be taken as soon as possible (preferably before the end of June) to avoid an adverse effect on the Chinese representation position in the UN and in any disarmament conference that may be called. Recent soundings by Marshall Green at our Embassy in Taipei and current conversations here with Taipei's DCM Ralph Clough indicate that now is probably the best time, as far as our relations with the GRC are concerned, to recognize Outer Mongolia. Our firm policy in Viet-Nam should allay any GRC fears that U.S. policy is softening, and the intelligence requirements dramatized by Communist China's second nuclear explosion are self-evident.

The Russians may be less inclined right now to be forthcoming about transit rights, but the virulence of the Chinese Communist attack upon them should stiffen their back and perhaps cause them fairly shortly to be seeking some indirect means to riposte. If our assumptions are correct, the Mongols will be urging the Russians to cooperate, and the USSR perhaps is not presently in the best position to deny favors to the Mongols. In November 1964 the British established a mission in Ulan Bator, and the French have recently recognized Outer Mongolia, so we are not breaking new ground.

Our generalized interest in self-determination argues that we recognize Outer Mongolia. To this may be added certain specific arguments. If negotiations lead to recognition, we shall have:

1) encouraged the Mongols' sense of national identity, both in Mongolia and the bordering areas of China, and promoted the further fractioning of the Communist world,
2) contributed to a deepening of Sino-Soviet hostilities,
3) increased our intelligence capabilities in an important area,
4) afforded better protection for the growing number of American tourists in Mongolia, and
5) deflected charges of racialism by recognizing for the first time a non-white Communist regime. (This small point may be useful in our efforts to counter the Chinese Communists' drive to polarize feelings between the white and non-white worlds.)

Even if they did not lead to recognition, negotiations with the Mongols would yield us certain advantages. We would gain a better reading of Russian/Mongol/Chinese relations at this juncture, we would have established communication with the Mongols, and we would have en-

---

[7] Unsigned and undated paper entitled "Precis of U.S.-GRC Exchanges on Mongolian Recognition Issue."

[8] The remainder of the tabs, consisting of unsigned and undated papers as described in the memorandum, are attached but not printed.

couraged their sense of nationalism and perhaps their irritation at the Russians. On the other hand, we also would have complicated our relations with the GRC.

A proposed scenario is at Tab H and answers to anticipated domestic criticism at Tab I, in the event you decide that this matter should be further explored. Ambassador MacArthur concurs in the recommendations but wishes to underline the importance of consultation with congressional leaders as spelled out in paragraph 2 of Tab H. As you are aware the Zablocki sub-committee has recommended that consideration should be given to recognition of Outer Mongolia.

Recommendation:

That you approve further exploration of the idea of resuming recognition negotiations with the Mongols in accordance with the scenario at Tab H.[9]

---

[9] The source text bears no indication of Rusk's approval or disapproval. A July 6 memorandum from Bundy to Thompson and Rusk transmitted additional material. (Department of State, Central Files, POL 16 MONG) A July 28 memorandum from Thompson to Bundy and EUR Assistant Secretary Leddy stated that Rusk did not wish to act on the matter at that time. (Ibid., ROC Files: Lot 75 D 76, Bundy Visit to ROC, March 10–12, 1966) An August 2 memorandum by Dornheim states that Thompson told Berger that Rusk did not want to take action at that time because it "would only invite hostility from President Chiang Kai-shek and we had enough governments critical of us at the moment." Rusk did, however, suggest that soundings be taken of Chiang's views when Chiang Ching-kuo visited Washington in September. (Ibid.)

345.   **Action Memorandum From the Assistant Secretary of State for East Asian and Pacific Affairs (Bundy) and the Assistant Secretary of State for European Affairs (Leddy) to Secretary of State Rusk**[1]

Washington, January 9, 1967.

SUBJECT

Diplomatic Recognition of the Mongolian People's Republic

Discussion

1.   In an action memorandum dated May 6, 1966 (Tab H),[2] the SIG forwarded a recommendation that we initiate steps to recognize Mongolia. No action was taken at that time, largely because the timing was considered unpropitious. The SIG recommendation stated that there were then more international advantages than disadvantages in recognizing Mongolia. (Tab F gives the arguments pro and con as presented to the SIG.)[3]

2.   There have been significant changes in the situation, leading us to reexamine the problem. We believe the time is now propitious to undertake steps which would lead to recognition of Mongolia. Factors supporting this view include the following:

a)   Chinese representation in the United Nations has been resolved for another year and will not come up again for several months;

b)   The Republic of China is pleased with the results of the Chinese representation issue in the United Nations which has strongly reaffirmed its international status, and this fact strengthens our position in countering expected GRC opposition to our recognition of Mongolia.

c)   We have demonstrated our opposition to Communist aggression in Vietnam, and recognition of Mongolia now would demonstrate our desire to work with and establish contacts with peaceful Asian Communist states;

d)   We have had a few recent indications from Mongolian officials through private channels that they continue to wish to establish relations with the U.S. [3 *lines of source text not declassified*] (INR has completed a

---

[1] Source: Department of State, Central Files, POL 16 MONG. Secret. Drafted by Franklin O. McCord of ACA. Concurred in by Jacobson, Bennett, Country Director for Soviet Affairs Malcolm Toon, Sisco, Country Director for Japan Richard L. Sneider, MacArthur, and Kohler. The Bureau of Far Eastern Affairs became the Bureau of East Asian and Pacific Affairs on November 1, 1966.

[2] The memorandum from Under Secretary Ball to the Secretary, undated but with a drafting date of May 6, 1966, stated that at the Senior Interdepartmental Group meeting on May 3, it had been agreed that Ball should inform Rusk of the SIG views: that there were more international advantages than disadvantages in recognizing Mongolia, that such a decision would require consulting some members of Congress and Japan and informing the GRC, and that the question of timing was important with respect to the GRC reaction.

[3] The remainder of the tabs, except Tab G, consisting of unsigned and undated papers as described in the memorandum, are attached but not printed.

study of probable reactions by Mongolia and certain other countries to a U.S. approach—Tab G.)[4]

3. We do not expect the Soviet Union to oppose establishment of a U.S. presence in Ulan Bator, although Soviet interests will undoubtedly be reflected in Mongol efforts to control the size and activities of our mission. At the present time, also, the prospect of Chinese Communist criticism will carry less weight with both the Mongols and their Soviet allies. We believe that the current situation in Communist China will have no effect on reactions to our approach to the Mongols.

4. One factor again urging speed is the prospective visit this May of the Vice President of the Republic of China. We should if possible progress to the point that we can make our approach to the Mongols a matter of public knowledge prior to his departure for the United States.

5. If the decision is taken to recognize Mongolia, certain members of Congress should be consulted and the GRC and Japan should be informed beforehand. Japan is also seriously considering early recognition of Mongolia after the January 29 elections and will wish to consult with us on the timing of our respective actions. We should also inform the Soviet Union shortly after approaching the Mongols. We may also wish to notify our NATO allies at an appropriate stage.

6. A recommended action schedule has been prepared by EA and EUR and is attached at Tab B. The talking points at Tab C and D, and draft telegram at Tab E, would be utilized in implementing this schedule following approval of the recommendation contained in the Memorandum for the President at Tab A.

7. We expect the GRC to protest, but we have already told the GRC that we had the step under review. We also believe we should be able to reassure the GRC that these actions do not in any way affect our continuing support for it and that we will play our move in low key. Our suggested action schedule allows the GRC time (two weeks) to make their views known.

8. Although we believe that the Mongols will respond favorably to our initiative, it is always possible that for some reason they will reject it. We believe that the risk on this score is minimal and that in any event the disadvantages that a negative Mongol response would entail do not outweigh the advantages of moving at this time.

---

[4] Tab G is not attached to the source text.

Recommendation

That you sign the Memorandum to the President at Tab A.[5]

---

[5] The source text is filed with a February 7 note from Under Secretary Katzenbach's Special Assistant Donald R. Morris stating that Katzenbach had discussed this memorandum with Rusk, who did not sign the memorandum to the President, and that it should be returned to EA on the basis of Katzenbach's conversation with Bundy. A memorandum from Bundy and Leddy to Rusk, undated but with a drafting date of July 5, states that in response to their January 9 memorandum, Katzenbach had suggested seeking to moderate the Republic of China's opposition to recognition of Mongolia by discussing with it some of the anticipated intelligence benefits. (Department of State, Central Files, POL 16 MONG)

---

346.   Telegram From the Embassy in the Republic of China to the Department of State[1]

Taipei, March 30, 1967, 1040Z.

2993. Eyes only Bundy. Ref: Taipei 2975.[2]

1. I had meeting March 29 with FonMin Wei at his request, which turned out to be on subject of Outer Mongolia.

2. FonMin said that President Chiang, who is very busy, had suggested that requested meeting with him to discuss Outer Mongolia could be handled by FonMin instead of President. FonMin said he could outline GRC position and that President Chiang would not give any different reaction from that he (FonMin) would give.

3. FonMin said that GRC viewed question of recognition of Outer Mongolia as matter of China's territorial integrity, and that recognition by US would be an act undermining GRC's basic position. He said that closeness of US–GRC relations meant that any US recognition would have a more serious impact on GRC than recognition by Australia, for instance. Australia is a "new friend" but US is a close ally who should not undermine GRC basic policy.

---

[1] Source: Department of State, Central Files, POL 16 MONG. Top Secret; Exdis.

[2] Telegram 2975 from Taipei, March 28, stated that McConaughy had a tentative appointment with President Chiang on March 31 to discuss Outer Mongolia. He planned to follow the instructions in telegram 142238, February 23, which instructed him to "take soundings with the Gimo" concerning the possibility of U.S. representation in Ulan Bator and possible intelligence advantages. (Both ibid.)

4. I emphasized that USG had not reached any decision on recognition, and that we wished at this stage only to place before President Chiang, and seek his reaction to, some of the possible advantages we think might accrue to US if we should open an Embassy in Ulan Bator. I said that my instructions were to seek the Gimo's views, and that I still wished if possible to have opportunity to do so, but that of course it would be up to Gimo whether he wished to receive me on this subject. I noted that in view of known high importance GRC attaches to entire subject of Outer Mongolia, it would seem appropriate for GRC reaction to be conveyed to US at highest level. I said there was no great urgency about appointment, and that USG was not on the brink of any quick decision, so that I could afford to wait until Gimo might have time to see me.

5. FonMin spoke at some length about impossibility, in GRC view, of getting any advantage from Embassy in Ulan Bator. He said Sovs would not permit US to set up any installations in Outer Mongolia capable of monitoring ChiCom nuclear or missile tests. I confined myself to saying that FonMin perhaps not aware of technological advances which might in fact enable us to obtain valuable technical information.

6. [*10 lines of source text not declassified*]

7. I reiterated request to discuss matter with Gimo at his convenience, and said I would stand by to see if Gimo would find it possible to give appointment. FonMin repeated that Gimo's views would be no different from what FonMin had already conveyed, but agreed to convey my renewed request to Gimo.

8. Today (March 30) in course of unrelated meeting with DefMin Chiang Ching-kuo (CCK) to exchange views on mainland situation, CCK brought up Outer Mongolia. He recalled that USG has expressed an interest in considering recognition, saying that this had been mentioned to him in September 1965 during his Washington visit. He said that while the matter was outside of his sphere of authority he would like to know of US view of relations between Outer Mongolia and ChiComs.

9. I said we had little independent information, but that Outer Mongolia seemed to be following anti-ChiCom stance similar to Soviets. Soviet influence was apparently strong, but Mongolia should not necessarily be considered merely their puppet. I recalled that Mongolians had recently reviewed alleged 1921 Chinese interference in Outer Mongolia, and I said we had information that Soviet SAMs installed near Ulan Bator. I said USG had reached no decision on recognition, was keeping an open mind, but that I had instructions see Gimo to get his views directly, as well as to convey to him our thoughts on certain advantages possibly to be derived from having an Embassy there. I said FonMin had conveyed to me that Gimo is very busy, but I had renewed my request for an appointment with Gimo because of USG desire to give full consideration to GRC views, and because I knew that Gimo's own views expressed by

him would get close high level consideration in Washington. I said I knew Gimo to be very busy, but that I felt it important for our joint interests for me to have appointment.

10. CCK said "I understand."

11. In obviously prepared reminiscences, he spoke of origin of Sino Sov Treaty of 1945, which was result, he said, of agreements at Yalta which GRC had not been party to. He said that during negotiations on that treaty he himself had spoken to Stalin, who said that an Outer Mongolia under influence other than Soviet would be threat to security of USSR. Stalin had also promised that there would be 30 years of peace in the area if Soviet proposals accepted by GRC, and that Soviets would not support ChiComs against ChiNats. (His intention was to say that Soviets not to be trusted.) He then referred to his third trip to Moscow in fall of 1945 to talk about an economic agreement privileges in Manchuria, not to be accorded to any other country. CCK had discussed this provision with Gimo, who had refused to sign, noting that treaty would have excluded US from economic opportunities in Manchuria. (His intention here was to say that GRC had protected US interests at that time.) He recalled that shortly afterwards in November Lin Piao's troops had begun attacking Mukden and Changchun, in violation of agreements.

12. *Comment:* We have recently had indications from middle level MOFA officers and others that GRC opposition to US or Japanese recognition of Outer Mongolia would be on "moral" grounds rather than on legal grounds, since MOFA officers recognize that GRC abrogation of Sino-Soviet Treaty after it was in force for eight years cannot from international law standpoint undo previous recognition of independence of Outer Mongolia. FonMin did place some emphasis on "territorial integrity" of Outer Mongolia, but major emphasis seemed to be on requesting USG not to undermine position of close ally. CCK has implied that past GRC actions in support of US interests deserve some recompense.

13. I am not sure whether my rather strong representations for appointment with Gimo will produce results, but believe next step should be to await reply from FonMin. If appointment again rejected, I would take it to mean that Gimo feels he already has received substance of this approach from Ambassador Goldberg on March 1 (Embtel 2623)[3] and does not wish to involve his prestige further at this preliminary stage. It would be quite an adverse indication.[4]

McConaughy

---

[3] See footnote 2, Document 245.

[4] McConaughy reported in telegram 3359, April 28, that he had discussed the possibility of U.S. recognition of Mongolia with Foreign Minister Wei the previous day and that Wei had reiterated GRC opposition. (Department of State, Central Files, POL 16 MONG)

347.   Action Memorandum From the Deputy Assistant Secretary of State for East Asian and Pacific Affairs (Brown) and the Assistant Secretary of State for European Affairs (Leddy) to Secretary of State Rusk[1]

Washington, May 27, 1968.

SUBJECT

    Recognition of Mongolian People's Republic

Discussion:

    1.   In response to our query of May 7, Ambassador Thompson has expressed the opinion that there is now a better-than-even chance that a direct approach to the Mongols on the subject of establishing diplomatic relations would elicit a favorable response (Tab A).[2] He continues to favor establishing relations with the MPR and does not believe the Soviets would oppose. Last August the Ambassador considered it inadvisable to approach the Mongolian Government on this issue because of indications that the Mongolian position on Vietnam ruled out ties with the United States at that time.[3]

    2.   We continue to believe that it is in our national interest to establish a diplomatic presence in Mongolia as soon as possible. It would improve our intelligence collection capabilities in that area. It would demonstrate in a timely fashion that the United States is willing to have normal relations with an Asian Communist state which leaves its neighbors in peace. It would not at this time have a significant effect on the attitudes of the USSR or Communist China.

    3.   In terms of timing, there are advantages in moving now while Vietnam negotiations are in an early stage. Progress towards peace talks has already served to ease existing political restraints, as demonstrated

---

    [1] Source: Department of State, Central Files, POL MONG–US. Secret; Exdis. Sent through Under Secretary of State Katzenbach. Drafted by J. Stapleton Roy of the Office of Soviet Union Affairs, and Kreisberg on May 14; and cleared by Bohlen, Sisco, Assistant Secretary of State for Congressional Relations William B. Macomber, Jr., Jacobson, Shoesmith, Sneider, and Assistant Legal Adviser for East Asian and Pacific Affairs George H. Aldrich.

    [2] Telegram 159927 to Moscow, May 7, and telegram 3782 from Moscow, May 8; neither printed.

    [3] Telegram 264 from Moscow, July 20, 1967, reported that the Austrian Ambassador to the Soviet Union had told Thompson this. (Department of State, Central Files, POL 16 MONG) This is apparently the telegram referred to in a July 20 note from Rusk's Special Assistant Harry W. Shlaudeman to Bundy file with the memorandum from Bundy and Leddy to Rusk cited in footnote 5, Document 345. In the memorandum, Bundy and Leddy renewed their recommendation for recognition of Mongolia. Shlaudeman's note states that Rusk wanted the memorandum returned to Bundy with a cable "which apparently disposes of the problem."

by Soviet ratification of the Consular Convention. In addition, the President and the White House staff have in recent weeks requested your suggestions on possible policy initiatives for the balance of the Administration. Recognition of Mongolia can usefully be considered in this context also.

4. We cannot expect to secure GRC concurrence in this move, and Nationalist Chinese opposition will continue to be vigorous. In March 1967 Ambassador Goldberg mentioned directly to President Chiang the intelligence aspect of our interest in recognition, and Ambassador McConaughy subsequently discussed the potential intelligence benefits in greater detail with GRC Foreign Minister Wei and other GRC officials reiterated their Government's strong opposition to recognition of Mongolia by the US. Ambassador McConaughy this month has reassessed the GRC attitude (Taipei 3177 at Tab C).[4] Although he recommends, from the standpoint of "best nourishment of our interests and relations" in Taiwan, that we postpone indefinitely any move toward recognition, he believes that GRC reaction now would be substantially that which he anticipated a year ago. We therefore conclude that recognition of Mongolia will create strains in our relations but that these strains will be largely temporary in nature and manageable in degree. Our actions over the past few years have probably conditioned Taipei to accept the inevitability of eventual US recognition of Mongolia, and the record shows we have given every consideration to GRC views. Moreover, unlike 1961, the GRC will not need to take any positive action suggesting acquiescence in our move.

5. The Japanese Government has made clear on several occasions its hope that the US would keep the GOJ informed of any US decision to move toward recognition of Mongolia. Embassy Tokyo's assessment (Tab D)[5] emphasizes that the GOJ would probably welcome such a move. We have indicated we would stay in close touch with the GOJ. The GOJ has informed the Mongolian Government of its willingness to enter diplomatic relations with Mongolia if the MPR would agree to waive the right to raise the question of war reparations, a condition the Mongols have thus far refused to meet. GRC opposition is also a factor in Tokyo's moves, as is the GOJ's desire to establish diplomatic relations with the MPR in advance of the US. In view of the sensitivity of the GRC and the GOJ on this issue, we intend to inform both governments in advance of any US decision to approach the Mongols on the question of recognition. Embassy Seoul (Tab E)[6] favors recognition providing the timing does not come on the heels of some unsettling development.

---

[4] Telegram 3177 from Taipei, May 22; not printed.

[5] Tab D, listed as telegram 8623 from Tokyo, is not attached to the source text. (Department of State, Central Files, POL 16 MONG)

[6] Tab E, listed as telegram 7443 from Seoul, is not attached to the source text. (Ibid.)

6.   Congressional support for this initiative will be essential. Our first move would be to take renewed soundings with key and discreet Congressional leaders. We have noted that key members of Congress, including the Chairmen of the House Foreign Affairs Committee and the Senate Foreign Relations Committee, have favored recognition of Mongolia.

Recommendations:

1.   That we in collaboration with H be authorized to sound out key Congressional opinion on recognizing Mongolia, drawing on information in Tab B.[7]

2.   That we then inform both the GRC and the GOJ that we intend to approach the Mongols to ascertain their position on exchanging diplomatic representation with the US.

3.   That we then sound out the Mongols in Moscow concerning their attitude toward establishing diplomatic relations with the US, and if their reaction is positive, that we then open formal discussions with the Mongols looking toward recognition and exchange of diplomatic representatives.[8]

---

[7] Tab B, listed as talking points for use with members of Congress, is not attached to the source text.

[8] The source text bears no indication of Rusk's approval or disapproval. Another copy is filed with a copy of a memorandum from Meeker to Rusk, undated but with a drafting date of June 20, stating that Read had asked the Legal Adviser's Office to review the 1961 exchanges with the Republic of China on the question of recognition of Mongolia to ascertain the nature and duration of any U.S. commitments. Meeker's memorandum concluded that there was no commitment binding on the United States in 1968 to refrain from recognizing Mongolia. An attached handwritten note of July 29 by Meeker states that Rusk "saw this after his return from Honolulu. He has in mind to let the Japanese act first, and is doubtful of our moving very soon." (Department of State, Central Files, POL 16 MONG)

Index

Albania. *See* Albanian resolution *under* UN representation issue.
Aldrich, George H., 193*n*, 254*n*, 308*n*, 374*n*, 496*n*, 567, 574*n*, 624*n*, 753*n*
Alldredge, Capt., 623*n*
Allen, Henry W., 733*n*
Allen, Ward P., 602*n*
Alphand, Hervé, 1–3, 5–7
Anderson (DOD), 374*n*, 496*n*, 633
Anderson, Donald M., 569*n*
Anderson, Jack, 683, 689
Armstrong, Oscar V., 671*n*, 690*n*, 700*n*
Arzac, Daniel N., 671*n*
Aughavin, Dennis F., 706*n*
Australia, 470, 611, 750
Ayub Khan, Mohammad, 174*n*

Bacon, Leonard L., 8*n*, 23*n*
Ball, George W.:
    Mongolia, 748*n*
    PRC nuclear capabilities, 109–110, 115*n*
    UN representation issue, 120, 313–314, 705
    U.S.–PRC relations, 129, 180, 228
Banning, Brig. Gen., 706*n*
Barber, Arthur W., 308*n*
Barnett, A. Doak, 513*n*, 634–636
Barnett, Robert W., 9, 27*n*, 562, 564–566, 700–701, 706*n*
    U.S. policy toward PRC, 61, 274, 680
Barton, William, 137
Battle, Lucius D., 739*n*
Beam, Jacob D., 308*n*
Beaulne, Yvon, 455
Belgium, 407, 432, 439
Belk, Samuel E., 125–128
Belman, Murray J., 666*n*
Bennett, Josiah, 129*n*, 142*n*, 245*n*, 281*n*, 286*n*, 402*n*, 437*n*, 443*n*, 539*n*, 572*n*, 574*n*, 745*n*, 748*n*
    Offshore Islands, 585
    U.S.–ROC relations, 562, 564, 566
Berger, Samuel D., 245*n*, 254*n*, 265*n*, 266*n*, 390*n*, 402*n*g, 403*n*, 407*n*, 436*n*, 453*n*, 539*n*, 601*n*, 602*n*, 623*n*
    Cultural Revolution, 526
    Offshore Islands, 585

Berger, Samuel D.—*Continued*
    ROC anti–mainland operations, 495
    UN representation issue, 261, 409, 418*n*
    U.S. policy toward PRC, 197, 200, 416–417
    U.S.–ROC relations, 226–228, 595
Berry, Col. Austin L., 209, 266*n*
Blouin, Adm., 245*n*
Blue Lion Committee. *See under* ROC anti–mainland operations.
Bohlen, Charles E., 1–2, 680, 739*n*, 753*n*
Brown, Elizabeth Ann, 289*n*
Brown, Winthrop G., 642, 690*n*, 700*n*, 706*n*, 718*n*, , 723*n* 753–755
Brubeck, William H., 56
Buffum, William B., 85*n*, 358*n*, 418*n*
Bundy, McGeorge, 3, 27*n*, 60, 142*n*, 230*n*
    Mongolia recognition, 220
    PRC nuclear capabilities, 23, 24*n*, 39*n*, 56–57, 109
    Congressional leadership meeting, 113–114
    Reconnaissance flights, 77–78, 94–96, 106
    U.S.–ROC discussions, 115*n*
    U.S.–Soviet discussions, 104–105
    ROC anti–mainland operations, 144, 190–191, 247
    ROC political situation, 25–26
    UN representation issue, 125–127, 223, 224*n*
    U.S. policy toward PRC, 55–56, 117, 130, 171, 249, 354*n*
    State–Defense studies, 183, 197, 199–201
    Travel restrictions, 195–196
    U.S.–PRC relations, 64, 75, 173–174
    U.S.–ROC relations, 55–56, 133, 160, 215–216
Bundy, William P., 65*n*, 70*n*, 84*n*, 129*n*, 142*n*, 144*n*, 174*n*, 296*n*, 308*n*, 358*n*, 364*n*, 374*n*, 420*n*, 430*n*, 443*n*, 476*n*, 496*n*, 500*n*, 567*n*, 574*n*, 624*n*, 670*n*, 686*n*, 733*n*, 747*n*
    Canadian PRC recognition, 681–683

Bundy, William P.—*Continued*
  Mongolia, 745–750
  Offshore Islands, 59
  PRC travel restrictions, 219–220, 229,
    281, 666–669
  ROC anti–mainland operations, 32,
    83, 240, 495
  ROC political situation, 271–272
  Sino–Soviet relations, 559
  UN representation issue, 120, 220,
    261, 313, 344n
    Canadian Two–China resolution,
      425, 427
  U.S.–ROC discussions, 271, 437
  U.S. policy toward PRC, 180, 183,
    249n, 251n, 281, 299–300, 410–411
    Cincinnati speech (Feb. *1968*),
      638–641, 643–644
    Trade, 541–543, 597–598, 639–640
    Travel restrictions, 174–176, 471–475
  U.S.–ROC relations, 216, 218–221, 286,
    595–596
    Cincinnati speech (Feb. *1968*),
      638–641
    ROC visit, 41, 271–273
    Status of Forces Agreement,
      193–195
    U.S. military aid, 272, 621–622
    Yen visit, 556, 562
  Vietnam conflict, 555n
  Warsaw talks, 203n, 206, 228–230,
    270n, 306–308, 492–494
Burma, 84–85, 336, 547, 675
Butterworth, W. Walton, 304, 372, 420n

Cabot, John M.. *See* Warsaw talks.
Cabot–Wang talks. *See* Warsaw talks.
Cambodia, 258, 336
Cameroon, 611
Canada (*see also Canadian and
    U.S.–Canadian subheadings under
    other subjects*):
  PRC recognition proposals, 681–683
Carter, Lt. Gen. Marshall S., 107
Cavender, Col., 671n
Central Intelligence Agency (CIA):
  Cultural Revolution, 360n, 361–364,
    399–402, 503–507
  PRC nuclear capabilities, 107–108
  Radio propaganda, 354–355
  ROC anti–mainland operations,
    476–478, 660–661

Central Intelligence Agency—*Continued*
  ROC political situation, 662
  Sino–Soviet relations, 33, 644
  Tibet, 731–733, 739–742
  U.S.–ROC relations, 595–596
Chamberlain (CIA), 107–108
Chang Chu–hsuan, 511
Chang Chun, 346–347
Chase, Gordon, 223–224
Cheng, Johnson, 9
Chen I, 34, 73, 174n, 321–323, 331, 384,
    402n
Chen Po–ta, 523
Ch'en Tung (*see also* Warsaw talks), 642
Chen Yi. *See* Chen I.
Chew, Vice Adm. John L., 688–689, 720n
Chiang Ching–kuo:
  Cultural Revolution, 392–394, 537,
    572, 599
  French PRC recognition, 19, 25
  French–ROC relations, 13–15, 25
  Health, 288
  Mongolia, 751
  Mongolia recognition, 220
  Offshore Islands, 688–689
  PRC military capabilities, 115–116, 662
  PRC propaganda, 537–538
  ROC anti–mainland operations, 141,
    240, 477, 495–496, 572
    Blue Lion Committee, 353–354
    Great Torch Five, 211–213, 221,
      224–226, 236–237, 242–249
    Intelligence cooperation, 403,
      599–601
    Political action plans, 553, 599–600,
      604–606, 660–661
    U.S.–ROC discussions, 242–245,
      402–403, 660–661
  ROC internal security, 662
  Rusk visits, 492
  Tibet, 660
  UN representation issue, 348, 454–455
  U.S. military aid, 141, 155, 157–159,
    297–298, 324, 538, 616–618, 697n,
    720n
  U.S. nuclear deterrent, 157–160
  U.S. policy toward PRC, 219–220, 270,
    297n, 411
  U.S.–ROC high–level talk proposals,
    221–223, 226–227
  U.S. visit, 202–203, 209–223
  Vietnam conflict, 29–30, 287

Chiang Kai–shek:
   Cultural Revolution, 531–532
   French PRC recognition, 4, 13–14, 15n,
      19–20, 22
   Health, 615
   Johnson correspondence, 25–29, 133,
      142–143, 212–213, 539–540
   Offshore Islands, 684–685
   PRC nuclear capabilities, 50–51,
      112–113, 116
   ROC anti–mainland operations, 239,
      248, 552–553
   Chiang–Johnson correspondence,
      133, 212–213
   Cline talks, 190–191, 202
   U.S.–ROC discussions, 43–45,
      48–49, 190–191, 236–237,
      350–351, 612–613
   ROC–Japanese relations, 53–54
   ROC political situation, 25–26, 31,
      271–272
   ROC security pact proposals, 20–21,
      29–30, 45–47, 49–51
   Sino–Soviet relations, 41–43, 531–532
   UN representation issue, 445–452
   Study committee proposals,
      457–467
   Successor state resolution
      proposals, 344–348, 350
   U.S.–ROC discussions, 53, 55,
      279–280
   U.S. military aid, 155–158, 692–694,
      697–700, 703–704
   U.S. nuclear deterrent, 51–52, 54–55
   U.S. policy toward PRC, 279–280,
      356–357, 410–411, 683–686
   Warsaw talks, 52–53, 270
   U.S.–ROC relations, 129, 227
   Rusk visits, 41–54, 344–348,
      350–352, 489–491
   Vietnam conflict, 20–21, 30, 234–239,
      351–352
Chiang Kai–shek, Madame, 41, 47, 288,
   296, 552
   PRC nuclear capabilities, 113, 116
   UN representation issue, 445, 462
   U.S. visit, 207–209
Chiba, Kazuo, 433
Ch'ien, Frederick, 445, 462, 552
Chile, 470

China, People's Republic of (see also PRC
   subheadings under other subjects;
   Sino–Soviet relations):
   Canadian recognition proposals,
      681–683
   Cultural Revolution, 363, 396
   China Panel meetings, 513–517
   CIA reports, 361–364, 399–402,
      503–507
   Jenkins reports, 388–389, 517–518,
      523–524, 527–530, 548–549, 580,
      590, 650–656, 659, 687–688,
      701–702, 712–715, 720–721,
      725–726
   Alexis Johnson speech, 519
   Military capabilities and, 696
   National Intelligence Estimates,
      573–574, 678–679
   Revolutionary Committees,
      725–726
   Rice papers, 326–332, 596–599
   ROC responses, 392–394, 525,
      571–572, 676
   Rostow reports, 360–364, 374,
      499–502, 521–522, 545–547,
      570–571, 663
   Rusk report, 646–647
   Sino–Soviet relations and, 479, 481,
      485, 512–513, 521, 531–532
   State–Defense studies, 333–335
   Tibet and, 739–740, 744
   UN representation issue and, 421,
      607–608
   U.S.–Japanese discussions, 433–435
   U.S.–ROC discussions, 392–394,
      537, 556–561, 599
   U.S.–Soviet discussions, 394–395,
      490–492, 526, 589
   U.S. trade with PRC and, 542–543
   Warsaw talks, 633
   Economic situation, 401–402, 506,
      694–695
   National Intelligence Estimates,
      15–17, 154, 241–242, 583–584
   State–Defense studies, 199–200, 334
   U.S.–Japanese discussions, 433–434
   U.S.–ROC discussions, 43–45
   Foreign policy, 168–170, 728
   French recognition, 1–15, 19–20,
      25–26, 31, 92

China, People's Republic of—*Continued*
Hong Kong, 252–253
Japan, relations with, 10, 258, 435
Military capabilities (*see also* Nuclear
capabilities *below*), 335, 553–555
National Intelligence Estimates,
152–154, 593–594, 695–697
Special National Intelligence
Estimates, 415–416
U.S.–ROC discussions, 212, 662
Nuclear capabilities, 57–58, 70, 131,
133
CIA memorandum, 107–108
Congressional leadership meeting,
113–114
National Intelligence Estimates,
146–148, 154
NSC discussions, 108–112
Soviet intervention possibility,
512–513
Special National Intelligence
Estimates, 78–81, 107, 415–416
State–Defense studies, 187, 335
U.S. military aid to ROC and, 155,
158
U.S. responses, 23–24, 39–40, 58,
144–146
Planning Group discussions,
96–99
Reconnaissance flights, 77–78,
94–96, 106, 134
Soviet joint action proposals,
94–95, 97–99, 104–105
U.S.–ROC discussions, 50–51,
112–113, 115–116, 155, 207–208,
410, 558
Warsaw talks, 136, 179
Political situation (*see also* Cultural
Revolution *above*), 43, 192–193,
200
Propaganda, 537–538
United States, relations with, 173–174,
256–259, 633–634
Fishing boat incidents, 229–230,
233, 234*n*, 265, 314, 316
Foreign minister meeting proposal,
285, 299–300, 307
Hainan incident (Feb. *13, 1968*),
641–642
Nan Hai incident (July *1966*),
377–378
U.S.–Soviet discussions, 726–728
Warsaw talks. *See* Warsaw talks.

China, People's Republic of—*Continued*
United States, relations with—
Continued
Yunnan aircraft incident (May *12,
1966*), 308–310, 314–316
U.S. policy (*see also* UN representation
issue):
Academic experts meeting, 634–638
Bundy Cincinnati speech (Feb.
1968), 638–641, 643–644
Congressional hearings, 274–275,
281, 318, 357
Containment, 119, 188–190,
215–216, 262, 338–341
Containment without isolation (*see
also* Travel restrictions *below*),
273–274, 281, 318–319, 356,
366–372
Manila declaration, 410–411
ROC reactions, 271, 279–280,
296–297, 356–357, 410–411
Thomson papers, 262–264, 274–275
Warsaw talks, 314–316, 383, 385
Covert action, 550
Goldberg position, 285–286
Japanese position, 367–368
Jenkins reports, 656–659, 709–718
Komer paper, 130–132
Mansfield visit proposals, 551
Radio propaganda, 284, 354–355
Reischauer appointment proposal,
249–251
Rice paper, 282–284
Rostow summary, 662–665
Rusk report, 645–650
Scientific exchanges, 627
State–Defense studies, 180–190,
332–343
Thomson papers, 117–120, 171–173,
262–264, 274–275
Tibet and, 744
Trade, 284, 364–366, 541–543, 597–598
Bundy Cincinnati speech (Feb.
1968), 639–640
Jenkins reports, 658, 680–681, 716
Rostow papers, 664, 729–730
Rusk report, 645–646
Thomson papers, 119, 264
Travel restrictions, 174–176, 416–417
Bundy paper, 666–669
Congressional hearings, 281
Revised regulations (*1966*), 471–475
ROC position, 271
Rostow policy summary, 664

China, People's Republic of—*Continued*
  Travel restrictions—*Continued*
    Rusk report, 645
    Thomson papers, 118–119, 171–173,
      263–264
    U.S.–ROC discussions, 219–220
    Warsaw talks, 36*n*, 229, 577–578,
      624–625
    White request, 195–196
  U.S.–ROC discussions, 683–686
China, Republic of (*see also ROC, ROC*
    anti–mainland operations, and
    U.S.–ROC subheadings under other
    subjects):
  Economic situation, 161, 163–164
  French PRC recognition, 4–5, 8–15
  French relations breakoff, 1, 7–8,
    10–15, 22
  Japan, relations with, 53–54
  Mongolia, 750–752, 754
  Political situation, 90–91, 160–163,
    271–272, 287, 338
    French PRC recognition and, 25–26,
      31
    Internal security, 618–621, 662
    U.S. Embassy reporting policy,
      162–163
  Tibet, 736–737
  United States, relations with, 26–27,
    129
    Bundy Cincinnati speech (Feb.
      1968), 638–641, 643–644
    Chiang Ching–kuo visit, 202–203,
      209–223
    Chiang–Johnson correspondence,
      25–29, 133, 142–143, 212–213,
      539–540
    High–level talk proposals, 221–223,
      226–228
    Madame Chiang visit, 207–209
    Rusk visits, 41–54, 319–321,
      344–352, 489–492
    Security pact proposals, 20–21, 26,
      29–31, 49–51
    U.S economic aid, 272–273, 351*n*,
      544–545, 588
    Yen visit, 556–564
  U.S. military aid, 266–269, 324–326,
    706–709, 718–720
    Country Team assessments,
      614–615, 675
    Jenkins reports, 703–704
    Offshore Islands, 585–587

China, Republic of—*Continued*
  U.S. military aid—*Continued*
    Sullivan proposals, 534
    U.S.–ROC discussions, 141,
      155–159, 212, 214, 287–288,
      538–539, 616–618, 621–622,
      692–694, 697–700
  U.S. military presence, 193–195, 623,
    671–672
  U.S. nuclear deterrent discussions,
    51–52, 54–55, 156–160
  U.S. policy:
    National Policy Papers, 55–56,
      86–94
    Shoesmith paper, 672–674
    Sullivan proposals, 532–536,
      564–566
    Thomson report, 160–164
China Panel, 513–517, 672
Chinn, Herman I., 624*n*
Chou Chung–feng, 605
Chou En–lai:
  Cultural Revolution, 400, 504, 514, 558
  Jenkins reports, 518, 523–524,
    528–529, 549, 590, 726
  Malley report, 546–547
  Rice papers, 328, 330
  Rostow reports, 500, 502
  Disarmament, 312, 316
  U.S.–PRC relations, 173–174, 256–257,
    315, 323
  Warsaw talks, 34, 134–135
  Vietnam conflict, 138, 546
Chou Hung–ching case, 8
Chow Shu–Kai, 207, 209, 215–216, 218,
  508
  UN representation issue, 425*n*,
    427–430, 437, 608–610
  U.S. military aid, 621–622, 703
  Yen U.S. visit, 556, 562
Christensen, Don T., 8*n*
Christian, George, 568*n*
Ciccolella, Maj. Gen. R. G., 688, 697*n*,
  699–700, 720*n*
Cleveland, J. Harlan, 120–125, 128, 137
Clifford, Clark M., 641–642
Cline, Ray S., 25–27, 286–288
  French–ROC relations, 12–15, 25
  PRC nuclear capabilities, 108–109,
    115–116
  ROC anti–mainland operations,
    190–191, 202
  Vietnam conflict, 231–232, 287

Clough, Ralph N., 54*n*, 59–60, 191*n*, 564,
    700*n*, 746
    ROC visit, 41, 49
Cobb, William B., Jr., 124
Colby, William E., 65, 476*n*, 495–496,
    550, 595
Congress, U.S.:
    PRC nuclear capabilities, 113–114
    U.S. policy toward PRC, 274–275, 281,
        318, 357
Cooper, Chester, 182, 207, 215–216
Couve de Murville, Maurice, 1–2
Cowherd, Col., 265*n*
Cox (Canada), 137
Cramer, Rear Adm. S. D., Jr., 641
Critchfield, James, 739*n*
Cultural Revolution. *See under* China,
    People's Republic of.
Cunningham, William J., 85*n*
Czechoslovakia, 703

Dalai Lama, 731–734, 736
Davidson, Daniel I., 726
Davis, Nathaniel, 388, 418*n*, 420
Davis, Richard H., 436*n*, 745*n*
Davydov, Boris, 726–728
De Gaulle, Charles, 1, 8, 10*n*
Dean, David, 34*n*, 65*n*, 228*n*, 265*n*, 281*n*,
    296*n*, 299*n*, 308*n*, 321*n*, 745*n*
    State–Defense studies, 180
    U.S. military aid to ROC, 718*n*, 720*n*
    Warsaw talks, 206, 265
Defense, U.S. Department of, 248, 379
    State–Defense studies, 180–190,
        332–343
Denmark, 439
Denney, George C., 495*n*, 660*n*
Dexter, John B., 83*n*, 84*n*
Dirksen, Everett M., 207
Disarmament, 264, 384, 386–387
    Warsaw talks, 134–135, 307, 312–313,
        316, 384, 626
Dobrynin, Anatoliy F.:
    Cultural Revolution, 394–395, 589
    PRC nuclear capabilities, 104–105, 115
Donald, Richard H., 402*n*, 493*n*, 541*n*,
    623*n*, 671*n*, 681*n*, 690*n*
Dornheim, Arthur, 737*n*, 745*n*, 747*n*
Dougall, Kathleen C., 743
Douglas, William O., 3
Downey, 578
Drexler, Robert W., 321*n*
Drumwright, Everett, 13*n*

Eckstein, Alexander, 513*n*, 634–637
Ecuador, 611
Eisenhower, Dwight D., 127, 303–304,
    586
Elder, Walter, 115*n*, 191*n*
Enders, Thomas O., 602*n*
Evans, Allan, 495*n*, 660*n*

Fairbank, John K., 274, 513*n*, 673
Fanfani, Amintore, 432, 438*n*
Fearey, Robert A., 9, 129*n*, 142*n*, 193*n*,
    224*n*, 245*n*, 266*n*, 281*n*, 296*n*
Fecteau, 578
Feldman, Mark B., 567*n*
Felt, Adm. Harry D., 567
Flynn, Lt. Robert, 629
Fong, Hiram L., 206
Ford (CIA), 595–596
Forrestal, Michael V., 27*n*, 56–57, 65*n*
Foster, William C., 39*n*, 137
France. *See French subheadings under
    other subjects.*
Freeman, Orville L., 544*n*
Fried, Edward, 729*n*
Friedman, Alvin, 224*n*, 245*n*
Fulbright, J. William, 318, 618*n*

Ganley, Oswald H., 574*n*
Gardner, James R., 495
Gaud, William S., 544*n*
Gentner, Adm. William E., 155, 235, 240,
    242, 298
Germany, Federal Republic of, 8
Getsinger, Norman W., 737*n*
Ghana, 470
Gim, Weaver, 569*n*
Givan, Walker F., 137
Gleysteen, William, 374*n*, 390*n*, 407*n*,
    425*n*, 427*n*, 453*n*, 469*n*, 602*n*, 608*n*,
    705*n*
Glick, Brig. Gen., 718*n*
Godley, G. McMurtrie, 671*n*, 706*n*
Goldberg, Arthur J., 344*n*, 358*n*
    Cultural Revolution, 531–532
    Mongolia, 754
    Tibet, 734–735
    UN representation issue, 285,
        293–296, 301, 303, 388
    Canadian Two–China resolution,
        418*n*
    Nov. *1966* statement, 420
    Presidential adviser meeting, 313
    Study committee proposals, 419,
        442

Goldberg, Arthur J.—*Continued*
    UN representation issue—*Continued*
        U.S.–Canadian discussions, 304–306
        U.S.–Soviet discussions, 404
        U.S. policy toward PRC, 219, 285–286,
            307
Goodby, James, 180, 183*n*
Grant, Lindsey, 61, 65*n*, 70*n*, 142*n*, 182,
    745*n*
Great Britain. *See* United Kingdom.
Green, Marshall, 4*n*, 23*n*, 27*n*, 34*n*, 61*n*,
    85*n*, 129*n*, 142*n*, 733*n*
    Mongolia, 746
    PRC travel restrictions, 182–183
Greene, Fred, 415*n*, 678*n*, 700*n*
Gromyko, Andrei A., 404, 490–492
Gronouski, John A. (*see also* Warsaw
    talks), 386–387, 642

Habib, Philip C., 595, 671*n*
Hagerty, Herbert G., 737*n*
Halperin, Morton, 379, 624*n*
Hamilton, William C., 495, 595
Handley, William J., 737*n*
Harman, Gary R., 124
Harriman, W. Averell, 4*n*, 13*n*, 25–27,
    70*n*, 142*n*, 374*n*
    French PRC recognition, 1–3, 5
    PRC nuclear capabilities, 98
    ROC anti–mainland operations, 81
    UN representation issue, 120
    U.S. policy toward PRC, 318–319
Harris, Gen., 240
Helms, Richard M., 60, 65, 99, 479*n*,
    573*n*, 695*n*
    Hong Kong, 568*n*
    U.S. policy toward PRC, 354–355, 550
Henry, David H., 745*n*
Herbert, Eugene T., 193*n*
Heymann, Philip B., 471–475
Hickenlooper, Bourke, 114
Hightower, Gen., 197
Holdridge, John H., 569*n*, 601*n*, 666*n*,
    670*n*
Holland (DOD), 496*n*, 574*n*
Holmes, Julius C., 513*n*
Hong Kong, 252–254, 374, 567–568
Hopson, Donald, 255, 321–323, 329, 331
Howard, Wally, 111
Hsi Sha Islands, 18*n*
Hsu Hsiang–chen, 548–549
Hsu Ju–ch'i, Gen., 240, 520
Hsu Wu–ch'iu, 585
Hu, Maj. Gen. S. K., 155, 157

Huang Chi–ming, 621
Hughes, Thomas L., 260, 403*n*, 415*n*,
    476*n*, 495, 550, 595, 660*n*, 678*n*, 728*n*
Hummel, Arthur W., Jr.:
    Cultural Revolution, 490–492
    Offshore Islands, 585–588
    ROC anti–mainland operations,
        239–240, 242–245, 259–260,
        507–508
        Cultural Revolution and, 571–572
        Political action plans, 552, 604
        Thailand/Burma irregulars,
            520–521
    ROC security pact proposals, 29
    UN representation issue, 445, 462,
        467–468
    U.S. policy toward PRC, 270, 279–280,
        297*n*
    U.S.–ROC relations, 221–223, 273,
        297–298, 319–321
    Vietnam conflict, 235
Humphrey, Hubert H., 238–239,
    274–275, 568*n*

Ikeda, Hayato, 10, 21
India, 337, 349
    Kashmir conflict, 199, 204
    Tibet, 660, 731, 735–738, 743
Indonesia, 336, 349, 470
International Telecommunications
    Satellite Corporation (INTELSAT),
    625–626
Iran, 470
Italy (*see also* Study committee proposals
    under UN representation issue):
    French PRC recognition, 8
    UN representation issue, 349,
        407–408, 432, 439

Jacobson, Harald W., 245*n*, 265*n*, 308*n*,
    321*n*, 436*n*, 441, 496*n*, 500*n*,
    564–565, 574*n*, 597*n*, 601*n*, 666*n*,
    670*n*, 748*n*, 753*n*
James, Leon, 629
Jao Shu–shih, 43
Japan, 366–372, 433–435
    China, People's Republic of, relations
        with, 10, 69, 258, 435
    French PRC recognition, 8
    Mongolia, 754
    Political situation, 10, 21, 51
    PRC nuclear capabilities and, 145
    ROC anti–mainland operations,
        612–613

Japan—*Continued*
  State–Defense studies, 181, 337–338,
    342
  UN representation issue, 368, 470
  United States, relations with, 366–367,
    710
  Vietnam conflict and, 181
Jenkins, Alfred LeS., 496*n*, 539*n*, 556*n*,
    728
  Cultural Revolution, 388–389,
    517–518, 523–524, 527–530,
    548–549, 580, 590, 701–702,
    720–721
    China Panel meetings, 513–517
    U.S. policy toward PRC and,
      529–530, 650–656, 712–715
  UN representation issue, 379–382,
    409–410, 606–608
  U.S. policy toward PRC, 656–659,
    709–718
    Academic experts meeting, 634–638
    Trade, 658, 680–681
    Travel restrictions, 416–417
  U.S. policy toward ROC, 672–674,
    703–704
Jenkins, Walter E., Jr., 677
Jessup, Peter, 354–355, 512–513, 550,
    731*n*, 739*n*
Johnson, Maj. Gen. D. B., 235
Johnson, Lyndon B., 650*n*
  Cultural Revolution, 326, 396, 501,
    503, 519, 531
    Jenkins reports, 523*n*, 527*n*, 548*n*,
      580*n*, 687*n*, 701
    Rice papers, 596, 598
    Rostow reports, 360–361, 374, 499,
      521, 545, 570
  French PRC recognition, 3–5, 25
  French–ROC relations, 12, 25
  Hong Kong, 568*n*
  Japan, 366*n*
  PRC military capabilities, 553
  PRC nuclear capabilities, 57*n*, 70, 77,
    94–96, 106, 109–110, 113–114
  ROC anti–mainland operations, 144,
    190
  ROC political situation, 31
  Sino–Soviet relations, 644
  Tibet, 733–734
  UN representation issue, 125–128,
    418, 420, 432
    Presidential adviser meetings,
      313–314, 387–388

Johnson, Lyndon B.—*Continued*
  UN representation issue—*Continued*
    Study committee proposals, 418*n*,
      457–461
    Successor state resolution
      proposals, 293–294, 301, 303
    U.S.–Canadian discussions, 372–373
  U.S. policy toward PRC, 195, 273, 285,
    551, 582–583, 662
    Academic experts meeting, 634–638
    Speech (July 12, 1966), 356
    U.S.–PRC relations, 173, 641–642, 729
    Warsaw talks, 151*n*, 232*n*
  U.S.–ROC relations, 216–218, 544,
    556–561
    Chiang correspondence, 25–29, 133,
      142–143, 212–213, 539–540
  Vietnam conflict, 238*n*, 555, 559–560
Johnson, Robert, 39*n*, 57*n*, 96*n*, 97–98
Johnson, Tom, 642
Johnson, U. Alexis, 34*n*, 181*n*, 254*n*,
    354–355, 642, 736, 737*n*
  Cultural Revolution, 519
  UN representation issue, 313–314
Joint Chiefs of Staff (JCS):
  PRC nuclear capabilities, 24*n*, 144–146
  ROC anti–mainland operations,
    224–226, 248
Jones, Betty Jane, 289*n*
Jorden, William J., 296*n*, 374*n*, 500*n*,
    672*n*
  Cultural Revolution, 388*n*, 517*n*, 519*n*,
    523*n*, 527*n*, 548*n*, 580*n*, 590*n*,
    596–597, 634*n*, 687*n*
  UN representation issue, 379, 409*n*
Judd, Thomas M., 425*n*

Kalb, Marvin, 281
Kao Kang, 43
Kashmir conflict, 199, 204, 217, 337
Katzenbach, Nicholas deB., 541*n*, 666*n*,
    753*n*
  Mongolia, 680, 750*n*
  UN representation issue, 407–408,
    412–414, 418*n*, 425*n*
  U.S. economic and military aid to
    ROC, 544, 621–622
  U.S. policy toward PRC, 597, 598*n*,
    683
Kearney, Richard D., 193*n*
Kennedy, John F., 13*n*, 55, 67–68,
    126–127
Khrushchev, Nikita S., 42, 112*n*

Kiang, Yi–seng, 9
Kimball, John W., 611n, 733n, 737n
King, Samuel L., 129n
Kintner, Robert E., 303n, 354
Kitchen, Jeffrey C., 180
Klaus, Josef, 583
Kohler, Foy D., 181, 515, 550n, 589, 745, 748n
Komer, Robert W., 56n, 129n, 366n, 733n
    Chiang–Johnson correspondence, 26–27, 133
    French PRC recognition, 12–13, 31
    PRC nuclear capabilities, 23–24, 96–99
    U.S. policy toward PRC, 130–132, 285–286
    Warsaw talks, 64n, 76n
Kono, Ichiro, 10
Korea, Democratic Republic of, 338
Korea, Republic of, 338
    ROC security pact proposals, 20–21, 26, 29–31, 49–51
Korean conflict, 2, 5–6, 36
Koren, Henry L. T., 260, 736
Kosaka, Zentaro, 433–435
Kosygin, Alexei N., 112n
Kreisberg, Paul H., 374n, 436n, 471n, 492n, 496n, 500n, 574n, 624n, 633, 638n, 666n, 690n, 700n, 706n, 723n, 753n
Kung, Dr., 207
Kuo Hsi–lin, 621
Ky, Nguyen Cao, 210

Lai Chia–chiu, 556, 562
Lakeland, William C., 495
Laos, 46, 336
    Warsaw talks, 67–68, 72–73, 101, 104
Leddy, Raymond G., 748, 753
Lemos, Adm., 402n
Lewin, Nathan, 624n, 666n
Lewis, Col. William F., 180, 197
Li Ching–Ch'uan, 504
Li Hsien–nien, 528
Li Kwoh–ting, 556, 562
Li Lien–pi, 511
Li Wen–huan, 520
Lin An–chi, 43
Lin Piao, 43, 204, 329–330, 573
    CIA reports, 399–400, 504–505
    Jenkins papers, 518, 523
    Rostow reports, 374, 500, 502
Lippmann, Walter S., 11
Liu Chieh, 437–440, 556, 562–564
Liu Chih–chien, 505

Liu Lan–t'ao, 504
Liu Ning–i, 504
Liu Shao–chi, 329, 399, 504, 528, 546, 549, 557, 560, 590
Lively, Lt. Col., 623n
Lo (PRC), 676–677, 722
Lo, Marshal, 559

MacArthur, Douglas, II, 471n, 745n, 748n
Macdonald, Donald S., 595–596
Macomber, William B., Jr., 666n, 753n
Malaysia, 336
Malley, Simon, 546–547
Manhart, Maj. Gen. A. H., 224–226
Mansfield, Mike, 551
Mao Tse–tung (see also Cultural Revolution under China, People's Republic of), 69, 192–193, 258
Mao Tse–tung, Madame, 502, 523
Marks, Leonard, 354–355, 683
Martin, Doyle V., 723n
Martin, Paul:
    UN representation issue, 137–140, 304, 358–360, 396–399, 432
    Two–China resolution, 408, 427, 455–457
Matsumura, Kenzo, 10
Matsu. See Offshore Islands.
Maurer, Ion Gheorghe, 582–583
Mayland, Col., 718n
McAfee, William, 403n, 476n, 495–496
McCain, Adm., 703n
McCloskey, Robert J., 471n, 690n
McConaughy, Walter P.:
    Appointment of, 314
    Bundy Cincinnati speech (Feb. 1968), 643–644
    Cultural Revolution, 392–394, 515, 537, 599
    Mongolia, 750–752
    Offshore Islands, 683–685, 688–689
    PRC propaganda, 537–538
    ROC anti–mainland operations, 350–351
        Blue Lion Committee, 353–354
        Country team assessments, 524–525, 591–592, 612–614, 674–676
        Matsu incident (Oct. 1966), 405–407
        Political action plans, 552–553, 599–600, 604–606, 660–661
        U.S.–ROC intelligence cooperation, 599–601
    ROC political situation, 618–621, 662

McConaughy, Walter P.—*Continued*
Tibet, 660
UN representation issue, 344–350,
427*n*, 430*n*
Study committee proposals,
440–441, 444, 454–455, 462–469
U.S. military aid to ROC, 538–539,
614–618, 692–694, 697–700, 703*n*
U.S. policy toward PRC, 356–357,
410–411, 445–452, 683–686
U.S. policy toward ROC, 534*n*, 564
Vietnam conflict, 351–352
Yen visit, 556, 562
McCone, John A., 33*n*, 77*n*, 106*n*, 231
French–ROC relations, 12–13, 25
PRC nuclear capabilities, 24*n*, 39*n*, 70,
113, 115*n*
NSC discussions, 109–111
Reconnaissance flights, 77–78,
94–96
McCord, Frank O., 541*n*, 748*n*
McDowell, Eleanor C., 193*n*
McNamara, Robert S.:
Hong Kong, 568*n*
PRC nuclear capabilities, 24*n*, 39*n*,
109, 114, 144
Reconnaissance flights, 77–78,
94–96, 106
ROC anti–mainland operations, 213,
224, 247–248
UN representation issue, 127, 379,
387*n*, 432*n*
U.S. policy toward PRC, 180*n*, 183,
197–201, 319
U.S.–PRC relations, 265*n*, 641–642
U.S.–ROC relations, 207–214, 324–326
McNaughton, John, 183, 197, 209, 211*n*
McNutt, Louise, 39*n*, 436n, 733*n*
Meeker, Leonard C., 177, 396, 418*n*,
443*n*, 567, 755*n*
Mehlert, Calvin E., 215–216, 218
Meloy, Francis E., 1*n*, 5*n*
Merchant, Livingston, 567
Meyer, Cord, 354–355
Meyers, Howard, 266*n*
Miki, Takeo, 10
Miller, Col., 671*n*
Miller, Robert H., 374*n*, 496*n*, 574*n*
Mongolia, 745–755
Sino–Soviet relations and, 220,
569–570, 752
U.S. recognition proposals, 172–173,
183, 220, 680, 745–749, 753–755
U.S.–ROC discussions, 750–752

Morris, Donald R., 412, 750*n*
Mountbatten, Lord, 567
Moyers, Bill D., 294*n*
UN representation issue, 303*n*, 387*n*,
432*n*
U.S. policy toward PRC, 274, 318,
354–355

National Intelligence Estimates:
NIE *10–2–64*, "Prospects for the
International Communist
Movement," 62–63
NIE *11–12–66*, "The Outlook for
Sino–Soviet Relations," 479–489
NIE *13–64*, "Economic Prospects for
Communist China," 15–17
NIE *13–2–65*, "Communist China's
Advanced Weapons Program,"
146–148
NIE *13–3–65*, "Communist China's
Military Establishment," 152–154
NIE *13–3–68*, "Communist China's
General Purpose and Air Defense
Forces," 695–697
NIE *13–5–66*, "Communist China's
Economic Prospects," 241–242
NIE *13–5–67*, "Economic Outlook for
Communist China," 583–584
NIE *13–7–65*, "Political Problems and
Prospects in Communist China,"
192–193
NIE *13–7–67*, "The Chinese Cultural
Revolution," 573–574
NIE *13–8–67*, "Communist China's
Strategic Weapons Program,"
593–594
NIE *13–9–65*, "Communist China's
Foreign Policy," 168–170
NIE *13–9–68*, "The Short–Term
Outlook in Communist China,"
678–679
NIE *43–64*, "Prospects for the
Government of the Republic of
China," 31
National Policy Papers:
"The Republic of China," 86–94
National Security Council (NSC):
PRC nuclear capabilities, 108–112
Sino–Soviet relations, 33
UN representation issue, 388
Neidle, Alan E., 624*n*
Nelson, 60, 116
Nenni, Pietro, 609
Ni Yue–si, Adm., 235, 298

North Atlantic Treaty Organization
(NATO), 140
Nuclear weapons (see also Disarmament;
Nuclear capabilities under China,
People's Republic of):
State–Defense study, 187, 190, 198
U.S. nuclear deterrent, 51–52, 54–55,
156–160
U.S.–ROC discussions, 44, 47, 51–52,
54–55, 350–351
Warsaw talks, 134–135, 307

Offshore Islands, 56, 59–60, 130n,
537–538
ROC statement request, 684–685,
690–692
Rostow policy summary, 664
Shoesmith paper, 700–701
Sullivan proposals, 533, 535–536,
565–566
U.S. military aid to ROC and, 692–693
U.S. presence, 585–588
U.S.–ROC discussions, 683–685,
688–689
Orwat, Maj. Gen., 706n

Pakistan, 199, 204, 337
Pearson, Lester B., 304–306, 372–373,
420, 424n
Pedersen, Richard F., 304
Peng, Gen., 155
P'eng Chen, 363, 399, 528
P'eng Te–huai, 43, 330
Philippines, 336–337, 470, 735
Pickering, Laurence G., 495
Planning Group, 96–99, 109n
Platt, Nicholas, 723n
Polansky, Sol, 115n
Policy Planning Council, 39–40, 57–58
Popper, David H., 469–470, 608n
Popple, Paul M., 4n, 8n, 23n, 27n, 34n, 61
Powell, Ralph L., 513n
Puhan, Alfred, 723n
Pye, Lucian W., 513n, 634–635, 673

Quemoy. See Offshore Islands.

Ramundo, Col., 193n
Read, Benjamin H., 109n, 293n, 296n, 490
Reedy, George, 125
Reichner, Col., 245n
Reischauer, Edwin O., 181, 249–251,
634–635, 663n

Rice, Edward E., 181n
Cultural Revolution, 326–333, 596–599
Hong Kong, 252–254, 568n
U.S. policy toward PRC, 64, 256–259,
282–284
U.S. policy toward ROC, 226, 228n,
534–536
Ridge, Col., 706n, 718n
Ridge, T. L., 324n, 623n, 671n
Riemer, Reynold A., 743
Ritchie, A. E., 304, 372, 396, 408n,
412–414, 681–683
Ritchie, Charles S. A., 124–125
Roberts, George B., Jr., 308n
Roberts, Peter M., 412
Robinson, Dana, 680
Robinson, H. Basil, 137, 372, 396
ROC anti–mainland operations:
Blue Lion Committee, 32, 82–83,
202–203, 246–247, 258–259, 403
JCS position, 225–226
U.S.–ROC discussions, 190–191,
202, 213, 226–227, 243, 245,
353–354, 393
Chiang–Johnson correspondence, 133,
212–213, 539–540
CIA role, 476–478, 495
Country team assessments, 81–82,
507–508, 524–525, 591–592,
612–614, 674–676
Cultural Revolution and, 392–394,
524–525, 571–572
Great Torch Five proposal (Sept. 22,
1965), 211–213, 221, 224–226
U.S. responses, 245–249
U.S.–ROC discussions, 236–237,
242–244
Grosbeak operation, 477–478, 495–496
Hong Kong and, 252
HU–16 incident, 239–240
Kwangtung raid, 612
Matsu incident (Oct. 1966), 405–407
Media involvement, 170–171
Political action plans, 552–553,
557–558, 572, 599–600, 602, 670
U.S.–ROC discussions, 604–606,
660–661
PRC fear of, 256–259
ROC propaganda, 612
Thailand/Burma irregulars, 84–85,
520–521, 675
U.S. policy, 91–92, 231–232, 259–260,
283

ROC anti–mainland operations—
  Continued
  U.S.–ROC discussions, 43–45, 48–49,
    141, 211, 236–237, 242–245,
    350–351, 402–403
  U.S.–ROC high–level talk proposals,
    227–228
  U.S.–ROC intelligence cooperation,
    403, 595–596, 599–602
  U–2 incident (Jan. *1965*), 144
Roche, John P., 512–513, 519, 634*n*
Romania, 582–583
Ropa, Donald, 388*n*, 409*n*, 517*n*, 523*n*,
    527*n*, 548*n*
Rosen, Samuel, 275
Rostow, Eugene V., 606*n*, 743–744
Rostow, Walt W., 286*n*, 293*n*, 308*n*, 531*n*,
    645*n*, 650*n*, 690*n*, 709*n*
  Cultural Revolution, 360–364, 374,
    396, 499–503, 521–522, 545–547,
    570–571, 663
  China Panel meetings, 513
  Jenkins reports, 388, 517, 523, 527,
    548, 580, 590, 687, 701–702, 720,
    725
  Alexis Johnson speech, 519*n*
  Rice papers, 598–599
  Hong Kong, 568*n*
  National Policy Papers, 56*n*
  PRC economic situation, 694
  PRC foreign policy, 728
  PRC military capabilities, 553–555
  PRC nuclear capabilities, 24, 39*n*, 57*n*,
    96*n*, 98–99, 109*n*, 512
  Sino–Soviet relations, 644
  UN representation issue, 120, 379,
    418*n*, 420, 432, 606
  Goldberg paper, 294–296
  Jenkins reports, 380, 409
  Presidential adviser meetings, 313,
    387*n*
  Study committee proposals, 457*n*
  Successor state resolution
    proposals, 294–295, 303–304
  U.S.–Italian discussions, 602–604
  U.S. policy toward PRC, 282, 416,
    550–551, 634
  Radio propaganda, 354–355
  Trade, 364, 680, 729–730
  U.S.–PRC relations, 630*n*, 641–642
  U.S.–ROC relations, 544–545, 672, 703
  Vietnam conflict, 555
Rowe, David N., 606–608

Rowen, Henry, 96–99
Roy, J. Stapleton, 374*n*, 402*n*, 496*n*, 569*n*,
    753*n*
Royster, Vermont, 206
Rubin, Alfred P., 193*n*
Rusk, Dean, 86*n*, 190*n*, 539*n*, 686*n*, 728*n*,
    747*n*, 755*n*
  Cultural Revolution, 433–435, 515,
    526, 560, 589
  French PRC recognition, 4–5, 23
  U.S.–French discussions, 1–3, 5–7
  U.S.–ROC discussions, 8–12
  French–ROC relations, 1, 7–8, 10–12,
    13*n*, 23
  Hong Kong, 568
  Mongolia, 173, 745, 748*n*, 753
  Offshore Islands, 690–692
  PRC nuclear capabilities, 39*n*, 50–51,
    109, 114–115
  Reconnaissance flights, 77–78,
    94–96, 106
  ROC anti–mainland operations,
    84–85, 245–247, 476, 601–602
  Political action plans, 602, 670
  U.S.–ROC discussions, 43–45,
    48–49, 350–351, 402–403
  ROC–Japanese relations, 53–54
  Sino–Soviet relations, 33, 41–43, 559,
    569–570
  Tibet, 733–734, 737–738
  UN representation issue, 120, 261,
    289, 301–303, 322, 432*n*
  Canadian position, 124–125,
    137–140
  Canadian Two–China resolution,
    413*n*, 418–419, 430–431
  ROC reactions, 427–430
  U.S.–British discussions, 425–426
  U.S.–Canadian discussions, 420–425,
    455–457
  U.S.–ROC discussions, 437–439
  Circular telegrams, 85–86, 390–391
  Goldberg paper, 296*n*
  Nov. 1966 General Assembly vote,
    469
  Nov. 1967 General Assembly vote,
    611
  Presidential adviser meetings, 387
  Study committee proposals, 409*n*,
    418*n*, 419, 430–431
  Circular telegram, 453–454
  ROC reactions, 441–445, 457–461
  U.S.–British discussions, 426

Rusk, Dean—*Continued*
  UN representation issue—*Continued*
    Study committee proposals—
        Continued
      U.S.-Canadian discussions, 423–424
      U.S.-ROC discussions, 428–430,
          437–440, 608–610
    Successor state resolution
        proposals, 301–303, 314, 344n,
        348–350
      U.S.-Canadian discussions,
          358–360, 396–399, 705
      U.S.-Italian discussions, 602–604
      U.S. position, 125–128
      U.S.-ROC discussions, 53, 55,
          562–564
  U.S. nuclear deterrent, 51–52, 54–55
  U.S. policy toward PRC, 645–650
    Bundy Cincinnati speech (Feb.
        1968), 638–641
    Containment without isolation, 271,
        281, 296–297
    Mansfield visit proposals, 551
    Reischauer appointment proposal,
        251n
    State–Defense studies, 180–183,
        197–201
    Trade, 541, 729–730
    Travel restrictions, 174, 196n, 281,
        471, 666
  U.S.-PRC relations, 285, 299, 641–642
  U.S.-ROC relations, 207–209, 271
    Bundy Cincinnati speech (Feb.
        1968), 638–641
    Chiang–Johnson correspondence,
        27–29, 142–143
    ROC visits, 41–54, 319–321,
        344–352, 489–492
    Security pact proposals, 49–51
    U.S. military aid, 266–269, 706–709,
        718–720
    U.S. military presence, 193, 623,
        671–672
    Yen visit, 556, 562–564
  Vietnam conflict:
    British–PRC discussions, 321–323
    ROC troop participation, 555n
    U.S.-ROC discussions, 45–47,
        351–352

Rusk, Dean—*Continued*
  Warsaw talks, 34, 36, 52–53, 203n, 265,
      632
    U.S. meeting guidance, 65–71,
        254–255, 306, 307n, 308–313,
        374–378, 492, 496–498, 500–501,
        574–579
Russell, Richard, 3–4

Salade, Pierre, 22
Salans, Carl F., 65n, 745n
Sanborn, Gen., 155, 157, 159
Sato, Eisaku, 612n, 613
Saudi Arabia, 470, 611
Saunders, Harold K., 380n
Scalapino, Robert A., 513n, 634, 637
Schneider, David T., 733n, 737n
Schultze, Charles L., 544
Schwartz, Abba, 177
Seaborg, Glenn T., 113–114
Seligmann, Albert L., 296n
Senegal, 470
Shannon, Brig. Gen. James A., 641
Sharp, Adm. U. S. Grant, 202–203, 298,
    534, 568n
Sharp, W. Mitchell, 681–683, 705
Shen, James, 19, 29, 53, 235
    U.S.-ROC relations, 41, 49, 209,
        215–216, 218
Shen, Sampson C., 240n, 297n, 520n, 556,
    562, 745
    UN representation issue, 440–441,
        445, 462, 467–469
Shen Chang–huan, 29–30, 41, 60n,
    115–116
    French PRC recognition, 10n, 19, 22n
Shepard, Adm., 718n
Shlaudeman, Harry W., 753n
Shoesmith, Thomas P. 564, 601n, 621n,
    623n, 638n, 666n, 670–671n,
    672–674, 690n, 700–701, 705n, 706n,
    718n, 723n, 753n
Shub, Anatole, 727
Sierra Leone, 470
Sieverts, Frank A., 624n
Singapore, 336
Sino–Soviet relations:
    Border areas, 569–570, 644
    Cultural Revolution and, 479, 481,
        485, 512–513, 521, 531–532

Sino–Soviet relations—*Continued*
French PRC recognition and, 6
Jenkins reports, 655–656
Mongolia and, 220, 569–570, 752
National Intelligence Estimates,
62–63, 479–489
NSC meetings, 33
PRC economic situation and, 16, 154
PRC nuclear capabilities and, 58, 70
ROC anti–mainland operations and,
44
Rusk report, 647–648
Soviet position, 105
UN representation issue and, 421
U.S. policy toward PRC and, 131
U.S.–ROC discussions, 41–43, 558–560
Vietnam conflict and, 483–484
Sisco, Joseph J., 129*n*, 289*n*, 308*n*, 390*n*,
418*n*, 420*n*, 430*n*, 441*n*, 443*n*, 453*n*,
539*n*, 733*n*, 748*n*
UN representation issue, 261*n*,
289–292, 314, 344*n*
Canadian Two–China resolution,
413*n*, 425–427
General Assembly resolutions (Nov.
1966), 437–439
Nov. *1967* General Assembly vote,
611
Presidential adviser meetings,
387–388
Study committee proposals,
291–292, 407–409, 426, 437–438
U.S.–British discussions, 425–426
U.S.–Canadian discussions, 304, 705
U.S.–ROC discussions, 437–440, 564
U.S.–ROC relations, 562
Warsaw talks, 307*n*
Smith (CIA), 245*n*, 495
Smith, Abbot, 399–402
Smith, Bromley, 151*n*, 190*n*, 326, 457*n*,
523*n*
Smith, Frederick, Jr., 666*n*
Smith, Jack, 111
Smith, Capt. Philip E., 278, 310, 316, 510,
578, 629
Smith, Rufus Z., 372, 412, 420*n*, 705*n*
Smith, William Y., 55*n*, 56*n*
Sneider, Richard L., 281*n*, 296*n*, 433,
748*n*
Snow, Edgar, 275
Solbert, Peter, 144
Sontag, John P., 569*n*

Southeast Asia. *See* Laos;
Thailand/Burma irregulars *under*
ROC anti–mainland operations;
Vietnam conflict.
Souvanna Phouma (Prince of Laos),
67–68
Soviet Union (*see also* Sino–Soviet
relations; *U.S.–Soviet subheadings
under other subjects*), 44, 53, 112, 180,
403
Cultural Revolution and, 394–395
Czechoslovakia occupation, 703
Mongolia, 749
State–Defense studies, 180, 185–186,
197
Tibet, 743–744
Warsaw talks eavesdropping, 255, 265
Spaak, Paul–Henri, 121
Sparkman, John J., 207
Special Group, 731
Special Memorandum No. *14–66* (CIA),
399–402
Special National Intelligence Estimates:
SNIE *13–4–64*, "The Chances of an
Imminent Communist Chinese
Nuclear Explosion," 78–81, 107
SNIE *13–8–66*, "Communist China's
Advanced Weapons Program,"
415–416
Spivy, Gen., 197–198, 200
Sprouse, Philip D., 513*n*
Stabler, Wells, 602*n*
Steadman, Richard C., 623*n*, 671*n*, 690*n*,
706*n*
Stephens, Robert P., 569*n*
Stevenson, Adlai, 115, 125–128
Stevenson, Robert A., 471*n*
Stewart, Michael N. F., 174*n*, 425–426
Stoessel, Walter J., Jr., 254*n*, 265*n*, 455,
471*n*, 722–723
Stover, Carl F., 634
Straus, Richard, 681*n*
Stuart, Richard K., 595–596
Stuart, Richard K., 737*n*
Sullivan, William H., 532–536
Sung Jen–ch'iung, 504
Sylvester, John, Jr., 569*n*
Symington, James W., 556, 562
Syria, 469, 611

Taiwan. *See* China, Republic of.
Taiwan Straits (*see also* Offshore Islands),
36, 277
Takasaki, Tatsunosuke, 10

T'ao Chen–lin, 528–529
T'ao Chu, 499, 504, 549
Taylor, George E., 513*n*, 634, 673
Taylor, Gen. Maxwell D., 127, 181*n*
Taylor, Rufus, 583*n*, 593*n*
Teng Hsiao–ping, 330, 504–505, 528, 549
Terruzzi (Italy), 602
Thailand, 84–85, 336, 470, 520–521, 675
Thant, U, 547
Thayer, Harry E. T., 681*n*, 700
Thomas, Cecil, 634–635
Thomas, William W., 436*n*
Thompson, Llewellyn E., 195*n*, 254*n*,
    745*n*, 747*n*
    Cultural Revolution, 394–395, 526
    Mongolia, 753
    PRC nuclear capabilities, 77–78,
        109–110, 114
    UN representation issue, 120
    U.S. policy toward PRC, 180–181,
        183–185, 188, 197–201
Thomson, James C., Jr., 61*n*, 65*n*, 70*n*,
    129*n*, 216*n*
    ROC anti–mainland operations,
        190–191, 247–249
    U.S. policy toward PRC, 117–120,
        171–173, 176–177, 182, 196*n*
        Containment without isolation,
            262–264, 274–275
        Reischauer appointment proposal,
            249–251
        Trade, 364–366
    U.S. policy toward ROC, 160–164
    Warsaw talks, 64, 75–76
Thondup, Gyalo, 734–738, 742–743
303 Committee, 77–78, 354–355, 550, 741
Tibet, 731–744
    CIA activities, 731–733, 739–742
    Indian policy, 660, 731, 735–738, 743
    UN resolutions, 733–736, 743–744
    U.S.–ROC discussions, 660
Toon, Malcolm, 748*n*
Tremblay (Canada), 137
Trueheart, William C., 65*n*, 84*n*, 660*n*
Tsiang Ting–fu, 8–12
Tuan Hsi–wen, 520
Tubby, Roger W., 436*n*
Two–China policy. *See* UN
    representation issue.
Tyler, William R., 5*n*, 7, 8*n*, 745*n*

United Kingdom (*see also British
    subheadings under other subjects*),
    252–254, 470, 567–568

United Nations (*see also* UN
    representation issue):
    Tibet, 733–736, 743–744
UN representation issue, 223–224
    Albanian resolution, 380–382,
        390–391, 407–408, 418, 430–432
        Nov. *1966* vote, 469–470
        Nov. *1967* vote, 611
        U.S.–Canadian discussions, 397,
            413–414, 423, 705
        U.S.–Italian discussions, 603
        U.S.–ROC discussions, 428,
            437–439, 443, 446–447
    British–PRC discussions, 322
    Canadian position, 124–125, 137–140
    Canadian Two–China resolution, 408,
        418–419, 430, 447
        ROC reactions, 425*n*, 427–430,
            437–439
    U.S.–British discussions, 425–426
    U.S.–Canadian discussions,
        412–414, 420–425, 455–457
    Circular telegrams, 85–86, 390–391
    Cleveland paper, 120–123
    Cultural Revolution and, 421
    Defense Department position, 379
    General Assembly vote (Nov. *1966*),
        469–470, 489
    General Assembly vote (Nov. *1967*),
        611
    Goldberg papers, 285, 293–296
    Goldberg statement (Nov. *1966*), 420
    Important Question Resolution, 423,
        430–432, 603
        Nov. *1966* vote, 469–470
        Nov. *1967* vote, 611
        U.S.–Canadian discussions, 414,
            423, 705
        U.S.–ROC discussions, 437–438,
            443–444
    Italian resolutions. *See* Study
        committee proposals *below*.
    Japanese position, 368
    Jenkins papers, 380–382, 658
    Komer paper, 132
    Mongolia recognition and, 748
    National Policy Papers, 92–93
    Presidential adviser meetings,
        313–314, 387–388
    Rostow report, 665
    Rowe paper, 606–608
    Rusk reports, 301–303, 645
    Sisco papers, 289–292

UN representation issue—*Continued*
  Soviet position, 139
  Stevenson position, 125–128
  Study committee proposals, 407–408,
    418*n*, 419, 430–432
    Circular telegram, 453–454
    Goldberg paper, 290–291
    Jenkins paper, 409–410
    Nov. *1966* vote, 469–470
    Nov. *1967* vote, 611
    ROC reactions, 440–452, 454–455,
      457–469
    U.S.–Canadian discussions,
      423–424, 705
    U.S.–Italian discussions, 602–604
    U.S.–ROC discussions, 428–430,
      437–440
  Successor state resolution proposals,
    290, 293–295, 301–304
    U.S.–Canadian discussions, 304–306
    U.S.–ROC discussions, 344–350
  Thomson paper, 117–119
  U.S.–Canadian discussions, 358–360,
    372–373, 396–399, 705
  U.S.–Italian discussions, 602–604
  U.S. position, 13, 118, 125–128
  U.S.–ROC discussions, 19, 53, 55, 220,
    271, 279–280, 287
  U.S.–Soviet discussions, 404

Valenti, Jack, 238*n*, 262
Van Lau, 547
Vance, Cyrus R., 77, 110
  U.S. policy toward PRC, 183, 188,
    197–198, 354–355, 550
Varg, Paul A., 513*n*, 673
Vietnam, Republic of (*see also* Vietnam
  conflict):
  ROC security pact proposals, 20–21,
    26, 29–31, 49–51
Vietnam conflict, 26, 119–120
  British–PRC discussions, 321–323
  Chiang–Johnson correspondence, 26,
    28, 133, 143, 540
  China Panel meetings, 515–516
  Cultural Revolution and, 396, 401
  French PRC recognition and, 20
  Hong Kong and, 252–253
  Mansfield PRC visit proposals, 551
  Mongolia recognition and, 748
  Peace offensive, 238, 244
  PRC fears of U.S. attack and, 256–257
  PRC policy, 65–66, 186, 546, 559–561

Vietnam conflict—*Continued*
  ROC anti–mainland operations and,
    44, 82, 231–232, 236, 242–245
  ROC security pact proposals, 20–21,
    26, 29–31
  ROC troop participation, 231–232,
    236, 555
  Sino–Soviet relations and, 483–484
  Soviet policy, 185–186
  State–Defense study, 184–186,
    189–190, 198
  UN representation issue and, 121,
    138–139, 398–399
  U.S. military aid to ROC and, 703
  U.S. policy toward PRC and, 131, 172,
    183, 335–336, 543, 716
  U.S.–ROC discussions, 45–47,
    210–211, 234–239, 287, 351–352,
    559–560
  U.S.–Soviet discussions, 589
  Warsaw talks and:
    Cabot/Wang Kuo–ch'uan (*1964*),
      72–76, 99–102, 104, 135
    Cabot/Wang Kuo–ch'uan (*1965*),
      148–149, 151, 165–168, 178–179,
      203–205
    Cabot/Wang Ping–nan (*1964*), 17,
      36–37, 66–68
    Gronouski/Ch'en Tung (*1968*), 633
    Gronouski/Wang Kuo–ch'uan
      (*1965*), 233
    Gronouski/Wang Kuo–ch'uan
      (*1966*), 276–278, 315, 383–384
    Gronouski/Wang Kuo–ch'uan
      (*1967*), 510, 581–582
    U.S. meeting guidance, 306,
      310–311, 376–377, 575–577, 627

Wabeke, Bertus, 396
Walsh, Thomas H., 578, 705*n*
Wang Bingnan. *See* Wang Ping–nan.
Wang En–mao, 557
Wang Kuo–chuan. *See* Warsaw talks.
Wang Meng–hsien, 467, 469
Wang Ping–nan, 17–19, 35–37
Ward, Barbara, 138
Warren, George L., 193*n*, 266*n*
Warren, Gen. R. H., 697–700, 706*n*, 718*n*
Warsaw talks:
  Change of venue proposals, 436, 497,
    500–501, 723–724
  Higher–level meeting proposals,
    493–494
  Jenkins paper, 658–659

Warsaw talks—*Continued*
Meeting reports (Cabot/Wang
    Kuo–ch'uan *1964*), 71–75, 99–104,
    134–137
Meeting reports (Cabot/Wang
    Kuo–ch'uan *1965*), 148–151,
    165–168, 177–179, 203–206
Meeting reports (Cabot/Wang
    Ping–nan *1964*), 17–19, 35–37
Meeting reports (Gronouski/Ch'en
    Tung *1968*), 630–634
Meeting reports (Gronouski/Wang
    Kuo–ch'uan *1965*), 232–234, 265*n*
Meeting reports (Gronouski/Wang
    Kuo–ch'uan *1966*), 276–278,
    314–317, 383–386
Meeting reports (Gronouski/Wang
    Kuo–ch'uan *1967*), 509–512,
    581–582
Paris, transfer to, 61
Peaceful co–existence agreement
    proposal, 35–38, 69, 71–72
Polish/Soviet eavesdropping, 255, 265
PRC breakoff possibility, 34
Schedule negotiations, 676–677,
    722–723
U.S. meeting guidance (*1964*), 65–71
U.S. meeting guidance (*1965*), 228–230
U.S. meeting guidance (*1966*),
    254–255, 306–313, 374–378, 436
U.S. meeting guidance (*1967*),
    492–494, 496–498, 500–501,
    574–579
U.S. meeting guidance (*1968*), 624–629
U.S. policy, 64, 75–76, 264, 665
U.S.–ROC discussions, 52–53, 270
Watson, Barbara M., 374*n*, 666*n*
Weiss, Seymour, 180–181, 183*n*, 197*n*
Wei Tao–ming, 492, 552
    Mongolia, 750–752, 754
    UN representation issue, 347–350,
        427*n*, 437, 442, 608–610
Wells, Bill, 503–507
Wheeler, Gen. Earle G., 202, 211*n*, 568*n*,
    641–642
    PRC nuclear capabilities, 144–146

Wheeler, Gen. Earle G.—*Continued*
    U.S. policy toward PRC, 183, 188,
        197–200
    Vietnam conflict, 234–237
White, John P., 193*n*
White, Paul Dudley, 195–196
Whiting, Allen, 65*n*
Wilson, Gen., 157, 159, 240
Wright, Adm. Jerauld:
    French PRC recognition, 4*n*, 10*n*, 12*n*,
        19–20, 22
    French–ROC relations, 13–15, 22
    Offshore Islands, 60*n*
    PRC nuclear capabilities, 112–113, 116
    ROC anti–mainland operations, 32,
        81–83, 141, 170–171
    ROC political situation, 162–163
    ROC security pact proposals, 20–21,
        29–30
    Thomson replacement
        recommendation, 164
    UN representation issue, 55
    U.S. nuclear deterrent, 54–55, 157–160
    U.S.–PRC relations, 129*n*
    U.S.–ROC relations, 41, 49, 141,
        155–160, 207
Wright, Marshall, 694–695
Wu Han, 363

Yager, Joseph A., 86*n*, 180, 182, 197–198
Yang (ROC), 437–438
Yang Hsien Chen, 363
Yang Shang–k'um, 505
Yarmolinsky, Adam, 266*n*
Yeh, Gen., 84, 495
Yen Chia–kan, 272, 288, 411, 553
    U.S. visit, 556–564
Yen Chien–ying, 548–549
Yu Pak–chuan, Gen., 235–237
Yu Ta–wei, 115–116

Zablocki Committee, 274–275, 281, 318,
    357
Zellmer, Ernest J., 107–108

*U.S. G.P.O.:1998–405–307:40001

ISBN 0-16-048811-7

9 780160 488115